DATE DUE

JE 16'04			

DEMCO 38-296

American Women's Track and Field

TO AN OLYMPIC HOPEFUL

By means of every race,
pacing, striding, pounding
through measured space,
prepared for reaching
by jogging over hills,
you slowly move
toward that far, difficult
high place
we only look at

and simply
through joy in running
and the will to do,
with a rueful smile
at the blinking star
you've hitched your wagon to.

An ardent acolyte
in a plain but sacred rite,
may you always serve
in satisfaction
your self-imposed ideal
(which makes you real)
with faith, friends, and exercise
to uphold you
just as Emerson told you.
— Lillian Morrison

American Women's Track and Field

A History, 1895 through 1980

by LOUISE MEAD TRICARD

McFarland & Company, Inc., Publishers
Jefferson, North Carolina, and London

Facing title page: Lillian Morrison's "To an Olympic Hopeful," from *The Break Dance Kids*, ©1985; reprinted by permission.

British Library Cataloguing-in-Publication data are available

Library of Congress Cataloguing-in-Publication Data

Tricard, Louise Mead, 1936–
    American women's track and field : a history, 1895 through 1980 / by
Louise Mead Tricard.
       p.   cm.
    Includes bibliographical references (p.) and index. ∞
    ISBN 0-7864-0219-9 (library binding : 50# alk. paper)
    1. Track-athletics for women — History. 2. Women athletes —
History. I. Title.
GV1060.8.T75 1996
796.4'2'082 — dc20   96-13463
                                                            CIP

Manufactured in the United States of America

McFarland & Company, Inc., Publishers
  Box 611, Jefferson, North Carolina 28640

Acknowledgments

During the course of the four years of collecting the mounds of material for this book, many people played a part. Susan Puretz first said, "get a computer," and Ruth Fountain, my technical adviser, guided me in the right direction with Don Miller's help. I wish in particular to thank the outstanding librarians who responded to my requests for information:

Violet Fallone, Montgomery County Department of History and Archives, Fonda, New York; Cindy Slater, Library, United States Olympic Committee; Jonathan Tee, Warner Library, Tarrytown, New York; Jan Kelsey, Rye Historical Society, Purchase, New York; Leo Flanagan, Silas Bronson Library, Waterbury, Connecticut; St. Louis Public Library; Richard Hart, Greenwich Library, Connecticut; New York Road Runners Club library; Gloria Poccia Pritts, Mamaroneck Historical Society; Wendy Thomas, Jane Knowles, Marie Gold, Arthur and Elizabeth Schlesinger Library, Radcliffe College; David Hinkley, New Haven Free Public Library, Connecticut; James S. Osbourn, Newark Public Library, New Jersey; Judith Jenkins George, DePauw University; Gail Grieb, duPont–Ball Library, Stetson University, DeLand, Florida; E. Timothy McGowan, Schenectady County Public Library, New York; Barbara James, Athletics Congress; Rochelle Evans, United States Olympic Committee; Steph Meyers, Laura Bell, Amateur Athletic Union, Indianapolis; Sylvia Berman, Charles E. Hayes, Hunter College; Mary Misch, National Cathedral School Library; Peter "Duffy" Mahoney, USA Track and Field; Jimmy Carnes, Florida Governor's Council on Physical Fitness; Barbara Irwin, UMD Libraries, Newark, New Jersey; Steve Vaitones, New England Athletics Congress; Teresa M. Brinati, Society of American Archivists; Carol Harris, Temple University, Conwellana-Templana Collection; Lee Sylvester, Choate Rosemary Hall Library; James Cartwright, University of Hawaii Archives; Dorothy Votaw, Meramec Valley Geneological and Historical Society; Nancy Mazmanian, University of Southern California; Dan McLaughlin, Pasadena Public Library; Linda Brown, Paterson Free Public Library; Robert Nelson, Dallas Public Library; Beth Howse, Special Collections, Fisk University; Joan Clark, Cleveland Public Library; John Andrus, *Sentinel-Ledger*, Ocean City, New Jersey; Mary Lou Cass, Montclair Public Library, New Jersey; Howard Schmertz, meet director, Millrose Games; Nancy Mackechnie, Special Collections of the Vassar College Libraries; Elizabeth Adams Daniels, Historian, Vassar College; Mary Riley, Special

Collections, Bates College; Sharon Garrison, College of William and Mary; Jean Brown, University of Delaware Archives; Marty Covey, University of Colorado at Boulder, Archives; Craig Fisher, Long Island University Library; David Stanley, East Shore Area Library, Harrisburg; Elizabeth Fitzgerald, Providence Public Library; Scot Van Jacob, Dickinson College; Dave Johnson, University of Pennsylvania Relay Carnival; Judy Bolton, Louisiana State University Library; Catherine Schlichting, Ohio Wesleyan University Library; Barry Bunch, University of Kansas Archives; Caroline Rittenhouse, Bryn Mawr College Library; Amy Doherty, Syracuse University Archives; Jan Davis, University of Arizona Special Collections; Clifford Muse, Howard University; Ruth Copans, Skidmore College Special Collections; Terry Birdwhistell, University of Kentucky Special Collections; Richard Popp, University of Chicago Library; Mark Woodhouse, Elmira College Archives; Wilma Slaight, Wellesley College Archives; Joseph Svoboda, University of Nebraska Library; Thomas Hamm, Earlham College; Frances Webb, Randolph-Macon Woman's College; Burt Altman, Florida State University Special Collections; Stacy Boales, Mills College Special Collections; Maynard Brichford, University of Illinois, Urbana-Champaign; Daniel Hass, University of Wisconsin–Madison Archives; Jane Lowenthal, Barnard College Library; Pamela Dunn, Stanford University Libraries Special Collections; Patricia Albright, Mount Holyoke College Library; Joan Clark, Rockford College Library; Elizabeth Nielsen, Oregon State University Archives; Smith College Archives; Doris Baker, Ector County Library, Odessa, Texas; Dorothy Frye, Michigan State University Archives; Patrick Quinn, Northwestern University Library; Bradford Koplowitz, University of Oklahoma Library; Gisela Schütler Terrell and Erin Davis, National Track and Field Hall of Fame Research Library, Butler University; Greg Ellis, Winthrop University Archives.

Special thanks go to Brevard Community College for its new, beautiful library and the librarian who connected the printer to the machine.

Thanks go to Lillian Morrison for permission to reprint her poem "To an Olympic Hopeful," on the page facing the title page.

When the writing began, Karen D'Aprix offered her grammatical expertise, and others made notable contributions: Dr. Edward H. Kozloff, Patricia Davis, Edward St. Martin, Sandy Pashkin, Doris Pieroth, Deidre Skinner, Julie Sandoz, Teddy Foy, Keith Davis, G. Forest Rucker, Lisa Downey, Kathy Wood, Carolyn Gill, Craig and Gretchen Gosling, Urla Hill, Robert Gilmore, Larry Bennett, June Wuest Becht, Bruce MacDonald, Cathy Catlin Van Leuven, Ken Doherty, Willye White, Dr. Bert Lyle, Walter Murphy, Ann Makoske, Dick Schultz, Fran Rizzi, Diana Sucich, Jocelyn Lowther, Richmond Davis, Laurie Urban, Patrick O'Connell, Pete Cava, Bill Pearson, Peggy Vetter, Dorothy Jennings, Hal Bateman, and Berny Wagner.

Last, but not least, I wish to thank my mother and those I have inadvertently forgotten.

Contents

Preface:
Another Stride Forward

In the past one hundred years of women's track and field in the United States, there was only one Wilma Rudolph. In 1960, standing tall on the top step of the Olympic victory stand while her national anthem echoed throughout the stadium in Rome, Wilma represented thousands of dedicated women in the United States who for sixty-five previous years faithfully trained and victoriously competed in track and field with little encouragement, support, opportunity, or recognition. But perform they did, despite obstacles too numerous and outrageous to list. Wilma's triumphs, with the whole world watching, symbolically and in reality were the phenomenon that broke the shackles that bound women's track and field and forced America to recognize and accept women in this sport.

This history began a century ago in 1895, when the women of the Vassar College Athletic Association ignored all of the athletic constraints placed upon females and inaugurated the first field day for women in the United States, with intense competition in five track and field events. The news flashed around the country like wildfire. It was only natural that other women aspired to break the first records established by the Vassarites.

By 1922, track and field for women was fashionable in colleges and schools around the nation. Dr. Harry Eaton Stewart organized a competition to select a United States team to compete internationally in the Women's World Games in Paris. The team was triumphant. On his return to the United States, Dr. Stewart was severely criticized by the leaders of the women physical educators, who sought to protect the girls in the United States from the "evils" of competition.

Track and field for women suffered. In response to the pressures of the physical education leaders, schools slowly snuffed out competition and along with it, track and field. All that survived were women's athletic clubs in a few cities around the country. It was not until 1962, inspired by Wilma's recent triumph in Rome, that a joint effort of the Olympic Committee and the physical educator's association led to the recognition and active development of track and field once again in the schools of the nation.

Little is known about the champions from Vassar's forty-two years of

1

uninterrupted field days, and less is known about the first international American team that competed against the world in Paris in 1922. Few people know about American national champions, Olympians, and record-holders from 1923 through the 70s.

This book is an effort to bring forth a 100-year history of women's track and field from materials scattered in brief articles in newspapers, magazines, books, and scrapbooks of those women who made this history.

The huge amount of research needed to bring this book to fruition was a labor of love. It began in the Vassar College library, where I scanned the *Physical Education Review* from 1898 through 1964, when the publication was called the *Journal of Health, Physical Education and Recreation*. I researched the *New York Times* from the late 1800s and then from 1923 to 1980 for the reports of the indoor and outdoor national championship meets, the Olympic Games from 1928 to 1980, the Pan American Games from 1951 to 1979, and other national and international competitions. I read the *World Almanac* for each national championship result, indoors and outdoors from 1923 to 1980. The Vassar library provided copies of the *Vassarion*, its yearbook, from 1895 to 1938 and the May *Miscellany* for the same years, carrying the results of Vassar's field days. Nancy Mackechnie produced for my perusal from the back recesses of the Special Collections of the Vassar libraries, hundreds of beautifully kept records and photos from boxes, folders and student scrapbooks.

As the recipient of the second annual Ken Doherty Fellowship, I did extensive research at the National Track and Field Hall of Fame Historical Research Library, a division of the Irwin Library at Butler University in Indianapolis. With the help of Gisela Schlüter Terrell, the librarian, I collected information from *Spalding's Official Athletic Almanac* 1904, 1905, 1909–12, 1916, 1919, 1925, 1927–41; the *A.A.U. Official Track and Field Handbook*, 1921–78; *Track and Field News* beginning with the inaugural 1948 issue and all available copies to 1980; track and field meet programs from the 1930s through 1980; available monthly issues of *Women's Track and Field World* from 1970 to 1980; the *DGWS Track and Field Guide* 1966–68, 1968–70, 1970–72, 1972–74, 1974–76, 1978–79, 1980–81; Olympic Committee reports for every Olympic Games from 1928 through 1980; and reports for other national and international meets such as the Pan American Games, the World Cup championships and the World University Games.

In Indianapolis, David Morton, the director of communications of the Amateur Athletic Union, offered me the opportunity to go through stacks of material on shelves in a closet at the AAU House. Material included copies of the *Amateur Athlete* magazine through 1950 (it began in 1921 as the *Athlete*). Minutes of the AAU conventions were read for the period 1930–78. Much of the information from the Women's Division came from Catherine Donovan Meyer's material when she was national chairwoman of women's track.

For the chapter on the other colleges, I wrote letters to the college archives librarian of each college.

For each of the indoor and outdoor national championship meets, I contacted local libraries in the cities or towns where the meets were held for results and write-ups from the local newspapers.

The United States Olympic Committee, through the courtesy of Cindy Slater, provided the listing of United States women Olympians.

The Historical Society in New Haven, Connecticut; Yale University; the University of Connecticut; and Central Connecticut College were contacted in hopes of obtaining Dr. Harry Eaton Stewart's papers, to no avail.

I also gained a pen pal in England. Eric Cowe and I exchanged many letters on the early ladies, and he generously shared the extensive research he used for his book, *International Women's Athletics 1890 to 1940*.

Books that were close at hand as reference material were Menke's *The Encyclopedia of Sports*, editor Hal Bateman's *American Athletics Annual*, Bateman's *America's Best*, Scott Davis and Dave Carey's *The United States National Record Progression for Women from 1892*, and David Wallechinsky's *The Complete Book of the Olympics*.

The story starts with the widely diverse, relatively inconsequential athletic beginnings in the United States in the late 1800s and then targets the historical events at Vassar College that launched organized track and field for females. This book documents the development of track as it spread throughout the nation's schools. Colleges and schools that reported records to *Spalding's Athletic Almanac* and the Women's Division of the National Amateur Athletic Federation were contacted, and archival material on field days was collected. Physical education journals were searched for reports of track and field programs in states across the nation.

After 1922, the organized attack on athletics designed by the Women's Division was captured from its letters and newsletters distributed throughout the United States and from articles and letters written by its officials that appeared in the professional journals.

This history reports the results of each of the Amateur Athletic Union Women's National Indoor and Outdoor Track and Field Championship meets beginning with the inaugural competition in 1923. The Olympic year chapters are highlighted with the names of the women Olympians and their performances in the games.

The story follows the significant setbacks and victories along the way to 1980. The tale of American women athletes is ongoing and still developing. They are catching up to their male counterparts surely but slowly. By 1980, because of Title IX, some rewards for athletic achievement in the sport were now being shared with women. Women were being awarded scholarships, and track and field was back in the nation's colleges once again.

This particular volume, a compendium of records and personality profiles, concludes at 1980 because the explosion of opportunity was well under way for women in track and field and because the women of the 1980 Olympic team symbolize through their outstanding level of achievement many of the earlier women who also did not get to compete.

Chapter 1

The Early Years

A study of women's athletic histories from various colleges indicates that walking was an activity that was unequivocally approved, encouraged, and required in the early years. In 1837, Mount Holyoke College required women to walk one mile a day. In 1860, one half hour of daily walking was required at Northwestern University, and in 1862, Elmira College required the same.

Walking clubs were started in 1891 at the University of Nebraska and in 1901 at Mills College. Walking required no instruction, no coaching, no unusual physical exertion, no clothing adjustment from the outrageous outfits women exercised in or wore out-of-doors, had no weather restrictions, no rules, no equipment, required no facility, and walking would not be labeled "masculine."

So, this was "our" sport. When women wanted to carry things a step further, walking competition followed. Barbara Walder, in her article in *womenSports* in June 1976 entitled "Walking Mania," said, "Marathon walking offered women a chance not only to demonstrate their prowess but also to earn fame and money." Women were entering a sports world formerly reserved for men.

Walder described Lulu Loomer's walk of more than seven hundred miles and said that she was one of "perhaps 35 women walkers, or 'peds,' who in the late 1870's helped make the East Coast a hotbed of the walking mania."

According to Walder, "By the mid–1870's women were competing for as much as $500 in prize money." She credits Ada Anderson with launching the women's "walking mania." In 1878, in Brooklyn's Mozart Hall, Anderson walked a quarter mile every fifteen minutes for a month. The majority of spectators were women, Walder said, who were there simply to see another woman walk. One reporter at Mozart Hall observed: "The women are so fascinated by the spectacle of a woman on the track performing a feat of which the majority of men would be incapable that they watch her for hours at a time, day after day, with unflagging interest and invariably beg to be allowed to stay and see her come out 'just once more, and then once more again' long after their male escorts have decided it time to go home." At one point in her walk, Anderson addressed the ladies, expressing the hope that her example would encourage them to "walk more and depend less on the horse cars." It was reported that after the twenty-eight days of walking 2,700 quarter miles in 2,700 quarter hours, Ada Anderson "walked" out of Mozart Hall with $10,000.

"Marathons and exhibitions for women sprang up all over the country. Within a year ten states had walking events." As the women's walking mania grew in popularity, so did bookmakers, managers, trainers and trainer's manuals. Other women began their long walks. Mae Marshall, a Chicagoan who had competed since 1875, began a 2,700-quarter-mile event in Washington. Ann Bartell began a 3,000-quarter-mile walk in Brewster Garden, New York.

The National Police Gazette of April 12, 1879, described in detail a match involving "the pretty pedestrians":

> The woman's six days walking match which began at Gilmore's Garden, on Wednesday night ... was brought to a conclusion. The conditions of the match were that it was a six days' contest, go as you please, for the champion belt and a prize of $1,000, the second prize to be $500, the third $250, and $200 for anyone covering 325 miles. ... At eleven o'clock on the night of the 26th, therefore, eighteen female aspirants for pedestrian honors started off on the prospective lengthy journey. This small army of more or less fair athletes consisted of Cora Cushing, Bella Killbury, Josie Wilson, Rosa Von Klamasch, Madame La Chappelle, Miss Lola, trapezist; Bertha Von Berg, Miss Henry, Marion Cameron, Madame Franklin, Fanny Rich, Eva St. Clair, Bessie Kohrn, Bella Brandon, Ada Wallace and Miss Farrand. Some of the walkers had records of two thousand or more quarter miles in as many quarter hours, but few were known to have walked any distance without frequent rests. ... They were a queer lot. Tall and short, heavy and slim, young and middleaged, some pretty and a few almost ugly. The number very speedily narrowed down materially. Henry and Franklin had withdrawn from the race before the first twenty-four hours was up. ... The next forty-eight hours carried off a half dozen more, and on the day before the finish at least four more, namely, Cushing, Mrs. Farrand, Williams and Rich.
>
> At the finish at five minutes past eleven P.M., on the 2nd, only five of the original eighteen showed up. A few incidents of interest occurred on the sixth and last day. Bertha Von Berg, who was twenty miles ahead on the score, walked as steadily as she did on the first day. She was the only one in the eighteen that started who was physically equal to the six days walk.
>
> The floor was cleared of the wrecks of the race by sending Williams to her home, and poor Farrand, who is fifty-four years of age, to Bellevue hospital....
>
> The struggle in the early part of the last day was between the young woman Killbury and middle-aged Mrs. Wallace. The girl of sixteen developed great endurance and pluck. She gained gradually on her opponent, who vainly endeavored to shake her off, until, at about 4 A.M., she passed Wallace. Then there were signs of war, and nearly a collision as the rivals labored around close together.
>
> Wallace said something spiteful, being worked almost to a frenzy. ... It nearly broke her heart to see the younger woman take second place. The effect on Killbury was like putting new life into her. She ran at times and walked at others with vigor. ... At one P.M., on her 325th mile, she carried a drum and beat a lively tattoo, with loud cheers for accompaniment.
>
> Madame Tobias walked in good form and made a fast mile occasionally; but she spent so much time in her tent that she dropped behind good-natured and plucky little Von Klamasch, who then stood fourth in the race. Von Klamasch is an Austrian. She speaks several languages fluently. Her father was a wealthy German. He gave his daughter a liberal education. She eloped with a rich Virginian, who squandered her fortune and then died, leaving her poor. They had six children, five of whom died. Unable to make a comfortable living by teaching

or sewing, she undertook walking without suitable training. She had walked 296 miles up to 10 P.M. ... She had already challenged Von Berg, the winner of the champion belt. Half of the female walkers in the country have announced their determination to do likewise. Among them, Mae Marshall desires a first place.

The contestants stopped walking at eleven o'clock and twenty minutes. The score then stood: Bertha Von Berg (Real name Maggie Von Gross), 372 miles; Bella Killbury, 352; Wallace, 336; Von Klamasch, 300; and Tobias, 292....

Von Berg was presented with the belt. This is to be held under the Astley rules, and $1,000 cash. Killbury received $300 and Wallace $250....

Tobias said, after the finish, that she did not enter the match to win anything, but merely to train and see what she could do. It was the general opinion that she was the best walker in the match.

There are very few accounts of women pedestrians after 1880.

Reports of women's running races are infrequent during the 1800s. A story about a women's race in the 20th Annual Brooklyn Caledonian Club Games appeared in the *New York Times* on July 6, 1886. A race of 220 yards for women was held. The race

excited immense enthusiasm, and the ropes were broken down in several places by the eagerness of the crowd to get a good view. There were nine starters, and prettier girls could not have been found in the whole park. They started off splendidly at the pistol shot, and for half a minute there was continuous applause and excitement. Miss Bessie Edwards led all the way, but somehow just as the tape was reached Miss Kate McDonald was found at her side, and a tie was declared for the first two places, with Miss Lily Fleming third. Misses Edwards and McDonald went again over the course and each tried her best to win the silver dinner service. Miss Edwards got to the tape two yards ahead.

Articles about women's athletics, in general, were scarce. The *Police Gazette* on January 26, 1895, had a story about the "Strong Gotham Girls." In applauding the fact that girls were now exercising in the gymnasiums, the reporter said:

There are some queer results of the invasion by young women of the athletic field. Eligible bachelors are selecting their wives from among this class. Physical strength in a woman attracts rather than frightens men. Some people think that a girl's capacity to ride thirty miles on a bicycle, to swing indian clubs and to punch a bag makes her strong minded; that muscle makes her masculine and lung power loquacious. This has been found to be a mistake. The up-to-date athletic girl who patronizes the gymnasiums that are now numerous and fashionable is not a blue stocking, although her stockings are often blue. She is essentially feminine. She does not as a rule want to vote, and the desire to command or govern, except in her own proper province, is furtherest from her thoughts.

The article acknowledged the popularity of basketball and cycling but stated that while playing basketball, any "excited thrust, any display of over eagerness or ill-nature counts three for the opposing side, while the ball in the basket counts one."

In the meantime, the Vassar College Athletic Association staged the first women's track meet in the United States, which it called a field day. The date was November 9, 1895. In May 1896 a second field day was held, and the number of track and field events was doubled from five to ten. With the success and excitement of the field days, teachers Harriet Ballintine and Eva May sought to improve their knowledge of track and field events by attending the Harvard summer session in July 1896.

In 1897, Harriet Ballintine spoke before the Bridgeport, Connecticut, Physical Education Society, where she described field day and its benefits to college women. In March 1898 her speech appeared as an article in the *American Physical Education Review*, a national journal. As a result of her association with the field days sponsored by the Women's Athletic Association of Vassar College, Harriet Ballintine was thrust into the position of becoming the first and lone spokeswoman for women's track and field in the United States. Fortunately, the Vassar athletes were unperturbed by statements in the magazine *Mind and Body* which Ballintine cited in her speech: "We lament it [field day] as one of the outgrowths of a wrong appreciation of what physical training should do and be."

Ballintine mentioned other criticism, but she maintained that track and field increased interest in all-out-of-doors sports and she pointed out that there was a growing demand among women for this type of activity. She maintained that these activities were no more fatiguing than many forms of exercise to which women had been accustomed. As the other colleges adopted track and field events, Ballintine's task eased.

The *American Physical Education Review* in September 1898 described the beginnings of physical education in the public schools of Manhattan and the Bronx. In 1896, two women supervisors were appointed. When exercise needed to be simple because of untrained teachers, rudimentary running, jumping, and throwing could usually be found. The predominant exercises were designed, however, to promote good posture and respiration.

Harriet Ballintine spoke to the physical educators of the nation a second time through another article in the *American Physical Education Review* in June 1901. This sole American female voice from prestigious Vassar College spoke in support of track and field for women: "There are hundreds of girls in our colleges who are well and strong, whose vigorous and normal conditions demand a certain amount of healthful excitement and really hard physical work."

By 1901 a few other colleges sparked by Vassar's fearless field days were creating their own field days and comparing their records to Vassar's records. Track and field for women was beginning to spread like wildfire to schools throughout the country.

In 1903, *Athletics and Out-Door Sports for Women* was published. A chapter on track athletics written by Christine Herrick Terhune was the first writing of its kind for women by a woman. She discussed aspects of serious training for track and field not previously considered and provided instruction for women in the track and field events.

Terhune stated that track was a "comparatively recent development in women's athletics." She viewed track as a means to develop physically, not "to enter the field against men. ... The career of the girl who takes up track athletics is leavened by self denial from the start." Terhune noted that the athlete may think it is fun before she begins, but that illusion soon vanishes. "Training can't be taken in broken doses, nor can it be discontinued and renewed at pleasure. The work must be followed day in and day out, if the athlete would not fall behind all other contestants." Terhune suggested that the male coach should recognize the athlete as a woman but deal with her as strictly as he would her brother. "Her work may be lighter, but her drill is as faithful, her practice as regular, as his."

Terhune described bending and stretching exercises done in the gymnasium in the winter and then the selection of the events in which the individual athlete should compete. She noted that different girls liked different events and some were suited to some events better than others. When it came to running, however, girls had little doubt about their ability to run. "They have always run, they will say."

In discussing sprinting, Terhune offered several tips. Run from the hips, not the knees, toe in rather than out, exercise for form, lift the knees high, and run on the toes. She described the "crouch" start for the sprints and the "standing" start for longer races and said that it was important to practice the sprint start. Photos of girls starting a sprint and a distance run, hurdling, jumping, and throwing accompanied her training tips. She covered all of the events.

As for spiked shoes, Terhune considered them a distinct advantage. They were always worn by men athletes, as she noted, but their use "is as yet by no means common among girls."

A second article in *Athletics and Out-Door Sports for Women* by Herbert H. Holton was entitled "Running." Holton was a member of the Boston Athletic Association and the instructor of running and hurdling at Wellesley College in 1902. He stated that "grace in form should be the objective" as opposed to "strenuous endeavor" when instructing girls in running. Regularity of practice three days a week was essential, and the athlete should have a preparation period of eight weeks of training prior to "making the track team." His students at Wellesley were coached using the "spiked shoe."

The May 30, 1903, *Montclair Times* reported the results of the first dual track meet for girls held in the state of New Jersey and quite possibly the nation. It was staged on May 29, 1903, between Montclair High School and the girls of the Pamlico Athletic Association of Pompton, the athletic group of the Pamlico School for Girls. The weather was perfect, and a crowd of two hundred friends and schoolmates poured into the athletic club grounds to watch the competition.

The first event was the 50-yard dash. Gertrude Giffen of Montclair High School won it in 7.0. Nine competitors in bloomers and blouses took part in the dash.

The second event, the eight-pound shot put, was won by Clara Mancini. Gertrude Giffen was second. Mancini's distance was 29' 1". Both girls represented Montclair High School.

The two-year-old record of 4' 2" was tied in the high jump. Again, Gertrude Giffen, clad in the blue and white colors of Montclair, emerged the victor with a leap of 4' 2".

The fourth event, the 75-yard dash, was a replica of the shorter sprint. Gertrude Giffen won easily in 10⅖.

Montclair was victorious in the 300-yard relay in the time of 42⅗. It was reported to be an exciting event which created great enthusiasm. Joining her three teammates and running the anchor leg was Gertrude Giffen.

The final event of the day was the running broad jump. It was the only event won by a Pamlico Athletic Association athlete. Marie Richards, wearing the red and gray colors of the school, jumped 14' 3". When the Pamlico team heard the results announced for this contest, the newspaper reported that they "gave vent to their feelings through countless horns they had brought for the purpose."

Medals of gold, silver, and bronze were awarded to the winning girls, and a silver trophy was won by Montclair High School. The performances were compared to those of Vassar College.

A listing of women's athletic records appeared for the first time in the 1904 *Spalding's Official Athletic Almanac*, a national publication. Ten of the fifteen records were from Vassar College, and those not from Vassar were in events not participated in by Vassar women, except for the high jump. Vassar College records were published separately for the first time in 1903. The 1904 *Spalding's* records follow:

50-yard run	6⅗	Miss Agnes Wood, Vassar College, Poughkeepsie, N.Y., (1903)
75-yard run	10⅖	Miss Giffen, Montclair, N.J., May 29, 1903 Miss Nina Ganung, Elmira, N.Y., June 6, 1903
100-yard run	13⅕	Miss Fannie James, Vassar College, Poughkeepsie, N.Y., May 17, 1903
220-yard run	30⅗	Miss Agnes Wood, Poughkeepsie, N.Y., May 17, 1903
40-yard hurdles	7⅕	Miss Marian Amick, Elmira, N.Y., June 6, 1903
120-yard hurdles	20	Vassar College record (Julia Lockwood, 1900)
60-yard hurdles	10⅗	Miss Nina Ganung, Elmira, N.Y., June 6, 1903
High jump	4' 3³⁄₁₀"	Miss Lydia Carpenter, Plattsburg, N.Y., May 18, 1903
Running broad jump	14' 6½"	Miss Evelyn Gardiner, Poughkeepsie, N.Y. (1903)
Standing broad jump	7' 7"	Miss Evelyn Gardiner, Poughkeepsie, N.Y. (1903)
Putting 8-lb. shot	29' 11½"	Vassar College record (Elsa White, 1902)
Fence vault	4' 10½"	Vassar College record (D.E. Merrill, 1900)

| Throwing baseball | 173' 6" | Vassar College record (Julia Lockwood, 1901) |
| Throwing basketball | 72' 5½" | Vassar College record (Harriet J. MacCoy, 1902) |

The names and dates in parentheses were added by the author. Vassar College set the standards in the events and established records for other colleges to follow.

From 1895 through the 1960s, the history of women's track and field in this country is closely intertwined with the attitudes and philosophies of the nation's women physical educators.

It is for this reason that along with the in-school and out-of-school development of women's track and field, the ideology of the leaders of the women's physical education association will be followed for that period.

It must be remembered that track and field competition for men was not questioned. A man did not have to justify his participation in a hundred-yard dash or a shot put event. Competition for men was considered "masculine" and was heralded as a desired attribute, an attribute even necessary at times in a man's workplace. No one questioned inter-collegiate competition for men; it was actively encouraged and developed. Competition made the champions and winning coaches important and powerful. It provided prestigious coaching positions with lucrative benefits. It furnished champion male athletes advantages that went far beyond the athletic arena. Year after year from the 1800s on, the colleges and clubs turned out men who were track and field champions. Some went on to be successful coaches who in turn produced more champions. This is how a program develops and becomes strong. The women's program never had that chance after the Women's Division, National Amateur Athletic Federation organized and executed plans which finally snuffed out competition and track and field from the schools of the nation from the 1930s through 1961.

In March 1904, the *American Physical Education Review* reported that a resolution was discussed by the Wisconsin Physical Education Society stating: "Inter-collegiate athletic contests for women are not approved." The resolution was passed at a conference of deans of women from nineteen colleges in the Middle West.

In September 1906, the *American Physical Education Review* reported on the first convention of the Public School Training Society. The topic of the convention was "Athletics for Girls." An exhibition at the convention included girls putting the shot and running relay races, but it was stated, "We do not approve of inter-school athletics for girls."

"The ability to run, to strike, and to throw is on the whole a masculine ability," Dr. Luther Halsey Gulick said in his presidential address at the first physical education convention on March 30, 1906. He was president of the society and director of physical training of the public schools in New York City. Dr. Gulick told the audience of distinguished physical educators, which included Dr. Dudley A. Sargent and Dr. J. H. McCurdy, how athletics tested manliness, and he ridiculed the athletic ability of Vassar College women by citing a small high school on Staten Island that recently had a field day. He said, "These high school girls, in their first field day, made better records in four of the events, so I am told, than ever had been made by the students of Vassar College." He concluded his address by acknowledging that a girl must be provided with outdoor exercise, which athletics furnished, but he stated his opinion that the strenuous training of teams was injurious to body and mind: "Let them have athletics for recreation, but not for serious, public competition."

Another address by Dr. Dudley Allen Sargent explored whether women should participate in the athletic games of men. He asserted: "The women who are able to excel in the rougher and more masculine sports, have either inherited or acquired masculine characteristics. ... Her relatively short legs and heavy hips and thighs would handicap her severely in all running, and jumping and vaulting contests. ... Women as a class cannot stand a prolonged mental or physical strain as well as men." Dr. Sargent did not forbid track and field activities for women, but he suggested modifying the hurdle heights and lessening the distance between them, lessening the weights of the shot and other "heavy weight appliances," and emphasizing good form rather than great records. "Exquisite grace" must enter women's athletic performances, according to Dr. Sargent. "Let her know enough about the rougher sports to be the sympathetic admirer of men and boys in their efforts to be strong, vigorous and heroic."

With philosophical beliefs like these held and disseminated by the physical education leaders of the time, what chance did women have?

The 1908 *Spalding's Official Athletic Almanac* listed the following women's athletic records:

50-yard run	6 ⅕	Miss Fanny James, Vassar College, Poughkeepsie, N.Y., May 7, 1904
70-yard run	6⅘	Miss Amelia H. Ware, Vassar College, Poughkeepsie, N.Y., May 9, 1908 (Ware won the 50-yard dash in this time in 1908. Vassar never had a 70-yard run.)
75-yard run	10¹⁄₁₀	Miss Helen Buck, Mt. Holyoke College, So. Hadley, Mass., May 10, 1905
100-yard run	13	Miss Fanny James, Vassar College, Poughkeepsie, N.Y., May 7, 1904
220-yard run	30⅗	Miss Agnes Wood, Poughkeepsie, N.Y., May 17, 1903
40-yard hurdles	7⅕	Miss Marian Amick, Elmira, N.Y., June 6, 1903
100-yard hurdles	16⅗	Miss Martha Gardner, Vassar College, Poughkeepsie, N.Y., May 12, 1906
120-yard hurdles	20	Miss J. B. Lockwood, Vassar College (1900)
60-yard hurdles	10⅗	Miss Nina Ganung, Elmira, N.Y., June 6, 1903

High jump	4' 6"	Miss Helen Schutte, Central High School, St. Paul, Minn., April 28 1905
		Miss Helen Aldrich, National Cathedral School, Washington, D.C., May 26, 1905
Running broad jump	14' 6½"	Miss Evelyn Gardiner, Poughkeepsie, N.Y. (1903)
Standing broad jump	7' 11¾"	Miss Edith Boardman, National Cathedral School, Washington, D.C., May 26, 1905
8-lb. shot	33' 1"	Miss M. Young, Bryn Mawr College, Bryn Mawr, Pa., 1907
Fence vault	4' 10¾"	Miss Mildred Vilas, Vassar College, Poughkeepsie, N.Y., May 11, 1907
Baseball throw	195' 3"	Miss Alice Belding, Vassar College, Poughkeepsie, NY, May 7, 1904
Basketball throw	72' 5½"	Miss Harriet MacCoy [corrected], Vassar College, 1902
Standing high jump	3' 6"	Miss T. Bates, Bryn Mawr College, 1905
Hop, step, jump	27' 5"	Miss H. Kempton, Bryn Mawr College, 1905

An article on physical training for high school girls written by Professor John M. Tyler of Amherst College appeared in the May 1909 *American Physical Education Review*. It stated:

> The average girl has no open air games. As a rule she never learns to play vigorously and properly, or to use the heavy muscles. She is very fortunate if her mother and aunts are not continually discouraging tom-boy play, and insisting on quiet, refined, dignified, and ladylike behavior. As a result of these differences of habit and sex, the development of the high school girl is quite different from that of her brother of the same age.

The 1910 records for women, published in the 1911 *Spalding's Official Athletic Almanac*, had the following changes:

75-yard run	8⅘	Ruth Spencer, Lake Erie College, and Ruth Baker, Lake Erie College, Painesville, Ohio, May 14, 1910
100-yard run	12	Marie Thornton, Lake Erie College, Painesville, Ohio, May 14, 1910
90-yard hurdles	14	Marie Thornton, Lake Erie College, Painesville, Ohio, May 14, 1910
Running high jump	4' 7⅝"	Carolyn Hale, Ingleside School, New Milford, Conn., June 13, 1910
Fence vault	5' 3¼"	Almede Barr, Vassar College, Poughkeepsie, N.Y., May 7, 1910
Standing high jump	3' 9"	Louise Fee, Lake Erie College, Painesville, Ohio, May 14, 1910
Hop, step, jump	29' 6½"	Charlotte Hand, Vassar College, Poughkeepsie, N.Y., May 7, 1910
Pole vault	4' 9"	Ruth Spencer, Lake Erie College, Painesville, Ohio, May 14, 1910

The *New York Times* on June 14, 1910, carried a small article on Carolyn Hale's world-record high jump on June 13. The field day meet was held in connection with graduation at Ingleside School for Girls. In addition to the high jump, Carolyn won five of the six events contested.

Field days were springing up in schools around the country. In June 1910, the *American Physical Education Review* reported that five thousand students took part in the third field day of the public schools of Philadelphia on May 21, 1910. The track and field events for girls were the standing broad jump, the basketball far throw, and the shuttle relay race.

St. Louis reported its first public school field day in the *American Physical Education Review* in October 1910. The grammar school girls were divided as follows: the "midget" class girls under 75 pounds participated in the 30-yard dash, broad jump, and throwing the basketball; the "lightweight" class, girls under 90 pounds, ran the 40-yard dash, did two standing broad jumps, and threw the basketball; the "middleweight" class, girls under 105 pounds, ran the 50-yard dash, did the running broad jump, and threw the basketball; and the "unlimited" weight class ran the 60-yard dash, threw the basketball, and did the running broad jump. Indications are that only high school boys competed in the 100-yard dash, shot put, and running broad jump. Eighty-seven grammar schools took part with a total of 644 girls participating.

The article concluded with the writer commenting upon

> the harmonious and friendly mingling of white and colored pupils from all parts of the city, entirely unknown to each other. The colored contingent, although in the minority, were given the glad hand unstintedly whenever one of them distinguished himself by a successful effort during the competition. No race prejudice was shown at any time during the whole day, which speaks as well for the good discipline as for the friendly feeling of the children. Everyone feeling as a part of the whole and trying to make the best showing for his or her school was in itself a valuable lesson in ethics.

While irrelevant issues such as masculinity, competition, and anything else that could be used to question women's participation in sports plagued college women and confused and sidetracked women's athletic development and progress, in February 1911, the *American Physical Education Review* stated that college men were consumed with consolidating their five existing sets of track and field rules into one, deciding upon orders of events, and establishing a permanent national track and field committee. Amos Alonzo Stagg was one of the three members of the first committee. Its self-imposed tasks were to receive and act on suggested rule changes, accept new records, promote the collection of records from the different districts in the association, and maintain records and summaries of meets. The technicalities of the growing sport were being addressed by the men; no one was questioning whether men should participate in track activities and competition. Progress was being made for men, whose events were the 100, 220, 440, 880, mile, 2 mile, 16-lb. shot, 16-lb. hammer, discus, high jump, broad jump, and pole vault.

Eight months later, in the October 1911 *American Physical Education Review*, an example of the attitude towards women was presented. It was reported: "Some of the young women who come to the University of Wisconsin are on the verge of a nervous breakdown because they do not know how to conserve their energy. ... The department of physical training for women ... has instituted classes in resting for this class of student. ... Nearly 175 young women were in these rest classes during the past school year."

On the elementary school level, the November 1911, *American Physical Education Review* said that both boys and girls had races in playground festivals and field days. A Grand Rapids, Michigan, playground festival had relay races and a 50-yard dash for "small boys and girls."

The November 1912, *American Physical Education Review* reported that the first annual field day of the Cambridge, Massachusetts, Public Schools was held on June 11, 1912, at Harvard University's stadium. The younger girls and boys had novelty races such as a bean bag race and shuttle flag race. On the high school level, the girls played dodge ball and had two novelty races, while the boys had a dual athletic meet. Cambridge High and Latin School boys competed in a track meet against the boys of Rindge Technical School.

The course of study in physical training for boys' and girls' high schools in Philadelphia allowed track and field work. The attitudes toward girls' participation is illustrated by a statement in the November 1913, *American Physical Education Review*: "In the track and field work ... the physical work demanded of girls should not be as great as that required of boys. For girls there should be little competitive track and field work."

A 1915 Preble County, Ohio, play day festival had track and field activities. The activities were divided into two categories: girls under 13 and over 13. The under-13 group had a basketball throw (for a goal), baseball throw, 40-yard dash, 40-yard relay, and potato race. The over-13 group competed in a basketball throw (for a goal), baseball throw, and eight-lb. shot in the field events and the 75-yard dash, 75-yard relay, and potato race in the running events. This was reported in the May 1915 *American Physical Education Review*.

On the adult level, a 1913 practical examination given to play leaders in Los Angeles required a woman to run a 50-yard dash, high jump, throw the basketball, and do the standing broad jump.

The 1912 *Spalding's Official Athletic Almanac* listed "Women's Athletic Records" and "Vassar College Records." The changes in the "athletic records" from 1910 follow:

100-yard hurdles	16⅓	Caroline Johnson, Vassar College, Poughkeepsie, N.Y., May 4, 1911
Running high jump	4' 9"	Isabelle Swain and Miriam Heermans, Wells College, Aurora, N.Y., May 16, 1911
Running broad jump	15' 1"	Carolyn Hale, Ingleside School, New Milford, Conn., June 3, 1911

Standing broad jump	8' ½"	Vassar College (was 8' 1½" Almeda Barr, (1910)
Baseball throw	204' 5"	Dorothy Smith, Vassar College, Poughkeepsie, N.Y., May 4, 1911
Basketball throw	77' 9½"	Vassar College (Milholland), 1909
Standing high jump	4'	Ruth Spencer, Lake Erie College, Painesville, Ohio, May 15, 1911
Pole vault	5' 8"	Ruth Spencer, Lake Erie College, Painesville, Ohio, May 15, 1911

In May 1915, Pauline Siebenthal of Indiana University set a record in the pole vault of 6' 1". The mark was made at a closed meet. The *New York Times* on May 21, 1915, reported that "a track meet for women athletes, something new in Indiana, is to be held soon."

Another article in the *New York Times* on May 19, 1915, headlined, "Vassar Record Beaten." In a dual meet between Howard Payne College of Mexico, Missouri, and Stephens College of Columbia, Missouri, Irene Chancellor of Howard Payne broke the broad jump record held by a Vassarite by leaping 15' 1".

A unique event took place on April 21, 1918, in California. The *San Francisco Call and Post* sponsored the first cross-country hike for women. The distance of the Dipsea hike was seven miles. The *San Francisco Call and Post* on April 22, 1918, reported, "To Miss Hickman goes the honor of winning the first cross country hike ever held in the United States in which women were the exclusive participants." Edith Hickman credited her coach, Eddie Stout of the Olympic Club, with her victory. He provided training and pacing advice to her. Three thousand enthusiastic spectators witnessed 177 girls start the hike. The women ran and walked the distance. Hickman's time was one hour, 18 minutes, and 48 seconds. Hikes were held in 1919, 1920, 1921, and 1922.

Chapter 2

Vassar College: Forty-two Years of Track and Field, 1895–1937

The crack of the starter's pistol and subsequent thunderous shouts from the student spectators gathered in the circle in the gardens ushered in this country's first continuous, well-documented annual track and field competition for women. The place was Vassar College, Poughkeepsie, New York, and the year was 1895. The field day competitions would take place every spring until 1937 — an unbroken span of forty-two years.

The stately pines today are deep green in color and stand more than 100 feet tall. These are the very trees that formed the hedge around the athletic circle in 1895. The circle is silent and empty now. The warm yellow sun overhead illuminates the field like a spotlight on a stage. A bird chirps, and two squirrels chase each other across the grass. A garden filled with fragrant flowers of all colors remains at the end of the circular athletic field.

A slow, lingering walk around the perimeter reveals the age of some of the pines. Under one towering tree is a plaque dated 1920, under another 1926. The thick, strong trunks grew each year that the girls ran and threw and jumped, and the pines remain surrounding the field like an ornate antique frame that circles a cherished painting.

I close my eyes and visualize that morning almost 100 years ago when it all began. So much excitement — sprinting, hurdling, and jumping — performances determined and confident. Shouts of victory saturate the circle. Cheers of support are chanted.

> Isn't that fine
> Isn't that fine
> All for the glory of '99

Perpetual activity abounds. Then the imagery ends abruptly when the silence is broken by the sound of a telephone coming from a nearby dormitory that recalls me to the present.

For years there was no plaque to tell of the beginnings of the forty-two historic years of women's track and field, just a grassy circle surrounded by steeples of deeply colored pines piercing the sky. Finally, to celebrate the 100th anniversary of field day, Vassar College placed a plaque on the field in November 1995.

The seed for field day was planted when Vassar College was created, said Harriet Ballintine in *The History of Physical Training at Vassar College 1865-1915*. Matthew Vassar's intent in founding a women's college was to provide for women what men already had. In regard to physical education, the college prospectus issued in May of 1865 made it clear that physical education was fundamental to all the rest of education. The first catalog stated, "A suitable portion of each day is set aside for physical exercise, and every young lady is required to observe it as one of her college duties."

One student's rebuttal to this philosophy was reflected in the following poem written during the academic year 1869-70 and published in *Letters from Old Time Vassar*.

"Sixty Minutes Every Day"

The shades of night were falling fast
as round the college quickly passed
a girl, who plods her weary way
because she heard the President say
"Sixty minutes every day."
Her brow was sad, her eyes below
were red and swollen as with woe;
but in her ear still sadly rung
the accents of that awful tongue
"Sixty minutes every day."
From the windows gleamed the light
of cozy rooms all warm and bright;
she thought it very hard to bear
that she must be in the open air
"Sixty minutes every day."

While the field days comprised of track and field events did not begin for another thirty years, "strolling" was an activity from Vassar's inception. The *Annual Report of the Department of Physical Training* for the school year 1876-77 documented a walking drill and also cited walking as a game. The drill involved 245 women in five classes enrolled in a walking class three times a week for fifteen minutes. In the classes that involved walking as a game, more women selected walking than cricket, gardening, boating, or ball.

Exercise was continually justified and fostered. The resident physician, Dr. Elizabeth Thelberg, in her annual report to President James M. Taylor in 1888 stated that "the opening of the new walks has been of great value in increasing the variety and interest of exercise." In the May 1889 annual report, she said, "This combination of exercise with true zest and enjoyment will I hope be further realized in the use of the new gymnasium during the coming year."

The Alumnae Gymnasium was the second gymnasium constructed on the campus. It was built in 1889, and Vassar College declared that it was the largest and best-equipped gymnasium in any American college for women. Nevertheless, Anna J. Bridgman, director of the gymnasium, in her *Annual Report of the Department of Physical Training 1890-91* cited the need for "more apparatus [and] a running track" and asked that "some good friend help us to make this department what it should be." It is interesting to note, though, that in order to keep within the budgeted $20,000 for constructing the gymnasium, the plan for the indoor running track had to be eliminated. The Alumnae Gymnasium became a reality because of the enduring belief in a diverse, contemporary physical education and sports program for the women of Vassar College.

Vassar girls participated in the following sports prior to the first field day: light gymnastics, swimming, skating, boating, croquet, shuttlecock, tennis, riding, baseball, basketball, fencing, bowling, golf, cycling, walking, and battle ball. Vassar's first annual tennis tournament was held in the spring of 1886.

> In *The History of Physical Training at Vassar College*, Harriet Ballintine reported how the students originated field day: Following basket and battle ball a demand was made for other out-of-door activities. The students became interested in hurdling, running and jumping, etc. They organized an Athletic Association, and in November, 1895, the first field day was held. This was the beginning of track and field sports for women. Before this time there is no record of girls taking part in such competitive events.
>
> In 1896, at the Harvard Summer School, a course in athletic training was opened to women. This first class was composed principally of teachers from schools and colleges whose students had asked for instruction in athletics. After Vassar's first field day many schools and colleges became interested in such contests. Previous to 1896 a course in athletics had been offered to women at the Chautauqua Summer School, but as there was no demand for it, the Harvard Summer School was, therefore, the first school to give systematic instruction to girls in track and field sports. This first class in athletics for women was in charge of Mr. James Lathrop, for many years athletic trainer at Harvard and instructor in the theory and practice of athletics at the summer school.
>
> He ordered for Miss Eva G. May, then an instructor in the gymnasium at Vassar, the first pair of spiked running shoes ever made for a woman. The Vassar College Athletic Association provided these running shoes for every student who entered field day.

James G. Lathrop was the coach of the Harvard track team from November 1884 until 1900.

The material taught at the summer session included "Suggestions as to Arranging Programs and Conducting Athletic Meetings, Methods of Starting and Training for Sprint and Long Distance Running and Practice in Field Games, Bicycling, Tennis, Shot Putting, Hammer Throwing, Pole Vaulting, Timing, Etc." The summer session was held from July 3 to August 8, 1896, and cost $50 for the full course or $25 for the theory or practice alone. Both Harriet Ballintine and Eva May attended the course in practice.

It is significant that two women, Harriet Ballintine and Eva May, represented Vassar College at the Harvard summer session which was for the first time open to men and women. Vassar was one of the only schools to send two teachers and the only institution in the United States that had track and field for women in the form of a field day. By the summer of 1896, Vassar already had had two field days within one school year, November 1895 and May 1896.

The attendance of Ballintine and May at the Harvard summer session demonstrated their desire to learn correctly the techniques of the many events in the track and field program even though they were not teaching track and field in the classroom at that time.

The Harvard summer group consisting of twenty-seven women and twelve men offered women the first formal instruction in track and field in the United States. The fact that this large group assembled at Harvard must have offered prestige and support to the women pioneers, who outnumbered the men in this track and field class. James G. Lathrop, the well-respected, successful Harvard coach added to their confidence in extending this male-dominated sport to women. Ballintine and May were instructed by an authority who imparted the most technical knowledge of the time for the events in which Harvard competed. The *New York Times* on May 31, 1896, reported the results of the men's 31st Annual Meet of the Intercollegiate Association of the Amateur Athletes of America. The events participated in by the male collegians were the 100-yard dash, 220-yard dash, 120-yard hurdles, 440, 880, and mile runs, one-mile walk, 16-lb. shot put, 16-lb. hammer, 220-yard hurdles, pole vault, high jump, and running broad jump. Vassar offered seven of these thirteen events and added others by 1898 to present an eleven-event program. In comparison to Vassar, other colleges did not have as substantial a field day, even in later years. One can say that the first national Amateur Athletic Union championships for women in the United States in 1923, twenty-five years later, were not as diverse or demanding as Vassar's program in 1898.

1923 AAU Program	*1898 Vassar Program*
50-yard dash	100-yard dash
100-yard dash	220-yard dash
60-yard hurdles	120-yard hurdles
440 relay	300-yard relay
High jump	High jump
Broad jump	Broad jump
Shot put	Shot put
Discus throw	Fence vault
Javelin	Standing broad jump
Baseball throw	Baseball throw
Basketball throw	Basketball throw

The Vassar program in 1898 contained eleven events, as did the AAU program in 1923. It was astounding, however, to find the 220-yard dash in the Vassar program because it was not added to the AAU program until 1926 or to the Olympic program until 1948, fifty years later. The fence vault was never part of the AAU program, and Vassar's 300-yard relay was not the standard 440-yard relay, undoubtedly because of the constraints of its athletic circle.

The Vassar Athletic Association was formed on March 27, 1895, with the purpose of expanding the scope of athletics, reported *The Vassar Miscellany* in October 1915. Maria Mitchell Champney was the first president. The idea for a field day originated with Ida Thallon of the class of 1897, who asked why girls could not have a track meet like men, recalled Miss Ballintine some time later. Thallon's novel idea was accepted by the Athletic Association, which began to make plans for the first field day for women in the United States. A newspaper announced on October 25, 1895, that the Athletic Association was scheduling events for a field day to include the 100-yard dash, the 220-yard dash, the running broad jump, the 120-yard hurdles, the high jump, and the standing broad jump. All of the aforementioned events were contested except for the standing broad jump.

November 9, 1895: The Bold Venture

A drizzling rain awaited all of the excited participants in America's first college field day for women. The date was November 9, 1895. The Athletic Association events were scheduled to begin at 10 A.M. By that time, all of the contestants and spectators, almost four hundred in number, had poured out of the red brick dormitories and assembled in the athletic circle.

The small Athletic Association program displayed an unusually organized and professional approach to field day. The five committee members provided for ample officials, including a referee, Dr. John Leverett Moore. All of the committee members, except for the chairman, participated in the meet. When not serving in her official capacity, Miss Ella Love, the starter, competed in the running broad jump, but the time keepers, judges, and scorer did not participate.

Twenty-two girls were listed as competitors in the five events. Miss Ida Thallon was entered in four events. Miss Spaulding, Miss Wilkinson, Miss Borden, and Miss Vassar were entered in three events. Seven girls were entered in two events and the remaining ten in one event.

Men were restricted from viewing the activities, except for Professor John Leverett Moore, the referee, who designed the competition area in the athletic circle. Professor Moore, a teacher of Greek and Latin language and literature, was a unanimously elected honorary member of the Athletic Association.

The curious event at the women's college in Poughkeepsie attracted the attention of many newspapers. Newspaper reports differed, however, and sometimes accounted incorrectly for the events listed on the official program.

News stories did agree on two items: the 100-yard dash was the first event, and it was won by Elizabeth Forbes Vassar. Her time was reported, however, as 11¾ seconds by one paper, 15½ seconds by a second and third paper, and 16 seconds by the *Daily Eagle*, a Poughkeepsie newspaper, and the *New York Times*. The official time, as recorded by Vassar College, was 16 seconds.

The actual story of the 100-yard dash, as pieced together with the help of

This page and opposite, top:
November 9, 1895, field day
program with results from the
scrapbook of Elizabeth Bishop.
(Courtesy of Special Collections, Vassar College Libraries.)

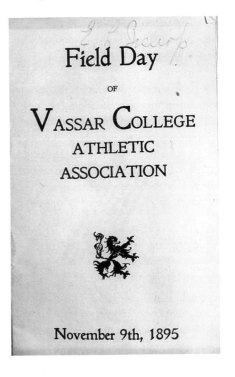

Field Day

OF

VASSAR COLLEGE
ATHLETIC
ASSOCIATION

November 9th, 1895

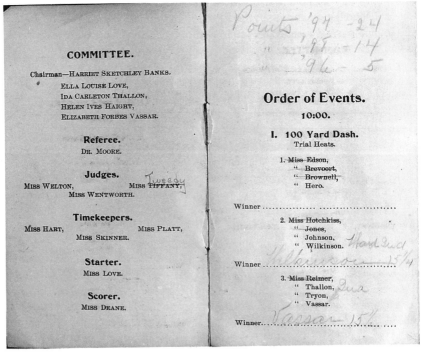

COMMITTEE.

Chairman—HARRIET SKETCHLEY BANKS.

ELLA LOUISE LOVE,
IDA CARLETON THALLON,
HELEN IVES HAIGHT,
ELIZABETH FORBES VASSAR.

Referee.
DR. MOORE.

Judges.
MISS WELTON,   MISS TIFFANY,
MISS WENTWORTH.

Timekeepers.
MISS HART,   MISS PLATT,
MISS SKINNER.

Starter.
MISS LOVE.

Scorer.
MISS DEANE.

Order of Events.
10:00.

I. 100 Yard Dash.
Trial Heats.

1. Miss Edson,
   " Brevoort,
   " Brownell,
   " Hero.

Winner ....

2. Miss Hotchkiss,
   " Jones,
   " Johnson,
   " Wilkinson.

Winner ....

3. Miss Reimer,
   " Thallon,
   " Tryon,
   " Vassar.

Winner...

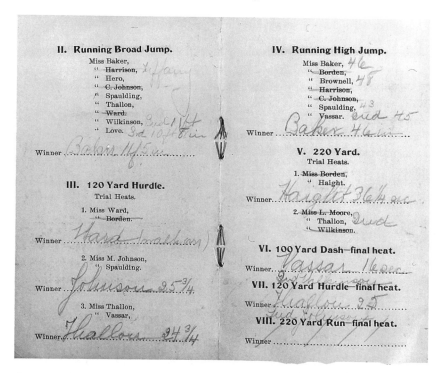

the meticulously kept programs from scrapbooks of students who were spectators, indicated that the first heat was to be composed of Misses Edson, Brevoort, Brownell, and Hero. All of them "defaulted" so that there was no first heat. The second heat was won by Miss Wilkinson in 15¼ seconds. The third heat was won by Miss Vassar in 15½ seconds. Miss Thallon was second. The final, scheduled as event number six, was won by Miss Vassar in 16 seconds, and Miss Wilkinson was second.

The *Eagle* report of the running broad jump had Baker winning in 11' 5" and said that she sprained her thumb jumping. The *Poughkeepsie News-Telegraph* had Baker winning in 11' 8". The *New York Tribune* and the *New York Times* said Miss Leslie (sic) Baker jumped 11' 5".

The girls' scrapbook accounts told this story about the broad jump: Miss Baker won the event with 11' 5", Miss Wilkinson was second with 11', and Miss Ella Love, the starter, was third with 10' 8".

The third event was the 120-yard hurdle race. One source, a newspaper fragment, described the heats and final:

> One of the most interesting events was the hurdle race of 120 yards, over hurdles 3 feet high and 12 yards apart. The girls proved themselves good jumpers. Miss Edith Ward had an easy victory in the first trial heat, and Miss M. B. Johnson won the next. The seconds were Miss Ida Carlton Thallon and Miss Haight, between whom the real contest lay, and who had saved themselves for the effort. Miss Haight got away well in the lead, but was overtaken by Miss Thallon. For

three hurdles they ran abreast. Then Miss Haight lost her stride, and fell behind, losing the race by a narrow margin. The time was 25½ seconds. The contest provoked the wildest enthusiasm, the girls yelling their class yells and shouting challenges to the others.

The Vassar scrapbooks indicated that since Fannie Borden defaulted, Miss Ward won the first heat in a walkover. No time was given. The second heat was won by Miss Johnson in 25¾ seconds, and Miss Spaulding was second. Miss Thallon beat Miss Vassar in the third heat in 24¾ seconds. The final was run as event number seven. Miss Thallon of Brooklyn beat Miss Johnson in 25 seconds.

The hurdle champion, Miss Thallon, returned to Vassar in 1906 to teach Latin and serve as a judge for many field days.

The running high jump was the fourth event. All of the newspaper reports had Miss Brownell winning.

The scrapbooks told the story of Miss Brownell, class of 1895, entering the field day as a postgraduate. Brownell worked as a laboratory assistant from 1895 to 1898. She did not represent any class, so even though she jumped higher (48") than the others, the first-place award went to Baker, who jumped 46". The scrapbooks also confirmed that Miss Baker dislocated her thumb while jumping. Dr. Elizabeth Thelberg was there to provide first aid. Miss Vassar was second with 45" and Miss Spaulding third with 43".

The final event was event number five, the 220-yard dash. Five reports had Miss Haight winning. The *Eagle* gave her time as 32½ seconds, but the student spectator account from the scrapbooks awarded first place to Miss Haight in 36¼ seconds, with Miss Thallon second.

Miss Ella Louise Love can be credited with being the first female starter in a women's track meet in the United States. The 1895 newspaper narratives about the woman starter included this account in the *Daily Eagle* on November 11, 1895: "All of the time the rain had dripped down slowly but surely. Once the cartridges for the starter's pistol grew so damp that they would not go off." Another report in the *Herald* said the athletes awaited "the firing of the pistol, which Miss Ella Louise Love, the starter, handled just like a man." The newspaper fragment proclaimed: "Miss Ella Love was the starter, and she fired the revolver with her eyes open. There was nothing timid in the way she did it, and she wasn't afraid it would go off."

Newspaper accounts were so detailed one has little option but to believe that reporters from everywhere were watching the events even though men were not supposed to be present. Did the newspapers send women reporters to cover this field day?

The weather was described as "mean" by one source. The article stated that no outsiders were admitted and then described in detail the costumes worn by the Vassarites. Divided skirts and kilts were worn with blouses or sweaters in distinctive class colors. The girls' hair hung in braids down their backs, tied with ribbons in the class colors.

The *Poughkeepsie News-Telegraph* said, "Saturday's results will be a sample to other female colleges which certainly will take a back seat when Vassar meets them in a great female inter-collegiate athletic tournament — date not yet fixed."

The Poughkeepsie *Daily Eagle* stated that it was "the first women's field day in the country." The reporter continued by describing Miss Vassar's high jumping: "Her gracefulness and the ease with which she jumped brought her rounds of applause." In commenting on the 220-yard race, she said, "Miss Haight looked as fresh after her run as if she had not run at all." The article concluded:

> Track events closed about 12 o'clock, when Dr. Moore, the referee, announced that the class of 1897 was the winner of the day. Then the students trooped back to the buildings — Strong Hall, where many of the juniors reside, echoed with their excited words. They had won the banner presented by the Athletic Association to the class that came off victor.
>
> Some prophetic soul said at the close, "I'm sure this marks an era in the history of women's colleges."

The *New York Tribune* noted that each girl who made a record would receive a medal. And the final comments in the newspaper fragment were "a splendid banner with the legend embroided on it: 'Vassar College, November, 1895, Field Day, Women's Class 1897' will hang in the gymnasium a trophy of envy and the first in honor among the many that will be ranged by its side in the years to come."

The *Tribune* commented upon the way the girls ran onto the circle: "There was no false modesty as they entered the field. ... One girl stopped to pull up her stockings. Another girded up her waist band. They were there to win."

And in conclusion, the reporter noted: "Here is a particular point to be marked by caviling critics: these same girls that ran so enthusiastically were dressed and ready for lunch at 1 o'clock, and showed no signs of fatigue from their violent exercise. They ate with the rest in Strong Hall ... and were the heroines of the hour."

Eleanor Belknap Humphrey's scrapbook contained a newspaper article entitled "Vassar's Champion Female Sprinter." It stated that "Vassar College is the proud claimant of the champion sprinter of the world." A drawing of Elizabeth Vassar in her starting stance with knee length bloomers and a full blouse accompanied the story.

One final note to that historic day. These same athletes who ran and jumped in the morning were back in the athletic circle after lunch for the class basketball championships. After basketball, they had dinner and several of them had parts in the evening play. A very busy fall Saturday for the bright young women of Vassar College.

The Second Field Day: May 1896

A second field day was held during the 1895-96 school year on May 16, 1896. Field day was subsequently held every May.

This page and next, top: May 15, 1896, field day program with results from the scrapbook of Elizabeth Bishop. (Courtesy of Special Collections, Vassar College Libraries.)

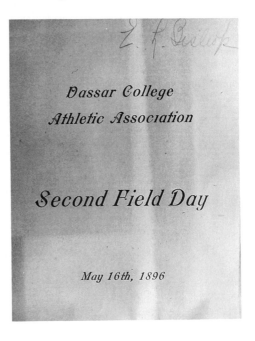

Dassar College
Athletic Association

Second Field Day

May 16th, 1896

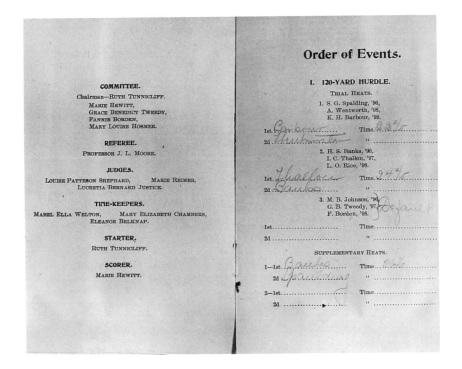

COMMITTEE.

Chairman—RUTH TUNNICLIFF.
MARIE HEWITT,
GRACE BENEDICT TWEEDY,
FANNIE BORDEN,
MARY LOUISE HOSMER.

REFEREE.

PROFESSOR J. L. MOORE.

JUDGES.

LOUISE PATTESON SHEPHARD,   MARIE REIMER,
LUCRETIA BERNARD JUSTICE.

TIME-KEEPERS.

MABEL ELLA WELTON,   MARY ELIZABETH CHAMBERS,
ELEANOR BELKNAP.

STARTER.

RUTH TUNNICLIFF.

SCORER.

MARIE HEWITT.

Order of Events.

I. 120-YARD HURDLE.

TRIAL HEATS.

1. S. G. Spalding, '96,
   A. Wentworth, '98,
   K. H. Barbour, '99.

1st........................ Time........................
2d........................ "........................

2. H. S. Banks, '96,
   I. C. Thallon, '97,
   L. O. Rice, '98.

1st........................ Time........................
2d........................ "........................

3. M. B. Johnson, '96,
   G. B. Tweedy, '97,
   F. Borden, '98.

1st........................ Time........................
2d........................ "........................

SUPPLEMENTARY HEATS.

1—1st........................ Time........................
   2d........................ "........................

2—1st........................ Time........................
   2d........................ "........................

II. RUNNING HIGH JUMP.

I. C. Thallon, '97,
G. B. Tweedy, '97,
A. Wentworth, '98

1st... *Thallon*   Height... *4ft 3½in.*
2d... *Morgan*   "
3d... *Wentworth*   "

III. FENCE VAULT.

S. F. Platt, '97,
M. H. Morgan, '98,
K. H. Barbour, '99.

1st... *Platt*   Height... *4ft 5in.*
2d... *Barbour*   "
3d... *Morgan*   "

IV. 100-YARD DASH.

G. B. Tweedy, '97,
A. L. Wilkinson, '97,
F. Borden, '98,
E. B. Hartridge, '98,
A. Wentworth, '98.

1st... *Wilkinson*   Time... *15*
2d... *Borden*   " *15.1*
3d... *Hartridge*   "

V. STANDING BROAD JUMP.

E. L. Love, '96,
S. J. Phillips, '97,
I. C. Thallon, '97,
M. H. Morgan, '98,
A. M. Day, '99,
H. E. Booth, '99.

1st... *Booth*   Distance... *8ft 1in*
2d... *Day*   " *8ft 1in*
3d... *Phillips*   " *8ft 0½in*

VI. THROWING THE BASKET BALL.

M. M. Champney, '96,
E. L. Darrow, '96,
L. Van Anden, '96,
B. L. Tiffany, '97,
I. C. Thallon, '97,
A. Wentworth, '98.

1st... *Champney*   Distance... *62-12½*
2d... *Van Anden*   " *49-8*
3d... *Wentworth*   " *41-1*

VII. 220-YARD RUN.

E. L. Love, '96,
M. M. Champney, '96,
F. Borden, '98,
H. I. Haight, '98,
A. M. Day, '99.

1st... *Day*   Time... *default*
2d... *Borden*   " *85*
3d... *Champney*   "

VIII. RUNNING BROAD JUMP.

S. G. Spalding, '96,   *9-7, 9-11*
S. J. Phillips, '97,   *9-8, 10-8*
I. C. Thallon, '97,   *10-5, 10-8*
A. L. Wilkinson, '97,   *10-6, 10-9, 11-3*
H. E. Booth, '99,
E. Nessenson, '99.

1st... *Wilkinson*   '97, *10-7, 10-9, 10-2, 10-5, 11-6* Distance... *11-6*
2d... *Thallon*   " *11-3*
3d... *Hardy*   " *11-1½*

IX. THROWING THE BASE BALL.

B. L. Tiffany, '97,
S. F. Platt, '97,
I. C. Thallon, '97.

1st... *Thallon*   Distance... *126th 2 in*
2d... *Platt*   " *111 3½*
3d... *Tiffany*   "

X. 120-YARD HURDLE—Final Heat.

1st... *Barbour*   Time...
2d... *Wilkinson*   "
3d... *Borden*   "

XI. 300-YARD RELAY RACE.

'96. A. E. Sill,   '97. S. F. Platt,
     H. S. Banks,   G. B. Tweedy,   *record*
     M. M. Champney.   A. L. Wilkinson.

'98. F. Borden,   '99. K. H. Barbour,
     H. I. Haight,   A. M. Day,
     A. Wentworth.   E. Nessenson.

46½ — ...

Points 97-42   96-13
*   99-26   98-8*

On April 15, 1896, Miss Ballintine requested and received a vaulting bar for the athletic circle. The *Vassar Miscellany* reported in May that a track department had been organized in the Athletic Association and Miss Love had been elected manager. These two pieces of information indicated that plans were in motion for a bigger and better field day. A remarkable change in the program occurred. The events doubled. Field day increased from five events to ten events in six months. The new events were the standing broad jump, fence vault, basketball throw, baseball throw, and 300-yard relay.

The field day committee also changed; four new Athletic Association members planned this day. Miss Tunnicliff was the chairman. New officials worked the event, except for Miss Welton, who moved from judge to timekeeper. Former officials Miss Tweedy, Miss Wentworth, Miss Platt, and Miss Love decided to compete rather than officiate. Professor Moore remained as the referee.

The competitors numbered twenty-four. Miss Thallon was entered in six events, Misses Wentworth and Tweedy, in five, and Fannie Borden in four. Elizabeth Vassar, the winner of the first 100-yard dash, left school prior to the second field day.

The weather was perfect on May 16. Four of the five original records were broken, and marks were established in the new events. Several athletes not in the first fall field day were victorious. Booth won both the standing broad jump and the running broad jump, establishing the record of 6' 11½" for the standing broad jump and breaking the record for the running broad jump. Barbour broke the record in the 120-yard hurdles. Platt won the fence vault, establishing that record. Miss Maria Mitchell Champney won the basketball throw, setting a record of 62' 10½", and Miss Day broke the record in the 220 with a 35-second clocking.

Miss Ida Thallon, the only repeat champion, won the high jump and the baseball throw and was second in the basketball throw and the hurdles. She established the record of 126' 2" for the baseball throw.

The 300-yard relay was won by the class of 1896. Three girls, each running 100 yards, ran on a team. There were four teams because every class was represented by a team. The relay was run in a shuttle fashion. The members of the winning 1896 team were Sill, Banks, and Champney.

The *Poughkeepsie-News Telegraph* on May 23 stated:

> There was more enthusiasm, more shouting, yelling, whistling … than at last year's events, and a general abandon of that dignity which surrounds the Vassar girl….
>
> The various classes grouped themselves on the grass and thundered forth their class crys. Every girl there seemed fired with college pride, and when the representatives of their classes came marching on the field in their brand new bloomers, some trimmed with red, some in white, with the letters V.C.A.A. blazoned on their sweaters, the wild shouts, cheers and confusion of a political convention couldn't "cut any ice" beside the reception given those athletic sportswomen by their classmates.

The Vassar records established at the field days were winning performance marks, not times from preliminary heats. When the 1896 spring field day was

May 15, 1897, Vassar College Field Day. Dr. Grace Kimball, assistant physician, starting a heat of the 100-yard dash. (From the scrapbook of Elizabeth Bishop; courtesy
of Special Collections, Vassar College Libraries.)

over, the only record remaining from 1895 was the 3' 10" high jump record set
by Emma Lester Baker.

The Third Field Day: May 1897

"One can hardly imagine a boy on entering college making the following
statement: 'Oh, I never take any exercise, I never have any time for it; I haven't
walked a mile in over two years.'" Harriet Ballintine made this point in her opening address to the Bridgeport, Connecticut, Physical Education Society in April
1897; her address was entitled "Out-of-Door Sports for College Women." She
said of Vassar's field days:

> Last year we brought upon ourselves some criticism from our colleagues ... by
> introducing track and field activities. ... Track and field athletics were intro-
> duced by the students themselves to meet a demand for them. It was an exper-
> iment, and so far had proved a satisfactory one. Training for these events has
> added greatly to the interest in all of our out-of-door sports by all classes of stu-
> dents. On the afternoons when the teams are practicing, "the circle" as our ath-
> letic field is called, becomes the most popular spot on the campus.

We do not advocate intercollegiate contests, or expect that other colleges will necessarily follow our example, but that we do endeavor to be most careful in our "choice of material" can be shown from the following rules and regulations imposed by the college authorities and athletic associations: any student entering for track and field athletics must have passed a creditable physical examination by the gymnasium director; have had her heart and lungs examined by the resident physician; have a written permission from parents or guardian, saying they are willing she should take part in the games, and come up to a certain standard in her work — for no deficient student is allowed to compete on field day.

There seems to be no physiological reason why a woman who can perform difficult and intricate exercises on the horse, vaulting bar or boom, could not jump hurdles, or, that a girl capable of riding forty or fifty miles a day on a bicycle, could not be trained for the 100 yard dash should she be inclined to that form of sport.

Comparing the records made by women with those of men is absurd. If women are to practice athletics, they must be content to establish their own standards. It may add to the interest of the feminine athlete to find that her record for the running broad jump is eleven feet nine, while Wescott of Yale has twenty-one feet five to his credit; but those most interested in her physical welfare do not consider records, but rather the physical and moral advantages she must necessarily receive from a systematic training in athletics.

The fact must not be overlooked that there are some objections to girls engaging in sports that until very recently have been regarded as only suitable for boys; objections which to some of us may seem unimportant, but to others very grave indeed. A frequent criticism, and perhaps a just one, is that girls indulging in active, competitive games, especially if they enter into them with genuine class spirit, have a tendency to become hoidenish [*sic*] ... but looking at the subject from a broader point of view, if refinement and quietness are but the results of weakness and inactivity, and a pronounced manner must necessarily be the outcome of a more vigorous life, we must be willing to sacrifice the former feminine attributes for the more precious possession of good health.

In her annual report to the president of Vassar College dated May 6, 1897, Harriet Ballintine discussed preparations for the field day and recommended future improvements in the grounds:

The students have entered into training for field day in a more systematic way than last year. The rules and regulations governing those entering are more strictly observed. All competitors must practice at least three, and not more than five hours each week. No student can enter for more than three events. A number of students interested in athletics are appointed to take charge of those in training. All the exercise in track and field athletics is under the direct supervision of Miss May.

If athletic games are to be practiced correctly the circle should be put in condition for all out of door sports. A running track would add to the interest in all out of door exercise. At present, the grass makes running difficult, and owing to the unevenness of the ground there is great danger of sprained ankles. Several such accidents occurred last year. This spring there has been but one so far. Especially should the ground be in better condition for the hurdle course: it should be a cinder track.

Situated as our gymnasium is, near the circle, it would be possible, even in winter — with suitable clothing — for the students to run out of doors. There is no better exercise, than systematic running in the fresh air.

Of course, the expense of a running track depends upon the amount of work put upon it — the soil, the amount of draining necessary.

The third field day was held on May 15. The *New York Tribune* reported that "the date had been kept secret, and the authorities have made great effort to keep the matter out of the newspapers." The track manager for 1897 was Annie Wilkinson, and Grace Tweedy was the chairman. The weather was perfect, and six hundred students and faculty assembled in the circle to cheer for the athletes. There were only seventeen contestants, but the performances continued to improve. Rowena Reed was the star of the day. She won three events, setting a new record in the 120 yard-hurdles of 22⅓ seconds. She also won the high jump and the running broad jump. Jean James' scrapbook revealed an unidentified article entitled "Athletics at Vassar" which stated that "Rowena Reed made 13' 3" in the running broad jump and broke the woman's record for the world."

Thallon, entering four events, won one, the basketball throw, placed second in the hurdles and standing broad jump, and third in the baseball throw. She was the only athlete to have won at least one championship in every field day to that date.

Bradley broke the record in the baseball throw, winning with a toss of 137' 8". Borden won two events, setting a new record in the 220 of 34½ seconds. An error occurred in the running of the 100-yard dash. The hurdle finish line was used which meant that Borden, in winning, ran 120 yards rather than 100 yards.

120-yard hurdles		Fence vault	
1. Reed	22⅓ seconds	1. Platt and	4' 3⅛"
2. Thallon		Ward	
3. Platt		3. Morgan	

High jump		220-yard dash	
1. Reed	3' 8¾"	1. Borden	34½ seconds
2. Tweedy		2. Wilkinson	36 seconds
3. Grefe		3. Day	

Baseball throw		Running broad jump	
1. Bradley	137' 8"	1. Reed	13' 3"
2. Johnson	127' 6½"	2. Grefe	11' 9"
3. Thallon	124' 5"	3. Wilkinson	11' 4"

120-yard dash (error in distance)		Standing broad jump	
1. Borden	17⅘ seconds	1. Day	6' 10"
2. Burnham		2. Thallon	6' 5¼"
		3. Morgan	6' 1½"

Basketball throw		300-yard relay	
1. Thallon	56' 6½"	1. Class of 1899	48 seconds
2. Bradley	49' 1½"		
3. Hosmer	45' 11"		

The starter was Dr. Grace Kimball, one of the few faculty members who belonged to the Athletic Association; she was an assistant physician at Vassar College.

On May 22, the *Poughkeepsie News Telegraph* published an interesting article written by May Blossom and entitled "Vassar Girls on Their Mettle." The writer reported a conversation between "an old fashioned woman" and a chic little maiden of modern tendencies:

> "Just see those girls actually tumbling on the ground, and hear their screams. ... I call it lunacy."...
>
> "Now, Aunty, now, aunty, you must be liberal — we are not Puritans any longer — higher education for women has worked a great revolution in the world."
>
> "Well, I should say so, if all this that I see be the result of higher education for women it's the most complete revolution I ever heard of— why, when a revolution advances so far as to send young women's heels and heads revoluting promiscuously through the air, I think it about time we revoluted back to the day of the modest Puritan maiden."...
>
> "There, there aunty — you just don't understand basketball — just because you never played it."

Blossom explained in her article that she never enjoyed anything more than that game of basketball:

> It was a complete contradiction of all that fogies have been saying for ages about the delicacy of women. The fraility of the girl, the tenderness of maidens and all that. I saw one of these young women actually laid out in a skirmish, a blow, a crush, or jam to the ground having rendered her unconscious for the moment. Suppose such a thing had happened to that girl's mother, in the not so very long ago, why she would have been physically helpless for the rest of the day. ... Did this young woman stay swooned? Not much. ... The disabled girl came back to activity and plunged right into the game again. Think you could your frail, blushing, unadvanced maiden of the sober ante–Matthew Vassar days, have done as much; or would not her superfluous shyness, her mistaken notions of girlish gentility, delicacy, precious physical construction and all that have taken her permanently out of the game, if, indeed, they would not have kept her out in the first place?
>
> But basketball was not the only delight of the day. The young women jumped hurdles like thoroughbreds. They ran foot races, and in such a manner as to emphasize the fact that there is no scientific reason for the timidity of gait, so-called gracefullness [*sic*] of walk and carriage which have set poets and doctors, and artists, and other sentimental people to clacking and scribbling about the alleged loveliness of woman as she steps across a velvet-like lawn, or as in fancied modesty she gathers her skirts about her ankles and steps carefully over the city crosswalk. There is, as I am now convinced, no reason whatever, either in science, ethics or physics, why a woman should not boldly run when she is in a hurry, and leap fences on a cross lot route when she is going to catch a train. ... Then I was so glad to see the contest in throwing a baseball. So much has been said, first and last, about the impossibility of a woman's throwing a stone, or of course, a baseball, that I observed with satisfaction the emphatic contradiction to all such nonsense which the girls at Vassar furnished. Some doctor has said that the reason why a woman cannot throw a ball is because of the way the creator formed her shoulders. Exploded theory. Another ... because she doesn't need

to and would be a fool if she tried. ... What stuff! Science, oh blissful science, how much we owe thee. Learning, oh precious thing, how many fogy notions have vanished before thy revolutionizing forces! and the end is not yet. ... It was a great day for Vassar.

The Fourth Field Day: May 1898

Fanny Borden, now a senior, was elected manager of track athletics for the school year 1897-98. Planning for the fourth field day, held on May 14, 1898, was in motion. A significant addition to the program was the shot put. If there was ever an event that could be classified as "unfeminine," the shot put was that event. This was the eleventh event on the field day schedule.

Dr. Grace Kimball remained as the starter. Photos in Bina Seymour's scrapbook clearly show men spectators scattered throughout the crowd at this field day.

Ida Thallon, Grace Tweedy, and Annie Wilkinson graduated in 1897, making room for new champions to surface with new records to their credit. Four records were set. The 100-yard dash record was lowered to 14 seconds by DeGraff. She broke the fence vault record by clearing 4' 7½", and the standing broad jump record was broken. The new mark was 7' 6", achieved by Calhoun in defeating Day, the previous champion. Lockwood raised the baseball throw record to 161' 2". DeGraff, Lockwood, and Calhoun won two events each.

Jean James' scrapbook contained the results of the 1898 field day from an unidentified newspaper article.

100-yard dash
1. B. DeGraff   14 seconds
2. E. C. Ward   15 seconds
3. I. Adams   Tie
   C. Paul

220-yard dash
1. I. Adams   35⅘ seconds
2. A. M. Day   37⅓ seconds

120-yard hurdles
1. J. Lockwood   22⅓ seconds
2. M. Calhoun   24 seconds

High jump
1. E. L. Johnson 3' 6½"
2. G. Burke   3'5"
3. E. C. Ward

Shot put
1. E.V. Jones   23' 5"
2. A. M. Day   19' 4½"

3. H. Hoy   18'

Baseball throw
1. Lockwood   161' 2"
2. Bradley   160' 1"
3. Jones

Basketball throw
1. E. Bradley   54' 6½"
2. G. Burke   52' 4"
3. E. V. Jones   49' 10"

Running broad jump
1. M. Calhoun   12' 6"
2. E. L. Johnson 10' 4½"
3. H. Hoy   9' 10"

Fence vault
1. DeGraff   4' 7½"
2. Ward   4' 3"
3. Morgan

Standing broad jump		Relay	
1. Calhoun	7' 6"	1. 1898	48 seconds
2. Day	6' 11"		
3. Hoy	6' 4"		

The Fifth Field Day: May 1899

The *New York Tribune* claimed that ninety Vassarites were in training for this field day. Thirty took part in the races.

The *World* described the circle that day:

> The contests were held on the oval within the thick hedge which conceals the girls from masculine gaze when they indulge in athletics. Four hundred or more students assembled to see the sports, every one of the four classes being represented by enthusiastic spectators. Each contingent tried to cheer louder and make more noise generally than its rival classes in encouraging its champions to their utmost endeavors in the various contests. The rooters wore the colors of their class, and carried banners to match. The seniors displayed green in profusion, the juniors showed yellow, the sophomores white and the freshmen red.
>
> The fair athletes were attired in the regulation gymnasium costume, consisting of loose fitting blue bloomers, blue blouse and black stockings. Everyone wore a sweater with the class number on its front, which was held by an admiring classmate while the contestant was engaged, and when the match was over the second would rush into the field and pull the sweater over her principal's head with all the gusto of a masculine football enthusiast. It was typical football weather, too, cloudy and damp, with just a sprinkle of rain toward the end of the exercises. The honors of the day fell to Miss Louise Sommer Holmquist, a New York girl, of the sophomore class, and captain of her class basketball team. Miss Holmquist won the running broad jump contest and the hundred yard dash in fine style.

The May 13 field day began at 10 A.M. and ended at noon. Four new records were produced. Holmquist, president of the Class of 1901, lowered the 100-yard dash record to 13⅘ seconds and won the running broad jump with a leap of 13' 1". Bradley recaptured her 1897 title in the baseball throw and set a record of 170' 3". She also won the basketball throw, making her the other double winner.

Lockwood repeated her previous year's victory in the 120-yard hurdles in the record time of 21⅖ seconds, clipping nearly a second from her old mark of 22⅕ seconds. The final record was set by the Class of 1900 in the three-person 300-yard relay. The new time was 43 seconds.

100-yard dash		300-yard relay	
1. Holmquist	13⅘ seconds	1. 1900	43 seconds
120-yard hurdles		Running high jump	
1. Lockwood	21⅖ seconds	1. Wells	3' 9"
		White	
220-yard dash		Running broad jump	
1. Fowler	38⅖ seconds	1. Holmquist	13' 1"

Standing broad jump		Baseball throw	
1. Bourne	6' 10½"	1. Bradley	170' 3"
Fence vault		Basketball throw	
1. Clark	4' 1"	1. Bradley	54' 2"
Shot put			
1. Long	18' 8"		

From these aggressive beginnings, the women of Vassar College, with great pride, conducted a very competitive track and field program for forty-two years, despite the fact that at the outset in 1895:

1) women did not compete in track and field
2) women did not participate in track and field events
3) women did not strive to set records
4) women did not train three hours a week for competition

The Vassar College women competed intensely in as many as thirteen track and field events, were amazingly organized right down to the printed program, had a woman starter that fired a starter's gun, wore spiked shoes, and pitted one class against the other every May for forty-two uninterrupted years. The competition was conducted complying with the Amateur Athletic Union rule book, which was written and observed by men, before the Amateur Athletic Union became the governing body for women's track in the United States in 1923.

Vassar's records were carefully kept and were publicly displayed in newspapers and magazines of the day; they appeared nationally for the first time in the 1903 *Spalding's Athletic Almanac*. Breaking records was important to Vassar women. Field day was not a play day. Record-breaking performances were rewarded with a "V." An example of the young women's dedication to excellence can be found in an 1910 article in the Vassar newspaper. "We have a high standard to live up to in the world's records of women's athletics, as Vassar already holds the majority of them."

From 1895 through 1903, the competition took place on grass despite the fact that students had asked for a track prior to 1900. The 1901 yearbook, the *Vassarion*, contained the following verse:

> We asked them for a running track
> But firm they stood and would not yield
> Because, they said, a track would spoil
> The beauty of the athletic field.

In 1904, their long awaited, student-funded, four-lane cinder track was completed.

With hundreds of long-skirted classmates crowding around the track, carrying class banners and shouting cheers of encouragement, records were smashed year after year. Six records fell in 1900 when the 4-foot barrier was broken in the high jump. In 1902, Evelyn Gail Gardiner leaped more than 14 feet in the broad jump. In 1903, Agnes Wood ran the 220-yard dash, in a circle, in the notable time of 30.6 seconds. In 1904, freshman Alice Belding threw the base-

May 9, 1914, Twentieth Field Day at Vassar College, M. Tilden winning the 50-yard dash. Note spiked shoes. (Courtesy of Special Collections, Vassar College Libraries.)

ball the amazing distance of 195' 3"and "forever silenced those male cynics who are fond of saying that a woman cannot throw anything."

In 1906, class track teams were organized for the first time. More than sixty girls were on the four class teams. In 1907, an indoor meet was held. The first records for the meet were kept in 1909. The indoor meet continued until 1921. The high jump and basketball throw were the field events contested.

Elizabeth Hardin was a freshman in 1913 and began her four-year winning and record-setting streak in the shot, basketball, and baseball throws. Elizabeth's records in these events were so outstanding that her 33' 11" shot put mark would have won the gold medal in that event in the 1923, 1924, and 1925 national Amateur Athletic Union championships. In the 1925 national championships, Elizabeth would have defeated Lillian Copeland, the 1932 Olympic gold medalist in the discus.

So many girls aspired to compete in the field days that participation standards were set by the four class managers in 1913. An athlete had to meet the standard in order to participate in the track and field events. In 1916, there were 121 girls training in anticipation of making the qualifying standards for field day.

In 1921, on the day that Madame Curie gave her first public address in the United States in the Vassar Chapel, Rita Fuguet captured three first places in the running broad jump, the 100-yard dash, and the hop, step, and jump. She was awarded the Shattuck Cup, first presented in 1909, for the individual scoring the greatest number of points.

Ever mindful of their place in the record books, the Vassar women compared their records to those of other colleges by sending questionnaires to Bryn Mawr, Mount Holyoke, and Wellesley. This was intercollegiate competition for women in the 20's. Vassar excelled in four events. Relative to men's and women's performances, the school newspaper commented, "The fact that women's college records bear any comparison at all with those of men's colleges shows that at least the day has gone by when women fainted gracefully at the mere thought of exertion."

The javelin throw was added to the program in 1926. Vassar's first spear thrower, Lucy Hall, threw further than our first two United States national champions.

As the years passed, Betty Buck reached the 5-foot mark in the high jump, Frances Preston soared past 15 feet in the broad jump, and Betty Woolsey bounded over 33 feet in the hop, step, and jump, an event that as of 1992, was not yet on the Olympic program for women.

A most memorable moment came in 1934 when Alice Egan broke the longest-standing record of thirty years in the 50-yard dash that had been set in 1904 by Fanny James, her mother.

The field days turned into sports days by 1934. In 1936, the event was called a dual track meet. When Peggy Davis threw the discus 88' 10" for the final track and field record in 1937, a distance that would have won the gold medal in the United States for the first three national AAU championships, the competition was called a physical education classes track meet. And then it disappeared. Track was finished at Vassar. It finally succumbed to the physical educators' philosophy of the times.

The 1908 *Vassarion* best captured the essence of field day by stating:

> [It was] a most exhilarating day of sport culminating weeks of training from the raw days of March to the softer days of April and May. It is a sudden return to the spirit of romping childhood to play about in the circle, to run a race as if your life depended upon the winning of it, and then to laugh and try again when you are beaten, to labor unceasingly at the broad jump, to exult as the bar creeps higher and higher in the high jump — to do all these things and to delight in the purpose and effort to do them well, this is the spirit of spring training.
>
> The day itself, both for those who actually enter the contests and for those who cheer them on, stands most completely for the spirit of true sportsmanship.

Chapter 3

The Other Colleges

Elmira College

The catalogue for the year 1862-63 states, "All the students are required to walk at least half an hour daily in the open air."

Physical Education at Elmira College traces the history of track and field activities at the college. The first field day was held on June 12, 1897. The activities included basketball, tennis, and a 50-yard dash.

Elmira continued to have annual field days, sometimes in the fall and other times in the spring. The track and field events fluctuated from year to year. On June 9, 1900, the events included the standing broad jump, 50-yard hurdle race, baseball throwing, the running broad jump, potato race, 50-yard dash, goal throwing, 100-yard dash, quarter-mile walk, tennis, and a basketball game.

Elmira's field day events as reported in the 1904 junior yearbook, the *Iris*:

50-yard dash	Nina Ganung	7⅕
Shot put	Clara Termansen	30'
40-yard hurdle	Marian Amick	7⅕
High jump	Nina Ganung	3' 9½"
Baseball throwing	Clara Banfield	129' 6"
75-yard dash	Nina Ganung	10⅖
60-yard hurdle	Nina Ganung	10⅗
Running broad jump	Nina Ganung	12' 4"
Basketball throwing	Nina Ganung	58'
Goal throwing	Linnette Adriance	Four goals out of six

The November 10, 1917, field day included tennis, field hockey, and track and field. The track and field events and winners were documented in *Physical Education at Elmira College*:

Hurdles	Grayce Searles	
50-yard dash	Dorothy Prechtl	
Shot put	Janet Preumers	24' 3"
High jump	Adelaide Noll	
Baseball throwing	Hannah Pickering	144' 8"
Relay race	Seniors	

During the 1922-23 season, a track team was organized. The 1924 field day included "races."

The 1926 report in *Physical Education at Elmira College* noted a "mass track meet in the form of a field day." It was to have been held in October of 1925 but was postponed twice because of bad weather. "This new event, sponsored by the Athletic Association was finally held in late May. It was the very first inter-class track meet at Elmira College." These results were cited:

Javelin throw	Elizabeth King	55' 11"
50-yard dash	Alta Brace	7⅖
Broad jump	Ernestine Bunnell	14' 3"
Discus throw	Elizabeth King	59'
High jump	Ernestine Bunnell	4' 7"
Hurdles	Alta Brace	
Baseball throw	Ernestine Bunnell	159' 10"

Mount Holyoke College

The *History of Physical Education at Mount Holyoke College 1837–1955* by Mildred S. Howard quoted *The Book of Duties* from 1837: "The young ladies are to be required to walk one mile per day till the snow renders it desirable to specify time instead of distance, then three quarters of an hour is the time required." According to Howard, "Half mile posts were set up on the nine roads leading out of South Hadley. A controversy soon arose as to whether one should walk up to the post or around it. In 1862 two miles a day were required."

Mount Holyoke's first field day was held in May 1897. The *Mount Holyoke* of June 1897 reported: "Wednesday, May 19, was chosen for field day and never were wind and weather more favorable. The sports began with a basketball game. ... The hundred yards dash was won by Jessie Harrington (1900), who made it in 12.7 seconds. May Lane made the best time in the boat race. ... Not content with this victory, May Lane also made the best record at throwing the baseball." Other events that day included tennis and a slow bicycle race, according to Howard.

The 1898-99 *Students' Handbook* included a paragraph about field day, calling it "one of the most pleasant features of the spring term."

In October of 1903, the *Mount Holyoke*, indicated that the Athletic Association declared that field day should be an annual occurrence and should be held on a fixed day in October. "An area for track and field was constructed behind the gymnasium," said Howard. The Mount Holyoke yearbook, the *Llamarada*, in 1905 reported the results of the October 28, 1903, field day:

50-yard dash		1. Helen Buck	31'	
1. Marion Keese	6½	2. Mary Allyn	26' 6"	
Shot put		Mary Beard	26' 6"	

Running broad jump
1. Helen Buck   12' 3"
2. Marion Keese   12' 2"
3. Eveline Lyle   12' 1"

75-yard dash
1. Marion Keese $9\frac{4}{5}$
2. Helen Buck   10

Running high jump
1. Faith Kelton   4'11"
    (reported height questioned by author)

2. Marion Keese   4' 1"
3. Alice Noyes   3' 10"

Hurdle race
1. Eveline Lyle $9\frac{1}{5}$
2. Alice Dodge $11\frac{3}{5}$

Throwing ball
1. Helen Buck   150'
2. Ruth Potwine   127'
3. Lottie Lane   122' 8"

The college records were also listed:

Running broad jump	Marion Keese	13'
Putting shot	Helen Buck	32' 9"
75-yard dash	Alice Cook	$9\frac{2}{5}$
Running high jump	Esther Heacock	4' 2"

    In 1904, the *Students' Handbook* described field day as "one of the most important events of the college year." The 1906 *Handbook* advised that field day had been changed back to the month of May, which gave the freshmen a better opportunity to compete equally with the other classes. "Class spirit runs high in competition for championship."

    The May 23, 1925, field day program lists track events starting at 9 A.M. Track shared the program with archery, cricket, swimming, tennis, and riding.

    In 1932, two new tennis courts were built in the space formerly occupied by the oval running track.

Wellesley College

    Wellesley College held its first field day on May 15, 1899. The Athletic Association–sponsored event featured golf, tennis, basketball, a slow bicycle race, four running races, a potato race, a three-legged race, an obstacle race, and a 50-yard dash. The *Boston Evening Record* said: "The 50-yard dash stirred the whole multitude up. All the classes raced in turn, but Miss Rockwell of 1900 won the championship. Miss Sanborn came in close at her heels and won great applause."

    The *Wellesley Magazine* in 1900 said: "Miss Hill has kindly consented to give instruction in running and jumping to such girls as may wish to train for field-day events. In place of gymnasium work cross-country running is to be offered. Instruction will be given by a man from the Boston Athletic Association." This was Herbert H. Holton, who was listed as "Instructor of Running and Hurdling" on the field day program in 1902.

    On October 29, 1902, the *College News* disclosed in an article written by

Lucille Eaton Hill that Wellesley had a "fine cinder track." Field day took on a new look that year. The "stunt" races were eliminated and replaced with low hurdling and a relay race. Each class entered four girls. The winner of the low hurdles was Maria Dowd. No time was given. The class of 1906 won the relay in 1 minute and 27 seconds. There were four girls on a team, and each girl ran one lap, about 300 yards. Other sports contested were basketball, tennis, hockey, and golf.

The shot put was added in 1903. The track and field portion of the 1903 field day program follows:

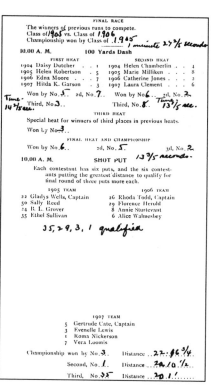

1903 Wellesley College field day program showing field day entries, events and results. (Courtesy of Wellesley College Archives.)

Randolph-Macon Woman's College

The 1899 yearbook, the *Helianthus*, reported:

> Our enthusiastic Director makes the girls enthusiastic, until the records in vaulting, running, hurdling, broad jump, standing high jump are above the average. And field day! How it is enjoyed! Not merely because of the holiday it affords, not only because we "get out of classes," but for the sheer love of the sports themselves. The morning for field day arrives; all are impatient to begin. "Who will be the champion?" is the remark heard on all sides. But, look; see that potato race; "practice makes perfect." "They must certainly have had lots of practice," one hears a bystander say. Now the three-legged race, the fifty yard dash, the hopping race, and, above all, the hurdle race — how it is all enjoyed. ... Now

the champion is carried triumphantly off the field on the shoulders of the perhaps envious, yet enthusiastic competitors.

The 1914 *Helianthus* listed the field day records:

50-yard dash	Margaret Rhea	6¾
75-yard dash	Eloise Parsons	10⅗
50-yard hurdle	Laura Argue	8⅖
8-lb. shot	Annie Whiteside	26' 2"
Basketball throw	Lillian Maben	69' 3"
Baseball throw	Elizabeth Griffith	148' 1"
Vault	Elise Paxton	4' 8"
Running high jump	Dorothy Cure	4' 4"
Running broad jump	Dorothy Cure	15' 2½"
Standing broad jump	Dorothy Cure	8' 2"
Hop-step-jump	Dorothy Cure	29' 10½"
Relay race	Class of 1914	25⅕

In 1915, Alice H. Belding was the starter for field day. Alice taught at the school after graduating from Vassar College. She was a field day champion at Vassar College and later returned to Vassar to teach.

The *Sun Dial* of May 7, 1926, reported the highlights of field day: "The most interesting event of the day was the discus throw, won by Borghild Prior with a record of 100' 2". This event gave to Randolph-Macon the honor of establishing a new intercollegiate record, and caused great enthusiasm among spectators and contestants. Prior also broke the Randolph-Macon record for baseball throwing." Prior's throw was 197' 4".

Bryn Mawr College

Bryn Mawr's Athletic Association was formed in 1892. An "annual sports and drill" held indoors early in the month of April produced a record in the high jump. The *Lantern* indicated in June 1892 that Mary H. Ritchie broke the record for jumping. Her high jump mark was 4' 1".

In 1893, the high jump ended in a tie between Miss Nicholson and Miss Bowman. The record was not broken as the winning height was 3' 10". The "indoor drill" consisted of rope climbing, high kick, high jump, and vault.

The *Lantern* indicated that interest in individual work was increased by establishing records. The records in jumping are usually made "on Thursday afternoons, and all the students who can make the effort take part. In the course of ten minutes the contest narrows down to some half dozen, and this number gradually dwindles to two or three." The record that Mary H. Ritchie broke in high jumping 4' 1" in April of 1892 was probably done on a Thursday afternoon, according to Caroline Rittenhouse, the Bryn Mawr College archivist.

Field day report from the 1909 *Helianthus*, the yearbook of Randolph-Macon Woman's College. (Courtesy Randolph-Macon Woman's College Archives.)

On April 27, 1894, the high jump record was broken again, the *Lantern* reported. Mary G. Frost jumped 4' 2".

By 1898, the standing and running broad jumps were on the indoor program. That year the high jump was won by Miss Phillips with a leap of 4' 1", the running broad jump winner was Miss Churchill with a jump of 10', and the standing broad jump was won by Miss Williams with an effort of 5' 10". Both broad jumps were records.

In 1899, the results of the indoor meet disclosed the first dash. It was a sprint of 15 yards. The standing high jump and a hurdle race were also new to the program. The 15-yard dash was won by Miss Houghton in 2 seconds. Miss Williams won the standing high jump with a leap of 3'. Miss Haines won the running high jump, leaping 3' 10". Miss Adams won the standing broad jump with a distance of 6' 8". Miss Haines also won the short hurdle race in 2.55 seconds.

The first field day was held in 1899. The *Fortnightly Philistine* of April 28 stated: "Field day is a welcome addition to the list of out-door sports, and has the further value of arousing interest in contests which were never entered into with much zest before. Although this field day suffered somewhat from being the first of its kind, ... its results were in no way discouraging."

The events and results follow:

Hurdle race (80 feet — 3 hurdles)		Hop, skip and jump		
1. M. Ayer	6	1. M. Ayer	22' ½"	
Walking race (235 feet)		Throwing the baseball		
1. H. Hunt	18	1. F. Sinclair	137' 1"	
Putting the shot		Throwing the basketball		
1. M. Ayer	21' 1"	1. E. Houghton	76' ½"	
235-foot dash		Running broad jump		
1. M. Ayer	11	1. M. Haines	11' 6"	

In 1905, the *Tipyn o' Bob* reported in January, February, and April that the members of the Athletic Association had decided to organize a track team in each class and had approved awarding letters for track. Following its indoor track meet in March, Bryn Mawr claimed that the class of 1905 held world records in the high jump, standing broad jump, and hop, skip, and jump.

During the 1906 year, track practice was held in the gymnasium on Tuesdays from 8:30 to 10 P.M.

In 1907, the *Lantern* said, "The track meet was noteworthy for the fact that the world's record for women in the shot-put was broken by Marjorie Young, '08, her distance being 33 feet 1 inch."

In 1912, Bryn Mawr adopted the events that were contested in Vassar's field day and moved the meet outdoors with the goal of beating Vassar's records, according to the *Lantern*.

Mary Churchman Morgan was a Bryn Mawr freshman in 1912. During the track meet that year, she won the 100-yard dash in 12 seconds and the 50-yard dash in 6⅕ seconds, setting college and world records. The Bryn Mawr high jump record was also broken. L. Mudge jumped 4' 4" for first place.

During her sophomore year in 1913, Mary Morgan set a record in the standing broad jump of 7' 9½". In her junior year, 1914, she established a hurdle record of 15⅖ and won the individual cup. Prior to the track meet in 1915, in her senior year, Mary Morgan left college.

When Mary died in 1972 at age seventy-eight, her obituary in the September 22 *Philadelphia Inquirer* said she "held three world records in track."

Barnard College

On April 18, 1904, Barnard College held its first field day with two track and field events. The events contested were basketball, baseball throw, quoits, basketball throw, and tennis, reported the April 25 *Barnard Bulletin*. The winner of the basketball throw was Fanny McLean, and Agnes Ernst won the baseball throw.

The *Barnard Bulletin* of May 8, 1905, recounted the results of the May 1, 1905, field day. Four track and field events were contested. Agnes Ernst repeated her victory in the baseball throw, winning the event with a toss of 169' 3". Eleanor Hunsdon won the high jump with a leap of 4' 1". The standing broad jump was won by Florence Mastin with a jump of 6' 4⅝", and the senior team won the relay. The other events held were basketball throwing for goals and a basketball game.

Seven track and field events were on the schedule for the May 14, 1906, field day. The high jump was won with a leap of 4' 1" by Marion Wilson. Grace McColl won the basketball throw. Fannie Rosenfelder jumped 7' 4" to win the standing broad jump. Agnes Ernst won the shot put, and Helen Williams won the dash. The class of 1906 captured the hurdles and the relay. Other events of field day included basketball, baseball, and tennis.

The field days with track and field events were held until 1934.

Northwestern University

"Every young lady is required to walk a half an hour a day," stated the first catalogue of the Northwestern Female College in 1860.

After the formation of the Women's Athletic Association in 1911, a major "N" was awarded to girls who scored a great number of points in the annual spring field day, which consisted of track and field, tennis, and baseball, according to *Women in Athletics*.

Results of the March 29, 1915, track meet, from the *Daily Northwestern* on March 31, follow:

Basketball throw	66' 11"	Esther Frisbee
220-yard dash	32⅗	Mabel McConnell
50-yard hurdles	7⅗ (record)	Josephine Holmes
50-yard dash	6⅕	Josephine Holmes
8-lb. shot	25' 6"	Dorothy Fargo
Standing broad jump	7' 2¾"	Mabel McConnell
High Jump	4' 2"	Millie Davis and Josephine Holmes

The *Daily Northwestern* added that Josephine Holmes and Mabel McConnell tied for high honors in scoring eighteen points. Miss McConnell scored points in six of the seven events of the meet.

Field day was discontinued in the early 1930s.

Mills College

"The walking club was organized in '01 as a branch of the Association," stated the *Chimes*, the Mills College yearbook, in 1914-15. By 1916, the Athletic Association was sponsoring track and field events.

The *Chimes* of 1919-20 stated:

> This year the field meet will have a very novel feature. The main events, such as the fifty-yard dash, seventy-five yard dash, broad jump, high jump and relay race will be run and the records will be compared with those made by the students at Bryn Mawr in a similar contest on the same day. Thus we will be able to get a rough estimate as to the comparative prowess of Eastern and Western girls. The results will be compared and the victorious college decided upon. It will be the first time any competition has taken place between an Eastern and Western woman's college.

Results of the March 26, 1923, meet from the *Chimes* for 1922-23 follow:

75-yard dash	Mildred Wescott	9⅘
High jump	Eugenia Grunsky	4' 3"
Discus	Eugenia Grunsky	76' 10"

| Running broad jump | Marian Buck | 14' 3" |
| Baseball throw | Marcia Hayes | 153' |

Although track was discontinued in 1923, the walking club continued through 1930. A pin was awarded to members completing 400 miles, 200 of which were to be covered in the first semester.

University of Nebraska

Walking was part of the early program. In 1891, senior Louise Pound originated a girls' walking club, according to Mabel Lee in her book, *75 years of Professional Preparation in Physical Education for Women at the University of Nebraska, 1898–1973.* Lee notes that the 1906 catalogue shows track and field as one of the department offerings.

The 1915 *Cornhusker* described the girls' attitude towards track: "When Coach Reed is rounding his track men into shape, the girls catch the fever and sprint along with the speed of a reese or top the bar with the grace of a ross."

The custom of awarding "N's" to the girls for their prowess in athletics was originated in 1912 when it occurred to those in charge that there should be some reward of merit for the girls. The requirements ... were a first, second, or third in some field or track event. The track and field records for 1915 follow:

25-yard dash	3⅘	1914	Florence Simmons
Shot put	29' 9"	1914	Blanche Higgins
50-yard dash	7⅓	1913	Florence Simmons
Basketball throw	71' 8"	1913	Lottie Savage
40-yard hurdles	7⅓	1914	Florence Simmons
High jump	4'	1914	Marie Clark
Baseball throw	168' 3"	1914	Mabel Longacre
Pole vault	5' 6"	1914	Eva Fisk

"It is interesting to note that practically all the records are as high or exceed those of Vassar, Wellesley, Smith and California, the other four schools at which a girls' track meet is an annual event," reported the 1915 *Cornhusker.*

Sweet Briar College

The first field day began in 1909 under the direction of Miss Martha Plaisted, a graduate of Bryn Mawr. A loving cup donated by the faculty was presented to the outstanding athlete, according to *The Story of Sweet Briar College,* written by Martha Lou Lemmon Stohlman.

In 1924, sport shirts and knee-length running pants were permitted for field day, which accounted for the high jump record being raised from 3' 6" to 4' 3".

Skidmore College

Skidmore's first field day was held on June 21, 1915. Their second annual field day was held on June 24, 1916. That day produced dramatic results. Headlines in the *Herald* on June 26, 1916, proclaimed that senior, Maude Devereux of Ludlow, Vermont, jumped 16' 9½" in the running broad jump. Other unidentified clippings heralded a new world's record by the Skidmore girl. The Vassar record at that time was 14' 6½".

The events and results follow:

50-yard hurdles		L. Dagenkolb
150-yard relay		Seniors
50-yard dash	6⅘	Maude Devereux
Baseball throw	147' 2"	N. Field
Basketball throw	63' 6"	J. Thompson
Discus	59' 7"	L. Dagenkolb
High jump	4' 3"	H. Carter
Running broad jump	16' 9½"	Maude Devereux
Standing broad jump	8'	Maude Devereux
Hop, step, and jump	33' 4½"	Maude Devereux

Skidmore also had an annual fall field day. The 1922 fall field day on November 4 produced another record. Martha Murdock of Poughkeepsie "threw the discus with great ease and skill, breaking the American women's record in this event." She threw the discus 100'. These reports were contained in unidentified newspaper clippings from the Skidmore library.

The events in both the spring and the fall field days were similar. Results of the fall field day follow:

50-yard dash	7	Marie Crowley
Hurl ball	66' 5"	Mary Saunders
Standing broad jump	8' 4¼"	Lois McAdams
Hurdle race		Adelaide Baumer
Baseball throw	191' 3"	Mary Saunders
Running broad jump	13' 7"	Emma Gammons
Discus throw	100'	Martha Murdock
Javelin throw	67' 11"	Martha Murdock
High jump	4'	Emma Gammons

Syracuse University

The first "Woman's Day" was held on May 16, 1914. Besides tennis and basketball, an interclass track meet was held. The *Syracuse Daily Orange* said, "a track meet in the forenoon furnished the most excitement of the day." The events and results follow:

High jump	4' 3"	Rita Parker
Shot put	26' 6"	Rita Parker
100-yard dash	13	Dora Ruland
Hurl ball		Ethel Stewart
Baseball throw		Margaret O'Brien
Running broad jump	13' 2"	Dora Ruland

The track meets continued to be held as part of Woman's Day until 1924, when the *Onodagan* reported that the "first annual track meet took place, consisting of hurdle, obstacle and relay events." It was also reported that Hendricks Field, with a quarter-mile oval track, was completed.

Oregon State University (formerly Oregon Agricultural College)

An athletic meet described in the Oregon Agricultural College *Daily Barometer* of December 11, 1917, included some races in addition to basketball games and a posture contest. The races were "a patriotic relay race, an obstacle race and a track relay." Each relay team consisted of four representatives from one class.

In March 1925, the *OAC Alumnus* said: "Since the women have been granted the privilege of practicing and holding track meets on Bell Field, track sports has taken long strides forward. The classes and practices have to be held in the early morning hours, but the girls don't mind that so much in the spring."

The 1926-27 *Beaver* exulted: "Picture a crisp spring morning! Out on Bell Field, girls may be seen running, jumping or practicing those events in which they are most interested. ... Women's track day is one of the big days of the year. Then it is that the faithful aspirant, who has practiced every morning and excelled in her event, is chosen to represent her class."

The 1927 interclass meet produced better results because a ruling was enacted to require every girl to have eight practice sessions in order to be eligible for the meet.

Records for the school were listed in the OAC *Daily Barometer* on May 8, 1926:

50-yard dash	6⅖	Discus	87'
100-yard dash	12⅖	Shot put	26' 9"
60-yard hurdles	9	Javelin	63' 1"
High jump	4' 7"	Baseball throw	180'
Broad jump	15' 8"	Basketball throw	70' 2"

Oregon State University field day photo published in the 1920 yearbook, *Beaver*, showing athletes competing in field day events and their records. (Courtesy of Oregon State University Archives.)

Florida State University (formerly Florida State College for Women)

In April 1919, sophomore Eleanor Brewer broke the national women's record in the discus throw during field day competition. The April 19, 1919, *Florida Flambeau* listed the record at 77'. Miss Brewer's throw was 80' 4". In addition to winning a sweater for best all-around, Miss Brewer was presented a small silver discus by the Athletic Advisory Board.

Classes were developed to teach skills and techniques in track and field events. It was decided that with proper form and training, breaking records would be easy.

New events in 1920 were the standing high jump, hurl ball, and the javelin throw according to the *Florida Flambeau* of March 6, 1920. On March 20, the paper reported that eighty-one girls entered the field day preliminaries and as at Vassar, the five girls with the best performances for a given event competed on field day.

Freshman Nell Carroll from Monticello, Florida, broke two national records in the two-day meet in 1920, the discus throw and the hurl ball, a new event. Yearbook accounts in the 1921 *Flastacowo*, have her marks in these events as 86' 7" in the discus and 104' 3" in the hurl ball event.

For her efforts, Nell Carroll became the first freshman at FSWC to win the coveted Spaulding sweater as the best all-around athlete. Nell won first place in the basketball throw, standing high jump, discus throw, and hurl ball. She placed second in the running hop, step, and jump and the javelin throw, and was third in the baseball throw.

Another outstanding performance was given by Antoinette "Tony" Mullikin. Tony, a sophomore, tied the world record in the 100-yard dash in 12 flat and the world record in the hurdles in 15⅖.

The records set were not officially accepted because of a three-foot grade in the athletic field where the competition was held. As a result, the college worked on the field in order to get credit for any future record set.

Prior to field day, national records were compared to the records of the Florida State College for Women. Florida State College was recognized nationally in the discus throw at 87' 7". Bryn Mawr held the hurl ball record at 85' 4½", however, even though Nell Carroll's record measured 104' 3", according to the *Florida Flambeau* of March 5, 1921.

During the field day of 1921, Nell Carroll bettered her personal records. The *Florida Flambeau* reported on April 2, 1921, that she set a world discus mark at 98' 2" and threw the hurl ball 112' 7".

The 1922 *Flastacowo* lists the records:

High jump	4' 3"	Dorothy Dodd
	4' 3"	Margaret Boyle
100-yard dash	12	Antoinette Mullikin
Hop-step-jump	30' 3"	Virginia Holland
Javelin	65' 11½"	Anne Harwick
Hurdles	15⅖	Antoinette Mullikin
50-yard dash	6⅗	Elizabeth Peschmann
Standing broad jump	7' 7"	Dorothy Richey
Basketball throw	73' 11"	Nell Carroll
Baseball throw	180' 10"	Anne Harwick
Shot put	27'	Anne Harwick
Standing high jump	3' 4"	Helen Harris
Running broad jump	16'	Emma Lee King
Discus (national record)	98' 2"	Nell Carroll
Hurl ball (national record)	112'	Nell Carroll

University of Illinois–Urbana

Copies of photographs obtained from the archives of the library at the University of Illinois–Urbana show the finish of a relay race and the high jump event in a girls' track meet on May 23, 1918.

A program for a women's track and field meet on May 15, 1923, included the following events:

50-yard dash	60-yard low hurdles	Baseball throw
Discus throw	Javelin throw	Half mile relay
High jump	100-yard dash	

The school catalogue for 1923-24 also lists a half-credit course in tennis/track.

University of Chicago

The 1919 *Cap and Gown*, the yearbook published by the junior class, reported that the Athletic Association took charge of the annual spring meet for the first time. The program for the day included tennis, baseball, long ball and university ball, relays, broad jump, and folk dancing.

The second annual spring meet was held on June 5, 1920. The events were tennis, baseball, and competitions in running, jumping, and dancing.

Rockford College

The 1917-18 *Rockford College Catalogue* mentions a fall field day sponsored by the Athletic Association, but the events scheduled for the day were not documented.

Walking was a prominent activity at this time. The walking club awarded a "500" pin to those walking 500 miles. Sixteen girls received the pin in the 1916-17 school year and twenty-two girls in the 1919-20 year, according to the yearbook.

An indoor meet was held on March 18, 1918, stated the 1918-19 yearbook, the *Cupola*. The events were marching, dancing, and the running high jump, which appeared under the heading of "apparatus work."

University of Wisconsin–Madison

Field days at the University of Wisconsin are described in the *Badger*, the 1923 yearbook:

> June 4, 1921, marked the culmination of the year's athletic achievements among women in the annual field day program at Camp Randall.
>
> For days before the final event, classes had practiced, preliminary track meets had taken place, and participants had been selected from the splendid material available.

Promptly at 2:30 o'clock, field day activities started with the championship tennis matches. ... Interest rose as the staccato report of a revolver set off the participants in the track events. Girls were throwing the baseball and basketball, hurling the javelin, and performing feats at broad and high jumping. ... Field day has a real significance, for it marks the progress of the women in the athletic life of the University.

University of Arizona

The Athletic Association was organized in 1920. In 1921, according to the yearbook, the *Desert*, a "girl's field meet" was held for the first time. The girls played hockey and captainball, however, while the walking relay and the running relay were interfraternal events.

The only event in the track and field program for women was to be a basketball distance throw, but high winds forced its cancellation.

University of Kansas

The Women's Athletic Association was formed in 1915, and the first track meet was held in 1917.

The *University Daily Kansan* of May 20, 1926, announced, "Telegraphic Meet Is First of Kind to Be Held Here." The events were a bicycle race, 50-yard dash, shot put, high jump, 60-yard high hurdles, basketball throw, discus throw, broad jump, 75-yard dash, baseball throw, 100-yard run, 60-yard low hurdles, hop, step, and jump, 220-yard relay, javelin throw, and 500-yard relay (10 runners).

Results of the meet were telegraphed to the offices of the Women's Collegiate and Scholastic Track Meet Association with headquarters in Long Beach, California. The rules required that the local meets be held between May 20 and May 30. The final report of the results was released on June 1. Amateur Athletic Union rules governed the competitions. No woman was allowed to enter more than three events. Each team had to enter the 500-yard relay, and a relay team consisted of ten runners running 50 yards each. Nine other events had to be entered, but the team selected any nine of the events.

Prior to the telegraphic meet, Kansas held meets for the first time in 1925 and established nine new records during the 1926 year. Marion Riley's baseball throw of 210 feet was within seven feet of the intercollegiate record, reported the May 23, 1926, *University Daily Kansan*. Miss Riley set three other records in the throwing events. Practice sessions for the telegraphic meet were held daily.

During the telegraphic meet on May 22, 1926, six of the university's records were broken. The 50-yard dash record was lowered to 6.8 by May Snead. She also lowered the 75-yard dash time to 9.9. Marion Riley threw the baseball 200' 7" and hurled the javelin 55' 8". Ruth Martin broke her own record in the 60-yard high hurdles, jumping the barriers in 9.8. Hila Church won the 100-yard dash in 13, which was 1.2 seconds faster than the previous record.

Top: **The University of Kansas field day. Athletes crossing the finish line. (Courtesy of University of Kansas Archives.)** *Bottom:* **Athlete from the University of Kansas hurdling. (Courtesy of the University of Kansas Archives.)**

Stanford University

Records from *A History of Physical Education for Women at Stanford University and a Survey of the Department of Physical Education for Women in 1943-44*, by Elizabeth Zimmerli, indicate that track and field was an activity from 1923 through 1931 at Stanford University, a period of nine years. The catalogue of 1922-23, the *Stanford Register*, lists track as a course for each of the four classes and the graduate level.

The *Daily Palo Alto* on April 20, 1923, had an article about the scheduled first field day. The article, "Women's Track Meet Should Prove Big Sensation of the Athletic World," contained many derisive statements:

> Sprinters have already hung up the mark of 7 seconds flat for the 50 yard dash. The time was taken with a cuckoo clock. ... Both high and low hurdles are to be run. Inclined ramps will be constructed to aid the weak sisters over the last gate. ... Loss of a hair-pin counts as a penalty of one second. ... The shot put is the only weight event adopted by the women. Beginning with an electric light bulb, the weightresses have already progressed to an orange and by the time of the meet they will be tossing a five pound bronze doorknob.

Many newspapers had had accounts of field days in colleges from coast to coast since 1895, but this was by far the most demeaning, sarcastic article written.

The field day on May 29, 1924, reported in the 1926 *Stanford Quad*, saw a Pacific coast intercollegiate record of 6⅗ in the 50-yard dash set by Lorraine Cleaveland. Alice Roth, who won the 65-yard low hurdles and the 60-yard high hurdles, was the high scorer of the meet.

The winners of the events follow:

50-yard dash	Cleaveland	Broad jump	Koeck
75-yard dash	Watson	Shot put	Williams
65-yard low hurdles	Roth	High jump	Watson
60-yard high hurdles	Roth	Baseball throw	Koeck

The 1928 *Stanford Quad* reported:

> After a season of daily practice, with timing and tryouts in the different events, and a series of interclass meets, the 1927 track season culminated with the interclass track meet on field day, May 26th. ... Both of the Stanford records broken in the meet were shattered by Marion Holley, '30, in the running broad jump and the high jump. Her distance for the former was 15' 5". ... In the high jump, she broke the record set two years before by Marie Manchee, going over at 4' 5½". Holley is now in training for the Olympic Games in these events.

50-yard dash	6.8 (new record)	Holley
100-yard dash	12.8	Fordyce
60-yard hurdles	12.5	Joyce Lyon
85-yard hurdles	12.5 (new record)	Joyce Lyon
Basketball throw	68' 3"	Watson
Baseball throw	174' 5½" (new record)	Watson
Shot put	26' 7"	Sutton
Hop, step, and jump		Sutton
Running broad jump	15' 5" (new record)	Holley
Standing broad jump		Mason
High jump	4' 5½" (new record)	Holley
Relay	38.6	Class of 1930

Smith College

The first track meet was held on the field day of 1926. So much interest was shown in the event that the June 3, 1926, *Smith College Weekly* proclaimed, "track will take an important place in sports here."

The results of the May 26, 1926, field day obtained from the Smith College archives follow:

75-yard dash	9⅘	G. Montgomery
High hurdles	10⅖	L. Cronin
50-yard dash	7	M. Kirk, A. Rodgers and M. Little
Running high jump	4' 7¾"	E. B. Pettee
Javelin	84' 8"	D. Bennett
Running broad jump	14' 5"	M. Hollister
Baseball throw	202'	E. B. Pettee
Hop, step, and jump	31' 11"	Agnes Rodgers
Low hurdles	10⅖	Agnes Rodgers
Standing broad jump	6' 7¾"	Jeanie Kerns
Discus	76' 11"	E. Warren

Freshman Agnes Rodgers accumulated 16 points, Pettee 13 points, and Warren 9⅓.

In 1927, Agnes Rodgers scored 31 points and was the high scorer for the second straight year. She won the 50-yard dash in 6⅘, the discus in 73' 2", the javelin throw in 82' 3", the baseball throw with a toss of 186' 3", and the standing broad jump with a leap of 7' 5". She placed second in the low hurdles and the hop, step, and jump.

The *Springfield Republican* on May 17, 1928, stated that the 1928 field day produced two intercollegiate records and six Smith College records. Agnes Rodgers from Buffalo, New York, accounted for the intercollegiate record of 9⅗ in the high hurdles (four hurdles — 2' 6" high). The other record was broken by Marion McInnis of Philadelphia in the hop, step, and jump. She jumped 32'. Once again, for the third straight year, Agnes Rodgers was the high scorer. Besides winning the hurdles in a new intercollegiate record, she won the baseball throw, discus throw, and low hurdles. She placed second in the 75-yard dash and the javelin throw.

In her senior year, Agnes Rodgers won the baseball throw, in 198' 5⅕", and broke her record in the javelin throw, tossing the spear 88'. For the fourth year, Agnes won the individual high score award.

As late as 1931-32, the *Physical Education Bulletin* listed track as a course offering, with Miss Aull as the instructor. In 1933, a newsletter stated, "No track this year" in reference to the field day.

Louisiana State University

According to the *Gumbo* in 1925, "The brightest jewel of the Tiger crown, as far as the girls' athletics is concerned, was placing fourth in the national telegraphic track and field meet, in which the Tigresses held their own with the best talent among the nation's women athletes."

Louisiana Tech University
(formerly Louisiana Industrial Institute)

In 1924 the Women's Athletic Association sponsored a team which entered the National Women's Telegraphic Track Meet. The team placed seventh out of many colleges and pledged to perform even better the following year.

The *Lagniappe* in 1925 reported that the Women's Athletic Association was celebrating its second anniversary and now had sixty members. Entrance into the organization was gained by making varsity teams in one of a number of sports, including track.

In 1926 the team placed second in the United States in the telegraphic meet.

The seventeen-member track squad of 1927 was coached by Miss Edna Arnold. To make the team, a girl had to enter at least three events.

Winthrop University
(formerly Winthrop College)

One of the colleges most involved in early track and field was Winthrop College. Field days were reported as early as 1901-02.

In 1922, Winthrop sent its outstanding athlete, Lucile Godbold, to the tryouts in Mamaroneck to compete for a place on the first international track and field team, which competed in Paris, representing the United States. Details of Lucile Godbold's international competitive experiences from the Winthrop College archives appear in the chapter on Mamaroneck and Paris.

Winthrop College was one of the first schools to participate in the National Telegraphic Track and Field Meet established in 1922. According to the May 8, 1927, *Charlotte Observer*, Mrs. Ruth Potwine Bartlett, a competitor in the 1903 field day at Mount Holyoke College and head of the physical education department, supported this event.

Eighty colleges throughout the United States held their track events during a certain time frame in May. The results were then wired to Howard G. Cleaveland, chairman of the committee for track results in Long Beach, California.

Winthrop won first place in 1923 and 1925 and placed third in 1924.

In 1925 Winthrop "received a telegram stating that ... Sarah Workman had won the most individual points." This placed her first in the United States in the National Telegraphic Track and Field Meet, with sixty-two colleges competing.

CLASS OF SERVICE | SYMBOL
Telegram
Day Letter | Blue
Night Message | Nite
Night Letter | N L

CLASS OF SERVICE | SYMBOL
Telegram
Day Letter | Blue
Night Message | Nite
Night Letter | N L

WESTERN UNION
TELEGRAM

NEWCOMB CARLTON, PRESIDENT   GEORGE W E ATKINS, FIRST VICE PRESIDENT

RECEIVED AT I5F   C   81 Collect   NL   I   Extra

Longbeach Calif May 22 1924

Mrs Ruth P Bartlett

Winthrop College Rock Hill SCar

REPORT TELEGRAPH MEET COLLEGE SECTION FINAL FIRST UNIVERSITY IOWA

THIRTY TWO SECOND GEORGE SCHOOL TWENTY SEVEN ONE HALF THIRD WINTHROP

COLLEGE TWENTY TWO ONE HALF FIRST PLACE SARA WORKMAN WINTHROP COLLEGE

FIFTEEN POINTS SECOND BLANCH BAILEY UNIVERSITY IOWA EIGHT POINTS DETAILED

LETTER FOLLOWS

HOWARD G CLEAVELAND   DIRECTOR 806A MAY 23

1924 Telegram from Telegraphic meet announcing third place finish for Winthrop College and first place win for Sara Workman from 1925 yearbook, *The Tatler*. (Courtesy of Winthrop University Archives.)

Winthrop sponsored a girls' meet for several years for the high schools in the northern part of the state. Its plan was to make the meet statewide in 1925, according to the *Johnsonian* of February 14, 1925.

Ohio Wesleyan University

The Women's Athletic Association was organized in 1918. In April 1926, the *Transcript*, the student newspaper, disclosed the start of women's track activities. The May edition announced the coming interclass track meet on May 28. Twelve practice sessions were required for participation in the meet. It was open to any woman in the university. During the halfway point of the meet, an intersorority 220-yard relay was scheduled.

On May 20, 1927, it was reported in the *Transcript* that the first-ever field day was to be held the following day. Field day events included shot, discus, javelin, baseball and basketball throws, high jump, and running events. Evelyn Ricard, the Women's Athletic Association president, was the high scorer, winning the baseball and javelin throws.

On May 28, 1927, fifty girls competed in the track meet. Twelve sororities ran the 220-yard relay, and seven other track events were held. The meet was a success as six records were broken in the baseball throw, javelin, 50-yard dash, high hurdles, quarter-mile walk, and interclass relay.

Results in the school newspaper did not include times, heights, or distances but emphasized that records were broken and that the junior class won.

Humboldt State University
(formerly Humboldt State College)

In 1926, Laura Herron left her position at Eureka High School and became a member of the faculty at Humboldt College. Under her guidance, the Women's Athletic Association was formed. Her star high school pupil, Elta Cartwright, enrolled at Humboldt in 1925. Working with Coach Herron, Elta became a national track star, making the 1928 Olympic team in the 100 meters, according to Joseph Forbes, *History of Athletics Humboldt State College 1914–1968.*

In a national women's telegraphic track and field meet in 1926, Humboldt placed first with 42 points, Louisiana Polytech, second; Battle Creek Normal, third; Ohio Wesleyan, fourth; Kansas University, fifth; Oklahoma University, sixth; Brena College seventh; Louisiana State, eighth; and Aberdeen Teachers ninth.

Records listed for Humboldt were:

50-yard dash	Elta Cartwright	5.9
100-yard dash	Elta Cartwright	11.8
60-yard hurdles	Ruth Stewart	9.0
220-yard relay	Mole, Stewart, Regli, Johnson	28.0
440-yard relay	Mole, Stewart, Regli, Johnson	58.1
High jump	Marie Howard	4' 8³⁄₁₆"
Broad jump	Elta Cartwright	16' 9"
8-lb. shot	Rose Mary Regli	30' 2¼"
Baseball throw	Eleanor Yocum	193' 8"

In an interclass contest in 1927, Elta Cartwright bettered the broad jump record. Her leap of 17' 10" in the annual play day was measured by four judges with a steel tape. Coach Herron intended to get the jump officially approved as a world record.

Mississippi State College for Women

The following records for 1929 appeared in October 1929 in the *American Physical Education Review* for Mississippi State College for Women:

50-yard dash	6¹⁄₁₀	Catherine Ward
75-yard dash	9⅓	Brunette Crawford
65-yard hurdles	10	Frances Howell
High jump	4' 8½"	Marion King
Basketball throw	72' 11"	Fannie Cox
Hurl ball throw	86' 8"	Ruth Martin
Javelin throw	70' 7"	Ruth Wallace
Discus throw	73' 1⅜"	Alcyone Warrington
Baseball throw	158' 5¾"	Ebbie Whitten

Earlham College

According to the *Sargasso*, the 1924 yearbook:

> Soon after spring vacation the attention of the coeds is drawn to track and with the first suitable weather, Comstock Field is covered with girls practicing the different throws and dashes. Track and field competition has gradually forged to the front. This year there has been adopted a new system here at Earlham. It is a program to perfect a schedule that will bring competition within the reach of every physical type represented in the Women's Athletic Association. Those unable to make a suitable time in the high or low hurdle races or the dashes, have under this new program, been given instruction in javelin, discus, baseball and basketball throws for distance.

College records were as follows:

Discus	78' 3"	Mary Windle
Javelin	67' 10"	Nellie Donovan
Baseball	154' 4½"	Mary Windle
75-yard dash	10	Elizabeth Parker
50-yard dash	6⅖	Elizabeth Parker
High hurdles	10	Margaret N. Taylor
Low hurdles	15⅓	Elizabeth Parker

The 1925 *Sargasso* said a special tribute was paid to the girl who attained the highest number of points in the track meet. The May Queen, chosen by the student body, crowned the victor of the meet and presented to her the Ray B. Mowe Medal.

Chapter 4

Dr. Harry Eaton Stewart

Perhaps the most significant person emerging in the 1915 time period was Dr. Harry Eaton Stewart, the physical director of Wykeham Rise School for Girls in Washington, Connecticut. Dr. Stewart, a medical doctor, supported and encouraged track and field competition for women and had the credentials to refute "unscientific" statements about women and track competition; he also had a talent for writing.

Dr. Stewart's article in the January 1916 *American Physical Education Review* cited track as one of the three activities that had increased steadily in popularity for women in this country. Its strenuous nature caused grave concern for parents and physicians, however. In order to alleviate this concern, Dr. Stewart conducted a study of the effect of vigorous exercise on the heart and blood pressure in girls. The results of the study were published in February 1914 in the *American Physical Education Review*. Dr. Stewart concluded that the girls' hearts were greatly improved by vigorous sports. He stated that track had an advantage over other sports because it provided for "different athletic types and in larger numbers."

His lengthy article included a listing of the standard track events and information on equipment, training, and coaching for sprinting. He said that the equipment needed for a track meet was "two stop watches, a steel tape, jumping standards with cross bar, two sets of eight hurdles two feet six inches high with cross sticks, a baseball, a basketball and shot."

Dr. Stewart described the jumping pit as having a 60' × 3' runway dug to a depth of 4" and filled with first coarse and then fine ashes, wet down and rolled. It was to be edged with a "heavy thick plank or log buried to the level of the ground and painted white." The pit itself was to be 10' × 8', with a 20' × 4' extension. The pit was to be dug to about a depth of 1 ½' and filled with dry, sifted sand and sawdust in equal parts. This provided a soft landing bed.

According to Dr. Stewart, hurdles could be built cheaply by any carpenter, and he described how the cross bar was to lay across the uprights.

Dr. Stewart stated that spiked shoes were of "great help in most events and should be obtained if possible."

Turning his attention to the shot put, Dr. Stewart recommended shots of two weights, six pounds for beginners and eight pounds for competition. He described the seven-foot circle with a raised toe board around the front half.

Dr. Stewart thought that for women to be successful in track, they needed trained coaches who knew correct form and would supervise their work closely. He believed that a male coach should work closely with the physical director and the school physician.

On the subject of training, Dr. Stewart's recommendations involved strict guidelines in matters of diet and sleep. His diet thoughts were interesting. The athlete was supposed to avoid eating between meals and avoid rich deserts and sodas. He thought that a little candy after dinner was permissible as long as there was consumption of fruit, but not bananas. A glass of water with meals was important. Tea and coffee drinking were to be reduced. Grapefruit, oranges, and cream were to be avoided at breakfast. Meat once a day was desirable, and water drinking between meals was to be encouraged.

While the athlete was doing track work, she was to be kept warm. Sitting or standing around in cold weather was not to be allowed. Work was to be easy to begin with and then gradually increased. Form was to be stressed and maximum effort exerted only on a few occasions.

Strains were likely to occur in the early part of the season. They were best treated by rest, massage, and baking. Dr. Stewart wrote that a strain healed more quickly with slight use and treatments than with complete rest.

Dr. Stewart suggested a few weeks of fall practice during which time the coach selected the team; during the winter work could then be continued in the gymnasium.

In Dr. Stewart's opinion, there was a great need to standardize the events, and he recommended the following selection of events for junior and senior athletes:

Junior events:	Senior events:
50-yard dash	50-yard dash
75-yard dash	100-yard dash
60-yard hurdles	100-yard hurdles
Standing broad jump	Standing broad jump
Running broad jump	Running broad jump
Running hop, step, and jump	Running high jump
Baseball throw	Running hop, step, and jump
Basketball throw	8-lb. shot put
	Baseball throw
	Basketball throw

Only the exceptional girl was to pole vault, run the 220, or put the 12-pound shot. Dr. Stewart included the discus and javelin as good events but thought the above list was adequate.

The last part of Dr. Stewart's article dealt with coaching the sprints. He described the individual who would be the best sprint type as a quick, nervous individual, with good staying power. Size was not essential, but the large girl who was quick had an advantage.

In sprinting, spiked shoes were necessary, Dr. Stewart said, because they made a difference of two- or three-fifths of a second in the 100-yard dash. The crouch start was harder to teach but preferable. He explained the crouch start positions and suggested practicing starts daily along with slow runs of two or three times the distance to be run. The whole distance was not to be run hard until late in the season and then the athlete was to run hard infrequently. Runners were to rest often to avoid staleness.

Dr. Stewart believed that six weeks of training was necessary to get girls into condition. A shorter time would suffice, however, for girls who had competed before or had just finished playing basketball or hockey.

A second article by Dr. Stewart, "A Survey of Track Athletics for Women," appeared in the February 1916 *American Physical Education Review*. It was a continuation of the preceding article and discussed hurdling, the running broad jump, the hop, step, and jump, the standing broad jump, the standing high jump, the running high jump, the shot put, basketball throw, baseball throw, javelin throw, and discus throw. The lengthy article was eleven pages. For each event, he discussed training and technique and included a list of United States records in the event.

Hurdling is appealing but difficult to teach, Dr. Stewart wrote. Hurdling requires the speed of the sprinter and the spring of a jumper. As can be seen by the records, girls were hurdling at distances from 40 yards to 120 yards. The heights of the hurdles varied from 14" to 2' 6", and the number of hurdles varied from 2 to 10. In his plea to standardize the event, Dr. Stewart called for 60 and 100 yards, with 4 and 8 hurdles respectively.

Dr. Stewart said that training was the same for the hurdles as for the sprints. An athlete had to practice, however, to get the stride right so that the same leg always led over the hurdle.

In the running broad jump, marking of the stride was the first thing to be learned. The jumper was to place a mark on the ground 20–25 feet from the takeoff board and be able to hit this mark with the jumping foot at top speed. When the mark was mastered it could easily be repeated each time the athlete jumped. Dr. Stewart said that a slow runner cannot be a good broad jumper because the distance is obtained by a high jump sustained by the speed of a fast sprint.

Dr. Stewart described the body position in the air and when landing and suggested placing a hurdle about 4 feet from the takeoff board to force the jumper to clear the height without losing the proper form.

According to Dr. Stewart, the running hop, step, and jump was an event "well suited to girls." Practice was needed to learn the right sequence, and speed was necessary while using the weaker leg for the hop and the jumping leg for the jump. The hop was to be moderately long, with the object being to keep up the speed through the step phase and to be able to use maximum effort for the jump.

Dr. Stewart described the standing broad jump next. He said it was an event not used much for men at that time. He described the form with the arms swinging and the body raising on the toes. The landing was similar to that of the broad jump but not as exaggerated.

The standing high jump was used less at that time, according to Dr. Stewart. The scissors jump was most prevalent, and the arm action was similar to that for the standing broad jump. Natural spring and courage were needed in the running high jump, he wrote. Even though the best men jumpers were not using the scissors style, he believed that it was still the best form for women. The bar was to be approached from the left side if the right leg was used. The run was to be of the bounding type, not too long or too fast, and the last three steps were to be quick, with a "gather" for the spring on the last step. The leading foot was to be kicked up higher than the bar. As the body reached the bar, the hips were to be jerked up by throwing the head back and the chest and arms up. Most jumpers cleared the bar in a "sitting position" and lost six to eight inches of height in so doing.

Dr. Stewart suggested the eight-pound shot as the weight to use but believed the six and the twelve were useful in practice. The six-pound shot was to be used to learn form and practice speed and the twelve-pound to build up strength. Dr. Stewart described the form and emphasized that the shot is not thrown.

Listed below is Dr. Stewart's compilation of best performances in the shot put:

Weight	*Distance*	*Athlete*	*School*
6 lb.	37' 2½"	M. Card	Sargent N.S.P.E.
	35' 4"	M. Miller	Randolph-Macon College
	35'	G. Wright	LaSalle Seminary
8 lb.	34' 1⅞"	F. Jackling	University of California
	33' 4"	E. Hardin	Vassar College
	33' 1"	M. Young	Bryn Mawr College
	32' 9½"	M. Card	Sargent N.S.P.E.
	30' 10"	M. Mitchell	Wykeham Rise School
	30' 1"	B. Randall	N.H.N.S.G.
	29' 9"	B. Higgins	University of Nebraska
	28' 11"	Maurice	Sweet Briar College
	27' 3"	Giessing	Western College
	27' ½"	M. Glass	National Park Seminary
	26' 7"	L. Elliott	Howard Payne College
	26' 4"	E. Emory	St. Mary's Hall
	26' 2"	M. Garford	Lake Erie College
	25' 1"	M. Miller	Randolph-Macon College
12 lb.	28' 5½"	M. Mitchell	Wykeham Rise School
	24' 7"		Wells College
	23' 4½"	M. Long	N.H.N.S.G.

Dr. Stewart advised a short run prior to throwing the basketball, even though some coaches preferred the standing throw. A high throw using the full arm was his suggested technique. The athlete's back was to be used as a baseball pitcher used his back.

Listed below is Dr. Stewart's compilation of some of the best performances in the basketball throw:

Distance	Athlete	School
88' 10"	E. Hardin	Vassar College
85' 10½"	L. Marshall	Sargent N.S.P.E.
83' ¾"	H. Kirk	Bryn Mawr College
82' 8"	F. Jackling	University of California

The form in the baseball throw was similar to that of the basketball throw, using the full arm swing and using the elbow very little. Listed below is the top performance in this event.

Distance	Athlete	School
205' 7"	E. Hardin	Vassar College

Referring to the javelin throw, Dr. Stewart noted: "Miss Maude Cleveland of the University of California, Mr. Carl Schrader of Harvard, and Dr. L. R. Burnett of the Sargent Normal School, all very rightly urge the wider adoption of this most interesting event for women." Only four schools had adopted this event, however. In an attempt to standardize the javelin, Dr. Stewart agreed with Dr. Burnett's suggestion of a special javelin two meters long and 600 grams weight. The javelin results were as follows:

Distance	Athlete	School
82' 2"	L. Davidson	Sargent N.S.P.E.
74' 6"	E. Kable	Northwestern University
68' 3"	M. Miller	Randolph-Macon College
61' 5½"	M. Scattergood	Bryn Mawr College

Dr. Stewart described the proper technique for throwing the discus:

> In the Greek style, the discus is thrown from a square pedestal or box of dirt, thirty inches by twenty-seven inches, two inches high in front and eight inches in back. A whitewash line is made fifteen inches from the front of the pedestal and parallel to it. The right foot is placed in front of this line and kept there. The measurements are made by extending the front line of the pedestal, fifteen feet to each side and then marking forward at right angles, one hundred and thirty feet.
>
> The form of the throw used is as follows: Place right foot in front and left in rear of cross line. Raise discus with both hands over the head, so that it is pointing forward and at right angles to the ground. Swing both arms down by the right side, right hand holding discus with fingers spread, palm toward body is carried back as far as possible; the left hand carried back as far as the right knee, which is bent. The left knee is nearly straight. The discus is delivered straight forward, arms passing close to the side. The competitor may leave the pedestal at the end of the throw in any direction.
>
> In the free style, the discus is held palm down and inward. The arm swings from the lower right side up and to the left, where it is steadied by the left hand.

The left foot is usually forward and the discus delivered after a quick, complete turn of the body to the left. It should scale evenly through the air.

These are the discus results cited:

Weight	Distance	Athlete	School
2 lb.	68' 6"	L. Elliott	Howard Payne College
		L. Volmar	Howard Payne College
4 lb.	65' 6"	W. Merrill	Merrill School
	61' 2½"	J. Miller	National Cathedral School
	54' 7"	M. Connelly	Lake Erie College

Records in two other events were listed, but with no description of the events or comments by Dr. Stewart.

Hurl Ball Throw

Distance	Athlete	School
67' 11"	M. Card	Sargent N.S.P.E.
58' 3½"		University of Wisconsin

Pole Vault

Height	Athlete	School
6' 3"	E. Fisk	University of Nebraska
5' 8"	R. Spencer	Lake Erie College
5' 6½"	J. Dunlap	N.H.N.S.G.
5' 5¾"	N. Bergami	Sargent N.S.P.E.
5' ½"	E. Drew	Lake Erie College

In his concluding statements, Dr. Stewart urged all directors of physical education to consider the sport for girls:

> It is my firm belief, after more than ten years' experience in track work for girls, that nearly all of the prejudice against track work for girls is traceable to injury due either to lack of medical examination, lack of proper training, poorly constructed jumping pits and hurdles, lax supervision, or to a girl's having done this work at a time when she knew she should not. If, on the other hand, these conditions of safety are strictly adhered to, the gain in health, strength, and confidence far outweighs any risk of danger involved....
>
> Women are entering in every line the broader and more exacting fields of competition. Let us urge then, under careful supervision, a vigorous training for women — not wholly for sport, not wholly for reasons of physical development, even, but for the acquirement of those sterling elements of character which must always mark the true sportsman.

Another article written by Dr. Stewart which appeared in the 1916 *Spalding's Almanac*, reprinted from the *American Physical Education Review*, recognized that the number of well-organized meets for women was increasing every year. Records were not being reported to the *Almanac*, however, and as a result, there was no complete compilation of records. Dr. Stewart took it upon himself to send forms to the physical director of every institution that had track activities to ask for record documentation. It was his desire to have all of the institutions that had women's track and field continue to send him documentation of records set.

Dr. Stewart divided the records into groups — American records, Lake Erie College records, collegiate records, Vassar College records, Bryn Mawr College records, and preparatory school records. Dr. Stewart's lengthy compilation was published in the *Almanac*.

The October 1916 *American Physical Education Review* reported that Miss Maude Devereux had broken the broad jump record by 4' ½". She jumped 16' 9½" at the field day at the Skidmore School of Arts at Saratoga Springs, New York, on June 24, 1916.

While Dr. Stewart was collecting and publishing track and field records and providing coaching information, women in colleges throughout the country were fiercely debating the issue of competition. In an article in the *American Physical Education Review* in January 1917, Florence C. Burrell recognized the need for a controlled type of intercollegiate competition for women in coeducational institutions. She identified three types of women, the skilled athletes who have come to college after being "man-coached" in a preparatory school and have the idea of winning "at all costs," the average athletes who play fairly well but could never make a varsity sport, and the beginners. She did say: "We must not limit the skilled player. She must be allowed to test and improve her ability." But the question arose whether "outside" competition was advisable. Stanford University seemed to think that it had the solution to women's desire for competition. The university encouraged intramural competition in each sport. At the end of the sport season, interclass matches were held. The same process was followed by the University of California. Burrell noted: "Each player who has won her numerals in her class team has, therefore, the additional joy of keen outside competition. No one team is responsible for the day; there are four teams to share the honors or losses and the 'nervous strain' of responsibility for winning is decreased greatly or is eliminated." This plan was used in 1915-16 in tennis and basketball and was to be extended to other sports thereafter.

Burrell concluded by stating: "The era of athletics is just beginning for women. ... It seems unwise to encourage the so-called varsity competition for women when the interclass intercollegiate sports offer such opportunities for sportsmanship and keen competition."

The Women's Athletic Associations of the Midwest held a conference on March 9 and 10 in 1917. After listening to addresses and reports from delegates of the University of Wisconsin, University of Chicago, University of Illinois, and University of Minnesota, the women resolved five issues which they said, "will be of interest to teachers of physical education." One resolution in particular was aimed at track and field and athletic competition:

> Resolved: That this body go on record as opposing intercollegiate athletic competition for women in so far as it involves the necessity of a team going from one college to another, but that the keeping of records of events be maintained by the conference secretary for competitive comparison between colleges.

In the meantime, schools and colleges all over the country had developed track and field programs. Many of the schools offered track and field as part of the physical training curriculum and were participating in interscholastic competition every spring as a culminating activity. One such school was the Oaksmere School in Mamaroneck, New York.

"The school, also known as Mrs. Merrill's Boarding and Day School for Girls, was founded in New Rochelle, New York in 1906, incorporated in 1911 as Merrill School, and moved to Orienta Point, Mamaroneck, New York in 1914. The school also had a branch in Paris, France which opened in 1921," stated a 1921-22 booklet describing the school for prospective students. Track and field was listed as part of the physical training program:

Track Athletics
All forms of track athletics are practiced in the Spring
Out-of-Door Season, season ending with track meets.
One hour a day

The *Mamaroneck Paragraph* reported the results of an interscholastic track meet on May 16, 1918. The Oaksmere girls traveled to Greenwich, Connecticut, for a dual meet with Rosemary Hall. The previous year Oaksmere had won the meet, this year the victory went to Rosemary Hall. An interesting note to the meet was that three Rosemary Hall girls cleared the bar in the high jump at 4' 8". The three girls were going to break the tie the following Saturday in a special competition.

50-yard dash
1. Madison — Rosemary Hall — 6⅘
2. Wright — Rosemary Hall

75-yard dash
1. Riddle — Oaksmere — 10⅕
2. Wright — Rosemary Hall

100-yard dash
1. Riddle — Oaksmere — 16⅘
2. Hyde — Rosemary Hall

Running Broad Jump
1. Robeson — Rosemary Hall — 14' 8"
2. Knox — Rosemary Hall — 13' 11"

Running Hop, Step, and Jump
1. Robeson — Rosemary Hall — 30' 3"
2. Grayson — Oaksmere — 30' 1¼"

Running High Jump
1. Robeson — Rosemary Hall — 4' 8"
Hyde — Rosemary Hall
Vincent — Rosemary Hall

Standing Broad Jump
1. Madison — Rosemary Hall — 7' 11¼"
2. Robeson — Rosemary Hall — 7' 8¼"

Baseball throw
1. Havermeyer   Rosemary Hall   195' 11"
2. Grayson   Oaksmere   172' 2"

Basketball throw
1. Hyde   Rosemary Hall   70' 9¼"
2. Johnson   Rosemary Hall   69' 9"

In 1919 the *Mamaroneck Paragraph* reported a second annual interclass meet in the public high school. Girls and boys participated. The girls had five events: the 60-yard dash, standing broad jump, running high jump, running broad jump, and the eight-pound shot put.

In 1920 the elementary school girls in Mamaroneck had interscholastic competition. In 1921 the high school meet was called an "inter-year track meet."

In 1921, Oaksmere had a meet with seven schools participating. The schools represented were St. Marys Hall, Burlington, New Jersey; Leonia High School, Leonia, New Jersey; St. Margaret's School, Waterbury, Connecticut; Rosemary Hall, Greenwich, Connecticut; Savage School for Physical Education, New York City; The Gateway School, New Haven, Connecticut, and Oaksmere. There were about eighty athletes. Oaksmere won the meet.

The *Mamaroneck Paragraph* of May 19, 1921, reported that Maude Rosenbaum had broken her own world record in the basketball throw. Her old mark was 89' 11", and the new mark was 94' 2". A second world record was set by Floreida Batson of Rosemary Hall. She ran the 60-yard hurdles in 9 seconds, and the other world record was in the 220-yard relay. The Oaksmere team ran 28⅖ seconds.

The 1919 *Spalding's Official Athletic Almanac* had a six-page section devoted to women's athletic records. Dr. Harry Eaton Stewart, now at the New Haven Normal School of Gymnastics, was the chairman of the newly formed National Women's Track and Field Committee. This was the first national committee to administrate track and field for women in the United States.

The National Women's Track and Field Committee held its first annual meeting in New York in 1918. The committee accepted five new American and collegiate records. Florence Somers, secretary of the committee, surveyed the schools that competed in events that were considered dangerous. The events in question were the 100-yard hurdles, 220-yard run, 12-pound shot, and pole vault. Twenty-one replies were received. Two to seven schools competed in each event and reported no injuries but said they were not worth retaining. The committee decided to drop them from the standard list and suggested to the schools that the events be discontinued.

The committee selected the first track and field rules to govern the sport, another significant step in the development of women's track and field. The committee declared that the Amateur Athletic Union rules would be followed.

They listed events which would be considered standard: 30, 50, 75, 100, and 220 yard dashes; 60, 65, and 100 yard hurdles; 220 and 440 yard relays (4 runners);

standing high and broad jumps, running high jump, broad jump, and hop, step, and jump; pole vault; baseball and basketball throws, hurl ball and javelin, discus and shot (6, 8, 12). In the committee's choice of events best suited for beginners and trained athletes, the 220, pole vault, and standing high jump were not on the list.

This committee, the first women's committee in the United States, consisted of Dr. Stewart, the only male, Florence A. Somers, Lakewood High School, Lakewood, Ohio; Alice M. Allen, Pratt Institute, Brooklyn, New York; Ina E. Gittings, University of Montana, Missoula, Montana; Mary DeWitt Snyder, Transylvania and Hamilton Colleges, Lexington, Kentucky; Eliza J. Foulke, public high school, Atlantic City, New Jersey; and Eleanor E. Greer, Oaksmere School, Mamaroneck, New York.

Records were listed, and Dr. Stewart entitled the first section "Standard Track Events — American Records."

The 1920 *Spalding's Official Athletic Almanac* published records again. Dr. Stewart, chairman of the National Women's Track and Field Committee, wrote in the introduction that the effect of the war lasted throughout the entire school year: "There were fewer track meets held and fewer national records broken this year than in any year since 1915." He continued, "The greatest year in the history of athletics has just been entered upon. ... Many schools are holding winter indoor meets and the committee hopes to publish next year the first official indoor records."

A change in the committee added Carl L. Schrader from the Sargent School for Physical Education, Cambridge, Massachusetts, replacing Eleanor E. Greer from Oaksmere School.

Another article appeared in the May 1922 *American Physical Education Review*. At this point in his career, Dr. Stewart had founded the New Haven College of Physiotherapy in New Haven, Connecticut. He stated that a sharp increase in athletics for girls had been noted within the previous two decades and that in the previous six years track and field growth in this country had been "phenomenal." He thought that it could not be "suppressed or eliminated, even if we wished it." Looking at competitive athletics from several viewpoints, Dr. Stewart stated that the physician is concerned with the effects upon the heart, blood pressure, and the eliminative mechanism. The parent is interested in how competitive athletics contribute to a good foundation for life's work. The educator is interested in using sports to build a sound body so the mind can function better and scholarship will be enhanced. He added, "Athletics ... have been of immense benefit to the participants in the development of self-control, vigorous health, and sportsmanship. They do not tend to make a girl less womanly." He compared girls and boys and said that the educator of boys realizes a direct positive correlation between the inducement to compete in sports and the need to attain good scholarship and the same should be recognized for the girls.

Dr. Stewart stated: "I am frankly one of those who believe most sincerely in interschool competition for girls, within reasonable limits." He acknowledged receiving letters from physicians stating that the effects of competitive athletics were not entirely clear to them. Again, he cited his study on the heart and blood pressure mentioned earlier and reiterated that injuries occurred as a result of lack of training and supervision and lack of medical examination. He blamed poor equipment for injuries. He was the first to mention that there is a "growing tendency to avoid complete inactivity" during menstruation. Another strong statement pertained to training: he said girls need as much time and care to get into condition for competition as do boys.

Dr. Stewart credited Vassar with being the place where track started "some twenty years ago" and mentioned Bryn Mawr too. He said it spread slowly to other colleges and preparatory schools. By 1915, increased public interest led to the publication of supposed records in newspapers and journals, but no collection of records had been made. Dr. Stewart sent record blanks all over the country and received replies from about eighty schools and colleges. They were tabulated and published for the first time in January 1916 in the *American Physical Education Review*. They were also then published in *Spalding's Almanac* and made a permanent record. Dr. Stewart again mentioned the fact that the committee worked to eliminate events that were not standard so that, for example, hurdle races did not vary from 40 yards to 120 yards. The committee in 1922 consisted of twelve persons:

Dr. Harry Stewart, chairman
Miss Eliza J. Foulke, secretary, high school, Atlantic City, New Jersey
Miss Suzanne Becker, high school, Leonia, New Jersey
Miss Clarice E. Bower, Gateway School, New Haven, Connecticut
Miss Sarah G. Blanding, University of Kentucky, Lexington, Kentucky
Miss Ina E. Gittings, Arizona State University, Tucson, Arizona
Miss Emma Ody Pohl, Mississippi State College for Women, Columbus, Mississippi
Miss Margaret Mitchell, Ethel Walker School, Simsbury, Connecticut
Miss Katherine Montgomery, Florida State College for Women, Tallahassee, Florida
Dr. L. Raymond Burnett, recreation commissioner, Paterson, New Jersey
Mr. Howard G. Cleaveland, Long Beach, California
Mr. Carl Schrader, state director of physical education, State House, Boston, Massachusetts

A follow-up article by Dr. Stewart appeared in the June *American Physical Education Review*. Much of the article was a repeat of a former article in the *Review*. It covered training, sprint and hurdle records, and all of the field event records. In his conclusion, Dr. Stewart asked for schools to submit records to him, and he informed the readers about the International Federation of Women's Athletics formed in Paris in October of the previous year. He said that it was the intention of this organization to hold an international meet in August of 1922, "in which meet it is hoped an American team will be entered." He concluded by recognizing that despite many accomplishments, there "still exists a marked degree of prejudice against track athletics in many quarters. … Let the girls have the joy of competitive athletics under proper restrictions and develop to the utmost her physical powers, every one of which will be of inestimable value to her in the complexities of modern life."

Chapter 5

1922:
Mamaroneck and Paris

The first profoundly significant women's track and field meet conducted in the United States was held on May 13, 1922, under a scorching sun at Oaksmere School, Mamaroneck, New York. The *New York Times* proclaimed that "Girls from the North and girls from the South, the greatest number of feminine athletes ever assembled for a track meet in the United States, today made their bow at the Oaksmere School as formidable competitors for the honors of the cinderpath, which in America previously have gone almost exclusively to men."

This track meet decided the American team that Dr. Harry Stewart took to Paris in August. This team was the first group of American women track and field stars to compete internationally as a team representing the United States. It was a bold and monumental stride in the development of women's track and field in the United States. It was Dr. Stewart's interest, organizational skills, dedication, and enthusiasm for the sport that made it all happen. He was the person that pulled everything together. A letter written by Suzanne Becker Young, an assistant coach on the International Team, said, "Dr. Harry Stewart was the real instigator of our United States participation and was a major contributor to advancing the cause of athletics for women."

One hundred and two girls representing twenty-two institutions from all over the East took part in the Mamaroneck track meet. The other interesting point is that while this meet took part in the East, similar meets took place in Los Angeles and the Middle West and results were compared.

The first event was the running broad jump. It was won with a leap of 16' by Elizabeth Stine, a high school girl from Leonia, New Jersey. Nancy Voorhees of East Hampton, New York, and the Ethel Walker School was second in 15' 3⅞". Martha Smith of Rosemary Hall was third with a jump of 14' 9¼". In a later event, Elizabeth Stine broke the world record in the hop, skip, and jump. The previous record was 33' 6". Her new world record performance was 33' 10¼".

Lucile Godbold of Winthrop College in Rock Hill, South Carolina, won the basketball throw with a distance of 88' 3¼". Kathryn Agar, Oaksmere School, threw 88' 3" for second, and Nancy Voorhees was third with 75' 7".

The record in the javelin throw using both hands was broken when Kathryn

Agar of Oaksmere threw 134' 3½". Anne Harwick, a graduate of Florida State College, was second with 127' 10", and Edith Easton of Leonia was third with 119' 8½".

Camelia Sabie hit the last of eight hurdles in the 100-yard hurdles, and as a result her record of 15⅕ did not count. Hester Smith of Rosemary Hall was second, and Mary McCune, also of Rosemary Hall, was third.

The world record was broken by Lucile Godbold in the eight-pound shot put. She tossed the shot 35' 11", breaking the record of 34' 1½".

Another world mark was set in the 440-yard relay by Leonia High School. The new mark of 57⅘ was 4 seconds faster than the old mark. The winning team was composed of Leila Hopper, Martha Nyquist, Janet Hobson, and Mabel Gilliland. Rosemary Hall was second, Ethel Walker School third, and Dasokol Gymnasium of New York City fourth.

Edith Easton of Leonia won the baseball throw with a toss of 200' 6½". Anne Harwick was second, tossing the ball 186' 7½", and Margaret Kirkner, Wykeham, was third with a throw of 186' 5".

The standing broad jump was won by Adeline Gehrig of the New York Turn Verein, who jumped 7' 7". Nancy Voorhees of Ethel Walker School was second, and Blanche Strebeigh, of St. Margaret's, and Edith Easton, of Leonia, tied for third.

The 300-meter run was held because it was scheduled as an event in Paris. It was the first time this distance was run. Mary McCune of Rosemary Hall won the event in 43⅗. Luella Mueller of Newark High School was second, and Blanche Dixon of the New York Municipal Employees Association was third.

Mabel Gilliland won the 100-yard dash in 12⅖. Lucile Godbold was second, and Elizabeth Stine third.

The 50-yard dash was also won by Mabel Gilliland in 6⅖. Camelia Sabie was second, and Ruth Wincoop was third.

The last event, the high jump, was won by Nancy Voorhees with a leap of 4' 7". Elizabeth Stine was second in 4' 6", and Josephine Stetson, of Rosemary Hall, and Emma Davis, of St. Mary's College, tied at 4' 5".

The team from Leonia High School won the trophy for winning the most points. Suzanne Becker, the coach, had been invited by Dr. Stewart to bring her team to participate in the meet. Becker said, "I was delighted when he asked me to bring a team from Leonia to the try-outs at Oaksmere and later to help him and be the Assistant Coach on the International Team."

The Leonia newspaper reported that Suzanne Becker was to be the United States representative of the Fédération Sportive Féminine Internationale, under whose auspices the Paris meet was held. She was a member of the National Women's Track and Field Committee. After her arrival home from Mamaroneck, she reported to the press that the Leonia girls had "only been training intensively for the last two weeks." Becker made efforts to raise money in order to defray the traveling expenses of the American women's team. She was waiting for a reply "from business men who are interested in seeing young women of the United States capture premier honors in Pershing Stadium on August 20."

The first American women's team to compete internationally was named:

Kathryn Agar	Chicago, Ill.	Oaksmere School
Floreida Batson	New Orleans, La.	Rosemary Hall–Smith College
Mabel Gilliland	Leonia, N.J.	Leonia High School
Lucile Godbold	Estill, S.C.	Winthrop College
Esther Green	Canal Zone	Balboa High School
Anne Harwick	Miami, Fla.	Florida State College
Frances Mead	Tarrytown, N.Y.	Rosemary Hall–Smith College
Camelia Sabie	Newark, N.J.	Newark Normal School
Janet Snow	Rye, N.Y.	Oaksmere School
Elizabeth Stine	Leonia, N.J.	Leonia High School
Louise Voorhees	East Hampton, N.Y.	Rosemary Hall
Nancy Voorhees	East Hampton, N.Y.	Ethel Walker School

Maude Rosenbaum, from Oaksmere School, was already in Paris and was scheduled to meet the team when they arrived.

Dr. Harry Eaton Stewart, coach	New Haven, Conn.
Suzanne Becker, assistant coach	Leonia High School, N.J.
Joseph D'Angola, assistant coach	Newark Normal School, N.J.

Mrs. Stewart and Mrs. Anita D'Angola, also a coach at Newark Normal, went along, as well as the mothers of two of the girls.

The *Newark Evening News* on August 1, 1922, had a photo of the entire team and staff and a detailed write-up on the team. Above the photo was the headline "Lassies and Coaches America is Sending Against the World for Track and Field Events."

The article was written as the *Aquitania* sailed towards Europe with the "members of the first team of lassies ever sent abroad to represent Uncle Sam in international track and field competition." The reporter quoted Miss Becker, who spoke about the girls in Weequahic Park after practice:

> This is our first trip across. It is most important that we come home with the goods, as the saying is. I would hate to appear over confident but I think the girls can do it. They are wonderful — wonderful spirit, you understand, willing to make any sacrifice that will bring victory to Uncle Sam, and you know they've really established a number of splendid marks, some of which they are quite sure of bettering when they get to Paris and the big test.
>
> It seems to me that the team we will have to beat is England. All is darkness so far as knowing anything about the Swiss, Belgians or Czechs. Our records are generally better than those of France, but England looms up as a genuine obstacle.

The newspaper article noted that practice was scheduled to be held on the deck of the *Aquitania* every morning. The ship's officers were going to provide hurdles, jumping posts, and running lanes. The reporter quoted the head coach:

> Dr. Stewart would promise nothing from his team members except their very best. "What we do over there must remain one big question until the day of the games. We know that the spirit of these girls can not be beaten — that they will

1922 United States athletes who participated in the Women's World Games in Paris. *Top:* Elizabeth Stine, Lucile Godbold, Camelia Sabie, Louise Voorhees. *Bottom:* Janet Snow, Captain Floreida Batson, Esther Green and Anne Harwick. (Courtesy of Choate Rosemary Hall.)

give the very best that is in them in every event and in every trial of every event. But you know we're facing quite a task."...

Just what events the girls will be assigned is something that will not be definitely settled until after the practice sessions in Paris. Miss Floreida Batson and Miss Sabie are certain starters in the hurdles and, barring accidents, are picked to win. But the real star of the team is expected to be a tall maid from South Carolina, Miss Lucile Godbold....

There was no wild send-off for the team as the ship sailed away from the dock. In truth, there was nothing to suggest the departure of an American Team of athletes, some of whom are actually paying their own expenses that they might be members of the first strictly girls' team which has ever represented the United States in track and field competition abroad. ... But they are a determined lot just the same, going over to 'clean up' and, as Captain Floreida Batson added, to "show Americans that the girls of the country are good athletes — just as good as the men."

The reporter next gave a brief account of some of the girls. Camelia Sabie was the world record holder in the 100-yard hurdles. She had established the record of 15 seconds in a special race on May 23 at City Field. Miss Sabie had been active in field sports since she was a student in East Side High School. She had graduated from Newark State Normal the previous month.

The other strong hurdler was Floreida Batson of New Orleans, formerly of Rosemary Hall, Greenwich, Connecticut, who was captain of the United States team. She was a freshman at Smith College the previous year. She held the world record of 9 seconds in the 60-yard high hurdles and the world record of 14⅖ seconds in the 100-yard low hurdles.

According to the reporter, Elizabeth Stine, a junior in high school, was to compete in the running broad jump and the sprints and might also run on the relay team. She had reached the seventeen-foot mark in the running broad jump in practice, and her coach, Miss Becker, thought she would break the world record in Paris.

Mabel Gilliland, who was going to return to high school as a senior in the fall, was to compete in the sprints and relay. She was one of the fastest runners on the team.

The pair of sisters on the team, Louise and Nancy Voorhees, did not come from the same school. Nancy was to compete in the high jump and broad jump, and Louise would also compete in the high jump. She was going to be a freshman at Bryn Mawr in the fall. Nancy, at fifteen, was reported to be the youngest of the girls on the team.

Two graduated representatives of Oaksmere School were Janet Snow and Katherine Agar. Janet was going to throw the javelin and shot and Katherine was to run in the relay and 300-meter race.

The *Daily Item*, the local paper in Rye, New York, Janet's hometown, stated: "Although but 17 she has already proven her right to be classed with the best girl runners in the country. ... She has been training hard for the past several months and her friends feel confident that she will be a big factor in helping to bring a victory to this country."

Esther Green, a distance runner, would probably also run the relay. "At home she is barred from all athletic meets because she has captured so many prizes that those in charge have decided some of the other contestants should be given an opportunity," reported the *Newark Evening News*.

The only South Carolinian was Lucile Godbold, who could broad jump and run distances. Frances Mead of Tarrytown, New York, and Rosemary Hall was scheduled to high jump and run a leg on the relay. Anne Harwick of Miami, a recent graduate of Florida State College, was to compete in the shot put, javelin, and 1,000 meter run. And lastly, Maude Rosenbaum of Oaksmere, who was already in Paris, was to compete in the high jump and broad jump.

A Spalding Company representative, Mr. Don Selbie, was an aid to the team in many ways, one of which was to help persuade his company to design the first women's international competition outfits. Suzanne Becker wanted new outfits for the team. The decision was made to "abandon" bloomers. Suzanne said, "I guess our team was the first in the United States to come out in shorts, rather long shorts, but at least better than those baggy bloomers."

On August 18, prior to the start of the games, the International Federation of Women's Athletics held its first congress. Mme. Milliat of France was elected president. Dr. Stewart was chosen vice president and Suzanne Becker a representative.

The *New York Times* on August 19 announced the start of the games in Paris.

> Seventy-seven women athletes, representing five countries, will compete in what is generally described as the first women's Olympics at Pershing Stadium Sunday....
>
> The United States and Panama have entered a team of 15, the members of which will be numbered 1 to 15. ... American girls are entered in one, two, three and in some cases four events. ... The fight on the whole is expected to be among England, France and the United States.

The trials were set to start in Pershing Stadium, just outside Paris, on August 20 at 9 A.M. in the 60 meters, 100-yard dash, hurdles, running high jump, running broad jump, standing broad jump, and 300-meter run. Four athletes from the trials in each event would run in the finals in the afternoon. During the meet, the American girls were to give an exhibition in the hop, step, and jump and throwing the baseball and basketball.

Dr. Stewart had arranged before the meet started to have the times recorded of all of the American girls for the purpose of possible American records.

In perfect weather a crowd of 20,000 assembled to view the games. According to the *New York Times,* the American girls "created an excellent impression in fitness and grace, earning generous applause when they won two events, tied in a third and broke two world's records." The article continued:

> In competition noteworthy for the number of new records set in the women's athletic world Miss Floreida Batson of the American team lowered the record for the 100 yards hurdles from $15\frac{4}{5}$ seconds to $14\frac{4}{5}$ seconds in a trial heat while Miss Sabie, another American, after lowering the same record to 15 seconds flat in the trials, reduced it to $14\frac{2}{5}$ in the finals.
>
> Miss Godbold of the Americans also set a new world's record for the shot put with 11 meters 27 centimeters for the right hand and 20 meters 22 centimeters for both hands.

The Americans were leading in the point score when half of the events were completed, but the English team won. Weakness in the sprints was blamed for the American loss.

The American relay team finished second but was declared "distanced" and placed fourth. Dr. Stewart filed a protest, even though the outcome of the relay would not have affected the scoring.

Before the afternoon session began, there was a parade of athletes. Lucile Godbold was selected to carry the American flag. The team made a striking appearance in size and costume. The members of the team wore a white blouse, blue trunks, and a red band, with the American emblem on their chest.

Complete results of how the Americans placed follow:

In the 60-meter dash, Gilliland was in heat one and finished fourth. Sabie was in heat two and finished third. Neither girl made the final.

In the 100-yard dash, Green was fourth in the first heat and Gilliland was third in the second heat. Neither girl qualified for the final.

In the first heat of the 100-yard hurdles, Batson won in a new world record. Sabie won the second heat. Sabie won the final in another world record time of $14\frac{2}{5}$. Batson, nursing an injured ankle, hit a hurdle and was forced to stop.

In the 300-meter dash, Harwick was third in the first heat, and Godbold was second in the second heat. Godbold was fourth in the final.

Godbold was fourth in the 1000-meters run, and Snow was sixth.

Stine was second in the running broad jump with a jump of 16' 5¾" and Sabie was a close third in 16' 3¼".

Nancy Voorhees tied for first place in the high jump, leaping 4' 9⅛". Mead was seventh.

In the javelin (using both hands), Godbold was third with 130' 3", and Agar placed fifth.

In the shot put (using both hands), Lucile Godbold won with a distance of 66' 4⅛", a world record, and Rosenbaum was fourth with 57'.

Sabie won the standing broad jump with a jump of 8' 1⅞". Camelia Sabie was the second highest point scorer in the meet and Lucile Godbold the third highest.

The United States was second to England in points scored.

When the team arrived home, the girls enjoyed enthusiastic welcome-home ceremonies. Newark State Normal College had a reception for nineteen-year-old Camelia Sabie. More than 1100 students and former schoolmates gave her three cheers as she entered the building. When school started, she assumed her duties as physical training director at the John Catlin School in Newark.

Perhaps one of the greatest welcome-home celebrations was at Winthrop College, Rock Hill, South Carolina. The *Winthrop College News* reported:

> On the morning of Saturday, October 7, Chapel was going as usual. ... The hymn was announced, the Scripture read, the Lord's prayer was repeated as usual, and then the announcements — but just as Dr. Johnson had begun to tell that the movie that night would show "Our Ludy" in action at the Paris Olympics, the marshals with their beribboned staffs appeared in the rear, and with their entrance a roar, a storm, a thunder storm, of applause swept down the student crowd. It was deafening, overwhelming. ... Someone said, "It's Ludy!" And so behind the marshalls there came a tall, graceful young woman, tastefully dressed in dark blue and evidently overwhelmed by her roaring reception. And how they did roar! ... Finally, the marshall reached the platform, where they presented the heroine to the President ... and then with his masterly directness and terseness [he] told of his trip to Paris, of the Olympic contest, and of the Winthrop victories.

According to the *Winthrop College News,* after the president presented Ludy to the audience, there was "more applause, more roaring from 1300 classmates." Lucile Godbold then spoke:

> Dr. Johnson, Faculty and Students of Winthrop College: Before I begin talking about myself I want to take the time to thank each and all of you, as well as those students who finished Winthrop last year, for the most wonderful and most pleasant trip of my life. Not just because you people raised the money to cover my expenses, but the way in which you did it and knowing that you wanted me to enjoy my trip as well as represent Winthrop College at the first international track meet for women. ... As you know, early in the spring, Winthrop had her annual track meet. At this meet I broke the American record in shot put and as a result, at the suggestion of Mrs. Bartlett, our physical director, you

Photo of Lucile Godbold in 1922 USA uniform putting the shot. Lucile was a Winthrop College student. (Courtesy of Winthrop University Archives.)

raised enough money to send me to Mamaroneck, New York, to take part in a "try-out" track meet which was held to select a team to compete in the International Meet. ... Then you raised money for my trip to Paris. I was told to practice four events, shot put, javelin throwing with both hands, the 300 meter run and the 1,000 meter run. I came to summer school and got up early every morning before breakfast and practiced these events. It wasn't so much fun practicing by myself with nobody for company except the dew and the birds that used to sit up on the grandstand and laugh at my attempts to throw the javelin. However, I stuck to it and after I had broken a couple of javelins and run 'round the track field so much till I could shut both eyes and run around backwards. Then the time came for me to go to New York.

We stayed in New York about a week, going over to Newark, New Jersey every day to practice. We had a grand time in New York, and the members of the team got to know each other before we sailed. ... It took just six days to cross and we had a wonderful trip. We enjoyed it so much that we hated to leave the ship. We got up every morning before breakfast and practiced on deck, one of which the Captain let us use. To practice the 1,000 meter run I had to go 'round the deck three times....

On August 7 we landed at Cherbourg, France. We had a time getting through the Custom House. They wanted to know if we had any tobacco or cigars in our baggage. Of course, they wouldn't take our word for it, so we had to give our clothes a coming out party. ... We went by rail from Cherbourg to Paris. We were in France two weeks. Every morning we would go to Colombes where we practiced for about two hours each day. In the afternoons or at night we went sight-seeing. ... We saw everything that was worth seeing and a heap that wasn't. We took a trip to the battlefields and visited different cemeteries and saw Quentin Roosevelt's grave.

We went to Versailles and went through the palace where the peace treaty was signed....

The meet was held in Pershing Stadium and began early on the morning of August 20. ... Each country was allowed two contestants in each event. In the morning they were cut down to the four best. I placed in the shot put, javelin throw, the 300 meter run and the 1,000 meter run.

The meet was run off very much like our track meets, but on a larger scale. Everything was announced in French.

We had lunch and Dr. Johnson ate with us. The meet began right afterwards. Just before it began the team marched around the track with one member carrying the nation's flag. I was chosen to carry Old Glory, and, believe me, I was proud to lead that American team around the track. There were 20,000 people to see us. The Americans were seated in the center of the stadium, and I could see Dr. Johnson very well.

My first event was shot put. I knew the French woman who held the record was going to give me a hard fight, so I was all keyed up, so to speak. I was taller than the French woman, but she was husky as an ox. She looked as though she could put that "iron pill" over the moon. Believe me, I was scared. If you had seen her, you would have been scared, too. ... When I stepped into the circle our coach, Dr. Stewart, shouted, "Now, ol' South Carolina Mountaineer, show 'em what the South can do!" I put the pill and I broke the world's record. I put it at twenty meters and more, twenty-two with both hands, and that is sixty-six feet. This beat the French woman's record by more than six feet, six inches. She looked as though somebody had pulled a chair out from under her kind of sudden-like. But she was a good sport, shook hands and congratulated me. The American flag was run up and the band played the "Star Spangled Banner" twice. I was one happy mortal! ... I can see those Americans yelling now. They opened their mouths so wide I was scared to death for fear the sun would warp their ribs or blister their tonsils.

Then when I looked up I was shut in by a circle of men with cameras, about four million of them, as it seemed to me. ... I grinned like a lunatic, and tried to make believe I was used to it — but you know better.

The next event was the 300 meter run. My coach told me I was just to trot around the track because that would give me fourth place, anyway, he wanted to save me for the 1,000 meter race. I couldn't picture myself not running my fastest and I urged him to let me do my best, but couldn't budge him. Worse than a balking horse! ... That race was the hardest thing I ever did in all my life. The rest started off at a rapid rate and I had to just jog along. ... I don't believe the judge knew whether I was last in that race or first in the next.

In the javelin throw I came in third.

I wish you could have seen the 1,000 meter race. Near the finish when you are supposed to speed up, the girl in front of me fell sprawling. The big hunk of mud! I could have murdered her. I was going pretty, and if somebody had offered me a million dollars to stop I could not have done it. I leaped over her (leap-frog-like) and in the leap thereof measured my length in that track of cinders. I thought I was through with this old world. However, I dragged my carcass to an upright position, coaxed my bruised bones to work and took third place. That gave me two more points....

After the International, the American team had a meet of its own to present some events that were not included on the regular program. I took first place in hop, step and jump and second in basketball throw.

We had lots of fun at the International banquet that night. Imagine five countries speaking five different languages. ... While in training we had to cut out all sweets, drinks, and so on, but at the banquet we turned loose. Did I drink wine? Can a fish swim? I ate so much French pastry I thought I would pop. In fact, I ate until there was no more....

The cup was awarded to England. ... The medals were awarded. I got six, three more than anybody else. Each time a name was called — all in French — a girl went forward, got her medal and some other article, from pictures to dishes. I am thinking of starting a hardware store.

The next morning we got up early and caught the train to Cherbourg. We sailed August 21 on the *Saxonia*. Who can keep from being seasick on a ship that thinks it's a cradle? About the third day out we got a little gale and we began getting six meals per day — three going and three coming.

On the *Aquitania* I had a room to myself, but coming back we existed four in a room. Our room was so small that half the furniture was painted on the wall. We had to back out in the hall to turn around and go on deck to even change our minds. As long as we stayed on deck it was O.K. I cultivated the deck, and my deck chair and I were stonewall buddies. I read so much I couldn't remember when I wasn't reading.

After creeping along for twelve days we got in sight of New York. Believe me, I was as glad to see the Goddess of Liberty as a Carolina mule is to see Sunday.

I didn't expect anybody to meet me, and when I saw Mrs. Bartlett I almost fell off the boat, I was so glad. After I had finished there [Customs] I saw my father. ... My father and I stayed in New York a day or two, and then went to my home in Estill, South Carolina.

The people in Estill were very nice to me and capped the climax by inviting Governor Harvey down and having what they called a Harvey-Godbold day. ... It was the first time a governor had ever spoken in Estill. I felt quite honored. Governor Harvey talked as though I had saved the country from smallpox, or some such animal. Everything was decorated in garnet and gold [the colors of Winthrop College] and we had a lovely time.

Before closing I want to say once more how much I appreciate all that you people — the girls who finished last year, the faculty and officers, Dr. Johnson and Mrs. Bartlett — did in connection with the trip to France. Especially do I want to thank Mrs. Bartlett before all of you for the part she played. If she had not been a regular live wire, had she not kept up with what was going on in other parts of the country, I doubt if I would ever have gone to Mamaroneck to take part in the try-out meet in the spring. I have much to thank her for.

As I said once before, what I did was not done for myself but for you people and for Winthrop, and because South Carolina and the South were looking to me to do my share in helping the U.S.A. win all she could in the first international meet for women.

Lucile Ellerbe Godbold was the first South Carolinian to qualify for an international track team. The *Greenville News* wrote: "It has remained for a South Carolina woman to do what no South Carolina man has ever done — win honors in an international athletic contest." In 1961 she became the first woman elected to the South Carolina Athletic Hall of Fame. In 1928 she was listed in *Who's Who in American Sports,* and she was listed in the first edition of *Who's Who of American Women* in 1957.

"Miss Ludy" taught physical education at Columbia College for fifty-eight years, retiring in 1980. She died in 1981 at the age of eighty.

Floreida Batson Gibbens, the captain of the first United States team, was ninety-three years old when I spoke with her on September 10, 1993. She was born in New Orleans and resides there today. Floreida recalled those days surrounding her historic trip to Paris and told me that prior to her schooling at Rosemary Hall, "I never hurdled before in my life." When she got to Rosemary Hall, she found that track and field was part of the program, "they were very much into athletics." Hurdling came naturally. She started hurdling with hurdles that were larger than the men's, but they weren't as heavy and "just had a little stick over them so that if you touched them, they would fall off."

"We didn't do it in the winter time because of the snow and it was pretty cold in Greenwich, Connecticut," Floreida recalled. "We started in the spring and had certain days to practice. We had competition against other schools but most of the schools came to Rosemary Hall."

When asked how she was selected for the Paris team, Floreida said:

> I had a world's record at Rosemary and I hadn't done anything at all in athletics because I was then a student at Smith College. They found me and asked me if I would go over and I said yes, I would, because I could afford it. I had to pay my own way. My mother and aunt went with me. This other girl who had been practicing all year and had her own coach was going to go too. In Paris, I was ahead at the fifth hurdle and my ankle just gave way. The hurdles were big heavy hurdles, they were men's hurdles.

Floreida remembers the trip over as being "very rough," which made training impossible.

> When we got there, I was hurdling over a man's hurdle, and they forgot to take the pins out. I hit the hurdle and sprained my ankle. But I had to keep going so I went to the doctor. It hurt a lot, but I had to get back into shape. I was in pretty good shape then because in the preliminaries I broke the world's record. When I got to the fifth hurdle in the finals, my ankle gave way. It was very disappointing. But in Rosemary you were taught to take your disappointments and not say anything about them. When we played basketball and we made a score, we weren't supposed to cheer because it's bad sportsmanship. So we were taught to be a sports person and not cry over losing or anything like that. I ran in the relay, but we weren't too good. We didn't win.

The team came home after the meet, but Floreida stayed in Europe with her aunt and mother. Upon her return she met her future husband of forty-five years at a dance. Her last hurdling was done in Paris. She spoke very highly of Rosemary Hall and loved it. She recalled Dr. Stewart as a very nice man.

The reception upon returning home to the United States was one of jubilation for the athletes. That was not the case for the adults. Suzanne Becker stated: "Upon our return to the States, I found a very considerable amount of criticism and opposition to competitive athletics for women. I attended a woman's Physical Education Association Convention in Washington at which several speakers claimed that participants were subjected to hazards that were a potential danger to their future life. Needless to say I took vigorous exception. (My two girls from Leonia later were happily married and had their children without trouble.)"

In June, before the team had even left for France, an article appeared in the *American Physical Education Review* that named a women's track and field committee appointed by the American Physical Education Association. The most prominent leader in women's track and field in the United States, Dr. Harry Eaton Stewart, was not named to this committee. The members of the committee were:

Chairman, Katherine Sibley, director of physical education for women, Syracuse University, New York

Alice Belding, director of physical education, Randolph-Macon College, Virginia

Gertrude Hawley, director of physical education for women, Northwestern University, Illinois

Janet Walter, director of women's athletics, public schools, Philadelphia

Carl Schrader, state supervisor of physical education, Board of Education, Boston

H. E. Brown, instructor of field and track, Department of Hygiene, Wellesley, Massachusetts

Dr. Stewart was appointed to the basketball committee. It is easy to see why he was not placed on the track and field committee. The *American Physical Education Review* reported that an informal meeting was held in New York's Hotel Astor on December 27, 1922. The committee members present discussed the relationship of their committee to the Amateur Athletic Union, to Dr. Stewart's organization, and to the National Amateur Athletic Federation. Dr. Stewart was not present. According to the report in the *Review:*

> The committee had received protests from societies and individuals against taking the women's athletic team to Europe last year and sent them to Dr. Stewart who stated that he was obligated, having gone as far as he had in the preparations, to carry through the athletic meet. He promised to cooperate with the committee of the American Physical Education Association after the meet. Disappointment was expressed that he should start an independent organization without consultation, upon his return from Europe.
>
> It was reported that the Amateur Athletic Union had appointed a committee, with Dr. Burdick as chairman, to investigate the problem of women's athletics. The committee presented its report, with a divided vote of five to five. Dr. Burdick and a number of Association leaders recommended that the A.A.U. refrain from taking over the women's athletics, leaving the matter for further study for the Women's Athletic Committee of the American Physical Education Association. The Amateur Athletic Union decided to go ahead without consultation. They were asking a number of the leading women to go on an advisory committee of their own. A number of the leaders at the meeting felt such a policy was undesirable, where they had already refused to cooperate.
>
> Resolutions were read from the Playground Congress, advocating the adoption of standards for women as follows:
>
> Atlantic City Recreation Congress
> October 9-12, 1922
>
> Whereas, athletics for girls and women have recently become of general interest and are in danger of exploitation and
>
> Whereas, we believe that athletics may provide good health and physical and social education for girls and women and
>
> Whereas, we believe that there are physical and social dangers which should be carefully avoided and
>
> Whereas, under well-organized physical training and recreation systems real progress is being made in the development of wholesome athletic activities for girls
>
> Be it resolved that: Conscious of our duty in the premises we recommend the appointment of a commission, representative of America's interest in girls' and

women's athletics, to study the physical and social problems involved in competitive athletics for women and report a policy and program.

During the course of discussion on the subject, it became evident that the following represented the consensus of opinion:

1. We disapprove strongly the exploitation of women in athletics.

2. We stand for the maintenance of the amateur spirit throughout all girls' athletic competitions and sports.

3. We believe that all girls' and women's athletics should be under trained direction and always under the immediate supervision or chaperonage of a woman.

4. We believe that an efficient and proper medical examination is required.

5. We believe that there should be some effective safeguard against girls competing when physiologically unfit.

6. We believe that proper and sufficient clothing should be required.

7. We believe that suitable restriction should be made in the number and type of events girls may enter in any one meet.

8. We regard the representation of America at the Women's International Athletic Games held in Paris in July, 1922, as inopportune and unauthorized by any national representative body and, in view of the present state of women's athletics in this country, we are not in favor of international competition at this time.

The committee asked that these resolutions be transmitted for approval to all organizations interested in girls' athletics, their cooperation solicited and the conclusions published broadly.

Dr. Burnett reported that there were three groups involved in women's athletics:

1) the public school and college group

2) the industrial group

3) the group that the AAU was arranging to organize

It was suggested that "the members of the Women's Committee accept positions on AAU committees. Miss Trilling, Miss Burchenal, and others thought that the committee should show its disapproval of their present methods of organization by withdrawing from the committees, or refusing to serve."

And so we see the downfall of Dr. Stewart, the split with the AAU, and the kindling fires of the fight that would rage for many years between the AAU, soon to be the governing body for women's track and field, and the women physical educators in the United States. It was a turning point for women's track and field in the United States.

The *New York Times* on July 20, 1922, had the following headline: "Women's Meet To Be Held By A.A.U." The story continued:

Preliminary steps looking forward to the direction and control of women's athletics in America were taken at a meeting of a special committee held at the Park Avenue Hotel last night. A resolution was adopted to the effect that the Metropolitan Association of the A.A.U. take control of women's athletic activities within its own district and to promote an athletic field meet either at the College of the City of New York Stadium or at Macombs Dam Park on September 16. The Metropolitan Association of the A.A.U. would issue sanctions to clubs to hold games in the future and furnish registration cards to contestants without fees.

The meet will be open to girls sixteen years of age and over. Entries will not be restricted to the metropolitan district, but will be open to contestants from any section of the country.

The program will include the following events: 50 yard dash, 100 yard dash, 440 yard relay race, standing broad jump, throwing the baseball, throwing the basketball, putting the 8-lb. shot and a one-half mile walk.

It was decided to restrict competitors to two events. Other matters taken up at the meeting was deciding upon a uniform dress for the contestants.

According to Mr. Rubien, President of the Metropolitan Association of the A.A.U., the meeting was initiated by the action of the International Federation abroad in taking control of women's athletics. It was pointed out that this was only a preliminary move, taken for the purpose of stabilizing women's athletics, which are now outside the jurisdiction of any national organization. The A.A.U., as a national organization does not recognize women's events at the present time, although it is possible that this sphere of sport will be included at the time of the annual meeting. The coming meet, however, will be purely under the direction of the metropolitan section of the national body.

On September 17, the *New York Times* announced that two records were witnessed by a crowd of more than 3,000. Miss Eleanor Churchill of Robinson Female Seminary, Exeter, New Hampshire, hurled the baseball 224' 2¼", and the Valcour Club of the Bronx eclipsed the 440-relay record in running 57⁴⁄₁₀ in the women's games. Camelia Sabie equaled her record in the 60-yard hurdles.

This meet was another important first. It was the first AAU meet held under the auspices of the Metropolitan Association of the AAU. More than three hundred athletes took part in Lewishon Stadium at City College, New York.

According to the *New York Times*, "The performances of the girls in the different events spoke volumes for the progress in women's athletics made in this country. ... The girls entered whole-heartedly into the spirit of competition and struggled through their respective events as if their lives depended on the result."

Some events were "open" competition, and some were restricted to the members of the Life Insurance Athletic League. In the 50-yard dash, Sabie beat McCartie, who was competing "unattached," by a yard. Her winning time was 6⁸⁄₁₀.

100-yard dash	
Rose Fisher, Valcour Club	12⁶⁄₁₀
Basketball throw (for Life Insurance athletes)	
Rose Walter, Prudential	76' 9½"
Baseball throw (for Life Insurance athletes)	
Florence Lesner	150' 8"
440 Relay	
Valcour Club	57⁴⁄₁₀
Standing Broad Jump	
Camelia Sabie, Newark Normal	8' 1¼"
Shot Put	
Rose Fisher, Valcour Club	31' 2"
Baseball throw	
Eleanor Churchill, Robinson Seminary	224' 2½"

Basketball throw
    Eleanor Churchill, Robinson Seminary   77' ⅔"
Javelin Throw
    Eleanor Churchill, Robinson Seminary   63' 5⅔"
50-yard dash (for Life Insurance athletes)
    Alice Kelley, Met Life   7¹⁄₁₀
440 relay (for Life Insurance athletes)
    Prudential   61⁶⁄₁₀
Standing broad jump (for Life Insurance athletes)
    Anna Kapalezynski, Met Life   7' 2½"
880-yard walk
    Florence Evans, Bridgeport A.A.   4:12

The third annual Pennsylvania Railroad System games were also held. The events for the women employees consisted of 50 and 75 yard dashes and the 440 relay.

The *Newark Star Eagle's* girls' meet was held on September 23 in Weequahic Park, Newark. The *New York Times* proclaimed, "Miss Sabie Breaks Two World's Marks." Camelia Sabie broke world records in the 60-yard hurdles and the standing broad jump before a crowd of 25,000. She equaled the American record of 12.0 in the 100. Five watches had Sabie in 8⅘ in the hurdles, breaking Floreida Batson's mark of 9.0. The Valcour Club of the Bronx set a record of 55⅗ in the 440 relay, bettering its time from the previous week.

The girls represented many different organizations, including the Valcour Club of the Bronx, Newark Normal Alumni, Edison Lamp Works, South Side High, New Haven School of Physiotherapy, Ladies' Auxiliary, St. Joseph's Catholic Church, Prudential A.A., West Orange Playground, Orange High, and Robert Treat School.

50-yard dash
1. Marion McCartie, Valcour Club   6⅖
2. Camelia Sabie, Newark Normal School
3. Cora Reed, unattached, Newark

100-yard dash
1. Camelia Sabie, Newark Normal School Alumni   12⅕
2. Elizabeth Theim, Edison Lamp Works
3. Luella Mueller, South Side High

Baseball throw
1. Mildred Crotty, New Haven School of Physiotherapy   213' 3"
2. May Quinn, Ladies' Auxiliary, St. Joseph's Catholic Club
3. Ruth Walters, Prudential A.A.

Basketball throw
1. Esther Behring, Prudential A.A., Newark   76' 4"
2. Ruth Walters, Prudential A.A.
3. Ethel Jackson, Orange Playground

8-lb. shot put
1. Gladys Booth, Prudential A.A.   28' 10½"
2. E. Loughlin, East Orange, unattached
3. May Quinn, Ladies' Auxiliary, St. Joseph's Catholic Club

Standing broad jump
1. Camelia Sabie, Newark Normal   8' 3¾"
2. Marie O'Dell, West Orange Playground
3. Hope Gardner, Newark Normal

440-yard relay
1. Valcour Club   55⅗
   (McCartie, Grant, Dixon, Kelley)
2. Prudential A.A.
3. Robert Treat School

In the fall of 1922, newspapers reported other records being broken. In Bridgeport, Connecticut, the Bridgeport Athletic Association bettered the record for the 440 relay in the American Legion Games. Their time was 56.0.

The *Athlete* was first published by the Metropolitan Association of the AAU in 1921. It was a monthly newsletter which fostered and improved amateur athletics in the New York area. Dan Ferris was on the editorial board. No mention was made of women's track activities in the inaugural issue.

Scattered reports of women's meets were reported in the *New York Times*. On May 24, 1920, a story appeared about the first girls' athletic meet conducted by the Morningside Athletic Club at Macombs Dam Park in New York.

Eleanor Smith, a record-holding swimmer, led her team to victory over four other clubs. Eleanor won the 100-yard dash by two yards in 12⅖ and anchored her 440-yard relay team to victory in 1:01⅗, equaling the American record. Other events were the 75-yard dash, basketball throw, running broad jump, and 50-yard potato race.

Chapter 6

1923:
Amateur Athletic Union

In 1923 the Amateur Athletic Union, now the governing body for women's track and field in the country, staged the first national track and field championships. This meet was the foundation which launched the annual women's national competition that exists today as the USA men's and women's national track and field championships.

The first historic meet was held in Newark, New Jersey, at Weequahic Park on September 29, 1923. Girls predominantly from Philadelphia, New York, and New Jersey representing more than twelve organizations fiercely vied to be crowned the first United States champion in one of the eleven events.

One world record was broken. The American record of 12.0 in the 100-yard dash was equaled by four girls during the trials, semifinals, and final, and the American record was shattered in the 440 relay.

Eleanor Churchill broke the world record in the baseball throw. The *New York Times* reported that she "heaved the horsehide the remarkable distance of 234 feet 5¾ inches," which broke her own record set the preceding year at City College, New York.

The 440-relay mark of 52⅖ was now owned by the foursome of Frances Ruppert, Dorothy Bough, Grace Rittler, and Madeline Adams, who represented the Meadowbrook Club of Philadelphia.

The 60-yard hurdles race was run on the grass infield for the first time. Hazel Kirk won and established a record for the event on a grass surface.

High jump
1. Catherine M. Wright, Bridgeport A.C. — 4' 7½"
2. Helen Dinnehey, Shanahan Country Club, Philadelphia — 4' 6¼"
3. Ida Robinson, Philadelphia Turngemeinde — 4' 5¼"

50-yard dash
1. Marion McCartie, City Bank Club, New York — 6⅗
2. Frances Ruppert, Meadowbrook Club, Philadelphia
3. Mabel Steel, Camp Almo, Horseshoe, N.Y.
4. Flora Ledgard, Board of Recreation, Paterson

8-lb. shot put
1. Bertha Christophel, German-American Turn Verein   30' 10½"
2. Roberta Ranck, Philadelphia Turngemeinde   29' 10⅝"
3. Gladys Booth, Prudential Insurance Co. A.A.   28' 3"
4. Freida O'Connor, Savage School, N.Y.   27' 11¾"

60-yard hurdles
1. Hazel Kirk, Prudential Insurance Co. A.A.   9⅗
2. Esther Behring, Prudential Insurance Co. A.A.
3. Rose Garlock, Newark Normal School
4. Bernice Ayer, Meadowbrook Club

100-yard dash
1. Frances Ruppert, Meadowbrook Club   12.0
2. Marion McCartie, City Bank Club, N.Y.
3. Madeline Adams, Meadowbrook Club
4. Mabel Gilliland, City Bank Club

Running broad jump
1. Helen Dinnehey, Shanahan Country Club   15' 4"
2. Alice Adams, Prudential Insurance Co. A.A.   15' ½"
3. Florence Bitner, Meadowbrook Club   15'
4. Marietta Ceres, Prudential Insurance Co. A.A.   14' 8⅛"

Basketball throw
1. Esther Behring, Prudential Insurance Co. A.A.   87' 6"
2. Eleanor Churchill, Robinson Female Seminary, N.H   86' 8"
3. Grace Castor, Philadelphia Turngemeinde   80' 7"
4. Freida O'Connor, Savage School, N.Y.   80'

440-yard relay
1. Meadowbrook Club, Philadelphia   52⅖
   (Ruppert, Bough, Rittler, Adams)
2. City Bank Club, New York
3. Board of Recreation, Paterson, N.J.
4. Prudential Insurance Co., Newark

Baseball throw
1. Eleanor Churchill, Robinson Female Seminary   234' 5¾"
2. Mildred Crotty, Bridgeport A.C.   222' 9½"
3. Grace Castor, Philadelphia Turngemeinde   204' 4"
4. Helen Wilson, unattached, Brooklyn   202' 2"

Discus throw
1. Babe Wolbert, unattached, Newark   71' 9½"
2. Roberta Ranck, Philadelphia Turngemeinde   70' 10"
3. Carrie Gerold, Bridgeport A.C.   65' 10½"
4. H. Haring, Savage School, N.Y.   65' 2"

Javelin throw
1. Roberta Ranck, Philadelphia Turngemeinde   59' 7¾"
2. Jeanette Casper, Bridgeport A.C.   59' 1½"
3. Gladys Booth, Prudential Insurance Co. A.A.   58' 8"
4. Carrie Gerold, Bridgeport A.C.   51' 2 1/2"

Team scores:
Prudential Insurance Company 22; Meadowbrook Club 19; Philadelphia Turngemeinde 17; Bridgeport A.C. 14.

In the December *AAU Bulletin*, Fred L. Steers, chairman of the Committee of Women's Athletics, presented the amended women's rules. Of significance were these items:

4. No woman shall be allowed to compete in more than three events in one day, of which three events not more than two shall be track events. The relay shall count as one track event.

6. No competitor shall permit herself to be massaged, or shall massage herself while on the track or field and no competitor shall take any exercise, or perform any feats not necessary to actual competition.

7. Women athletes shall wear a uniform consisting of brassiere, over-blouse with small neck band, quarter length sleeves or longer, loose fitting running breeches reaching within two inches from the knee caps, or bloomers.

8. The Annual Track and Field Championships for women shall be as follows:

a. Outdoor Meeting — Order of Events:

50 Yards run	Throwing the Javelin
60 Yards Hurdle Race	b. Indoor Meeting
100 Yards Run	40 Yards Run
440 Yards Relay	50 Yards Hurdle Race
Running High Jump	440 Yards Relay
Putting 8 lb. Shot	Running High Jump
Throwing the Discus	Putting 6 lb. Shot
Running Broad Jump	Standing Broad Jump
Throwing the Baseball	Throwing the Basketball

With the AAU having jurisdiction over women's track, men's meets, both indoors and outdoors, added selected women's events to the program. The opportunity for competition was exploding.

The women shared the headlines in the *New York Times* with the men. A combined meet in Chicago on September 3 saw the women break four records, while one record was broken by a male competitor. The women broke two world records and two American records. Five women's events were held on the last day of the men's AAU annual championship games.

Helen M. Filkey, a fifteen-year-old Chicago schoolgirl, leaped 16' 6⅜" in the broad jump for the new world record and sprinted the 100 yards in 11⅗ for a new American record. Katherine Lee, also from Chicago, cleared 4' 10⅞" for a world record in the high jump. Two girls, Marion McCartie and Rose Fisher, ran 11⅗ in the 100 in qualifying heats.

McCartie and Fisher later combined with Adams and Kirk to make an Eastern team and ran to a new 440-relay record of 53⅗. Of the five events that the women competed in, every event culminated in a record except the 75-yard hurdles. This event was won in 11⁶⁄₁₀ by Hazel Kirk, Prudential Insurance Company, Newark, New Jersey.

Less than a week later, on September 8, the Wilco Athletic Association Games were held at Yankee Stadium before a crowd of 8,000. Again, the American 440-relay record was broken. The Meadowbrook Club ran 52⁴⁄₁₀. The team was composed of Frances Ruppert, Dorothy Bough, Grace Rittler, and Madeline Adams. This was the only woman's event in the men's meet of fifteen events.

In the minutes of the Metropolitan Association Meeting, the following comment appeared under the heading of "Women's Athletics":

> Due to the great success athletically of the women's meet which was conducted a year ago greater interest has been aroused, and our association has developed some of the greatest women athletes in America, if not in the world. Through the courtesy of Park Commissioner Hennessy of the Bronx, special provisions have been made at Macomb's Dam Park for dressing and training privileges for women athletes.

In the same Metropolitan Association minutes, the following is recorded in the report of the Women's Athletic Committee given by Martin Klein, chairman:

> A great deal of interest has been shown by various industrial houses, banks and athletic clubs in helping along athletics for women.
>
> The Amateur Athletic Union having taken over the jurisdiction of women's athletics will no doubt stimulate a great deal of interest during the coming year than ever before.
>
> During the past year various athletic clubs holding athletic meets in the various armories have catered somewhat to women's athletics, by putting on one or two events for them; a fairly good entry was always received, and keen competition shown.
>
> I have tried very hard to put on a women's track and field handicap meet.
>
> I have approached various newspapers and clubs looking for aid financially from them. I have still to hear from two newspaper reporters, one of whom I am almost sure will finance a meet of this sort.
>
> The Women's Athletic Committee met on several occasions, and has shown pronounced interest in athletics for women. Each and everyone of this committee was and is very much interested in women's athletics and the committee has thrashed over various subjects and were very careful to slowly but surely bring women's athletics to the fore.
>
> I look for big things for the coming indoor meets.
>
> There was some opposition from various members as well as clubs of the A.A.U. in regard to high and broad jumps for women, and by furnishing data and reports from various capable doctors and physical instructors, the committee has overcome this objection, and I hope to see in the coming indoor meets, the running high jump for women as one of the features.

On May 24, the *Mamaroneck Paragraph* reported the results of another Oaksmere track meet. Miss Helen Meffert broke the interscholastic record for the shot put. She tossed the shot 34' 6¾". More than 150 girls competed in the interscholastic meet, including two prominent athletes from the 1922 Paris meet, Mabel Gilliland and Elizabeth Stine. Gilliland won the 50-yard dash, the 100-yard dash, and the basketball throw.

Late in 1922, the subcommittee on track and field of the American Physical Education Association met in the office of Mr. Carl Schrader in Massachusetts; Katherine Sibley presided. The first discussion was concerned with adding two more members to the committee, one to represent the YWCAs and one from the field of industrial work, or the National League of Girls' Clubs. After hearing other reports and suggestions, the committee decided that there was a need for instruction and standardization of events. Dr. Stewart did this work in 1919. They basically decided upon his list but eliminated the 440 relay in lieu of the 220 relay. They were to send the list of events to a committee of women physicians to be investigated from a medical standpoint and to be approved by them.

The subcommittee recommended the following guide books: *Spalding's Official Rules*, Murphy's *Athletic Training*, Graham and Clark's *Track and Field Athletics*, Clark's *Track Athletics Up-To-Date*, Hjertberg's *Athletic Theory and Practice*, and Carl Schrader's articles on coaching.

In the meantime, with track and field competition exploding for girls and women around the country and with the loss of jurisdiction over the sport, a Conference on Athletics and Physical Recreation for Women and Girls was called by Mrs. Herbert Hoover at the suggestion of the National Amateur Athletic Federation of America. It was held in Washington, D.C., on April 6–7, 1923. Sessions included "Limitations for Women and Girls in Athletics," "Inter-school versus inter-mural athletics," and "Standard Ideals and Avoidance of Exploitation." The outcome of the conference, as reported in the *American Physical Education Review,* stressed the fact that the program for women depends upon women experts. The women physical educators wanted their committee to deliberate, investigate, legislate, promote, and control national sports for girls and women. A statement was made that schools and other organizations should stress enjoyment of the sport and development of sportsmanship and minimize the emphasis which was being placed upon individual accomplishment and the winning of championships. Publicity given to the event should stress the sport and not the individual or group competitors. Subcommittee members also went on record again saying:

> Whereas, certain international competitions for women and girls have already been held, and
> Whereas, we believe that the participation of American women and girls in these competitions was inopportune. Be it resolved, that it is the sense of this conference that in the future such competitions, if any, be organized and controlled by the national organization set up as a result of this conference.

The information from the conference was released to all members, the Associated Press, and the American Physical Education Association.

The position of the Amateur Athletic Union was stated in the first issue of its newsletter. A report by William C. Prout of Boston, the newly elected president of the AAU, was delivered at the 35th annual convention in Detroit in November and included this passage:

> During the past year, through the medium of a most efficient committee, we have given deep consideration to the question of women competing in track and

THE NATIONAL AMATEUR ATHLETIC FEDERATION OF AMERICA

Please send reply to

2300 S Street,
Washington, D. C.

March 15th, 1923.

Dr. Elizabeth B. Thelberg,
Vassar College,
Poughkeepsie, N. Y.

My dear Doctor Thelberg:

In furtherance of the program adopted on December 29, 1922, at the annual meeting of the National Amateur Athletic Federation of America, I have been designated by the Executive Committee of the Federation, as the only woman vice president of the organization, to call a meeting in Washington on April 6 and 7 of those especially interested in athletics and physical recreation for women and girls.

The purpose of the conference is to afford opportunity for the discussion of the three following major topics:

1. Standards and tests, and their coordination.
2. Mass activities and their effect on
   (a) The individual.
   (b) The community.
3. Competitive athletics.

There will also be opportunity to discuss any outstanding problems connected with the general subject.

We desire to have at this conference recognized leaders in the various related fields of hygiene, physical education and physical recreation. We therefore very much hope that you yourself will be able to attend. If that is quite impossible, can you send a substitute?

May I also ask whether you will consider the subjects in question and send me suggestions as to any points you think particularly desirable to include in the discussion?

It would greatly facilitate our effort if you could let me know your decision immediately.

Yours sincerely,

Mrs. Herbert Hoover
Vice President, National Amateur Athletic Federation of America.

Letter from Lou Henry Hoover (Mrs. Herbert Hoover) calling the meeting on April 6 and 7, 1923. (Courtesy of Special Collections, Vassar College Libraries.)

field sports. This is admittedly a rather perplexing problem and while it may be said it is still in its experimental stage from the work accomplished thus far we can look forward to the future with the feeling of confidence that comes to us in recalling the splendid success that the A.A.U. has had in every activity which has thus far been entrusted to its keeping.

Chapter 7

1924

The second women's national AAU outdoor championship track and field meet was held on September 20, 1924, at Forbes Field in Pittsburgh, Pennsylvania.

50-yard dash
1. Christine Pylick, Pennsylvania R.R., Cleveland   6.2
2. Grace Rittler, Meadowbrook Club
3. Christine Joseph, Meadowbrook Club
4. Marietta Ceres, Prudential A.C.

100-yard dash
1. Frances Ruppert, Meadowbrook Club   12.0
2. Christine Pylick, Pennsylvania R.R., Cleveland
3. Marietta Ceres, Prudential A.C.
4. Nanette Dowling, Pennsylvania R.R., Cleveland

60-yard hurdles
1. Hazel Kirk, Prudential A.C.   9.0
2. Clara Farley, Prudential A.C.
3. Esther Behring, Prudential A.C.
4. Ida Robinson, Philadelphia Turngemeinde

440-yard relay
1. Meadowbrook Club, Philadelphia   57.0
   (Ruppert, Rittler, Adams, Dickson)
2. Pennsylvania R.R., Cleveland
3. Prudential A. C.

Running broad jump
1. Dorothy Walsh, Rocky River, Ohio   15' 3"
2. Marietta Ceres, Prudential A.C.
3. Nanette Dowling, Pennsylvania R.R., Cleveland
4. Ida Robinson, Philadelphia Turngemeinde

8-lb. shot put
1. Esther Behring, Prudential A.C.   30' 1½"
2. Gladys Booth, Prudential A.C.
3. Bertha Christophal, German-American Turn Verein, N.Y.
4. Roberta Ranck, Philadelphia Turngemeinde

Javelin throw	
1. Esther Spargo, Boston Swimming Club	72' $5\frac{3}{4}$"
2. Roberta Ranck, Philadelphia Turngemeinde	
3. Catherine Donovan, Prudential A.C.	
4. Gladys Booth, Prudential A.C.	
Discus throw	
1. Roberta Ranck, Philadelphia Turngemeinde	70'
2. Minnie Wolbert, Millrose A.A.	
3. Clara Farley, Prudential A.C.	
4. Gladys Booth, Prudential A.C.	
Baseball throw	
1. Mabel Holmes, board of education, Paterson, N.J.	199' 10"
2. Alberta Bauman, unattached	
3. Florence Eggleston, Rocky River, Ohio	
4. Miss Donnelly, unattached	

The Prudential Athletic Club won the team title.

Spalding's Official Athletic Almanac listed the American records and women's world records:

30y	$3\frac{4}{5}$	Betty Brown, New Haven Normal School of Gymnastics
50y	6.0	Eleanor Macbeth, New Haven Normal School of Gymnastics
75y	$8\frac{3}{5}$	L. Haydock, Bryn Mawr College
100y	$11\frac{3}{5}$	Helen Filkey, Chicago, Aug. 2, 1923 Norma Zilk, Chicago, Oct. 11, 1924
220y	$28\frac{2}{5}$	Lucile Godbold, Winthrop College
300m	$43\frac{3}{5}$	Mary McCune, Rosemary Hall
880y	$2{:}35\frac{4}{5}$	Lucile Godbold, Winthrop College
1000m	$3{:}28\frac{3}{5}$	Lucile Godbold, Winthrop College
60yh (four, 2')	8.0	Josephine Schessler, Agnes Scott College, 1923
60yh (four, 2'6")	$8\frac{4}{5}$	Camelia Sabie, New Jersey Normal School
65yh (six, 2'6")	11.0	Mary Worrall, Sargent School of Physical Education
100yh (eight, 2')	$14\frac{2}{5}$	Floreida Batson, Rosemary Hall
100yh (eight, 2'6")	$14\frac{2}{5}$	Camelia Sabie, New Jersey Normal School
220yr	$28\frac{2}{5}$	Oaksmere School (Agar, Suydam, Snow, Metzger)
440yr	$52\frac{4}{5}$*	Meadowbrook Club (Ruppert, Joseph, Rittler, Adams), Sept. 8, 1923
440yr	$54\frac{1}{5}$*	National City Bank Team (McCartie, Carlson, Hassard, Gilliland), March 11, 1924
HJ	4' $10\frac{7}{8}$"	Katherine Lee, Chicago, 1923
SHJ	3' 8"	Natalie Wilson, Sargent School of P.E.

SBJ	8' 3¾"	Camelia Sabie, New Jersey Normal School
RBJ	16' 9½"	Maude Devereux, Skidmore College
H,S,J	33' 10¼"	Elizabeth Stine, Leonia High School, New Jersey
PV	7' 2"	Mildred Carl, New Haven Normal School of Gymnastics
6lb. SP	43'	Leslie Perkins, Sargent School of P.E.
8lb. SP	36' 11¾"	Lucile Godbold, Winthrop College
8lb. SP (both hands)	68' 8"	Lucile Godbold, Winthrop College
12lb. SP	28' 4"	Margaret Mitchell, Wykeham Rise School, Connecticut
Discus (free style)	98' 2"	Nell Carroll, Florida State College for Women
Javelin	98' 4"	Kathryn Agar, Oaksmere School
Javelin (both hands)	135' 3½"	Kathryn Agar, Oaksmere School
Basketball	94' 2"	Maude Rosenbaum, Oaksmere School
Hurlball	104' 2½"	Nell Carroll, Florida State College for Women
Baseball	234' 5¾"	Eleanor Churchill, Robinson Seminary, 1923

* indoor record

The National Women's Collegiate and Scholastic Track Athletics Association listed women's records. Dr. Stewart was president of this organization, Howard Cleaveland was vice president, Joseph D'Angola was treasurer, and Suzanne Becker was secretary. Preparatory school and collegiate records were listed. American women accounted for eight world records in the running events and thirteen in the field events.

A national AAU Women's Track and Field Committee was listed in the February 23, 1924, *AAU Bulletin*.

Fred Steers, Chairman (Central)
Miss M.C. Hagan (Middle Atlantic)
George Vreeland (Metropolitan)
Miss Ada Taylor (Middle Atlantic)
Martin Klein (Metropolitan)
Mrs. E. Fullard Leo (Hawaiian)
John Magee (New England)
Miss Charlotte Epstein (Metropolitan)
Dr. William Burdick (South Atlantic)
Dr. deNaouley (Metropolitan)

Five American track and field records were accepted by the committee. The new records appeared in the December 19, 1924, *AAU Bulletin*. An indoor record for the 440 relay of 54⅕ was recognized. It was set on March 11, 1924, in New York City by the National City Bank team of McCartie, Carlson, Hassard, and Gilliland.

Outdoor records approved were 440 relay, 52⅘, Meadowbrook Club, Philadelphia (Ruppert, Joseph, Rittler and Adams), at Yankee Stadium, N.Y., September 8, 1923; 70-yard low hurdles, 10⅕, Nellie Todd, Chicago, October 11, 1924; 100 yards, 11⅗, Norma Zilk, Chicago, October 11, 1924, and Helen Filkey, Chicago, August 2, 1923.

On April 4, 1924, an indoor meet was held in the armory in Paterson, New Jersey. The *Paterson Morning Call* referred to it as a "monster indoor meet." Four AAU events for women were on the program. The headlines the next day proclaimed, "Two Records Go In Meet At Armory." Of the four women's events, two women broke records, and the other two events were won by "local" girls. Marion McCartie, National City Bank, bettered the 50-yard dash mark, sprinting the distance in 6⅖. Hazel Kirk set a new record of 8⅘ in the 60-yard hurdles. Eleanor Egg of the Paterson Recreation Club won the high jump at 4' 6", and the Paterson Recreation Club won the 440 relay in 56.0. Eleanor Egg was a member of the relay team.

The *New York Times* on September 21 had a photograph of six American girls who competed in an Athletic Day Meet in Toronto. The girls were Marie Teichman, Norma Zilk, Nellie Todd, and Helen Filkey, all of Chicago, and Esther Behring and Hazel Kirk of Newark.

Meanwhile, the struggle in the academic circles continued. Mabel Lee, a leading physical educator, wrote an article, published in the January 1924 *American Physical Education Review*, entitled "The Case For and Against Intercollegiate Athletics for Women and the Situation as it Stands Today." Suggestions were made by Lee as alternatives to interscholastic competition, such as making the athletic girl an "assistant instructor" and scheduling "inter-collegiate interclass activity with very close neighbors" or even participating in telegraphic meets in track. In a small survey conducted with fifty colleges, eleven had intercollegiate athletics. Only two directors of physical education were "ardent advocates" of intercollegiate competition. Over 90 percent opposed intercollegiate competition for women.

The workshop group of the Women's Division of the National Amateur Athletic Federation met on February 6 and decided to devote the next session to designing "standards for a field meet." The subject was to be considered from an "intra"-institutional viewpoint and topics for consideration were the following:

I. Eligibility for participation
    1. physical examination
    2. training
    3. behavior — should a girl be disqualified for such things as poor
       spirit, uncontrolled temper, etc.?

II. Program
    The events listed are merely suggestions.
    Running
       dashes   25, 50, 75 yard dashes

hurdles   2' and 2' 6" high — distances up to 75 yards
relays   up to 75 yard limit for each runner
walking races

Throwing
    basketball
    baseball
    hurlball
    discus
    javelin

Jumping
    running high jump
    running broad jump
    standing high jump
    standing broad jump

III. Uniforms
    We recommend a modest uniform, suitable for track needs.
    What shall it be?

The workshop group suggested women officials, prizes of little intrinsic value, limited audiences by invitation only, and no publicity. Group events and scoring should be emphasized rather than individuals or record breaking.

Lillian Schoedler, the executive secretary, stated that "groups from all parts of the country are looking to the Women's Division for guidance and help in the problems of girls' and women's athletics."

Katherine Sibley, chairman of the subcommittee on track and field, gave her first report on April 15, 1924. It was presented at the Eastern District Convention in Atlantic City, New Jersey, and published in the October *American Physical Education Review*.

Sibley began by emphasizing that the preliminary report given at the previous year's convention offering suggestive programs for those institutions that were looking for guidance in the way of events and rules were not final recommendations but "safe" suggestions. She then discussed possible approaches to track and field for women:

> Many schools and institutions have barred this sport [track and field] because in the minds of the teachers it is connected with ideas of prolonged training with intense individual competition. To many people and teachers track and field athletics means a track meet. But it has been demonstrated both in the army camps and industrial athletic clubs that it may be used as a satisfactory form of daily exercise. It was the consensus of opinion of those who are interested in and who teach athletics for women, that this particular branch of sport needed revision and standardization. Competition may be desirable if only against one's own record.

Sibley's report indicated that investigation and study into track were necessary and that selected colleges all over the country were testing events for uniformity in athletics. Randolph-Macon was studying the dashes, with Bryn Mawr and Vassar assisting. The University of Wisconsin was measuring the distance of the hurdle race and heights, with Mt. Holyoke and Earlham assisting. The University of Arizona was testing the throws, with Washington State and Western Reserve helping. Northwestern had the jumping events, with Ohio and Syracuse assisting. Miss Frost of Columbia was investigating the value of spiked shoes. The schools were to use the spring track season to do the research and submit reports.

Eleanor Egg: A Pioneer Track Star

My interview with Eleanor Egg Krattiger took place in December 1991, when she was eighty-two years old and living in Florida. She told me that she was born on February 3, 1909, in Wilkes-Barre, Pennsylvania. Her family was on the stage at the time and were called "The 3 Spauldings." Eleanor recalls:

> We were on the stage when I was a child. I joined my family's act at one year, seven months and I was billed all over the country as the smallest acrobat in the world. Theatrical people didn't challenge each other unless they didn't like you. Maybe I wasn't the smallest in the world but I seemed to be. I've had a wonderful life. Just gorgeous.
>
> I started running in the seventh or eighth grade. Two men from Paterson, Dr. Burnett and Harry Gourley, started a club for boys. The two men were arguing with a physical education teacher from School Number Five in Paterson that they had the four best girls around. They could beat anybody, even the women around. We were children, I was less than fourteen when we started. In fact, we got put out of the AAU because we weren't fourteen. We had to wait a year to compete again. They started yelling at us after we won. We were children beating women.
>
> I competed for the Paterson Recreation Club. In our town we had four separate teams, and all the girls were good. I still see the girls, one of them was here a week ago. They come down to Florida for a vacation. Ellen Brough Post, who ran the two-twenty, is still a friend. We once had a Paterson runner's reunion. I moved to Florida in nineteen seventy-nine.
>
> My mother and father were definitely with me. They were there all the time. They did lots of things with me. My father paid the fare for the girls who didn't have any money and stuff like that. I'm the only one who ran in my family.
>
> I did everything. I was all around. At one time the papers called me "iron girl." As for the Olympics, I had the best chance in 1932. But in 1931, I got hurt. I tore the ligaments in my foot and leg, and I was out of competition for two years. So I missed the best chance that I ever had. I'll never know what I might have done.
>
> In 1931, I beat Stella Walsh. Let me tell you about that. Everybody gets excited over it. I know what happened. I felt very sorry for her. I beat her that day in a hundred in Jersey City. I don't count that race like everybody else does. They all get mad at me, and they say I shouldn't tell anybody. Well, I'm sorry, it's the way it is. She had been in the discus throw just before our race. The discus slid out of her hand and she fractured a man's skull and for a while there was talk of her being brought up on charges. I know that had to throw her. I beat her that day but I didn't beat her record so I, personally, don't count it. And I get yelled at for it. That's my claim to fame. That was the last time I had a chance to run against her.

Eleanor's track accomplishments are chronicled in two New Jersey history books, *Past and Promise: Lives of New Jersey Women* and *New Jersey History*. J. Thomas Jable's article "Eleanor Egg: Paterson's Track and Field Heroine" in *New Jersey History* was particularly enlightening and supplemented Eleanor's information.

Imagine having a bronze plaque of yourself depicting a run to victory in a national championships enshrined on a wall of the stadium in your home town. The commemorative plaque of Eleanor captures her "form, speed and grace" in sprinting to the 1931 United States 100-yard championship. The plaque is on the northwest wall of Hinchliffe Stadium in Paterson, New Jersey. It is inscribed "Eleanor Egg — Champion of America." It represents the "supreme honor that the city of Paterson bestowed upon its track and field heroine of the 20's and 30's."

Eleanor's introduction to major competition began in 1923. Track and field was growing rapidly in the United States, and the first national championships were staged in Newark.

The Paterson girls' relay team finished third in the inaugural AAU competition. Fourteen-year-old Eleanor was the star, and her career was launched. In the Osceola Games in New York early in 1924, she beat Marion McCartie in the 75-yard dash. From 1924 through 1926, the indoor 50-yard dash record changed hands several times. Eleanor, Marion, and Rosa Grosse of Canada vied for the American and world record. Eleanor set a record of 6⅖ in Paterson on December 6, 1924.

Entering a number of events from the sprints to the jumps and throws, on February 13, 1926, in the Metropolitan Indoor Championships, Eleanor jumped 4' 10⅜" in the high jump for an American record. She captured first place in the 50-yard dash, too. Outdoors, she placed in five different events in a dual meet with the Prudential Insurance Athletic Association. She won the high jump, 50 and 100 yard dashes, and took second in the broad jump and shot put.

At times, Eleanor's mother acted as the team chaperon during trips to competitions out of town. Her mother went with the team to the Pasadena nationals, and in addition to chaperoning and "rubbing down" the girls, she competed in the shot put. Perhaps they were the first mother-daughter duo to compete in a track meet.

When the national meet was held in Pasadena in 1925, the Metropolitan AAU did not have enough money to send Eleanor and her three relay teammates to California. The Paterson Chamber of Commerce raised the money because it expected the relay team to be the "Champions of America." On the way to California, the "flying four," as they were known in Paterson, defeated their rivals in an exhibition in Chicago. The Paterson press was jubilant. The *Paterson Evening News* proclaimed that sixteen-year-old Eleanor was "one of the finest specimens of womanhood that any city in this meet can boast of." In Pasadena, the team finished second, and Eleanor was third in the high jump and 50-yard dash. On their way home from Pasadena, they competed in a meet in San Francisco for the Pacific Coast championships.

The city of Paterson celebrated upon their return home. Led by Eleanor, the girls were the heroines of New Jersey.

On February 4, 1926, the United States team of Gilliland, Egg, Ruppert, and McNeil set an American record of 52.9 in the 440 relay. In the Metropolitan outdoor championships that year, Eleanor won the high jump at 4' 9" and finished second in the 100, thereby earning the right to go to the nationals in Philadelphia. In that meet, she placed third in the 100, behind Rosa Grosse of Canada and Helen Filkey of Chicago.

The last two meets of the season were in Connecticut; the Paterson club won both of the dual meets.

Eleanor's career peaked in 1927. She set metropolitan records in the shot put and broad jump, said Jable. Her teammate Ellen Brough broke the American record in the 220. At the nationals in Eureka, California, both Eleanor and Ellen starred. Eleanor jumped 17 feet 1¾ in the broad jump, for a new American record, and Ellen won the 220 in 26⅘ seconds. Eleanor also captured the medal for second in the 50 and fourth in the shot put.

In 1928, despite an injury, Eleanor was "determined to compete," according to Jable. When the first Olympic tryouts were held in Newark in 1928 in conjunction with the nationals, she competed in the high jump but did not place. An interesting story evolved from her plight. Elta Cartwright, the 100 meter champion, asked the officials to name Eleanor to the squad. She said, "If I can do anything or say anything, Miss Egg will be a member of the team for I know that she can help us win points if she gets to Amsterdam." Elta established a fund for Eleanor with a hundred dollar donation and asked her teammates to do likewise. This would cover Eleanor's expenses to Amsterdam. Eleanor thanked Elta but declined knowing that physically she was not capable of performing at her best.

She competed in the 1929 and 1930 National Championships, her seventh and eighth Nationals. In 1929 in Chicago, she placed second to Rena MacDonald in the shot and third behind Olympian Jean Shiley in the high jump. In 1930 in Dallas, she finished fourth to Stella Walsh in the 100 and placed third in the shot put and broad jump.

In the fall of 1930, a meet was held in Pershing Field as one of the celebrations of Jersey City's tercentenary. A Canadian-American relay match was to be held. Eleanor was invited to be part of the United States team. However, when the gun sounded and Eleanor sprinted off the starting line, it was not for the American team. She was the lead-off leg for the Canadians! It seems as though while traveling to New Jersey, Rosa Grosse had an attack of appendicitis. Mel Sheppard, coach of the Millrose AA, "confident that his athletes were unbeatable, 'loaned' Eleanor to the Canadians." This put her in an awkward position, especially in her home state of New Jersey. She wanted to run her best but on the other hand did not want to be a "traitor." She handed the baton to the second Canadian girl two yards ahead of the American team! The officials voted her the outstanding athlete of the meet for her unselfish efforts.

In the 1931 nationals in front of 15,000 spectators, the Stella Walsh story, as told by Eleanor, unfolded. Eleanor beat her in the 100-yard final in 11.4. Evelyn Furtsch was second and Stella third.

The ankle injury recurred after the 1931 season, and Eleanor competed in only a few meets. In the 1932 Olympic tryouts, she was eliminated in the preliminary heats. Although Eleanor had planned to compete longer, the constant problem from the old injury led her to retire. She had amassed 227 medals, 22 silver cups, 6 trophies, and numerous other awards.

Following her retirement from competition, after nearly ten years, Eleanor organized and coached a track club for Paterson school girls and taught dance at her mother's studio. She spoke to school students and groups about track and field technique and her own experiences. Eleanor's athletic achievements alone would have made her a popular person but, "her attractive personality and 'stage presence' bolstered her image" in Paterson. "She was both a fine athlete and a colorful sports personality," concluded Jable.

Chapter 8

1925

Three years had passed since the Amateur Athletic Union voted to assume jurisdiction and control of women's track and field. Fred Steers, the chairman of the women's committee, said that although the initial response was weak and came from only two localities, the enthusiasm had become widespread and competitions were being sponsored and encouraged throughout the United States.

Steers said that the prejudice against competition had almost entirely disappeared. He maintained that three years of competitions had shown that no physical harm came to the participants and women did not exhaust their physical strength.

One request to add the pole vault to the program was received, but the committee, by a majority male vote, refused to concur with the proposal.

The national championship meet was held in Pasadena on July 11. This was the first nationals and the largest meet held for women on the West Coast. The Pasadena Athletic and Country Club appropriated the sum of $2000 to apply primarily to the expenses of competitors, and this enabled a large number of athletes to come to the competition from all parts of the country. One hundred girls from twelve teams from states around the country were represented at Paddock Field. The national pentathlon championships and a special 100-meter dash and 440 relay were held for men in conjunction with the women's meet.

For days before the meet began, the local newspapers had articles about the meet and photographs of many of the athletes in action. Exciting stories about the arrival by train of the first group of thirty-four eastern athletes graced the papers. The names of "noted men" officials were released by Aileen Allen. Fred Steers was "honorary" referee. Robert Weaver, Dean Cromwell, and George Eastman, big names in men's track, all had official positions.

One woman journalist described the girls as she saw them after a practice session in the locker room. The article, "Sports Fail to Conquer Femininity," was in the *Pasadena Evening Post* prior to the meet. She saw the girls as "daintily feminine" and said that even though they were devoted to their sport, they were faithful followers of dame fashion. Colors of orchid and apricot apparel were evident. The girls called each other by their first names and were not "boisterous" or "offensive." They were between seventeen and twenty-five, and some were older. Eleanor Egg's mother, Mrs. Lena Egg, was described as a "womanly woman."

A beautiful photo of Elizabeth Stine winning the high jump at 4' 10" at the AAU national championships July 11, 1925. Elizabeth held the American record of 4' 10½ in 1923 and was a memeber of our first international team that competed in Paris. (UPI/Bettmann)

She served as the team chaperone for the girls of Paterson in their purple bloomers and gold sweaters, rubbed them down, and also put the shot.

The Pasadena Athletic and Country Club entertained the visiting athletes. Seventeen of the athletes were taken on a tour of the Hollywood studios. "It was clearly displayed that the social, sportsmanship and athletic features of such a contest have a beneficial and far-reaching effect upon the participants," concluded the *Pasadena Evening Post.*

Before a crowd of about 3,000 spectators, six records were set. The headlines of the evening newspaper read, "Girl Star Breaks World Hurdle Record." Seventeen-year-old Helen Filkey, who three years earlier had been sent from Chicago to California to regain her health, was the first athlete to break a record at the meet in the morning trials.

100-yard dash
1. Helen Filkey, Chicago A.C.   11⁴⁄₁₀ (ties WR)
2. Elta Cartwright, Eureka A.C.
3. Frances Ruppert, Meadowbrook A.C.
4. Mabel Gilliland, Savage School

High jump
1. Elizabeth Stine, Savage School   4' 10"
2. Marci Howard, Eureka A.C.

Pasadena Athletic and Country Club team. *Left to right:* Nellie Doerschlag, Kate Moore, Ethel Nichols, Alice Ryden, Elvira Peterson, Lillian Copeland and MayBelle Reichardt. (Courtesy of Pasadena Public Library and Pasadena Athletic Club.)

3. Eleanor Egg, Paterson A.C.
4. Anna Koll, Wiltz A.C.

50-yard dash
1. Elta Cartwright, Eureka   6⅒ MR
2. Mabel Gilliland, Savage School
3. Eleanor Egg, Paterson A.C.
4. Ethel Nichols, Pasadena Athletic and Country Club

Discus throw
1. MayBelle Reichardt, Pasadena   87' 2¾"
2. Aurelia Brown, San Jose
3. Lillian Copeland, Pasadena
4. Estelle Moloss, Eureka A.C.

60-yard hurdles
1. Helen Filkey, Chicago A.C.   8⅗ WR
2. Hazel Kirk, Prudential Insurance Club
3. Alta Huber, Eureka
4. Alda Silva, Vallejo

8-lb. shot
1. Lillian Copeland, Pasadena   32' 10⅝"
2. MayBelle Reichardt, Pasadena
3. Rena Acquistapace, Vallejo
4. Marie Bulce, Vallejo

Javelin throw
1. Alda Silva, Vallejo   105' 8"
2. Estelle Moloss, Eureka
3. Margaret Proctor, Luxenbury
4. Katherine Young, Anaheim

Baseball throw
1. Ann Harrington, Eureka   232'
2. Lillian Copeland, Pasadena
3. Mabel Holmes, Paterson
4. Evelyn Maxon, unattached

Running broad jump
1. Helen Filkey, Chicago A.C.   17' WR
2. Elvira Peterson, Pasadena
3. Lois Reed, Pasadena,
   and Elizabeth Stine, Savage School

440 Relay
1. Pasadena   52⅘₁₀
   (Nelson, Nichols, Ryden, Doerschlag)
2. Paterson
3. Vallejo
4. Eureka

The clubs and schools represented at the meet were Eureka Athletic Club, Vallejo Athletic Club, San Jose Athletic Club, Chicago Athletic Club, Kern County High School, Berkeley Athletic Club, Paterson Recreation Athletic Club, Anaheim Athletic Club, Los Angeles Athletic Club, New Orleans, Pasadena Athletic and Country Club, Meadowbrook Athletic Club, and the Savage School.

While Pasadena won the point total, the star of the meet was Helen Filkey, who wore a bright red uniform. Heralded as the best athlete in the world, Helen won three events, all in record-breaking performances. Headlines in the *New York Times* on July 12 read, "Miss Filkey Sets 3 World Records."

The Pasadena Athletic and Country Club was the first Southern California club reported Lynne Emery in *The Pasadena Athletic Club and Sport for Southern California Women in the 1920's*. Soon after the nationals were awarded to Pasadena, forty women began training that December for the big national meet. Enthusiasm was high when after only two months of training, the 440 relay team of Doerschlag, Nelson, Nichols, and Ryden ran 53.3 for an American record. In another meet prior to the nationals, the relay team bettered its own record, running 52.7.

"For the first time women's events were included in the May AAU Southern California championships and Elizabeth Nelson won the 220 yard dash in 27.8 seconds setting the Club's first world record," said Emery. On July 18, she ran 27.2.

When the Pasadena nationals were over, the Pasadena Club, competing in national championships for the first time, had won the title, but not until the points from the last event, the 440 relay, were tallied.

At the annual AAU convention in November, Chairman Steers said that the committee had voted to add the 220-yard dash to the indoor and outdoor national championship program. In view of this addition, the rules read, "Provided, however, no competitor in a race of over 110 yards shall be allowed to compete in any other event." Another significant proposal was to add the 8-lb. shot to the indoor program to replace the 6-lb. shot.

In a report from the second meeting of the Women's Division of the National Amateur Athletic Federation of America in Chicago in 1925, the women took action "in opposition to the present tendency toward the wearing of track pants in girls' and women's athletics. It was moved, seconded, and carried that the 'Women's Division as here represented go on record as opposed to the wearing of track pants or their equivalent in public meets and public performances.'"

Since Dr. Harry Stewart was not on a track committee, his articles no longer appeared in the journals. L. W. Sargent, of the Sargent School for Physical Education, wrote on the technique of hurdling in the May 1925 *American Physical Education Review*.

Chapter 9

1926

The outdoor national meet was on July 9-10, under a blazing sun in Philadelphia. This was the first two-day championships. The *New York Times* announced on July 10 that three United States marks fell in the championship meet and one world and two American records were equaled.

Lillian Copeland shattered two of the records, throwing the discus 101' 1", which broke the record set by Nell Carroll of Florida State College for Women, and putting the shot 38' ¾", eclipsing Lucile Godbold's record. Ellen Brough of Paterson won a heat in the 220-yard dash in 27⅘, equaling the record set by Elizabeth Nelson of Los Angeles in May of 1925. It was the first year that the 220-yard dash was an event in the program. Betty Siska equaled the American record in a heat of the 50-yard dash.

The second day of competition saw two more record-breaking performances. The *New York Times* said, "A pitiless sun drove pedestrians off the street here ... but the athletes went on to break the world's record, one American record, and tie one world's and one meet mark. ... The world's record went when Lillian Copeland of Pasadena, the outstanding star of the two days of competition, won her third title today." Lillian had no competition in the event (javelin) and broke the existing record by almost 6 feet. She was the only triple winner of the day.

Prior to Lillian's record-breaking performances at this meet, she had a throw in the discus in May of 103' 5½", a shot put toss in June of 40' 4¼" and a June javelin throw of 116' 7½".

The *New York Times* article gave further details of the championship meet:

> The American mark to go by the board fell in the running high jump when Catherine Maguire of St. Louis cleared the bar at 4 feet 11¼". The old mark was 4 feet 10⅞". This event was a fight between the winner and Elizabeth Stine of Paterson, who was barely a quarter of an inch below her.
>
> The closest fight on the track came in the 220 yard run, when Frances Keddie of Northern California and Ellen Brough, unattached, came out of the chute running neck and neck.
>
> At the 100 yard point, Miss Brough took a slight lead, but the California girl had a lot left and in the last few yards nosed out Ellen Brough. The time of the final was 28⁶⁄₁₀, a little slower than Miss Brough's time yesterday.

50-yard dash
1. Elta Cartwright, No. Calif. A.C.   6.1

2. Betty Siska, Midwest A.C.
3. Mary Weime, unattached

100-yard dash
1. Rosa Grosse, Toronto Ladies' A.C.   11.8
2. Helen Filkey, Midwest A.C.
3. Eleanor Egg, Paterson Recreation Club

220-yard run
1. Frances Keddie, No. Calif. A.C.   28.6
2. Ellen Brough, unattached, New Jersey
3. Ethel Nichols, Pasadena Athletic and Country Club

60-yard hurdles
1. Helen Filkey, Midwest A.C.   8.7
2. Hazel Kirk, Prudential Ins. Co.
3. Nellie Todd, Midwest A.C.

Running high jump
1. Catherine Maguire, New Coliseum A.C.   4' 11¼" AR
2. Elizabeth Stine, Paterson Recreation Club
3. Ruth Brinton, Meadowbrook Club

Running broad jump
1. Nellie Todd, Midwest A.C.   16' 7⅜"
2. Helen Filkey, Midwest A.C.
3. Elta Cartwright, No. Calif. A.C.
4. Catherine Maguire, New Coliseum A.C.

8-lb. shot
1. Lillian Copeland, Pasadena Athletic and Country Club   38' 3¾"
2. Rena MacDonald, Boston Swimming Assn.
3. Aurelia Brown, No. Calif. A.C.
4. Florence Wolf, VVV Girl's A.C., Detroit

Discus throw
1. Lillian Copeland, Pasadena Athletic and Country Club   101' 1"
2. MayBelle Reichardt, Pasadena Athletic and Country Club
3. Dee Boeckmann, New Coliseum A.C.
4. Florence Wolf, VVV Girl's A.C., Detroit

Javelin throw
1. Lillian Copeland, Pasadena Athletic and Country Club   112' 5½"
2. Pauline Hascup, Paterson Recreation Club
3. Alice Ryden, Pasadena Athletic and Country Club
4. Clara Ballard, McGill College

Baseball throw
1. Mabel Holmes, Paterson Recreation Club   212' 9"
2. Margaret Watson, Wilmerding YWCA
3. Lillian Kelly, Brooklyn Edison Co.
4. Jean Godson, unattached

440-yard relay
1. Toronto Ladies' A.C. (Davies, Glover, Belle, Grosse)   51.0

2. Pasadena Athletic and Country Club
3. No. Calif. A.C.

Pasadena won the team title for the second straight year. Performances improved, as can be seen by the above results. Lillian Copeland became the nation's best thrower, setting American records in the shot, discus, and javelin. The relay team, in addition to the 440 relay, ran all of the listed distances for women's relays and broke the record for every distance. The club set eight national records.

Helen Filkey of Chicago shaved a fifth of a second from her own indoor American record time and equaled the world mark for the 70-yard dash when she raced the distance in 8⅖ at the American Institute of Banking track and field games.

The December *A.A.U. Bulletin* listed the "Women's Athletics" committee with Fred Steers as chairman. The associations represented were Allegheny, Connecticut, Florida, Hawaii, Indiana-Kentucky, Inter-mountain, Metropolitan, Michigan, Middle Atlantic, New England, Niagara, Ohio, Pacific, South Atlantic, Southeastern, Southern, Southern Pacific, and Western. There were ten women and twelve men in this group.

In this same year, Steers visited Texas and met with several people representing the Southwestern District of Playgrounds and Recreation who played leading parts in athletics and recreation in the Southern district. He spoke at the meeting, endeavoring to show how competitive sports provided physical and mental benefits and how the champion athletes were role models who imparted incentive and encouragement to other women.

The AAU associations in different parts of the country conducted meets prior to the nationals. Results for 1926 appear in the 1927 *Spalding's Almanac*. The Metropolitan Association had indoor and outdoor championships, the New England Association had outdoor championships, the Allegheny Mountain Association had outdoor championships (a list of their records appeared in this *Spalding's Almanac*), and the Southern Association and the Southern Pacific Association had outdoor championships. The Southern Pacific Association also had a record listing.

The American records from *Spalding's Official Athletic Almanac* were as follows:

30y	3⅘	Betty Brown	New Haven Normal School
50y	6.0	Eleanor Macbeth	New Haven Normal School
		Katherine Mearls	Boston, June 13, 1926
50y	6⅖*	Marion McCartie	Paterson, April 4, 1924
		Eleanor Egg	Paterson, Dec. 6, 1924
75y	8⅗	L. Haydock	Bryn Mawr College
100y	11⅖	Helen Filkey	Chicago, July 20, 1925
220y	27⅘	Elizabeth Nelson	Los Angeles, May 16, 1925
220y	28⅘*	Ellen Brough	New York City, Dec. 9, 1925

300m	43⅗	Mary McCune	Rosemary Hall
880y	2:35⅘	Lucile Godbold	Winthrop College
1000m	3:28⅗	Lucile Godbold	Winthrop College
60yh	8.0	Josephine Schessler	Agnes Scott College, 1923
(4 — 2')			
(4 — 2'6")	8.3	Helen Filkey	Chicago, July 20, 1925
	8.⅗*	Hazel Kirk	Newark, February 13, 1926
65yh	11.0	Mary Worrall	Sargent School of P.E.
100yh	14⅖	Floreida Batson	Rosemary Hall
(8 — 2'6")	14⅖	Camelia Sabie	N.J. Normal School
HJ	4' 10⅞"	Katherine Lee	Chicago, 1923
	4' 10⅜"*	Eleanor Egg	Newark, February 13, 1926
SHJ	3' 8"	Natalie Wilson	Sargent School
BJ	17'	Elizabeth Stine	Paterson, June 20, 1925
		Helen Filkey	Pasadena, July 20, 1925
SBJ	8' 3¾"	Camelia Sabie	New Jersey Normal School
	7' 6½"*	Ethel Emmons	Brooklyn, February 13, 1926
Hop, Step, Jump	33' 10¼"	Elizabeth Stine	Leonia High School, N.J.
Pole Vault	7' 2"	Mildred Carl	New Haven Normal School
6lb. SP	43'	Leslie Perkins	Sargent School
8lb. SP	40' 4¼"	Lillian Copeland	Pasadena, June 26, 1926
	31' 9"*	Gladys Booth	Newark, Feb. 13, 1926
8lb. SP	68' 8"	Lucile Godbold	Winthrop College
(2 hands)			
12lb. SP	28' 4"	Margaret Mitchell	Wykeham Rise School
Discus	103' 5½"	Lillian Copeland	Pasadena, May 15, 1926
Javelin	116' 7½"	Lillian Copeland	Pasadena, June 26, 1926
(2 hands)	135' 3½"	Katherine Agar	Oaksmere School
Basketball	94' 2"	Maude Rosenbaum	Oaksmere School
	85' 9"*	Esther Behring	Newark, February 20, 1925
Hurlball	104' 2½"	Nell Carroll	Florida State College for Women
Baseball	234' 5¾"	Eleanor Churchill	Robinson Seminary, 1923

* indoor record

While the Amateur Athletic Union was sponsoring the national championships, the colleges were condemning the idea of competition for women and sponsoring play days. The *American Physical Education Review* described a triangular sports day held by Stanford, Berkeley, and Mills College on the Berkeley campus. The idea of interclass and intercollegiate competition between these colleges was abandoned several years before when the Athletic Conference of American College Women voted against intercollegiate competition.

The women were assigned to "color squads" and participated in events such as a shuttle relay. They had lunch together after the events and heard speeches on the value of sports days. The women thought that play days were a solution to the "difficult problems in athletic activities for women and girls." That was the program adopted in California and carried out in the high schools.

The "play day" concept, emanating from the West Coast, provided the physical educators an answer to competition for girls. A very powerful paper presented at the Third Annual Meeting of the Women's Division of the National Amateur Athletic Federation of America described the impact that this organization was having on girls' competition in the whole country. Clare Small, director of physical education for women at the University of Colorado, stated that "leadership flows naturally from the colleges and universities" in the area of sports and said that "leadership in physical education is greatly needed at the present time. ... One of the most striking evils growing out of an uncontrolled play life is the interscholastic situation with which we are all familiar. The question of intercollegiate activities for women seems to be largely solved, at least for the present, but interscholastic competition for high school girls and even younger girls is still uncontrolled and wide-spread."

Small's specific goal was to set a plan in motion to eliminate interscholastic competition. While basketball was the major culprit, track with its myriad of other problems posed a great threat too. She outlined the plan to "engineer" the elimination of competition.

Pamphlets were distributed to high school principals suggesting that state leagues of high school girls' athletic associations be organized and that play days be held as alternatives to competition. Two schools that were leaders in this area were Illinois State Normal University and the University of Colorado. In Illinois, a school that had interscholastic competition could not join the organization, but in Colorado, all schools could join and then the schools with interscholastic competition were educated towards "better ways."

Michigan, Texas, and Iowa emulated these plans, and Florida had already abolished all interschool tournaments for girls. Other states taking steps in 1926 were Indiana, Washington, Nebraska, Missouri, Oregon, Kentucky, Ohio, and North Carolina.

Clare Small stated that Florida State College had held the first track meet for girls in 1922. She read a report from Katherine Montgomery, director of physical education for women at Florida State. "The results of our work were not what we had hoped for. Instead of encouraging all girls to take part in such activities, it stimulated some girls to specialize in the form of athletics in which they already excelled, while the average girl preferred to be a spectator."

From the same meeting in 1926, Lillian Schoedler reported:

> On the whole, except in the basket ball field, I think I would say that there is not a very great deal of destructive work, comparatively, being done throughout the country in girls' athletics. Track and field athletics, and swimming, offer possibilities for exploitation and over-doing which are not being altogether missed, as witness a report only last month of a girl in a university track meet (where there was a woman physical director at that!) who was allowed to take part in eight events in a strenuous co-educational field day program — four speed and two jumping events, discus and shot put — in one afternoon. ... Most of the people in those track and swimming meets are now the same ones who were in them two or three years ago (unless they have fallen by the wayside since!) ...

The numbers attracted don't really increase in any marked proportions. ... [Here is the thinking, relative to basketball.] Girls fainting in games from heart attacks or over strain, and being put back into the game if they could be revived ... (I heard recently of a case where the administering of aromatic spirits of ammonia to one of the team leaders whose heart always gives out was one of the regular parts of each game's routine!)

What chance did the girls have with this attitude from the leader of girls' athletics in the United States? Other written material said, "Three girls were removed from the floor in fainting and hysterical condition."

Catherine Maguire: Another Pioneer

Catherine Maguire Horsfall was born on February 4, 1906. In an article entitled "My Sister, Kay," her brother Dan described her background:

Kay was number four to be born into the family of Barney and Jenny Maguire. ... She was a healthy, alert, pleasant and rather care-free child, although she did have a bout with scarlet fever as a youngster.

In 1912 at age 6, Kay began walking two and a half miles to school. ... Somewhere along the way, Kay, along with Irene and Anna began participating in girls basketball as well as track and field events at a time when such activities for girls was something new. By that time, all the walking began to pay off and the "Maguire Sisters" helped the girls Pacific athletic teams win many Franklin County medals and trophies.

Kay found that her best event seemed to be the running high jump. In this event she went on to compete in many national meets and was national girls champion for two years.

In 1982, Catherine told the *Meramec Valley Transcript*:

I graduated in 1925 [from Pacific High School] and went to the Olympics in 1928. ... 1928 was the first time they had track and field events for women. My event was the high jump, and after competing in county, district and state meets, the coach thought that I did well enough to compete in the National and Olympic trials. That year they were held in Newark, New Jersey. There was an Amateur Athletic Union in St. Louis which paid most of our expenses.

Two girls were from St. Louis, of which I was one, one from Chicago, one from Philadelphia, the remainder of the team were from California and the East, mostly New York. It was a case of being at the right place at the right time in my career. It was a glorious experience, one which I have always remembered. ...

I was born and raised on a farm. ... There were six children in our family, three boys and three girls, so we always had companionship....

My two sisters were also on the teams from Pacific High, but didn't get to go as far as I did in athletics.

When I first started to compete I wasn't very good at any event. ... The coach in high school believed in athletics and encouraged me to go out for the team. I didn't do very well until my junior year, by then I could run as fast and jump as high as most of the others in school.

Catherine, the tallest and youngest of the Maguire sisters, was thoroughly sold on athletics for women. She said that she would rather practice high jumping than go to a movie. People had said that track and field was too strenuous

1920 The girls of Pacific High School — champions in track and basketball. *Front row:* Anna and Irene Maguire, Flora Bell Langenbacher and Hazel McKee. *Middle row:* Catherine Maguire, Esther Seeinhaus, Gladys Maher, Elda Zitzman, Lorene Roemer, Mabel Long, Bunny Beth Scott. *Back row:* Gladys Dillon and Gladys Fisher. (Courtesy of Meramec Valley Geanealogical and Historical Society.)

for women, but Catherine said, "that is not true." She credited her interest and success in athletics to hurdling fences on the farm as a child.

Articles from local newspapers in 1923 report that Pacific High School, with the three Maguire sisters, won the team trophy in the second annual municipal athletic meet. There were eighty entries representing twelve organizations.

With W. T. Leezy as the coach, Pacific High School had not lost a track meet in or out of the county in five years. The individual stars of the team were the Maguire sisters and Bunny Beth Scott. Irene Maguire won three firsts: the standing broad jump in 7' 4½", the 60-yard low hurdles in 9.1 seconds, and the 75-yard dash in 9.6 seconds. Bunny Beth Scott set a new American record in the high jump with a leap of 4' 9". Anna Maguire won the 50-yard dash, and Catherine was third in the high jump with a leap of 4' 7". Dolores Boeckmann was second with 4' 8".

> On May 19, 1923 this same team practically won everything at the first annual track and field meet under the auspices of the women's division of the Western Amateur Athletic Union, held on the Maplewood High School campus. Catherine Maguire won three firsts out of the eight events, Irene two and Anna one. This showing will probably take them to the national meet at Newark, N.J. whence one may have a chance at the Olympic Games [women's] to be held in Paris next year.

Typical newspaper reports of scholastic meets reported results of Irene and Anna getting 1-2 in the 100 and standing long jump and Catherine winning the broad jump and tying with Bunny Beth Scott in the high jump. Irene's time in the 100 was 11⅗. The three Maguire sisters also ran the relays.

Catherine won her first national high jump championship in Philadelphia in 1926. She repeated the victory in Eureka, jumping 5' ½", a new American record. She attributed her success to constant training using a jumping pit at home and running the two miles from home to school. Her training began about a month and a half before the meet. She built up her "wind" by short runs and exercised to limber up her muscles.

When Catherine returned home from Eureka, an auto parade of more than fifty cars drove through the streets. The Maguire sisters led. Professor Leezy introduced speakers, who praised the athletes. Catherine and Irene were presented a gift. One of the other athletes was called to the stage, and all of the sisters were presented with the medals won at the Caledonian games in St. Louis the day before the two sisters left for California. A local paper published Catherine's record:

1922	County H.S. meet	first in high jump
1923	County H.S. meet	first in running broad jump, second in high jump
	Herman meet	2d in broad jump, tied for 2d in high jump
	AAU meet in Maplewood	1st in high jump, broad jump, and basketball throw
	Municipal meet	3d in high jump and basketball throw
1924	County H.S. meet	1st in broad jump, 2d high jump
1925	County H.S. meet	1st in broad jump, high jump, 100, shot put — won individual cup
1926	AAU meet at Coliseum	1st in high jump
	AAU national meet in Philadelphia	1st in high jump
	Dual meet between St. Louis and Pacific	1st in broad jump, high jump, shot put 3d in 60, discus, baseball throw
1927	AAU meet, Washington University	1st in high jump, 2d in broad jump
	National AAU meet, Eureka, California	1st in high jump (American record), 3d in shot put

A song was dedicated to Catherine:

I'm a High Jumper Because I'm on a Frog-Leg Diet

Kate, jumps high —
She's always going higher,
Kate, jumps high —
She always clears the wire;
When she jumps —

> She never slumps —
> And when she's on the track boy;
> She's full of pep and joy, boy.
> She's in to win.
> Just for her own school team
> And for her own home town;
> She went out West —
> Done her best —
> Now she's champ of all the rest,
> Kate, jumps high that's all
>   Words by Elmer and Ralph
>   (Tune: "She's Got It")

In 1928, competing for the Headlight Athletic Club with Harry Riddick (a past distance great) as coach, Catherine placed third in the high jump in the nationals, qualifying her for the first women's Olympic track and field team. She recalled her Olympic experience: "We lived aboard the steamer (for seven weeks). Our meals consisted largely of fresh vegetables, boiled and baked meats and there was an absence of pastry. We had to be in bed by 9 o'clock and up at 6:30 or 7. Our chaperone made the rounds every night. On the way home we were allowed to stay up until 10 P.M." Her roommates were Elizabeth Robinson and Dee Boeckmann. Catherine, eliminated in the trials, jumped 4' 10¼" in Amsterdam.

A parade and celebration was held in St. Louis when the two famous Olympians, Catherine and Delores, arrived home. They were presented with huge bouquets and boxes of candy.

In the 1932 tryouts, Catherine was fourth. She said that even then, Babe was using an illegal jump which should have disqualified her (Didrikson's jump in the Olympic Games was ruled illegal). Robert Probst, president of the Western AAU, filed a protest, contending that Didrikson, who tied with Shiley, used an illegal diving finish and should have been disqualified, thus raising Kay Maguire to third place and a position on the 1932 team. The protest was not honored.

Dan Maguire's story about his sister Kay provides information about her life after her days as a track star:

> Kay taught one term at Indian Creek elementary school, a one-room facility so common in those days. Later she went on to business school and worked as a comptometer operator. ... Kay met and married Frank Horsfall in 1940. ... To this union one child was born, but unfortunately she died as an infant.
>
> To help fill their empty arms, Kay and Frank opened their home and hearts to tiny babies waiting to be adopted. Those babies came and went over a period of several years, some boys, some girls. They came, some for only a few weeks, some for months, but all thirteen came to receive the love and nurture of two ordinary, yes extraordinary people it has been my good fortune to know. Kay continued to enjoy competition in bowling and golf most of her life.

Kay died on April 19, 1991, at the age of 85.

Chapter 10

1927

The important 1927 outdoor championship meet was held on September 3 in Eureka, California. This was the final outdoor championships prior to the 1928 Olympic Games which introduced the first track and field events for women.

In Eureka, two world records and five national records were smashed. Margaret Jenkins accounted for a world record in the javelin with a throw of 127' 3½". Helen Filkey set a new world record in the 60-yard hurdles with a time of 8⅕.

The national record breakers were Lillian Copeland in the shot put with a throw of 39' 6⅜" and in the discus with a toss of 103' 8⁵⁄₁₆", Catherine Maguire in the high jump at 5' ½", Ellen Brough in the 220 with the excellent time of 26⅘, and Eleanor Egg in the broad jump with a leap of 17' 1¾".

Lillian Copeland bettered her javelin record again this year. She finished behind Margaret Jenkins in that event in the nationals, however.

The Pasadena Club added about twenty new members during the year, and two of them shared the spotlight in the national championships. Fanny Burt was second in the discus and shot put and third in the javelin. Ann Vrana placed second in the long jump and was a member of the winning 440-yard relay. The Northern California Athletic Club, with seventy-two athletes in the meet, won the team championship, and Pasadena was second.

From Catherine Maguire's scrapbook came the following yell, printed in a California paper:

> Rickety, rick, rickety rack,
> American girls are on the track!
> Hurling the discus, putting the shot;
> Heaving the baseball all over the lot;
> Over the hurdles and through the jump,
> Putting the shades on Andy Gump.
> Pretty good Egg, see her stride,
> Regular girl, New Jersey's pride
> Fast enough is Ellen Brough
> Right from New York and not a bit tough,
> New Orleans pats Miss Dora Katz,
> For there is a girl who is rough on rats.
> Isn't it odd that Nellie Todd
> Would leave Chicago's windy sod?

Spirit of St. Louis, her name is Dee
She'll hurl that discus across the sea.
Keddie and Cartwright, Huber, Maguire-
They'll soon be speeding and rising higher.
Atta girl! Atta girl! Show your stuff;
You cut out the candy, and didn't chew snuff.
Up on your toes,— Crack! goes the gun!
Zowie, Whoopee! Has California won?

50-yard run
1. Elta Cartwright, No. Calif. A.C.   6⅕
2. Eleanor Egg, Paterson A.C.
3. Minnie Meyer, No. Calif. A.C.
4. Margaret Ritchie, Paterson A.C.

60-yard hurdles
1. Helen Filkey, Chicago   8⅕
2. Belle Owens, No. Calif. A.C.
3. Alda Silva, No. Calif. AC
4. Nellie Todd, Chicago

100-yard run
1. Elta Cartwright, No. Calif. A.C.   11⅖
2. Minnie Meyer, No. Calif. A.C.
3. Margaret Ritchie, Paterson A.C.
4. Helen Filkey, Chicago A.C.

220-yard run
1. Ellen Brough, Paterson A.C.   26⅘
2. Alta Huber, No. Calif. A.C.
3. Frances Keddie, No. Calif. A.C.
4. Martha Scarlett, No. Calif. A.C.

440-yard relay
1. Pasadena A.C.   52⅗
   (Kate Moore, Elizabeth Grassie, Ethel Nichols, Anne Vrana)
2. No. Calif. A.C.

High jump
1. Catherine Maguire, St. Louis   5' ½"
2. Marion Holley, No. Calif. A.C.
3. Margaret Clay, No. Calif. A.C.
4. Doris Metcalf, No. Calif. A.C.

Broad jump
1. Eleanor Egg, Paterson A.C.   17' 1¾"
2. Anne Vrana, Pasadena A.C.
3. Nellie Todd, Chicago A.C.
4. Elta Cartwright, No. Calif. A.C.

8-lb. Shot put
1. Lillian Copeland, Pasadena A.C.   39' 6⅛"
2. Fanny Burt, Pasadena A.C.   34' 6⅜"

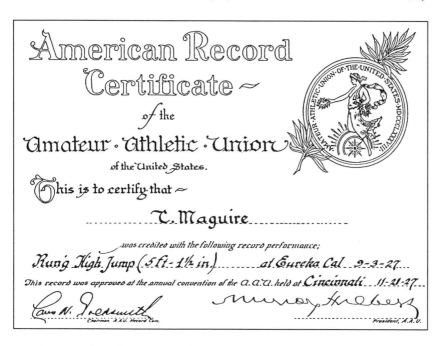

American record certificate 1927 Catherine Maguire, high jump 5' 1½". The certificate was incorrectly filled out. Maguire's record was 5' ½".(Courtesy of Dan Maguire and Sandra Maguire Weaver.)

3.	Catherine Maguire, St. Louis	34' 1½"
4.	Eleanor Egg, Paterson	33' 5½"

Discus throw
1. Lillian Copeland, Pasadena A.C.   103' 8⁵⁄₁₆"
2. Fanny Burt, Pasadena A.C.
3. Dee Boeckmann, St. Louis
4. Rena Acquistapace, No. Calif. A.C.

Javelin
1. Margaret Jenkins, No. Calif. A.C.   127' 3½"
2. Lillian Copeland, Pasadena A.C.
3. Fannie Burt, Pasadena A.C.
4. Agnes Acquistapace, No. Calif. A.C.

Baseball throw
1. Margaret Jenkins, No. Calif. A.C.   233' 11½"
2. Vivian Hartwick, No. Calif. A.C.
3. Gloria Russell, No. Calif. A.C.
4. Henrietta Godfrey, No. Calif. A.C.

800-meter run (special event)
1. Marcelle Barkley, No. Calif. A.C.   2:36⅗
2. Irene Sand, No. Calif. A.C.

3. Rea Strickland, No. Calif. A.C.
4. Chelis Carson

Team scores:
Northern California A.C. 54; Pasadena A.C. 29; Paterson R.C. 14.

The Indoor Nationals

The results of the first indoor meet on March 26 at the Armory in Boston, Massachusetts, follow:

40-yard dash	
1. Rosa Grosse, Canada	5.2 AR
2. Eleanor Egg, Paterson R.C.	
3. Mary Weime, Paterson R.C.	
4. Katherine Mearls, Boston Swimming Assn.	
High jump	
1. Mildred Wiley, Boston Swimming Assn.	4' 9⅜" AR
2. Eleanor Egg, Paterson R.C.	
3. Mae Magill, Boston Swimming Assn.	
Standing broad jump	
1. Katherine Mearls, Boston Swimming Assn.	7' 11¾" AR
2. Ethel Emmons, Savage School	
3. Bernice Hurley, Paterson R.C.	
8-lb. shot put	
1. Rena MacDonald, Boston Swimming Assn.	32' 1" AR
2. Ethel Stuart, Savage School	
3. Mae Magill, Boston Swimming Assn.	
Basketball throw	
1. Eleanor Churchill	87' 3" AR
2. Ruth Kohler, Posse Nissen Gym	72' 9½"
3. Anna Sullivan, Malden A.C.	72' 1¾"
440-yard relay	
1. Paterson (Egg, Weime, Oltar, Brough)	51⅕ AR
2. Boston Swimming Assn.	
3. Pennsylvania Rail Road A.A.	

The annual AAU convention was held in November in Cincinnati, Ohio. Fred Steers gave a lengthy report in which he acknowledged that like all other innovations, "women's athletics has met with a storm of protest and the wrath of those, who refuse to progress." He cited the results of mailings sent around the country to ask if any results of "ill health or physical or mental harm was reported." Not one case was reported. The reports showed just the opposite. Athletic competition was beneficial to the participants. Steers said that there would be athletic competition: "We cannot, even if we wished, suppress or eliminate it."

Steers stated that opponents of the sport said that it tended to make a girl "bold and coarse" but he had found the majority of girls taking part to be gentle, refined young women. He said that the group of athletes represented a group far superior to the average American girl.

In order to have a worthy group of athletes represent the United States in 1928 at Amsterdam, Steers requested the help of the whole country in backing the sport. He said, "Patriotism is on our side and it is time that we challenge those, who for imaginary and fantastic reasons seek to hinder us in the next Olympiad."

Steers said that the championship meet of the Central Association showed women's interest in track and field. Three hundred and sixty-eight women competed, making it the largest meet ever held in the United States.

Then Steers spoke about the nationals in Eureka. He was satisfied with the events that were to appear on the Olympic program except for the 800 meters. He said that the 2:36⅗ time of the winner of the nationals was not comparable to times made by European women. Everyone did finish in good condition.

This was the second year that the 220-yard dash was contested. According to Steers, competition had shown that it was not too long a distance for women, provided that the competitors were limited to that race only.

The first indoor championships events were held at different places and at different times. The New England Association held the 40-yard run, high jump, 8-lb. shot put, and standing broad jump. The committee recommended that in the future all of the indoor events be held at one time and in one place.

The *A.A.U. Bulletin* had two announcements about women's track that year. One announced the June 4 meet of the Allegheny Mountain Association in Pittsburgh. The other announced the national meet in Eureka. The meet was originally scheduled to be in Pasadena.

On the scholastic track scene, Winthrop College of Rock Hill, South Carolina, boasted of having the best program in the South. Since there was no participation in intercollegiate sports, eighty women's colleges took part in a telegraphic track meet. Winthrop was one of the first to take part. Each college had to hold its meet before a certain date in May. The results were then wired to Howard G. Cleaveland in Long Beach, California. Winthrop was first in 1923 and 1925 and was third in 1924. In 1925, Sara Workman of Winthrop was first in the total point score, surpassing athletes from the sixty-two colleges entered.

Elizabeth Ardrey broke the American record in the pole vault by clearing 7' 2½".

Reports of AAU association meets were becoming commonplace. Associations reporting results were the Metropolitan, both indoor and outdoors; Allegheny Mountain Association; Southern Association; Indiana-Kentucky; Western Association, indoor and outdoor; and Southern Pacific Association. Some of the associations like the Metropolitan Association, the Allegheny Mountain Association, and the Southern Association conducted only women's meets, while the others had special women's events within the men's meet.

On the college front, the Women's Athletic Association of Temple University reported:

> The death knell for women's varsity teams has been sounded. "Wonder teams," Championship aggregations and other teams have now become a matter of history never more to be revived at the Cherry and White institution.
>
> This decision was announced recently when the Women's Athletic Association of Temple University decided that varsity competition for girls should pass out of the picture. "Play days" will replace the heavy schedule formerly arranged for the favored few who were able to make the grade and fight for the honor of the Cherry and White.

Margaret Jenkins: A Field Event Pioneer

Margaret Jenkins was born on July 2, 1903, in Santa Clara California. Through many postcards and letters from her home in Campbell and her summer home in South Lake Tahoe as well as articles that Margaret sent to the author, the story of her life in track and field can be pieced together.

Margaret's athletic career started in grade school in about the 5th grade. She played baseball on the boys' team since she could throw farther than any of the boys on the team. In high school in Santa Clara, she pitched for the girls' team. In her four high school years, the team lost only one game.

Track started for Margaret when she was in college. She entered San Jose Teachers College in 1921. She also competed in baseball, basketball, hockey, volleyball, and tennis. Margaret was an all-around athlete. Between 1924 and 1926, she held the Santa Clara County singles, doubles, and mixed doubles tennis titles.

In the early 1920s, women were still wearing long pants to play in. Margaret thought that they were too restrictive and wore shorts, a very daring move for the 20s. Since shorts made sense, however, others soon followed.

In 1924, as a college junior, Margaret was asked by Laura Herron, the director of the women's physical education department and one of Margaret's coaches, to compete in a telegraphic meet. She threw the baseball and basketball and the javelin. She got second in the javelin throw but in error threw the men's javelin. She had never thrown the javelin before and liked it.

Margaret graduated in 1925 and began teaching, a job that she held for thirty years. After work, she practiced the javelin, shot put, and other throwing events. She competed in three or four meets a year, mainly in the summer, but still had no coach.

In the spring of 1927, she asked R. L. "Dink" Templeton, the well-known track coach at Stanford, to work with her. After due consideration, because she was a female, he agreed. When she learned that the javelin would not be on the Olympic program for women, she then persuaded Coach Templeton to teach her how to throw the discus just two months before the trials. At 5'6" and 142 pounds, Margaret was a natural athlete.

Johnny Myrra, the 1920 and 1924 Olympic champion in the javelin from Finland, saw her throw and offered to make her a customized javelin. It was this javelin that caused the furor at the 1927 National Championships in Eureka, California, on September 3. The javelin did not have an official stamp burned into the wood. Lillian Copeland was Margaret's main competition and the defending champion in all three throws, the javelin, shot, and discus. Lillian's coach, Aileen Allen, objected to the javelin. The dispute was settled when the officials excluded the Myrra javelin from the competition and placed all of the other javelins in a pool that anyone could use. Margaret angrily picked up Lillian's javelin and threw it to a new world record of 127' 3½".

Margaret wrote that the trials in 1928 ended in a terrific storm:

> Everyone who was in the later events like me, in the discus and javelin, were drenched. They turned the javelin event around for some reason — everyone who threw, threw the javelin up that-a-way, the thing floundered in the wind and fell to the ground. I pegged my throw to second base and won easily at, I think 112 feet [112' 5⅝"]. No one else lasted more than a few feet. After the discus competition I hurried to get inside as I was on the national committee from the West Coast. I was anxious to see if they'd recognize the three throws — and when I found out "yes" I was satisfied — it meant I made the 1928 team. Some of us were wet, I mean wet so we got out of there as soon as we could to get something dry on.

Twenty-four-year-old Margaret remembers the long trip to Amsterdam with one day spent on the Grand Canal. She was unable to practice during the trip. She said that the royal family did not come to the opening ceremony because the queen was "miffed" that it was on a Sunday. Margaret came in eighth in the discus. When the Olympic Games were over, she competed in Belgium. She was the first woman from Santa Clara county to participate in the Olympics.

Margaret continued to teach physical education and work out for the 1932 Olympic team. She said that during most of her college years she was criticized by women in physical education, especially from Wisconsin. Margaret said at an alma mater luncheon in 1984:

> How different now that women are accepted in the world of sports and competition. In days long gone by, you were frowned on if you took part in sports anything heavier than croquet. ... In looking back at the curious notion that women should hold back female talent, it reflected a fear of change on the part of teachers who had been trained to accept traditional roles for women. Winning requires aggressiveness and a healthy dose of ego, expected of men, but unacceptable at that time in a woman.

Memories of the 1932 tryouts at Evanston are still vivid for Margaret:

> The discus throwers went "over there" out of the stadium, of course. We took some warm-ups and one throw and there we sat for about an hour. Finally, a couple of us got to "yakking" and naturally we wanted to know what was holding things up. Heard from "certain horses mouths" was that the discus was being held up so that "a certain" person could take part in all events. Well, finally after more "yakkin" a certain party, I believe his name was McCombs [Didrikson's coach], was given an alternative by the officials, choose three events or get out of here. After selecting the hurdles, javelin and high jump, the meet went on.

Margaret's family was athletic. Her uncle, Doug Helm, was a football coach at Los Gatos High School, and the field was named for him. Her nonconforming mother, Mala Helm Jenkins, was a champion cyclist in the 1890s when the bicycle became an appropriate vehicle for women and girls. In 1896, when Margaret's mother was seventeen, she belonged to a San Jose bicycle club. Women were held in high esteem in Margaret's family, and her parents freely and generously supported her athletic involvement. Her mother saw her compete in the Olympic Games.

The collection of medals Margaret won exceeds one hundred, and she is in three Halls of Fame. The Halls have two of her javelins — one is the Johnny Myrra javelin. The fondest memories of her track participation are the unique experiences she had and the great people she met. The meet in Eureka, where the Johnny Myrra javelin caused the "stink," remains her favorite meet memory. The whole controversy backfired, and Margaret threw the new world's record, as she remembered with a laugh.

In looking for a future Olympian, Margaret said: "They would have to have the personality for it, be reliable, have the interest and attitude and 'mind' the coach. The difference between the star and the average person is because of interest and perseverance, good training and good living. The most important attributes of an athlete are reliability and stability."

Elta Cartwright: A Pioneer Sprint Sensation

Elta Cartwright Henricksen was born in California on December 21, 1907. An article written by Richard P. Mann, "They Called Her Cinder-Elta," published in the *California Living Magazine* of the *San Francisco Sunday Examiner & Chronicle* on March 18, 1984, said that she was the fourth of five daughters and credited her mother for her sprinting ability. Her mother had five brothers, and she could beat them all in running.

Elta's running career began in elementary school, according to Mann. "I'd always win," she said. During high school in 1923, national telegraphic meets were in vogue. Eureka would win the telegraphic meets all of the time. Eureka high school girls were the first to wear shorts in competition. Laura Herron was her high school coach and then her coach in college.

In 1925, Elta graduated from high school. It is this year that her name begins to appear in the results of the national AAU championships. Pasadena was the site of the nationals that year. When the meet was over, Elta had captured second place in the 100-yard dash and became the USA champion in the 50-yard dash.

In 1926, with Laura Herron now coaching her at Humboldt State, Elta successfully defended her crown in the 50-yard dash, placed third in the broad jump, and was a member of the second-place 440-yard relay team, according to Mann.

In 1927 at Eureka, Elta won the national 50-yard dash crown for the third year in succession. She won the 100-yard dash title and placed fourth in the broad jump.

At the Olympic tryouts the next year, Elta became the first woman in the United States to be named to the Olympic team after winning the first final, the 100-meter dash. In addition, she won her fourth consecutive 50-yard dash championship.

On the way to Amsterdam, Elta became ill. Although she competed in the 100 meters and got to the semifinal round, she did not have the speed to get into the finals. "I just didn't run fast enough" she said. Her last disappointment of the Olympic Games came when she was not selected to run on the relay team. She thought that the coach favored the girls from the East. The first three legs of the relay team were from his club, the Millrose Athletic Association in New York.

Upon arrival home from Amsterdam, Elta was given a parade through the town of Eureka.

Elta taught school for many years, and at age seventy-three, she became the first woman selected for her college Hall of Fame.

Chapter 11

1928: Amsterdam, the First Olympic Year

The final Olympic trials were held on July 4 at City Field in Newark, New Jersey, under the auspices of the Metropolitan Association of the Amateur Athletic Union. When the trials were over, the following nineteen women were the first United States Olympians in track and field in the five-event Olympic program in Amsterdam, Holland:

Name	*Olympic Event*	*Olympic Place*	*Olympic Performance*
Boeckmann, Dee	800m	DNQ	
Cartwright, Elta	100m	DNQ	
Copeland, Lillian	Discus	2	121' 7⅞"
Cross, Jessie	400mr	2	48.6
Hasenfus, Olive	100m	Reserve	
Holley, Marion	HJ	9 tie	4' 10¼"
Jenkins, Margaret	Discus	19	88' 9¾"
McDonald, Florence	800m	6	2:22.6
MacDonald, Rena	Discus	15	99' 3"
Maguire, Catherine	HJ	8	4' 10¼"
McNeil, Loretta	400mr	2	48.6
Reichardt, MayBelle	Discus	7	109' 11¾"
Robinson, Elizabeth	100m	1	12.2
	400mr	2	48.6
Sayer, Edna	100m	Reserve	
Shiley, Jean	HJ	4	4' 11½"
Vrana, Anne	100m	DNQ	
Washburn, Mary	100m	DNQ	
	400mr	2	48.6
Wiley, Mildred	HJ	3	5' 1⁷⁄₁₆"
Wilson, Rayma	800m	DNQ	
Steers, Fred	Manager		
Sheppard, Mel	Coach		
Allen, Aileen	Chaperone		

The team sailed from New York on the S.S. *President Roosevelt* on July 11 to participate in the first Olympic Games having track and field events for women. The *New York Times* on July 12 had a photograph of the ship leaving New York for Amsterdam with an article describing the exciting noon departure. The ship had "American Olympic Team" blazoned on the side in immense letters.

A crowd of 2,000 jammed pier 86. Cheers rang out as athletes were recognized. Major General Douglas MacArthur, president of the American Olympic Committee, welcomed everyone aboard. The 268 athletes departed amid waving flags, blowing whistles and clicking cameras.

A program of the passenger list pictured United States Olympians in competition uniform on the cover. Each team was listed separately and by event. The competition uniform consisted of blue shorts with a red, white, and blue stripe down the side and a white top. The large USA emblem was on the left top side, and a stripe of red, white, and blue ran diagonally across the front. The sweats were navy blue.

The Olympic Results

100 meters. The 100 meters was the first women's track event. Mary Washburn, Elta Cartwright, and Betty Robinson were all second in their respective heats. Anne Vrana was third in her heat and did not advance to the semis. Elta and Mary were eliminated in the semifinal round. Only Elizabeth Robinson, who won the second semifinal, beating Canada's Myrtle Cook, progressed to the final.

Following the third day of the Olympic Games, headlines on the front page of the *New York Times* on August 1 exclaimed, "Americans Capture 2 Olympic Events, Setting New Marks." The article included a picture of Elizabeth Robinson, one of the two winning athletes, with the following story:

> An American girl helped restore the prestige of the Olympic team today and again brought the Stars and Stripes fluttering to the central flag staff. [In winning, Elizabeth set a world record of 12⅕ seconds for the 100 meters.] The 100 meter dash for women was by far the most interesting event on the program, inasmuch as it provided, aside from the race itself, other scenes entirely feminine, and never before witnessed in any Olympic stadium. Six girls were at the starting line when the event was called. All were extremely nervous and jumpy, several breaking ahead of the gun. Myrtle Cook of Canada, the second favorite, a slight attractive lass, wearing red shorts and a white silk blouse, then made a second break. Under the Olympic rules she was disqualified.
>
> When the starter waved her out she seemed not to comprehend for a moment and then burst into tears. She soon had company on the sidelines when Fraulein Schmidt, a buxom German blonde, also made a second break. But instead of tears, the German girl shook her fist under the starter's nose and the spectators for the moment thought she might stage a face-scratching and hair pulling act.
>
> The harassed official backed away, waving the irate sprinter off the track, at the same time trying to comfort Myrtle Cook, who had sat down too near the starting line and was sobbing lustily. The starter, fearing the bad effect on the other girls, succeeded in getting the Canadian girl removed to a pile of cushions

Betty Robinson winning the first U.S. women's gold medal in track and field in the 100 meters in the 1928 Olympic Games in Amsterdam, the first Olympic games to have track and field events for women. (Courtesy of the National Track & Field Hall of Fame Historical Research Library at Butler University.)

on the grass, where she remained, her head buried in her arms and her body shaking with sobs, for at least half an hour.

After the race the other Canadian girl sprinters sat with their arms about her, trying vainly to comfort her. Meanwhile Fraulein Schmidt departed from the scene, vowing vengeance upon the race official the next time they meet.

Betty Robinson's Olympic victory began with several false starts and two disqualified runners. She was not nervous and jittery, as were the others, but she was worried about lane assignments. She wanted Fanny Rosenfeld of Canada to be in a lane next to her so she could see her out of the corner of her eye. Betty thought that she was the one to beat in the final because Fanny had beaten her "by a whisker" in the seventh semifinal. As it turned out, Fanny was to Betty's right. When the gun sounded, Fanny was out fast. Near the halfway mark, Betty had pulled up even with her. From that point on they were even, stride for stride. At the finish, Betty forged ahead by a half stride. It was close, but enough for first place and a world record.

An unidentified newspaper said: "What Charlie Paddock, who holds more sprint records than any other man who ever ran, could not do; what Jackson Scholz, the St. Louis sprinter who won the 100 meter sprint in the games four years ago, could not do, and what Lloyd Hahn, the Boston flyer, could not do, slim Elizabeth Robinson, 15 year old Chicago girl ... has done. The American boys who were so easily outrun by pretty much all the rest of the world, ought to buy Elizabeth a big box of candy."

Discus throw. The discus throw for women was also held on July 31. Of the four U.S. entries, Lillian Copeland was the only athlete to make the finals and win a medal. She placed second, throwing 121' 7⅞", her best throw of the year to that date. The winning throw was 129' 11⅞". MayBelle Reichardt tossed the discus 109' 11¾" in the trials and remembers that she missed the finals by ½ inch. Her throw of 116' 9¼" in Newark at the trials would have placed her fifth in the finals.

800 meters. The women's 800 meters was held on the next day, August 1. The *New York Times* reported:

> In the first heat of the women's 800 meter event Dolores Boeckmann of the United States ran well on the first lap, but withdrew before entering the homestretch....
>
> In the second heat the former Frau Radke won by inches from the Japanese star K. Hitomi, while the American girl Rayma Wilson finished seventh....
>
> Florence McDonald of the United States qualified in the third and last heat, placing second three yards behind Jean Thompson of Canada. Miss McDonald was fourth entering the stretch, but finished gamely to take second, although she was near exhaustion. The time was 2 minutes 23⅕ seconds.

On August 3, the *New York Times* said: "Miss McDonald, in finishing sixth in the 800 meters, also bettered the world's record. She was timed in 2:23⅖ seconds, ⅖ of a second better than the former record." The winning time, 2:16⅘, was more than seven seconds faster than Frau Lina Radke's best time.

Anne Vrana commented on the 800 meters, saying that the girls were tired and of course, they were winded. "But they certainly weren't collapsing all over the track the way they described it. It's just too bad that that impression has been allowed to grow because it kept women's track from getting into distances for many, many years. I was there and they were winded, I'll guarantee you that, but I have seen men that were winded at the end of a 220 just as badly."

400-meter relay. On August 5, the *New York Times* carried the story of the women's relay trials. The American team of Mary Washburn, Jessie Cross, Loretta McNeil, and Elizabeth Robinson equaled the world record in the second heat, beating the German team by almost two feet in 49⅘ seconds.

The last day of the Olympic Games saw the women first on the program. The relay produced a world record for the Canadian team, with the Americans, anchored by Betty Robinson, four yards behind in second place.

High jump. The high jump results were also reported in the newspaper. The four American entries did well. Marion Holley was ninth, and high-school-girl Jean Shiley was fourth, Mildred Wiley was tied for second but lost the silver medal in the jump-off, and Catherine Maguire was eighth.

When the women's events were completed, most of the team went to Brussels for a post-Olympic meet.

The *New York Times* on August 13 reported: "Miss Copeland Sets Mark in Shot Put; American Girls Triumph." Before a large crowd in Belgium, Lillian Copeland put the shot 38' 5½" for a new world record and won the discus and javelin throws also. The United States girls won the meet by winning four first places in a nine-event meet. Mary Washburn won the 80-meter hurdles. Mildred Wiley tied for second in the high jump, and Rena MacDonald was a close second in the shot put and finished third in the javelin. Margaret Jenkins finished second in the discus and the javelin. Anne Vrana placed second in the broad jump, and Jean Shiley was third. Vrana was second in the 100 yards also. In the 800-meter run, no Americans placed.

The *New York Times* article dated August 15 noted that the Olympic ship the S.S. *President Roosevelt* sailed from Southampton at noon. A stop was to be made in Cherbourg to pick up members of the team who were competing in other areas of the continent. Much of the athletic apparatus had been dismantled on the ship, but the running track remained so that the athletes could continue training for a meet in the States.

When the athletes arrived home, New York City provided a gala celebration. Fire boats shooting water into the air met the ship as it pulled into the harbor. The mayor greeted the athletes, and they were presented medals.

In the *Report of the American Olympic Committee* after the Games, the women's coach, Mel Sheppard, made the suggestion that the "units" travel separately. He thought that supervision, communication, training, diet, and team spirit needed for a higher morale would be improved. The team could sail on smaller, faster steamers, and the athletes would maintain the "keen edge to which they had risen for the tryouts."

Mrs. Allen, the chaperone, also regretted the "slow boat" and recognized what she termed "the biggest mistake"—a number of coaches who had no connection with the games were allowed to go over on the same boat as the athletes. She praised the meals on board ship and was glad that the athletes did not need to adjust to a different diet, but she believed that staying in a good hotel in Amsterdam would have broken up the monotony. She praised the girls for the wonderful showing, stating, "We remember the few years we have followed this branch of sport compared to the other countries." All in all, she noted, "It was a trip worthy of the time and effort; one that each participant will remember in all the years to come."

Mel Sheppard, the coach of the women's team, was the undisputed leader of the middle-distance runners of the world in his prime. He was the head of the personnel department of the New York John Wanamaker store. "Peerless Mel," which was his title from 1907 to 1913, won the 800 and 1500 meters events at the Olympic Games in London in 1908. At one time, he held all of the world records from 500 yards to ⅔ of a mile.

The Olympic Trials

The sixth annual national championships served as the final trials for the Olympic team. Twelve events were held, but only five of the events were rewarded with the historic honor and lifelong memory of being selected to represent the United States as a member of the first women's Olympic track and field team.

The heroine of the meet was Elta Cartwright, a twenty-year-old school teacher. She accounted for three victories, winning the 50 and 100 yard dashes and the running broad jump. Of the more than 250 athletes competing, three women set records. Rayma Wilson broke the 800-meter run record, MayBelle Reichardt established a new American record in the discus throw, and Lillian Copeland equaled her American record in the shot put. This was the first time that the European discus was used in the United States. It weighed nine ounces less than the discus that the women were used to throwing.

The *New York Times* on July 5 said that Rayma Wilson ran an impressive 800 meters in the last heat. "She stayed with the pack at the start, and conserved her speed for the final dash." Dee Boeckmann won the first heat, running against Catherine Donovan, considered the best of the eastern girls. Dee had too much speed for Catherine and won comfortably over Ruth Martin in 2:33$\frac{4}{5}$. Miss Boeckmann also broke the American record.

Florence Wright, running the 220 "around one turn," captured the second heat in 27$\frac{1}{5}$ and won the final several yards ahead of Alice Williams.

The high jump was closely contested. Both Mildred Wiley and Jean Shiley cleared 4 feet 11$\frac{3}{4}$. A jump-off was necessary to determine first place. Wiley won by clearing 4 feet 11$\frac{3}{4}$ again.

50-yard dash

1. Elta Cartwright, No. Calif. A.C.	6$\frac{3}{5}$
2. Maybelle Gilliland, Paterson R.C.	
3. Ruth Waldner, Pennsylvania A.A.	
4. Josephine Farnsworth, No. Calif. A.A.	

100-meter run

1. Elta Cartwright, No. Calif. A.A.	12$\frac{2}{5}$
2. Elizabeth Robinson, Illinois Women's A.C.	
3. Anne Vrana, Pasadena Athletic and Country Club	
4. Mary Washburn, Millrose A.A.	

220-yard run

1. Florence Wright, Headlight A.C.	27$\frac{2}{5}$
2. Alice Williams, San Francisco Girls A.C.	
3. Martha Scarlett, No. Calif. A.A.	
4. Emma Hearn, Paterson R.C.	

800-meter run

1. Rayma Wilson, Pasadena Athletic and Country Club	2:32$\frac{3}{5}$
2. Dee Boeckmann, Headlight A. C.	2:33$\frac{4}{5}$
3. Florence McDonald, Boston Swimming Assn.	2:36.0
4. Ruth Martin, San Francisco Girls' A.C.	
(Places decided by time trials in three heats)	

60-yard hurdles

1. Helen Filkey, Illinois Women's A.C.	8$\frac{2}{5}$
2. Belle Owens, No. Calif. A.C.	
3. Alda Silva, No. Calif. A.C.	
4. Dorothy Watson, Prudential A.A.	

440-yard relay
1. No. Calif. A.C.   52⅕
     (Minnie Meyer, Ruth Stewart, Myra Parsons, Delores Henders)
2. Millrose A.A.
3. Pasadena Athletic and Country Club
4. St. Bonaventure Lyceum

High jump
1. Mildred Wiley, Boston Swimming Assn.   4' 11¾"
2. Jean Shiley, Haverford H.S.   4' 11¾"
3. Catherine Maguire, Headlight A.C.
4. Marion Holley, No. Calif. A.C.

Broad jump
1. Elta Cartwright, No. Calif. A.C.   16' 10¾"
2. Elizabeth Grobes, Scotch Plains H.S.   16' 5"
3. Dorothy Furth, Paterson R.C.
4. Alta Huber, No. Calif. A.C.

8-lb. shot put
1. Lillian Copeland, Pasadena Athletic and Country Club   40' 4¼"
2. Rena MacDonald, Boston S.A.   37' 6½"
3. Alda Silva, No. Calif. A.C.
4. Eleanor Egg, Paterson R.C.

Discus
1. MayBelle Reichardt, Pasadena Athletic and Country Club   116' 9¼"
2. Lillian Copeland, Pasadena Athletic and Country Club   115' 1½"
3. Margaret Jenkins, No. Calif. A.C.
4. Rena MacDonald, Boston Swimming Assn.

Javelin
1. Margaret Jenkins, No. Calif. A.C.   112' 5⅝"
2. Gloria Russell, No. Calif. A.C.   97' 7½"
3. Estelle Hill, Prudential A.A.
4. Theodora Schmidt, Prudential A.A.

Baseball throw
1. Vivian Hartwick, No. Calif. A.A.   228' 8½"
2. Margaret Jenkins, No. Calif. A.A.   223' 6"
3. Gloria Russell, No. Calif. A.A.
4. Lillian Kelly, Unattached

Team scores:
Northern California A.C. 52; Pasadena Athletic and Country Club 17; Boston Swimming Association 9; Illinois Women's A.C. 8; Paterson Recreation Club 7; Headlight A.C. 7; Millrose A.A. 4; Prudential Insurance Co. A.A. 4; Haverford Township H.S. 3; Scotch Plains H. S. 3; San Francisco Girls' A.C. 3; Pennsylvania R.R. A.A. 2; St. Bonaventure Lyceum 1.

his certifies that

C. Maguire

was a competitor in the Try-outs at Newark
held by the American Olympic Committee to prepare
a team to represent the United States of America at the
IX Olympiad~Amsterdam~Holland~1928
and won 3 place in Run'g High Jump

7-4-28

Secretary   *President*

1928 certificate of Catherine Maguire's participation in 1928 Olympic try-outs. (Courtesy of Dan Maguire and Sandra Maguire Weaver.)

The Indoor Nationals

The second indoor track and field championship meet was held in Boston on March 10. Six events were contested, and the *New York Times* reported that three world marks were set. This was the first time that the 50-yard hurdles was held. The national champions in the first indoor meet hosting all of the events were as follows:

40-yard run
1. Katherine Mearls, Boston Swimming Assn.   5⅖
2. Mary Washburn, Millrose A.A.

220-yard run
1. Irene Moran, Brooklyn Edison Co. A.A.   30⅘
2. Catherine Donovan, Prudential A.A.

50-yard hurdles
1. Mary Washburn, Millrose A.A.   7⅗
2. Rose Huysentruyt, Paterson R.C.

High jump
1. Mildred Wiley, Boston Swimming Assn.   4' 10⅝"
2. Olive Huber, St. George Club

Standing broad jump
1. Katherine Mearls, Boston Swimming Assn.   8' 3"
2. Ethel Emmons, Paterson R.C.

8-lb. shot
1. Mabel Travers, Brooklyn Edison Co. A.A.   33' 3½"
2. Mae Magill, Boston Swimming Assn.

Women's indoor records were reported in the 1929 *Spalding's Almanac* for the first time.

40y	5⅕	Rosa Grosse, Toronto, March 26, 1927
220y	30⅘	Irene Moran, Brooklyn Edison Club, March 10, 1928
High jump	4' 10⅝"	Mildred Wiley, Boston Swimming Assn. March 10, 1928
Broad jump	8' 3"	Katherine Mearls, Boston Swimming Assn. March 10, 1928
8lb. shot	33' 3½"	Mabel Travers, Brooklyn Edison Club, March 10, 1928
50yh	7⅗	Mary Washburn, Millrose A.A., March 10, 1928
(three — 2'6")		

The Metropolitan Championships were held on June 23. The *New York Times* headlines the following day proclaimed, "U.S. Record in 440 Yard Relay." The Millrose relay team of Mary Washburn, Jessie Cross, Carrie Jensen, and Loretta McNeil won the relay in American record time of 51⅕ at Weequahic Park, in Newark, New Jersey. The team beat Pasadena's record of 52⅕ set in 1927.

Eleven events were held along with a special 800-meter run, won by Catherine Donovan of the Prudential A.A. in 2:38⅘.

In describing the race, the *New York Times* reported:

> A field of seven started in the 800-meter run, Mrs. Dorothy Wallace of the Red Men's A.C. being rated as Miss Donovan's principal rival, though she has lost to Miss Donovan on previous occasions.
> Miss Donovan allowed Miss Celia M. Dolan of the Loughlin Lyceum to make the early pace, staying about two yards behind. As they rounded the first lap Miss Dolan led, Miss Donovan came next and Mrs. Wallace was fourth. Mrs. Wallace began to move up here. On the last turn, however, Miss Donovan came with a rush and finished five yards in front of Mrs. Wallace. Miss Dolan came in third, rather exhausted, and Miss Miller barely jogged over the line fourth.

The *New York Times* reported that all of the eleven defending champions were present. Those retaining their title were Emma Hearn in the 220, Mabel Travers in the shot, Caroline Lowe in the discus, and Lillian Kelly in the baseball throw.

The new champions were Mary Washburn in the 60-yard hurdles, Loretta McNeil in the 50-yard dash, Jessie Cross in the 100-yard dash, Dorothy Furth in the running broad jump, Estelle Hill in the javelin throw, and Olive Huber in the high jump. (In 1958, while attending Hunter College in the Bronx as a physical education major, the author was a student in Professor Olive Huber's physiology of muscular activity class. I remember her as being almost six feet tall and an interesting and dynamic teacher, well-liked by her students. Knowing that I competed in track, she remarked to me casually one day that she too had competed.)

Besides the Metropolitan Association in New York City, *Spalding's Almanac* reported championships in the following associations: New England, indoor and outdoor; New England junior, indoor and outdoor; Allegheny Mountain Association, outdoor; Southern Association, outdoor; Western Association, outdoor; and Southern Pacific Association, outdoor.

The major indoor meets had women's events. The most distinguished of the meets was the Millrose Games.

In 1992, Howard Schmertz recalled:

> My father, when he graduated from high school, went to work for Wanamaker's. It was nineteen hundred seven. He then went to Law school at night and eventually, sometime in nineteen eighteen or nineteen nineteen, became the store [Wanamaker's] attorney. He was the store attorney until he retired in nineteen fifty-five. Although he was running the [Millrose] games from the late nineteen twenties, he officially became the meet director in nineteen thirty-four. He was the meet director until he was eighty-five years old in nineteen seventy-four — for forty-one years. I gradually helped him out after I graduated from law school in nineteen forty-eight. I became more and more involved with the meet, and when he got sick in nineteen seventy-four, I took over the meet in nineteen seventy-five. Between the two of us, this [1991] is the Schmertz's family fifty-ninth year as meet directors....
>
> Some of the meets were held outdoors in the spring on the roof of the old John Wanamaker garage building, where they had a board track. I know they trained there, and they had some informal meets up there.
>
> The first actual printed records that we have of the meet are in nineteen eleven, when they were in one of the New York armories in nineteen eleven, nineteen twelve, and nineteen thirteen. The meet got too big. They couldn't fit all of the people into the armory that wanted to attend, so they moved into Madison Square Garden in nineteen fourteen. The Millrose Games have been in Madison Square Garden now for seventy-nine consecutive years.
>
> As far as the women are concerned, I don't know whether they were there at the very beginning, but certainly by the twenties the Millrose Athletic Association had a women's track team and they competed quite favorably in the late twenties. A number of the Millrose women were on the 1928 Olympic team in Amsterdam. Mel Sheppard was appointed the women's track coach. He was the Millrose A.A. women's coach. Sheppard was the only American to win the fifteen hundred–meters in the Olympics [1908] and was a great athlete. We have had a Mel Sheppard "six hundred" in the Millrose Games which we named for him when he died. He was the Millrose coach from the late nineteen twenties until sometime in the early forties. The club, the Millrose Athletic Association is still in existence, comprised mainly of road runners. Joe Kleinerman is the coach. The club was the strongest in the twenties and thirties as far as very good runners were concerned. It's probably the second oldest, after the New York Athletic Club, still in existence in the United States. [It is the oldest club in the United States that sponsored both men and women at different periods of time.]

In 1928, four Millrose members did make the Olympic team. Three of the four were women: Loretta McNeil, Mary Washburn, and Jessie Cross. All three ran on the silver medal 440-relay team anchored by Betty Robinson. Mel Sheppard was named coach of the women's team.

In Fred Schmertz' book *The Millrose Games Story*, he stated:

> Our girls, too, did very well, scoring many points in A.A.U. competition, with Carrie Jensen the leader, closely followed by Loretta McNeil. Our girls relay team also accounted for six new relay records, the 220, the 330, the 440 medley, the 440 indoor and outdoor and the 440 Canadian record. A prominent member of our 1932 Millrose girls team was red haired Alice Arden (now Mrs. Russell Hodge). She was the 1933, 1934 and 1935 national high jump girls' champion breaking the national high jump record in 1933 with 5' 3½ inches, a record which stood for twenty-two years and was finally eclipsed in 1955. Alice was a member of the 1936 Olympic team.

Schmertz summarized the highlights of the 1930 Millrose meet: "This year marked the only time in Millrose history when a girl athlete was voted the outstanding performer of the meet. Stella Walsh, the great Polish star, received this honor. She came from Cleveland, and before a great crowd of 16,000 won two 50 yard races, breaking the world's indoor record in both heat and final. Miss Walsh defeated Myrtle Cook, Canada's star woman sprinter, who was the 1928 and 1929 Millrose winner."

Schmertz noted that in 1931, "The girls too had a field day, for that night our Millrose girls relay team, composed of Misses Cross, Jensen, Gilliland and McNeil, was returned the victor in a quarter mile relay, establishing a new world record of 52 seconds in the International Girls Relay, defeating Canada's great girl's team anchored by their star sprinter, Myrtle Cook."

February 2, 1928, marked the 21st Annual Indoor Games. A page from the program lists the entries in the international 50-yard dash for girls and the heat winners and their times. The winner of the final was number 205, Myrtle Cook of Canada.

Two other girls' events were on the program — a 440-yard relay for John Wanamaker girls and an international girls' 440-yard relay.

Meets flourished around the country in 1928, the first Olympic year for women in track and field. Eric Cowe's listing of 1928 "best performances" by women included meets in these locations throughout the United States:

Month	*Location*
January	Newark
February	Boston, Los Angeles, Newark
March	Boston, Evanston, St. Louis, and Burlingame
April	San Jose, San Francisco, and Fairfax Park
May	Sacramento, Los Angeles, Claremont, Philadelphia, Stockton, Kennywood Park, Pasadena, and Painesville
June	Abingdon, Philadelphia, Eureka, Chicago, St. Louis, Dorchester, New York, New Orleans, Newark, Los Angeles, and Chelsea

July   Olympic tryouts in Newark, New Jersey, and Boston
August   Olympic Games, Schaerbeek, Belgium, Boston, and Chicago
September   Chicago, West Roxbury, Cicero, Kearney, and Boston

In a November 1928 letter to the members of the Women's Division, the executive committee chairman, Ethel Perrin, reported that Mrs. Hoover gave up the chairmanship of the committee because of her obligations as the First Lady. Mrs. Henry Alvah Strong replaced her as chairman of the board of directors. Both Mrs. Strong and Mrs. Hoover were underwriting the Women's Division for $3,000 for the 1928-29 year, however. The small budget prevented the Division from launching its bulletin, but Ethel Perrin said, "We have been building in a quiet way." Many influential women from all over the country were members of the board of directors.

In the schools, the March *American Physical Education Review* reported on interscholastic athletics for girls in 141 schools in 28 states. Nebraska and Illinois were not represented because they prohibited girls' athletics. Interscholastic athletics were conducted in track in fifteen schools in the survey. Basketball presented the greatest problem at this time because sixty-five schools had interscholastic activity.

In the April *Physical Education Review,* a state-by-state report on athletics revealed:

South Dakota — the high school association voted to prohibit state basketball championships for girls;

Michigan and Virginia — the state departments of education very definitely discouraged interscholastic competition for girls;

Wisconsin — voted in September 1926 to abolish all interscholastic competition for girls;

Missouri — prohibited interscholastic basketball competition for girls;

New Jersey — supported the principles of the Women's Division;

West Virginia and New York — took similar steps as Wisconsin;

California — placed emphasis on play days. Approved field day events were listed: dashes and relays up to 75 yards, hurdles up to 60 yards, jumping into a soft pit (not broad jump) and throwing the basketball and baseball. The events not approved were shot put, long runs for speed, and jumping without a soft pit.

In the May *Physical Education Review,* Frederick Rand Rogers, the state director of physical education of New York, made his views clear:

> School administrators and physical educators are confronted constantly with requests for the sanctioning of interschool athletics for girls. Sometimes girls even demand that they be permitted to ape boys' sports. ... Above all, we say, the competitive element in girls' activities should be minimized almost to the point of rendering it a negligible factor during the senior high school period....
>
> At this point, physical educators of girls should abandon high standards of

athletic accomplishment (as measured by tapes and stopwatches) as proper objectives and increase their emphasis on graceful execution of exercises as girls' physical activities.

Elizabeth Robinson Schwartz: The Nation's First Olympic Champion

Betty was born in Riverdale, Illinois, on August 23, 1911. In a phone conversation with me on August 20, 1992, she told me something of her history:

Prior to high school, anytime anyone was having races I was in them. I liked to run. At the church picnic, the school picnic, or at my father's lodge in another town, if there were races, I would run and I would win. I knew I was a fast runner, but I didn't know it would come to what it did. I probably was twelve or even younger when I first raced, but I was not aware of how much I was running.

In high school I used to compete in everything. I even went out for swimming. We always had swimming competition between the various schools. I used to go into rifle competition. Anytime there was competition, I was in it.

I went to a high school in another town because Riverdale was a small town. I went to Thornton Township High School like everyone else did from around that area.

It meant I had to take the train when I first started because I didn't have a car. I'd take the train every morning to Harvey. I lived in Riverdale, and it was just two stops on the train to Harvey. The station in Harvey was elevated, and the story that is told about the teacher seeing me run for the train, well, he was up on the station and a train was coming. I was still down on the street. I had to run up that flight of stairs. So, when I got on the train and sat down next to him, he was so surprised. He said tomorrow we're going to time you in a fifty. That's what started it. I made the train, and he didn't think I was going to. He was the one who started the whole thing. I had Mr. Price as a teacher. I was in Mr. Price's eleventh grade home room, and he was my biology teacher. In the morning when I came to school, he told me that he would like to have Bob Williams, a senior, time me in the fifty-yard dash in the halls when school was out. That day, I went up in my tennis shoes, and Bob timed me in the fifty. It wasn't accurate, but when he gave the time to my teacher, Mr. Price, he knew that the time would warrant me entering some kind of competition. Mr. Price was not a track coach. He was interested in track, and he knew about it. He might have run in college. He recognized the fact that I was a fast runner and I should do something about it. Mr. Price knew that there were women's meets in Chicago. I didn't know that they had track meets for women in the city of Chicago. It was the nearest big town. He watched the newspapers. He told me about it and made the arrangements for me to take part in the meet three weeks later. It was all his doing and the young man that worked with him. My family didn't know anything about it. My dad knew I was a fast runner because he was. He was fast when he was young. Bob took me downtown to register me because my folks didn't know what to do. So it was Mr. Price and Bob Williams who did the whole thing up to my first meet. It was an indoor meet in March.

The young man who timed me knew exactly what to do. He took me downtown to a store where I could get my track shoes. He really helped me all the time along with my teacher. We were good friends.

At the indoor meet, I placed second to Helen Filkey and was asked to join the Illinois Women's Athletic Club, which was in Chicago. So that meant that after school three times a week I would go all the way in to the north side of Chicago to work out. When I got into the city, I would have to take a bus or walk a couple of miles. I did a lot of traveling back and forth. I would go downtown, after school, and get there around four o'clock and wouldn't get home until seven or eight by the time I got to the track and worked out and got dressed again and took a bus back to the train to go home again. I really had a long trip. But it was worth it because I enjoyed it. The coach of the club was a woman. Workouts included warm-ups and starting practice. There were two track men who were at the park that were helping the girls start. They had experience. They advised me as to what the best thing was that I could do if I wasn't starting fast enough or if my feet weren't close enough together or whatever. Any correction that they could give me that would better my track record was helpful. So I really had a lot of help when I got started.

My second meet was outdoors at Soldier Field. I broke the world's record in the hundred meters, running it in twelve flat. I always ran on the relay in the last position.

My third race was at the Olympic tryouts. The club sent me to the tryouts. I never had to pay my own way. The hundred final was close with Elta Cartwright. I thought I could win the Olympic hundred meters. I was running good times, and I had broken the record in the first race I ran in. So, my coach expected me to make the team. It was exciting and I get excited now, just thinking about it. There was so much tension, but it was fun.

On the boat to Amsterdam, they had a track around the deck, and the Olympic team took over the boat. There were so many of us. They didn't have a pool. Johnny Weismueller was on the team. There was no pool for the swimmers to work out in, so they erected a big wooden square thing that they put a sack in. There was water in it so that Johnny could tie himself to one side and swim away from it. It was like four feet bigger than he was. That's how the swimmers worked out. It was something to see. In nineteen thirty-six there was a pool on board. But, I'll never forget seeing Johnny in this square thing swimming away from one side and going nowhere.

We were on the boat nine days. We did not compete for at least a week after we arrived. The boat anchored out in the water, and we took a water taxi to town. All of the runners went together to work out in the field. The field was adjacent to the stadium.

There were three rounds in the hundred. I knew I had won the hundred. I broke the tape first. Just talking about the awards ceremony gives me duck bumps when I think of my standing in the middle of the stadium with all these people there and the Star Spangled Banner playing because I had just won the hundred meters. I get duck bumps now. I was so thrilled at having won and so pleased that I was there and all the people were singing because I had won. It was a wonderful sensation. I left the field alone because all of the other girls were up in the stands, but I walked out of the track and an elderly man, as I was walking over to the bus, came up and said, "Thank you very much for winning for America." Even when I think of it now I get duck bumps. He was so nice. He and I were the only people around. It was thrilling. I remember it often how delighted I felt when he said this.

The city of Chicago had a parade for me when I returned home. So did the little town and the school and of course Mr. Price.

After the nineteen twenty-eight Olympic Games, I continued to train and race. I graduated from Thornton Township High School the following year. I was working towards a degree in physical education at Northwestern University. The day of the accident, in nineteen thirty-one, I was training. It was so hot, and we weren't allowed to swim as runners. I decided to ask my cousin, who was part-owner of a plane, to take me up. That's why I went up, to cool off. I was hoping to make the nineteen thirty-two Olympic team. But I made the mistake of flying. I was destined to go to Los Angeles and would be expected to win.

The flight ended in a crash in a marshy field near Harvey in June. A news report said that the plane had gained an altitude of 400 feet when it appeared to stall and go into a spin. The soft ground may have saved their lives. Betty was hospitalized for more than eleven weeks. She suffered facial lacerations and a crushed arm. The most serious of the injuries was a cracked hip and a broken leg that required a silver pin to hold the bone together. As a result, her left leg is slightly shorter than her right leg and her knee has always been "stiff." The doctors told her that she would walk with a limp and that she would not compete again. After the accident, she eventually went to work. Medical expenses and continued rehabilitation ended her college years.

Betty explained to me how she succeeded in returning to running:

> During my recuperation, three years later, I went out to run for the sake of the exercise. When I found out that I could run o.k., not as fast as I used to, but fast enough to make a team, of sorts, I decided to go for it. I started training again, hoping I'd make the nineteen thirty-six Olympic team. I went back with the Illinois Athletic Club and the girls I used to run with and worked out with them until it was time to try out in nineteen thirty-six.
>
> I have such fond memories of everything. After I was in the airplane accident, I didn't think I'd run again. When I made the team again in nineteen thirty-six, I got duck bumps then because I made the team and was going to be able to run on the relay. It was really a struggle to make the team in nineteen thirty-six. I had to work overtime. I still have a stiff knee....
>
> [In the 1936 Olympic 400-meter relay final] I saw the German team drop the baton. They were a little ahead of us. We were depending on Helen Stephens, who was so fast, to make up what time the other girls had not made up. We were sure she could. The German girl was just passing me as she dropped the baton. I had just passed the stick to Helen. They were out of it, and we were winners. I hated to see that, I'd rather have won it the other way. Helen would have passed her. The victory ceremony was thrilling because I didn't expect to ever be able to run again after the accident. I was glad to have made the team. But when we won and I was going to get another first place medal, it's indescribable how lucky I felt to be there and getting another medal. It was hard to watch the hundred. That's what I liked best. I didn't like the two hundred.

After 1936, Betty stopped running, but she occasionally officiated at track meets. She was one of the youngest on the team in 1928 and one of the oldest in 1936. She is 5' 6" tall and her running weight was 128 pounds. She said, "I always weighed a lot."

Betty's parents were very supportive, and her father always said she took after him. She had two sisters that were older than her. Both of her children were good athletes but did not have the interest to compete. She said, "Rick could have been a terrific sprinter but he just didn't want to specialize."

"It's fun for me to talk about these things because I relive them. I get duck bumps when I think about it," Betty concluded.

Elizabeth Robinson was the first woman to win an Olympic gold medal in track and field. She did it at 16 as a high school junior, in the first Olympic Games to have women's track and field events. It was only her fourth track competition.

Betty's accomplishments in addition to the two Olympic gold medals and one Olympic silver medal are the following:

American Records

50y	5.8	Chicago, July 27, 1929
50y	6.0	Chicago, March 19, 1931
60y	6 4/5	March 2, 1929
100y	11 1/5	Chicago, July 27, 1929
220y	25.1	Milwaukee, Wisconsin, June 20, 1931
100m	12.0	Chicago, June 2, 1928 (first outdoor meet — world record)

Established first 100m Olympic record of 12 1/5
Voted into Helms Hall of Fame
Charter member and officer in the Mid-Western Chapter of U.S. Olympians
Hostess at 3d Pan American Games in 1959
First woman to win an Olympic championship in track
First American woman to win a track and field gold medal
First track and field woman to win two medals in one Olympic Games
Only woman on 1928 team to win a gold medal
Only woman on 1928 team to win two medals
Voted into U.S.A. Track and Field Hall of Fame
Only U.S.A. woman in Spalding's Almanac world record list for 1928

USA outdoor champion in 1929	50y 5 4/5 (record)
USA outdoor champion in 1929	100y 11 1/5 (record)
USA championships in 1930	second to Stella Walsh in 100y

MayBelle Reichardt Hopkins: 1928 Olympian

MayBelle Reichardt Hopkins spoke with me in November 1991 when she was eighty-four years old. She was born in Los Angeles, California, on May 27, 1907. In the interview, she recalled:

> I always was interested in all kinds of sports from the day I was born. I was a real "tom boy," I was into everything. When I went to high school, I competed in almost every sport for the four years. The first sport I played was field hockey. That was the first year that they had a freshman on the varsity team. We had interclass teams, and we had a few interschool competitions. I competed in the shot and discus in high school and made the varsity team every year in a number of things. I graduated in nineteen twenty-five.
>
> In nineteen twenty-six, I was on the Los Angeles Athletic Club basketball team, and we won the national championship. I was interested and still am very interested in basketball. In track I won two national championships in the discus and came in second twice in the shot put. So track and basketball were my best sports.

I had just a general coach for track in high school, no one that specialized in it. I just sort of did as I could. I competed for the Pasadena Athletic and Country Club for probably a year. Then the coach moved to the Los Angeles Athletic Club, and I competed for them until I retired. Aileen Allen was the coach of the team. She was like a real friend, but she did not know too much more than we did in the discus. Someone just showed me how to throw the discus, and I tried to improve my technique. I think one of the men showed me how to throw it. He did not coach me, he just showed me the form. We had lots of competitions in the local cities. We went to San Francisco and a lot of little towns around the Los Angeles area. I had a shoe box full of medals, most of them were gold and silver. One or two were bronze. I got a medal in everything I competed in. I was always in the discus and shot put, if it was offered. I ran in nineteen twenty-five. Paavo Nurmi came to the United States, and they had a big track meet at the Coliseum in Los Angeles. I ran in a relay, and we broke the world record. But, in those days it wasn't much. They were just starting track, so there weren't too many fast times. There was quite a bit of interest in women's sport. We ran all winter. The sportswriters were very generous, and I have loads and loads of newspaper pictures. But all of the pictures are disintegrating.

I never thought I would make the nineteen twenty-eight Olympic team. I was in nurses' training in nineteen twenty-five. I went into nurses' training at the hospital right after graduating from high school. I didn't see or go to any athletic functions. I never saw a discus for over two years since I had retired. I didn't have time for anything because we had eight hours of work every day, three hours of classes and the other hour between twelve hours was for lunch and dinner at night. I had no place to practice and of course, no coach, or anyone to tell me if I was doing anything right or wrong. I didn't even know that they were having women in field events in the Olympics.

Three weeks before the tryouts, Mrs. Allen called me and she said, "Would you like to try out for the Olympic Games?" I said, "I haven't seen a discus in over two years. I don't know if I could even hold one!" She said, "It's an opportunity," but I said I couldn't possibly do it. She said there will be lots of girls who would be very happy to have an opportunity to try out. But, she said, "If you're not interested, that's all right." She knew that would irritate me. So, I thought, well, I'm gonna do it. So I went to train. Sometimes I had to walk five miles because I didn't have the nickel for a bus. Then I would practice, and I'd be the only one around. I'd throw it, and then go get it and throw it back. I didn't know if I was doing anything right or wrong. Finally, I did well enough to qualify to go to New Jersey. The superintendent of nurses told me that if I didn't make the Olympic team that I must be on duty the following Monday. She said, "If you make it, you can have a leave of absence from the hospital. If you don't make it, you either be on duty that day or you will never have a chance to get your registered nurse's degree." So, I just begged Mrs. Allen, the week before our tryouts, I begged her to buy my ticket home because I didn't have the money for it. I said I had already put in three years of work toward my registered nurse's degree and I can't give that up. I want to do that for my life's work. She said, "Nope, I'm not going to because you could make the team." There were four girls that were doing better than I, and they were only going to take four girls. I thought that it was a losing cause, and she didn't get my ticket.

It just happened that I was very lucky that day. I won the national championships, and I set a record that lasted four years. It was a real thriller. Most of all I was happy that I wasn't going to get kicked out of nursing. It was like a dream come true.

We went by boat to Amsterdam. I went by rail. I was in bed the whole time; I was terribly sick. When I wasn't in bed, I was on the rail. That left me pretty weak. I don't offer that as an alibi or an excuse that I didn't do better in Amsterdam. I had only trained for three weeks and all by myself. I had no coaching criticism to help me. Dean Cromwell, the coach of the men's team, tried to help me on the ship. He was a very good friend of mine. He told me if I did it a little differently, I could do a lot better. That was the most coaching that I had. I tried to change. Then in the competition I couldn't do it his way, and I couldn't do it my own way.

The discus record I set in the United States was a hundred and sixteen feet, nine and a quarter inches. I missed getting into the finals in the Olympic Games by a quarter of an inch. I was upset about that because I think I would have done better in the finals. It was a great experience. I had a wonderful time. Something you never could get any other way except competing.

I remember the opening ceremony at the Olympic Games. I was very proud. The stadium was filled. The ceremony was very impressive; it was gorgeous. The closing ceremony was too. The awards presentations were the same as today. The three finishers were on a podium, and the medals, which were on a ribbon, were placed around their necks. The women were treated equally as well as the men, even though this was the first Olympics that women's track was on the program. We had a marching uniform and a competition uniform which fit very well because they took our measurements ahead of time.

When the Olympics were over, some of the team went to another country. I came right home because of nursing. I figured that she wanted me back as soon as possible, but I found out I could have stayed longer. But I had a chance to study after arriving home. A funny thing happened on the ship coming back. Lillian signed up for the captain's bridge party. When the time came to play, she was in Brussels but had asked me to take her place. I said no because I couldn't play very well. But I went anyway. One hundred and sixty people played. I won first prize. Now I play three or four nights a week.

I earned my nursing license when I got home. I only needed three more months. I took my state boards and got my registered nurse's degree and was very happy about that.

In nineteen thirty-two, I went to Chicago to defend my championships. I had just gotten married and was very much in love and didn't care about competing. Nursing now was much more important to me. I remained in nursing for fifty years in California.

In looking back, when I see the facilities and coaching and advantages the people have now, I wonder how we ever did anything. I have two televisions, and I watch all sports. They asked me to accompany some of the school children in the nineteen eighty-four Olympic Games. I did go to that. I wonder what we could have done if we had the facilities and the coaching because I had absolutely nothing of either one. None of us did. I was five foot seven and a hundred and thirty-five to a hundred and forty pounds. I think I could really have done well. I would have liked to try the javelin.

Lillian Copeland was on my team, she took second in Amsterdam and won the discus in Los Angeles in nineteen thirty-two. We were teammates for many years. She was on the Pasadena and Los Angeles teams, but we didn't practice together because I was in Pasadena and she was in Los Angeles. She was in college. Dean Cromwell was the coach at her college and worked with Lillian.

We met as a club sporadically. There were two or three girls that were in the field events. Maybe there were eight to ten runners. One of the runners who made the team was Anne Vrana.

My parents were very proud of everything I did. I was the "baby" of thirteen children. I had eleven sisters and one brother. I was the only athlete. They were happy to see me compete even though no one was at the Olympics. They could not afford to go.

I was married in nineteen thirty-one. I have two sons. Both of them are professors. One is at the University of Southern California and is a composer. The other is at the University of Houston and teaches physics. One received his doctorate from Princeton and the other from Harvard. They've got my brains! I tried to interest them in track.

My advice to a young girl just beginning track and field is to have a goal. It may take a lot of time but persevere and work towards the goal.

Mary Washburn: 1928 Olympian

Mary Washburn Conklin was born on August 4, 1907, in Hudson Falls, New York. Her track experience began when she was in grammar school. Mary said in a letter on March 2, 1992:

> I lived in Hempstead, Long Island. The store merchants celebrated the 4th of July by giving prizes of articles that they sold in their stores, in a track meet for children. I won a pen and a pencil set and a string of pearls. The next race was at a Sunday school picnic at Belmont race track. The whole group traveled from Hempstead by trolley car to Jamaica. I won a 50 yard dash at that affair. The prize was a box of candy. The Carle Place school in Long Island had a track meet at their school and gave medals to the winners.
>
> I was on the high school track team in Hempstead. There were only three girls on the team. We practiced with the boys and the boys coach. As a junior, I competed in the Nassau County Interscholastic track meet and joined the AAU in 1924.
>
> I went to DePauw University for three years. I won a first prize in the hurdles in a University Invitational Telegraphic Meet and broke the national intercollegiate 60 yard hurdle record. While at DePauw, I competed in soccer, swimming and basketball as well as track.
>
> I transferred from DePauw in 1927, in my junior year, to New York University so that the opportunity for track participation would be increased. We had some track meets there, held at Macombs Dam Park in New York City. That was the year that I competed on the NYU team and evenings and week-ends I competed with the Millrose Track Club, a group that was financed by Millrose and supported by Wanamaker's store.
>
> We practiced on the roof of the Wanamaker store garage between 5 and 8 P.M. A board track of 1/10 of a mile was constructed on the roof. We had quite a few meets sponsored by the Metropolitan AAU that were climaxed by larger AAU meets, Brooklyn Edison, National City Bank, Knights of Columbus, etc.
>
> On the 4th of July, 1928, the tryouts for the Olympics were held in Newark, New Jersey. I qualified for a place in the 100 meter dash. Two other Millrose girls made the team by placing in the 100 meters as extras and had gone to Amsterdam. They did run the relay. Loretta McNeil, Jesse Cross and I qualified for the Olympic relay team. I ran number one, the Millrose girls ran two and three and Betty Robinson, fourth. Canada won the gold and we were second.

MayBelle Reichardt, member of the first United States women's Olympic track and field team in 1928 throwing the discus, her Olympic event, in the United States uniform. (Courtesy of MayBelle Reichardt Hopkins.)

[Mary placed second in her heat in the 100 meters, advancing to the semifinal round. In the semifinal, she placed fourth and was eliminated.]

We all traveled on the S.S. *President Roosevelt* and shared a stateroom on the ship. It was a happy time. A Dutch masseuse came in every day to give massages. The coach of the girls was Mel Sheppard, former Olympic winner. He was the only athlete to win firsts in two events in the Olympics. In 1908 he won the 1500 meters and 800 meters. He was on the team in 1912 also.

The competition uniforms were red, white and blue. The shorts were blue with stripes of red, white and blue down the sides. The tops were white with a large USA emblem on the left side and red, white and blue stripes on a diagonal across the front. The sweats were blue.

After the Olympics were over we were invited to take part in an Invitational meet in Brussels against Great Britain, Belgium and Germany. There I won the 80 meter hurdles, my best event but not included in the 1928 Olympics. It was run on grass. Then they gave us a tour of Brussels. It was most interesting to see the effects of the war after World War I.

Mary Washburn Conklin's family added to her story:

Clearly, the most significant person in Mary's life was her mother, Edith Washburn. Edith was widowed at an early age and raised and supported her three daughters by working as the manager of the Western Union office in their town. Edith was a strong and loving mother who instilled in her daughters a great respect for education. All three girls graduated from college — an amazing feat for a single mother in that era. Mary's sister Louise, four years younger, followed in Mary's footsteps and competed in track. She went to the Olympic trials in 1932.

After many years of teaching physical education and coaching track, basketball, field hockey and lacrosse at Beaver College in Philadelphia, Mary became the coach and manager of the United States and British women's lacrosse touring team in 1969. This team traveled for four months to Philadelphia, Honolulu, Fiji, New Zealand, Australia, Singapore, Tokyo, Hong Kong, Rome, Amsterdam and England.

Carrying on his mother's tradition in athletics, Deke Conklin competed in track and field in high school and college. At Rutgers University, Deke held the pole vault record from 1955 to 1962.

Judith Jenkins George, a member of the faculty of DePauw University, said in a lengthy article about Mary that during her freshman year at DePauw, she entered eight track and field events in the women's intracampus meet during the May Day festival. She came in first in five of the events, scoring enough points on her own to defeat the senior class team. Her other activities at DePauw included playing the violin in the university orchestra, serving as coed sports editor for the school newspaper, and working on the yearbook.

George noted: "It was not easy for a woman to be an athlete in those days. Washburn reminisced about an incident at New York University in 1927 when the head of the School of Education lectured her on how women should not compete in intercollegiate sports. Washburn thus chose to register at the Washington Square College, another branch of N.Y.U. because it offered field hockey, basketball, and swimming teams."

In discussing the Olympic 800-meter run with George, Mary Washburn Conklin recalled:

> A couple of old fogies were there from Columbia and Barnard College, and when they got back they capitalized on that [800-meter run] because they were against all competition for women. I went to a confer-

MayBelle Reichardt, member of the first United States women's Olympic track and field team in 1928 putting the shot. MayBelle is wearing the USA uniform. (Courtesy of MayBelle Reichardt Hopkins.)

ence at NYU about a year after the Olympics. These women were there and they got up and gave this spiel and everyone who knew me looked at me as if to say, "What are you going to say about this?" So I got up and defended it, the girls on the team. Nobody did any harm. They were just pretty exhausted after running the 800 meters.

Conklin has received many awards for her contributions to sport and physical education, among them:

1975 — Nassau Area Certification of Recognition, Association of Women in Physical Education of New York State

1979 — Women's Varsity Hall of Fame, New York University
1984 — Empire State Woman of the Year in Sports, presented by Governor Mario
   Cuomo
1986 — DePauw University Hall of Fame

Delores Boeckmann

In 1928 when "Dee" Boeckmann made the Olympic Team in the 800-meter run, she was a physical education teacher at Loretto Academy in St. Louis. At the age of sixteen, in 1920, she held all ten of her AAU association's track and field records, according to an article by June Wuest Becht in the *St. Louis Globe-Democrat* on May 21, 1978. Dee was a member of the first women's Olympic track and field team, and she competed in the first and last 800-meter run in the Olympics until 1960. She was the first United States woman to be an Olympic coach in 1936 and was the first woman to coach service teams during World War II. Dee was the first woman to serve as chairman of a national AAU sports committee (basketball), was the first woman to "chair" in 1940 a national Olympic committee (track and field), was the first woman national chair of the AAU track and field committee, and was the first American woman to coach a foreign national team. Her first athletic award was won in 1919 and her last in 1937. She participated internationally in four sports — track, basketball, fencing, and field hockey.

Dee's mother was of Irish descent and her father German. Dee reported that he was her first coach at the age of eight and taught her to "run like a boy." Every time that there was a race at school or Sunday school, she was in it. Her sister was also an excellent athlete. She played with Dee on the basketball team and was also on the Washington University rifle team. Dee also had a brother Ed, whom she dragged to the track so he could run with her.

In 1927, Dee broke the world record for the indoor 50-yard dash, running 6.1. While training for the 1928 Olympics, the 5'9" middle-distance runner set a record of 2:31 for the 880-yard run.

In 1928, Dee paid her own expenses to the Newark tryouts, as did three other St. Louis women. She said that in those days it was lucky if there were three track meets in a season.

Making the team was like an answer to a prayer for Dee, Becht wrote in her article. Dee Boeckmann anticipated competing in Paris in the 1924 women's Olympics, but the United States Olympic Committee decided not to enter what they considered to be a weak contingent. Dee was disappointed at this lost opportunity to compete, and she joined other women athletes in a letter-writing barrage to the Olympic Committee vigorously supporting the addition of women's events in the 1928 Olympic Games.

Dee did not place in the 800 meters in 1928. At the finish of the final, many of the runners "collapsed." Dee thought that the runners "collapsed" more from emotion than fatigue. The display at the finish caused the opponents of this event to have it eliminated from future Olympic Games.

On the way back to the United States, as Dee recalls, General MacArthur presented a gold globe to each member of the team.

Upon returning to St. Louis, Becht continues, Dee returned to teaching, coaching, and participation in sports. She held the position of superintendent of the St. Louis community centers and playgrounds.

In 1936, Dee was selected to coach/chaperone the women's Olympic track and field team. This was the first time that a woman served in the capacity of coach of an Olympic track and field team. It was advantageous for her to coach the team because she had Olympic experience in 1928 and had professional sports training. She helped plan menus to include foods which the girls were accustomed to. Other coaches followed her lead for their teams.

After the 1936 Olympic Games, Dee received many job offers. She left St. Louis to teach and coach in Pennsylvania and then in New Orleans. When the New York sportswriters chose six outstanding sportswomen who were pioneers in American women's sports, Dee was selected the All-Around Sportswoman.

In 1937, in New Orleans, Dee won the International Fencing Championship.

In 1941, Dee returned to St. Louis to become the first woman superintendent of recreation for the city. International events led her to become a Red Cross recreation director for the armed forces overseas.

Dee first served in Iceland, where she helped improve the recreational facilities, organized athletic teams, and coached. Her second post was in China. There she set up boxing rings, baseball fields, and other recreational facilities for the servicemen. For a period of time, she served as the director of the Red Cross Club in Shanghai.

When the war ended, Dee returned to the United States to lecture at colleges about her experiences. While lecturing in Washington, D.C., she was asked to join the U.S. Army Special Services as a recreation director. She accepted a position in Korea but never got there. She stopped in Japan and was coaxed into working there.

In 1950, General MacArthur asked her to coach the Japanese women's track and field team. She remained in Japan for years. During the 1964 Olympic Games in Tokyo, she served as activities director for the United States team. She retired from government work in 1972.

As a retiree, Dee's activities in Arizona included walking two miles a day. In 1976 Dee and Mae Faggs Starr were inducted into the National Track and Field Hall of Fame. Helen Stephens gave Dee's induction presentation. In 1977, she was inducted into the Missouri Track and Cross Country Coaches Association Hall of Fame.

Dee coached all over the world. Becht quoted her 1976 statement: "I still feel like an 18 year old. I see kids running on the street, stop them and tell them what's wrong with their form. They look at me as if I'm crazy. About her induction into the Hall of Fame she said, I'm glad it happened while I'm still alive, and not after I'm pushing up daisies. I'm so excited, it's the highest honor you can get after the Olympics."

Her most humorous experience in athletics, Dee said, was being presented to the king and queen of Belgium in Brussels at the International Track and Field Meet. "The queen presented us with flowers — not a large bouquet — but a large funeral spray, it tickled we teenagers and we all laughed! This was in 1928."

Delores Boeckmann was listed in the 1965-67 *Who's Who*; *The Royal Blue Book*, England 1969; *International Biography* 67, 68, and 69; *Blue-Book*, London, 1970; *National Register of Prominent Americans & International Notables 1970-71*.

Anne Vrana

In 1987, Anne was interviewed by George Hodak for the Amateur Athletic Foundation of Los Angeles. This profile is based upon his interview.

Anne Vrana O'Brien was born in Schenectady, New York, on August 22, 1911. She began running "from the time that I was born." Every time that her mother sent her to the store, she would run, rather than walk. At picnics, she'd run and beat the boys.

Anne's formal training began in high school in California. Play days were popular at the time, but there were no competitive sports for girls. "Competition … was a no-no in those days." She sat in the stands after school each day and watched the boys run track. One day, after wondering why Anne was always around, the coach, Otto Anderson, asked her why she was there. She told him she wanted to run. He invited her to run a 440 with the boys. In her long black gym bloomers, a midi-blouse, and black cotton stockings she accepted Coach Otto's invitation. She paced herself with the group and then decided she could do better. So off she went towards the finish and beat the whole boys' team.

Can you imagine Coach Anderson's surprise? The captain of the track team, Howard O'Brien, came over to find out who she was and why she beat the boys.

Coach Anderson told Anne to see Dean Cromwell, the coach at USC, who would be able to advise her, so Anne and her sister headed to USC. Anne took her sneakers, bloomers, and midi-blouse with her but left the stockings at home.

Running at USC, Anne again beat some of the boys. Charlie Paddock and Charlie Borah were there training. Dean Cromwell was impressed and referred her to Aileen Allen, the coach of the Pasadena Athletic Club.

The following Saturday Anne went to Paddock field to try out for Coach Allen's team. All she had to do, Coach Allen said, was to keep up with the other girls, but she beat the whole team. Needless to say, she made the team.

On September 3, 1927, in Eureka, California, at the national championships, Anne placed second to Eleanor Egg in the broad jump and ran on the winning 440-yard relay team. In the 100, she was disqualified for two false starts. The 100 was her best event, and she thought that she might have won because in practice she was running equal to world record times. The Eureka nationals was Anne's first track meet. It was also the first time that she broad jumped. The coach told her to just run down the runway, hit the board, and jump. With one jump, she placed second in the nationals.

Aileen Allen wanted women from her club on the Olympic team. Everything the club did in 1927 was geared for the trials in 1928. At the same time that Allen coached the track team, she also coached swimmers. Four track and field women did make the team, and Aileen Allen was the chaperone.

Anne placed third in the 100 meters in the trials, qualifying her for the first women's Olympic track and field team.

In Amsterdam, Anne celebrated her seventeenth birthday. In the third heat of the 100 meters, she placed third and did not advance to the semifinal round.

When the women's events were over, before the Olympics ended, the team left for a meet in Belgium. Anne finished second in the 100 and second in the broad jump. This was the second time she competed in the broad jump. After leaving Belgium, the team stopped in Paris for a visit and then joined the ship, the S.S. *President Roosevelt,* in Cherbourg for the trip back to the United States.

Anne returned home with sights set on the 1932 team. In 1930 she married the captain of her high school track team, Howard O'Brien. He continued to push and support her athletic endeavors.

In 1932, Anne was hurdling. Coach Cromwell, Jim Tevan, and her husband were coaching her. At the trials in Evanston in the first heat, she hit the second hurdle. She went over two more but had a bad fall on the fourth hurdle.

She ran in the 100 meters and beat Babe Didrikson to get first place in the heat. Because of the fall on the cinders during the hurdles, however, she had abrasions on her knees and hands and had to have a tetanus shot. It made her violently ill and forced her to drop out of the 100 meters. She was named an alternate to the team and trained with the girls during the Olympic Games. Afterwards, she competed in San Francisco as a member of the United States team, placing second in the hurdles.

As a spectator at the 1932 Olympic Games, Anne saw the controversial final of the hurdles. She thought that Evelyne Hall had won the event even though the decision was awarded to Babe Didrikson.

Anne was in training for a meet in conjunction with the Chicago World's Fair in 1933 when she discovered that she was pregnant.

After her daughter was born in 1934, she started training again for 1936.

The tryouts were in Providence, Rhode Island. This time Anne won her heat, semis, and finals of the hurdles and was ready for the trip to Berlin aboard the S.S. *Manhattan.*

The ship, which was nicer than the S.S. *President Roosevelt,* was well equipped for all of the athletes. They landed in Hamburg and were driven to Berlin at 125 miles an hour on the autobahn.

In Berlin, the women were housed in a building that was later used for the military, two athletes to a room. The dorms were right next to the stadium, and the men were housed in the Olympic Village.

In the 80-meter hurdles, Anne placed second in her heat, but she did not qualify for the finals. After the Olympic Games, the women's team went to the southern German town of Wuppertal for a post-Olympic competition.

Upon arriving back in the United States, the team had a ticker tape parade down Broadway.

Anne planned to compete in 1940 in Japan, but the war ended all Olympic Games competition until 1948. Anne's daughter was then in high school. Anne got a girls' team together and took them to Freeport, Texas, for the nationals in 1950. Her daughter ran the sprints and put the shot. Anne also entered the meet and competed. If Eleanor Egg and her mother were first, this was probably the second mother-daughter competitive duo. Anne also competed a few years later at age forty-two in the Coliseum Relays. Her daughter was in the meet also. Anne ran one more hurdle race at age forty-five.

Chapter 12

1929

The *Amateur Athletic Union Bulletin* in August had a relatively lengthy article on the outdoor nationals. The meet was held on July 27 in Grant Park Stadium (Soldier Field) in Chicago. Fred Steers, the chairman of the national committee on women's athletics, reported that despite the 93-degree weather, 4,000 spectators witnessed the breaking of five world records. According to Steers:

> Betty Robinson, Illinois Women's A.C., America's only feminine winner in the 1928 Olympic Games at Amsterdam provided the most sensational performances of the meet setting new world's records in the 50 and 100 yard dashes. The slim, smiling Chicago girl, who runs like a man, clipped ⅕ of a second from her own 50 yard dash mark, sprinting the distance in 5⅘ seconds. In the longer dash she broke the existing mark of 11⅖ seconds held jointly by herself and Helen Filkey Warren, a clubmate, in the semi-final heat by ⅕ of a second and equalled the performance in the final.

A new world record was set by Helen Filkey Warren in the opening event of the meet, the 80-meter hurdles. Returning to competition after a year's absence, Helen ran 12⅗ to break a record set in 1927 by a German athlete.

Other record-breaking performances were Rena MacDonald's 42' 3" in the shot put, which broke Lillian Copeland's meet record, and Gloria Russell's baseball throw of 258' 1", the last mark to go. Maybelle Gilliland tied the 220 yard dash meet record with her performance of 27⅖.

50-yard dash
1. Betty Robinson, Illinois Women's A.C.   5⅘
2. Loretta McNeil, Millrose A.A.
3. Delores Henders, No. Calif. A.C.
4. Genevieve Brick, Orr Playground

100-yard run
1. Betty Robinson, Illinois Women's A.C.   11⅕
2. Jessie Cross, Millrose A.A.
3. Ethel Harrington, Illinois Women's A.C.
4. Margaret Whitcomb, Golden A.C., Dallas

220-yard run
1. Maybelle Gilliland, Millrose A.A.   27⅖
2. Ruth Waldner, Pennsy A.C.

3. Florence McDonald, Boston Swimming Assn.
4. Catherine Capp, Globe A.A.

80-meter hurdles
1. Helen Filkey Warren, Illinois Women's A.C.   12⅗
2. Evelyne Hall, Illinois Women's A.C.
3. Nellie Todd, Illinois Women's A.C.
4. Catherine Donovan, Prudential A.A.

440-yard relay
1. Millrose A.A.   51⅓
   (Gilliland, Cross, Jensen, McNeil)
2. Prudential A.A.
3. Illinois Women's A.C.
4. South Parks A.C.

High jump
1. Jean Shiley, Meadowbrook Club   4' 9⅞"
2. Genevieve Valvoda, South Parks A.C.
3. Eleanor Egg, St. Bonaventure's
4. Anna Polcik, South Parks A.C.

Broad jump
1. Nellie Todd, Illinois Women's A.C.   17' 3¼"
2. Margaret Whitcomb, Golden A.C., Dallas
3. Eleanor Towler, Pennsy A.C.
4. Lillian Janat, Finnish American A.C.

8-lb. shot
1. Rena MacDonald, Boston Swimming Assn.   42' 3"
2. Eleanor Egg, St. Bonaventure's
3. Evelyn Ferrara, Illinois Women's A.C.
4. Fanny Weisinger, Golden A.C., Dallas

Discus
1. Rena MacDonald, Boston Swimming Assn.   113' 4"
2. Dee Boeckmann, Western A.A.U.
3. Evelyn Ferrara, Illinois Women's A.C.
4. Gloria Russell, No. Calif. A.C.

Javelin
1. Estelle Hill, Prudential A.A.   100' 5"
2. Fay Langford, Golden A.C., Dallas
3. Rena MacDonald, Boston S.A.
4. Gloria Russell, No. Cal. A.C.

Baseball throw
1. Gloria Russell, No. Cal. A.C.   258' 1"
2. Fay Langford, Golden A.C., Dallas
3. Lillian Kelly, Millrose A.A.
4. Dorothy Orgren, Board of Education

The Illinois Women's A.C. won the team title with 31 points.

Martin Klein, in his report to the Metropolitan Association said that the meet was run in fairly good fashion. The only fault he found was that there were many people running around with officials' badges on, but when they were asked to work the field events, they made themselves scarce. Mr. Klein had to help with the field events and also serve as a timer. When reported to Mr. Steers, the national chairman, that he had no stop watch with him, Mr. Steers told him to go to the judges' table, and get one. At the judges table he found the watches in a bag with a collection of measuring tapes. When he chose two of them, he found a timing variation with them and pointed this out so that in the future, the delicate watches would be properly handled.

The Indoor Nationals

The national indoor meet was held on March 31 in Boston.

40-yard run
1. Mary Carew, Medford Girls' A.C.   5⅗
2. Katherine Mearls, Boston Swimming Assn.
3. Loretta McNeil, Millrose A.A.
4. Olive Hasenfus, Boston Swimming Assn.

220-yard run
1. Catherine Donovan, Prudential A.A.   29.0
2. Florence McDonald, Boston Swimming Assn.
3. Mabel Morrissey, Boston Swimming Assn.
4. Jessie Cross, Millrose A.A.

50-yard hurdles
1. Catherine Donovan, Prudential A.A.   8.0
2. Marietta Ceres, Prudential A.A.
3. Dorothy Watson, Prudential A.A.
4. Rena MacDonald, Boston Swim A.

440-yard relay
1. Millrose A. A.   54⅕
   (Jensen, Cross, McNeil, Gilliland)
2. Boston Swimming Assn.
3. Prudential Insurance A.A.

High jump
1. Jean Shiley, Meadowbrook Club   5' 3⅛"
2. Mildred Wiley, Boston Swimming Assn.   5' ¼"
3. Olive Huber, St. George Club   4' 11½"
4. Mary Scully, W.S.A. Brookline

Standing broad jump
1. Katherine Mearls, Boston Swimming Assn.   8' 2¾"
2. Jean Shiley, Meadowbrook Club   7' 11½"

3. Marion Raymond, Simmons College
4. Esther Laing, Prudential A.A.

8-lb. shot
1. Rena MacDonald, Boston Swimming Assn.   39' 3⅝"
2. Bertha Poetschke, Warinanco A.A.   33' 11⅞"
3. Lillian Dennon, Medford Girls' A.C.
4. Mae Magill, Boston Swimming Assn.

Basketball throw
1. Marietta Ceres, Prudential A.A.   85' 5¾"
2. Rena MacDonald, Boston Swimming Assn.   81' 8¾"
3. Esther Laing, Prudential A.A.
4. Carrie Jensen, Millrose A.A.

Martin Klein gave the women's athletic committee report for the Metropolitan Association. He was pleased with the improved cooperation that year from the various clubs that added women's events to their program.

The senior metropolitan outdoor championship meet was held in Brooklyn at Wingate Field on July 13. The *New York Evening Journal* paid for all of the printing and the prizes. It also paid for the winners to travel to Chicago and compete in the national championships. A check for $1,200 was received to help defray the cost of sending fourteen girls to Chicago: Loretta McNeil, Jessie Cross, Dorothy Furth, Lillian Kelly, Maybelle Gilliland, Louise Washburn, Carrie Jensen, and Dorothy Meyers, all of the Millrose A.A.; Eleanor Egg, Estelle Hill, Catherine Donovan, Marietta Ceres, Esther Laing, and Catherine Capp. Mrs. Loesch, the women's handicapper, acted as the chaperone of the team, and Martin Klein went as manager.

Klein reported on an historic first for women. He stated that on August 10, the North Jersey Athletic League conducted a pentathlon for women at Weequahic Park in Newark. "This is the first time in the history of women's athletics in America that this event has been staged and I hereby want to give full credit to George Vreeland of the Prudential Insurance A.A. through whose efforts the pentathlon was put on at this meet." Seven girls participated and completed the contest. Estelle Hill won the event, Eleanor Egg was second, Catherine Capp third, Catherine Brown fourth, Marietta Ceres fifth, Steffie Kuczynski sixth, and Shirley Daniels seventh.

The *Amateur Athletic Union Bulletin* reported several women's events. The February-July *Bulletin* announced the Third International Track Meet in Prague. The meet is scheduled for September 6, 7 and 8th in 1930 and in order for the United States to compete, notification of intent to participate must be received by the secretary of the Fédération Sportive Féminine Internationale by the end of December 1929.

The International Slovak Championships were held in Prague on July 4. Miss Wilhelmina Swetlik, of Schenectady, New York, was "crowned the world's all-around athlete," reported the August *Amateur Athletic Union Bulletin*. Two thousand women and girls took part, representing France, Germany, Belgium, Canada, Switzerland, the Slovakias, and all of the Balkan states. The five events competed in were the shot, running broad jump, 60-meter hurdles, marching, and calisthenics.

The *Schenectady Gazette* of July 17 reported:

> "Minnie" is 22 years of age and considered to be the best athlete of the Czechoslovakians throughout the world. Youngstown, Ohio hosted the games to select the United States participants.
>
> Minnie has been active in athletics since the age of nine, and participated in meets in Binghamton, Johnstown, Branville, Albany and Bridgeport, Connecticut. She graduated from Schenectady high school in 1926 and was employed in the office of the International General Electric Company at the time of her world's pentathlon victory in Prague.

A second article in this *Bulletin* entitled "Athletics For Women Will Help Save the Nation" is a rebuttal to the 1928 article by Dr. Frederick Rand Rogers. The article by Bernarr MacFadden said: "It is regrettable that a man of the intelligence and experience of Dr. Frederick Rand Rogers, state director of health and physical education, should feel that women have no place in competitive sports. Many women athletes the world over will disagree with his contention that competitive athletics make women 'manly.' MacFadden also maintained that health is a prime reason to engage in athletics. The shocking condition of the male population revealed during the last war appalled the nation. He said that if our young women were tested, conditions far worse would be revealed.

According to MacFadden, exercise develops "suppleness" and "symmetry" characteristics that women crave:

> Athletics properly used makes a woman more beautiful, makes her a far better sweetheart, a more alluring wife, and a more dependable mother. ... Strong, vigorous, vital women are badly needed....
>
> The hour-glass figure of a generation ago has been discarded. Women no longer tighten their waists until they look like a dressed up wasp.
>
> Athletics of every kind should be encouraged. The evils associated with athletics should be discouraged, but every friend of womankind who is able to look into the future will use every possible endeavor to encourage the interest of women everywhere in every kind of muscular exercise that will help make her a more vital specimen of humankind."

The August 1929 *Bulletin* had a reprint of an article written in *Sport Story* magazine by Mrs. Ada Taylor Sackett, who served as the chaperone of the women's Olympic swimming team in 1928. She was a swimmer known for her eight mile swim in the ocean from Atlantic City to Brigantine and back. Here's what she said about track:

> In the case of women's participation in track and field events, we have not had time to give the situation a complete study, and it is these events that are now under fire. There is not yet a general participation in this type of athletics, notwithstanding the fact that we had a track and field team of girls in the Olympic Games last summer. Only a comparatively few girl athletes tried for representation on our team. However, it was because of an incident at Amsterdam when a girl running in the 800 meter race collapsed at the tape, that this

hue and cry had been heard. Immediately, the Olympic committee decided to take this event off the program for 1932.

Unpleasant as it is to see any one collapse at the end of a contest, it is not an uncommon sight. Young men have been doing it by the hundreds these many years, but I am glad we are not yet hardened to seeing a woman collapse. It shows that chivalry is not entirely extinct yet. But in this particular case, some in authority believed that the young woman collapsed because of nervousness and because of tenseness of her task was relieved, and not because of physical exhaustion. She was herself almost immediately and did not display any ill after effects.

Mrs. Sackett said that if one measured a woman's health by the number of children she bore, the women swimmers would shine. She cited these women and the number of children they had had and then stated:

It will not surprise me to find that track and field competitors, after their competitive days are over, will show a record similar to that of their water-loving sisters. Nor will it surprise me that 800 meter races for women will some day be considered much less of a strain than that of a woman swimming the English Channel.

I do not think it time to raise a scare over women competitors in track and field. However, it is always good time to use good judgment in training. Not any slipshod, ignorant method will produce the right results, but wise training, carefully thought out and worked out, will give us healthy women and star athletes.

The Women's Division, NAAF, held its fifth annual meeting in New York City January 3-5. The Olympic problem surfaced everywhere. Miss Ethel Perrin, chairman of the executive committee of the Women's Division, spoke of the problem confronting the women of America in the Olympics to be held in Los Angeles in 1932 and the importance of the Women's Division taking a stand regarding them. She outlined the three alternatives:

1. The Division could ask to be included in the planning committee of the AAU.

2. It could oppose the participation of girls and women in the Olympic Games.

3. It could conduct an educational campaign to discourage participation in the Olympics.

Of these choices, Miss Perrin pointed out, "the third offers the most hopeful method of approach to the problem and presents a constructive program which, with its emphasis on the play day idea and its stressing of the values of joyful play for all, would make it possible for all girls to take part in a play program in local communities to the exclusion of intensive training for a few. A brief discussion followed in which some of the delegates from California pointed out the seriousness of the problem."

The minutes of the meeting summarized the end of the conference:

Throughout the entire conference the problem of the Olympic Games had been raised at every session and it was inevitable that before the meeting closed the group, representing women throughout the country responsible for the leadership of activities for girls, should take a definite stand on the participation of girls and women in the Games. The latter part of the last session of the conference was accordingly given over to a discussion of the stand which the Women's Division should take. The following resolutions were passed:

I. Whereas competition in the Olympic Games would among other things
   (1) entail the specialized training of the few,
   (2) offer opportunity for the exploitation of girls and women, and
   (3) offer opportunity for possible over-strain in preparation for and during the Games themselves,
   Resolved that the Women's Division of the National Amateur Athletic Federation go on record as disapproving of competition for girls and women in the Olympic Games.

II. Whereas the United States will be acting in the capacity of host to the other nations participating in the Games in 1932, in order that we may not seem to be inhospitable to the girls and women who may take part in the Games, especially those from foreign countries,
   Resolved that the Women's Division send a letter to the proper committee or authority offering to assist in every way possible in the entertainment of the women participants in the Games in 1932.

III. Whereas the Women's Division is interested in promoting sports and games for girls and believes absolutely in competition of the right kind under the proper conditions,
   Whereas, the Women's Division is interested in promoting the ideal of Play for Play's sake, of Play on a large scale, of Play and recreation properly safeguarded,
   Whereas it is interested in promoting types and programs of activities suitable to girls as girls,
   Resolved that the Women's Division or whomever it shall designate shall ask for the opportunity of putting on in Los Angeles during the Games (not as part of the Olympic program) a festival which might include singing, dancing, music, mass sports and games, luncheons, conferences, banquets, demonstrations, exhibitions, etc.
   Whereas as a result of the discussions which took place during the convention, realizing that a crisis is at hand whereby the platform and principles of the Women's Division will be severely tested,
   Be it resolved that the members of the Women's Division and all of those who are interested in the Federation and its ideals, go back to their communities determined to do all in their power to more actively spread the principles advocated by this Division and to work unceasingly toward putting on for girls, a program of sports and games in their individual situations which shall
   (1) include every member of the group;
   (2) be broad and diversified;
   (3) be adapted to the special needs and abilities and capacities of the participants: with the emphasis put upon participation rather than upon winning.

A committee was to be appointed to study the Olympic situation as it related to girls and women.

The April letter of the Women's Division stated that on May 1, Miss Perrin broadcast a speech over WJZ, with a national hook-up.

As a result of the January conference, so many letters and reports were received that a newsletter became a necessity. The February newsletter had reports from the following states:

Alabama — "Our plans now are to hold a district play day in place of the district tournament and a state play day for the winner of the state letter to take the place of the state tournament."

St. Louis, Missouri — "I should say here that Dr. Curtis has done excellent work in eliminating girls' basketball tournaments in this state."

The March newsletter contained further reports:

Texas — "This month a letter, with Miss Perrin's pamphlet of Play Days, is being sent to those colleges urging them to organize inter or intra college, or community play days this spring."

Oregon — "For the past three years the State Physical Education Association has, through a State Point System, been building up a feeling against interschool competition. Such competition has been practically eliminated in the larger high schools."

Kansas — "We have a sectional college and a sectional high school play day this year at Emporia."

Georgia — "In a radio announcement of meetings of the Southern Section of American Physical Education Association and of the Georgia Physical Education Association, Miss Leonora I. Ivey of Georgia State Women's College states: … 'Do you belong to the National Athletic Federation? Are you familiar with and in sympathy with the policies of the Women's Division of the National Amateur Athletic Federation?' She closed the announcement with the New York address to which to send for the particulars in promoting 'safe, sound, and wholesome athletics for girls.'"

Pennsylvania — "The State Teachers College in Indiana, Pa. is planning a Play Day at their college for high school girls of the nine neighboring towns. We wish this to inspire the high schools to have Play Days with each other instead of basketball tournaments and also to discourage competition, such as training for the coming Olympics."

Oklahoma — Established a "point system."

Also, Buffalo and Cleveland have no inter high school competition in girls' basketball. However, Pittsburgh allows the best class team to play against the best class team of another high school.

The November newsletter included still more information from the states:

Alabama — "The Central Board … voted to discontinue basketball tournaments held for high school girls."

Florida — "We carried on the customary telegraphic track meet for high school girls — one part of which is a group score (25%) in three events."

Kentucky — The first Play Day to be held for colleges was on May 23, at the University of Kentucky. All of the Kentucky Colleges were represented. The first high school Play Day was held on May 11th at Kentucky College for Women.

Missouri — St. Louis county with its eleven schools that are within a radius of ten miles have inter school competition. A play day was held with eight schools. The girls were divided into color teams. Relays, basketball, volleyball, baseball, folk and square dancing were participated in.

New York — Rochester plays no interschool games for girls in Junior and Senior High Schools.

Ohio — No inter-school competition in Junior or Senior High Schools in Toledo.

Rhode Island — The Providence City Schools keep their competition within their own system. The old League of High Schools has disintegrated.

Texas — Houston and Austin are not going to enter teams in the Women's State Basketball Tournament this year and will try to stop plans for one.

This November newsletter also announced that Miss Lena Walmsley, Bates College, Lewiston, Maine, was the chairman of the National Committee on Track and Field.

The December newsletter added:

California — The principal of San Jose High School reported:

Play Days at home	2
Schools participating	15
Number of participants	959
Cost	$32.50
Play days at other schools	4
Number of schools	12
Number of participants	429
Cost to San Jose H.S	$153.72

The total cost for interscholastic competition for girls at San Jose H.S. during 1924-1925..........$902.16

The total cost of intermural program with Play days 1928-1929..........$186.22

Saving $715.94

Nevada — "We have abolished the High School Basketball Tournament but not interschool competition in basketball. We are working toward your goal."

New Jersey — "We are doing away with interschool basketball in Neptune."

New York — "We had two play days in New Rochelle last spring."

Ohio — The Director of the Ohio State High School Athletic Association said, "whatever the women of the State want, we will do."

In the June *American Physical Education Review,* Alice Belding of Vassar College said that in 1922 a committee was formed to study the kinds of track and field events which were suitable to the capacities of women because "The track and field 'urge' was beginning to expand. Track meets were springing up everywhere and with a strong tendency to produce more harm than good."

According to Belding, "It is the very earnest desire of the committee that this fairly new form of athletic competition involving the fundamental forms of activity (running, jumping, throwing, and climbing) may be so used that the best development of the individual will result, and that it may be so guarded that the pleasurable satisfaction of achievement comes through effort minus strain."

Chapter 13

1930

The outdoor national championship meet was held on July 4 at Southern Methodist University Stadium in Dallas, Texas. Two thousand spectators witnessed the first national championships to be held in the South. Stella Walsh stole the show by setting three of the six new world records under ideal weather conditions.

The *Times Herald* featured a story about the meet on July 4, predicting that thousands of Dallasites would be celebrating the 4th of July at the Southern Methodist University stadium. A world record chart of the events was published. Also printed was the list of entries and the numbers that the girls would be wearing. Stella Walsh was number one. The paper on July 5 referred to Stella as "Cleveland's 20th Century Limited" because of her record-shattering performances in the 100, 220 yard straightaway, and broad jump.

In the 100-yard dash, Stella was pressed from the gun to the tape by Betty Robinson. Both women ran stride for stride for the distance, and inches separated them at the finish. It was one of the most exciting events of the day. Walsh also won the 220, beating the defending champion by five yards, and then on her first jump, she leaped 18' 9⅜" in the broad jump.

This meet also saw the national debut of Mildred Didrikson, who set new records in the baseball and javelin throws. Her close second-place broad jump of 18' 8¼" also broke the existing record. Her three throws with the baseball were so close that the officials had to measure them to decide which was best. Had she been able to enter more than three events, she might have beaten Stella in the point score. The other record was set in the 440-yard relay by the Millrose A.A. of New York.

Helen Filkey of Chicago was leading by five yards in the 80-meter hurdles with four hurdles to go when she caught her foot on a hurdle, fell, and got up, only to fall again. Evelyne Hall won the event.

After winning the high jump, Jean Shiley attempted a height of 5' 2¾". On her final attempt, she cleared the bar, but a slight brush caused it to fall before she was out of the pit.

50-yard dash
1. Mary Carew, Medford Girls' A.C.   6.2
2. Olive Hasenfus, Boston Swimming Assn.

3. Annette Rogers, Illinois Women's A.C.
4. Nellie Todd, Illinois Women's A.C.

100-yard dash
1. Stella Walsh, N.Y. Central A.A.   11.2
2. Betty Robinson, Illinois Women's A.C.
3. Olive Hasenfus, Boston Swimming Assn.
4. Eleanor Egg, Duffy League

220-yard dash
1. Stella Walsh, N.Y. Central A.A.   25.4
2. Florence Wright, Illinois Women's A.C.
3. Mary Carew, Medford Girls' A.C.
4. Catherine Capp, Globe Indemnity A.A.

80-meter hurdles
1. Evelyne Hall, Illinois Women's A.C.   13.0
2. Ruth Boswell, Boswell Dairies
3. Anna Koll, Wiltz A.C.
4. Anne East, Employers' Casualty

440-yard relay
1. Millrose A.A.   49.4
   (Gilliland, Cross, Jensen, McNeil)
2. Illinois Women's A.C.
3. Eureka Junior A.A.
4. Boswell Dairies

High jump
1. Jean Shiley, Meadowbrook Club   5' 1"
2. Genevieve Valvoda, South Park
3. Annette Rogers, Illinois Women's A.C.
4. Ruth Reilly, Western Association

Broad jump
1. Stella Walsh, N.Y. Central A.A.   18' 9⅜"
2. Mildred Didrikson, Employers' Casualty
3. Eleanor Egg, Duffy League
4. Nellie Todd, Illinois Women's A.C.

Shot put
1. Rena MacDonald, Boston Swimming Assn.   38' 11½"
2. Evelyn Ferrara, Illinois Women's A.C.
3. Eleanor Egg, Duffy League
4. Lucy Stratton, Employers' Casualty

Discus
1. Evelyn Ferrara, Illinois Women's A.C.   111' 6"
2. Rena MacDonald, Boston Swimming Assn.
3. Lucy Stratton, Employers' Casualty
4. Dee Boeckmann, Western Association

Javelin
1. Mildred Didrikson, Employers' Casualty   133' 3"

2. Katherine Mearls, Watertown, Mass.
3. Lucy Stratton, Employers' Casualty
4. Mary Neederman, Employers' Casualty

Baseball throw
1. Mildred Didrikson, Employers' Casualty   268' 10"
2. Mabel Cutchins, Boswell Dairies
3. Katherine Rutherford, Illinois Women's A.C.
4. Jane Monju, Wiltz A.C.

Team scores:
Illinois Women's A.C. 30; Employers' Casualty 19; N.Y. Central A.A. 15.

The Indoor Nationals

The indoor national championship meet was held on April 19 in the Boston Garden. The *Amateur Athlete* reported in May that three world's indoor records had been shattered and another equaled in the meet. Six of the 1929 champions successfully defended their title.

Stella Walsh won the 220 by fifteen yards in 26.2, shattering the accepted world indoor record of 28.8. Jean Shiley bettered her existing indoor record by clearing 5' 3½" on her third attempt. Katherine Mearls broke her standing broad jump record with a leap of 8' 3¾".

The first team championship title in the indoor championships was won by the Millrose A.A.

220-yard dash
1. Stella Walsh, N.Y. Central A.A.   26.2 MR
2. Catherine Capp, Globe Indemnity A.A.
3. Ruth Smith, Prudential A.A.
4. Ellen Post, Duffy League of Paterson

50-yard hurdles
1. Catherine Donovan, Prudential A.A.   7⅕ MR
2. Mary Smith, New Haven Harriers A.C.
3. Nellie Sharka, Prudential A.A.
4. Hazel Hanzakas, Duffy League

440-yard relay
1. Millrose A.A.   55.0
   (Gilliland, Cross, Jensen, McNeil)
2. Medford Girls' A.C.
3. Duffy League

Standing broad jump
1. Katherine Mearls, Watertown   8' 3¾" MR
2. Gertrude Mayer, Millrose A.A.   8' 2"
3. Stella Walsh, N.Y. Central A.A.   8' 1½"
4. Mary Carew, Medford Girls' A.C.   7' 11½"

Running high jump
1. Jean Shiley, Meadowbrook A.C.   5' 3½" MR
2. Elizabeth Stine, Millrose A.A.   4' 10"
3. Nellie Sharka, Prudential A.A.   4' 7"
4. Sylvia Broman, Brockton A.C.   4' 5½"

8-lb. shot
1. Rena MacDonald, Boston Swimming Assn.   38' 1¼"
2. Katherine Mearls, Watertown   35' 6"
3. Eleanor Egg, Duffy League   35' 3"
4. Bertha Poetschke, Warinanco A.C.   33' 6¾"

Basketball throw
1. Gertrude Mayer, Millrose A.A.   82' 8¼"
2. Steffie Kuczynski, Warinanco A.C.   78' 1½"
3. Marietta Ceres, Prudential A.A.   77'
4. Sylvia Broman, Brockton A.C.   76' 8"

40-yard dash
1. Mary Carew, Medford Girls' A.C.   5.2 ties MR
2. Stella Walsh, N.Y. Central A.A.
3. Loretta McNeil, Millrose A.A.
4. Katherine Mearls, Watertown, Mass.

The minutes of the AAU convention in November reported that the indoor meet would be in Newark in 1931. Money for travel was not provided. There was no definite bid as yet for the 1931 outdoor championships.

The first life membership for the AAU went to Mrs. Richard S. Folsom of the Illinois Women's Athletic Club of Chicago, reported the March 1930 *Amateur Athlete*. An active member of the Central District, Mrs. Folsom was responsible for much of the interest in women's sport in Chicago.

The metropolitan indoor championship meet was held on February 19 in the 113th Regiment Armory in New York City. Winners of the events were the following:

50 yards
1. Loretta McNeil, Millrose A.A.   6⅘

220 yards
1. Catherine Capp, Globe Indemnity A.A.   28⅖

50-yard hurdles
1. Catherine Donovan, Prudential A.A.   8⅕

440 relay
1. Millrose A.A.   54⅘
   (McNeil, Jensen, Cross, Gilliland)

High jump
1. Elizabeth Stine, Millrose A.A.   4' 9½"

Standing broad jump
1. Gertrude Mayer, Millrose A.A.   8' 2¼"

Shot put
1. Bertha Poetschke, Warinanco A.C.   34' ¾"

Basketball throw
1. Steffie Kuczynski, Warinanco A.C.   83' 9"

The metropolitan outdoor meet was on June 28 at Newark School Stadium.

Reports of other meets included the Queens and Richmond County championships, with one running event for girls. The New England Association had its outdoor championships for girls, which included a senior and junior outdoor meet and a senior indoor meet. The Connecticut Association had four women's events in its meet, and the Adirondack Association had one women's event. The Allegheny Mountain Association, the Southern Association (with Didrikson winning the broad jump, baseball throw, and javelin throw), New Orleans meet, Southeastern Association, Central Association, Rocky Mt. Association, and Western Association reported women's results. The Ohio Association reported Stella's 220 yard run record of 26.4, on March 22, in Cleveland.

The February 8, 1930, Millrose Games had four women's events: the girls' 440 relay between the women employees of the New York and Philadelphia Wanamaker department stores, the international girls' sprint of 50 yards, a women's international high jump, and an international girls' relay between Canada and the United States.

Another early annual indoor meet in New York City was the fourth annual Knights of Columbus, Columbus Council, 126, meet on January 4, 1930, at the 106th Infantry Armory in Brooklyn.

The official program lists a large committee entitled "program girls." The one women's event was the 440 relay, handicap, a race in which the slower teams started ahead of the faster team. Six teams were entered; the Millrose A.A. and the Globe Indemnity fielded two teams. The female handicapper was Alice May Adams of the Prudential Insurance A.A.

The *Newark Evening News* on February 19 featured three photos of women. The headlines said that they were running in the Prudential Meet. The article included pictures of five members of the Globe Indemnity relay team (Miller, Dohmeyer, VanPelt, McCann, and Capp) warming up on the outdoor track atop the Globe building; Carrie Jensen, a member of the Millrose team; and the Prudential relay team (Laing, Ceres, Smith, Donovan). The same photo of the Globe Indemnity women appeared on the back page of the *Daily News* on January 30.

The *Amateur Athlete* in June reported the results of the Allegheny Mountain Association track and field championships. The only new record was the shot put of 30' 10" by Ann Anderson.

Two other articles dealing with women's athletics appeared in the July and November issues. The first article was a second notice of the third World Championships to be held in Prague September 6-8. It was an invitation to compete and said, "We beg you … to send your very best sports women to Prague." The United States did not enter a team, but the *Dallas Morning News* of July 20, 1930, carried the headline: Babe Didrikson, Local Girl, Named Member American Team for International Track Go" followed by this account:

> Babe Didrikson, brilliant athlete of the Employers' Casualty Cyclones Squad, was selected as one of seven girls to represent the United States in the international women's track and field meet at Prague, Czechoslovakia in September against twenty-two other nations....
>
> On the American team with the Dallas star are some of the most prominent feminine athletes in the country. The roster of the team will include Betty Robinson, Helen Filkey and Evelyn Ferrara of Chicago, Stella Walsh of Cleveland, Jean Shiley of Philadelphia and Rena MacDonald of Boston....
>
> Fred Steers, secretary of the Central AAU, will be in charge of the team and will coach them while en route and at the meet. The team will sail from New York about August 15 and will return to this country about October 15.

The follow-up article in November stated:

> Stella Walsh, Cleveland girl track champion and holder of many world's running records, came home from her record breaking tour of Europe to encounter a rousing reception in New York City and her home town of Cleveland, Ohio.
>
> Reaching New York on October 7, the girl athlete was taken off the Atlantic liner, placed aboard a tug on which was a welcoming committee which had come from Cleveland to greet her, and thence to meet Mayor Walker, and to be the guest of honor at a luncheon given by the New York Central AA....

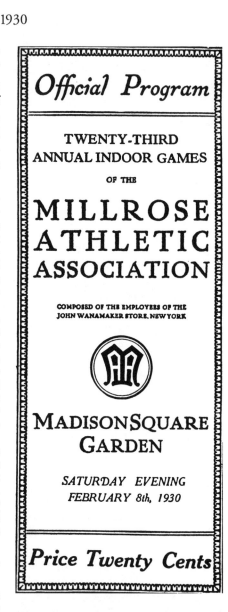

Official Program

TWENTY-THIRD ANNUAL INDOOR GAMES

OF THE

MILLROSE ATHLETIC ASSOCIATION

COMPOSED OF THE EMPLOYEES OF THE
JOHN WANAMAKER STORE, NEW YORK

MADISON SQUARE GARDEN

SATURDAY EVENING
FEBRUARY 8th, 1930

Price Twenty Cents

Program cover from the Millrose Games, February 8, 1930. (Courtesy of the National Track & Field Hall of Fame Historical Research Library at Butler University.)

EVENT NO. 2

GIRL'S RELAY—440 YARDS

(New York and Philadelphia Stores)

MILLROSE	MEADOWBROOK
Edna Carson	Gladys Perry
Edith Carson	Gladys Michael
Elizabeth Innes	Eleanor Gray
Anna Struncius	Marie Brobst
Florence Purcell	Marjorie Perry
Jane Hanna	

Won by .... Time..............

4

EVENT NO. 7

INTERNATIONAL GIRLS SPRINT - 50 YARDS

(1st and 2nd qualify for final)

Heat No. 1

Comp. No.	Reg. No.	Name	Club
160	3516	Olive Krueger, A. B. C., Chattanooga
161	134	Kay Griffiths, Canada
167	2934	Mary Ladenig, Meadowbrook
91	3210	Stella Walsh, Cleveland N. Y. C. A. A.
163	....	Peggy Mathieson, Canada

Won by ...*91*... 2nd.*161*... Time.*6*...

Heat No. 2

162	129	Myrtle Cook, Canada. (winner 1928-1929)
164	....	Jane Bell, Canada
90	14182	Esther Laing, Prudential
89	10716	Louise Washburn, Millrose A. A.
476	....	Dallas Creamer, Toronto

Won by ....*162*.. 2nd.*164*... Time.*6.3*...

EVENT NO. 20

50 YARD DASH—GIRLS INTERNATIONAL

FINAL HEAT

Won by *91*.. 2d.*161*. 3d.*164*. Time.*6 1/5*..

EVENT NO. 11

WOMEN'S INTERNATIONAL HIGH JUMP-SCRATCH

Comp. No.	Reg. No.	Name	Club
186	....	Eva Dawes, Toronto
188	2975	Jean Shiley, Meadowbrook, U. S. Champion
187	16	Constance Colston, Toronto, Canadian Champion
189	10722	Elizabeth Stein, Millrose A. A.

Won by ...*188*...Height...*5*...Feet...*2 3/4*...Inches

Second by ..*186*.Height..*5*...Feet..*1 3/4*...Inches

Third by ..*187*.Height...*4*...Feet..*11 3/4*...Inches

8

EVENT NO. 27

INTERNATIONAL GIRL'S RELAY

(Teams of 4 Each Girl to Run 110 Yards)

CANADA

162	129	Myrtle Cook
161	....	Kay Griffiths
163	134	Peggy Mathieson
164	....	Jane Bell
165	....	Jean Thompson
166	....	Kay Flanagan

UNITED STATES

95	11597	Mabel Gilliland
94	10717	Jessie Cross
93	10828	Carrie Jensen
92	10718	Loretta McNeil
Prov. Starter—Olive Krueger		
Prov. Starter—Stella Walsh		

Won by ....*U S*........ Time.*52*...

Millrose Games, February 8, 1930, showing the entries in the four women's events. (Courtesy of the National Track & Field Hall of Fame Historical Research Library at Butler University.)

Present besides the welcoming committee from Cleveland and the NYCAA were representatives from the Millrose AA, the Prudential Insurance AA, and the Polish Falcons Club, Martin Klein president of the Metropolitan AAU, and Daniel J. Ferris, Secretary-treasurer of the AAU....

A luncheon attended by fifty prominent Clevelanders, including Mayor John Marshall, was tendered Miss Walsh at the Cleveland Athletic Club ... on October 9th, ... where President Hopkins presented Miss Walsh with a beautiful wrist watch.

None of the other girls went to this meet. Apparently, a decision was made to cancel the trip.

The *Amateur Athlete* in January 1931 stated that Stella, a girl of 19 years of age, defeated the best sprinters in the world the previous September in Prague, winning the 80, 100, and 200 meter championships of the world. The article said that she was "ineligible to represent the United States in the Third International Women's Championships ... because she will not be a fully naturalized citizen of the United States until July of 1932,—although a resident of the United States since she was 10 months old,—she accepted the invitation of Poland,—where she was born, to wear the Polish colors in the Prague games." At the last minute, Stella was told that she might not be able to represent the United States in the Olympics in 1932 if she competed for Poland in this meet. She returned home to Cleveland after hearing this news but was later assured by the international athletic governing body that this would not be the case. She sailed to Europe after receiving positive assurances.

Other association championships reported in *Spalding's Almanac* were the Pacific Association championships held at Vallejo High School on June 1 and the Hawaiian championships held on May 18. The two reported women's events from Hawaii were the 60-yard run and the 440-yard relay.

A notable event occurred on the scholastic side of the picture. Alice Frymir wrote *Track and Field for Women*, which was billed as "the only complete book on the subject" and contained action photographs and diagrams. The June *Journal of Health and Physical Education* listed the chapters:

1. History	11. Javelin Throw
2. Training	12. Discus Throw
3. Form	13. Shot Put
4. Methods	14. Hurl Ball
5. Sprinting	15. Basket Ball Throw
6. Hurdling	16. Baseball Throw
7. Relay Racing	17. Programs
8. Running High Jump	18. Classifications and Scoring Systems
9. The Broad Jumps	19. Organization of a Formal Meet
10. Hop, Step and Jump	20. Competition

Principles of Women's Athletics by Florence Somers was published in 1930. Somers wrestled with the problem of competition:

> It seems as though a greater part of the civilized world is divided today upon the question of the desirable method of conducting athletic activities for girls; argued on the one hand by the people who think of athletics as a factor of education and enrichment of life; the other side dominated by the spectator element and the coach who seems to believe it is his especial province to develop athletic ability for the purpose of winning, whether in boys or girls.
>
> A constructive effort is now being made by educators ... to obtain "mass participation" in sport by which they mean every girl playing the types of games which are of interest to her and fitted to her needs.

Referring to the Olympic Games, Somers stated:

> Organizations have adopted resolutions disapproving the participation of women in such forms of international competition, with the hope that they can make educators and parents realize the much greater benefit of a home program of sports for girls. Among the latter organizations are the Women's Division, National Amateur Athletic Federation, Section on Women's Athletics, American Physical Education Association, and the Association of Directors of Physical Education for Women in Colleges and Universities.
>
> It seems reasonable to place some of the blame for this difference of opinion on the fact that an organization primarily interested in the athletics of men has assumed the privilege and the right to conduct athletic competition for girls and women. This is an undesirable procedure. ... How entirely unnatural, then, is the condition which has arisen today in the field of girls' athletic activities.

Spalding's Athletic Library in 1930 included *Athletic Activities for Women and Girls*, a booklet containing official rules for track and field. The resolutions of the National Section on Women's Athletics of the American Physical Education Association were stated:

> WHEREAS, Training for formal spectator athletic events like the Olympic Games tends to restrict interest and limit the use of public facilities, such as schools, colleges, parks, playgrounds, and other civic recreational systems to those practicing for such special events; and
>
> WHEREAS, The exploitation of individuals coincident with such contests tends to subordinate an interest in athletic activity and accomplishment in such activity to an interest in awards, such as public adulation, financial gain, or both; and
>
> WHEREAS, Certain recognized medical authorities in the physiology of activity state that formal spectator contests in athletic activities are physiologically undesirable for girls and women; and
>
> WHEREAS, A large number of trained women in the field of physical education hold the opinion, based on practical experience, that formal spectator athletic contests in any athletic activity bring about detrimental effects upon the physiological processes and emotional reactions of girls and women participating:
>
> RESOLVED, That the Section on Women's Athletics of the American Physical Education Association, which is interested in the adaptation of athletic activities to the varied types of interests and ability of all girls and women, and encouraging participation in the activities suited to the individual needs, go on record as being opposed to girls and women entering the Olympic Games; and
>
> RESOLVED, That unless and until scientific research establishes the fact that formal contests in any type of athletic event are beneficial or at least not detrimental to the health and character of the girls and women participating, the Section on Women's Athletics of the American Physical Education Association is opposed to the entering of girls and women in such formal spectator athletic contests.

Agnes Wayman defined the position of the Women's Division on competition by stating that the organization believed in competition but "disapproves of ... the highly intense specialized competition such as exists when we have programs of inter-school competition, inter-group open track meets ... with important championships at stake."

Another blow to the women's Olympic track and field movement was struck by J. E. Rogers in his "Around the Country" column in the June *Journal of Health and Physical Education* when he stated:

> One of the most beneficial changes ever made in Olympic regulations is the elimination of several women's events. A congress of physicians met during the course of the Games, and decided to discontinue the 800 meter run, broad jump, shot put, and the proposed 200 meter run. It was pointed out that these events are too strenuous for women and were becoming a menace rather than a benefit to their physical well being and growth. When we consider that the three women who finished the 800 meter run collapsed at the tape, it is not surprising that the doctors provided as a substitute for the barred events, the following—100 meter run, 400 meter relay, 80 meter hurdles, discus throw and high jump. This change will become effective at the next Olympic Games to be held in Los Angeles, California in 1932.

Newsletter No. 10 of the Women's Division summarized what was happening in various states:

Colorado: "We have had several successful play days during the past three years."

Massachusetts: "We, in Haverhill have in the last year dropped varsity sports for girls and put in quite an intensive point system."

Michigan: "The Playtime of a Million Girls or an Olympic Victory — Which?" by Blanche M. Trilling was published in the February 1930 issue of the *Michigan Journal of Physical Education*.

New Hampshire: "The first play day was held during the winter term of 1923. The second play day was held in February of 1929. The third play day was held this fall. Almost all high schools in New Hampshire have inter-school athletics which we are trying to discourage."

New York: "The health and physical education departments of the schools of New York State went on record, September 27, 1929 as supporting … the platform of the Women's Division of the N.A.A.F."

North Carolina: Durham, "We have a very nice system of inter-class athletics. …The games are played after school. We have a class tournament and from the class teams the honorary varsity is chosen. Sometimes just for the stunt and novelty the varsity plays a faculty team during an auditorium period."

Chapter 14

1931

Two hundred and thirty-five women took part in the ninth national track and field championships on July 25, 1931, at Pershing Field in Jersey City, New Jersey. Eleven of the women were defending champions, and eight Olympians competed.

Babe Didrikson won three victories, and Eleanor Egg beat Stella Walsh in the 100-yard dash before a crowd of 15,000 fans.

Arthur Daley of the *New York Times* wrote on July 26: "A new feminine athletic marvel catapulted herself to the forefront as an American Olympic possibility ... yesterday when 19 year old Miss Mildred (Babe) Didrikson of Dallas broke the world's record for the 80 meter high hurdles, shattered the American mark for the baseball throw and topped off her activities with a victory in the running broad jump."

The crowd gasped as Babe hurdled to a world record that was two-tenths of a second faster than the existing world mark. Five of the six watches caught her in 12 seconds flat. The other was stopped at 11.8. Unbelieving officials even measured the 80-meter distance with a steel tape. It proved to be 2' 4" too long.

In her bright orange outfit, Babe then went to the broad jump and won that event. The third mark she shattered was done with the baseball. She eclipsed her record by more than 20 feet, throwing the ball 296'.

Didrikson overshadowed Stella Walsh, who came into the meet as a three-event defending champion and left with only one title, the 220-yard dash. In the 100, she was beaten by Eleanor Egg, the twenty-two-year-old hometown favorite.

Jean Shiley bettered her previous year's mark in the high jump by one inch to win in 5' 2". She was the first of the defending champions to repeat a victory.

Mary Carew was running against her doctor's orders, having been ill for a few weeks. She placed third in her semifinal and did not qualify for the final.

The Amateur Athlete in August 1931 had a write-up on the meet and reported the complete summaries.

50-yard dash
1. Alice Monk, Newark Women's A.C.   6.4
2. Ethel Harrington, Illinois Women's A.C.

3. Mary Ladewig, Meadowbrook Club
4. Louise Stokes, Onteora Club

100-yard dash
1. Eleanor Egg, Duffy League   11.4
2. Evelyn Furtsch, Los Angeles A.C.
3. Stella Walsh, N.Y. Central A.A.
4. Mrs. Anne Vrana O'Brien, Los Angeles A.C.

80-meter hurdles
1. Mildred Didrikson, Employers' Casualty   12.0 WR
2. Nellie Sharka, unattached, Newark
3. Evelyne Hall, Illinois Women's A.C.
4. Mary Carter, Employers' Casualty

220-yard dash
1. Stella Walsh, N.Y. Central A.A.   26.4
2. Olive Hasenfus, Boston Swimming Assn.
3. Catherine Capp, Newark Women's A.C.
4. Ellen Brough Post, Duffy League

440-yard relay
1. Illinois Women's A.C.   51.0
    (Hall, Todd, Harrington, Rogers)
2. Millrose A.A. (Cross, Jensen, Gilliland, McNeil)
3. Duffy League
4. Meadowbrook Club

Running broad jump
1. Mildred Didrikson, Employers' Casualty   17' 11½"
2. Nellie Todd, Illinois Women's A.C.   17'
3. Alice Monk, Newark Women's A.C.   16' 7"
4. Eleanor Towler, unattached, Pennsylvania   16' 6"

Shot put
1. Lillian Copeland, Los Angeles A.C.   40' 2⅜"
2. Evelyn Ferrara, Illinois Women's A.C.   36' 3¾"
3. Mildred Yetter, Meadowbrook Club   36' ¾"
4. Rena MacDonald, unattached, Mass.   34' 11¾"

High jump
1. Jean Shiley, Meadowbrook Club   5' 2" AR
2. Annette Rogers, Illinois Women's A.C.   4' 11"
3. Genevieve Valvoda, unattached, Chicago   4' 10"
4. Helen Phillips, Boston Swimming Assn.   4' 9"
    and Sylvia Broman, Brockton Girls' Club

Discus throw
1. Evelyn Ferrara, Illinois Women's A.C.   108' 10⅝"
2. Lillian Copeland, Los Angeles A.C.   108' 7¹⁄₁₆"
3. Lucy Stratton, Employers' Casualty   100' 9½"
4. Augusta Coleman, Millrose A.A.   95' 1¼"

Baseball throw
1. Mildred Didrikson, Employers' Casualty   296' AR
2. Mabel Cutchins, Employers' Casualty   252' 9"
3. Lillian Tresselt, Hand H.S., Madison, Conn.   250'
4. Verna Coleman, Penn Railroad A.A.   233' 5"

Javelin throw
1. Lillian Copeland, Los Angeles A.A.   116' 1½"
2. Elsie Sherman, Newark A.C.   110' ¾"
3. Nan Gindele, Illinois Women's A.C.   108'
4. Inez Paterson, unattached, Philadelphia   105' 8½"

Team scores:
Illinois Women's A.C. 26; Employers' Casualty 19; Los Angeles A.C. 17.

The *New York Times* had a report of the discus accident involving Stella Walsh beyond the sports section on page 25. The small article was entitled "Discus Hits Onlooker; Women Athlete Held." Stella Walsh was arrested after the discus slipped from her hand and struck twenty-eight-year-old James McBride of Jersey City. The discus hit him in the head, rendering him unconscious, and he was taken to Jersey City hospital with a possible skull fracture. The park commissioner announced that "he would place the girl under arrest, but was prevailed upon to withhold action until after she had competed in the 220 yard dash. ... She was then arrested and paroled in the custody of the commissioner." The accident occurred when, as a contestant in the discus throw, she was in the outfield returning the discus to the athletes near the circle.

The Indoor Nationals

40-yard dash
1. Mary Carew, Medford Girls' Club   5.2
220-yard dash
1. Stella Walsh, N.Y. Central A.A.   27.2
50-yard hurdles
1. Evelyne Hall, Illinois Women's A.C.   7.6
440-yard relay
1. Millrose A.A.   54.0
    (Washburn, Stanczuk, Jensen, McNeil)
High jump
1. Jean Shiley, Meadowbrook Club   5' 3"
Standing broad jump
1. Katherine Mearls, Boston Swimming Assn.   8' 2⅞"
Shot put
1. Rena MacDonald, unattached   37' 6"
Basketball throw
1. Carolyn Dieckman, So. Paterson Girls' Club   96' 2"

The second team championship title was won by the Medford Girls' Club.

The August *Amateur Athlete* reported the activities of the Central AAU More than 1,100 took part in the central track and field championships for women on July 18 at Soldier Field. The meet was sponsored by the *Chicago Evening American*, and the winners were the following:

100m	12.6	Annette Rogers, Illinois Women's A.C.
220y	26.9	Lois Collar, Illinois Women's A.C.
50y	6.1	Annette Rogers, Illinois Women's A.C.
80mh	12.3	Helen Filkey, Illinois Women's A.C. (Central AAU record)
Javelin	79' 11½"	Evelyn Ferrara (Central AAU record)
Discus	107' 10"	Evelyn Ferrara, Illinois Women's A.C. (Central AAU record)
HJ	5' ⅛"	Annette Rogers, Illinois Women's A.C. (Central AAU record)
SP	35' 9"	Evelyn Ferrara, Illinois Women's A.C. (Central AAU record)
Baseball	245' 1"	Nan Gindele, unattached (Central AAU record)
RBJ	17' 6½"	Nellie Todd, Illinois Women's A.C.
400mr	51.1	Illinois Women's A.C. (Hall, Todd, Harrington, Rogers, Central AAU record —first time held)

The September *Amateur Athlete* featured a story on Babe Didrikson. Her accomplishments in the two national championships were cited, and then a question was raised, "Is it necessary to say that Miss Didrikson expects to win all of the individual track and field events for women in the Olympic Games at Los Angeles next summer?" The article listed some of her claims: "She claimed that she can throw the discus 140'. The Olympic record is 129' 11⅞". She has reached a height of 5' 4" in the high jump. The Olympic record is 5' 3". She already holds the world record in the 80-meter hurdles and threw the javelin 133' 5½" for a world record last year. She has run the 100 yards in 11 flat! With only five individual events for women in the Games, will 'Babe' win them all?"

The *Amateur Athlete* reported the results of the Central AAU championships on March 27 in Oak Park, Illinois. Betty Robinson set a new world record in the 60-yard dash, running it in 6⁹⁄₁₀, and Genevieve Valvoda set a new American record in the high jump by clearing 5' 1⅛".

A final note in the *Amateur Athlete* in May reported Katherine Mearls' record in the standing broad jump of 8' 4⅜" in defending her New England standing broad jump title on March 24.

The physical educators continued to sabotage the Olympic program as 1932 loomed in the near future. The "Evils of Sports for Women" was a radio talk in Cincinnati, and it then appeared in the January 1931 edition of the *Journal of Health and Physical Education*. Helen Smith, the director of physical education for women at the University of Cincinnati, stated:

> Although athletics have done a vast amount for the health of the youth of America, there are danger signs ahead. Commercialization has overwhelmed the world of sport. Competition is stressed over play and enjoyment. Great national organizations have developed whose members are, for the most part, men who are dependent upon sports for a livelihood, and who need record breakers, winning

teams and star performers to boost their trade. These men include news gatherers, heads of sporting goods houses, heads of athletic associations, coaches and trainers....

In days gone by a few women indulged in croquet, in a bit of lawn tennis, and perhaps golf. Today, however, we must deal with the hundreds of girls who are in schools and colleges, and with the thousands who are in factories and industries. These girls want opportunity for athletic activities. ... Numerically the college undergraduates form a small proportion of the mass of girls who are interested in athletics. Almost every large concern (banks, factories, offices, etc.) offer sporting activities for their employees, and it is from the girls in industries that the material comes which makes up our women's Olympic teams every year. The colleges and universities have succeeded in conducting a sane and wholesome program of athletics for girls, but it is the great mass of American girls who are in industry who are more likely to be injured if the present trend in men's athletics continues to seep into women's athletics.

In the colleges and universities at the present time there are no inter-collegiate sports for women because the authorities in these institutions believe that there should be a broad program of sports activities with opportunities for every girl in the university to indulge and reap their benefits, rather than a narrow program....

In 1932 the Olympic Games will be held in Los Angeles. Already the AAU is canvassing the high schools of the country for material. They are not interested in seeing that every girl has a chance to take part in the Olympic Games, but they will take one or two "star" performers, train them intensively, and boost them and America to their best ability.

On May 22nd the following article appeared in a Cincinnati newspaper:

"Battling for retention of women's track and field events in the Olympic Games, the International Amateur Athletic Federation indicated today it would go as far as to declare a walk-out of all male athletes if its demands were not met. The Federation at its closing session today adopted a resolution proposed by the American delegate, Gustavus T. Kirby, of New York, providing that the I.A.A.F. shall remain in Berlin in recess ready to be reconvened in case the International Olympic Congress, meeting here next week, turns thumbs down on feminine competition.

"What action would be taken in such a case was not stated in the resolution, but it was understood that recalling the I.A.A.F. into session would mean voting to withdraw from the Olympics. Abandonment of the feminine track and field events which were inaugurated in the Amsterdam Olympic of 1928 would be accepted by the Federation only on condition that all other women's competition such as fencing and swimming should be eliminated.

"Acquiescence then would be given with keen regret. That such drastic measures probably will not be necessary, however, was indicated by Murray Hulbert, former president of the Amateur Athletic Union of the United States, who joined Kirby in leading the fight. Hulbert pointed out to the Associated Press that the Olympic Games in this case are to be held in the United States, which is strongly in favor of allowing the girls to compete at Los Angeles in 1932. He added that France, England, Italy and Hungary appeared to be the only nations opposed to women's participation.

"Most of the opposition to feminine competition arose after the 800 meter event in Amsterdam where several of the girls collapsed."

In connection with this 800 meter run, let me quote from Mr. John R. Tunis again:

"Obviously at the present time one cannot dogmatize upon the physical ability of women to stand the strain and stress of athletic competition; but one can say conservatively that in competitive sport women are far more in need of medical supervision than men. Those who doubt this statement should have stood beside me during the eight-hundred meter run in the Olympic Games at Amsterdam last summer. Below us on the cinder path were eleven wretched women, five of whom dropped out before the finish, while five collapsed after reaching the tape. I was informed that the remaining starter collapsed in the dressing room shortly afterward."

And yet the American delegates insist on the retention of these unwholesome activities. The women of America do not want these events, and by women, I mean those trained educators who have had experience in athletic coaching and training. Who then is promoting these events? A small group of men who are again interested in promotion and commercialization, and not in a sane, wholesome program for all girls and women.

Smith's last few paragraphs deal with her solution to the problem — a play day.

The September *Journal of Health and Physical Education* reported that Amy Howland, of the public schools in Mt. Vernon, was the track and field chairman. The Women's Division *Newsletter* in January stated: The following resolution, "in opposition to women competing in the 1932 Olympic Games," was passed at the convention of the National Council of Catholic Women held in Denver, Colorado, October 1, 1930:

Whereas: The Women's Division of the National Amateur Athletic Association has recorded its opposition to competition of women and girls in the Olympic Games, and

Whereas: The National Council is in full accord with the standards for athletics for girls as set forth by this federation,

Resolved: That the National Council endorse the action of the Women's Division N.A.A.F, and

Further Resolved: That the National Council of Catholic Women record its disapproval of the entering of girls and women in such formal spectacular athletic contests.

Chapter 15

1932: The Los Angeles Olympic Year

The final Olympic trials were held at Dyche Stadium, Northwestern University, Evanston, Illinois, on July 16. Seventeen women were selected as the second group of women track and field champions to represent the United States in the Olympic Games at Los Angeles from July 30 to August 14:

Name	Olympic Event	Olympic Place	Olympic Performance
Carew, Mary Louise	400mr	1	47.0
Copeland, Lillian	Discus	1	133' 2"
Didrikson, Mildred	80mh	1	11.7
	HJ	2	5' 5"
	Javelin	1	143' 4"
Furtsch, Evelyn	400mr	1	47.0
Gindele, Nan	Javelin	5	124' 6⅛"
Hall, Evelyne	80mh	2	11.7
Harrington, Ethel	100m	DNQ	
Jenkins, Margaret	Discus	9	99' 1¾"
Osborn, Ruth	Discus	2	131' 8"
Pickett, Tidye	400mr		reserve
Rogers, Annette	400mr	1	47.0
	HJ	6	5' 2"
Russell, Gloria	Javelin	6	120' 6⅜"
Schaller, Simone	80mh	4	11.9
Shiley, Jean	HJ	1	5' 5¼"
Stokes, Louise	400mr		reserve
Von Bremen, Wilhelmina	100m	3	12.0
	400mr	1	47.0
Wilde, Elizabeth	100m	6	12.5

Steers, Fred	Manager
Klein, Martin	Assistant Manager
Vreeland, George	Coach
Allen, Aileen	Chaperone

Three women, Jean Shiley, Lillian Copeland, and Margaret Jenkins, were the only athletes from the first women's team in 1928 to make the 1932 Olympic team. In his report, manager Fred Steers said:

> The United States Women's Track and Field team of 1932 was the strongest aggregation of its kind in the history of athletics. ... Our team succeeded in winning five of the six events on the program and established world's Olympic records in each of them. In addition, American women succeeded in taking three second places and one third place, thus easily outclassing the combined Women's Track and Field Teams of the world.
>
> Coach George H. Vreeland gave his entire time and attention to bring the several members of the team on the field in the various competitions in the best physical condition. The magnificent showing was due, in great measure, to his unselfish efforts....
>
> During the period of competitions, the morale of the team was high, individually and collectively....
>
> The housing and management of the team separately from other American teams proved very satisfactory. It permitted elasticity and freedom of movement and conflict which could not have been obtained under any collective arrangement. I recommend that in future Olympic Games the several American teams be handled individually.
>
> Raiment of various kinds other than parade and dress uniforms was given to the team. Very little of the clothing received fitted the individuals for whom it was intended. As a result for a time there was considerable irritation amongst the members of the team. I recommend that hereafter no clothing be given to the women's team, except parade uniforms and the necessary athletic clothes and equipment, and that such clothing and equipment be placed with the manager at the earliest possible moment after the arrival of the team at the place of the games, so that there will be ample time for the making of necessary alterations, if any be required.
>
> I further recommend that all matters pertaining to the team be transacted and carried on through the Manager only. This was not done in many cases and as a result, considerable confusion was caused which might otherwise have been avoided.

All of the women's teams were housed at the Chapman Park Hotel. Women were not allowed into the Olympic Village.

Stella Walsh of Cleveland, who competed as Stanislawa Walasiewicz representing Poland, won the 100 meters in 11.9, surpassing the old world mark of 12.0 and the Olympic record of 12.2. She ran the same time in the heat, semi, and final. Wallechinsky stated in his *Complete Book of the Olympics*:

> As a result of the worldwide depression, her job with the New York Central Railroad had been eliminated. She was offered a position with the Cleveland Recreation Department, but taking it would have made her ineligible for the Olympics, since Olympic regulations at the time disqualified athletes who made their living from physical education or recreation. With no help forthcoming from her adopted country, Stella Walsh made a major decision in her life. Twenty-four hours before she was scheduled to take out United States naturalization papers, she accepted a job offer from the Polish consulate in New York and decided to compete for Poland.

Stella was granted her naturalization papers in 1947.

The Olympic Results

100 meters. Wilhelmina Von Bremen, Elizabeth Wilde, and Ethel Harrington represented the United States in the 100 meters. Von Bremen placed second in the first heat, qualifying for the semis. Elizabeth Wilde easily won the fourth and final heat. Ethel Harrington ran in heat three but did not qualify for the next round.

In the semis, Elizabeth Wilde placed second in the first semi, and Wilhelmina Von Bremen placed second in the second semi. Stella was pressed by Von Bremen in this semi.

Von Bremen was in second place in the final until Stella Walsh caught everyone and forged ahead in the last ten yards. She beat the Canadian girl by inches, and Von Bremen was a foot back in third place with a time of 12.0. Wilde placed sixth.

80-meter hurdles. The finish of the 80-meter hurdles was disputed for years. All three American women made the final. Didrikson and Hall won their heats, with Schaller second to Babe in heat one. In the final, Babe was given first, by three inches say some reports, Evelyne Hall second, and Simone Schaller, who started hurdling three months prior to the games, fourth. The time of 11.7, a new world record, was given to both Evelyne and Babe. The hurdles was the prettiest event of the first, somewhat drab, day of Olympic competition, stated one reporter. The *New York Times* on August 5 said:

> With two fences yet left to be cleared, Miss Didrikson had a two foot advantage. Not quite as finished a timber-topper as Mrs. Hall, the Texas star was much faster between hurdles. Her lead began to slip away as Mrs. Hall advanced and they were absolutely even as their forward feet touched the ground, just before the tape.
>
> Then with a magnificent closing burst, Miss Didrikson pounced over the last stretch to hit the tape a scant two inches ahead of her teammate in the new world's record time of 11.7.

400-meter relay. The relay was a resounding success. Six teams were entered: Canada, Great Britain, Holland, Japan, Germany, and the United States. Our team members were Mary Carew, Evelyn Furtsch, Annette Rogers, and Wilhelmina Von Bremen. Mary was the lead-off leg and had a small lead over the Canadian runner. During the next two legs, the Canadians gained a two-yard lead. The third baton pass between Annette Rogers and Von Bremen was flawless, giving Von Bremen a slight lead over the 100-meter silver medalist from Canada. She maintained the lead in an exciting stride for stride race to the tape to win by a foot, and the time of 47.0 shaved 1.4 seconds off the world record. (They were actually timed in 46.9, but women's relays were not timed in tenths of a second unless even figures are bettered by more than a tenth.) Mary Carew represented the team on the victory platform as the national anthem was played. In her hand she held the relay baton which she still has.

High jump. The high jump finish provided even more controversy, according to the press, than the finish of the hurdles. Again, Babe Didrikson was in the

1932 Olympic champions and world record holders, 400-meter relay. *From left to right:* Wilhelmina Von Bremen, Annette Rogers, Evelyn Furtsch and Mary Carew. (Courtesy of Evelyn Furtsch and Mary Carew.)

center of the controversy. Both Jean Shiley and Babe tied for first place. Since no ties were allowed in the Olympic Games, a jump-off ensued. Babe cleared the bar first. Jean then cleared the bar. At that point, Babe was disqualified for jumping illegally. In 1932, diving over the bar was a foul. She used the Western roll but in women's athletics, the shoulder could not precede the body over the bar. This should have been detected in the trials. A disqualification would have moved Babe out of the competition. Annette Rogers would have been fifth (5' 2") instead of sixth. Jean's winning jump was 5' 5¼", which was a new Olympic, world, and American record.

Javelin throw. The javelin was the first of the women's track and field events held on the first day's program. One reporter said that it fell to a feminine contestant to put on the really spectacular show of the first day. He described the scene:

> A lot of girls come out for the javelin throw in this big concrete stadium shaped like a bowl. The Olympic brass hats stick out a flag which tells you that this marks the best that a woman has ever done in the event.
> Then Babe grabs hold of the javelin and lets loose. Swoosh! The javelin lands in the grass about 10 yards past the neat little flag. Cheers rang out because everyone knew something special had just happened. The girls, Babe too, tried all afternoon to do better. No one even came close. Babe Didrikson set an American and Olympic record with her winning toss of 143' 4". Her throw also broke the existing world's record. However, the second place finisher from Germany had a pending record which was eventually accepted. Babe's comment was, "If my hand hadn't slipped I could easily have tossed it out a few more feet. I just went out with the idea I was going to win and did."

Jean Shiley, 1932 Olympic champion, clearing the bar in the high jump during the Olympic Games, Los Angeles. (Courtesy of Jean Shiley Newhouse.)

Nan Gindele was fifth with 124' 6⅛", and Gloria Russell was sixth with a toss of 120' 6⅜". This was the first staging of the javelin event in the women's program of the Olympic Games.

Discus throw. The discus was another United States highlight. Lillian Copeland won with a toss of 133' 2" again, a world, Olympic, and American record. *The Journal of Health and Physical Education* in November had an article on the Olympic Games. A part of the story dealt with Lillian Copeland's throws in the discus. The writer said that on her first throw, Ruth Osborn outdistanced the Polish record-holder. He noted that the women were now throwing like the men, using the three turns. Miss Copeland followed Miss Osborn but did not match her throw. Lillian made all of her subsequent throws without moving into first place. The writer described her last throw:

> Finally she stepped into the circle for what she must have felt to be the last time that she would ever represent her country in the women's Olympic events. She stood concentrating every faculty on the final effort which she was about to make, and manifestly attempting to relax in preparation for a supreme effort. Evidently she determined to abandon the technique of taking turns in the circle, and fall back on the method of launching the discus which she had formerly used — that of standing in position. Twisting with arm extended to gain the largest possible arc, while her feet were planted in position, she swayed backward

and forward several times, crouching and straightening as she brought the discus up and forward, and finally, putting everything she had behind it, she launched the most perfect throw which I have ever seen, or am likely to see, from a standing position.

It was really a thrilling sight to me to see an athlete put so much power into one supreme effort, and then to observe the discus sailing perfectly out to a new world's record. ... I do think that women perfecting the turns in the circle, as men have done, are likely to break this record; but no woman, in my opinion, standing planted in the circle, is ever likely to get away with a more perfect throw than Miss Copeland scored that afternoon. ... She is a woman of perfectly calm demeanor and poise, but when she went back to her seat on the bench, after winning laurels as a new world's record holder, she burst into tears and had a good cry over it.

With this win, the athletic career of Lillian Copeland was over, reported a correspondent. "This is the end. I'm through with all competition now, and I am very happy and satisfied to have made the record I did this afternoon," said Lillian, who was in her third year of law school at the University of Southern California. She planned to enter the law profession or governmental work in Washington. Her career had started in junior high school in 1922 while she was watching a boyfriend throw the discus.

Twenty-year-old Ruth Osborn placed a close second in 131' 8". Standing 5' 11" tall, she just began throwing the discus in April of 1932.

After the games, the October *Amateur Athlete* featured an article entitled "Spirit," written by the manager of the team, Fred Steers. He described the evening after the trials:

Seated in a room in Chicago on a hot night in mid–July was a group of young women from all parts of the United States, ages ranging from seventeen to twenty-nine, from different creeds, sprung from dissimilar races, of different stations in life, the best of the land in their several athletic endeavors. ... Young women from the east, west, north and south, from the city and the farm, from high schools and colleges, from shops and offices, home girls, a housewife, bookkeepers, stenographers, and school teachers. Some had never been outside their home state before. A cross cut of the young womanhood of our land.

One by one the ladies were being interrogated regarding the date and place of their birth and other information for the purpose of filing their entries with the International Olympic Committee, and were being measured for their parade and athletic uniforms. It was a quiet and serious scene. The collection of individuals was a team in name only with no cohesion, no uniformity of spirit of purpose.

These ambitious young ladies, bound together only by the spirit of sport and their American citizenship, met at the train at the appointed hour still merely a collection of strangers — a team in name only. A stop over in Denver for a visit and training and efforts of those in charge of the party and three girls who were members of the American Women's Team at Amsterdam in 1928, brought the group closer together and their arrival in Los Angeles found a happy and friendly crowd of young women, all ambitious to win.

Training periods together under a competent coach, social hours and life together at their hotel brought about a spirit of co-operation and a desire that the team win rather than the individual. Practice periods found girls of superior knowledge and technique giving the benefit of their experience to their teammates possessing less skill and knowledge, but in many instances having greater potentialities....

In this spirit the American Women's Track and Field Team went into the Games to outdo the entire women's athletic world combined, and succeeded in their effort....

The spirit of sportsmanship — that great leveler, which knows not nationality, language, race, creed, color, poverty, riches, social position, or any of those accidental and fictitious distinctions, which arbitrarily and ruthlessly separate humans.

The respect, understanding and friendships, which the Olympic Games created amongst the women of all nations, who took part, will remain after the results of the competition are forgotten. As long as there are mothers of statesmen, diplomats and soldiers, women's participation in the Olympic Games will not be in vain.

Lillian Copeland, 1932 Olympic Champion, discus throw. (Courtesy of the USOC Photo Library.)

The Olympic Trials

Mildred "Babe" Didrikson was the sensation of the combined national championships and Olympic trials on July 16 at Northwestern University. She captured five first places, tied in one event, and placed fourth in another. She won the "team" title by herself.

A crowd of 5,000 watched her run from event to event, breaking the world record in the javelin and sharing a new high jump world record with Jean Shiley.

High school girl Ruth Osborn won the discus in a new world record.

The *Chicago Defender* on July 23 reported a problem in the running of the 100 meters:

> Miss Pickett will have to thank George T. Donoghue, member of the South Park commission and one of the judges, for her success. Miss Pickett had qualified for a berth, being sixth, when one of the girls was disqualified for stopping before reaching the finish line. But when the latter athlete was allowed to compete in the finals, Miss Pickett became seventh and was thus automatically out of it. Then Mr. Donoghue stepped up and fought for Tidie's [sic] place in the finals in view of the charity being shown the other girl. Mr. Donoghue, white, is to be congratulated for his fairness in the girl's behalf.

Tidye Pickett from Chicago and Louise Stokes from Massachusetts were the first black women to represent the United States in Olympic track and field competition.

50-yard run
1. Dorothy Nussbaum, St. Bernard, Ohio   6.3
2. Mary Ladewig, Meadowbrook Club, Philadelphia
3. Alice Monk, Newark Women's A.C.
4. Mary Hawkins, Pasadena, Calif.

100-meter run
1. Ethel Harrington, Illinois Women's A.C.   12.3
2. Wilhelmina Von Bremen, Western Women's Club
3. Elizabeth Wilde, Kansas City, Mo.
4. Louise Stokes, Onteora Club, Mass.,
      and Mary Carew, Medford Girls' A.C., Mass.
6. Tidye Pickett, Chicago Park District

220-yard run
1. Olive Hasenfus, Boston Swimming Assn.   26.5
2. Marie DeMay, Rankin, Pa.
3. Olive Kruger, Chattanooga, Tenn.
4. Lillian Janat, Chicago

80-meter hurdles
1. Mildred Didrikson, Employers' Casualty   12.1
2. Evelyne Hall, Illinois Women's A.C.
3. Simone Schaller, Pasadena A.C.
4. Lois Collar, Illinois Women's A.C.

440-yard relay
1. Illinois Women's A.C.   49.4
      (Hall, Harrington, Terwilliger, Rogers)
2. Illinois Women's A.C., "B" team
3. Tower Grove Quarry A.C., St. Louis
4. South Park, Chicago

High jump
1. Mildred Didrikson, Employers' Casualty   5' 3³⁄₁₆"
      and Jean Shiley, Meadowbrook Club
3. Annette Rogers, Illinois Women's A.C.
4. Wilhelmina Von Bremen, Western W.C.,
      Frances Anderson, Michigan State Normal School,
      Catherine Maguire, Tower Grove Quarry A.C.,
      and Genevieve Valvoda, South Parks.

Broad jump
1. Mildred Didrikson, Employers' Casualty   17' 6⅛"
2. Nellie Todd, Illinois Women's A.C.
3. Margaret Jordan, Carter Playground, Chicago
4. Ruth Jacques, Chicago

Shot put
1. Mildred Didrikson, Employers' Casualty   39' 6¼"
2. Rena MacDonald, Boston Swimming Assn.
3. Carolyn Yetter, Meadowbrook Club
4. Lillian Copeland, Los Angeles A.C.

Discus
1. Ruth Osborn, Shelbyville, Mo.   133' ¾"
2. Margaret Jenkins, No. Cal. A.C.
3. Lillian Copeland, Los Angeles A.C.
4. Mildred Didrikson, Employers' Casualty

Javelin
1. Mildred Didrikson, Employers' Casualty   139' 3"
2. Nan Gindele, Illinois Women's A.C.
3. Gloria Russell, Western Women's Club
4. Gertrude Sterling, Puyallup, Wash.

Baseball throw
1. Mildred Didrikson, Employers' Casualty   272' 2"
2. Gloria Russell, Western W.C.
3. Nan Gindele, Illinois Women's A.C.
4. Frances Kanzius, Burgettstown, Pa.

Team scores: Employers' Casualty Company Club ("Babe" Didrikson) 30; Illinois Women's Athletic Club 22; Western Women's Club 13; Meadowbrook Club 9.

Fred Steers in his committee report stated that the four American and world records broken were in the Olympic tryout events. No records were broken in the other events. It was evident that the desire to make the Olympic team was greater than the desire to win a national championship.

The 1932 *Spalding's Athletic Library* published the *Official Handbook of the A.A.U.* containing the general rules of track and field. Under women's athletics, rule 4 stated: "No woman shall be allowed to compete in more than three events in one day, of which three events not more than two shall be track events except competitors in the Pentathlon who shall not be allowed to compete in any other event. The relay shall count as one track event." This rule was in effect when Babe Didrikson competed in the combined national championships and Olympic tryouts.

The Indoor Nationals

The national senior indoor championship meet was held in Newark Armory in Newark, New Jersey, on March 12. Rena MacDonald won her third successive title in the shot put, and Jean Shiley won her fourth straight high jump title.

"Another champion to retain her crown was Mary Carew of the Medford Girls' Club," stated the *New York Times* on March 13. "When she broke the tape in 5⅖ ahead of Miss Mary Ladewig of the Meadowbrook Club and Miss Helen Fairbanks, the latter's team-mate, it marked the fourth time in a row that Miss Carew had captured the title. The sprint was keenly contested, Miss Carew winning by less than two feet."

40-yard dash
1. Mary Carew, Medford Girls' Club   5⅖
2. Mary Ladewig, Meadowbrook Club
3. Helen Fairbanks, Meadowbrook Club
4. Harriet Matthews, Meadowbrook Club

220-yard dash
1. Catherine Capp, Newark Women's A.C.   28⅕
2. Grace Rittler, Meadowbrook Club
3. Eleanor Egg, Duffy League
4. Esther Laing, Newark Women's A.C.

50-yard hurdles
1. Nellie K. Sharka, Newark Women's A.C.   7⅘
2. Emily Smith, Millrose A.C.
3. Flora Stoepker, Duffy League
4. Ethel Gowen, Newark Women's A.C.

440-yard relay
1. Medford Girls' Club   54⅕
      (M. Carew, C. Carew, McCarthy, Wendt)
2. Millrose A.A.
3. Meadowbrook Club
4. Paulist A.C.

High jump
1. Jean Shiley, Meadowbrook Club   5' 1¾"
2. Effy Oord, Newark Turn Verein   4' 9¾"
3. Virginia Ewald, Newark Women's A.C.   4' 8¾"
4. Dorothy Hayes, Paulist A.C.,   4' 4¾"
      and Regina Curtis, German-American A.C.

Standing broad jump
1. Kay Ungemach, N.Y. and Queens Electric Co. A.A.   8' 1"
2. Mary Carew, Medford Girls' Club   7' 11"
3. Louise Washburn, Millrose A.A.   7' 9¾"
4. Jean Shiley, Meadowbrook Club   7' 8½"

Shot put
1. Rena MacDonald, Karhu A.C.   38' 6½"
2. Mildred Yetter, Meadowbrook Club   37' 10½"
3. Effy Oord, Newark Turn Verein   35' 3"
4. Marie Wegener, unattached   34' 1¾"

Basketball throw
1. Carolyn Dieckman, So. Paterson Girls' Club   87' 3"
2. Elizabeth Lichtfuss, Turn Verein   85' 6½"
3. Inez Patterson, unattached   84' 10"
4. Mildred Yetter, Meadowbrook Club   84' 2¾"

Team scores:
Meadowbrook Club 21; Newark Women's Club 14; Medford Girls' Club 13½; Millrose A.A. 8.

A report on the junior indoor championships was given. The event was held on January 23, 1932, in Boston.

40-yard run
1. Louise Stokes, Onteora Club   5⅖
2. Helen McCarthy, Medford Girls' Club
3. Patricia Cahill, Boston Swimming Assn.

High jump (held April 16, in Boston)
1. Helen Philips, Boston Swimming Assn.   4' 11"
2. Patricia O'Brien, Boston Swimming Assn.
   and Sylvia Broman, Brockton Girls' A.C.
4. Virginia Blomerth, Onteora Club

Standing broad jump
1. Dorothy Lyford, Boston Swimming Assn.   8' 6³⁄₁₆"
2. Louise Stokes, Onteora Club
3. Mary Carew, Medford Girls' A.C.

Shot put
1. Marie Wegener, Winthrop, Mass.   35' 10½"
2. Alice Morris, Boston Swimming Assn.
3. Margaret Tierney, Boston Swimming Assn.
4. Helen Hakkanen, Karhu Club

The 220-yard run, 50-yard hurdles, basketball throw, and 440-yard relay were not held.

The Millrose Games celebrated its Silver Anniversary Games in 1932. Mary Carew won the sprint. The meet program included a story on remembrances from the past. One of the highlights was the 50-yard victory of Stella Walsh in the 1930 Games. She was voted the outstanding performer of the meet. A lengthy write-up on Stella appeared in the program. She said that the greatest thrill of her athletic career came the evening that she broke the record in the Millrose Games. She was the only American competitor in the final. The three other girls were Canadian. Just before the final, she had been told that Canadian girls had won this race for the past five years. She felt that rather than representing herself, she was representing every American girl.

Stella described her coming to America at ten months of age, twenty-one years earlier. At fourteen, she was the best all-around athlete in Cleveland. She said that the real secret of her running goes back further. Her mother was always athletic in Poland and her maternal grandfather even more so. She said that when she visited him the previous year, he challenged her to a 100-yard run. She just nosed him out. "And, he's well over sixty years old!"

Stella started to compete in track in 1929. She competed in Europe with the Polish Falcons of America in the Pan-Slovanic World Meet. She won the 60 and 100 meters, was third in the high jump, fourth in the shot put, and ran the anchor leg on the American relay team. After the meet, she was invited by the Polish government to represent Poland in its international meets against Austria and Czechoslovakia. She said, "I won every race I was in and lowered one world's record."

After returning from Europe, she began training for the Millrose Games in 1930. This was her first American appearance.

With the honor of being voted the meet's outstanding athlete came the placing of her name on the coveted Rodman Wanamaker Trophy.

In 1930, Stella competed in fifteen indoor and outdoor meets across the country and Canada. She equaled or bettered seventeen American, Canadian, or world records.

The World Games were held in Prague in 1930, and after it was decided that the United States would not send a team to these games, Stella was permitted by the AAU of the United States to accept an invitation from the AAU of Poland to represent them. She won the 60, 100, and 200 meters, beating women from seventeen nations.

The program write-up concluded by stating that Stella was now waiting for her naturalization papers making her an American citizen so that she would be eligible to represent the United States in the Olympic Games in Los Angeles.

Headlines in the *New York Times* on December 6 read, "Babe Didrikson Barred by A.A.U." Babe was barred because a photo of her hurdling and her name were used in an auto advertisement. She denied authorizing the ad.

Avery Brundage, president of the AAU, in publicly discussing the Didrikson case in the *New York Times* on December 25 said: "You know, the ancient Greeks kept women out of their athletic games. They wouldn't even let them on the sidelines. I'm not so sure but they were right."

The March 1932 *Journal of Health and Physical Education* reported the continued work of the Women's Division. Agnes Wayman recapitulated the resolutions adopted in the 1929 meeting opposing the participation of girls and women in the 1932 Olympic Games and then displayed the petition that the Women's Division sent to M. le Comte de Baillet-Latour, president of the International Olympic Committee in April 1930. The resolution read in part:

> Whereas, participation in the Olympic Games, particularly participation in Track and Field Events,
> (1) Entails the specialized training of the few,
> (2) Offers opportunity for exploitation and commercialization,
> (3) Stresses individual accomplishment and winning of championships,
> (4) Places men in immediate charge of athletic activities for girls and women,
> (5) Offers opportunity for possible over-strain in preparation for and during the games themselves; and
> Whereas, Pierre de Coubertin, founder of the modern Olympic Games, said to the Athletes and all taking part at Amsterdam in the IXth Olympiad Games, "As to the admission of women to the Games, I remain strongly against it. It was against my will that they were admitted to a growing number of competitions"; and
> Whereas, it is the understanding of the Women's Division, National Amateur Athletic Federation, that it is within the power of this International Olympic

Congress to veto the participation of women in track and field events in the Xth
Olympiad at Los Angeles, California, U.S.A., in 1932.

Therefore, the Women's Division, National Amateur Athletic Federation,
petitions this International Olympic Congress to vote to omit Track and Field
Events for Women From the 1932 Program.

The Eighth Annual Meeting of the Women's Division was held at the Bilt-
more Hotel in Los Angeles July 21-23, 1932.

The December newsletter carried this statement by Anne Hodgkins, field secretary: "The more I saw of the Games ... the more convinced I was that women
had no place in them, and that we must work with renewed enthusiasm to inter-
pret our standards to all nations until we shall be able to prevent the exploitation of women for such spectacles."

Mary Carew: The Lead-off Leg

Mary Carew Armstrong was a junior high school student when she first
started to run. In a conversation with her on February 13, 1993, in her home just
outside of Orlando, Florida, Mary said to me:

> My gym teacher thought I showed promise. Track was coming along then. She
> had me join the YWCA in Malden, Massachusetts, because they had a track team.
> I didn't compete in the AAU meets but I used to run in Malden with this woman
> who also thought I had promise. Then, when I got to be a year older, they
> entered me in the junior events in the AAU. I think it was under fourteen, and I
> used to "clean up." I didn't like not being a senior, so the next meet I said,
> enter me in both. At that point, I could win both, seniors and juniors. That
> really started my interest. Then when I got to high school, there was an orga-
> nization starting, the Medford Girls' Club. I joined that. Everybody pushed me.
> They said, that's just made for you. And the coach liked me. He is responsible
> for me coming along. He took a great interest in me. He was the high school
> boys' coach. He was good. He was dedicated to his work. Sometimes we would
> shovel the snow off of the track at Tufts College so we could practice. It was a
> banked quarter mile board track, outdoors. When I trained during the winter
> with him, I went to the high school where he coached the boys. We opened the
> double doors in the lunchroom, and we could make a nice fifty-yard straight-
> away right down through the doors. I trained with the boys all of the time. I
> was the only girl there. Nobody thought it was different. When spring came, we
> used to run outdoors on a cinder track. We had to dig our holes for the start. The
> coach really did take great pride in me. He taught me everything I knew. The
> combination of my natural ability and expert coaching produced my success.
>
> When the nineteen twenty-eight Olympic team came home from Amsterdam,
> Boston had four women on the team. I knew them a little bit, I was one of their
> admirers. They were heroines to everybody in the area. When I saw those girls,
> I decided right then and there, that's what I want. And I was only a kid. But,
> it did inspire me to see those four women. Later on I competed against them.
> Olive Hasenfus was a sprinter, Florence McDonald was an eight hundred-meter
> runner, Rena MacDonald was a shot putter, and Mildred Wiley was a high
> jumper. They got a large press notice. The write-ups about any meet were only
> about those people. That encouraged me. I said to myself, I didn't dare say it

to anybody else, but I had decided, the next Games I'm going to be on that team. Of course, I had such wonderful support from my coach. I was pretty good then. I was just entering high school, tenth grade. My coach would point to them at a track meet and say, "look what you could do." They were an inspiration to me.

I was in all of the meets the Olympians were in. I had to compete against them. In those days, there were a lot of meets. I competed in Nova Scotia, New York City, Philadelphia, Paterson, New Jersey, Dallas. The AAU had to pay the sectional champions' way to the national meets. That's how you got your expenses paid.

I won my first nationals in the Boston Garden. I had more success indoors probably because I was better at fifty yards. I ran the one hundred meters all of the time. I was better at fifty yards probably because my start was so good. I could beat anybody in ten yards. There's no man or woman that could be in front of me in ten yards. I used to run the two hundred twenty too. And I always broad jumped unless it was a special meet and the coach thought I might get injured.

Four or five girls on my team went to all of the meets, and we'd travel with the men of the Boston Athletic Association. On the Medford team, there were about twenty-five girls. We worked out during the week and weekends. I was dedicated, and I had a competitive spirit.

I was frightened when I went to the Olympic trials, when I thought of all those girls from all over the country. It was quite a performance to make the finals. You could make the finals after having run four times and not make the team. It's heartbreaking.

We ran and finished in one afternoon. It's a lot of work. I was psyched up for something. Maybe I was too modest to even dare think that I wanted it. But I knew I was just as good as anyone else, until the race was over. That was my attitude. I knew it would be hard for me. It was my goal. I knew almost every girl in it. I had been on that circuit. It was a wonderful experience. I was there alone without a coach. He had said to me, don't sit with those other girls. Don't even listen to them. Now, I know how they'll talk, he said, they'll un-psych you. I tried to do what he said because I figured he had my interests at heart and he knew more about it than I did. So, I just found a shady place and sat by myself and thought about how great it would be. The minute that race was over, all your troubles are over. The Olympic Committee was there, and they just scooped you up and took you to the nicest hotel, measured you for clothes. That was it. Period. You didn't go home. Isn't that wonderful for a kid?

I'm the biggest flag-waver you ever heard of. I did want it so bad. I was dedicated to that race for four years. That's all I had in the back of my head was that race — you're gonna make it. When you think of how long ago that was. There were a lot of women in it. To have quarter finals — those tracks were eight lanes.

I kept hoping not to be seeded against anyone who was good, like Babe Didrikson, but I think she was eliminated early. I didn't have to run against her. She didn't make the team in the sprints. I didn't run against Billie Von Bremen in the heats.

I don't remember much about the final except, this is it. I was steady on my mark. I don't like talking about being tied for fourth. But they took six so I was definitely on the team. I thought I did my very best performance that day, and I couldn't have beaten Billie Von Bremen and Elizabeth Wilde. I felt I had run well and I had accomplished what I went out there for. I ran to the phone; you

Left: Mary Carew in "start" position showing form used as lead-off leg of 1932 United States 400-meter relay team that ran a world record time of 47.0 for the gold medal. (Courtesy of Mary Carew Armstrong.) *Right:* Mary Carew Armstrong, 1993, in "start" position.

don't call your family, you call the coach. Isn't that awful? He was delirious. He could hardly talk. He knew I was going to make it. It was a happy day. He didn't go to Los Angeles.

No one in my family got to Los Angeles. That was bad, but the money was scarce. I knew they were behind me. They were supporting me but they didn't get out there.

George Vreeland was the coach. That was hard too. Getting to know us, all our idiosyncrasies. We used to practice at a junior college in Santa Ana.

We left from the trials. Never came home. We got out there quite a while before the opening day, it might have been almost two weeks. We worked out together every day. We were housed at the Chapman Park Hotel. The Japanese women were already there. We had a big dining room for everyone. We had the whole hotel.

I knew Louise Stokes from Massachusetts. I knew who most all of the girls were.

In Los Angeles I roomed with Babe Didrikson. I had nothing to say about it. Our chaperone was Fred Steers' wife. I had met Babe in Dallas. But it wasn't because we were friends or anything. It seemed to me that I was so insignificant and modest and retiring that they thought I would be good for this big bragger. Maybe that had nothing to do with it. It turned out that we got along very well. It was a perfect combination, the two of us. The mousy one taken care of by Babe. She was very good to me. I learned to like her and to respect her, and everything that she bragged about, she could do. And she bragged all of the time. She wasn't liked by the other girls because nobody likes a bragger, but she didn't care, evidently. And I liked her because she was so good to me and I got to know her. If you live with someone, you do. She was the one that used to say, "Hey, kid, you're just as good as anyone else until the race is over, don't forget that." But, she didn't say that to me. I think she was the greatest athlete, I'm thinking of all the current ones, that we have ever seen. She had something, charisma. I was seventeen, and she was probably about nineteen. She was not that much older. She played basketball for an insurance company and then got interested in track.

The four hundred-meter relay was staggered, and I was in a middle lane. That was a good pick, it was the best. It was hard to tell if you gave them a lead. I

Mary Carew displaying her 1932 Olympic gold medal in 1993.

was first. It seemed to me that I at least held my own. I passed the baton to Evelyn Furtsch of Los Angeles. Annette Rogers of Chicago was third, and fourth was Billie Von Bremen. She must have increased the lead. It wasn't a close finish. We won by about three yards. We knew we won. We set a new Olympic record. Bedlam broke loose. We were hugging and kissing, jumping, turning somersaults. Yeah, it was really something to behold. In relay teams only one person stood on the podium. For some reason or another, I don't know why, they chose me. That increased my dilemma. It was terrible that the others couldn't be on the podium. They stood in front of the podium on the ground.

That overwhelmed me, that victory ceremony. I turned to jelly. It is, it's amazing. It's hard to tell you how it feels to see a hundred thousand people standing at attention and hear the national anthem because of you. Just to see that flag going up the pole. You've had it all. I watch those ceremonies today, and I see them crying. Yeah, that's it. I feel today that was the greatest accomplishment in my entire life. And look at all of those ordinary things that I did, like getting married and having kids, and all that. It is an accomplishment. You have to look at it that way. Maybe when you get old like this, you get more emotional. But I don't think that's it at all. I really don't. Any Olympian will tell you that, there's a spirit, I tell the kids when I speak to them in schools, that must be carried over from the ancient Greeks, to run those games with honor and pride and for your country. It's a wonderful feeling. Exultation. I felt so proud. And when will the people back home know that we've done this. I wonder if I could get to a phone. You're thinking of how proud they'll be of you. And they were. They didn't let me down.

I called the coach. It got all over town. Two weeks later when I got back to Boston, the mayor was waiting and a great big hook and ladder fire engine, clanging and everything. Making noise. It almost knocks you out. You step out from those revolving doors and oh. They had a reception for me on the front porch where I lived. All the neighbors came. That was the same day. Afterwards they had an official greeting. Amelia Earhart was from my town. She was invited, I was invited, and so was the swimmer Helen Johns. The Kiwanis Club game me a scholarship for the four-year college. My town had three people on the Olympic team. Two of them were women and one was a marathoner. Helen Johns won a gold medal in swimming.

Gold medal winners were invited everywhere. As the saying goes, to the victor belongs the spoils. We were invited to radio shows in Los Angeles and across the country too. We were invited to the world's fair; to the national air races in Cleveland and we went somewhere in Denver. We were invited guests. It took me quite a while to get home. We got off the train every day to do something. None of us flew. It was through the telephone that they knew I was on the train.

I started college that September. There were six kids in the house. They were not my brothers and sisters. I was an orphan. But that's the way my family thought in those days. You just didn't quit school after high school. The schol-

MARY CAREW SCHOLARSHIP CERTIFICATE

GIVEN BY THE CITIZENS' COMMITTEE OF MEDFORD

AND

SPONSORED BY MEDFORD POST 45, AMERICAN LEGION

* * * * * * * * * * * * * * * * *

This certificate will entitle Mary Carew to a Scholarship in any School of Physical Education that she may select.

This Scholarship may be obtained when Mary Carew enters the school of her selection and satisfies the Committee to that effect.

Rufus H. Bond
Commander, Medford Post 45,
American Legion

Patrick N. McNally
Chairman, Citizens' Committee

Evans H. Larkin
Mayor of Medford

Certificate of Scholarship Award presented to Mary Carew, 1932 Olympic Gold Medalist, 400-meter relay. Possibly the first athletic scholarship for a woman track and field athlete. (Courtesy of Mary Carew Armstrong.)

arship was from the Kiwanis Club. You don't appreciate it at the time. You just think that was good, they thought of me. When you look back at it, it really is something. This was the depression. When I got out of college, even though I was well known, I couldn't get a job. It was a wonderful thing that they did. I ran for about a year during college. I was a big shot at school. Everybody knows you. No one else at school ran. I did learn about track, field hockey, swimming, and lacrosse as a physical education major.

I graduated from college in nineteen thirty-six and got married in nineteen thirty-eight. A gym teacher broke her leg and was out for a long time. I got temporary work there in the middle school, but it was for a few months. I had a license to referee and umpire in swimming, hockey, and basketball. That gave me spending money, and it was easy for me. I helped to coach the Medford Girls' Club. I had people write for advice. Some came over, and I would show them how to start. That goes with being an Olympic champion. I followed the meets.

I always said that my kids were brought up in a gymnasium or stadium rather than a nursery. My whole family was very supportive. All my aunts and uncles had all these kids and the Olympic champion. You're the special one. My Olympic life, even now, is like something apart from the rest of my life. I go with my kids to their affairs, but then on the side I travel to Colorado Springs and meet all those Olympians. Sometimes people seem jealous of that. Oh, you're going off again. ... But they don't realize, I don't talk about it much to them. It is a very special life you have in addition to being a housewife. Can you understand that? It's special. Just going to that Olympic Congress in October. All my friends here can't understand that. It is a different, special, nice thing. Olympians do have that bond. It's probably because of the ideals of the Olympic Games. The commitment to excellence ... you don't get on an Olympic team by chance. ...I never knew of anyone that did....

I was glad that I was on a track team. I'd say to my daughter, I was on the real Olympic team and she'd say, what's the matter with figure skating? Track is where it started in Greece. The real, authentic games was track. My granddaughter is a figure skater, and they know that I don't consider the winter games as being nearly up to Barcelona. Poor kid, she's fourteen. But she knows that I do appreciate what she does. The summer Games are it. When you get right down to it.

My husband was my biggest press agent. During two Olympics he tried to have his wife carry the pillow out with the medals on it for her event, the 400-meter relay. When he was turned down for one Games, he'd start all over for four years later. They claim that's protocol. They claim that I couldn't do that even if I were Bill Clinton. It has to come through the International Committee. My husband thought that there wasn't anybody on the face of the earth more deserving to do it than an Olympic champion in that event. I don't know why I haven't written to the president of the Olympic committee myself.

In nineteen eighty-four, the gold medalists were going to march in the opening ceremony. They measured us. They were going to have us in gold uniforms. The whole thing was in order. I don't hold it against Peter Ueberroth, but he said the opening ceremony was too long, so they cut that.

Alice Lord Landon was in the opening ceremony in nineteen eighty-four. The flag from nineteen twenty, she was in those Olympics, [swimming] was paraded in those games. It was the original flag from Antwerp. She was thrilled.

Boston is special. I was favored so by the press. They were really wonderful to me.

I ran against Stella every year. I ran against her, and I was so young. She was so big. The press used to call me the auburn-haired school girl running against this big woman. She never beat me in the Boston Garden. I don't think I ever beat her in a hundred meters outdoors. I ran against her a lot. She wasn't friendly. People don't like pushy women; she seemed so big and aggressive and didn't know her place, according to us girls. That's unfair too. I was not pushy at all. I was timid, and they picked that up and multiplied it a hundred times in the Boston papers. Young, unsophisticated kid was competing against this manly woman. The only physical we ever had in those days was to have your heart checked. The doctors told me I'd be dead by the time I was forty. I probably have an enlarged heart. Slow pulse. There hasn't been anyone healthier through the years. I haven't had any surgery. I was told it would be very difficult to have children. I didn't have any trouble there either. Even a physical education major being trained by the most knowledgeable teachers in the world — and you go along with it. I was shocked when I heard the women were running a four hundred meters. That would kill them. And to run while you were menstruating.

Oh, horrors to Betsy. My daughter says I'm a women's-libber right from the start. She recognizes that in me. But, it isn't that at all, I'm just defensive. I'm just saying it the way it is. I'm a perfect example, aren't I? The women physical educators, boy, they were all on the other team. They didn't think it was right for a person like me to be out there training for an Olympic Games. That used to bother me something awful. I felt it all along, more or less. I knew they must be right. After all, they're the leaders, the educated people. Who am I? I can remember this in college. This was being instilled in me. I was the future teacher. Don't forget, women are different from men. I was the underdog in college. They didn't like it. I read it in my books. I'd go to class, and I'd read that I was doing all the wrong stuff. I was on one team, and they believed just the opposite. I was automatically in that group because I was a physical education teacher. It was my professional organization.

When I went out to meet the high school physical education teacher, I always felt inferior. I felt it personally that they were down on me. And yet on the other hand it was very confusing, because they did admire what I had done, making a new world's record. They had to hand it to me. But, that's changed I think.

I taught for a year and then couldn't get a job. My minor was physiotherapy. I worked for a doctor. I finally got a job at Medford High School. I worked for about five years until I started my family.

I officiated at the nineteen thirty-six Olympic trials in Providence. I picked third place in the sprints. That was the last meet I officiated in. It was a bad day for me because when I saw how they did, I always felt I could have made that team. I was married and I didn't have the time for track.

They didn't have track in my high school. I was lucky. Those boys didn't resent me. The coach was compassionate and dedicated. Someone did it for me. Someone believed in me. I'm a believer in the Olympic movement. I was also extra lucky because I was an orphan. I lost both my parents when I was five years old, and I was pushed from pillar to post. Maybe that helped me. Boy, you'd have to be defensive if you're the extra wheel there. They don't mean to be mean to you, but it's human nature. I learned to duck, run out of the way, play with the boys. It has its advantages even though it was awful for me to be an orphan and to be raised like that. Maybe that developed the instinct in me that I had to take care of myself— go for all — do what I could. ... I don't know.

My parents were in their thirties. My mother was pregnant, and my father died in the flu epidemic. That penicillin is great stuff, and you never lose anyone with the flu today. My father worked on Friday and died on Sunday. It was the tragedy of the neighborhood. My Uncle Larry took the baby. My sister Rita was two. He kept an eye on affairs, and he could see that something was going wrong in Greenwich, Connecticut, where I was. I was there two years. I was noticeably abnormal from this experience. It left me timid and shy. He took me out and brought me back with him. He had nine in his family. He told all of the relatives that I was up for adoption — did anyone need another kid? I can remember one of my aunts saying, when he was trying to get a home for me and she didn't have any children, isn't she homely? Look at those freckles and that red hair. All the relatives were the same age as my own parents, bringing up their kids. It was pretty tough; he couldn't get anyone to take me. In the meantime I lived with him. I just became the tenth member of his family. It was a happy home. When I went to school, there were two Miss Davises — one was a special class — and I got put in that room by mistake. He had five kids of his own, but none of them were taking sewing and coming home early. So he went down and found the error.

He had a son the same age as me. We became very close. He got a basketball scholarship to college.

> I was lucky that I didn't go to a foster home. I was lucky. It's tough being an orphan. That was a big, loving family. I was the star of the family. We didn't have much money. If the milk was low, Mary got it because she was the athlete. I had my own bed. I didn't have my own bedroom.
>
> I taught kindergarten for twenty-six years. The superintendent couldn't get anyone, and I told him I wasn't trained in that field. He said, "Try it."

Mary spends her time now as a volunteer in Osceola Regional Hospital. She has been doing this for ten years.

Mildred "Babe" Didrikson

Mildred died in 1956 when I was a junior in college. I can still remember that September day because my dad was saddened by the news and that left an impression on me. He told me about her.

The *New York Times* obituary said that hundreds of residents of her home town of Beaumont, Texas, joined with sports celebrities for the service at Bethlehem Lutheran Church. She lost her three-year battle with cancer and died at the age of 45. Imagine, the greatest woman athlete of all time, the winner of Olympic medals and breaker of world records in running, jumping, and throwing events, dying that young.

In *This Life I've Led*, Babe's autobiography published in 1955, she talked about her childhood, when she was the sixth of seven children:

> Before I was even into my teens, I knew exactly what I wanted to be when I grew up. My goal was to be the greatest athlete that ever lived. I suppose that I was born with the urge to get into sports, and the ability to do pretty well at it. And my dad helped to swing me in that direction. He followed the sports news in the papers, and he'd talk to us about it. I began reading the sports pages when I was very young myself....
>
> In the summer of 1928 the Olympic Games were being held in Amsterdam, Holland. Poppa kept reading about the Olympics in the newspapers, and telling us about the star athletes over there.
>
> I got all steamed up. I said, "Next year I'm going to be in the Olympics myself."
>
> Poppa said, "Babe, you can't. You'll have to wait four years."
>
> It sounded like the greatest thing in the world to me — that free trip across the ocean and everything. I didn't know that the 1932 Olympics would be held in this country in Los Angeles. ... Lillie and I started training for the Olympics right then and there.
>
> Anyway, back in 1928 when we started thinking about the Olympics, ... I was going to be a hurdler and jumper. ... I didn't seem to want to stay on the ground. I'd rather jump some obstacle.
>
> There were hedges in the yards along our block — seven of them between our house and the corner grocery, I used those hedges to practice hurdling. But there was one of them that was higher than the others. I couldn't get over it. ... So I went to the people who lived in that house. ... I asked Mr. King if he'd mind cutting his hedge down to where the rest of them were, and he did it.

Babe played basketball for Employers' Casualty. When the season was over, the coach asked her if she'd like to see a track meet. Colonel McCombs explained the different events to her. As they left the field, they decided to organize a track team during the summer. The president of the company agreed, and everyone selected events. When it was Babe's time to pick an event, she asked the colonel how many events there were in track and field. When he said about nine or ten, she said, "Well, I'm going to do them all."

Everyone laughed, but she was serious. In a meet against the Bowen Air Lines girls in Fort Worth, she won seven out of the nine events she entered. She won the shot, discus and javelin, broad jump, high jump, 100 and 220 yard dashes. She was second in the 50 and was on the losing relay team.

Babe trained extra hours. An hour's practice

Babe Didrickson, 1932 Olympic Champion, 80 meter hurdles, javelin. (Courtesy of the USOC Photo Library.)

was not good enough for her. When the women's national championships were held in Dallas in 1930, she was ready. She won the javelin and baseball throw and was leading in the broad jump with a leap of 18' 8½" until Stella Walsh jumped a quarter of an inch further.

In 1931, Babe was the leading scorer in the Jersey City nationals. She won three first places: the broad jump, the baseball throw, and the 80-meter hurdles.

Before the 1932 combined nationals and Olympic tryouts, Colonel McCombs told her that she could win the meet all by herself.

The day came. After an almost sleepless night, Babe barely made it to the field in time. During the opening ceremonies, as the teams were announced, the girls ran onto the field and were given a round of applause. Babe said that when they announced her "team," she "spurted out there all alone, waving my arms, and you never heard such a roar. It brought goose bumps all over me. I can feel them now, just thinking about it."

She was entered in eight events. "For two and a half hours I was flying all over the place. I'd run a heat in the 80 meter hurdles, and then I'd take one of my high jumps. Then I'd go over to the broad jump and take a turn at that. Then they'd be calling me for the javelin or the eight-pound shot."

When the meet was over, she had done it. She had won the meet all by herself. She placed in seven of the eight events. She won five of them and tied for first in the sixth. She scored thirty points. The Illinois Women's Athletic Club was second with twenty-two points.

This was when the press began referring to her as the "super athlete" and "wonder girl." She stood 5' 5" and weighed 105 pounds. "Winning that 1932 national championship track meet singlehanded was the thing that first made my name big — that and the Olympic Games that followed."

The Olympics were a couple of weeks after the tryouts. Babe and the rest of the Olympians boarded a train for Los Angeles. She said that while most of the girls were sitting around and watching the scenery pass by, she was working out in the aisle. Several times a day, she jogged the whole length of the train and back. People remarked, "Here she comes again!"

The team stopped in Denver and worked out. Then they went on to Los Angeles. George Vreeland, the coach, attempted to change Babe's hurdling and javelin form. She refused to change. Her own coach had told her to stick to her natural style.

Babe described the thrill of the opening ceremony on August 1. The dress and stockings and white shoes which were part of the parade uniform were uncomfortable, however. She had never worn stockings in her life, and the shoes hurt her feet.

While standing in the hot sun for an hour or so, she slipped her feet out of the shoes. And so did everyone around her.

The javelin throw was that first day. It began late in the afternoon, as Babe recalls in her autobiography:

> We all got out there to warm up. I was watching the German girls, because they were supposed to be the best javelin throwers. I could see that they'd been taught to loosen up by throwing the spear into the ground. I'd been told that this was the way to practice, but I never could agree. It seemed to me that this gave you the wrong motion. You'd feel a tug that wasn't right. I always thought you should warm up with the same swing you used in competition.
>
> There were too many of us around for me to risk throwing any spears up into the air the way I wanted to. Rather than have no warm up at all, I thought I'd practice that other way, throwing the javelin into the ground. I tried it, and I almost put it in a German girl's leg. I decided I better stop.
>
> The event started. They had a little flag stuck in the ground out there to show how far the world record was. It was a German flag, because a German girl had set the record. It was some distance short of my own world's record.
>
> When my first turn came, I was aiming to throw the javelin right over that flag. I drew back, then came forward and let fly. What with the coolness and my lack of any real warm-up, I wasn't loosened up properly. As I let the spear go, my hand slipped off the cord on the handle.
>
> Instead of arching the way it usually did, that javelin went out there like a catcher's peg from home plate to second base. It looked like it was going to go right through the flag. But it kept on about fourteen feet past it for an Olympic and world's record of 143' 4".
>
> In practice I'd made throws of close to 150 feet. Nobody knew it, but I tore a cartilage in my right shoulder when my hand slipped making that throw. On

my last two turns, people thought I wasn't trying, because the throws weren't much good. But they didn't have to be. My first throw stood up to give me the gold medal for first place.

Two days later we had the qualifying heats for the 80 meter hurdles. ... The finals of the 80 meter hurdles followed the next day, a Thursday. I was so anxious to set another new record that I jumped the gun, and they called us all back. Now in Olympic competition, if you jump the gun a second time they disqualify you. I didn't want that to happen, so I held back on the next start until I saw everybody taking off. It wasn't until the fifth hurdle that I caught up, and I just did beat out Evelyne Hall of Chicago. If it was horse racing, you'd say I won by a nose. Even with the late start, I set another new record with a time of 11.7 seconds.

Now all I needed was to win the high jump the next day to make a clean sweep of my three events. The high jump turned into another contest between Jean Shiley and myself, like the one we had in the Olympic tryouts. Both of us were better this day than we'd ever been. The cross bar moved up to 5' 5", which was nearly 2 inches higher than the record Jean and I had set in Evanston. We both cleared it. Now I'd beaten the world's record in all three of my Olympic events.

Both Jean and Babe missed the bar at 5' 5¾", so they lowered the bar to 5' 5¼" to break the first-place tie. Babe later recalled:

Well, my Western roll was a little confusing to the judges. They weren't used to seeing it, especially with women jumpers. And the Western roll had to be performed just right to conform with the high jump rules of the day. Your feet had to cross the bar first. If your head went over first, then it was a "dive" and didn't count.

We took our last jumps. Jean Shiley made hers this time. I made mine too. Then all of a sudden the judges disallowed my jump. They ruled that I had dived....

I'd been jumping exactly the same way all afternoon — and all year, for that matter. I told the judges so, but they said, "If you were diving before, we didn't see it. We just saw it this time."

When Babe returned to Dallas, the mayor and throngs of fans were there to greet her, along with her mother and father. She was given a ticker tape parade through the city followed by a party at one of the hotels.

A post-Olympic meet followed in Chicago, where Babe won the high jump and was second in the discus.

Babe was voted the world's greatest woman athlete of the first half of the twentieth century in a poll conducted by the Associated Press. She was named six times as "Woman Athlete of the Year" (1931, 1945, 1946, 1947, 1950 and 1954).

Evelyn Furtsch

Evelyn Furtsch Ojeda was born in San Diego on April 17, 1914. In a conversation on November 21, 1991, she told me that she started running seriously in high school, although she has earlier recollections of running at picnics as a youngster:

I ran where my father worked and at picnics sponsored by other organizations. It was the big thing in the summer. I always won every race I was ever in. I just kind of ran all my life. I loved to run. But I never trained until I was seventeen and a junior in high school. My gym teacher in Tustin High School thought that I was a fast runner. She had the men's track coach watch me run, and as a result he decided to write for information about the nineteen thirty-two Olympics. He also began to coach me with the boys' track team. This was in nineteen thirty-one. I was the only girl that he was working with, and I did just what the boys did. Mr. Humeston was training me for the one hundred meters. I ran the one hundred, two hundred, and the fifty. The main reason I did the two hundred meters was to train for the one hundred. It gives you the extra endurance. I never ran a four hundred. I used to start out in January, jogging. I would jog twice around the track just to build up. Then I'd go through stretching exercises and push-ups like the boys did. Before the Olympics, I was in just a few meets. I was very amateur. Mr. Humeston entered me in the meets. I was in the tryouts to go to the national meet in nineteen thirty-one, and the nineteen thirty-one national meet. There were few meets in California.

My parents were very supportive of what I was doing. My father was always interested in sports. So I had a lot of encouragement. They were all there at the Olympic Games. You could just walk up to the window and buy a ticket, no lottery, no drawings. I have a brother who was older, and he's still excited about what's happened to me in the last four years.

I represented the City of Tustin. I did train with the Los Angeles Athletic Club in nineteen thirty-one. I went up on Sundays to Pasadena. There were about a dozen girls there. Several of the winners, like Lillian Copeland, were there. In nineteen thirty-two, with the depression, they ran out of money. So they informed me that they were not going to sponsor anyone for the Olympics. The people in Tustin went door to door and sent me to the trials. They raised one hundred ninety dollars and my mother, coach, and I drove to Chicago. No one had any money at that time to sponsor anybody. They had to take the money out of their own pockets. So I did run for the Los Angeles Athletic Club for a short time. I was by myself because they really didn't have another runner.

In nineteen thirty-two, I had qualified for the Olympic team by being one of the six fastest girls who made it to the final of the one hundred meters. I fell when I was crossing the tape so I was disqualified for the one hundred meters in the Olympics. I don't know how it happened, I may have leaned too far forward or I just lost my balance. The girls were all packed in together. We had run three races within three or four hours. It was just one afternoon for all the races. The track was pretty beat up. I had won my preliminary and my semifinal race. I was always considered a potential winner. I was running record times.

I came out to Los Angeles with the team and the Olympic coach had me run in the second position on the relay team. Mary Carew led off, I was second, Annette Rogers third, and Wilhelmena Von Bremen last. It was too hard to tell if we were in first when I got the baton because of the stagger. I have read conflicting reports. It was a very close race. I could tell that we had won because there was a stride difference.

Evelyn told the *Tustin Weekly* on November 22, 1991:

We four girls had never run together before. The Canadian team had won the 400 meter relay four years before. They had been practicing constantly. We knew we were going to have competition, but everything clicked....

Our technique then was we'd slap the baton into the girl's hand. The second you could feel they had a hold of it you let go.

Evelyn Furtsch, 1932 Olympic gold medalist and world record holder, 400-meter relay, starting to sprint. (Courtesy of Evelyn Furtsch Ojeda.)

After the Olympic Games, I went to Santa Ana College for two years. There weren't any track meets or activities for four years and during that time I had married and had a baby in 1935. There were no organizations for women in southern California between Olympics. There were no opportunities.

For fifty years no one knew where I was or anything about me. Then when the Olympics returned to Los Angeles in 1984, they started digging up their old, early athletes. I attended the 1984 Olympics. We had a reunion also. It was the first time we saw each other since 1932. So, I've really had more recognition since 1984 than I ever had in 1932. They didn't make so much out of it then. There was no T.V., and nobody knew who you were. In 1985 I was voted into the Orange County Sports Hall of Fame, and in 1984 I was given another Orange County award. It was lucky I lived a long time. We still get fan mail from all over the world. I get a lot from Germany and Australia. There are a lot of track and field enthusiasts all over the world.

Track is so completely different today. It's hard to imagine what they have to go through today. It's so much more advanced in training and everything. My daughter-in-law is a dietitian and she's going to have a radio show. I'm going to be on to show the difference between 1932 and now in training and diet. We didn't even mention diet.

The meets look very much more professional today. I do watch the meets and enjoy seeing the relays.

Evelyne Hall

Evelyne couldn't do enough to help with the research of finding some of her old teammates. She had their addresses, and she freely volunteered information on where to get information. Evelyne Hall Adams was born on September 10, 1909, in Minneapolis, Minnesota. At the time of our conversation, she said that she was the oldest living American Olympic medalist at eighty-two years of age. Evelyne died in April 1993.

In an interview on November 11, 1991, Evelyne recalled how she started running:

My mother was athletic and she approved of my running. Even though it wasn't ladylike then, my mother used to run around the flat iron building in Minneapolis with some of the other girls and said, "I was pretty good at it, too." It was never considered a sport for her, just a game.

The first race that I ran was in nineteen twenty-six, and I stopped competing in nineteen thirty-six. I competed for the Illinois Women's Athletic Club and then for the Chicago Park District. Besides the hurdles, I competed in the running broad jump and the relays. Indoors I competed in the standing broad jump. It's interesting, I was just reading a book that was printed in London, I don't know where on earth I got the book, but it was talking about some of the early girls that were running and it mentioned the long jump then. So it's been called the long jump a long time, and I guess Americans called it the broad jump until finally they changed over. They called it the long jump in Europe right from the beginning.

There were usually from six to twelve girls on the Illinois Athletic Club team. We really didn't have any coach in the beginning. We'd go up to the playground or parks and practice by ourselves and then different athletes would help. They'd start us and give us ideas. My husband was my coach. He was also an athlete, a pole vaulter.

We found out about track meets through a woman who was in charge of the exercises for overweight women, and she would somehow get the information because the team had some good swimmers and divers. She evidently belonged to the AAU and probably got information from them. She would tell us that there was a track meet, and they would pay our entry fee. There were very few meets. We went mostly to picnics. The picnics were company picnics which would be advertised in the newspaper. There would be races. The German club, Polish club, or Gaelic club would sponsor a track meet and a picnic, always a picnic in conjunction with it. There would just be dashes in the picnic races.

I was working in a correspondence school, Nellie Todd worked there. She was a broad jumper, and she was also a hurdler. She was representing the Illinois Women's Athletic Club. One day she invited me to come down there with her. So I went. A woman was in charge. She said, "Go over a hurdle." They only had one because the space was so small. It was only big enough for one hurdle. So I went over the hurdle, and she said, "Good, I'll enter you in the hurdle race." That's how I became a hurdler. I liked it because it was hard for most girls to go over an obstacle straight forward. I used to like to play jump rope because we didn't have enough money for too many other things. We would play higher and higher. We used to go straight forward over the rope. That's why it didn't phase me too much to go straight forward over the hurdles. I was about 5' 3½" and I weighed 118 or 120 pounds. I started hurdling in about nineteen twenty-eight. I can remember one hurdle race on a circular board track.

I worked out two times a week but did not start training for the Olympics until March or April. It was my own workout. I did wind sprints. I never did have any endurance, but I was very quick. My husband ran with me, but he was a pole vaulter. Since I was a hurdler, there was only one place where I could get all of the hurdles. That was on the north side of town, a long way from where I lived. We had a little car but no money for gas. It was really more recreation than anything else.

As 1932 approached it looked like I would make the team but not easily. I heard different reports of so many girls here and there who were running so well. I was hoping I would make it, and I kind of planned on it.

For years it had been the rule that girls were allowed two track and one field event, or two field and one track event. We all had to limit ourselves. I went into the hurdles, and the relay was my second event. That's why everyone was aghast at the thirty-two tryouts, which was governed by the same rule. Babe Didrikson competed in nine events, I don't know who permitted it. That's where she got the title of "superwoman." Everyone was very concerned and wanted to know what was going on. People were ready for the heats of the fifty or one hundred, and they had to wait for Didrikson to come from someplace. Everything stopped until she got to the event. No one understood what it was all about. All the clubs had about six or seven girls competing, and we all spread out as well as we could. We were all fighting for the team trophy, and Didrikson won it because she was allowed to compete in all of those events. That's where she got the title, and she beat the whole Illinois Women's Athletic Club. I'll tell you, most of the girls, in those days, including myself, were very naive, we didn't know the rules. We didn't know about the politics and all that was behind it.

Evelyne Hall hurdling, 1932 Olympic silver medalist and world record holder, 80-meter hurdles. (Courtesy of the National Track & Field Hall of Fame Historical Research Library at Butler University.)

At the Olympic tryouts in the hurdles, she was on one end of the track and I was on the other end, the far end, and when we got to the finish line, I stood at the finish waiting for the clerk of the course to announce the time, because that's what I was most interested in. The clerk of course said, "Who was first?" The two judges who were judging first said, "Hall." Then he asked the two who were judging second and they said, "Hall." So he said, where the heck was the Babe? They said, "well, she must have been first." And that's the way it was. I couldn't tell that I had won because she was on the other side of the track. I knew we were close because I could almost feel her, but I couldn't tell. My husband was in the stands, and he couldn't tell either.

We were all dumbstruck when all the publicity came to Babe when we got to California. I was very, very shy. I always shied away from publicity. I didn't want my picture taken. I was so afraid that something might happen and I might not win.

When we got to Los Angeles, all the women from the different countries were housed at the Chapman Park Hotel. All the men were in the village.

The support for the women from the media was poor. There was one newspaper reporter who was very harsh on the women. At that time they were playing up to Babe. She got a lot of attention because her manager–publicity agent was taking all of the reporters out and treating them to dinner. Babe was a marvelous athlete, but we were embarrassed by her actions. Most of the girls were ladylike. She was very brash. She roomed with Mary Carew, a young, naive high school girl.

They handed us men's track shirts with low-cut arm holes. I wasn't going to wear that for love nor money, and neither were a couple of the other girls. They had to get a tailor in quick to sew up the sides. Then we had loose shorts. As a hurdler, I wasn't going to wear loose shorts. So, I went out and bought elastic to put in the bottom of mine.

In the hurdles in the Olympics, the only name they knew was Didrikson. At the tape, she put her arm up and turned her shoulder and that was how the race was decided. I had a real cut, and my neck was bleeding in a semicircular pattern from the finish line.

The movie that was taken of the race looked like the photo. It was very quick. I did see a movie that was taken by a fan in the stands. That showed Didrikson very much on my side. She hit me on a couple of hurdles. That caused me to break my stride a little. That's what they wanted me to protest. Whoever took that film wanted five dollars for it, and I didn't even have the money to give to him. Every once in a while, someone says that they have a film of the race and I always hope it will be that one — but it hasn't shown up.

In nineteen thirty-six, I tried out again for the Olympic team. The four finishers were close. I was fourth. Because finances were next to nothing for women's track and field, the girls who made the team wired home for about a thousand dollars that they'd need in order to go. It was easier for the girls who were from small towns. I tried to get money from the Parks Department, but I didn't get it. The winning time in Berlin was the time I ran in Los Angeles, four years earlier.

I was a professional after nineteen thirty-six because I was teaching. I coached girls for the Chicago Park District for twelve years. I had kids under ten, juniors, and a senior team. Dorothy Dodson, a nineteen forty-eight Olympian was one of my athletes.

I moved to California in nineteen forty-seven and expected to coach a team that was already established but there were none. I was Central AAU chairman, so out there I was elected Pacific Coast chairman for women's track and field.

In a men's meet in California, I asked for a women's one hundred meters. The women's physical education teachers got so uptight that they threatened to boycott the whole affair if they permitted women to run. So the men asked if they could rescind their offer. Then about in nineteen forty-nine to nineteen fifty I organized a team from Glendale. The Glendale Lions Club sponsored us. They gave us uniforms. Since I was Pacific Coast chairman, they agreed to put on a relay and one hundred meters in the Coliseum Relays. I was given permission to invite Fanny Blankers-Koen, four-time Olympian, to come. She and her husband came over as guests of the Coliseum Relays. She loved it, and she stayed at my house part of the time. I had to get competition for her, so I wrote to my friend Myrtle Cook in Canada. She brought her relay team down. We had her relay team and my relay team. Fanny won the one hundred, and they paid for it.

I was the manager for the nineteen fifty-one Pan American team. It was a difficult assignment because I didn't meet some of the athletes until I was on the plane. Some of the athletes practiced in the morning, some in the afternoon, and some at night. I was going night and day.

The games were in Argentina when the Perons were in power. The thing I remember best is that I was selected to present the Perons with flowers opening night. I had this huge, I never saw such a huge bouquet, of red roses that had real long stems. The stems must have been thirty-six inches long. I walked from one end of the field, across the field in an aisle of flag bearers with flags from all of the countries. There was a spotlight on me as I walked all the way across the field. Then I had to walk up the red-carpeted stairs because they sat higher than everybody else. I had to present those roses to Evita. As I climbed those stairs, I kept thinking, how am I going to get down? I couldn't turn around and there was no banister. I thought, what if I slipped going backwards. Evita could speak English, we had spoken several times at some receptions. Most of the time she was there, and some of the time both of them were there. We were at a boxing match after the track was completed, and Evita was there. She had on this enormous, gorgeous, brilliant emerald. It was oblong. It seemed that it was almost as big as a postage stamp. She sat in the balcony. I was near her and whenever she turned the slightest bit, that emerald sparkled and hit the wall and bounced back. It was unbelievable how huge it was. It was just a single emerald with no decorations around it. I liked her very much. She was very courteous and very gracious.

After the Pan American Games were over, some of us were invited to Chile for a meet. They were very hospitable.

One of the most memorable times I remember was my first trip to the East Coast. That was the first chance I had to travel. That gave me a zest for traveling.

If I hadn't gone to the Olympic Games, I would not have started teaching or coaching. It gave me the incentive to obtain an education. I loved teaching and coaching. I would have worked for nothing. It didn't seem like work at all. It was a tremendous experience, and I give the Chicago Park District a lot of credit.

I have a daughter who is a school teacher and a son who was born in nineteen fifty-one, an attorney. My daughter competed for a while when she was a youngster and I was coaching.

Jean Shiley Newhouse: High Jump Gold

My conversation with eighty-year-old Jean Shiley Newhouse took place on October 21, 1992. Oddly enough, it was also the night that she was being inducted into her hometown Hall of Fame.

Jean was born in Harrisburg, Pennsylvania, on November 20, 1911. She related to me how her track and field career had started in Haverford Township High School:

The school was about seventy-five years ahead of its time because they had a girls and boys' program that was equally subsidized. We were treated equally. We had our schedule the same as the boys had their schedule. I had an opportunity to compete in hockey, basketball, track and field, and tennis. I also could have done golf and swimming if I could have fit it in. I ended up doing hockey, basketball, track and field, and a little tennis in between. I had one coach for all the sports, Ethel David, the physical education teacher. She was a very good teacher from a very good physical education college in New England. We had competitions with about twelve schools in Delaware County.

I did not have any competition in grammar school, just free play. There was nothing outside of school. There were very few places that a girl could go to belong to a club or be sponsored by someone. A few places in the country had programs like New York, New England, Chicago, Texas, California, and St. Louis. Those were the centers where people came from back in those days. There was nothing in between. There might have been a lot of good people out there. They just didn't have the opportunity.

In nineteen twenty-five I started high school. I began track in April of my freshman year. I did everything. I threw the baseball, did the running broad jump, standing broad jump, and high jump. There were about fourteen girls on the track team. It was a small school. I loved any sport. I'd do sports at the drop of a hat.

I was playing basketball in nineteen twenty-seven for the state championship. We received very good coverage from the Philadelphia newspapers. There were female reporters with bylines from the *Record*, the *Inquirer*, and the *Bulletin*. The girl from the *Inquirer*, whose name was Dora Lurie, was there reporting on the game that day. She sort of inadvertently spoke out and said, "My goodness, that girl jumped so high, the forward can't get the ball." A little boy sitting next to her, and I wish I knew who he was, I'd love to thank him, said to her, "That girl jumped four feet, ten inches last year." Well, at that time, that was a very good height, and this reporter was a very knowledgeable reporter. She said, "I'll call her." She called me the next day and asked me if I'd like to compete in the Olympics. I said, what's that? First of all that was the first year that women were in the Olympics, but I didn't even know what the Olympics were. I said, sure, I would jump. It was just another track meet to me, and it was something I loved to do. She made an appointment for me to go to see the coach at the University of Pennsylvania, who was Lawson Robertson. He subsequently became the head men's coach for the nineteen twenty-eight and nineteen thirty-two Olympic teams. He took me as a pupil. So if it hadn't been for my school and the reporter and the principal of my school who let me off school every Wednesday morning and Lawson Robertson giving me all of his free time and remarkable training, nothing would have happened. I worked with him alone. He was a very difficult man to get to. When I did go down to "audition," sort of, he scared the daylights out of me. He was a very gruff man. I did my thing and went to get dressed, and Dora came screaming in the door, "He's gonna take you, he's gonna take you." From then on, which was sometime in April, that's how I did it. All my life I wondered who that little boy was, I owe him so much.

[Dora Lurie, a Temple graduate and member of their Hall of Fame, played basketball for undefeated Temple from 1919 to 1922. From 1923 to 1926, she played pro basketball in the United States and Canada. For 23 years she reported on men's and women's sports for the *Philadelphia Inquirer*.]

The four foot ten inch jump was done as a sophomore. I won all of the track meets. The high jump was easy. I was five-feet ten and a half-inches tall and weighed one hundred thirty-three pounds. I had no training. I was jumping in sneakers, and the conditions were primitive. We didn't have all of the nice conditions they have today. The sand was damp, and the ground was murky. I had the natural ability. I was not taught. The learning process started when I met Lawson Robertson. He taught me concentration and the form. A gun could go off beside me, and I wouldn't have heard it. I once competed in the center field in New Jersey, where they were having horse racing in the outfield. It didn't bother me. I never even heard them. Things were very primitive then.

I worked with Lawson during April, May, and June. The tryouts were on July fourth, in Newark. I was second. I jumped four feet, eleven and three-quarters inches. I used the scissor jump, but then I hitched my hips a little, to get them out of the way. I still went up with one foot and landed on the other. No one knew anything about me. I competed unattached. I was jumping in a pair of pants that my mother made for me, and she wasn't a very good seamstress. I was afraid I was going to split them. I had my brother's shirt on and a pair of sneakers.

I was excited about making the team. My father and family had trouble with it because I was only sixteen. I was a little country girl. My Pennsylvania Dutch grandmother thought, "You're going to let this sixteen year old go to Europe without a chaperone, without a chastity belt."

My aunt was at the meet when I made the team. My mother and father never saw me compete. My aunt and my uncle were the ones. My father had a hard time with his only daughter in a family of boys. He didn't know just what I was all about. I was doing all of the things that the boys should have done, and the boys weren't doing them. My father's eyebrows would go up. He didn't encourage me but he didn't discourage me either. It was like two trains going down the track and not meeting. Women were still submissive. My mother and father were good people, but they were not prepared for their rogue daughter. My brothers were younger than I. I was the oldest.

After the tryouts, I went home and got a trunk and clothes. I had to be back in a week to set sail. My mother and my father and my aunt and uncle did see me off. But it was my aunt and uncle that were really interested in everything that I did. They encouraged me.

I had no schedule for training on the boat. The first night, I was so naive that when I sat down to the table with all of those knives, forks, and spoons in front of me, I didn't know what to do with them. I learned very fast. It was very interesting. It was one of the best things that ever happened to me. It taught me an awful lot in the four to five weeks we were gone. It took seven days to get over there by ship. We had a woman chaperone and a manager who took care of us. "Babe" Robinson was also sixteen.

The whole Olympic team went on the ship. The swimming team and the track team were on one level. I was worried about the horses on the ship. The equestrian team had their horses, and we had a five-day storm on the way over. Nobody was in the dining room. The Olympic team was taken very good care of. We lived on the boat even when we were over there. The food and the service was luxurious. It was my first experience so it seemed that way to me.

I did not get sick on the way over. I guess I didn't even know that I should get sick. Some of the girls were sick before we even got out of the harbor. There wasn't too much we could do on the ship except jog around and do stretching exercises. I didn't high jump at all. They didn't have stabilizers then either. When you sat in the middle of the dining room and looked from side to side, you see the ship go down and all you see is water, then it goes up and all you see is sky. And it keeps doing that. There was one girl who was so sick, MayBelle Reichardt.

When we arrived in Amsterdam, we had water taxis that took us to the track to train. They came and went all day long. We could leave the ship anytime. There was no security, no drugs, no anything. We were perfectly free to come and go as we pleased, except for the time that we trained. The coach set up the training time, and we would meet and then go to train. I competed in the high jump in the Olympics about a week after we arrived.

I don't remember a lot of things about the trip because I was learning so much, so fast. I was so curious about everything. Art, architecture, cultural patterns, music, geography, just everything, and as my uncle said, from a small child I always asked why and what and how. I had an insatiable curiosity about anything. I was a risk-taker. I wanted to know about everything.

The other girls were willing to help each other in the Olympics. Even between nations we helped each other. It's not like today. It was a damp, cold day of the competition. I was elated at getting fourth, I didn't even think I placed. I couldn't believe it.

The trip home was marvelous. We had a ticker tape parade. My little town gave me a parade. I was a junior in high school. It's like ancient history. In those days the Olympics were not a big deal. News didn't travel very fast. There was no television. The newspapers provided the coverage. I received very good coverage. Many people who have visited me and have gone through my memorabilia are surprised at the amount of coverage that our teams got in basketball, hockey, and track around the Philadelphia area. The worst part of the welcome home celebration was getting up in the assembly and speaking. I never did get used to it.

I did get a small scholarship to Temple. It was a scholastic scholarship, not an athletic scholarship. There was no track program at Temple. That was the time when they felt that girls should not be competing in sports and all they had was intramural sports and they were just dull, dull, dull. I had to do everything outside of college. My professors, through the whole four years I was there, every time they would meet me in the hall or we had any close contact, would say, "When are you going to quit?" It was terrible. They took advantage of me. Whenever they had some important event, they would drag me out of class or make appointments for me to appear here or there. But those were the days of the depression, and without Temple I would not have been able to go to college. I had to work all of the time and finally had to borrow money to finish. I was so grateful to just be able to go.

After coming back from the Olympics, the following winter I went to an indoor track meet. I just happened to be standing next to a man, and we got to talking. It turned out that he competed for the Meadowbrook Club, which was sponsored by Wanamaker's in Philadelphia. He suggested that I go down and speak to the coach and see if they would take me on. But in order to compete for Wanamaker's you had to work for them. So I did what he suggested. It wasn't easy. There was no place for women, and the men were running around in all sorts of nothing, and I couldn't even get to the office to get to talk to the coach. I finally got up my nerve to ask one of them to ask the coach if he would come out to talk to me. Anyway, after talking to him, he said yes. He arranged for me to work on Saturdays in the summers so that I could compete on the Meadowbrook team. From then on, they sponsored me.

There weren't as many meets as there are today. We competed in all outdoor and indoor nationals and other meets. But there weren't that many. In the indoor season, we competed in Boston, one of my favorite cities, Philadelphia, New York. Outdoor we competed in Toronto, Chicago, Dallas, New York, New Jersey, quite a few. But not as many as there are today.

I gradually got better. Just by practicing I got better and better. I relied on what my first coach told me. It worked very well. The coach of the Meadowbrook Club would come and watch me, but he really couldn't give me much more than what I had because I had the best. I practiced indoors up on the top floor where all of the imports and goods were; it was like a warehouse. I put up a couple of standards and a crossbar and a couple of mats. That would be it. I had three months of coaching.

The nineteen thirty-two tryouts were in Evanston, Illinois. I had been winning all along, but I never went into a meet with expectations. I just went to do the best I could, and it turned out very good. I was just very lucky. I put the pressure on myself to do the best I could. In the tryouts I won. [Jean tied with

Babe Didrikson.] I jumped five feet, three and three-sixteenths inches. Babe and I were friends. Even after the games, we kept in touch. The tryouts were on the sixteenth of July and the Olympics were August seventh. We left the next day for Los Angeles from Chicago.

In nineteen thirty-two, I was better able to savor the conditions surrounding me, so it was a lot more fun. The women were all in one hotel. They took the hotel over for us. We had lovely accommodations. It was really very nice. We could see all of the other girls from the other countries. We would eat together. We would visit back and forth. It was just great. Remaining on the ship in nineteen twenty-eight limited us because we ate and slept on the ship.

The competition was tough at the Olympics. Babe and I held the world's record together, you know, five feet, five and a quarter inches. But you

Jean Shiley preparing to high jump in the 1932 Olympic Games in Los Angeles. (Courtesy of Jean Shiley Newhouse.)

probably have some knowledge of what they called a controversy. There was no controversy really. The fact is that the rules were very rigid on how you could jump. You had to take off with one foot and land on the other. Your shoulder could not precede your body over the bar. The other thing was that there were no ties in the Olympic Games at that time, so you had to jump it off. Babe was using a form of jump that was called the Western roll, that was coming into effect, the men had been doing it for a while, which is sort of a lay out on top of the bar. I had tried that out with Robbie [Lawson] and he said no, it was too dangerous because if you get your shoulder on the bar, you foul out. That's what happened to Babe. It became a controversy because most people did not know the rules, even the reporters like Grantland Rice and Paul Gallico, who were the top reporters in those days. They really didn't know the rules. So it became a controversy which wasn't really a controversy. She herself said, "How's this, why, because I've been jumping that way all afternoon." She had been. The Dutch girl and the girl from Toronto, Eva Dawes, wanted to claim a foul, and I said no, I wouldn't do that. I had good training in high school. That was one thing our coach would not stand for — poor sportsmanship or anything like that. You were penalized. You didn't play the next week. I didn't do that. It happened on the jump-off. The bar went up to five feet, six and one quarter inches, and we both missed it three times. They put it down to five feet, five and one quarter inches, I made it and then Babe jumped and that's when they called the foul. Aside from that you have five judges, each of them speaking a different language, so it takes them a while to getting around to making a decision. And so, it was just one of those things. Many of those kind of things have happened over the years. I held the record until nineteen forty-eight. Alice Coachman broke it.

I knew that I was jumping correctly. I didn't know Babe was jumping incorrectly in the tryouts. I did not know the precise rules either. I knew that there were no ties in the Olympic Games. I knew I won as soon as they claimed the foul. The other girls were complaining.

I felt great because America had gotten the first two places. I couldn't call home because the phone system was a relay system. It would go through about six cities before it would get to the East Coast. I couldn't even call my mother and father to tell them. They found out from Walter Winchell. Everybody listened to Walter Winchell in those days. He announced it on his program, and that's how they found out.

The victory ceremony was the same as we see today. You really don't know how emotionally involved you are until you stand up there on that victory stand and they play the Star Spangled Banner. Something just wells up inside of you, and I cried, I just cried. There was nothing I could do about it. It just happened that way. When I see an ice skater up there now, and she's crying, I cry. Some of them gulp and try to stop from crying and they can't, then I cry. Tears just well up, there's no way you can stop it.

I was a junior at Temple at the time. When I came back, I had to speak before the entire student body at the orientation meeting when the school term started. It was awful. When I went back, they still had no sports for women. The next year I didn't compete. I did want to go to the Olympics in nineteen thirty-six because I was jumping higher than the girl they sent. But I had taught swimming. That made me a professional. I had to eat. I had to earn money. I went to New York to see Dan Ferris. He just said a plain no. That was the rule then. My little town made up a little purse for me of five hundred dollars after the nineteen twenty-eight Games and I had to return it.

I just loved doing it. I was the biggest tomboy in town, I guess. I just loved doing anything that the boys did. My brothers fixed cars, and I learned to fix cars too.

Between nineteen twenty-eight and nineteen thirty-two we had to go underground to play basketball. It wasn't organized. It was semiorganized. I majored in physical education and history in college. I really didn't want to be a physical education teacher. I wanted to go into medicine. A lot of our courses in college were taken with the medical students. I figured maybe somehow, after I got out, I might be able to work and then go into medicine. But, it just never worked out that way.

In spite of the fact that I've become somewhat disenchanted, I watch the Olympics. I love perfection. I like to see the things they do today in other sports like gymnastics, swimming, and diving. I'm just fascinated by it. The good part is the strides that women have made in sports. I'm happy about that. Yes, I'd love to do the Fosbury Flop with those nice cushions to land on. I had to jump down into a hole. The shoes were so heavy. Today they're so light. I bought my first pair of shoes in Spalding's in Philadelphia from my babysitting money. When I went to the nineteen twenty-eight Olympics, they gave me these lovely, soft leather shoes. They felt like moccasins on my feet. I was so surprised, I couldn't believe the difference. They were high jump shoes with the spikes in the heel.

I would have loved to compete in the hurdles. I loved the hurdles. The hurdles are too dangerous for a high jumper. But, in local meets, I did the hurdles. The coach said, no hurdles, no tennis, no swimming. I would have done both events if I had the opportunity. I would have done the running broad jump and the running hop, step, and jump. I liked to do that. Believe it or not, I competed in one indoor meet in nineteen twenty-nine in the standing high jump in New York. I never saw it after that.

I have three children, two girls and a boy. I gave them every opportunity. I gave them tennis lessons and swimming lessons. They were really pretty good, but they didn't have the dedication and the discipline for it. You just have to be dedicated. You have to want to really do it.

If I were giving advice to a young girl just starting out in track and field, I'd tell her to go for it. If she had the will and the dedication and the discipline and she loves it. You have to love it, I think. Training isn't easy. You give up a lot of things when you're training. But I never thought I was giving up anything. If I had a choice between going to a party or training, I would do the training. I didn't feel like I was giving anything up at all.

Chapter 16

1933

The outdoor track and field championship meet was held at Soldier Field, Chicago, on June 30. Alice Arden and Annette Rogers were the only record breakers. Arden won the high jump with a jump of 5' 3¼", breaking Babe Didrikson and Jean Shiley's meet record by ⅟₁₆th of an inch. The *New York Times* called the performance by nineteen-year-old Alice Arden "astounding." Alice was competing in her first outdoor national meet. Annette Rogers ran the 100 meters in 12.2, one tenth of a second faster than the record of the previous year.

Two defending champions retained their titles — Olive Hasenfus, a 1928 Olympian, in the 200 meters and lanky Ruth Osborn in the discus.

The Illinois Women's Athletic Club had to win the 400-meter relay twice. In the first running of the race, the team ran 48 seconds, which would have been a new world record. Because of a foul, however, the event was rerun the following afternoon on a rain soaked track. Their new time was 49.5.

Catherine Rutherford was the only double winner of the day and the individual high point winner.

---

50 meters
1. Louise Stokes, Onteora Club, Mass.   6.6
2. Wilhelmina Von Bremen, Western Women's Club, San Francisco
3. Ethel Harrington, Illinois Women's A.C.
4. Doris Anderson, Illinois Women's A.C.

100 meters
1. Annette Rogers, Illinois Women's A.C.   12.2
2. Louise Stokes, Onteora Club
3. Harriet Bland, St. Louis
4. Elizabeth Wilde, Webster College, Kansas City

200 meters
1. Olive Hasenfus, Boston Swimming Assn.   26.2
2. Elizabeth Wilde, Webster College, Kansas City
3. Lois Collar, Illinois Women's A.C.
4. Elizabeth Munsey, Board of Education, Chicago

400-meter relay
1. Illinois Women's A.C.   49.5

(Hall, Anderson, Terwilliger, Rogers)
2. Laurel Ladies A.C., Tornoto
3. Newark N.J. Women's Club
4. Dragon Club, Brooklyn

80-meter hurdles
1. Simone Schaller, Bailleaux Health System, Pasadena   12.1
2. Lois Collar, Illinois Women's A.C.
3. Roxy Atkins, Laurel Ladies A.C., Toronto
4. Nellie Sharka, Newark Women's A.C.

Shot put
1. Catherine Rutherford, Illinois Women's A.C.   38' 11"
2. Rena MacDonald, Alpha A.C., Mass.
3. Evelyn Ferrara, Illinois Women's A.C.
4. Effy Oord, Newark, N.J., Turn Verein

Broad jump
1. Genevieve Valvoda, So. Parks, Chicago   17' 2¾"
2. Nellie Todd, Illinois Women's A.C.
3. Mildred Schworm, Concordia Turners, St. Louis
4. Margaret Jordan, Board of Education, Chicago

High jump
1. Alice Arden, Dragon Club, Brooklyn   5' 3¼"
2. Genevieve Valvoda, So. Parks, Chicago
3. Annette Rogers, Illinois Women's A.C.
4. Doris Anderson, Illinois Women's A.C.

Discus throw
1. Ruth Osborn, Shelbyville, Mo.   123' ¼"
2. Catherine Rutherford, Illinois Women's A.C.
3. Wilhelmina Von Bremen, Western Women's Club
4. Rena MacDonald, Alpha A.C., Mass.

Baseball throw
1. Catherine Rutherford, Illinois Women's A.C.   232' 2"
2. Ann Brebeck, German-American A.C., N.Y.
3. Mildred Monju, Wiltz A.C., New Orleans
4. Sue Daugherty, Philadelphia

Javelin throw
1. Nan Gindele, Illinois Women's A.C.   130' 2¼"
2. Sue Daugherty, Philadelphia
3. Evelyn Ferrara, Illinois Women's A.C.
4. Katherine Ferrara, Illinois Women's A.C.

Team scores:
Illinois Women's A.C. 47; South Parks, Chicago 8; Onteora Club, Massachusetts 8;
Dragon Club 6; Bailleaux Health System, California 5.

A total of eighteen clubs scored points.

The Indoor Nationals

The indoor national meet was held on February 25 in Madison Square Garden. This was the first time in the history of women's events that both the men's championships and the women's were held at the same time. The women's meet was in the afternoon. Another innovation was the use of women officials to officiate the meet.

There were eight heats in the 50-meter dash, four quarter finals, and two semifinals.

50-meter dash
1. Pearl Young, Newark Women's A.C.   6⁸⁄₁₀
2. Mary Carew, Medford Girls' A.C.
3. Mary Terwilliger, Illinois Women's A.C.
4. Doris Anderson, Illinois Women's A.C.

50-meter hurdles
1. Evelyne Hall, Illinois Women's A.C.   7⁶⁄₁₀
2. Alda Wilson, Silverwood Lakeside Club, Canada
3. Nellie Sharka, Newark Women's A.C.

200-meter run
1. Annette Rogers, Illinois Women's A.C.   26⁸⁄₁₀
2. Mary Anderson, Boston Swimming Assn.
3. Olive Hasenfus, Boston Swimming Assn.

400-meter relay
1. Newark Women's A.C. (Monk, Young, Sharka, Capp)   50⁸⁄₁₀
2. Silverwood Lakeside Club, Canada
3. Carter Playground, Chicago
4. Illinois Women's A.C.

8-lb. shot put
1. Rena MacDonald, unattached, Massachusetts   37' 10"
2. Mildred Yetter, Meadowbrook Club   37' 7"
3. Catherine Rutherford, Illinois Women's A.C.   35' 11"
4. Effy Oord, Newark, Turn Verein   32' 2½"

Standing broad jump
1. Dorothy Lyford, Boston Swimming Assn.   8' 6¾"
2. Anna Paluszek, Dragon Club, Brooklyn   8'
3. Nan Gindele, Illinois Women's A.C.   7' 10"
4. Mary Carew, Medford Girls' A.C.   7' 8¼"

High jump
1. Annette Rogers, Illinois Women's A.C.   5' 1¹⁄₁₆"
2. Frances Anderson, Michigan Normal, Detroit   5' ¹⁄₁₆"
3. Alice Arden, Dragon Club   4' 11¹⁄₁₆"
4. Pearl Young, Newark Women's A.C.   4' 10¹⁄₁₆"
   and Doris Anderson, Illinois Women's A.C.

Basketball throw
1. Nan Gindele, Illinois Women's A.C.   101' 6¾"
2. Lillian Tresselt, Arnold College   97' 9¼"
3. Carolyn Dieckman, So. Paterson Girls' Club   92' 1"
4. E. O'Brien, Boston Swimming Assn.   91' 5½"

A suggestion was made by Fred Steers to send a women's team to the 1934 women's world games in London. The track and field committee believed that the United States should be represented.

The Women's Track and Field Committee for the AAU follows:

Fred Steers (Central), chairman; Jean Shiley (Middle Atlantic), vice chairman, Cecile Daly (Pacific), vice chairman; Dee Boeckmann (Western), vice chairman.

Adirondack	Mrs. Hugh Morrison
Allegheny Mountain	Frances G. Taylor
Atlantic Seaboard	Marian Wood
Central	William C. Larson, Leo Fischer
Connecticut	Anna Tracy
Gulf	Doll Harris, Elizabeth Finley
Indiana-Kentucky	Dr. Carl B. Sputh
Inter-Mountain	Frances Lund
Metropolitan	M. A. Klein, William H. Moseley, Henry Blaul
Michigan	Elsie Erley
Missouri	Dr. H. J. Huff
New England	Mrs. Pauline Bromberg, Mrs. Georgina McLellan
New Jersey	G. H. Vreeland, Estelle F. Hill, Mrs. Catherine D. Meyer
Niagara	Elbert Angevine
Ohio	James H. Cunningham
Pacific Northwest	Evelyn Ryer
South Atlantic	Mora Crossman
Southeastern	J. D. Alexander
Southern	L. diBenedetto
Southern Pacific	Mrs. Aileen Allen

Chapter 17

1934

This was the only year in the history of outdoor championships that the national senior outdoor championship meet in track and field was not held for women.

The Indoor Nationals

The ninth annual national indoor championship meet was held on April 14 in the Second Naval Battalion Armory in Brooklyn, New York. Jesse Abramson's article about the meet in the May *Amateur Athlete* stated that the girls traveled all night in buses and automobiles to get from places like Chicago and Toronto to New York. He noted that the Lincoln Park team from Chicago won the team trophy and were the same girls who won the title in Madison Square Garden the previous year as the Illinois Women's Athletic Club, which had been disbanded.

Betty Robinson made a comeback to sprinting in this meet. It was her first competition since the airplane accident. Abramson noted: "She did not win a prize of any sort and her racing was hardly noticed in the excitement of the relay. She started training a month ago and this was her first competition in three years. Although she ran only in the relay she intends to compete in the outdoor nationals and hopes to go to London this summer for the women's world international meet and then make the 1936 Olympic team."

The *New York Times* headlined the world 50-meter-dash mark made by Stella Walsh, and in the 200 meters she led from the gun to the tape and finished twelve yards ahead of Annette Rogers.

Rena MacDonald, a 1928 Olympian, set a world indoor record in the shot put, bettering her own record set in 1929.

50 meters
1. Stella Walsh, Cleveland   7.0
2. Mildred Fizzell, Laurel Ladies A.C., Toronto
3. Louise Stokes, Onteora Club
4. Miriam Nelson, Boston Swimming Assn.

200 meters
1. Stella Walsh, Cleveland   26.0 WR
2. Annette J. Rogers, Chicago Park District

3. Olive Hasenfus, Boston Swimming Assn.
4. Mary Terwilliger, Chicago Park District

50-meter hurdles
1. Mrs. Edna Roxy Atkins, Laurel Ladies A.C.   8.2
2. Mrs. Evelyne Hall, Chicago Park District
3. Leora Johnson, Chicago Park District
4. Tidye Pickett, Chicago Park District

400-meter relay
1. Laurel Ladies A.C.   52.6
   (Fizzell, Lamb, Atkins, Norton)
2. Meadowbrook Club
3. Dragon Club
4. Chicago Park District

High jump
1. Alice Arden, Dragon Club   5' 1"
2. Doris Anderson, Chicago Park District,   5'
   and Genevieve Valvoda, Chicago Park District
4. Pearl Young, unattached, Williamsburg, Va.   4' 8"

Standing broad jump
1. Dorothy Lyford, Boston Swimming Assn.   8' 5½"
2. Anna Paluszek, Nassau Collegiate Centre, L.I.   7' 11⅝"
3. Dorothy Ott, Dragon Club   7' 9¼"
   and Alice Helm, Shore A.C., Belmar, N.J.

Shot put
1. Rena MacDonald, Alpha A.C., Quincy, Mass   40' 11" WR
2. Catherine Fellmeth, Chicago Park District   38' 9½"
3. Mildred Yetter, Meadowbrook Club   36' 7"
4. Thora Pawley, Dragon Club   33' 4¾"

Basketball throw
1. Nan Gindele, Chicago Park District,   95' 9¼"
2. Evelyn Ferrara, Chicago Park District   94' 7¾"
3. Catherine Fellmeth, Chicago Park District   88' 3"
4. Mildred Yetter, Meadowbrook Club   86' 9½"

Team scores:
Chicago Park District 29; Laurel Ladies A.C. 13; Dragon Club 9½.

Fred Steers, the national chairman, said that the meet was an athletic success but a financial failure. He added that this was the second time in the history of the indoor championships that a full corps of women officials, assisted by a few men, handled the meet.

According to Steers, at the women's track and field committee meeting it was resolved to request a rejection of the amendment to rule #30, which has to do with the number of events in which a woman is permitted to compete in one meet. The proposed amendment would have made it possible for a woman to compete in four events. The committee requested that the policy remain as it was at that time — a woman was allowed to compete in three events.

Dee Boeckmann, chairman of the AAU Women's Sports Committee, gave a report on a questionnaire that was sent to the chairmen of the AAU districts and to the chairmen of the women's district sports committees. Twenty-two districts reported, and eleven of those had track championships. She found varying age requirements for the different sports and suggested that the age requirement for track and field be eighteen. This would not apply to Olympic trials, just to national championships.

A small article appeared in the January *Amateur Athlete* about the New York City Police Athletic League. It announced its formation, with 7,000 youngsters enrolled. The group joined the Metropolitan Association of the AAU.

A second article appeared in the March *Amateur Athlete* about the fourth Women's World Games in London in August. The Durant girl's basketball team expected to compete in the games, and some of their players planned to participate in the track and field events.

The February *Amateur Athlete* featured a lengthy story about Dee Boeckmann being appointed the first woman chairman of the women's basketball committee, a major national AAU sports committee.

The *New York Times* on August 12 stated that Anna Paluszek of Baldwin, Long Island, competed in the Polish Olympic Games in Warsaw. She won two first places, which aided the United States team to lead the other countries in the final point score. Stella Walsh was the only woman to beat Anna Paluszek in the number of first places. Anna won the shot with a put of 30' 2¼" and the broad jump in 16' 8¾".

Another small article in the *Amateur Athlete* in August indicated that Gertrude Webb would be the track representative of St. Louis and of the Western Association in the Women's World Games in London.

Chapter 18

1935

New York University's Ohio Field in the Bronx, New York, was the site of the national championship meet on September 14. The star of the meet was seventeen-year-old Helen Stephens, a tall, speedy farm girl from Fulton, Missouri. She raced to sensational victories in the 100- and 200-meter dashes, winning both with ease and setting a new world record of 11.6 in the 100 meters. Her time of 24.6 in the 200 meters was a half second off Stella Walsh's world record. Helen also placed second in the discus throw. She was easily the high point scorer of the meet. Dan Ferris, secretary of the AAU, commented that she was a potential Olympic champion.

The *New York Times* stated on September 15 that Helen "combines the speed of Stella Walsh with the field versatility of Babe Didrikson."

Several hundred people braved the chilling winds and threatening weather to see the three-hour championships. Only one defending champion retained her title — Louise Stokes of Malden, Massachusetts. She was just one tenth of a second off of her American record in the 50-meter dash. The other defending champions were less fortunate: Olive Hasenfus was beaten by Helen Stephens in the 200 meters, and Alice Arden was forced out of the high jump competition because of a sprained neck vertebra.

---

50 meters
1. Louise Stokes, Onteora Club, Mass.   6.7
2. Miriam Nelson, Boston Swimming Assn.
3. Charlotte Rafferty, Onteora Club
4. Pearl Edwards, Mercury A.C., N.Y.

100 meters
1. Helen Stephens, Fulton, Missouri, H. S.   11.6
2. May Brady, St. Louis A.C.
3. Harriet Bland, St. Louis A.C.
4. Josephine Warren, Boston Swimming Assn.

200 meters
1. Helen Stephens, Fulton H. S.   24.6
2. Olive Hasenfus, Boston Swimming Assn.
3. Marion Thompson, German-American A.C., N.Y.
4. Agnes Gerrity, St. George Dragon Club, Brooklyn

80-meter hurdles
1. Jean Hiller, St. George Dragon Club   13.0
2. Jane Santschi, St. Louis A.C.
3. Anna Lebo, Newark N.J. Women's A.C.
4. Evelyn Wright, News A.A., Paterson

400-meter relay
1. St. Louis A.C.   51.0
   (Bland, Santschi, Webb, Brady)
2. Boston Swimming Assn.
3. St. George Dragon Club
4. Mercury A.C.

High jump
1. Barbara Howe, Boston Swimming Assn.   4' 11"
2. Ruth Timmerman, St. George Dragon Club   4' 10"
3. Dorothy Davis, St. George Dragon Club,   4' 7"
   and Ruth Reilly, St. Louis A.C.

Broad jump
1. Etta Tate, unattached, N.Y.   16' 6"
2. Dorothy Ott, St. George Dragon Club   15' 10¾"
3. Sylvia Broman, Brockton Girls Club, Mass.   15' 9¾"
4. Margaret Wright, Brockton Girls Club   15' 6¾"

8-lb. Shot put
1. Rena MacDonald, Abington Alphas, Mass.   38' 3⅞"
2. Effy Storz, Newark, N.J.   34' 4¾"
3. Evelyn Ferrara, Lake Shore Park Club   34' 1"
4. Jane Hesslein, Boston Swimming Assn.   33' 3¾"

Discus
1. Margaret Wright, Brockton Girls Club   113' 9½"
2. Helen Stephens, Fulton H.S.   111' 6¾"
3. Evelyn Ferrara, Lake Shore Park Club   110' 7¾"
4. Rena MacDonald, Abington Alphas   103' 10⅝"

Javelin
1. Sylvia Broman, Brockton Girls Club   102' 7⅝"
2. Rose Auerbach, unattached, N.Y.   102' 6⅝"
3. Evelyn Ferrara, Lake Shore Park Club   97' 11⅞"
4. Sylvia Rothenberg, unattached, N.Y.   88' 6½"

Baseball throw
1. Carolyn Dieckman, unattached, N.J.   223' 6"
2. Josephine Sally, Boston Swimming Assn.   219' 10¾"
3. Beatrice Larson, St. George Dragon Club   210' 7¾"
4. Mildred Dugan, Eastern Women's A.C.   210' 5"

Team scores:
Boston Swimming Assn. 19; Dragon Club 17 ½; St. Louis A.C. 14 ½; Fulton, Missouri High School 13; Brockton Girls Club, Massachusetts 13.

The *Amateur Athlete* in October had a full-page photo of Helen Stephens winning the 100 meters in the national championships. She was the first female to grace the cover of the national magazine.

The May issue of the same magazine featured an article by Dee Boeckmann, chairman of the National AAU Women's Track and Field Committee. Would Helen Stephens become a member of the 1936 Olympic team? Did she really defeat Stella Walsh on March 22? Dee said she had been asked those questions a hundred times.

The Indoor Nationals

The indoor national meet was held on March 22 in the St. Louis Arena. Before a surprised crowd of 4,000, Helen Stephens burst onto the track scene in a big way by beating Stella Walsh in the 50 meters in 6.6. The *New York Times* featured headlines which read, "Miss Walsh Bows in 50-Meter Dash." Helen also won the shot put with a toss of 40' 11" and jumped 8' 8¼" to win the standing broad jump.

Three defending champions retained their title: Alice Arden in the high jump, Stella Walsh in the 200 meters and basketball throw, and the Laurel Ladies Club of Toronto in the 400-meter relay.

All of the premeet newspaper stories were about Stella Walsh's first appearance on a track in St. Louis. The possibility never occurred to anyone that Stella would be beaten. Apparently, W. B. Moore, Helen's coach at Fulton High School had told officials in advance of the meet that he had someone who was breaking the world broad jump record in practice. He didn't say anything about her sprinting. Even if he had, no one would have taken him seriously about his girl beating Stella, the 100-meter Olympic champion.

When Helen lined up at the start in the heats, not many people paid attention. Then came the final. Helen, wearing a blue gym suit, was out in front with the gun. Everyone kept watching, knowing that Stella would reel her in. But the tall girl in blue barreled to the tape a yard ahead of Stella on the clay track. Stella protested the start, claiming that Helen "broke," but her protest was not upheld.

As people congratulated Helen for beating Stella, the naive teenager said, "Who is Stella Walsh?"

The victory came after only two weeks of serious training. Helen was tall, strong, and wiry and had a powerful stride.

50-meter dash
1. Helen Stephens, Fulton H.S.   6.6 ties AR
2. Stella Walsh, Cleveland
3. Thelma Norton, Laurel Ladies A.C., Toronto
4. Olive Hinder, Laurel Ladies, A.C., Toronto
200-meter run
1. Stella Walsh, Cleveland   26.1
2. Mary Jane Santschi, St. Louis A.C.

3. Gertrude Webb, St. Louis A.C.
4. Mildred Holmberg, Brunswick, Missouri

400-meter relay
1. Laurel Ladies A.C., Toronto   56.8
    (Hinder, Atkins, Creamer, Norton)
2. Chicago Park District
3. German-American A.C.
4. St. Louis A.C.

50-meter hurdles
1. Evelyne Hall, Chicago Park District   8.1
2. Leora Johnson, Chicago Park District
3. Shirley Barrington, New York
4. Dolores Glenn, Chicago Park District

8-lb. shot put
1. Helen Stephens, Fulton H.S.   39' 7¼"
2. Evelyn Ferrara, Chicago Park District
3. Kathryn Ferrara, Chicago Park District
4. Helmut Story, Newark, N.J.

High jump
1. Alice Arden, Dragon Club   4' 11¾"
2. Helmut Story, Newark, N.J.
3. Catherine Maguire, St. Louis A.C.
4. Leora Johnson, Chicago Park District

Standing broad jump
1. Helen Stephens, Fulton H. S.   8' 8¼"
2. Effy Storz, Newark, N.J.
3. Nan Gindele, Chicago Park District
4. Alice Arden, Dragon Club

Basketball throw
1. Stella Walsh, Cleveland   96' 5⅓"
2. Nan Gindele, Chicago Park District
3. Evelyn Ferrara, Chicago Park District
4. Ruth Wucher, Missouri

Team scores:
Chicago Park District 25; Fulton Missouri High School 15; Toronto Laurel Ladies
A.C. 8; Newark Turn Verein 7; Brooklyn Dragon Club 6.

On May 4, Helen ran in a special race in connection with the Missouri State
Interscholastic Track Championships. She was timed in 5.9 seconds for 50 yards,
faster than the world record of 6.2, but officials did not think that the mark would
be recognized because she used starting blocks, which were taboo under both AAU
and Olympic rules. She ran the 100-yard dash in 10.8, which tied the world mark.
Helen commented that she would have done better if the weather had not been
so cold and rainy.

On May 11, Helen ran the 100 meters in 11.9, equaling the American record. Her 200-meter time was 24.5. She won the 50 meters in 6.3 and won the shot with a put of 36' 9". She placed second in the discus.

Helen Stephens ran the 220 yards in 23.9 on a straightaway track at Toronto on August 31.

The Ninth Annual Tuskegee Relays were held under a bright sun before 6000 fans on May 17 with these women's results:

50-meter dash	
1. Vesta Crayton, Tuskegee Institute	6.8
Running broad jump	
1. Mabel Smith, Booker Washington H.S.	17' MR
Shot put	
1. Florence Wright, Tuskegee Institute	
80-meter hurdles	
1. Cora Gaines, Tuskegee Institute	13.4
Discus throw	
1. Florence Wright, Tuskegee Institute	98' 11½" MR
High jump	
1. Mamie Harder, Booker Washington H.S.	4' 9"
100-meter run	
1. Gertrude Webb, Tuskegee Institute	13.0
Javelin throw	
1. Ruth Kidd, Tuscaloosa County H.S.	92' 10½"
Baseball throw	
1. Asie Smith, Russell County H.S.	224' 11" MR
440-yard relay	
1. Tuskegee Institute (Webb, Burns, Gibson, Crayton)	51.7 MR

Chapter 19

1936: The Berlin Olympic Year

The Olympic trials were held on July 4 in Providence, Rhode Island. Upon their completion the following women were the members of the 1936 Olympic team:

	Olympic Event	*Olympic Place*	*Olympic Performance*
Arden, Alice Jean	HJ	9	Tied — 4' 11"
Bland, Harriet C.	100m	DNQ	
	400mr	1	46.9
Burch, Betty L.	Javelin	12	98' 6⅜"
Ferrara, Evelyn L.	Discus	18	106' 8"
Hasenfus, Olive B.	400mr		Reserve
Kelly, Kathlyn	HJ	9	Tied — 4' 11"
O'Brien, Anne Vrana	80mh	DNQ	11.8
Pickett, Tidye Anne	80mh	DNQ	Fell in semis
Robinson, Elizabeth	400mr	1	46.9
Rogers, Annette Jean	HJ	6	Tied — 5' 1½₂"
	400mr	1	46.9
	100m	5	12.2
Schaller, Simone E.	80mh	DNQ	
Stephens, Helen H.	100m	1	11.5
	Discus	10	112' 7½"
	400mr	1	46.9
Stokes, Louise	400mr		Reserve
Warren, Josephine F.	400mr		Reserve
Wilhelmsen, Gertrude	Discus	9	112' 11½"
	Javelin	7	122' 6½"
Worst, Martha V.	Javelin	9	120' 4½"
Steers, Fred Lewellyn	Manager		
Boeckmann, Delores H.	Coach-Chaperone		
Dunnette, Katherine V.	Asst. Coach-Chaperone		

The Games of the XIth Olympiad took place from August 1 to August 16 in Berlin, Germany. The report of the American Olympic Committee written by Fred Steers, the manager of the team, reveals information about the trials and the Games.

Steers said that the performances in several events were not as good as in previous Olympic years. Complicating matters were the means by which funding for the team was handled. Gate receipts from meets were not enough to fund the team, and Steers indicated the resultant problems:

> A short time before sailing a mad scramble started. Contributions were made by towns, communities, clubs friends and relations of those who had qualified for the team, and in some cases very substantial sums were given by the athletes themselves. This caused complications, as certain persons felt they had a direct interest in individual athletes, athletes felt they had to force issues promoting themselves, because of such direct contributions and some of those who had helped finance themselves assumed an attitude of independence which was not of the best interest of the group. These conditions led to considerable embarrassment to the coach of our group, particularly in the selection of a relay team. No athlete should be permitted to finance himself, nor should anyone be permitted to earmark his contribution for any particular athlete or athletes.

Steers said that the facilities for training aboard ship during the trip were, "as good as the circumstances permitted." Two girls were seasick, however.

During the first ten days after the team's arrival in Berlin, the weather was cold and rainy. This made for difficulties in training even though the training facilities were excellent and close by. The track was located about two hundred yards from the team's living quarters.

Steers stated that the American women were much weaker in the field events than in previous Olympics. For the first time, we failed to place in any field event.

Steers concluded his report with two major recommendations: the first was that standards be established for each event and the second was that a representative should survey the site of the Games and report on housing, training facilities, food, water, and climate prior to the arrival of the team.

The track and field events began on August 2 and continued until August 9.

The Olympic Results

100 meters. Thirty-one competitors from fifteen countries took part in the women's 100-meter event.

In the heats, Harriet Bland finished fourth in the first heat and was eliminated. Helen Stephens won the second heat in 11.4. The world record time was not allowed because of the aiding wind, but it did earn her a front-page headline in the *New York Times* and a short write-up that called her performance "dazzling." Annette Rogers placed second in the fourth heat in 12.8 and moved into the semis.

Helen Stephens (second from right) 1936 Olympic 100-meter champion and world record holder winning the finals of the 100 meters in 1936 in Berlin, Germany. On far left is Stella Walsh, representing Poland, second. Annette Rogers, who placed fifth, is fourth from left. Helen's world and Olympic record time of 11.5 remained for twenty-four years as an Olympic record until broken by Wilma Rudolph in 1960. (Courtesy of Helen Stephens.)

Three qualified from the semis for the final. In the first semi, Helen won and established the new Olympic and world record of 11.5. Annette Rogers placed third in the second semi with a time of 12.1 and moved on to the final.

In the final, Helen again ran 11.5. The defending Olympic champion, Stanislawa Walasiewicz (Stella Walsh) representing Poland, was second in 11.7, two yards back. Annette Rogers was fifth. A German account of the race indicated that Helen left her competitors behind at the 50-meter mark and sprinted in a style which would be many a man's envy.

Fred Steers, the manager, cited Helen Stephens as the outstanding athlete, stating that her performance in the 100 meters defeated the former Olympic champion by a wide margin and in record time, making her the best sprinter "the world has ever known."

80-meter hurdles*.* In the 80-meter hurdles, the three American women made the semifinals. Tidye Pickett was third in 12.4 in the second heat, Mrs. Anne Vrana O'Brien was second in 12.0 in the third heat, and Simone Schaller won the fourth heat in 11.8. In the semifinal round, Anne Vrana O'Brien placed fourth in the first semi and was eliminated. In the second semi, Simone Schaller placed fourth, and Tidye Pickett fell. Both girls were eliminated from the final round.

"The United States was represented by three excellent hurdlers," commented Steers. Two of the girls were eliminated in the semifinals and the third, little Tidye Pickett, fell at the second hurdle and was out of the running. Simone Schaller was eliminated after the judges studied the photographs and reversed their decision, awarding the third-place qualifying position to another girl.

High jump. Although Jean Shiley held the world, Olympic, and American record in the high jump, the best that an American could do in a field of seventeen competitors was finish in a triple tie for sixth place. Annette Rogers jumped 5' 1½₂" for that place. Both Kathlyn Kelly of Seneca, South Carolina, and Alice Arden of New York City finished in a five-place tie for ninth with jumps of 4' 11".

Javelin. The javelin throw produced similar results. Nan Gindele held the world record of 153' 4½", which she set before the trials, but she missed making the team because she finished fourth in the trials with a poor throw of 118' 2½". The three U.S. entries in this event placed seventh, ninth, and twelfth out of fourteen competitors. Gertrude Wilhelmsen finished seventh with a throw of 122' 6½", Martha Worst placed ninth with a toss of 120' 4½", and Betty Burch threw 98' 6⅜" and finished twelfth.

Discus. Lillian Copeland's 1932 Olympic discus record was broken, but not by an American. The three U.S. girls were not in the top three this time. Mrs. Gertrude Wilhelmsen was ninth with a throw of 112' 11½", Helen Stephens placed tenth with a toss of 112' 7½", and Evelyn Ferrara did not qualify for the final in the eighteen-woman group of competitors.

400-meter relay. The 400-meter relay produced unexpected results. The American team of Harriet Bland, Annette Rogers, Elizabeth Robinson, and Helen Stephens easily won the first heat in 47.1. The second heat was won by the German team in the world record time of 46.4. In the final, the German team had about a ten-yard lead at the fourth exchange. It appeared that the Americans would place second, even though Helen Stephens was running the anchor leg for the United States team. After the exchange, the anchor leg for the German team dropped the baton (the *New York Times* called the team "stage-struck" because they were awed by the presence of Hitler). Helen zoomed into first and finished eight yards ahead of the British team. The winning time was 46.9. The *New York Times* on August 10 said, "Stephens, the wonder runner from Missouri who probably could have won anyway for the United States, was able to take things a bit more easily."

"In the relay," Fred Steers said, "the German team had a lead at the finish of the third leg when they dropped their baton. However, judging from her race in the final of the one hundred meters, Miss Stephens could have overcome the lead easily had the German girls not met with this misfortune."

On August 10, the *New York Times* reported:

> The women's relay was a huge disappointment for the German crowd. The Reich's standard-bearers were at the head of the procession all the way and the spectators were going wild with joy when Marie Dollinger zoomed up to Ilse Doerffeldt eight yards ahead of Betty Robinson. To the Germans the champi-

onship already was won. They split the air with their cheers and then suddenly there was an awkward and embarrassing silence. One girl had dropped her baton and instead of a medal Germany got nothing at all from the race.

The chances were that the Reich would not have triumphed anyway. Miss Doerffeldt could not have beaten Miss Stephens even with an eight-yard lift in the getaway.

The National Championships and Olympic Trials

The national championships served as the final Olympic trials. They were held on July 4 at Brown University Stadium, Providence, Rhode Island, before a crowd of 4000 under perfect weather conditions.

The *Providence Journal* quoted Dee Boeckmann, the coach of the team:

> The track and field are very fast, both are in A-1 condition and I expect a number of new American records.
>
> We have the fastest field of women athletes ever to grace our women's championship. Indeed, I term this group the fastest field of women track stars ever assembled anywhere....
>
> The group that qualifies for the Olympic team, which is the first three finishers in the six Olympic events, and the extras for the 400 meter relay team, picked from the showing in the 100 meter dash, will go with me to New York Sunday afternoon. We'll remain at the Lincoln Hotel until time to sail on July 15th, along with the other members of the Olympic team not already in Europe.

Boeckmann stated that athletes from sixteen states were represented in the trials: Washington, Massachusetts, California, Alabama, Utah, New York, Illinois, New Jersey, Ohio, Missouri, Indiana, Mississippi, Pennsylvania, Rhode Island, Oklahoma, and Oregon.

Prior to the competition, the athletes were taken on a tour of the State House in Providence. About seventy-three of them were received by Governor Theodore Francis Green in the State Reception Room. According to the *Providence Journal*: "Governor Green greeted the visiting athletes and urged them 'to uphold American ideals of democracy and freedom, not apologetically but proudly,' when they go to Berlin this summer."

The governor reminded them: "Some of you are going to a country where the principles of political equality and religious liberty established here in Rhode Island by Roger Williams are denied. ... But, stand up for your American ideals there ... proudly."

The *New York Times* headlines read "World Record Set by Miss Stephens," and the article detailed her success:

> Miss Helen Stephens, the Fulton (Mo.) farm girl who is rapidly becoming a second Babe Didrikson in women's track and field circles, continued her habit of winning three events in the national championships on Brown University Field today. And in doing so she became our Olympic hope in two of these events, the 100 meter dash and the discus throw.
>
> By equalling the world record of 11.8 in her semi-final heat and then taking the final in 11.7 without being extended, Miss Stephens gave warning to Miss

Stella Walsh of Poland and Miss Kaethe Krauss of Germany that the United States will be ready for an Olympic victory in Berlin.

Miss Stephens loped to the tape a good three yards in front of Annette Rogers of the Illinois Catholic Women's Club of Chicago and five yards ahead of Miss Harriet Bland of the St. Louis Athletic Club. And the tall, long-striding Missourian gave the definite impression that she could unleash far greater speed if pressed.

Miss Stephens walked from the cinder track to the discus enclosure and with hardly a pause for breath won the final with a toss of 121 feet 6 1/2 inches.

Helen did not defend her title in the 200 meters.

The Providence Sunday Journal reported that the tall, eighteen-year-old Helen qualified in three of the six Olympic events and also won the national shot put title.

Anne O'Brien, married six years and the mother of a child, was a member of the 1928 Olympic team. Her comeback after eight years in winning the 80-meter hurdles was an outstanding achievement.

Little Tidye Pickett hit the seventh hurdle in the trials and severely bruised her ankle. Her second-place finish in the final was brilliant considering the ankle injury. Her coach was John Brooks of the University of Chicago.

---

100 meters (first three to qualify for team)
1. Helen Stephens, William Woods College   11.7
2. Annette J. Rogers, Illinois Catholic Women's Club
3. Harriet C. Bland, St. Louis A.C.
4. Olive Hasenfus, Boston Swimming Assn.

80-meter hurdles
1. Anne Vrana O'Brien, Los Angeles   12.0
2. Tidye A. Pickett, Chicago Park District
3. Simone E. Schaller, Los Angeles
4. Evelyne Hall, Chicago Park District

Running high jump
1. Annette J. Rogers, Illinois Catholic Women's Club   5' 2½"
2. Alice J. Arden, St. George's Dragon Club, Brooklyn 5' 1½"
3. Kathlyn Kelly, Keowee High School, S.C.   5' ½"
   Ida Myers, Chicago Park District
   (Miss Kelly won jump-off for third place at 5' 1½")

Discus throw
1. Helen Stephens, William Woods College   121' 6½"
2. Gertrude Wilhelmsen, Washington A. C., Seattle   116' 9"
3. Evelyn L. Ferrara, Chicago Park District   116' 1¾"
4. Margaret Wright, unattached, Brockton, Mass.   113' 8¾"

Javelin throw
1. Martha V. Worst, Metro Social and A. A., Calif.   125' ¼"
2. Betty L. Burch, Boston Swimming Assn.   119' 7½"
3. Gertrude Wilhelmsen, Washington Athletic Club   119' 3"
4. Nan Gindele, Chicago Park District   118' 2½"

[Non-Olympic events contested]

50-meter dash
1. Ivy Wilson, Mercury A.C.   6.7
2. Genevieve Brick, Illinois Catholic Women's Club
3. Marguerite Jones, Salt Lake City, Utah

200-meter dash
1. Beverly Hobbs, Greenwood, Miss.   26.6
2. Cora Gaines, Tuskegee Institute
3. Marion Thompson, German-American A.C., N.Y.

400-meter relay
1. Illinois Catholic Women's Club   48.0
    (Robinson, Harrington, Terwilliger, Rogers)
2. Boston Swimming Assn.
3. Tuskegee Institute

Broad jump
1. Mabel B. Smith, Tuskegee Institute   18'
2. Etta Tate, Mercury A.C.   17' 5¼"
3. Sylvia Broman, Brockton, Mass.   17'

Baseball throw
1. Josephine Lally, Boston Swim Assn.   237' 3"
2. Catherine Fellmeth, Illinois Catholic Women's Club   224' 8"
3. Betty Burch, Boston Swim Assn.   218' 3½"

8-lb. shot
1. Helen Stephens, Fulton, Missouri   41' 8½"
2. Florence Wright, Tuskeegee Institute   39'
3. Catherine Fellmeth, Illinois Catholic Women's Club   36' 11¼"

Team scores:
Illinois Catholic Women's Club 22½; Boston Swimming Association 15½.

The Indoor Nationals

In her report to the AAU at the convention in Houston, Texas, national track and field chairman Dee Boeckmann stated that the indoor championship meet was held on February 12 in St. Louis, Missouri, in the Arena under the auspices of the St. Louis Athletic Club. A large entry participated, and all of the national champions were there to defend their titles. Because of an ice storm at about 6 P.M. that evening, the crowd was small, however.

The Southern Association had its first athlete in a national indoor meet — Sally Core, a high school student from Covington, Louisiana.

Premeet publicity in the *St. Louis Post-Dispatch* headlined, "Helen Stephens Hopes to Break Two Records Tonight." Burton Moore, her coach, predicted that the 50-meter dash and shot put marks would be broken.

The newspaper noted:

It was at last year's National Indoor meet here that the unheralded girl now known as the "Flash from Fulton" made her debut in a sanctioned meet. Only her coach, Burton Moore of Fulton, predicted bright things for her, but his prophecy was as a voice crying in the wilderness. Nobody paid any attention, and all were totally unprepared for the shock when Miss Stephens defeated the great Stella Walsh of Poland at 50 meters for the national title at that distance. To round out a perfect evening she also won national championships in the standing broad jump and the eight pound shot put. ... Has she improved? Will she break some records? These and other questions were put to Moore by the *Post-Dispatch* in a telegram to him at Fulton yesterday. His answer, in part, and perhaps somebody will listen this time.

"I believe Helen will better her record of 6.6 seconds in the 50 meters by two-tenths of a second if the track is good. She will also better her shot put mark of 39' 7¼" by two or three feet. She shouldn't have any trouble winning the broad jump at 8' 6". I kept her out of the 200 meters because she is recovering from a very severe cold and I do not wish to tax her strength."

Before a crowd of 1000, Burton Moore's prediction was validated when eighteen-year-old Helen Stephens, a freshman at William Woods College, ran a new American indoor record in the 50-meter dash. Her time of 6.4 was exactly the time that he stated she would run, and a nine-foot gap separated her from the second-place runner at the tape. As Moore had calculated, Stephens broke the shot put record with a put of 41' 7" and won the standing broad jump with a leap of 8' 8".

For the third year in a row, the Chicago Park District won the team title.

---

50 meters
1. Helen Stephens, William Woods College   6.4 ties WR
2. Harriet Bland, St. Louis A.C.
3. Mae Brady, St. Louis A.C.

200 meters
1. Annette Rogers, Illinois Catholic Women's Club   27.9
2. Hilda Cameron, Toronto, Laurel Ladies A.C.
3. Jane Santschi, St. Louis A.C.

50-meter hurdles
1. Tidye Pickett, Chicago Park District   7.9
2. Roxy Atkins, Toronto, Laurel Ladies A.C.
3. Evelyne Hall, Chicago Park District

400-meter relay
1. St. Louis A.C.   53.3
   (Bland, Crain, Gustavson, Brady)
2. Toronto, Laurel Ladies A.C.
3. Illinois Catholic Women's Club

High jump
1. Ida Myers, Illinois Catholic Women's Club   5' 1¼"
   and Annette Rogers, Illinois Catholic Women's Club
3. Loretta Murphy, St. Louis A.C.   5'
   and Eula Fortune, Toronto, Laurel Ladies A.C.

Standing broad jump
1. Helen Stephens, William Woods College   8' 8"
2. Nan Gindele, Chicago Park District
3. Anne Vucich, St. Louis A.C.

8-lb. shot
1. Helen Stephens, William Woods College   41' 7"
2. Katherine Ferrara, Chicago Park District
3. Catherine Fellmeth, Illinois Catholic Women's Club

Basketball throw
1. Nan Gindele, Chicago Park District   94' 4¾"
2. Evelyn Ferrara, Chicago Park District   91' 6¾"
3. Marilon Garrison, Wood River High, Ill.   88' 6¾"

Team scores:
Chicago Park District 22; Illinois Catholic Women's Club 18; St. Louis A.C. 17;
William Woods College 15.

In January, an article by Charlotte Epstein, chairman of the AAU Women's
Sports Committee, reported discussions from the committee meeting at the AAU
convention and noted:

> A survey of the country showed that Track and Field for women, in most sec-
> tions of the country has not only failed to progress as it should, but in several
> districts, formerly active, has practically ceased to exist. The general feeling of
> the meeting was that if the A.A.U. District Associations would appoint on their
> several Women's Track and Field Committees, people with sufficient time and
> interest to push this sport, it could and would be elevated to the high plane which
> it should occupy in the field of sport.

The "Women's Sport Committee Report" at the AAU convention related
answers in response to the following question regarding Olympic participation:
"Do you think the women's track and field program should be increased in number of events. If so, what new events would you suggest?" One member suggested
that archery and more relays be added to the program, and a second recommended the 8-lb. shot, the running broad jump, and the 200-meter run be
included.

The 1936 AAU *Handbook* lists an extensive women's track and field committee. The chairman of the committee was Delores Boeckmann, representing
the Ozark region. The vice chairmen were Racine Thompson of the Central
region, Jean Shiley Reps of the Middle Atlantic area, and Irene Sand of the Pacific
region. The committee had twenty-six members representing the following regions
of the country: Adirondack, Allegheny Mountain, Atlantic Seaboard, Central,
Connecticut, Gulf, Indiana-Kentucky, Inter-Mountain, Metropolitan, Michigan, Midwestern, Minnesota, Missouri Valley, New England, New Jersey, Niagara, Northeastern Ohio, Ohio, Oregon, South Atlantic, Southern Pacific, and
Wisconsin. Seventeen of the members were women.

The Women's Division of the NAAF in a June *Newsletter* reported on the
states. Tennessee, California, Texas, Maine, Indiana, Rhode Island, Alabama,

Wisconsin, Nebraska, and Pennsylvania informed of play days followed by social interludes with milk and graham crackers — softball, tennis, archery, volleyball, bowling, paddle tennis, gymnastics, swimming, basketball, hockey, and dancing were listed, but track activities in the schools was extinct.

Harriet Bland Green

"The Forgotten Champion" was published in the *St. Louis Globe-Democrat* in 1978. The author, Robert L. Burnes, states that Harriet's Olympic team members from 1936 have been remembered and honored, but Annette Kelly and Harriet Bland, the other members of the gold medal 400-meter relay team, have been forgotten. It was Harriet's dream to have the entire relay team named to the National Track and Field Hall of Fame. Her close friend and 1936 relay team anchor, Helen Stephens, agreed.

In one of her first races, red-headed and freckled Harriet ran 12.1 seconds for the 100 meters.

Harriet retired from track in 1938, when she married. She believed that she had achieved her goal of making an Olympic team and winning a gold medal. According to Burnes,

> Her track career was brief and Harriet herself is not quite sure how it all started. "The only thing I can remember is that as a teenager at Mary Institute, I enjoyed running. ... I could run fast, I knew that. I won every race I was in."
>
> She tried out for the 1932 Olympic team at the age of 17. ... She thought she had qualified. ... No one told Harriet why she didn't make the team after apparently having qualified. There was talk of "politics" and she was bitterly disappointed. But she was determined to make it four years later.
>
> Harriet joined the Ozark A.A.U. women's track squad. ... The Bland family employed Dee Boeckmann to give special attention and training to Harriet.
>
> In addition to this, Harriet remembers working out on her own a lot. "We lived on Washington Avenue just west of Kingshighway and I can remember walking to Sherman Park and just running on my own. I ran and ran, all by myself, until I was so exhausted that I barely had enough strength to crawl home."
>
> Making the team was one thing. Making it to Berlin was something else and suddenly there was a new crisis. Each competitor was responsible for his or her own expenses. If Harriet Bland couldn't come up with $500, as good as she was, she couldn't make the trip.
>
> Her plight became known to *The Globe-Democrat* which took it upon itself to raise the funds, starting with a $100. contribution of its own.
>
> (This writer remembers as a cub reporter he was assigned to go to the Bland home and break the good news on a warm evening in June. Neighbors and friends sat on the front porch and celebrated with cake and conversation.)
>
> "It was a wonderful trip," said Harriet Bland Green. "The relay itself was exciting. I had been sick the week before but finally regained my strength and was the lead off runner. I could always break fast and I had the lead when I handed the baton to Annette Kelly. ... It still has to be, I think, the greatest thrill of my life."...

During her stay in Berlin, Harriet made friends with many German children and corresponded with them ever since. There was a triumphant journey home, civic ceremonies in St. Louis for Dee, Helen and Harriet and then two years later, when she married, Harriet Bland put all track competition behind her. When she returned from the Olympic games she was appointed the first director of the St. Louis playgrounds.

Harriet Bland Green graduated from Washington University and spent twenty years as an interior designer.

Harriet died at the age of 77 on November 6, 1991, in Ft. Worth, Texas.

W. Burton Moore

Burton Moore was the person who "discovered" and coached Helen Stephens.

He graduated from Westminster College and became a coach and teacher in the Pleasant Hill, Missouri, high school. He wrote in a letter dated November 15, 1991:

I was the boys coach, but there was no girls coach so I coached both the boys' and the girls' teams.

The only other female coaching experience I had was at Fulton, Missouri High School, and I stumbled onto Helen, who was a student there. Since I was the coach, and had a stopwatch, I was putting a group of girls through some physical tests. I had noticed Helen's great athletic ability and speed in ordinary physical education activities. So, I was anxious to time her in the 50 yard dash, which was one of the tests the girls were working on to win a state badge or medal.

Helen was in a group of twelve to fourteen girls. She didn't know that I was especially interested in her time for 50 yards and how it would compare with national or world records. I didn't want to put any undue pressure on a young high school sophomore. She had never had any coaching or competitive experience in running form or practice. When she ran, starting from a standing start, she tied the world record for women, 5.8 seconds.

It quickly ran through my mind to not mention world records or anything that might be pre-mature. So I lied to her and told her that her time was 6.2, which was better than anyone else anyway. A year or two later, when I talked to Helen about trying actual competition, I told her that I lied to her in the Badge Test and that was the first time that she knew that she had unofficially tied the world record.

When this story is repeated several times, usually somebody along the line lets their imagination get the best of them, and they say things that are not true. I'm referring especially to the statement that I had Helen run the 50 yards a second time and that I took my watch to the jeweler to have it checked for accuracy. Neither of those statements are true. The only person I told the truth about Helen's time was my wife after I got home. She and I were the only persons who knew that Helen was probably one of the fastest runners in the world.

We kept the secret until about two years later when we decided to take Helen to the AAU meet in St. Louis, if she were willing. She readily agreed to practice and compete and the road to the 1936 Olympics began.

I coached Helen up to and including the Olympic tryouts. As she practiced running at various speeds, jogging, half speed, sprinting, etc., I had her run slightly pigeon-toed. I wanted her to toe in slightly so that her feet were not pointed out. This made it more likely that she would push off of all five toes instead of just the big toe. Even world class runners, not all, but many of them, plant their foot down with each step slightly turned out. This promotes lost motion because movement is side wise with each step rather than straight ahead. My college track coach, Brutus Hamilton, taught us that technique, and I'm sure it helped me in my coaching. Brutus Hamilton, also in the Track and Field Hall of Fame, was on the United States Olympic teams of 1920 and 1924 and after coaching at a small college, Westminster, he coached at Kansas University, where he coached Glenn Cunningham. From Kansas University he went to the University of California where he coached until he retired. He was the head United States Olympic track and field coach in 1952 in Helsinki. He was an assistant men's coach for the United States in 1936 at Berlin when Helen was the women's star.

When they returned from Berlin, they had a ticker-tape parade in New York. Jesse Owens rode in the lead convertible, and Helen rode in the second convertible.

It would be difficult to determine how much impact they had on women's athletics in America and also the world, but the performances of such big stars as Babe Didrikson and Helen surely had some influence on women's participation.

Helen Stephens

In a conversation on October 24, 1991, Helen related to me some of her history:

> I was born in Fulton, Missouri on February third, nineteen and eighteen. I began competing in nineteen thirty-five and competed until nineteen thirty-seven, totaling two and one half years of amateur competition. When I first started out, in nineteen thirty-five, I represented Fulton High School. I was a senior in high school. Then I competed for the Fulton Athletic Club and then William Woods College.
>
> I was fifteen when I started running. It was an accident. My coach was holding a tryout for high school girls to run fifty yards to qualify for a Missouri State letter. The qualifications were that you had to run it in seven seconds. Which to me, is pretty fast. I ran it in five point eight seconds, which equaled the world record for the fifty, the time held by Betty Robinson of Chicago, who was on the nineteen twenty-eight team. She won the first gold medal in Amsterdam and became my roommate in nineteen thirty-six. She was a good friend, and we still are friends. I didn't have any track in elementary school. I just ran against all the boys and beat them. I lived on a farm. When I ran the five point eight seconds, Coach Moore didn't believe it. What he had was a tiger by the tail, and he didn't know what to do with it at that time. Then, in a couple years, we knew the Olympics were coming up. That's when he entered me in this meet in St. Louis over opposition of the school official, who said "You'll just go down there and make a fool out of yourself." We came down to St. Louis, a hundred miles away, and came back the next day with three gold medals. I had set an indoor record for the fifty meters and beat Stella Walsh.
>
> I wouldn't have amounted to anything if it hadn't been for Mr. Moore. I would have been the proverbial diamond that went down the drain. He had a

winner, and all he had to do was to get me on the track. I was lucky that he took an interest in me. He gave me lots of advice. He coached me right up to when I got on the boat. Our coach in the Olympics was Dee Boeckmann. She was from St. Louis. Long before I got on the team, she and I became great friends and kept our friendship up through the years. She just died the year before last here in St. Louis in a nursing home. She was the first woman coach of an Olympic team.

I competed in the shot put, discus, broad jump, the fifty meters, the one hundred meters and the two hundred meters. I was a one-woman team representing Fulton High School and William Woods College. My coach was a gentleman named W. Burton Moore, who lives in Ames, Iowa, and is in his eighties. I got a letter from him yesterday. Mr. Moore was head of athletics. He coached the boys, taught girls physical education, and coached football. As for the discus, Mr. Moore may have bought me a discus when I was fifteen. I played with it on the farm. Then when I got a chance to enter something, two years later, I entered the shot put, standing broad jump, and the fifty meters. From then on I competed in both the shot and discus. Of all the events, I liked running the best. I always wanted to throw the javelin. I've taken that up as a senior. In the Olympic Games, I couldn't have won, but I thought I could have gotten a bronze medal. I had thrown about one hundred twenty-seven feet. It wasn't my day, but my mind was on the run anyway. The final of the one hundred meters was on the same day as the discus, August fourth, nineteen thirty-six.

I competed in National Championships in nineteen thirty-five, nineteen thirty-six, and nineteen thirty-seven. We had indoor and outdoor championships. My first competition was indoors and against Stella Walsh. I was seventeen years old. I ran against her five times in the fifty meters, one hundred meters, and two hundred meters and beat her in all five races. She never forgot me. I have fourteen national championship medals.

I ran a lot of exhibition races at boys' track meets. I went to Canada a couple of times to compete indoors and at the Canadian National Exhibition. I competed around here in Missouri, in Kansas City, and in New Orleans in the Sugar Bowl Games. In the exhibition meets, sometimes the races were handicapped, I'd give them forty-five yards. The races didn't count, even though you set a world record.

In nineteen thirty-six, the qualifications were held in St. Louis, and the final tryouts were in July in Providence, Rhode Island.

I'm in about seven or eight Hall's of Fame. These Halls of Fame are a state of mind. They always do this stuff with a great flurry but then in a few years something happens, and some of then end up in boxes. The St. Louis Sports Hall of Fame wound up in boxes.

I used the track at Westminster College in Fulton for training. It was the only track in town. We didn't even have a gym, let alone a track. I ran against the Westminster College boys, and I ran against the high school boys in training. They all claim that I beat them, but I don't know. I trained at least three times a week. The only other sports that they had in that town was church-sponsored basketball. I was the star on the Methodist church basketball team.

I never followed any special diet. They often told me to and I was supposed to, but I never believed too much in that. My coach tried to keep me on toast and tea and that stuff. I had to eat what I had.

My mother and father came to a couple of meets. I took my mother to Canada once. They were supportive after I started. They were a little suspicious at first, but they let me do my thing. My brother always felt that he was in my shadow. He went to a different high school than I did. He was a pretty good basketball player. Because of the age difference, I was gone before he got into it. He's a good bowler and a good golfer.

In my active days, the only injury that I had when I was an amateur was when we went on board ship to the Olympics in Germany. They had us working out on the deck, running, jogging, and they didn't have the cushioned shoes that they have today. I developed a bad case of shin splints. When I got in to Berlin, I could hardly walk, let alone run. After about a week of therapy by a German masseuse, I was running like a colt by the time the Olympics came around. I ran eleven point five in the one hundred meters, which was an Olympic and world record. It stood for twenty-four years until Wilma Rudolph wiped it out.

After the 100-meter final, I was interviewed by CBS for a broadcast being heard in America. In the meantime, a messenger from Hitler came and said that Hitler wanted to meet me and he wanted to take me

Helen Stephens, 1936 Olympic champion, 100 meters, winning a heat of the 100 meters in Berlin, Germany. (Courtesy of Helen Stephens.)

to his box. We postponed him, and he picked me up after we got out of the broadcast. The station was on the top of the stadium. We (Dee Boeckmann, the coach) started down to the room and that's when the blackshirts came in. They checked the room over, and then Hitler, with an interpreter, came in. He gave me a "Nazi" salute. I didn't return it. I just gave him a good old Missouri handshake. And I put a squeeze on it, and I think he must have misinterpreted it because immediately he began to pat my fanny and feel my leg. He wanted to know if I wouldn't want to go with him for the weekend to his hide-a-way in the mountains. Dee told him I was in training and you were too, running your country. He nodded his head and winked at me. I was getting his autograph then, and that's when the photographer came out of nowhere and snapped our picture. The guard seized him, shook him and kicked him, and threw him out, camera after him. Hitler had jumped up and down and slapped him with his gloves. Oh boy, then the next day that photograph appeared on a postcard. Only Hitler and the storm troopers, the interpreter, the little photographer, and us two chickens were in the room. I was there about ten minutes. He asked me what I thought of the Games, what I thought of Germany. I told him it looks good. He liked that. He said, well, you should be running for Germany. You're a true Aryan type, tall, blonde, blue eyes. You should be running for Germany. I was six feet tall and about one hundred sixty-five pounds. I was all bone and muscle. Didn't carry any fat on me. Hitler came to the stadium every day. You could set your watch by him. He was visible. I was at the swimming pool one day, and he was over there. Some woman ran up and kissed him and threw her arms around him. I don't have any regrets. I'm glad I met him. The first event on the program was won by a German. He had him up to his box, he got up and kissed him on both cheeks and gave him an iron cross and all that stuff. It disrupted the Olympic program. So, the officials asked the Germans to ask him not to do that anymore, that he was just a guest in that stadium. He didn't meet her publicly but I think he did drive around one night with that Eva Braun. ... I think Eleanor Holm met him ... but no other track women except the Germans, of course. He had them up there consoling them after they lost that relay.

They were leading by about eight yards. The girl that was running the last leg was the slowest. They had thought that I was going to lead off. When they said, on your mark, I ran down and took that last leg and they were in utter confusion. Oh, there are those who thought I could have won it anyway. I don't know. I had a nine-foot stride. That's a pretty good stride, you know. I saw it happen out of the corner of my eye. I knew it was happening. As the teams came around, I figured I was going to have to run for my money. Our baton passes were good. You see, that happens quite often where they screw up on the baton pass. In Germany, we worked out with me starting it off. The Germans watched, and they thought I was going to run first. I didn't have any idea of running first. We did it to fool them. Dee outfoxed them. Annette was pretty fast. She got into that 100-meter run. Here's what the 1936 Olympic book says: "In the final the German team had a ten yard lead going into the home stretch and it appeared that the American team would have to be content with second place. The last exchange proved disastrous for the German team, however, when Miss Doerffeldt dropped the baton causing disqualification. ... Miss Helen Stephens, the Olympic 100 meter champion, ran the final leg for the United States and won by 8 yards over the British team. The winning time of 46.9, though a half of a second slower than the world's record, established by Germany in the qualifying heat, bettered the previous Olympic record by a tenth of a second." The Germans were favored in the relay. They thought they were going to get it. They counted their chickens.

There were one hundred ten thousand people in the stadium almost every day. Sold out. That was the first time that they used electronic timing. The people in Germany could not get tickets to see a lot of the events. They had television downtown in one of the big theaters for the German people. Did you know that? Or they were filming it and running it down like the news, or something.

They gave us a crown of olive leaves, that's something they cut out. No one took a victory lap. Back in those days, that was showing off, and it was frowned on. We were subdued. Now, if I had run around the track, I'd probably got a lot of cheers, true. But, I'd probably have gotten reprimanded like heck. And they'd give me a good verbal spanking.

I arrived home in September. We came back to New York, and we had a whole week on the town. We could do anything we wanted and go anywhere we pleased. It was just the city of New York. Then we went up to Canada. Then Dee and I went down to Washington for a track meet that the Department of Agriculture was behind. Babe Didrikson came to see me and J. Edgar Hoover. From there, Dee and I drove, in her car that she had in New York the whole time, to St. Louis. They gave us a victory parade, and then I went down to my hometown and had a big celebration at the college. They paraded me through town. Coming back was the hardest because you've been in another world. I was in demand, and they'd call me. I continued then until the spring of nineteen thirty-seven. I competed in the National AAU indoor championships and won three more medals. And that was the end of my medals because the last race I ran was in August of nineteen thirty-seven, when I went to Chicago on Irish-American day and ran a fifty or one hundred and that was my last race as an amateur.

In nineteen thirty-six, there were a lot of rumors that Hitler was mistreating the Jews. It did turn out that there was supposed to be a Jewish girl on the German Olympic team. They sent her to the country so she wouldn't be around any reporters. She later came to this country and became a doctor. She's told her story a number of times, but I don't remember her name. But she also was aware of the fact that the Germans had a man on their team. She was a high jumper. She/he didn't win a medal. It wasn't known at that time, but the woman that I was telling you about who they wouldn't let on the team, she was aware of this guy, masquerading as a woman. She had roomed with him on some of the trips with the German track team, so she knew firsthand. Anyway, their scheme didn't work. I can get you the name if you have time to listen. I have to go downstairs. O.K., his name, her name was Dora Ratjen, placed fourth. Now, after the war, she, I don't know whether she was involved in a sex change operation or not, possibly not. But she went to Holland, got married, and had several kids. And became a Dutch citizen. That's what happened.

As for the two hundred meters, the girl who won the two hundred from Holland in nineteen forty-eight, Fanny Blankers-Koen, she competed in Berlin and didn't even get in the finals. She was the same age I was. Twelve years later, married and a couple of kids, boy she got heavy. I could have beaten her in forty-eight based on her times. But, of course, in the meantime, I did the cardinal no-no. I took a few dollars. In nineteen thirty-seven, in about August, there were a lot of pressures on me. I had come to St. Louis, and my Olympic coach had gotten me a job with a company that sponsored a world champion softball team. I played a few games with them. There was a lot of pressure on me to turn pro and "see if you can make some money." So I turned pro with a fellow out of Chicago. I guess I didn't give him time enough to get a lot of things jelled because I took a job with that All-American Redhead Team. They were paying me pretty good. Actually, when I announced I was pro, I hadn't even received a dime. I announced I was pro, and they wrote my obituary. I had let the country down. I let everybody down. But I needed the money. My folks needed money. We were in the process of buying a farm. They had lost the farm. Hard times. They were renting one and they had a chance to buy it and they didn't have the money. I was able to get the money. That sort of thing. It was a great investment. Back in those days, they were so damned persnickety about that pro business. Look what they did to Thorpe over a nine-dollar baseball game. Today they're putting those millionaires in there which I think is wrong. I don't think it's right. I think they should reserve that for the young kids coming up, the college kids. Hey, these professionals already have it made. And that goes for all sports.

I majored in "running" in college. That's what I always tell 'em. I entered there on a scholarship because of running. My grades were good at that time in high school. I was a one-woman track team in the all-girl's college. The understanding was that Mr. Moore would oversee me. They formed an athletic club in Fulton to defray my expenses. There was no competition in those days in college. In nineteen seventy-six, after I retired from the government, I went back to the college and worked with the track team. I spent four years with them. Then when the new president came in, they eliminated track because they did not have enough bodies to go around for spring sports.

I also helped with the AAU program in St. Louis. I had my own basketball team that I coached and managed too. After the Olympics, I toured the country with the All-American Redheads. They played all over the country. Then another girl and I started our own team. We ran that team from nineteen thirty-eight to nineteen forty-one. Then I came back to St. Louis and dropped out of basketball. When the war years came along, I changed companies I was working for. The aircraft plant had girls' basketball and softball, and I got involved in that. We were city champs. Then in nineteen forty-five, the war ended, and that fall I came back to St. Louis and started up my old coeds again and kept them going until nineteen fifty-two. All the girls had jobs. We played on weekends, Sundays — one year we played eighty games. The teams were men's town teams mainly. They wouldn't draw flies, girls playing girls. We beat a lot of the teams. A lot of them still remember it. And I'd run the fastest man across the floor, twenty yards. And tossed the shot put onto floor mats. Many a superintendent or high school principal, or whoever was in charge of the gym, was just about to have a heart attack. But I hit it most of the time. It was padded, it didn't go through the floor. We did this at half time.

I worked for the federal government from nineteen forty-five until nineteen seventy-six. I wound up as a librarian in a technical library for twenty-six years. The space center does all the mapping for the branches of the service. They were very active in the Persian Gulf thing. They know every sand dune in Saudi Arabia.

I went to the Montreal Olympics. I watch football and basketball on TV now. I was with those Chicago Bulls last year. They went all the way. But I kind of jump around a lot. A lot of those basketball players were former track people and football players too. A lot of the baseball players were former track people. Of course, in baseball, I watch the St. Louis Cardinals. I kinda watch Denver football and follow them.

I kept in touch with Betty Robinson and Annette Rogers. Of course, Harriet Bland lived here, but she's in Texas living with her son. She's in bad health.

A lady friend of mine came this week, and we packed trophies. I'm in the process of getting them up to my school. We got several boxes full. They gave trophies and medals as awards. Sometimes they promised medals, and they never gave them to us. They gave nice prizes in Canada, and they gave nice prizes in Germany. There were two post–Olympic meets in Germany. I was invited to go to a lot of places, but they only wanted me. They did not want the team. So they wouldn't let me go by myself. I was invited to London, Norway, and some of the European countries. Boy, I would've liked that. But that was one of those trips that Jesse Owens made, and they took his amateur status away from him. Although later they gave him every honor that they could give him through the years. But, anyway those were difficult times.

Helen Stephens, the 1936 Olympic champion and world record holder in the 100 meters, died on January 17, 1994.

Chapter 20

1937

September 25, 1937, was the date of the women's national outdoor championships. The meet was held in Trenton, New Jersey, at the Trenton Central High School Field. One thousand fans witnessed the events sponsored by the *Trenton Times* Athletic Association.

While the greatest number of athletes came from the Metropolitan Association, Tuskegee Institute, Alabama, fielded the second largest delegation.

The headlines in the *Trenton Sunday Times-Advertiser* read, "Tuskegee Takes Women's Track Championship." Their team score was more than double that of each of the two teams which tied for second. Tuskegee scored points in ten of the eleven events and won the championship title for the first time. The newspaper stated that the Tuskegee team of seven girls was a well-balanced squad.

George Vreeland, chairman of the national women's track and field committee, reported in the *Amateur Athlete* in November that the stars of the meet were sixteen-year-old Claire Isicson, unattached, of Brooklyn, and Margaret Bergmann. Isicson, a senior in high school, won the 50 and 100 meter dashes and placed fourth in the broad jump. In the second heat of the 50, she equaled the national record of 6.6 set by Louise Stokes in 1933. Bergmann won the high jump and shot put. She competed unattached because she had come to this country just five months earlier from Germany.

Vreeland said that an outstanding performance was turned in by Mrs. Gertrude Johnson of the Mercury Athletic Club, a Negro club from New York. She bettered the championship citizen's mark of 26.8 in the 200 meters by winning in 26.0.

50-meter run
1. Claire Isicson, unattached, Brooklyn, N.Y.   6.8
2. Lula Hymes, Tuskegee Institute
3. Josephine Warren, Boston Swimming Assn.
4. Fanny Vitale, Park Central A.A.

100-meter run
1. Claire Isicson, unattached, Brooklyn   12.8
2. Josephine Warren, Boston Swimming Assn.
3. Esther P. Dennis, Mercury A.C., N.Y.
4. Jessie Abbott, Tuskegee Institute

200-meter run
1. Gertrude Johnson, Mercury A.C.   26.0
2. Fanny Vitale, Park Central A.A., N.Y.
3. Rose Cea, Eastern Women's A.C., Brooklyn
4. Mabel Smith, Tuskegee Institute

80-meter hurdles
1. Cora Gaines, Tuskegee Institute   12.8
2. Sylvia Rothenberg, Glencoe A.C., N.Y.
3. Anna Lebo, Warinanco A.C., Elizabeth, N.J.
4. Elizabeth Saunders, Park Central A.A.

400-meter relay
1. Mercury A.C.   51.2
   (Wilson, Bynoe, Dennis, Johnson)
2. Tuskegee Institute
3. Park Central A.A.
4. Fifth Street M.E., Harrisburg, Pa.

High jump
1. Margaret Bergmann, unattached, N.Y.   4' 11½"
2. Cora Gaines, Tuskegee   4' 10½"
3. Rose Harley, Park Central,   4' 5½"
      and Lucile Harris, West Philadelphia A.C.

Broad jump
1. Lula Hymes, Tuskegee Institute   17' 8½"
2. Mabel Blanch Smith, Tuskegee Institute   17' 4"
3. Esther Dennis, Mercury A.C.   16' 11"
4. Claire Isicson, unattached, Brooklyn, N.Y.   16' 10¼"

Shot put
1. Margaret Bergmann, unattached, N.Y.   37' 6¾"
2. Florence Wright, Tuskegee Institute   37' 5"
3. Florence Blasch, Polish National Alliance, Chicago   35' 5¼"
4. Sylvia Rothenberg, Glencoe A.C.   33'

Discus
1. Elizabeth Lindsay, German-American A.C.   107' 11"
2. Florence Wright, Tuskegee Institute   105' 11"
3. Betty Laughlin, unattached, Bayonne, N.J.   100' 8"
4. Florence Blasch, Polish National Alliance   98' 9½"

Javelin
1. Rose Auerbach, Eastern Women's Club, Brooklyn   123' 5½"
2. Sylvia Broman, Brockton Girls' Club, Mass.   108' 6¾"
3. Florence Blasch, Polish National Alliance   105' 8¾"
4. Sylvia Rothenberg, Glencoe A.C.   101' 2¼"

Baseball throw
1. Rose Cea, Eastern Women's A.C., Brooklyn   249' 8¼"
2. Malisa Fitzpatrick, Tuskegee Institute   229' 5½"
3. Lee Ordine, Eastern Women's A.C.   227' 6¼"
4. Beatrice Larson, Park Central A.A.   204' 11"

Team scores:
Tuskegee Institute 33 points; Mercury A.C. 14; Eastern Women's A.C. 14; Park Central A.A. 9½.

The Indoor Nationals

The St. Louis A.C. won the team title on April 23 in St. Louis, Missouri.

50-meter run	
1. Helen Stephens, William Woods College	6.5
220-yard dash	
1. Helen Stephens, William Woods College	28.5
50-meter hurdles	
1. Jane Santschi, St. Louis A.C.	7.7
400-meter relay	
1. St. Louis A.C.	56.0
(Santschi, Crain, Gustavson, Brady)	
High jump	
1. Loretta Murphy, unattached	4' 9"
Standing broad jump	
1. Claire Isicson, unattached, N.Y.	8' 2"
Shot put	
1. Helen Stephens, William Woods College	44' 11½"
Basketball throw	
1. Evelyn Ferrara, Chicago Park District	97' 4"

The May 15 edition of the *Amsterdam News* reported results of the 11th Annual Tuskegee Relays held in the Alumni Bowl in Tuskegee, Alabama. Four thousand spectators saw Lula Hymes, a Tuskegee sophomore from Atlanta, Georgia, the outstanding athlete of the meet, broad jump 17' 4", beating national broad jump champion Mabel Smith, nineteen, by ½". She also set a meet record in the 100 meters of 12.4, and her leg on the winning Tuskegee relay team enabled Tuskegee to win the Julius B. Ramsey Revolving trophy for the second consecutive year.

Florida A&M College was second, and Booker T. Washington School of Atlanta was third in the point score.

Cora Bently won the 50-meter dash in 6.9. Helen Brown won the 200 meters, a new event, in 27.0.

Cora Gaines of Tuskegee equaled her 1936 record of 13.2 in winning the 80-meter hurdles. Cora also won the high jump with a leap of 4' 9¾".

Ruth Wright won the javelin throw with a toss of 87' 2" and twenty-one-year-old Florence Wright of Tuskegee won the shot put with a toss of 33' 2".

A junior division championships was conducted in which Tuskegee Institute High School placed second in the point score.

A listing of women's world records appeared in the 1937 *Almanac*. Five American women held world records: Helen Stephens in the 100 meters, Jean Shiley and Babe Didrikson in the high jump, Dorothy Lyford in the standing broad jump, and Nan Gindele in the javelin.

The AAU convention was held in November. In his track and field report, George Vreeland said of the championships:

> The apparent lack of interest in the championships may be attributed to the usual post–Olympic let-down — but more likely a general disinterestedness in women's track and field events.
>
> Reports from committee members indicate but fair activity in districts usually most active, with little or no action in other sections of the country.
>
> Opposition to women participating in track and field sports continues from most teachers of physical education notwithstanding repeated efforts to win over this group by strictly adhering to a code which we feel adequately safeguards the health and morals of those taking part.

Mrs. E. J. Allison, chairman of the AAU Women's Sports Committee, verified Vreeland's report in stating, "Track and field events show inactivity in all but a very few sections."

Following the meeting of the track and field committee, Dee Boeckmann reported that an informal discussion was held on how best to stimulate interest in the United States in women's track and field. It was agreed that the members of the national committee should devote at least one hour a week towards this goal.

It was suggested that subcommittees be developed to provide coaching for girls and find facilities, develop track athletic organizations for girls fifteen years of age and older, insure that one or more events for girls were added to an already established men's meet, and contact newspapers to enlist their help in giving publicity to the girls' track and field program.

The efforts made at this convention appear to be the first attempts by the AAU's women's track and field committee to counteract the long-time thrust of the Women's Division to eliminate track and field competition from the national scene and the Olympic Games.

On September 28, Mrs. Herbert Hoover attended a tea held at the Women's University Club with the members of the executive committee and board of the Women's Division. Her "loyal and active support" as honorary president of the federation began in the "pioneer days" of the organization. The Women's Division cherished the privilege of her support "for the best standards in athletics for girls and women in our country and throughout the world." For fourteen years the Women's Division had been at work enforcing its platform.

The 1936-37 executive committee annual report contained the following statement: "The Olympic Questionnaire: At the time of each Olympiad the N.A.A.F. discusses what attack it can make on the participation of women. This time we have determined to begin early, to secure the opinion of thousands of women and not just our own membership, so that any protest we make can be backed up by a much larger voice of women. To this end a questionnaire study is being made. In Berlin last summer we had a group of unofficial observers whose confidential reports have been of great help to the Executive Committee."

Alice Schriver from Missouri was reported to be the new track and field chairman. In June, a revised edition of the *Athletic Handbook* was ready. The guide, called the *Handbook on Games*, included recreational games, active sports for small spaces, games for large groups, games for the handicapped, inexpensive and homemade equipment, and track and field.

The thinking of the day can be understood by reading an article entitled "Must Women in Sports Look Beautiful?" written by Alice Sefton of the Metropolitan Life Insurance Company. It appeared in the October *Journal of Health and Physical Education*. Sefton referred to one critic who would have eliminated nearly all sports for women because he thought they should look beautiful in sports and should not participate in anything that did not permit this. The critic's list of approved sports included swimming, archery, shooting, flying, speed and figure skating, angling, and riding horseback. Skiing might be placed on the list if happy landings were guaranteed. If the woman fell, she must be sure to fall in a graceful and dignified position.

Alice Sefton demonstrated where such an attitude could lead:

> If we all held this point of view, conversations might run somewhat like this:
> He: Hello, Betty. Come on out and play eighteen holes of golf with me.
> She: Oh, I can't, Tom. The stance is so unbecoming.
> He: How about a game of tennis?
> She: To look knock-kneed — pigeon-toed? Not for me.
> He: Well, surely you can come for a swim. You look swell in a bathing suit.
> She: Oh, the only stroke on the approved list for a lady is that "back-hand crawl"; other strokes are said to be unbecoming.
> Imagine a girl deciding her sports program with only the criterion of beauty to guide her!

Sefton added, "Girls are born with the same fundamental instincts for physical activity and with the same urge to run, throw, and climb as boys."

Cleve Abbott

Cleve supposedly started the team at Tuskegee so his daughter Jessie could compete. His team entered national competition in the 1936 combined national championships and Olympic trials in Providence, Rhode Island. His athletes did well in the non–Olympic events. Cora Gaines placed second in the 200 meters, Florence Wright placed second in the shot put, Mabel Smith won the championships in the broad jump with a leap of 18', and the 400-meter relay finished third.

The next year, 1937, Tuskegee Institute won its first team title, and then it won again in '38, '39, '40, '41, '42, '44, '45, '46, '47, '48, '49, '50, and '51. These were the outdoor titles; the indoor titles were won in '41, '45, '46, and '48. There would have been more indoor titles if the meets had been held.

Cleve coached Olympians Mabel Walker, 1948; Nell Jackson, 1948; Theresa Manuel, 1948; Mary McNabb, 1952; gold medalist Alice Coachman, 1948; and gold medalist and world-record-holder Mildred McDaniel, 1956.

Cleve was born on December 9, 1894, and died April 16, 1955.

Chapter 21

1938

Naugatuck, Connecticut, hosted the national outdoor championships on August 7, attracting about one hundred athletes to Naugatuck, a last-minute switch from Waterbury.

About 3,000 spectators witnessed two star athletes perform. Claire Isicson of Long Island University equaled the world record of 6.4 in the third heat of the 50 meters, and Lula Hymes of Tuskegee Institute won the 100-meter dash and the broad jump and anchored the winning relay team. Isicson's 50-meter time matched that of the time established in 1922 in Paris and equaled in 1933 by Stella Walsh. Helen Stephens had equaled the mark twice indoors. Lula Hymes was voted the outstanding individual athlete of the meet.

A second double winner was Catherine Fellmeth from Chicago. She won the shot and discus shortly after arriving by plane.

Six new champions were crowned, and Tuskegee Institute defended its title by scoring thirty points, double the score of the second-place Eastern Women's Athletic Club of New York.

Chairman Dee Boeckmann said that three Connecticut girls were entered in the meet but failed to medal. This was the first time that girls from this state were in the national meet.

50-meter dash
1. Claire Isicson, Long Island University   6.6
2. Ivy Wilson, Mercury A.C.
3. Olive Hasenfus, Boston Swimming Assn. ·
4. Josephine Warren, Boston Swimming Assn.

100 meters
1. Lula Hymes, Tuskegee Institute   12.4
2. Olive Hasenfus, Boston Swimming Assn.
3. Claire Isicson, Long Island University
4. Josephine Warren, Boston Swimming Assn.

200 meters
1. Fanny Vitale, Park Central A.C.   26.7
2. Esther Brown, Tuskegee Institute
3. Marie Cotrell, German-American A.C.
4. Gertrude Johnson, Mercury A.C., N.Y.

80-meter hurdles
1. Marie Cotrell, German-American A.C.   13.0
2. Cora Gaines, Tuskegee Institute
3. Sylvia Rothenberg, unattached, N.Y.
4. Sybil Cooper, German-American A.C.

400-meter relay
1. Tuskegee Institute   52.0
    (Birge, Abbott, Brown, Hymes)
2. Polish National Alliance, Chicago
3. Tuskegee Institute, "B" team

High jump
1. Margaret Bergmann, Park Central A.C.   5' 2"
2. Mildred Pufundt, Polish National Alliance, Chicago
3. Beulah Clark, Crystal City A.C., St. Louis,
    Frances Sobczak, McDonnell A.C., Cleveland,
    and Mildred Kosick, Polish National Alliance, Chicago

Broad jump
1. Lula Hymes, Tuskegee Institute   17' 2"
2. Dorothy Catocci, German-American A.C., N.Y.
3. Esther Dennis, Mercury A.C.
4. Leila Perry, Tuskegee Institute

Shot put
1. Catherine Fellmeth, Dvorak Park, Chicago   38' 5¾"
2. Florence Wright, Tuskegee Institute
3. Margaret Bergmann, Park Central A.A.
4. Amy Dreyer, Brockton Girls A.C.

Discus
1. Catherine Fellmeth, Dvorak Park, Chicago   126' ¼"
2. Frances Sobczak, McDonnell A.C., Cleveland
3. Elizabeth Lindsay, German-American A.C.
4. Amy Dreyer, Brockton Girls' A.C.

Javelin
1. Rose Auerbach, Eastern Women's A.C.   121' 6¾"
2. Margaret Barnes, Tuskegee Institute
3. Rose Cea, Eastern Women's A.C.
4. Sylvia Rothenberg, unattached, N.Y.

Baseball throw
1. Betsy Jochum, unattached, Cincinnati   261' 7"
2. Rose Cea, Eastern Women's A.C.
3. Alice Ordine, Eastern Women's A.C.
4. Blanche Zambransky, Dvorak Park, Chicago

Team scores:

Tuskegee Institute 30; Eastern Women's A.C. 15; German-American A.C. 12½; Park Central A.C., 12; Dvorak Park, Chicago 12; Long Island University, Boston Swimming Assn. 7; Polish National Alliance 7; Mercury Club 6; McDonnell A.C. 4; Brockton Girls' A.C. 2½; Crystal City 1; unattached 7.

There was no national indoor competition in 1938.

On May 13, the 10th annual women's junior and senior championship meet was held in Tuskegee, Alabama. Tuskegee won with record-breaking performances from Lula Hymes in the 100 meters in 12.1 and in the broad jump with 18' 4½" and from Mabel Smith, who high jumped 5' ¾", three inches higher than the old mark.

Six records fell in the Metropolitan AAU meet on September 24-25 at Macombs Park in New York. Claire Isicson of Long Island University won the 50-yard dash in 6.0, and Ivy Wilson of the Mercury A.C. won the 100-yard dash in 11.6 and the 220 in 26.5. Elizabeth Lindsay of the German-American A.C. threw the discus 102' 7¾", and Rose Auerbach of the Eastern Women's A.C. tossed the javelin 114' 7½". The Mercury A.C. team captured the 440-yard relay in the record time of 50.9. That club won the team title, scoring 41 points. The Eastern Women's A.C. was second with 34 points.

The national track and field committee, with Boeckmann as chair, had five vice chairmen, which included former Olympic gold medalist Lillian Copeland from the Southern Pacific Association. The committee had twenty-six members from all around the country, including Olympic gold medalist Jean Shiley Reps.

In its April newsletter, the Women's Division stated: "The Executive Committee of the Women's Division, N.A.A.F. sent a protest to the International Olympic Committee at its recent meeting in Cairo, asking the women be withdrawn from Track and Field events and that girls 16 years of age and under be not allowed to participate in any activities of a competitive nature."

It was again requested that track and field be omitted from the 1940 Olympic Games. A reply came from Count Baillet-Latour, president of the International Olympic Committee: "The International Olympic Committee has heard with great interest the opinion expressed in your letter, which is shared by quite a number of my colleagues. Unfortunately, the majority is in favor of the participation of women in track and field events, and the question of the right age for participation, being a technical question, is in the hands of the International Federations."

The Women's Division worked actively to support its "platform" during the 1938 year. It held forty-four state committee meetings, gave nine radio broadcasts, and sponsored a record number of 127 talks throughout the country. Twenty-nine articles were written for journals in Louisiana, New Hampshire, North Dakota, Michigan, Utah, Oklahoma, and Missouri, there were 72 newspaper releases, 150 schools in Hawaii, were contacted through questionnaires.

Another significant article appearing in the November issue of *Health and Physical Education* addressed the lack of a competition policy within the Women's Division. Gladys Palmer, professor of physical education at Ohio State University, cited an excerpt from a book entitled *Athletics in Education*: "The present leadership in women's athletics which refuses to sanction interschool competition is not receiving the full support of the women in the field and of the girls themselves."

Palmer quoted opinions of college directors stated in this book. One said, "I do not believe that women should be on the Olympic team," while another stated, "I believe that women should participate in the Olympic Games but I do not approve of the present setup and conditions." Another expressed a strong view: "We do not favor national or international competition in any form. Our plan is to try to eliminate these events and to provide in school and community the kind of programs that will satisfy all kinds of girls and women."

Palmer then cited a new magazine, the *Eastern Sportswoman*. The three professional groups from which Palmer gave sample opinions earlier all had members on the advisory council of the new publication. Some of the activities reported in the magazine were results of squash racquet tournaments in New York and New Jersey, fencing competition in Massachusetts, and other competitive endeavors, including a report on national and international tennis competition. Palmer noted, "This is perhaps sufficient evidence that our professional group has no clear conception of what it approves or disapproves in competition for women."

The most astounding statement Palmer made was the following:

> I venture to suggest that they [Women's Division] might have become a more powerful factor in the conduct of all sports competition for women had they not, from their inception, taken a stand against state, national, and international competition in any form. Had they set up an additional platform and lent their guidance in this area we would perhaps have no problem of policy at this time. Since 1923 there has been a greater increase in organized state, national, and international events than ever before. This has been due, in part, to the very platform which calls for "every girl in a game and a game for every girl." It is impossible to legislate out of an individual the instinctive urge to compete — competition is the very soul of athletics.

Chapter 22

1939

September 3 was the date of the outdoor national championships. Water-bury, Connecticut, hosted the meet at the new municipal stadium. The *Sunday Republican* featured four large photos of Tuskegee athletes taken at Hamilton Park while they were practicing for the meet. Lulu Mae Hymes, the "brilliant all around performer," was pictured in the "on your mark" position.

The following day, the *Waterbury Republican* headlined, "Stella Walsh Tops Own Running Broad Jump Mark to Feature A.A.U Meet." A crowd of 2500 watched "the first girls' track meet here in history" and saw Stella Walsh better her American record in the broad jump with a leap of 19' 4". Her previous record of 18' 9⅜" was set in 1930 in Dallas.

The *New York Times* also headlined this performance. The *Waterbury Republican* continued: "Olive Hasenfus, blonde Boston lass, who has worn Uncle Sam's colors in two Olympics (1928 and 1936) and admits she's getting a 'little old' for another bid for international fame, scored an unexpected victory in the 100 meter run over Lucy Newell, new fleet star of the Tuskegee team in 12.6 seconds, two tenths of a second slower than last year's performance at Naugatuck when Miss Hymes was the victor. The latter finished fourth in a strong field."

In her annual track and field report, chairman Dee Boeckmann recounted that Stella Walsh had broken her nine-year-old American record in the broad jump with a leap of 19' 4". She also won the 200 meters and anchored her club's relay team, moving them into third place. The other double winner was Catherine Fellmeth from Chicago. She repeated 1938 victories in the shot put and discus.

Tuskegee Institute ran away with the team championship. The team scored more than double the number of points scored by the Chicago Park Hurricanes, the team placing second. Their winning 440-relay team crossed the line in semi-darkness.

---

50 meters
1. Gertrude Johnson, Mercury A.C.   6.7
2. Ivy Wilson, Mercury A.C.
3. Jeanette Jones, Harrisburg A.A.
4. Ernestine Rogers, Tuskegee Institute

100 meters
1. Olive Hasenfus, Boston Swimming Assn.   12.6
2. Lucy Newell, Tuskegee Institute
3. Elizabeth Kinnard, Missouri Racing Club
4. Lula Mae Hymes, Tuskegee Institute

200 meters
1. Stella Walsh, Polish Olympic C.   25.5
2. Hester Brown, Tuskegee Institute
3. Hilda Plepis, Philadelphia Moose Lodge
4. Jewell Cole, Prairie View College, Texas

80-meter hurdles
1. Marie Cottrell, German-American A.C.   12.5
2. Sybil Cooper, German-American A.C.
3. Leila Perry, Tuskegee Institute
4. Sylvia Rothenberg, German-American A.C.

400-meter relay
1. Tuskegee Institute   49.4
   (Birge, Abbott, Harrison, Hymes)
2. Mercury A.C.
3. Polish Olympic C.
4. Chicago Park Hurricanes

High jump
1. Alice Coachman, Tuskegee Institute   5' 2"
2. Mary Haydon, Ottawa, Ontario   5' 1"
3. Barbara Howe, Boston Swimming Assn.   4' 10"
4. Thelma Lalumondier, Crystal City H.S., Mo.

Broad jump
1. Stella Walsh, Polish Olympic C.   19' 4"
2. Lula Hymes, Tuskegee Institute   18' 1½"
3. Lucy Newell, Tuskegee Institute   17' 3¾"
4. Thelma Lalumondier, Crystal City H.S.   17' 1½"

8-lb. shot put
1. Catherine Fellmeth, Chicago Park Hurricanes   41' 1¾"
2. Ramona Harris, Mercury A.C.   37' 8¾"
3. Florence Wright, Tuskegee Institute   37' 1"
4. Carolyn Yetter, Philadelphia Moose Lodge   36' 4¾"

Discus
1. Catherine Fellmeth, Chicago Park Hurricanes   113' 7½"
2. Hattie Hall, Tuskegee Institute   104' 1¼"
3. Florence Wright, Tuskegee Institute   99' 4½"
4. Betty McLaughlin, unattached   98'

Javelin
1. Dorothy Dodson, Chicago Park Hurricanes   130'
2. Rose Auerbach, Eastern Women's A.C.   123' 5"
3. Jean McGunnegle, Hope H.S., Providence, R.I.   122' 3"
4. Margaret Barnes, Tuskegee Institute   113' 8"

Baseball throw
1. Catherine O'Connell, Boston Swimming Assn.	233' 3¹⁄₁₀"
2. Jean McGunnegle, Hope H.S.	233' 2"
3. Irene Romano, Eastern Women's A.C.	232' 4⁷⁄₁₀"
4. Margaret Myers, Harrisburg A.A.	220' 8⁸⁄₁₀"

There was no indoor competition this year.

The *Amateur Athlete* published a list of women's world track and field performances compiled by Sol Goldstein, the coach of the Eastern Women's A.C. He commented, "The United States is way behind in women's athletics and unless we unearth a Didrikson, or a Stephens this year we will fare badly in the 1940 Olympics."

The AAU rule book for 1939 listed the women's track and field rules. One of the more interesting was "Women athletes shall wear a uniform consisting of brassiere, overblouse with small neck band, quarter length sleeves or longer, loose fitting running breeches reaching to within two inches from the knee caps, or bloomers."

Chapter 23

1940

Ocean City, New Jersey, hosted the national meet on July 6 on a new track. One hundred and forty-one athletes representing eleven states were entered. High-point scorer Stella Walsh was the star of the meet, winning the 200 meters and the broad jump and placing second in the 100 meters. Seventeen-year-old Jean Lane of Wilberforce University defeated Stella in the 100 meters and won the 50-meter dash. Headlines in the *New York Times* on July 7 read, "Miss Walsh Stars in National Meet."

Catherine Fellmeth defended her titles for the third time in the shot put and discus throw. The other repeat champions were Alice Coachman in the high jump, Dorothy Dodson in the javelin, and Tuskegee Institute in the 400-meter relay and team championship.

50 meters
1. Jean Lane, Wilberforce University   6.6
2. Lucy Newell, Tuskegee Institute
3. Jeanette Jones, Harrisburg A.A.
4. Claire Isicson, Long Island University

100 meters
1. Jean Lane, Wilberforce University   12.0
2. Stella Walsh, Polish Olympic Women's Club
3. Lula Hymes, Tuskegee Institute
4. Rowena Harrison, Tuskegee Institute

80-meter hurdles
1. Sybil Cooper, German-American A.C.   13.1
2. Nancy Cowperthwaite, German-American A.C.
3. Lillie Purifoy, Tuskegee Institute
4. Leila Perry, Tuskegee Institute

200-meter dash
1. Stella Walsh, Polish Women's Olympic Club   26.1
2. Edna Gustavson, St. Louis A.C.
3. Hester Brown, Tuskegee Institute
4. Hilda Plepis, Philadelphia Moose Lodge

400-meter relay
1. Tuskegee Institute, "A" team   49.3
    (Newell, Abbott, Harrison, Hymes)

2. Tuskegee Institute, "B" team
3. Philadelphia Moose Lodge, "A" team
4. Mercury Athletic Club, N.Y.

High jump
1. Alice Coachman, Tuskegee Institute   4' 11"
2. Gerda Gottlieb, Canton, Massachusetts
3. Betty Henning, Philadelphia
4. Leila Perry, Tuskegee Institute,
   Frances Sobczak, Polish Olympic Women's Club
   Mary Homler, Jacksonville, Florida

Discus throw
1. Catherine Fellmeth, Chicago Park Hurricanes   114' 11"
2. Evelyn Taylor, Taylor A.C., Illinois
3. Frances Sobczak, Polish Olympic Women's Club
4. Hattie Hall, Tuskegee Institute

8-lb. shot put
1. Catherine Fellmeth, Chicago Park Hurricanes   38' 3⅝"
2. Ramona Harris, Mercury A.C.
3. Frances Sobczak, Polish Olympic Women's Club
4. Mildred Yetter, Philadelphia Moose Lodge

Baseball throw
1. Angela Mica, St. Louis A.C.   241' 9½"
2. Irene Romano, Eastern Women's A.C.
3. Katherine O'Connell, Boston Swimming Assn.
4. Jean McGunnegle, Boston Swimming Assn.

Broad jump
1. Stella Walsh, Polish Olympic Women's Club   17' 7½"
2. Lucy Newell, Tuskegee Institute
3. Betty Charters, Philadelphia Moose Lodge
4. Lula Hymes, Tuskegee Institute

Javelin throw
1. Dorothy Dodson, Chicago Park Hurricanes   126' 1"
2. Miriam Melton, St. Louis A.C.
3. Marie Sostar, Harrisburg A.A.
4. Margaret Barnes, Tuskegee Institute

Team scores:
Tuskegee Institute 85⅓; Polish Olympic Women's Club 42⅓; Philadelphia Moose
Lodge 34.

There was no indoor championship meet in 1940.

The national track and field chairman, Catherine Donovan Meyer, had six
vice chairmen, including Olympian Evelyne Hall. Two of the other seventeen
members of her committee were Cleve Abbott from Tuskegee Institute, representing the Southeastern Association, and Dee Boeckmann, representing St. Louis,
Missouri.

The National Section on Women's Athletics conducted a track and field survey, which it published in the *Health and Physical Education Journal* in February 1940. In this survey, Alice Schriver reported:

> An effort was made during the year 1937-38 to secure opinion regarding the desirability of track and field events with particular emphasis on the anatomical structure of certain recognized types of individuals. A brief questionnaire was circulated to one hundred and ten college directors, high school teachers and supervisors covering the entire United States. Seventy-nine questionnaires were returned. A brief summary of the returns follow:
>
> Two types of individuals were described, both of which were to apply to the adolescent and adult levels: feminine type — narrow sloping shoulders, broad hips, short legs; masculine type — broad square shoulders, narrow hips, long legs.
>
> Question 1. Athletic activities for girls and women should be selected for the typical feminine girl (not a sissy type).
>
> yes — 50
> no — 12
>
> Question 2. Athletic activities for girls and women should be selected for the more masculine type of girl (not the mannish type).
>
> yes — 12
> no — 45
>
> Question 3. Present athletic activities planned for girls and women tend to favor the more masculine type of girl.
>
> yes — 26
> no — 37
>
> Question 4. Present athletic activities planned for girls and women tend to favor the typical feminine type of girl.
>
> yes — 18
> no — 37
>
> Question 5. Track and field events at the college level are best adapted to the more masculine type girl.
>
> yes — 59
> no — 8
>
> Question 6. Track and field as separate events should be confined to grades: 1–6, 1–8, senior high school, college.
>
> grades 1–6 — 19
> grades 1–8 — 17
> high school — 16
> college — 16
>
> Question 7. Track and field events should be combined with other field events at grades 1–6, 1–8, high school, college.
>
> 1–6 — 16
> 1–8 — 32
> high school — 28
> college — 11
>
> Question 8. Greater interest in running and throwing is found while participating in games such as hockey and basketball in junior high school, senior high school and college.
>
> junior high school — 27
> high school — 46
> college — 27

Question 9. Jumping events being somewhat questionable, they are best omitted at level of: elementary school, junior high school, high school, college.
    elementary school — 16
    junior high school — 43
    high school — 45
    college — 16

Question 10. I would favor discontinuing the use of track and field as individual events at the level of: elementary, junior high school, high school, college.
    elementary — 23
    junior high school — 36
    high school — 38
    college — 36

The article ended with this conclusion:

It appears that schools and colleges, taken the country over, now place track and field at the bottom of the sports list, but at the same time they seem unwilling to drop them from the program. In some instances, particularly at the college level, they are included only as electives.

Chapter 24

1941

The national outdoor meet was held on July 5 at the recreation center in Ocean City, New Jersey, the same location as the year before.

The *New York Times* on July 6 headlined, "Miss Lane Breaks U.S. Sprint Record." The highlight of the 150-girl meet was eighteen-year-old Jean Lane's defeat of Stella Walsh in the 200 meters in the meet record time of 25.2, despite inclement weather and poor track conditions that forced a rearrangement of the events. Jean, a senior at Wilberforce University, also blazed to first place in the 100 meters. Jean and Stella were the only double winners in the meet.

50 meters
1. Lucy Newell, Tuskegee Institute   6.6
2. Jeanette Jones, Harrisburg A.A
3. Claire Isicson, Long Island University
4. Mamie Taylor, Tuskegee Institute

100-meter dash
1. Jean Lane, Wilberforce University   12.4
2. Alice Coachman, Tuskegee Institute
3. Rowena Harrison, Tuskegee Institute
4. Margaret Wigiser, Eastern Women's A.C.

200-meter dash
1. Jean Lane, Wilberforce University   25.2
2. Stella Walsh, Polish Olympic Women's A.C.
3. Hester Brown, Tuskegee Institute
4. Betsy Carey, Tuskegee Institute

80-meter hurdles
1. Leila Perry, Tuskegee Institute   13.2
2. Lillie Purifoy, Tuskegee Institute
3. Hilda Plepis, Philadelphia Moose Lodge
4. Nancy Cowperthwaite, German-American A.C.

400-meter relay
1. Tuskegee Institute   50.0
   (Newell, Perry, Harrison, Coachman)
2. Tuskegee Institute, "B" team
3. Philadelphia Moose Lodge
4. St. Claire A.C., Toronto

8-lb. shot put
1. Catherine Fellmeth, unattached, Chicago   37' ⅜"
2. Dorothy Dodson, unattached, Chicago
3. Hattie Hall, Tuskegee Institute
4. Caroline Yetter, Philadelphia Moose Lodge

Broad jump
1. Stella Walsh, Polish Olympic Women's A.C.   18' 6¾"
2. Lucy Newell, Tuskegee Institute
3. Betty Charters, Philadelphia Moose Lodge
4. Jeanette Jones, Harrisburg A.A.

High jump
1. Alice Coachman, Tuskegee Institute   5' 2¾"
2. Norma Jeffrey, Chicago Park Hurricanes
3. Leila Perry, Tuskegee Institute
4. Jean Harvey, Philadelphia Moose Lodge

Discus throw
1. Stella Walsh, Polish Olympic Women's A.C.   113' 10⅜"
2. Evelyn Taylor, Taylor A.C., Illinois
3. Catherine Fellmeth, unattached, Chicago
4. Hattie Hall, Tuskegee

Javelin throw
1. Dorothy Dodson, unattached, Chicago   128' 7⅛"
2. Marian Twining, Philadelphia Moose Lodge
3. Marie Sostar, Harrisburg A.A.
4. Angela Mica, St. Louis A.C.

Baseball throw
1. Angela Mica, St. Louis A.C.   260' 10⅞"
2. Betsy Jochum, unattached, Cincinnati
3. Jean McGunnegle, Boston Swimming Assn.
4. Margaret Wigiser, Eastern Women's A.C.

Team Scores:
Tuskegee Institute 100; Philadelphia Moose Lodge 43; Polish Olympic Women's Athletic Club 31½; Wilberforce University 20; Harrisburg Athletic Association 19; St. Louis Athletic Club 14; Eastern Women's Athletic Club 11; Boston Swimming Association 10; Chicago Park Hurricanes 8; Taylor Athletic Club 8; St. Claire Athletic Club, Toronto 7; Long Island University 6; German-American Athletic Club 5½; Red Diamond Athletic Club 3; Rhode Island Cinder Lassies 2; Philadelphia Turners 1; unattached 42.

The Indoor Nationals

The indoor meet had not been held since 1937. This year the meet was held on Easter Saturday, April 12, at the municipal auditorium in Atlantic City, New Jersey. The national junior championships for men were held in conjunction with the meet. Preliminaries for both meets were in the afternoon, with the finals at night. Highlighting the meet was Jean Lane's world-record-breaking performance in the 200 meters, beating Stella Walsh by several yards.

Large, bold headlines appeared on the front page of the sports section of the *Atlantic City Press* proclaiming Jean Lane's world record in the 200 meters. The story read:

> Eighteen year old Jean Lane, of Wilberforce University, broke the first record of the evening when she carried off the 200 meter event in the spectacular time of 25.1 bettering the mark of 25.7 set by Stella Walsh, of the Polish-Olympic Club of Cleveland, during the trials in the afternoon....
>
> The Wilberforce representative defeated Miss Walsh by a couple of yards. ... Miss Lane earned a double victory when she breezed off with the 50 meter run in 6.8.

The *New York Times* also headlined Jean's world-record-breaking performance.

Prior to the meet, the *Atlantic City Press* featured an article on Jean Lane's arrival in Atlantic City:

> The Wilberforce University star, who will compete in the 50 meter run, pulled into town yesterday and spent part of the afternoon limbering up. She inspected the Big Hall and will probably do some light running today.
>
> Miss Lane is the holder of two records. One is the Southern Intercollegiate Athletic Association mark of 26.0 for the 200 meter event and the others are the Ohio Association and the National Citizens' mark for the century of 10.9.
>
> C.J. Newsome, chairman of the Convention Bureau of the Atlantic City Board of Trade, acted as host for Miss Lane and her father, Dr. Aubrey Lane.

---

50 meters
1. Jean Lane, Wilberforce University   6.8
2. Jeanette Jones, Harrisburg A.A.
3. Lucy Newell, Tuskegee Institute
4. Rowena Harrison, Tuskegee Institute

200 meters (record disallowed — no border on track)
1. Jean Lane, Wilberforce University   25.1
2. Stella Walsh, Polish Olympic Women's Club
3. Hester Brown, Tuskegee Institute
4. Jeanette Jones, Harrisburg A.A.

50-meter hurdles
1. Lillie Purifoy, Tuskegee Institute   8.1
2. Hilda Plepis, Philadelphia Moose Lodge
3. Nancy Cowperthwaite, German-American A.C.
4. Leila Perry, Tuskegee Institute

Standing broad jump
1. Lucy Newell, Tuskegee Institute   8' 1⅞"
2. Lillie Purifoy, Tuskegee Institute
3. Jean Harvey, Philadelphia Moose Lodge
4. Betty Charters, Philadelphia Moose Lodge

Basketball throw
1. Marian Twining, Philadelphia Moose Lodge   95' 10¼"
2. Mildred Yetter, Philadelphia Moose Lodge
3. Evelyn Taylor, Taylor A.C.
4. Marie Sostar, Harrisburg A.A.

High jump
1. Alice Coachman, Tuskegee Institute   5'
2. Jean Marie Harvey, Philadelphia Moose Lodge
3. Nancy Cowperthwaite, German-American A.C.
4. Frances Gorn, Polish Women's Olympic Club

400-meter relay
1. Tuskegee Institute   50.1
   (Newell, Perry, Brown, Harrison)
2. Philadelphia Moose Lodge
3. Tuskegee Institute, "B" team
4. Philadelphia Moose Lodge, "B" team

8-lb. shot put
1. Dorothy Dodson, Chicago Hurricanes   35' ⅝"
2. Hattie Hall, Tuskegee Institute
3. Frances Gorn, Polish Women's Olympic A.C.
4. Mildred Yetter, Philadelphia Moose Lodge

Team scores:
Tuskegee Institute 84; Philadelphia Moose Lodge 68; Polish Olympic Women's Athletic Club 26; Wilberforce University 20; Harrisburg Athletic Association 17; German-American Athletic Club 13; Chicago Hurricanes 10; Taylor Athletic Club 6; Boston Swimming Association 2; York Athletic Club 1.

The indoor championship records appeared in the *Amateur Athletic Union Handbook*:

40y	5⅕	Rosa Grosse, Toronto Ladies A.C.	3/28/27
		Mary Carew, Medford Girls' A.C.	4/19/30
			3/14/31
		Stella Walsh, N.Y. Central AA	4/19/30
50m	6.4	Helen Stephens, Wm. Woods College	2/12/36
200m	26.0	Stella Walsh, Poland	4/14/34
200m	26.8	Annette Rogers, Illinois Women's A.C.	2/25/33
220y	26⅕	Stella Walsh, N.Y. Central AA	4/19/30
50yh	7⅗	Nellie Sharka, Newark W.A.C.	3/12/32
50mh	7.6	Evelyne Hall, Illinois Women's A.C.	2/25/33
HJ	5' 3½"	Jean Shiley, Meadowbrook Club	4/19/30
SBJ	8' 8¼"	Helen Stephens, Fulton H.S.	3/22/35
8lb.SP	44' 11½"	Helen Stephens, Wm. Woods College	4/23/37
Basketball	101' 6¾"	Nan Gindele, Illinois Women's A.C.	2/25/33
400mr	50.8	Newark Women's A.C.	2/25/33
440yr	54.0	Millrose A.A.	3/14/31

Chapter 25

1942

The outdoor championship meet was held on July 4 for the third consecutive year at the Municipal Recreation Center in Ocean City, New Jersey. National track and field chairman Catherine Donovan Meyer remarked that "despite the difficulties of transportation in a gas rationed zone, the meet drew a fine entry including a team from the Laurel Ladies Club of Toronto, Canada."

On July 5, the *New York Times* reported that thirty-one-year-old Stella Walsh had again captured three crowns. Had it not been for the Amateur Athletic Union rule allowing only three events, Stella would have run the 100 meters also. She was the high point scorer.

Word was received at the last minute that Jean Lane would be unable to defend her sprint titles, according to the *Atlantic City Press*.

For six straight years, Tuskegee Institute captured the team championship. Alice Coachman was its outstanding star, winning the high jump and the 100 meters. After the meet, the Tuskegee athletes were informed of the death of their coach, Mrs. Christine Evans Petty. The news was received earlier but was withheld by Cleve Abbott, club athletic director, who accompanied the team in Mrs. Petty's place.

---

50 meters
1. Jeanette Jones, Harrisburg A.A.   6.7
2. Janet Ellicott, St. Claire A.C.
3. Mamie Taylor, Tuskegee Institute
4. Rita Corrigan, Polish Olympic Women's A.C.

100 meters
1. Alice Coachman, Tuskegee Institute   12.1
2. Rowena Harrison, Tuskegee Institute
3. Jean Lowe, Laurel Ladies, Toronto
4. Jeanette Jones, Harrisburg A.A.

200 meters
1. Stella Walsh, Polish Olympic Women's A.C.   25.4
2. Jean Kaplan, Chicago Park Hurricanes
3. Katherine Geary, Philadelphia Turngemeinde
4. Alice Jagus, Polish Olympic Women's A.C.

Alice Coachman in "get set" position, gold medalist in the high jump and national AAU champion in the 100 meters. (Courtesy of the National Track & Field Hall of Fame Historical Research Library at Butler University.)

80-meter hurdles
1. Lillie Purifoy, Tuskegee Institute   12.6
2. Nancy Cowperthwaite, German-American A.C.
3. Leila Perry, Tuskegee Institute
4. Roxy Atkins Campbell, Laurel Ladies, Toronto

400-meter relay
1. Tuskegee Institute   50.7
    (Perry, Coachman, Harrison, Purifoy)
2. Laurel Ladies, Toronto
3. Philadelphia Moose Lodge
4. German-American A.C.

8-lb. shot put
1. Ramona Harris, unattached, N.Y.C.   37' 10½"
2. Dorothy Dodson, Chicago Park Hurricanes
3. Frances Gorn, Polish Olympic Women's Club
4. Margaret Wigiser, Eastern Women's A.C.

Broad jump
1. Stella Walsh, Polish Olympic Women's A.C.   17' 11"
2. Rowena Harrison, Tuskegee Institute

3. Betty Moore, Philadelphia Moose Lodge
4. Betty Charters, Philadelphia Moose Lodge

High jump
1. Alice Coachman, Tuskegee Institute   4' 8"
2. Norma Jeffrey, Chicago Park Hurricanes
3. Frances Gorn, Polish Olympic Women's A.C.,
    Catherine Bowden, Tuskegee Institute,
    and Leila Perry, Tuskegee Institute

Discus throw
1. Stella Walsh, Polish Olympic Women's A.C.   110' 11¾"
2. Frances Gorn, Polish Olympic Women's A.C.
3. Anne Pallo, Polish Olympic Women's A.C.
4. Dorothy Dodson, Chicago Park Hurricanes

Javelin throw
1. Dorothy Dodson, Chicago Park Hurricanes   122' 10½"
2. Marie Sostar, Harrisburg A.A.
3. Marian Twining, Philadelphia Moose Lodge
4. Katherine Geary, Philadelphia Turngemeinde

Baseball throw
1. Irena Romano, Eastern Women's A.C.   259' 7"
2. Hattie Turner, Tuskegee Institute
3. Marian Twining, Philadelphia Moose Lodge
4. Margaret Wigiser, Eastern Women's A.C.

Team scores:
Tuskegee Institute 80; Polish Olympic Women's Athletic Club 64½; Philadelphia
Moose Lodge 41½; Chicago Park Hurricanes 39; Harrisburg A.A. 24; Toronto Laurel
Ladies 22½; Eastern Women's Athletic Club 18; Philadelphia Turngemeinde 12; German-American Athletic Club 11½; St. Claire Athletic Club 8; Unattached 21.

The indoor championship meet was not held in 1942.

1942 American Outdoor Records

50y	5⅘	Elizabeth Robinson	Chicago	7/27/29
50m	6.4	Claire Isicson	Connecticut	8/7/38
100y	10.8	Stella Walsh	Philadelphia	5/30/30
100y	10.9c	Jean Lane	Cincinnati	5/20/40
100m	11.6	Helen Stephens	Kansas City	6/8/35
			NYC	9/14/35
200m	24.1	Stella Walsh, Poland	Chicago	8/18/32
200m	24.4c	Helen Stephens	St. Louis	6/1/35
220y	24.3	Stella Walsh	Cleveland	6/9/35
220y	25.1c	Elizabeth Robinson	Milwaukee	6/20/31
60yh	8.0	Josephine Schessler	Agnes Scott Col.	1923
60yh	8.0	Helen M. Filkey	Chicago	6/2/28
80mh	11.7	Mildred Didrikson	Los Angeles	8/4/32
		Evelyne Hall		

Tuskegee Institute Team with the National Championship 400-meter relay team in the front row. From left, Lillie Purifoy, Leila Perry, Rowena Harrison and Alice Coachman. (Courtesy of Richmond Davis and Alice Coachman.)

HJ	5' 5¼"	Jean M. Shiley	Los Angeles	8/7/32
BJ	19' 4"	Stella Walsh	Waterbury	9/3/39
BJ	18' 1½" c	Lula Hymes	Waterbury	9/3/39
SBJ	8' 7¾"	Dorothy Lyford	Worcester	6/4/32
8lb.SP	42' 3"	Rena MacDonald	Chicago	7/27/29
Discus	115' 6½"	Lillian Copeland	Los Angeles	2/18/28
Discus (2lbs., 3¼ oz)		Lillian Copeland	Los Angeles	8/2/32
Javelin	153' 4½"	Nan Gindele	Chicago	6/18/32
Baseball	296'	Mildred Didrikson	Jersey City	7/25/31

Relays

220y (4x55)	24⅘	Millrose A.A.	Elizabeth, N.J.	9/28/30
300y (4x75)	34.0	Millrose A.A.	Elizabeth, N.J.	9/28/30
300m (4x75)	39.0	Pasadena A.C.	Pasadena	6/27/26
400m	46.9	U.S. Team	Los Angeles	8/7/32
440y	49.4	Millrose A.A.	Dallas	7/4/30
		Illinois W.A.C.	Chicago	7/16/32

c — citizen's record

Fred Steers, one-time women's track and field chairman and now first vice president of the AAU, wrote an article for the *Amateur Athlete* stating that "women's athletics should be encouraged and extended."

An interesting letter written by Ann Avery Smith of Wellesley College appeared in the March *Journal of Health and Physical Education*. She said, "Track work is a rarity in our usual collegiate and scholastic sports program. And if the fine art of running well is not taught to women and girls in sports classes, where will it be taught?"

In a second article in the February *Journal of Health and Physical Education* entitled "Track and Field in a Program of Physical Education for Girls," Gertrude Moulton, M.D., director of physical education for women at Oberlin College, stated that track and field events have great value in a sports program.

Chapter 26

1943

The senior outdoor national championship meet was held in Cleveland, Ohio, on August 15. Stella Walsh won three events, thus scoring the highest individual point score ever attained in national competition. Her score propelled her team to victory over Tuskegee Institute, the first defeat for Tuskegee Institute in its six-year reign as team champions. Stella, in winning the 100 meters in 11.6, equaled Helen Stephens' American record set in 1935. It was an exciting race as both Stella and Alice Coachman, the defending champion, sped together, side by side, towards the finish line. In a last desperate surge, Stella beat Alice to the tape. Alice Coachman was second high scorer with twenty-eight points. In addition to placing second in the 100 meters, she again won the high jump and the 50 yard dash.

Dorothy Dodson joined Walsh and Coachman as a repeat champion in winning the javelin throw.

Tuskegee's defending 400-meter relay team was upset by the Laurel Ladies Club of Toronto.

50m
1. Alice Coachman, Tuskegee   6.5
2. Jeanette Jones, Harrisburg A.A.
3. Lillian Young, Chicago Central Association

100 meters
1. Stella Walsh, Polish Olympic Women's A.C.   11.6
2. Alice Coachman, Tuskegee Institute
3. Rowena Harrison, Tuskegee Institute

200 meters
1. Stella Walsh, Polish Olympic Women's A.C.   26.3
2. Alice Jagus, Polish Olympic Women's A.C.
3. Mary Cummins, Laurel Ladies A.C., Toronto

80-meter hurdles
1. Nancy Cowperthwaite, German-American A.C.   12.3
2. Joan Davis, St. Clair A.C.
3. Leila Perry, Tuskegee Institute

400-meter relay
1. Laurel Ladies A.C., Toronto   50.6
2. Tuskegee Institute
3. German-American A.C.

8-lb. shot put
1. Frances Gorn, Polish Olympic Women's A.C.   37' 11"
2. Dorothy Dodson, unattached, Chicago
3. Mildred Yetter, Philadelphia Moose Lodge

Broad Jump
1. Stella Walsh, Polish Olympic Women's A.C.   19' 1"
2. Rowena Harrison, Tuskegee
3. Betty Dummeldinger, Philadelphia Moose Lodge

High jump
1. Alice Coachman, Tuskegee Institute   5'
2. Adrienne Robinson, Chicago Central Assn.
3. Bernice Robinson, Chicago Central Assn.

Discus throw
1. Frances Gorn, Polish Olympic Women's A.C.   109' 6¼"
2. Betty Weaver, unattached
3. Ann Pallo, Polish Olympic Women's A.C.

Javelin throw
1. Dorothy Dodson, unattached, Chicago   111' 3"
2. Marian Twining, Philadelphia Moose Lodge
3. Bessie Leick, Polish Olympic Women's A.C.

Baseball throw
1. Elaine Grothe, Chicago Central Assn.   260' 6¼"
2. Marian Twining, Philadelphia Moose Lodge
3. Hattie Turner, Tuskegee Institute

Team scores:
Polish Olympic Women's A.C. 87⅙; Tuskegee Institute 77½; Chicago Central Association 30; Philadelphia Moose Lodge 28; Toronto Laurel Ladies A.C. 16; German-American A.C. 16; Harrisburg A.A. 8; St. Clair A.C. 8; unattached 26.

The indoor championship meet was not held this year.

Under the leadership of chairman Meyer, approval was received from the track and field committee to select an annual All-America Team. Certificates and awards were given to the following who were the first women selected for this honor.

The first All—America Women's Track and Field Team

50-meter run	Alice Coachman
100-meter run	Stella Walsh
200-meter run	Stella Walsh
Broad jump	Stella Walsh
High jump	Alice Coachman
80-meter hurdles	Nancy Cowperthwaite

Discus throw	Frances Gorn
8-lb. shot put	Frances Gorn
Javelin throw	Dorothy Dodson
Baseball throw	Elaine Grothe
400-meter relay	Stella Walsh, Alice Coachman, Rowena Harrison, Jeanette Jones

The track and field committee had three vice chairmen and twenty members, including Stella Walsh, representing northeastern Ohio, and Olive Hasenfus Sparks, a 1928 Olympian, representing Needham, Massachusetts.

In the section on rules, the *AAU Handbook* addressed the track uniform: "Women athletes shall wear uniforms consisting of blouse with small neck band and cap or short sleeves to be worn with brassiere. The trunks shall be halfway between knee and hip, and shall have an inner leg closely fitted, or with elastic in the hem."

Chapter 27

1944

The national senior outdoor track and field championship meet was held for the first time in Harrisburg, Pennsylvania, on July 8 at William Penn High School.

The *Amateur Athlete* reported that the phrase "six in succession" seemed to mark the meet. Stella Walsh, Alice Coachman, and Dorothy Dodson won their events for the sixth year in succession. Stella captured her sixth title in the broad jump, Alice in the high jump, and Dorothy in the javelin throw.

The *New York Times* headlines on July 9 read, "3 U.S. Track Titles Go to Miss Walsh." The 100 meters proved to be the most exciting and the closest race of the day. At age thirty-three, Stella again scored triple wins. She battled Alice Coachman, stride for stride, to the finish line and won in 12 flat, only four tenths off her own world record. In the broad jump, Rowena Harrison, an army cadet nurse, was in first place with only one jumper left. On her final attempt, Stella leaped 17' 11⅛" to win by a margin of slightly more than four inches.

Stella's easiest victory was in the 200 meters. She beat Rowena Harrison by about five yards on the 200-meter straightaway in 24.6, a new meet record and within a second of her world record.

In addition to her sixth consecutive victory in the high jump, Alice Coachman defended her 50-meter dash title, equaling the world record of 6.4 set by Stella Walsh eleven years previously.

Dorothy Dodson's second victory was in the shot put; the third double winner was Hattie Turner of Tuskegee, who was victorious in the discus and baseball throw.

Four girls won nine of the eleven events at this meet. Tuskegee Institute recaptured the team championship after its 1943 loss, their first loss in six years.

---

50 meters
1. Alice Coachman, Tuskegee Institute   6.4
2. Lillian Young, Forrestville Playground, Chicago
3. Viola Myers, Laurel Ladies Club, Toronto
4. Betty Dummeldinger, Philadelphia Moose Lodge

100 meters
1. Stella Walsh, unattached, Cleveland   12.0
2. Alice Coachman, Tuskegee Institute

3. Jean Lowe, Laurel Ladies Club, Toronto
4. Kay Geary, Philadelphia Turners

200 meters
1. Stella Walsh, unattached   24.6
2. Rowena Harrison, Tuskegee Institute
3. Mary Cummins, Laurel Ladies Club, Toronto
4. Jean Walraven, unattached, Cleveland

80-meter hurdles
1. Lillie Purifoy, Tuskegee Institute   12.8
2. Jean Walraven, unattached
3. Leila Perry, Tuskegee Institute
4. Dolores McElduff, Philadelphia Moose Lodge

400-meter relay
1. Laurel Ladies Club, Toronto   52.8
2. Tuskegee Institute
3. German-American A.C.
4. Philadelphia Moose Lodge

8-lb. shot put
1. Dorothy Dodson, unattached, Chicago   36' ¼"
2. Carolyn Yetter, Philadelphia Moose Lodge   32' 3½"
3. Cleo Davis, Tuskegee Institute   32' 2½"
4. Pauline Ruppeldt, Philadelphia Moose Lodge   29' 7¾"

Broad jump
1. Stella Walsh, unattached, Cleveland   17' 11⅛"
2. Rowena Harrison, Tuskegee Institute   17' 7"
3. Jean Kaplan, Riis Park, Chicago   16' 2⅜"
4. Betty Dummeldinger, Philadelphia Moose Lodge   16' 1½"

High jump
1. Alice Coachman, Tuskegee Institute   5' 1⅝"
2. Nancy Cowperthwaite, German-American A.C.   4' 6"
3. Nellie Stafford, Tuskegee Institute,   4' 5"
    and Clara Schroth, Philadelphia Turners

Discus
1. Hattie Turner, Tuskegee Institute   101' 7¾"
2. Betty Weaver, unattached, Bayonne, N.J.   93' 6"
3. Pauline Ruppeldt, Philadelphia Moose   92' 8⅖"
4. Mildred Yetter, Philadelphia Moose   88'

Javelin
1. Dorothy Dodson, unattached, Chicago   123' 1½"
2. Lillian Davis, Philadelphia Moose Lodge   103' 11½"
3. Marie Sostar, Harrisburg A.A.   101' 11"
4. Hattie Turner, Tuskegee Institute   101' 8¾"

Baseball throw
1. Hattie Turner, Tuskegee Institute   214' 6"
2. Harriet Mitchell, Harrisburg A.A.   206' 6"

3. Marie Sostar, Harrisburg A.A.   198' 4"
4. Lillian Carrig, Harrisburg A.A.   194' 7"

Team scores:
Tuskegee Institute 110; Philadelphia Moose Lodge 51; Laurel Ladies Club 30; Harrisburg A.A. 29; German-American A.C. 16; Forrestville Playground 11; Philadelphia Turners 8; Riis Park 6; unattached 75.

The indoor championship meet was not held this year.

1944 All-America Women's Track and Field Team

50-meter run	Alice Coachman
100-meter run	Stella Walsh
200-meter run	Stella Walsh
Broad jump	Stella Walsh
High jump	Alice Coachman
Discus throw	Hattie Turner
Baseball throw	Hattie Turner
8-lb. shot put	Dorothy Dodson
Javelin throw	Dorothy Dodson
80-meter hurdles	Lillie Purifoy
400-meter relay	Stella Walsh, Alice Coachman, Kay Geary, Elizabeth Peel

For the first time, a women's relay team appeared on the cover of the *Amateur Athlete*. A photograph of the Laurel Ladies Club team of Toronto, the winners of the 400-meter relay in the national championships, graced the prime spot. The girls were Doris Wright, Viola Myers, Nancy Mackay, and Jean Lowe, captain of the team and president of the club, pictured with their coach, Albert Foster.

A second issue of the *Amateur Athlete* featured a story on Dee Boeckmann. She had just returned by chartered plane to the United States after spending eighteen months in Iceland as athletic director for the Red Cross. Dee was the only American passenger on the plane of "Swenn Bjornsson, newly elected President of the world's newest independent state." She spent time in Iceland organizing basketball, softball, tennis, golf, and track teams and coaching basketball.

Rachael Yocum of Utah State College was chairman of the six-woman track and field committee of the NSWA. The October issue of the *Health and Physical Education* journal featured an article by Yocum entitled "Track and Field for Girls in Secondary Schools," in which she said:

> Track and field once held a prominent position in our physical education programs for girls ... [but have] all but disappeared from the physical education programs for girls in many sections of the United States. Due to the present war emergency, the popularity of the Victory Corps program and the emphasis on physical fitness, track and field for girls may once come into its own. ... Let us then examine critically the values offered by a track and field program in the light of the individual, the war emergency, physical fitness, and activity in general.

Chapter 28

1945

The national outdoor track and field championship meet was held for the second consecutive year at Fager Field in Harrisburg, Pennsylvania, on July 30. Twenty-one-year-old Alice Coachman produced the outstanding accomplishment and excitement of the day by beating defending champion Stella Walsh in the 100-meter dash. Only a week before, Stella lowered the world record for the 100 meters to 11.2, breaking the nine-year-old mark of 11.5 set by Helen Stephens in the 1936 Olympic Games in Berlin. In the 100-meter final, Coachman got the lead at the sound of the gun and led all the way. Coachman won the high jump for the seventh straight year and captured a first in the 50-meter run. Coachman's victories and thirty points led her team to another title and earned her the high point trophy over Walsh, who scored twenty-eight points.

Walsh repeated her victory in the broad jump for the seventh year and won the 200 meters in 26.6. Dorothy Dodson repeated as seven-year champion in the javelin throw, and Frances Gorn Sobczak scored a double in the shot and discus. Lillie Purifoy retained her crown in the 80-meter hurdles.

---

50 meters
1. Alice Coachman, Tuskegee Institute   6.5
2. Lillian Young, Forrestville Playground, Chicago
3. Rowena Harrison, Tuskegee Institute,
    and Viola Myers, Laurel Ladies A.C.

100 meters
1. Alice Coachman, Tuskegee Institute   12.0
2. Stella Walsh, Polish Olympic W.A.C.
3. Jean Lowe, Laurel Ladies A.C.
4. Lillian Young, Forrestville Playground

200 meters
1. Stella Walsh, Polish Olympic W.A.C.   26.6
2. Nell Jackson, Tuskegee Institute
3. Gwendolyn Taylor, Harrisburg A.A.
4. Alice Jagus, Polish Olympic W.A.C.

80-meter hurdles
1. Lillie Purifoy, Tuskegee Institute   12.5
2. Nancy Cowperthwaite, German-American A.C.

3. Marie Wingo, West Side A.C., Asbury Park, N.J.
4. Jean Walraven, Polish Olympic W.A.C.

400-meter relay
1. Laurel Ladies A.C., Toronto   51.4
2. Tuskegee Institute
3. German-American A.C.
4. Harrisburg A.A.

8-lb. shot
1. Frances Gorn Sobczak, Polish Olympic W.A.C.   37' 9⅞"
2. Helen Steward, Harrisburg A.A.   35' 11¼"
3. Dorothy Dodson, Chicago Park Hurricanes   35' 8½"
4. Pauline Ruppeldt, Philadelphia Moose Lodge   35' ¼"
   and Estelle Kestenbaum, German-American A.C.

High jump
1. Alice Coachman, Tuskegee Institute   5'
2. Marie Wingo, West Side A.C.,   4' 6"
   and Nancy Cowperthwaite, German-American A.C.
4. Jean Walraven, Polish Olympic W.A.C.,   4' 4"
   and Clara Schroth, Philadelphia Turners

Broad jump
1. Stella Walsh, Polish Olympic W.A.C.   18' 3"
2. Rowena Harrison, Tuskegee Institute   17' 9½"
3. Lillian Young, Forrestville Playground   16' 2"
4. Alice Crowell, Tuskegee Institute   16' ½"

Discus
1. Frances Gorn Sobczak, Polish Olympic W.A.C.   103' ¾"
2. Hattie Turner, Tuskegee Institute   98' 11¼"
3. Dorothy Dodson, Chicago Park Hurricanes   98' 2¾"
4. Marie Sostar, Harrisburg A.A.   95'

Javelin
1. Dorothy Dodson, Chicago Park Hurricanes   124' 10"
2. Marian Twining, Philadelphia Moose Lodge   114' 11"
3. Marie Sostar, Harrisburg A.A.   108' 2½"
4. Hattie Turner, Tuskegee Institute   104' 5"

Baseball throw
1. Marian Twining, Philadelphia Moose Lodge   237' 9"
2. Hattie Turner, Tuskegee Institute   224' 8"
3. Peggy Anderson, Polish Olympic W.A.C.   220' 7½"
4. Christine E. Long, Lincoln Air Field   218' 9"

Team scores:
Tuskegee Institute 102; Polish Olympic W.A.C. 68¾; Harrisburg A.A. 32; Philadelphia Moose Lodge 27¼; German-American A.C. 24; Chicago Park Hurricanes 22; Laurel Ladies A.C., Toronto 21; Forrestville Playground, Chicago 20; West Side A.C., Asbury Park, N.J. 13; Philadelphia Turners 10; unattached 4.

The Indoor Nationals

The indoor championship meet was held in Buffalo, New York, on March 31. This was the first indoor meet to be held since 1941. The *New York Times* carried the story, but because men's events were featured, the women's write-up consisted of three small paragraphs at the end of the article. Mentioned in these paragraphs were Alice Coachman's two-title win, Stella Walsh's win in the 220, Dorothy Dodson's victory in the shot put, and Tuskegee's defense of its team championship.

50-yard dash
1. Alice Coachman, Tuskegee Institute   6.1
2. Lillian Young, Forrestville Playground, Chicago
3. Rowena Harrison, Tuskegee Institute
4. Kay Geary, Philadelphia Turners

220-yard run
1. Stella Walsh, Polish Olympic W.A.C.   26.3
2. Nell Jackson, Tuskegee Institute
3. Gwendolyn Taylor, Harrisburg A.A.
4. Muriel Millheiser, German-American A.C.

50-yard hurdles
1. Nancy Cowperthwaite, German-American A.C.   7.6
2. Lillie Purifoy, Tuskegee Institute
3. Clara Schroth, Philadelphia Turners
4. Edith Barber, German-American A.C.

440-yard relay
1. Tuskegee Institute   53.6
   (Jackson, Purifoy, Harrison, Coachman)
2. German-American A.C.
3. Forrestville Playground
4. Chicago Hurricanes

High jump
1. Alice Coachman, Tuskegee Institute   4' 8"
2. Pauline Ruppeldt, Philadelphia Moose Lodge   4' 7"
3. Clara Schroth, Philadelphia Turners,   4' 6"
      and Nancy Cowperthwaite, German-American A.C.

Standing broad jump
1. Clara Schroth, Philadelphia Turners   7' 11¾"
2. Lorraine Boesen, Chicago Hurricanes   7' 10⅛"
3. Corrine Winston, Forrestville Playground   7' 8½"
4. Rowena Harrison, Tuskegee Institute   7' 7⅞"

8-lb. shot put
1. Dorothy Dodson, Chicago Hurricanes   35' 1⅝"
2. Kay Geary, Philadelphia Turners   33' 9½"
3. Hattie Turner, Tuskegee Institute   31' ¾"
4. Pauline Ruppeldt, Philadelphia Moose Lodge   30'

Basketball throw
1. Marian Twining, Philadelphia Moose Lodge   94' 10½"
2. Dorothy Dodson, Chicago Hurricanes   89' 10¾"
3. Hattie Turner, Tuskegee Institute   88' 7⅞"
4. Katherine Jones, Copernicus Playground   82' ⅝"

Team scores:
Tuskegee Institute 28; Philadelphia Turners 12½; Chicago Hurricanes 12; German-American A.C. 11½; Philadelphia Moose 9; Forrestville Playground, Chicago 7; Polish Olympic W.A.C. 5; Harrisburg A.A. 2; Copernicus Playground, Chicago 1.

1945 All-America Women's Track and Field Team

50 meters	Alice Coachman
100 meters	Alice Coachman
200 meters	Stella Walsh
50-yard hurdles	Nancy Cowperthwaite
80-meter hurdles	Lillie Purifoy
High jump	Alice Coachman
Standing broad jump	Clara Schroth
Running broad jump	Stella Walsh
8-lb. shot put	Frances Gorn Sobczak and Dorothy Dodson
Discus throw	Frances Gorn Sobczak
Javelin throw	Dorothy Dodson
Basketball throw	Marian Twining
Baseball throw	Marian Twining
400-meter relay	Alice Coachman, Stella Walsh, Lillian Young, Lillian James

The *Amateur Athlete* featured several articles on women's track. Roxy Atkins Campbell wrote "Fashions in Feminine Sport," outlining a brief history of women in sport from 776 B.C. to the days of Esther Williams, the swimming star and movie actress. Roxy's main thrust was to state that beauty and glamour can be displayed through the medium of sport.

Campbell's second article, "U.S. Girls Wake Up!" compared the winning times, heights, and distances from our national championships to the best performances from the European championships. Not one American woman was in the top three in any event.

The November issue of *Amateur Athlete* included a photograph of the Central Association's Outdoor Women's Track and Field Committee, the only all-woman track and field officials group. Evelyne Hall and Annette Rogers, both 1932 Olympians, were members of the group of thirty-seven women.

The December *Amateur Athlete* had a photograph of the Chicago Hurricanes. The coach and manager of the fifty-eight girls was 1932 Olympian, Evelyne Hall. Dorothy Dodson, seven-time national javelin champion, was a member of the team.

American Records

40y	5⅕*	Rosa Grosse	March 26, 1927
		Stella Walsh	March 12, 1930
			April 19, 1930
			February 12, 1931
		Mary Carew	April 19, 1930
			March 14, 1931
50y	5⅘	Elizabeth Robinson	July 27, 1929
50y	6.0*	Stella Walsh	February 8, 1930
50y	6.1*c	Jeanette Jones	April 6, 1940
50y (dirt track)	6.0*	Elizabeth Robinson	March 19, 1931
50m	6.4	Claire Isicson	August 7, 1938
50m	6.4	Alice Coachman	July 8, 1944
50m	6.4*	Helen Stephens	February 12, 1936
			March 25, 1936
50m (dirt track)	6.6*	Helen Stephens	March 22, 1935
100y	10.8	Stella Walsh	May 30, 1930
100y	10.9c	Jean Lane	May 29, 1940
100m	11.6	Helen Stephens	June 8, 1935
			September 14, 1935
		Stella Walsh	August 15, 1943
200m	24.1	Stella Walsh (Poland)	August 18, 1932
200m		Helen Stephens	June 1, 1935
200m	25.8*	Stella Walsh	March 16, 1941
200m	25.8*	Annette Rogers	February 25, 1933
220y	24.3	Stella Walsh	June 9, 1935
220y	25.1c	Elizabeth Robinson	June 20, 1931
220y	25.8 *	Stella Walsh	March 16, 1941
220y	28.7*	Helen Busch	April 6, 1940
50yh	7.4*	Evelyne Hall	March 18, 1932
50mh	7.6*	Evelyne Hall	February 25, 1933
60yh		Josephine Schessler	1923
60yh	8.0	Helen Filkey	June 2, 1928
60yh	8⅗*	Hazel Kirk	February 13, 1926
80mh	11.7	Mildred Didrikson	August 4, 1932
		Evelyne Hall	August 4, 1932
HJ	5' 5¼"	Jean Shiley	August 7, 1932
HJ (dirt track)	5' 1¼"*	Annette Rogers and Ida Meyers	February 12, 1936
HJ	5' 3½"*	Jean Shiley	April 19, 1930
SHJ	4' 1"*	Gerda Gottlieb	March 15, 1941
RBJ	19' 4"	Stella Walsh	September 3, 1939
RBJ	18' 1½"c	Lulu Mae Hymes	September 3, 1939
SBJ	8' 7¾"	Dorothy Lyford	June 4, 1932
SBJ	9' ¼"*	Dorothy Lyford	January 25, 1933
8lb.SP	42' 3"	Rena MacDonald	July 27, 1929

8lb.SP	41' 11"*	Helen Stephens	March 25, 1936
Discus	115' 6½"	Lillian Copeland	February 18, 1928
(2lb. 12½ oz.)			
Discus	133' 2"	Lillian Copeland	August 2, 1932
Javelin	153' 4½"	Nan Gindele	June 18, 1932
Basketball	101' 6¾"*	Nan Gindele	February 25, 1933
Baseball	296'	Mildred Didrikson	July 25, 1931

Relays

220y	24⅘	Millrose A.A.	September 28, 1930
300y	34.0	Millrose A.A.	September 28, 1930
300m	39.0	Pasadena Athletic & C.C.	June 27, 1926
400m	46.9	USA team	August 7, 1932
	50.0	Pasadena A. & C.C.	June 16, 1928
	50⅕*	Newark W.A.C.	February 25, 1933
440y	49.4	Millrose A.A.	July 4, 1930
		Illinois W.A.C.	July 15, 1932
440y	51.5*	Millrose A.A.	March 12, 1930
440ymr	53.0	Millrose A.A.	September 13, 1930
(50,60,110,220)			
440ymr	52.4*	Mercury A.C.	June 26, 1939
500y (10x50)	58.5	Pasadena A & C.C.	
800m	1:49.6	Mercury A.C.	October 16, 1938
880y	1:49.6	Mercury A.C.	October 16, 1938
880ymr	1:57⅗	N.Y.C.R.R.A.A.	September 28, 1929

* indoor record
c citizen's record

Chapter 29

1946

All-High Stadium in Buffalo, New York, was the site of the outdoor national championships on August 4. Alice Coachman and her Tuskegee Institute team dominated the meet. For the second straight year, Coachman was a triple winner, and Tuskegee won the team title, scoring 95 points. Coachman captured the high jump and the 50 meters, and she led Walsh by four feet in the 100 meters, bringing a tumultuous ovation from the crowd of more than seven thousand.

Dorothy Dodson was the other triple winner. The 5' 2", 124-pound athlete scored victories in the javelin, shot, and discus.

Thirty-five-year-old Stella Walsh captured two events, the 220 and the broad jump. These were her twenty-ninth and thirtieth national titles. She was second to Coachman in the 100 meters. In the 220, she beat Nell Jackson by nine yards.

Malvernette Athletic Club, known the previous year as the Laurel Ladies Athletic Club of Toronto, won the 440-yard relay in the good time of 50.0.

Twenty-five-year-old Nancy Cowperthwaite, a New York socialite, scored the only upset of the meet by beating defending champion Lillie Purifoy in the 80-meter hurdles by a yard. A photograph of Nancy winning the hurdles appeared in the *New York Times* on August 5. Cowperthwaite tied with Jean Walraven for second place in the high jump. In her third event of the day, she helped her team place second in the 440-yard relay.

Since there was a tie for high scorer, Dorothy Dodson and Alice Coachman "tossed" for the trophy. Dorothy won, but the Niagara Association planned to award gold medals to both women.

---

50 meters
1. Alice Coachman, Tuskegee Institute   6.5
2. Katherine Geary, Philadelphia Turners
3. Lillian Young, Forrestville Playground, Chicago
4. Shirley Eckel, Malvernette A.C., Toronto

100 meters
1. Alice Coachman, Tuskegee Institute   12.3
2. Stella Walsh, Polish Olympic W.A.C.
3. Nancy Mackay, Malvernette A.C.
4. Ruth Harrigan, Malvernette A.C.

220-yard dash
1. Stella Walsh, Polish Olympic W.A.C.   26.3
2. Nell Jackson, Tuskegee Institute
3. Jeanette Jones, Harrisburg A.A.
4. Mildred Martin, unattached

80-meter hurdles
1. Nancy Cowperthwaite, German-American A.C.   12.2
2. Lillie Purifoy, Tuskegee Institute
3. Jean Walraven, Polish Olympic W.A.C.
4. Theresa Manuel, Tuskegee Institute

440-yard relay
1. Malvernette A.C., Toronto "A" team   50.0
2. German-American A.C.
3. Tuskegee Institute, "A" team
4. Tuskegee Institute, "B" team

Broad jump
1. Stella Walsh, Polish Olympic W.A.C.   17' 3"
2. Lillian Young, Forrestville Playground   16' 6⅛"
3. Jean Walraven, Polish Olympic W.A.C.   15' 7⅓"
4. Fannie Johnson, Tuskegee Institute   15' 6⅛"

High jump
1. Alice Coachman, Tuskegee Institute   5'
2. Nancy Cowperthwaite, German-American A.C.   4' 6"
   and Jean Walraven, Polish Olympic W.A.C.
4. Verna Myers, Malvernette A.C.,   4' 4"
   and Bessie Leick, Polish Olympic W.A.C.

Javelin throw
1. Dorothy Dodson, unattached   120' 2"
2. Marian Twining, Philadelphia Turners   114' 1"
3. Hattie Turner Palmer, Tuskegee Institute   112'
4. Bessie Leick, Polish Olympic W.A.C.   105' 5"

8-lb. shot put
1. Dorothy Dodson, unattached   38' 10¾"
2. Elaine Bradford, Tuskegee Institute   32' 7"
3. Florence Blasch, unattached   32' 5¾"
4. Josephine Wilkowski, Kay Daumet Hurricanes   31' 5½"

Discus
1. Dorothy Dodson, unattached   102' ½"

Baseball throw
1. Marian Twining, Philadelphia Turners   242' 10¼"

Team scores:
Tuskegee Institute 95; Polish Olympic W.A.C. 64¼; German-American A.C. 38½.

The Indoor Nationals

One hundred and twenty-nine athletes gathered for the indoor championship meet on March 31 at the Central Armory in Cleveland, Ohio, under the sponsorship of the Polish Olympic Women's Athletic Club.

For the first time in the history of women's track and field, a junior national championships was held in conjunction with the senior meet on March 30, the day before the senior meet. It drew an entry of 180, which was 51 more women than the senior championships. Many athletes participated in the two championships, like Lorraine Boesen of Chicago, who won the standing broad jump in both meets.

Chairman Meyer reported in the May *Amateur Athlete* that Tuskegee Institute won the senior and junior meet. The team was led by Alice Coachman, who successfully defended her high jump and 50-yard dash crowns, and Lillie Purifoy, who nipped defending champion Nancy Cowperthwaite in the 50-yard hurdles.

Alice Coachman, the only double winner in the meet, and Walsh tied in points with ten each, but Coachman won the trophy because of her two first places to Walsh's one first in the 220, a second in the broad jump, and a third in the shot put.

50-yard dash
1. Alice Coachman, Tuskegee Institute   6.4
2. Kay Geary, Philadelphia Turners
3. Lillian Young, Chicago Bureau of Recreation
4. Eleanor Millheiser, German-American A.C.

220-yard run
1. Stella Walsh, Polish Olympic W.A.C.   28.6
2. Juanita Watson, Tuskegee Institute
3. Fannie Johnson, Tuskegee Institute
4. Gwendolyn Taylor, Harrisburg A.A.

8-lb. shot put
1. Dorothy Dodson, unattached, Chicago   34' 6½"
2. Helen Steward, Harrisburg A.A.
3. Stella Walsh, Polish Olympic W. A.C.
4. Katherine Geary, Philadelphia Turners

High jump
1. Alice Coachman, Tuskegee Institute   4' 6⅞"
2. Jean Walraven, Polish Olympic W.A.C.
3. Eleanor Millheiser, German-American A.C.
    and Bessie Leick, Polish Olympic W.A.C.

Basketball throw
1. Marian Twining, Philadelphia Turners   101' 4¼"
2. Hattie Turner, Tuskegee Institute

3. Harriet Mitchell, Harrisburg A.A.
4. Theresa Manuel, Tuskegee Institute

Standing broad jump
1. Lorraine Boesen, unattached, Chicago   8' 1⅛"
2. Stella Walsh, Polish Olympic W.A.C.
3. Mildred Martin, unattached, Chicago
4. Nancy Cowperthwaite, German-American A.C

50-yard hurdles
1. Lillie Purifoy, Tuskegee Institute   7.8
2. Nancy Cowperthwaite, German-American A.C.
3. Jean Walraven, Polish Olympic W.A.C.
4. Theresa Manuel, Tuskegee Institute

440-yard relay
1. Philadelphia Turners   59.8
   (McKee, Twining, Geary, McClurken)
2. Chicago Bureau of Recreation
3. Tuskegee Institute, "A" team
4. Tuskegee Institute, "B" team

Team scores:
Tuskegee Institute 29; Polish Olympic W.A.C. 16½; Philadelphia Turners 14; German-American A.C. 6½.

The First National Junior Indoor Championships

The *Cleveland Plain Dealer* reported that Jean Walraven "beat both the American Indoor and national A.A.U. records" in the hurdles. Nancy Cowperthwaite was the high point scorer.

200-yard run
1. Juanita Watson, Tuskegee Institute   30.2
2. Nell Jackson, Tuskegee Institute
3. Marian Twining, Philadelphia Turners
4. Nancy Cowperthwaite, German-American A.C.

50-yard hurdles
1. Jean Walraven, Polish Olympic W.A.C.   7.3
2. Theresa Manuel, Tuskegee Institute
3. Loretta Blaul, German-American A.C.
4. Bessie Leick, Polish Olympic W.A.C.

50-yard run
1. Katherine Geary, Philadelphia Turners   6.3
2. Nancy McClurken, Philadelphia Turners
3. Lillian Young, Bureau of Recreation, Chicago
4. Dorothy Jacobs, unattached, Chicago

Shot put
1. Helen Steward, Harrisburg A.A.A.   34'
2. Katherine Geary, Philadelphia Turners
3. Pauline Ruppeldt, Philadelphia Turners
4. Rose Przybylski, Polish Olympic W.A.C.

High jump
1. Nancy Cowperthwaite, German-American A.C.   4' 7¾"
2. Eleanor Millheiser, German-American A.C.,
      and Pauline Ruppeldt, Philadelphia Turners
4. Jean Walraven, Polish Olympic W.A.C.,
      Bessie Leick, Polish Olympic W.A.C.,
      and Loretta Blaul, German-American A.C.

440-yard relay
1. Tuskegee Institute, "B" team   61.0
2. Chicago Bureau of Recreation
3. Tuskegee Institute, "A" team
4. German-American A.C.

Basketball throw
1. Peggy Anderson, Polish Olympic W.A.C.   87' 11½"
2. Harriet Mitchell, Harrisburg A.A.
3. Theresa Manuel, Tuskegee Institute
4. Helen Lasch, Ranger A.C.

Standing broad jump
1. Lorraine Boesen, unattached, Chicago   7' 9½"
2. Nancy Cowperthwaite, German-American A.C.
3. Theresa Manuel, Tuskegee Institute
4. Corrine Winston, Bureau of Recreation, Chicago

Team scores:
Tuskegee Institute 22; Philadelphia Turners 17½; German-American A.C. 14⅚; Polish Olympic W.A.C. 12⅔.

1946 All-America Women's Track and Field Team

50-meter run	Alice Coachman
100-meter run	Alice Coachman
200-meter run	Nell Jackson
50-yard hurdles	Lillie Purifoy
80-meter hurdles	Nancy Cowperthwaite
High jump	Alice Coachman
Broad jump	Lillian Young
Standing broad jump	Lorraine Boesen
8-lb. shot put	Dorothy Dodson
Discus throw	Dorothy Dodson
Javelin throw	Dorothy Dodson
Basketball throw	Marian Twining
Baseball throw	Marian Twining

| 400-meter relay | Alice Coachman, Katherine Geary, |
| | Lillian Young, Eleanor Millheiser |

The September *Amateur Athlete* reprinted an article appearing in the *New York Times* entitled "U.S. Crushes Canada in Resumption of International Track Competition." The first international dual meet with Canada was on August 3 in Molson Stadium, McGill University, Montreal, Canada. Three women's events were on the program: the 100 meters, the 440-yard relay, and the high jump. The American team consisted of Alice Coachman, Kay Geary, Eleanor Millheiser, and Nancy Cowperthwaite. The *New York Times* description of the meet centered around the men's events but mentioned Alice Coachman's double victory.

Alice Coachman won the 100-yard dash in 11.5. Canadians placed second and third, and Kay Geary was fourth.

The United States won the 440-yard relay (Geary, Millheiser, Cowperthwaite, Coachman) in 50.2, a new Canadian record.

Alice Coachman won the high jump in 5' ⅜". Nancy Cowperthwaite placed second, jumping 4' 11", and Eleanor Millheiser was fourth with a jump of 4' 7".

The girls left Canada for Buffalo to compete in the national outdoor championships the following day.

The Second Annual *Philadelphia Inquirer* Indoor Track Meet was held on January 25. The twenty-five cent program included an article by Dora Lurie, the *Philadelphia Inquirer*'s feature sportswriter who played an important role in launching Jean Shiley's high jumping career.

Dora highlighted several women in her article, "Women in Track and Field," in which she stated:

> American women's track and field activity is due for a big postwar boom that promises to inspire a new generation of athletes like Jean Shiley, Philadelphia's 1932 Olympic captain and holder of the Games' high jump record, and Helen Stephens, the lone Yankee maid who still holds a world mark — that being the 100 meter dash....
>
> One of the few girls ever to defeat Miss Walsh in the early 1930's was Elizabeth Robinson, the Chicago flash, pretty enough to be a "Cover Girl." ... Miss Robinson was the first American girl to win an Olympic title and our only woman winner in the 1928 Games at Amsterdam when she captured the 100 meters.

Chapter 30

1947

Alamo Stadium in San Antonio, Texas, was the site of the national outdoor junior and senior championships on June 27-28. The meet was held in conjunction with the Army Air Corps Meet. It was the first time in more than a decade a money bid was made for the championships. This enabled thirty-one contestants to receive financial help in order to defray expenses to and from Texas. Reasonable housing was provided at Kelly Field. These factors made for the largest entry in the history of the championships.

For the tenth year, Tuskegee won the senior team title. Dorothy Dodson and Alice Coachman tied for individual high point honors, as they did in 1946. Both took two firsts and a second, for a total of 28 points. The *San Antonio Express* stated: "It remained for the 'big three' of women's track — Dorothy Dodson, Alice Coachman and Stella Walsh — to capture the fancy of the crowd of 2,553. The trio, that last year won eight of the eleven championships, didn't dominate the picture so completely last night, but they performed in such a manner to leave little doubt who the boss women of the cinderpath really are."

Thirty-six-year-old Stella Walsh came from behind to win the 200-meter dash. Alice Coachman, now transferred to Albany State College, Georgia, was upset in the 100 meters by Tuskegee athlete Juanita Watson.

---

50 meters
1. Alice Coachman, Albany State College, Ga.   6.8
2. Katherine Geary, Philadelphia Turners
3. Mabel Walker, Tuskegee Institute
4. Shirley Eckel, Malvernette A.C.

200-meter dash
1. Stella Walsh, Polish Olympic W.A.C.   26.2
2. Audrey Patterson, Wiley College, Texas
3. Nell Jackson, Tuskegee Institute
4. Gwendolyn Taylor, Tuskegee Institute

High jump
1. Alice Coachman, Albany State College   5' 1"
2. Emma Reed, Tennessee A. & I.   4' 11"
3. Gertrude Orr, Tuskegee Institute,   4' 10"
    and Rebecca Oprea, Cleveland

285

Broad jump
1. Lillie Purifoy, Tuskegee Institute   17' 6"
2. Nancy Cowperthwaite, German-American A.C.
3. Lillian Young, Chicago Hurricanes
4. Stella Walsh, Polish Olympic W.A.C.

100-meter dash
1. Juanita Watson, Tuskegee Institute   13.1
2. Alice Coachman, Albany State College
3. Mary Griggs, Tuskegee Institute
4. Elaine Burgess, Mississippi

80-meter hurdles
1. Nancy Cowperthwaite, German-American A.C.   12.6
2. Theresa Manuel, Tuskegee Institute
3. Lillie Purifoy, Tuskegee Institute
4. Jean Walraven, Polish Olympic W.A.C.

400-meter relay
1. Tuskegee Institute, "A" team   50.5
     (Walker, Watson, Griggs, Jackson)
2. Malvernette A.C.
3. Tuskegee Institute, "B" team
4. German-American A.C.

Javelin
1. Dorothy Dodson, Chicago Hurricanes   122' 5"
2. Hattie Palmer, Tuskegee Institute   113' 9½"
3. Marian Twining Barone, Philadelphia Turners   105' 11"
4. Bessie Leick, Polish Olympic W.A.C.   102' 11¼"

8-lb. shot put
1. Dorothy Dodson, Chicago Hurricanes   37' 11"
2. Francis Kaszubski, Polish Olympic W.A.C.   36' 8"
3. Katherine Geary, Philadelphia Turners   35' 9½"
4. Josephine Wilkowski, Chicago Hurricanes   33' 7½"

Discus
1. Francis Kaszubski, Polish Olympic W.A.C.   110' 4¾"
2. Dorothy Dodson, Chicago Hurricanes   107' 1¾"
3. Pauline Ruppeldt, Philadelphia Turners   98' 10"
4. Hattie Palmer, Tuskegee Institute   96' 5"

Baseball throw
1. Marian Twining Barone, Philadelphia Turners   252' 8"
2. Hattie Palmer, Tuskegee Institute   250' 11"
3. Peggy Anderson, Polish Olympic W.A.C.   240' 5"
4. Juanita Watson, Tuskegee Institute   225' 11"

Team scores:
Tuskegee Institute 106; Polish Olympic W.A.C. 55; Philadelphia Turners 39; Chicago
Hurricanes 35; German-American A.C. 30; Albany State College 28; A & I State Col-
lege, Nashville 11; Wiley College, Texas 10; Forrestville Playground, Chicago 8; Uvalde

H.S., Texas 8; Malvernette A.C., Toronto 4; Army Air Corps, Ohio 4; Brookhaven H.S., Mississippi 5; Ozark Women's Sport Club, Missouri 2; San Antonio Recreation 1.

The Junior Nationals

The *San Antonio Express* reported: "Climaxing their performance by finishing first and second in the final event of the evening — the 400 meter relay — a well-balanced team representing Tuskegee Institute of Tuskegee, Alabama captured the 1947 women's National AAU junior team championship Friday night in Alamo Stadium."

Katherine Geary was the high-point scorer in the junior meet.

50 meters
1. Mabel Walker, Tuskegee Institute   6.9
2. Elaine Burgess, Brookhaven High, Miss.
3. Nancy McClurken, Philadelphia Turners
4. Eleanor Millheiser, German-American A.C.

100-meter run
1. Mary Griggs, Tuskegee Institute   13.2
2. Cleo Reece, Prairie View A & M College, Texas
3. Audrey Patterson, Wiley College, Tex.
4. Nancy Mackay, Malvernette A.C., Toronto

200-meter run
1. Audrey Patterson, Wiley College   26.1
2. Nell Jackson, Tuskegee Institute
3. Nancy Cowperthwaite, German-American A.C.
4. Gwendolyn Taylor, Tuskegee Institute

80-meter hurdles
1. Theresa Manuel, Tuskegee Institute   12.8
2. Loretta Blaul, German-American A.C.
3. Raynice Eads, Uvalde H.S., Tex.
4. Verna Myers, Malvernette A.C., Toronto

400-meter relay
1. Tuskegee Institute, "A" team   51.0
2. Tuskegee Institute, "B" team
3. German-American A.C.
4. Chicago Hurricanes

High jump
1. Emma Reed, A & I State College, Nashville   4' 11"
2. Unar Martin, Phoenix, Arizona   4' 10"
3. Gertrude Orr, Tuskegee Institute   4' 9"
4. Barbara Mewes, Ozark Women's Sports Club   4' 8"

Broad jump
1. Lillian Young, Forrestville Playground, Chicago   16' 2½"
2. Shirley Stanley, Brookhaven H.S.   15' 9"
3. Lillie Purifoy, Tuskegee Institute   15' 7½"
4. Fannie Johnson, Tuskegee Institute   15' 6¼"

Javelin
1. Katherine Geary, Philadelphia Turners   103' 11"
2. Bessie Leick, Polish Olympic W.A.C.   100' 4"
3. Bonnie Reed, San Antonio Recreation   87' 3"
4. Torchi Blasch, Chicago Hurricanes   83' 9"

Baseball throw
1. Juanita Watson, Tuskegee Institute   229'
2. Estelle Kestenbaum, German-American A.C.   219' 9"
3. Josephine Wilkowski, Chicago Hurricanes   209' 7"
4. Frances Narcissus, San Antonio Recreation   194' 5"
   (Peggy Anderson of the Polish Olympic W.A.C. won with 238' 7", but it was
   later discovered that she had won the national junior indoor basketball throw
   and was therefore ineligible for competition in the junior throwing class. Once
   an athlete won a national title as a junior, they were no longer eligible to compete in that junior event again.)

8-lb. shot put
1. Katherine Geary, Philadelphia Turners   34' 1½"
2. Verda Crawford, Prairie View College
3. Torchi Blasch, Chicago Hurricanes
4. Josephine Wilkowski, Chicago Hurricanes

Discus throw
1. Verda Crawford, Prairie View College   102' 5¾"
2. Rosia Nettles, Tuskegee Institute   97' 1¼"
3. Estelle Kestenbaum, German-American A.C.   96' 3¾"
4. Marvis Smith, Prairie View College   91' 11¾"

Team scores:
Tuskegee Institute 99; German-American A.C. 38; Prairie View College 33; Philadel-
phia Turners 31½; Chicago Hurricanes 25; Brookhaven High School 18; Wiley Col-
lege 16; Polish Olympic W.A.C. 14; San Antonio Recreation 13; A & I State College,
Nashville 11½; Malvernette A.C. 11; Forrestville Playground, Chicago 10; Phoenix,
Arizona 8; Ozark Women's Sports Club 4.

There was no national indoor competition this year.

1947 All-America Women's Track and Field Team

50-meter run	Alice Coachman
100-meter run	Juanita Watson
200-meter run	Audrey Patterson
80-meter hurdles	Nancy Cowperthwaite
High jump	Alice Coachman
Broad jump	Lillie Purifoy

8-lb. shot	Dorothy Dodson
Javelin throw	Dorothy Dodson
Discus throw	Frances Kaszubski
Baseball throw	Marian Twining Barone
400-meter relay	Juanita Watson, Alice Coachman, Mary Griggs, Elaine Burgess

The twenty-three member track and field committee was headed by Catherine Donovan Meyer, and Evelyne Hall was one of three vice chairmen. Committee members were Olympians Annette Rogers, Olive Hasenfus Sparks, and Alice Arden Hodge, coaches Cleve Abbott from Tuskegee and Aileen Allen from California, and athlete Frances Kaszubski.

The 1947 *AAU Handbook* listed an Olympic Track and Field Committee. The members were Cleve Abbott of Tuskegee, Roberta Ranck Bonniwell of Philadelphia, Mrs. Frances Gorn Sobczak Kazubski of Cleveland, Fred Steers of Chicago, Harry Hainsworth of Buffalo, and Evelyne Hall of California. This appears to be the first women's Olympic track and field committee.

Chapter 31

1948: The First Post-War Olympic Year

Brown University Stadium in Providence, Rhode Island, was the site of the final women's track and field trials. The meet was scheduled from 5 P.M. to 7:30 P.M. on July 12. When the trials were over, the following twelve women were on the fourth United States women's Olympic track and field team, which competed in the Olympic games in London from July 29 to August 14.

	Olympic Event	*Olympic Place*	*Olympic Performance*
Coachman, Alice	HJ	1	5' 6⅛"
Dodson, Dorothy	Discus	16	113' 9½"
	SP	DNQ	
	Javelin	4	137' 7½"
Faggs, Mae	200m	DNQ	26.0
Jackson, Nell	200m	DNQ	25.8
	400mr	DNQ	48.3
Kaszubski, Frances	Discus	11	119' 8½"
	SP	DNQ	
Manuel, Theresa	80mh	DNQ	
	Javelin	12	110' 11½"
	400mr	DNQ	48.3
Patterson, Audrey	100m	DNQ	12.8
	200m	3	25.2
	400mr	DNQ	48.3
Reed, Emma	BJ	12	15' 10¼"
	HJ	14	Tied — 4' 7⅛"
Robinson, Bernice	80mh	DNQ	
	HJ	11	Tied — 4' 11"
Walker, Mabel	100m	DNQ	12.8
	400mr	DNQ	48.3
Walraven, Jean	80mh	DNQ	
	BJ	DNQ	
Young, Lillian	100m	DNQ	13.0
	BJ	DNQ	

Meyer, Mrs. Catherine D.	Coach
Hainsworth, Harry	Manager
Hainsworth, Mrs. Evelyn E.	Chaperone

The 200-meter dash, broad jump and the 8-lb. shot put were new events added to the 1948 Olympic track and field program.

Following the tryouts on July 12, the team left Providence by train for New York on July 13. The young women sailed to London on July 14 on the S.S. *America* with the other members of the Olympic team. Mrs. Meyer reported that the team was "truly representative," made up of high school, college, and business women.

Ideal weather made shipboard training possible, and a small gymnasium was available for indoor work. The team had a 10:30 P.M. curfew, and the conduct of the team was excellent. The food, training facilities, and housing in England were inferior to those of the ship, however.

Only three of the team placed among the first four in their events. The outstanding performance was that of Alice Coachman. She established a new Olympic record of 5' 6½" for the high jump while 65,000 spectators in Wembley Stadium watched the final event on the last day of the track and field competition.

The Olympic Results

100 meters. Nine heats were conducted in the 100 meters. There were forty-one contestants. Audrey Patterson was third in the third heat in 12.8 seconds. Mabel Walker was third in the fourth heat in the same time. Lillian Young placed third in the fifth heat in 13.0. Only the first two in each heat qualified for the semifinal round, so the United States did not have anyone in the final.

200 meters. There were thirty-two starters and seven heats. Two qualified for the semifinal.

Mae Faggs was third in the first heat of the 200 meters in 26.0. In the fourth heat, Nell Jackson was third in 25.8, and the fifth heat was won by Audrey Patterson in 25.5.

Audrey Patterson was second in the first semifinal in 25.0. She placed third in the final in 25.2, bringing home the bronze medal.

80-meter hurdles. Jean Walraven, our only athlete to qualify for the semifinal round, placed third in the fourth heat in 12.6. In the first of the four heats, Theresa Manuel was sixth, and in the third heat, Bernice Robinson was fourth. In the first semifinal, Jean Walraven came in sixth and did not advance to the final.

400-meter relay. Ten teams were entered in this event. The United States team composed of Nell Jackson, Theresa Manuel, Audrey Patterson, and Mabel Walker, was third in the third heat in 48.3. They did not make the final, nor did they break the American record of 46.9 set in the 1932 Olympic Games by Carew, Furtsch, Rogers, and Von Bremen, a time that would have won the 1948 gold medal.

High jump. The only gold medal won by the United States women was in the high jump, which proved to be one of the most exciting events of the entire Games. Few of the nineteen contestants had trouble with the lower heights. The six place winners were from five different countries, and all cleared 5' 2¼". As the bar was raised, the three survivors were Alice Coachman, Dorothy Tyler of Great Britain, the runner-up in the 1936 Olympics, and Michelene Ostermeyer of France, who had already won the discus and shot put. Ostermeyer failed at 5' 4½" and finished third. Coachman and Tyler then both cleared 5' 4½", setting a new Olympic record. At 5' 6¼", Coachman cleared the bar on her first attempt; Mrs. Tyler cleared it on her second attempt. The bar was then raised to 5' 7". Both women failed at this height.

While the high jump competition was still in its final stages, all of the other events had been concluded, but about 65,000 fans remained in the stadium to witness the dramatic conclusion. Alice Coachman became the new Olympic champion because of fewer misses. Tyler, for the second time, took home the silver medal.

Our other two entrants, Bernice Robinson and Emma Reed, failed to place.

Kieran and Daley's book, *Story of the Olympic Games*, reports Coachman's victory in one sentence: "In the only other women's event Alice Coachman of the United States won the high jump at the record height of 5' 6⅛", winning the crown from Mrs. Dorothy Tyler of Great Britain on fewer misses."

The August 21 *New York Amsterdam News* featured a story on Alice Coachman:

> American womanhood was due for a sad let-down so far as Olympic competition was concerned, until a brown-skinned girl from the heart of Dixie set a new world record on the last day of the event, and emerged the high jump champion.
>
> This victory was so significant that the *Atlanta Constitution* ran the following editorial, which also tells the story of Alice Coachman:
>
> "Georgia had one athlete in the Olympic Games, the track and field events of which have just been concluded at London. That was Miss Alice Coachman, of Albany, a young Negro woman, graduate of Albany State College.
>
> "She won the high jump, defeating the favorite, a young woman from Great Britain. In winning she established a new Olympic record. Twenty-six years old, she has won 25 gold medals in national track and field events for women. In the 50 and 100 meter races she held the title for two years, defeating the famous Stella Walsh, of Poland, to win those championships.
>
> "She is the only member of the United States women's Olympic squad to win a gold medal in the field events. We are sure Georgia is proud of her and that her native city will arrange a program in which all citizens can participate in honoring her when she returns."
>
> For the first time in history, this south Georgia town is going to have a parade for a Negro — Alice Coachman, Olympic champion.
>
> The plans were being made today and just about every big wig in the community is planning to be on hand to honor the 25 year old daughter of a laundry worker.

Alice was the first black woman to win an Olympic gold medal.

Broad jump. Twenty-nine women were entered in this event. Of the three

Alice Coachman, 1948 Olympic champion in the high jump, showing her style in the high jump. (Courtesy of Richmond Davis and Alice Coachman.)

entries from the United States, only Emma Reed reached the finals but she did not place. Jean Walraven and Lillian Young did not qualify for the finals.

Shot put. We had two entries in the shot put, Frances Kaszubski and Dorothy Dodson. Neither qualified for the final round.

Javelin throw. There were only fifteen contestants in the javelin throw, but the competition was good. Dorothy Dodson finished fourth with a throw of 137' 7½". Theresa Manuel did not place.

Discus throw. Our two entries in this event, Dorothy Dodson and Frances Kaszubski, did not make the finals.

When the Olympic Games were over, invitational meets were held in London on August 12 and in Paris on August 15 and 16. Two events, the 80-meter hurdles and the 440-yard relay, were held in the USA vs. Commonwealth meet at White City Stadium. The United States finished second in the relay.

In addition to all of the Olympic events, an 800-meter run for women was held in the Paris meet. Audrey Patterson won the 200-meter dash in 25.2, Bernice Robinson was fourth in the 80-meter hurdles, Lillian Young placed third in the broad jump, the United States 400-meter relay team finished second to France, and no one placed in the women's shot put. On the second day of competition, Patterson won her second gold medal in the 100 meters, finishing first in 12.1.

Coachman won the high jump with a leap of 5' 3", Emma Reed was third, and Bernice Robinson was fourth. None of the American women placed in the discus throw, but Dorothy Dodson finished fourth in the javelin throw.

The Olympic Trials

For the first time, the United States Olympic Committee instructed each sports committee to establish standards of qualification for membership on the Olympic team. The standards were to be based on the eighth place performance of the previous Games. The track and field committee established the standards at a meeting held on December 5, 1947, at Omaha, Nebraska:

100-meter dash	12.4
80-meter hurdles	12.3
Broad jump	17' 10¼"
Shot put	39' 1½"
Discus throw	123' 4"
Javelin throw	128' 4"
High jump	5' ½"
200-meter run	26.0

At the meeting, Mrs. Meyer was elected chairman, Mrs. Roberta Ranck Bonniwell, the 1923 national javelin champion, was elected secretary, and Mr. Hainsworth was elected representative to the United States Olympic Committee. The committee established the standards, secured the tryouts, and made plans for fundraising. At a later meeting, Mrs. Meyer was named coach of the team, Mrs. Bonniwell chaperone, and Mr. Hainsworth team manager. Several weeks prior to sailing, Mrs. Bonniwell resigned because she was selected as team leader for women's gymnastics. The committee was contacted and asked to submit names for the chaperone assignment. Several were nominated, and the chairman conducted a mail vote. With the understanding that she defray part of her expenses, Mrs. Harry Hainsworth was named chaperone.

After an impressive opening ceremony, just before the Olympic trials began, a quartet of Navy jets zoomed over the stadium, performing a series of low-flying maneuvers.

Twenty-nine-year-old Dorothy Dodson shattered the championship javelin record set by Babe Didrikson sixteen years before, and Frances Kaszubski won both the shot and discus events.

An unofficial American record was set in the 880-yard medley relay (110-110-220-440) by Tuskegee running against a team from the New York City Police Athletic League. Walker, Griggs, Jackson, and Manuel ran 1:54.0 to better a 1929 mark.

With a mob of fans surrounding the pit, Alice Coachman high jumped an inch and a half over the present championship record set in 1933. She was trying to clear the Olympic record height of 5' 5¼", but it got too dark to continue jumping.

Only ten athletes of the seventy-four competing qualified for the Olympic team under perfect weather conditions, but the United States Olympic Committee notified the track and field committee that the winner of each event should be selected. On this basis, a team of eleven was named at the completion of the trials. Upon the committee's recommendation, a twelfth girl, Jean Walraven, was added to the team. She had barely missed making the standard.

Newly married socialite Nancy Cowperthwaite Phillips declined to make the trip to London.

---

100 meters
1. Mabel Walker, Tuskegee Institute   12.3
2. Audrey Patterson, Tennessee State College   12.4
3. Lillian Young, Forrestville Playground, Chicago   12.6
4. Mary Griggs, Tuskegee Institute   12.8
5. Juanita Watson, Tuskegee Institute   12.8
6. Nancy McClurken, Philadelphia Turners   13.2

200 meters
1. Audrey Patterson, Tennessee State College   25.3
2. Nell Jackson, Tuskegee Institute   25.8
3. Mae Faggs, New York Police Athletic League   25.9
4. Janet Moreau, Red Diamond A.C.   26.6
5. Dorothy Klein, N.Y. Police Athletic League   28.5
6. Gwendolyn Taylor, Tuskegee Institute   28.5

80-meter hurdles
1. Bernice Robinson, Washington Park, Chicago   12.4
2. Nancy Cowperthwaite Phillips, German-American A.C.   12.4
3. Theresa Manuel, Tuskegee Institute   12.6
4. Eleanor Millheiser, German-American A.C.   12.7
5. Jean Walraven, North Olmsted-Westlake A.C, Ohio   13.3
6. Loretta Blaul, German-American A.C.   14.0

Running broad jump
1. Emma Reed, Tennessee State College   18' 4⅝"
2. Lillian Young, Forrestville Playground   17' 9⅜"
3. Nancy C. Phillips, German-American A.C.   17' 5"
4. Jean Walraven, North Olmsted-Westlake A.C.   17' 3"
5. Lillie Purifoy, Tuskegee Institute   17' 2"
6. Jeanette McKay, Harrisburg A.A.   16' ⅛"

Running high jump
1. Alice Coachman, Albany State College   5' 4¾"
2. Bernice Robinson, Washington Park, Chicago   5' 1¼"
3. Emma Reed, Tennessee State College   5' ¾"
4. Mary Rebecca Oprea, No. Olmsted-Westlake A.C.,   4' 8"
       and Bessie Leick, No. Olmsted-Westlake A.C.   4' 8"
6. Barbara Mewes, Unattached, St. Louis,   4' 6"
       and Geraldine Gross, LeDroit Falcons, Washington, D.C.   4' 6"

Discus throw
1. Frances Kaszubski, No. Olmsted-Westlake A.C.   122' 6½"
2. Dorothy Dodson, J. T. Dempsey Hurricanes   113' 11"
3. Pauline Ruppeldt, Philadelphia Turners   104' 10¾"
4. Amelia Bert, Little Rhody A.C., Providence   100' 9¾"
5. Estelle Kestenbaum, German-American A.C.   100' 9¼"
6. Torchi Blasch, J. T. Dempsey Hurricanes   93' 4"

Javelin throw
1. Dorothy Dodson, J. T. Dempsey Hurricanes   140' 4"
2. Theresa Manuel, Tuskegee Institute   115'
3. Bessie Leick, No. Olmsted-Westlake A.C.   102' 6"
4. Torchi Blasch, J. T. Dempsey Hurricanes   86' 1"
5. Anita Schriver, unattached, West Virginia   76' 4"

8-lb. shot put
1. Frances Kaszubski, No. Olmsted-Westlake A.C.   38' 8¼"
2. Dorothy Dodson, J. T. Dempsey Hurricanes   38' 4½"
3. Ramona Harris, unattached, New York   37' 3¾"
4. Amelia Bert, Little Rhody A.C.   36' 8"
5. Doris Sutter, unattached, Los Angeles   33' 4"
6. Torchi Blasch, J. T. Dempsey Hurricanes   33' 2"

The Outdoor Nationals

The national championship meet on July 5 and 6, a week before the Olympic trials, was held in Grand Rapids, Michigan, at Houseman Field. The meet raised funds for financing the team to England. The men's track and field committee and the basketball committee aided greatly in helping with the monetary problems.

More than 3,000 spectators witnessed the outdoor championships, where world and American records were expected to be set. None were, even though athletes and members of the track and field committee complimented the officials on the well-run meet and thought that the track was in excellent condition. Stella Walsh won three events. Six foot, one inch Frances Kaszubski won two events, the shot and discus, and five foot, two inch Dorothy Dodson won the javelin and was runner-up to Kaszubski in the shot and discus. Tuskegee won the team title.

50-meter dash
1. Mabel Walker, Tuskegee Institute   6.7
2. Alice Coachman, Albany State College
3. Mary Hardaway, Tennessee State College
4. Dolores Dwyer, German-American A.C.
5. Bessie Barfield, N.Y. Police Athletic League
6. Marie Taylor, N.Y. Police Athletic League

200-meter dash
1. Stella Walsh, Polish Women's A.C.   25.5

2. Audrey Patterson, Tennessee State College
3. Nell Jackson, Tuskegee Institute
4. Mae Faggs, N.Y. Police Athletic League
5. Dorothy Klein, N.Y. Police Athletic League
6. Jean Lowe, Tuskegee Institute

High jump
1. Alice Coachman, Albany State College   5'
2. Emma Reed, Tennessee State College,
    and Bernice Robinson, Washington Park, Chicago
4. Mary Oprea, No. Olmsted-Westlake A.C.
5. Doris Hill, Tuskegee Institute,
    and Bessie Leick, No. Olmsted-Westlake A.C.

Broad jump
1. Stella Walsh, Polish W.A.C.   17' 8½"
2. Lillian Young, Forrestville Playground, Chicago
3. Nancy Phillips, German-American A.C.
4. Jean Walraven, No. Olmsted-Westlake A.C.
5. Jean Lowe, Tuskegee Institute
6. Loretta Blaul, German-American A.C.

100-meter dash
1. Stella Walsh, Polish W.A.C.   12.9
2. Mary Griggs, Tuskegee Institute
3. Juanita Watson, Tuskegee Institute
4. Dorothy Jacobs, J.T. Dempsey Hurricanes
5. Claudine Young, Standford Park, Chicago
6. Bessie Barfield, N.Y Police Athletic League

80-meter hurdles
1. Bernice Robinson, Washington Park   12.1
2. Lillie Purifoy, Tuskegee Institute
3. Theresa Manuel, Tuskegee Institute
4. Nancy Cowperthwaite Phillips, German-American A.C.
5. Eleanor Millheiser, German-American A.C.
6. Jean Walraven, No. Olmsted–Westlake A.C.

400-meter relay
1. Tuskegee Institute   50.3
2. N.Y. Police Athletic League
3. Tennessee State College
4. German-American A.C.
5. Tuskegee Institute, "B" team
6. J.T. Dempsey Hurricanes

Javelin
1. Dorothy Dodson, J. T. Dempsey Hurricanes   125' 10⅜"
2. Theresa Manuel, Tuskegee Institute
3. Bessie Leick, No. Olmsted–Westlake A.C.
4. Torchi Blasch, J. T. Dempsey Hurricanes
5. Eleanor Repinski, Polish W.A.C.

8-lb. shot put
1. Frances Kaszubski, No. Olmsted-Westlake A.C.   40' 5⅞"
2. Dorothy Dodson, J. T. Dempsey Hurricanes
3. Pauline Ruppeldt, Philadelphia Turners
4. Doris Sutter, City of Glendale
5. Josephine Wilkowski, J. T. Dempsey Hurricanes
6. Mellie McKee, Tuskeegee Institute

Discus
1. Frances Kaszubski, No. Olmsted–Westlake A.C.   124' 3⅜"
2. Dorothy Dodson, J. T. Dempsey Hurricanes
3. Herta Rand, unattached, San Rafael, Calif.
4. Pauline Ruppeldt, Philadelphia Turners
5. Estelle Kestenbaum, German-American A.C.
6. Torchi Blasch, J. T. Dempsey Hurricanes

Baseball throw
1. Juanita Watson, Tuskegee Institute   218' 6"
2. Bessie Leick, No. Olmsted–Westlake A.C.
3. Estelle Kestenbaum, German-American A.C.
4. Audrey Sturm, unattached, Phoenix
5. Josephine Wilkowski, J. T. Dempsey Hurricanes
6. Barbara Mooney, unattached, Schenectady, N.Y.

Team scores:
Tuskegee Institute 80½; North Olmsted–Westlake A.C. 44½; J. T. Dempsey Hurricanes 40; Polish W.A.C. 32; German-American A.C. 29; Tennessee State College 27; Albany State College 18; New York Police Athletic League 17; Washington Park, Chicago 17; Philadelphia Turners 10; City of Glendale, Calif. 4; unattached 11.

Individual scores:
Stella Walsh 30; Dorothy Dodson 26; Frances Kaszubski 20; Alice Coachman 18; Bernice Robinson 17; Juanita Watson 16.

The Indoor Championships

Only two of the 1946 defending champions (meet was not held in 1947) competed on April 24 at the University of Chicago field house. Both Dorothy Dodson and Lillie Purifoy were unsuccessful in retaining their titles. New champions were crowned in the eight events.

American indoor records were broken on the dirt track in the 50-meter hurdles and the 50-meter dash. Both former records were set in the 1930s — the hurdle record in 1933 by Evelyne Hall and the 50-meter mark in 1935 by Helen Stephens. The citizen's record for the 200 meters was lowered. The former record was held by Annette Rogers, chairman of the Central AAU women's track and field committee, who was at the meet and saw her 1933 record of 26.8 broken.

200-meter run
1. Audrey Patterson, Tennessee State College   26.4

2. Nell Jackson, Tuskegee Institute
3. Jean Lowe, Tuskegee Institute
4. Katherine Geary, Philadelphia Turners

50-meter hurdles
1. Theresa Manuel, Tuskegee Institute   7.4
2. Bernice Robinson, Washington Park, Chicago
3. Nancy Cowperthwaite, German-American A.C.
4. Lillie Purifoy, Tuskegee Institute

50-meter run
1. Juanita Watson, Tuskegee Institute   6.5
2. Lillian Young, Forrestville Playground, Chicago
3. Mabel Walker, Tuskegee Institute
4. Katherine Geary, Philadelphia Turners

400-meter relay
1. Tuskegee Institute, "A" team   51.8
2. Tennessee State College
3. German-American A.C.
4. J. T. Dempsey Hurricanes, "A" team

High jump
1. Emma Reed, Tennessee State College   4' 11⅜"
2. Bernice Robinson, Washington Park
3. Rebecca Oprea, No. Olmsted-Westlake A.C.
4. Evelyn Lawler, Tuskegee Institute

8-lb. shot put
1. Frances Kaszubski, No. Olmsted–Westlake A.C.   38' 4⅛"
2. Dorothy Dodson, J. T. Dempsey Hurricanes
3. Katherine Geary, Philadelphia Turners
4. Torchi Blasch, J. T. Dempsey Hurricanes

Standing broad jump
1. Nancy Cowperthwaite, German-American A.C.   7' 11½"
2. Mildred Martin, J. T. Dempsey Hurricanes
3. Evelyn Lawler, Tuskegee Institute
4. Bernice Robinson, Washington Park

Basketball throw
1. Stella Gorka, Whittier Playground, Chicago   93' 7"
2. Eva Pikal, Gary Playground, Chicago
3. Frances Kaszubski, No. Olmsted–Westlake A.C.
4. Theresa Manuel, Tuskegee Institute

Running broad jump (added event — nonchampionship)
1. Nancy Cowperthwaite, German-American A.C.   17' 2⅜"
2. Lillian Young, Forrestville Playground
3. Bernice Robinson, Washington Park
4. Lillie Purifoy, Tuskegee Institute

Team scores:
Tuskegee Institute 27; Tennessee State College 13; German-American A.C. 9; No.

Olmsted-Westlake A.C., Cleveland 9; J. T. Dempsey Hurricanes, Chicago 8; Washington Park, Chicago 7; Whittier Playground, Chicago 5; Philadelphia Turners 4; Forrestville Playground, Chicago 3; Gary Playground, Chicago 3.

Individual scores:
Nancy Cowperthwaite 7; Frances Kaszubski 7; Bernice Robinson 7; Theresa Manuel 6.

1948 All-America Women's Track and Field Team

50 meters	Juanita Watson
100 meters	Audrey Patterson
200 meters	Audrey Patterson
50-meter hurdles	Theresa Manuel
80-meter hurdles	Bernice Robinson
High jump	Alice Coachman
Broad jump	Emma Reed
Standing Broad jump	Nancy Cowperthwaite
8-lb. shot put	Frances Kaszubski
Discus throw	Frances Kaszubski
Javelin throw	Dorothy Dodson
Basketball throw	Stella Gorka
Baseball throw	Juanita Watson
400-meter relay	Audrey Patterson, Mabel Walker, Lillian Young, Stella Walsh

---

Meyer, in her annual committee report to the AAU, indicated that the increased interest in women's track and field in the United States was expected because of the Olympic Games. She thought that adding women's events to many of the major indoor men's meets was also a contributing factor to this growth.

An example of this increased interest can be seen in the program of the Sixtieth Annual American Indoor Track and Field Championships held in Madison Square Garden on February 21. Seventeen women were entered in a 60-yard dash. Eight of the seventeen were from the Mercury Athletic Club of Montreal, Canada.

Kay Geary of the Philadelphia Turners won the event in 7.3. Nancy McClurken of the same club was second. Bessie Barfield of the New York Police Athletic League was third, and Mae Faggs of the same club was fourth.

A second event on the program was the women's 440-yard relay. Five teams competed. First place went to the Philadelphia Turners in 52.9, followed by the German-American A.C. and the Police Athletic League.

The *Amateur Athlete* reported in February that Stella Walsh had won what she considered to be "her greatest race." After trying for fifteen years to become an American citizen, she at last obtained her citizenship. Although she had suffered a leg injury in Texas in July, Stella was setting her sights on the 1948 Olympic Games. She wrote in a letter to Dan Ferris: "My boyfriend told me to give competition one more try before I hang up my track shoes. After all it's been a long twenty-two year grind. I expect to become engaged soon and to get married. It's about time I settled down, is it not?" Stella had won sixty-four world and national titles.

Track and Field News was published for the first time in February. The first issue reported some of the best performances in the world of women athletes for 1947. The list was ten deep in most of the eight events, but no American girl was on any list.

An article in the *Amsterdam News* on May 8 reported the results of the 20th Annual Tuskegee Women's Sports Day. Six meet records were broken, and a world record was tied. Tennessee State College was second to Tuskegee in point score. Other colleges participating were Arkansas A.M. and N. College, Grambling College, and Prairie View College.

An effort was made to add some women's events to the following indoor meets: the *Philadelphia Inquirer* Invitation Meet, the Cleveland Knights of Columbus Meet, the *Chicago Daily News* Relays, the Millrose Games, and the National AAU Indoor Meet.

Alice Coachman

Alice was born in Albany, Georgia, in 1922. When she was a young girl, she played with the boys, challenging them to running and jumping contests. "The girls were no fun to play with as they were always trying to act cute," said Alice in an interview on June 9, 1995, in Philadelphia, Pennsylvania.

Her only high jump bar at the time was a jump rope with each end held tightly by two friends. Her style was to approach the rope straight on, and she always beat the boys.

When she tried to join the track team, the coach did not really need her because he had all the sprinters he wanted. He figured he could use field event people, however, so he let her high jump. The first time Alice jumped over a high jump bar was that summer when her coach took the team to the Tuskegee Relays. She won the event.

Cleve Abbott saw her jump and asked her to become part of his Tuskegee track team, which had competed each year since 1936 in the national AAU championships. The year was 1939, and the national meet was in Waterbury, Connecticut. Sixteen-year-old Alice won her first of many national titles in the high jump. In her interview, she continued the story of her track and field history:

> I went back to school after that in Albany, Georgia. I finished the next year of school, and Coach Abbott asked me again to compete with his team. Again, my parents somehow agreed on it. The national meet was in Ocean City, New Jersey, and I won the high jump for the second straight year.
>
> I returned home, and about two weeks later, Coach Abbott and Miss Petty came to my house to convince my mother and father to let me come to Tuskegee to live on the campus like the college students. At that time Tuskegee taught a lot of trades, and they housed high school students as well as college students,

but the high school students didn't have the privileges that college students had. Two other high school girls had been invited, Lillian Purifoy and Rowena Harrison. Rowena went into nursing, so she had to stay on the campus in the nursing dorm. But Lillie and I stayed out in the community, and we went to all of the activities there. After that I was on my own. I had to work for my tuition. I was on a work scholarship. I worked and did things on the campus that would give me some credit so I could pay my room and board. I never did get home much because of that.

During the early years that I was high jumping, there were only two or three styles — Eastern roll, Western roll and scissors. I was jumping straight across in front of the bar. When I got to Tuskegee, they tried to change me from jumping straight at the bar to doing a forty-five degree angle from the left and then going into a roll — which would have been a Western roll. But, I never did get that style.

In 1948, when I made the Olympic team, I knew all of the other girls. We were just like close friends. Many of us were in the same dorms at meets. Both black and white were living together then. Wherever we went we were together. The only differences were that the girls were in different clubs and in different events.

I didn't really want to go to England. I had qualified to go, and when the boat pulled out, I started crying like a baby. But I couldn't let my country down, I couldn't let my school down, and I couldn't let my folks down, so I had to go. After being champion for nine or ten years, I had no choice even though I was sick. I had an ailment that was corrected by the doctor placing a plastic tube in me to turn my ovary around. It was twisted. That was dangerous in high jumping. To jump when your back was hurting was terrible. My doctor gave me a letter to give to the doctor on board the S.S. *America*. He told him to take care of me. He knew what to do the day before I jumped. He had to take the tube out to give me some relief.

I went to the doctor every day on the boat. He examined me and said I'd be o.k. after a while. It hurt my back. Every time I jumped it seemed as though I'd get a catch in my back. The day before I jumped, the doctor took the tube out. I went out and stretched and took a couple of laps.

Everyone on the team failed. Only Mickey Patterson got a third place. So here I was, the last person to try to bring America through. I said to myself as I saw my other teammates coming in last in the first round — not the second round, but the first round, whoever beats me is going to have to put up some because I'm going to sure try to win my event.

When I walked out on the field, King George and Queen Elizabeth were there. Eighty-five thousand people were watching me jump because there never had been a black woman win a gold medal or even attempt to win one.

There were only three people left in the high jump — Dorothy Tyler, me, and Ostermeyer from France. The people just sat there and watched, and every time I would miss, I could hear the crowd say Ohhhhh! And then I looked around and saw nothing but all of those people in the stadium, when I got ready to jump, I didn't hear them, but I could hear their sighing afterward.

I went on and I was lucky enough to win. I won because I had fewer misses. Every time I went over that bar I tried to make the first one count. It took the other athletes sometimes two or three jumps to do it. Tyler jumped the same height, but I was lucky enough to win it.

My Olympic team coach was mad that I didn't work out the day before I jumped. I said to her that my school coach told me never to work out the day before I compete — save that strength in your legs. I heard that each time I got ready to jump she walked out of the stadium and then came back in and said, "Did she make it? Did she make it?" It was the last event, and everyone was staying around to see who was going to win this battle between the United States and England. I was the only one to bring her bacon in.

I did not know I won. Someone came out there and told me. I had my hair braided across my head. Someone said, "Come on. I looked up there and saw A. Coachman — USA. They said, "Come on, you've got to get up on the stand." So, I just took my hair down and brushed it back and went on the stand. King George presented me with the medal. I was happy to get my medal awarded to me by King George because I had read so much about the king and queen of England.

We went to Paris after the games. I won the high jump and relay. Then we went on a tour of southern France.

When we returned home, it was all over. I hung up my shoes after that.

Nell C. Jackson

Nell was always there, wherever there was women's track. She was the hub of the national wheel of women's track and field. There was not a thing the soft smiling, gentle lady did not do athletically, educationally, administratively, or as a coach in our sport.

Nell was born in Athens, Georgia, on July 1, 1929. Her introduction to national competition was in the 1944 championships. In 1945, indoors and outdoors, at the age of sixteen, she placed second in the two meets to Stella Walsh in the 200 meters.

In 1946, Nell was second to Stella again in the 200 meters and won the 200 meters in the first junior national championships. She was named to the United States All-America team in the 200.

In 1947, Nell was second in the outdoor junior nationals and third in the senior nationals.

In 1948, Nell was a member of the Olympic team. She finished second in the trials in 25.8. In London, she was eliminated in the second round of the 200 meters.

In 1949, Nell set a championship record of 24.2 in the 200 meters, an excellent time even by world standards.

In 1950, Nell won the national title in the 200 meters, beating Stella Walsh in 25.0, and she anchored her winning 400-meter relay team.

In 1951, Nell was third in the outdoor nationals and made the Pan American team, placing second in the 200 meters in 25.7. The U.S. 400-meter relay team, of which she was a member, won the gold.

Nell graduated from Tuskegee Institute in 1951. Her master of science degree was from Springfield College, Massachusetts, in 1953, and her doctor of philosophy degree was earned at the University of Iowa in 1962.

Nell's teaching and coaching career began in 1953 at her alma mater, Tuskegee Institute. Her professional pathway continued to the University of Iowa, Illinois

Alice Coachman in June 1995.

State University, University of Illinois, and Michigan State University, where she was the assistant director of athletics. In 1981, she moved to the State University of New York at Binghamton, where she was the director of physical education and intercollegiate athletics and a professor in the Department of Physical Education.

Nell wrote many articles on women's track and field for professional journals and directed motivational track and field films for girls. In 1968 she wrote a book entitled *Track and Field for Girls and Women*.

The positions Nell held include chairman of the U.S. women's Olympic track & field committee, national chairman of women's track and field, member of the board of directors, U.S. Olympic Committee, consultant to the 1968 Olympic team, and coordinator of track and field sections for the First and Fifth National Institutes on Girls' Sports (1963, 1968). She was secretary and vice president of The Athletics Congress.

Nell coached the 1956 and 1972 women's Olympic track and field teams and managed ten United States teams nationally and internationally. I was appointed to work with Nell as assistant manager on her last assignment at the 1987 Pan American Games in Indianapolis. We worked together during the days and in the evenings reminisced over chocolate sundaes about the thirty-five years since we met in 1952 at the Olympic trials.

Dr. Jackson coached national-level athletes — Mildred McDaniel, Neomia Rodgers, Sue Latter, and Judy Brown King, to name a few. She conducted more than fifty workshops and clinics throughout the country and was a coordinator of regional track and field camps for women.

Tuskegee University honored her with the Alumni Merit Award and the National Alumni Merit Award, the NSGWS (National Section on Girls and Women's Sports) gave her a Presidential citation, she was inducted into the Black Sports Hall of Fame, she was a recipient of the 1980 Joseph Robichaux Award, she was inducted into the first Sudafed International Women's Sports Hall of Fame in 1980, and she was enshrined into the National Track and Field Hall of Fame in 1989.

Nell Jackson worked her whole life to promote and develop women's track and field. Dr. Bert Lyle, coach at Texas Woman's University, has spoken of her important contributions:

> [Nell] became instrumental in developing the DGWS collegiate women's sports program in track and field. Nell served as the first rules chairperson of the Track

and Field Committee as well as Games Committee Chairperson and within a few years elevated the rules of competition to a state of usability and acceptance by all within the track community. I had the privilege of serving on the committees during these years and admired her patience and leadership as she constantly sought the best approaches for advancing women's collegiate track and field. ... She was the quiet stable one who could be depended upon to offer quality insight for she listened so well to individuals and groups that the consensus she achieved was very satisfying to all. Her qualities of reserved but confident mannerisms — control and quiet drive — understanding and trust — intelligence and loyality — insight and acceptance contributed to her effective guidance.

Nell Jackson was fifty-eight years of age when she died on April 1, 1988.

Chapter 32

1949

The national championship meet was held in Bronco Stadium, Odessa, Texas, on August 12 and 13. After a barbecue at the Shrine Club for the more than one hundred athletes, coaches, and officials, the athletes gave singing and dancing performances. The climax of the evening was Bernice Robinson's singing of four songs, including her rendition of "Summertime" and "Some Enchanted Evening."

The next day the highlight of the meet was the new championship record set by Bernice Robinson in the 80-meter hurdles. Her time of 11.9 broke the record of 12.0 set in 1931 by Babe Didrikson and equaled by Anne Vrana O'Brien in 1936. It was the first time that the 12-second barrier was eclipsed in the nationals. Robinson was also high scorer, placing second in the high jump and broad jump.

Juanita Watson was the only double winner, and Stella Walsh lost all three of her events. Nell Jackson ran away from the field, including Stella, in the 200 meters and posted the excellent time of 24.2.

Tuskegee won the team title, scoring five firsts and placing in every event but the javelin throw.

Shot put
1. Amelia Bert, Little Rhody Club, Providence   39' 8¼"
2. Frances Kaszubski, Cleveland
3. Dorothy Dodson Kenny, Chicago Dempsey Hurricanes
4. Herta Rand, Takoma Park, Md.

High jump
1. Gertrude Orr, Tuskegee Institute   5'
2. Bernice Robinson, Washington Park, Chicago
3. Evelyn Lawler, Tuskegee Institute
4. Nancy Phillips, German-American A.C.,
    and Cynthia Booker, Washington Park

50-meter dash
1. Juanita Watson, Tuskegee, Institute   6.5
2. Jean Patton, Tennessee State College
3. Dolores Dwyer, German-American A.C.
4. Gladys Tally, Tuskegee Institute

200-meter dash
1. Nell Jackson, Tuskegee Institute   24.2 MR
2. Stella Walsh, Cleveland
3. Audrey Patterson, Tennessee State College
4. Jean Lowe, Tuskegee Institute

80-meter hurdles
1. Bernice Robinson, Washington Park   11.9 MR
2. Theresa Manuel, Tuskegee Institute
3. Mildred Martin, Chicago Dempsey Hurricanes
4. Constance Darnowski, German-American A.C.

Discus throw
1. Frances Kaszubski, Cleveland   123' 9"
2. Herta Rand, Takoma Park, Md.
3. Concepcion Villaneuva, Mexican Athletic Federation, Mexico City
4. Dorothy Dodson Kenny, Chicago Dempsey Hurricanes

100-meter dash
1. Jean Patton, Tennessee State College   12.1
2. Audrey Patterson, Tennessee State College
3. Dorothy Jacobs, Chicago Dempsey Hurricanes
4. Dolores Dwyer, German-American A.C.

Javelin throw
1. Dorothy Dodson Kenny, Chicago Dempsey Hurricanes 123' 1"
2. Herta Rand, Takoma Park, Md.
3. Maria Julia Perez, Edison Institute, Havana
4. Elsa Atzumi, Mexican Athletic Federation

400-meter relay
1. Tuskegee Institute (Jackson, Lowe, Manuel, Watson)   50.0
2. San Angelo
3. Mexico City
4. Havana Edison Institute

Baseball throw
1. Juanita Watson, Tuskegee Institute   233' 8"
2. Amelia Bert, Little Rhody A.C.
3. Eva Pikal, Gary Playground, Chicago
4. Mrs. J. C. Freeman, Loop, Texas

Broad jump
1. Mabel Landry, Chicago   17' 5"
2. Bernice Robinson, Washington Park
3. Stella Walsh, Cleveland
4. Evelyn Lawler, Tuskegee Institute

Team scores:
Tuskegee Institute 81; Chicago Dempsey Hurricanes 34; Tennessee State College 32; Washington Park, Chicago 26; German-American A.C. 23; Little Rhody Club, Providence 20; Mexican Athletic Federation and Polish Falcons 16; Edison Institute of Havana 13; San Angelo 9.

The junior meet was held in conjunction with the senior championships on August 12. Tuskegee won the team title.

Shot put
1. Amelia Bert, Little Rhody Club   37' 2"
2. Doris Sutter, So. Calif. Lions Club
3. Melie McKee, Tuskegee Institute
4. Pauline Amey, Tuskegee Institute

High jump
1. Gertrude Orr, Tuskegee Institute   4' 11½"
2. Cynthia Booker, Madden Park, Chicago
3. Evelyn Lawler, Tuskegee Institute
4. Ella Spears, Blue Bonnet Belles,
   and Loretta Blaul, German-American A.C.

50-meter dash
1. Gladys Tally, Tuskegee Institute   6.7
2. Jean Patton, Tennessee State College
3. Mabel Landry, unattached, Chicago
4. Cynthia Booker, Madden Park, Chicago

Discus throw
1. Doris Sutter, So. Calif. Lions Club   109' 4½"
2. Concepcion Villaneuva, Mexican Athletic Federation
3. Amelia Bert, Little Rhody Club
4. Mellie McKee, Tuskegee Institute

200-meter dash
1. Pauline Amey, Tuskegee Institute   26.3
2. Jean Lowe, Tuskegee Institute
3. Nancy Phillips, German-American A.C.
4. Constance Darnowski, German-American A.C.

Broad jump
1. Mabel Landry, unattached, Chicago   17' 3½"
2. Loretta Blaul, German-American A.C.
3. Mildred Martin, Chicago Dempsey Hurricanes
4. Evelyn Lawler, Tuskegee Institute

80-meter hurdles
1. Mildred Martin, Chicago   12.6
2. Constance Darnowski, German-American A.C.
3. Aleda Surret, Havana Edison Institute
4. Loretta Blaul, German-American A.C.

100-meter dash
1. Jean Patton, Tennessee State College   12.3
2. Betty Lawrence, So. Calif. Lions Club
3. Dorothy Jacobs, Chicago Dempsey Hurricanes
4. Mary McNabb, Tuskegee Institute

Javelin throw
1. Elsa Atsumi, Mexican Athletic Federation   99' 11¼"
2. Maria Julia Perez, Edison Institute, Havana
3. Theresa Bobadilla, Mexican Athletic Federation
4. Billy Smith, Loop A.C., Texas

400-meter relay
1. Tuskegee, "A" team (Amey, Lawler, McNabb, Tally)   50.0
2. So. Calif. Lions Club
3. Tuskegee, "B" team
4. Mexican Athletic Federation

Baseball throw
1. Amelia Bert, Little Rhody A.C.   216' 6"
2. Eva Pikal, Gary, Indiana
3. Barbara Dean Clayton, Lorraine A.C., Texas
4. Mrs. J. C. Freeman, Loop A.C., Texas

Individual scores:
Amelia Bert 26; Jean Patton 19½; Doris Sutter 18; Mildred Martin 16.

Team scores:
Tuskegee Institute 87; Southern California Lions Club 37; German-American A.C. 36; Mexican Athletic Federation 29 2/3; Little Rhody Club 26; Chicago Dempsey Hurricanes 22; Edison Institute 21½; Tennessee State College 19½; Madden Park, Chicago 12; Loop A.C., Texas 10; Gary Playground 8; Lorraine A.C. 7; Blue Bonnet Belles 5⅓; Blackshear H.S. 2.

"Stella Walsh Will Retire After A.A.U. Track Meet" proclaimed the *New York Times* on August 12. Stella's first national championships were won in Dallas in 1930. She said she wanted to retire in Texas, the state in which she started.

The Indoor Nationals

The indoor national meet was held in New York City in the Third Engineers Group Armory on March 26. Sixteen-year-old Mae Faggs of the New York Police Athletic League provided the excitement of the meet by defeating Stella Walsh in the 220-yard dash in the meet record time of 25.9. The time also bettered the American citizens' mark of 28.7 set by Helen Busch in 1940. The May 1949 *Amateur Athlete* proclaimed, "16-Year Old Beats Famed Stella Walsh." Catherine Meyer, cochairman of the AAU Women's Track and Field Committee, wrote the article.

Mae, the youngest member of the 1948 Olympic track team, led from the gun. At the finish she was six yards ahead of Stella. The Police Athletic League won the 440 relay in record time with Mae running the anchor leg.

Bernice Robinson broke Evelyne Hall's 50-yard hurdle record set in 1932. Evelyne was officiating at this meet and witnessed her old record topple.

The only double winner was Nancy Cowperthwaite Phillips, who leaped 4' 7" to win the high jump and retained her standing broad jump crown with a jump of 8' 3½".

50-yard dash
1. Dolores Dwyer, German-American A.C.   6.4
2. Joan Salmon, N.Y. Police Athletic League
3. Joyce Fleming, N.Y. Police Athletic League
4. Bessie Barfield, N.Y. Police Athletic League

220-yard dash
1. Mae Faggs, N.Y. Police Athletic League   25.9 AR
2. Stella Walsh, Cleveland
3. Marie Taylor, N.Y. Police Athletic League
4. Audrey Patterson, Tennessee State University

50-yard hurdles
1. Bernice Robinson, Washington Park, Chicago   7.2 AR
2. Nancy Phillips, German-American A.C.
3. Constance Darnowski, German-American A.C.
4. Lillie Purifoy, Tuskegee Institute

440-yard relay
1. N.Y. P.A.L. (Salmon, Barfield, Taylor, Faggs) 51.4 MR
2. N.Y. Police Athletic League, "B" team
3. German-American A.C.
4. Tuskegee Institute

Basketball throw
1. Ottilie Barth, N.Y. Police Athletic League   94' 4½"
2. Ramona Massey, N.Y. Police Athletic League   86' 8"
3. Theresa Manuel, Tuskegee Institute   79' 10½"
4. Betty Herrmann, N.Y. Police Athletic League   78' 10⅞"

High jump
1. Nancy Phillips, German-American A.C.   4' 7"
2. Evelyn Lawler, Tuskegee Institute   4' 6"
3. Loretta Blaul, German-American A.C.   4' 5"
4. Clara Schroth, Philadelphia Turners   4' 4"

8-lb. shot put
1. Ramona Massey, N.Y. Police Athletic League   38' 3"
2. Amelia Bert, Little Rhody   33' 2"
3. Pauline Ruppeldt, Philadelphia Turners   31' 6"
4. Katherine Geary, Philadelphia Turners   30' 4"

Standing broad jump
1. Nancy Phillips, German-American A. C.   8' 3½"
2. Bernice Robinson, Washington Park   8' 2⅜"
3. Evelyn Lawler, Tuskegee Institute   8' 4"
4. Janet Moreau, Red Diamond A.C., Boston   7' 11⅜"

Team scores:
New York Police Athletic League 35; German-American A.C. 24; Tuskegee Institute 9; Washington Park, Chicago 8; Philadelphia Turners 4; Little Rhody A.C. 3.

1949 All-America Women's Track and Field Team

50-yard run	Dolores Dwyer
100-meter run	Jean Patton
200-meter run	Nell Jackson
50-yard hurdles	Bernice Robinson
80-meter hurdles	Bernice Robinson
400-meter relay	Jean Patton, Audrey Patterson, Dorothy Jacobs, Mae Faggs
High jump	Gertrude Orr
Broad jump	Mabel Landry
Standing broad jump	Nancy Phillips
8-lb. shot	Amelia Bert
Discus throw	Frances Kaszubski
Javelin throw	Dorothy Dodson Kenny
Baseball throw	Juanita Watson
Basketball throw	Ottilie Barth

An item in the February 1949 *Journal of the American Association for Health, Physical Education and Recreation* listed Mrs. Mary Conklin, Beaver College, Jenkinstown, Pennsylvania, as the track and field representative to the Rules and Editorial Committee. Mary Washburn Conklin was a member of the 1928 Olympic team.

Chapter 33

1950

The national women's senior outdoor championship meet was held in Freeport, Texas, on August 26.

Six defending champions retained their title in a meet in which no records were broken. Tuskegee Institute retained its team title. Amelia Bert was the high-point scorer with twenty-six points.

200-meter run
1. Nell Jackson, Tuskegee Institute   25.0
2. Stella Walsh, Polish Falcons
3. Catherine Johnson, Tuskegee Institute
4. Josephine Gilmore, Tuskegee Institute

50-meter dash
1. Dolores Dwyer, German-American A.C.   6.7
2. Jean Patton, Tennessee State College
3. Janet Moreau, Little Rhody A.C.
4. Juanita Watson, Tuskegee Institute

100-meter run
1. Jean Patton, Tennessee State College   13.3
2. Dolores Dwyer, German-American A.C.
3. Janet Moreau, Little Rhody A.C.
4. Evelyn Lawler, Tuskegee Institute

80-meter hurdles
1. Evelyn Lawler, Tuskegee Institute   11.9
2. Nancy Phillips, German-American A.C.
3. Constance Darnowski, German-American A.C.
4. Mildred Martin, Chicago Catholic Youth Organization

400-meter relay
1. Tuskegee Institute   50.2
    (Johnson, Tally, Lawler, Jackson)
2. German-American A.C.
3. Tuskegee Institute, "B" team
4. Catholic Youth Organization, Chicago

Shot put
1. Frances Kaszubski, Sandy's Club, Cleveland   39' 3⅞"

2. Amelia Bert, Little Rhody A.C. — 38' 3⅞"
3. Doris Sutter, Glendale Lions Club — 36' 7⅞"
4. Carolyn Nave, Little Rhody A.C. — 33' 1¼"

Javelin throw
1. Amelia Bert, Little Rhody A.C. — 115' 1¾"
2. Carolyn Nave, Little Rhody A.C. — 109' 1¼"
3. Stella Walsh, Polish Falcons — 108' 9"
4. Margarene Harrell, Tuskegee — 97' 2"

Discus throw
1. Frances Kaszubski, Sandy's Club — 113' 4¾"
2. Amelia Bert, Little Rhody A.C. — 102' 11¾"
3. Pauline Ruppeldt, Philadelphia Turners — 99' 6½"
4. Eva Pikal, Catholic Youth Organization Chicago — 98' 6½"

Broad jump
1. Mabel Landry, Chicago Catholic Youth Organization — 17' 5⅞"
2. Nancy Phillips, German-American A.C. — 17' ¾"
3. Loretta Blaul, German-American A.C. — 16' 6¾"
4. Mary McNabb, Tuskegee Institute — 16' 5⅜"

Baseball throw
1. Juanita Watson, Tuskegee Institute — 239' 2⅜"
2. Pat Sanicky, Sandy's Club — 231' 6⅜"
3. Frances Tolin, Sangu Club, Ohio — 203' 2"
4. Marianne Rothhaas, Sandy's Club — 200' 4"

High jump
1. Dorothy Chisholm, Tuskegee Institute — 4' 8¾"
2. Nancy Phillips, German-American A.C. — 4' 5"
3. Loretta Blaul, German-American A.C., — 4' 5"
   Judy Broomell, Tustin, Calif.
   and Evelyn Lawler, Tuskegee Institute

Team scores:
Tuskegee Institute 91; German-American A.C. 73; Little Rhody A.C. 50; Sandy's Club 34; Chicago Catholic Youth Organization 26½; Tennessee A. & I. College 18; Polish Falcons 15; Sangu Athletic Club 8; Glendale Lions Club 7; Tustin, Calif. 6½; Philadelphia Turners 6; Poe Playground 3.

The junior meet was held in conjunction with the senior meet. Evelyn Lawler of Tuskegee tied the American record in the 80-meter hurdles and led her team to an easy victory. Evelyn ran her heat in 11.7 and the final in 12.0.

The Indoor Nationals

The senior indoor championship meet was held on February 13 in New York City under the auspices of the Police Athletic League.

Mrs. Nancy Phillips won her ninth national title. She captured the standing broad jump and the 50-yard hurdles and tied for second in the high jump. These victories made her the individual high scorer.

The Police Athletic League retained the team title. Ottilie Barth of the P.A.L. was the only record breaker of the meet. Her basketball throw of 101' 9½" set a new American indoor record. the former record, set in 1933 by Nan Gindele, was 101' 6¾".

Mae Faggs, P.A.L., retained her 220-yard dash title. Stella Walsh, in her twenty-first year of competition, took second in the 220 and third in the standing broad jump and 100-yard dash.

Standing broad jump
1. Nancy Phillips, German-American A.C.   8' 3⅝"
2. Janet Moreau, Little Rhody A.C.   8' 3½"
3. Stella Walsh, Polish Falcons   8'
4. Mildred Martin, Chicago Catholic Youth Organization   7' 11½"

8-lb. shot put
1. Amelia Bert, Little Rhody A.C.   38' ¼"
2. Ramona Massey, N.Y. Police Athletic League   36' ⅝"
3. Doris Sutter, Glendale Lions, Calif.   34' ¼"
4. Carolyn Nave, Little Rhody A.C.   32' 1⅛"

100-yard dash
1. Jean Patton, Tennessee State College   11.8
2. Dolores Dwyer, German-American A.C.
3. Stella Walsh, Polish Falcons
4. Bessie Barfield, N.Y. Police Athletic League

Basketball throw
1. Ottilie Barth, N.Y. Police Athletic League   101' 9½"
2. Marian Barone, Philadelphia Turners   90' 9⅛"
3. Amelia Bert, Little Rhody A.C.   89' 11¾"
4. Pat Monsanto, N.Y. Police Athletic League   89' 8⅞"

50-yard dash
1. Dolores Dwyer, German-American A.C.   6.5
2. Joyce Fleming, N.Y. Police Athletic League
3. Edna Rogowski, N.Y. Police Athletic League
4. Mabel Landry, Chicago Catholic Youth Organization

220-yard dash
1. Mae Faggs, N.Y. Police Athletic League   27.0
2. Stella Walsh, Polish Falcons
3. Marie Taylor, N.Y. Police Athletic League
4. Lena Acosta, N.Y. Police Athletic League

50-yard hurdles
1. Nancy Phillips, German-American A.C.   7.7
2. Mildred Martin, Chicago Catholic Youth Organization
3. Constance Darnowski, German-American A.C.
4. Janet Moreau, Little Rhody A.C.

440-yard medley relay (220, 110, 60, 50)
1. N.Y. Police Athletic League, "A" team   53.6
2. Tennessee State College
3. N.Y. Police Athletic League, "B" team
4. Chicago Catholic Youth Organization

440-yard relay
1. N.Y. Police Athletic League, "A" team   51.8
2. German-American A.C.
3. Chicago Catholic Youth Organization
4. N.Y. Police Athletic League, "B" team

High jump
1. Marion Boos, N.Y. Police Athletic League   4' 7"
2. Nancy Phillips, German-American A.C.,   4' 6"
   and Marilyn Vowles, Little Rhody A.C.
4. Loretta Blaul, German-American A.C.   4' 5"

Team scores:
N.Y. Police Athletic League 41; German-American A.C. 26½; Little Rhody A.C. 14½;
Chicago Catholic Youth Organization and Tennessee State College 8; Polish Falcons
7; Philadelphia Turners 3; Glendale Lions, Calif. 2.

1950 All-America Women's Track and Field Team

50-meter dash	Dolores Dwyer
100-meter run	Jean Patton
200-meter run	Nell Jackson
50-yard hurdles	Nancy Phillips
80-meter hurdles	Evelyn Lawler
400-meter relay	Jean Patton, Dolores Dwyer, Nell Jackson, Janet Moreau
440-yard medley relay	Dolores Dwyer, Jean Patton, Joyce Fleming, Mae Faggs
High jump	Marion Boos
Broad jump	Mabel Landry
Standing broad jump	Nancy Phillips
Shot put	Amelia Bert
Javelin throw	Amelia Bert
Discus throw	Frances Kaszubski
Baseball throw	Juanita Watson
Basketball throw	Ottilie Barth

A national pentathlon championship was held on October 15 in Queens,
New York. Stella Walsh scored 1,929 points to capture first place. The runner-
up was seventeen-year-old Dolores Dwyer with 1,824 points. The November
Amateur Athlete commented that this was Walsh's thirty-sixth win in a national
championship.

Running broad jump
1. Stella Walsh, Polish Falcons   16' 3½"   (337 points)
2. Nancy Phillips, German-American A.C.   15' 6½"   (293 points)
3. Dolores Dwyer, German-American A.C.   14' 9⅝"   (249 points)
4. Mae Faggs, N.Y. Police Athletic League   14' 4"   (226 points)

Javelin throw
1. Amelia Bert, Little Rhody A.C.   126' 11⅛"   (394 points)
2. Stella Walsh, Polish Falcons   99' 4⅞"   (265 points)
3. Carolyn Nave, Little Rhody A.C.   94' 9¼"   (244 points)
4. Patricia Monsanto, N.Y. Police Athletic League   93' 10"   (240 points)

60-meter dash
1. Dolores Dwyer   7.9   (475 points)
2. Stella Walsh   8.2   (386 points
   and Mae Faggs   8.2   (386 points)
4. Constance Darnowski   8.4   (333 points)

Discus throw
1. Stella Walsh   105' 1"   (491 points)
2. Amelia Bert   98' 6¼"   (440 points)
3. Dolores Dwyer   91' 11⅛"   (391 points)
4. Carolyn Nave   85' 3⅝"

200-meter dash
1. Dolores Dwyer   26.0   (473 points)
2. Stella Walsh   26.3   (450 points)
3. Janet Moreau   26.7   (421 points)
4. Mae Faggs   27.6   (362 points)

Final scores:
1. Stella Walsh   1929
2. Dolores Dwyer   1824
3. Nancy Phillips   1418
4. Janet Moreau   1373
5. Constance Darnowski   1330
6. Mae Faggs   1253

Evelyne Hall, chairman of the track and field committee, had six vice chairmen and twenty-one committee members.

There were no women's events scheduled in the men's nationals in February.

The September *Amateur Athlete* featured a story entitled "Women's Track and Field Needs Promotion," which was written by Evelyne Hall. She pointed out that from a nation of over 146,000,000 in population, just twelve women represented the United States in women's track and field in the Olympic Games. She claimed that the biggest problem facing the sport was "the lack of interest and the amount of insufficient promotion and build up to the public in general."

Evelyne pleaded with officials of the AAU to include one or two women's events in the local and regional men's meets. She praised the Junior Olympic program for providing excellent ways to discover young talent. She pointed out that despite the fact that former track stars were leading normal, healthy lives, there were still those who thought the sport was harmful to women.

The October *Amateur Athlete* stated that 12,000 spectators watched 2,000 boys and girls compete in the fourth annual New York City Junior Olympic Sports Festival held at Randall's Island. The meet was sponsored by the *New York Mirror* and the Department of Parks.

This issue also featured "So You Want to Be a Coach," by Roxy Atkins Andersen. She stressed teaching fundamentals, developing each athlete individually and gradually, involving the athlete's parents, and learning the etiquette of the sport.

Another article followed in the November issue entitled "Girls Thrive on Sport." In a fast-reading, comical dialogue, Roxy extolled competition and attacked reporters for making disparaging comments about women in competition. She said that the "present day objectors are using the same old words and ideas that have been used by all those who have carried the banner inscribed, 'I hate women's sports.'"

Roxanne Atkins Andersen

Roxy Atkins Andersen, who was born on June 26, 1912, in Montreal, Canada, was inducted into the National Track and Field Hall of Fame in December 1991. I interviewed her in New Orleans on December 3, 1991. When I asked how she got started in track and field, the answer came quickly:

> This is going to kill you! At the age of nine another little girl and I were having what you might call a difference of opinion — in other words an argument. I can't remember what it was over at this belated stage of the game. Anyway I must have pressed the wrong button because she pushed me. For a moment — never having been pushed by anyone before — I wasn't too sure how I was supposed to react. But react I did by pushing her right back. I must have had some punch in my push for she sat down real hard. This took place in front of her house. Well, she started screaming bloody murder. Her papa rushed to the door, took in the situation, and with blood in his eye started toward me. I decided not to wait to see what turn this was going to take. I took off with him in hot pursuit. We must have gone around the block a time and a half — a scrawny little girl being chased by a big six-footer. He ran out of steam just before I did, so he never did catch me. The only comment he made after the incident was discussed throughout the neighborhood — "Boy, could that brat run!" His remark gave me the feeling that perhaps I had something in the way of athletic talent. But where could I go for any training program that embraced track and field since I was under fourteen? Nowhere. So I, like hundreds before me and probably thousands after me, drifted from sport to sport that did have programs for kids. I sampled swimming, volleyball, tennis, basketball, even speed skating. I never did find myself until I was about sixteen. Once a year my high school had a field day. I won the all-around school championship. Once a year there would be a Sunday school picnic where they would have a few crazy little races such as potato races or a short sprint which had no meaning — just something to do on the spur of the moment. That was track way back when.
> With the advent of the Olympics in nineteen twenty-eight with its induce-

ments of free travel and fame athletically, inclined women became interested and female athletic clubs sprang up.

I got seriously started in women's track when a girl I went to school with invited me to join the Canadian Ladies Athletic Club. It was coached by Myrtle Cook, who was a member of the Canadian Olympic team that won the relay at Amsterdam in nineteen twenty-eight. Women's track was in its infancy. It seemed the whole world was against women participating in competitive sport — any sport.

Practice in those days was twice a week with the weekends reserved for meets. For over a year, I competed in the sprints against Olympians without making a final. It just so happened at the Ontario [Provincial] Championships that the only entry in the hurdles was a girl who had competed in that event at the nineteen twenty-eight Olympics. When they came looking for volunteers to fill in the race, the starter announced that there were two medals to compete for. Did I ever come to life! I entered even though I didn't know anything about technique. I ran that woman into the ground even though I was just jumping high over the hurdles and going like hell in between. She retired right after that. I decided I was going to become a hurdler even though I didn't have anyone to coach me. I bought men's hurdle instruction books and studied the form of the men hurdlers in all their races. I tried so many styles before I found the best one for me. It was with amusement that everyone wondered what form I would come up with at the next meet.

We practiced behind the billboards at the old Maple Leaf Baseball Stadium. My idea of a warm-up was jogging a quarter mile and a few hurdle exercises. Before the baseball team showed up, I filched four of the baseball seats that I folded up in lieu of hurdles. One of the men's clubs took pity on me and loaned me four real hurdles to work out over. Eventually I was the owner of both Canadian records — eighty meters outdoor and fifty yards indoor.

I got to know Dan Ferris, secretary of the Amateur Athletic Union of the United States, from competitions in Paterson, New Jersey, and Buffalo, New York. He brought my Laurel Ladies Athletic Club down to New York for the United States Indoor Nationals. Those were the depression days. He gave us fifty dollars to cover our travel, food and hotel expenses. We had to dig up the rest. He was so open-minded and far-sighted. We ran in Brooklyn in a little roped-off gym in nineteen thirty-four. I won the hurdles from nineteen thirty-two Olympian Evelyne Hall and was a member of our winning club relay team — two gold medals. Nineteen thirty-four was my best year — I finished fourth in the hurdles at the British Empire Games in London and sixth in the Women's World Games that followed.

Our Canadian Olympic tryouts in nineteen thirty-six were in Montreal. It rained cats and dogs. The starting holes we dug filled with water faster than we could empty them. What a blessing when starting blocks finally came in. In Berlin we had heats and semi-finals. The seeding was pathetic — I ran twelve flat in a heat that contained two medal winners and a semifinalist. The two other heats were won in 12 flat. After Berlin I competed until 1938, when I retired after an appendix operation at the age of twenty-six.

In August of nineteen forty-six I came to the United States. We had not been able to travel because of the war. Then everything opened up, and I decided I wanted to see what I had been champion of. I bought the longest train ticket round trip from Toronto all the way down to my girlfriend in Los Angeles, up through San Francisco, on to Vancouver, and across Canada to home. Only I met my husband at the Grand Canyon, and we hit it off beautifully. He promised to court me the rest of my life if I married him. He didn't even ask me if I could

Roxanne Atkins Andersen on December 3, 1991, at the time of her induction into the National Track and Field Hall of Fame. (Author's photo.)

cook. We got married nearly forty-eight years ago. I never did get home from that trip [laughter]. My greatest supporter and helper is my engineer husband. I owe him so much.

When Dan Ferris discovered that I had settled in California, he came after me with a couple of projects. He asked me to run for two offices — the national chairmanship and the women's Olympic chairmanship. I thought that was a pretty big bite for a little greeny fresh out of a district association. I asked our chief track man here which one I should go for. (The women's track and field chairman was appointed, which would have been easy for me, while the Olympic chairmanship was elected.) He advised me to take the Olympic, which would keep me in office four years, while the national chairmanship might last only one year, the politics being what they are. I chose the elective one. Talk about a baptism by fire — the politics in track and field — Washington should take lessons.

There were seven people on that committee eligible to vote. Frances Kaszubski (who received the appointive national chairmanship) went to work on Cleve Abbott and pinned his vote down for me. Along with Nell Jackson's vote, that gave me three. Nominated against me was Lucile Wilson, with supporting votes from Kay Myer and Alice Arden Hodge. To break the tie, I had to vote for myself [laughter]. When I got home and told my district that I had voted for myself, they said: "What did you expect? That's what we all do." I never saw so much backbiting in my life, but it's just the same in men's track. Out on the coast, I was chairman of the whole shebang — men's, women's, long distance, and age-group. I was still coaching my Laurel Track Club of San Francisco (named after the Laurel Ladies A.C. in Toronto, Canada).

Another one of the projects Dan Ferris had lined up for me — he wanted someone to head up a committee to study the effect of athletic competition on girls and women. Dan gave me the names of some marvelous specialists. I had to dream up all of the questions to ask them. It wasn't difficult — I just picked out all the prejudices that I had run up against in my competitive life. It was written for the United States to stifle prejudice in all sports — not just track. They didn't think women should be competing — period. Brutus Hamilton [head track coach at the University of California at Berkeley] had invited coaches from fifty countries to a world track and field clinic. He had seen my book and invited me over, even though I'd be the only woman coach there. I introduced the book and spoke on women's track. That book went to forty-seven countries and was translated into nineteen languages. The book was completed in nineteen fifty-three. Thousands were issued during its three printings.

When I got through with all of the things that Dan Ferris had cooked up for me to do, I suddenly realized one day decades later there was still no track program for youngsters under the age of fourteen. This river of athletic talent was drifting to other sports that offered them programs, bypassing track and field. I realized throughout all those years when I was involved in other projects that this is where we were losing out terribly in track and field. Much of that talent should have been coming to us. In the early fifties I called up a school principal whose senior girls were competing in our track meets. I told him I knew how to reach girls under fourteen because I've given clinics galore to school, recreation, and playground directors. In those days I was trying to sell women's track because Dan Ferris wanted women's track started out on the West Coast. (That was another of his little jobs for me.) I told the principal at El Cerritos that I can get the little girls if he could provide boys under fourteen if we put on a track meet for them. Well, we put on our introductory meet. That track was just jam packed with kids, starting with ten-eleven year olds. We found out that the boys needed it just as much as the girls for they didn't have any program either. This was the first joint program despite the fact that men and women were not allowed to compete on the same program. It was a huge success. The meet ran so long we practically saw the moon rise and made us realize we had to have separate girls and boys age-group meets. So age-group was born. Many, many years later age-group got started because I recollected my own experience as a kid looking for a place to take my talent to be nurtured and developed. That made me the "Mother of Age-Group" as they named me.

My first managerial position was to the Melbourne Olympics in 1956; then I managed the team to the World Cross Country Championships in Belgium, an international meet in Toronto, two trips to China, a trip to Japan, the multi-event team to Estonia, the Trinidad Invitational in 1963, Europe vs. the Americas (Montreal) in 1967, the 1971 Pan American Games in Colombia, the Taiwan Invitational in 1979, and the 1983 Pan American Games in Venezuela.

I represented both the United States and Canada in Olympic Games. The Olympic experience is a very moving one. It really gets to you. Watching your country's team swing into the stadium makes you tingle inside. I wrote an Olympic poem that's been published several times. It now hangs in the National Track and Field Hall of Fame in Indianapolis, along with the Canadian Maple Leaf from my sweats and the logo from my USA uniform on either side. The other item in the Hall which I authored is "Effect of Athletic Competition on Girls and Women."

Chapter 34

1951

Waterbury, Connecticut, hosted the senior women's national track and field championships on August 11-12.

The *New York Times* reported:

> Miss Mary McNabb, 17 year old enrollee at Tuskegee institute, stamped herself as an outstanding 1952 Olympic prospect today by winning two events and running on a victorious relay quartet....
>
> Although Mrs. Nancy Cowperthwaite Phillips of New York, a 1948 Olympic star, won the outstanding individual trophy by capturing a first and two seconds, she was forced to share the leading role with Miss McNabb....
>
> Miss McNabb, who comes from Atlanta, Georgia, and ran for Tuskegee, won the 50 meter race in 6.6, added the 100 meter title in 12.2 and was on the Tuskegee team that won the 400 meter relay in 49.8.

200-meter run
1. Jean Patton, Tuskegee Institute   25.4
2. Mae Faggs, N.Y. Police Athletic League
3. Nell Jackson, Tuskegee Institute

50-meter run
1. Mary McNabb, Tuskegee Institute   6.6
2. Catherine Hardy, Fort Valley, Ga.
3. Dolores Dwyer, German-American A.C.

80-meter hurdles
1. Nancy Phillips, German-American A.C.   12.2
2. Evelyn Lawler, Tuskegee Institute
3. Constance Darnowski, German American A.C.

100-meter run
1. Mary McNabb, Tuskegee Institute   12.2
2. Catherine Hardy, Fort Valley
3. Jean Patton, Tennessee State

280-meter shuttle hurdle relay
1. Tuskegee Institute (Bell, Chisholm, Davenport, Lawler)   41.2
2. German-American A.C.
3. N.Y. Police Athletic League

400-meter relay
1. Tuskegee Institute, "A" team   49.8
   (McNabb, Johnson, Lawler, Jackson)
2. Tuskegee Institute, "B" team
3. N.Y. Police Athletic League

High jump
1. Marion Boos, N.Y. Police Athletic League   4' 9¾"
2. Lolita Mauer, So. Calif. Lions,
   Ora Lee Allen, Chicago Catholic Youth Organization,
   and Nancy Phillips, German-American A.C.

Baseball throw
1. Amelia Wershoven, Equitable Life, N.Y.   225' 1¾"
2. Marion Murphy, Libra A.A., Waterbury, Conn.
3. Barbara Queary, N.Y. Police Athletic League

8-lb. shot put
1. Amelia Bert, Little Rhody Club   41' 3"
2. Janet Dicks, Harrisburg A.A.
3. Ramona Massey, N.Y. Police Athletic League

Discus throw
1. Frances Kaszubski, Polish Falcons   121' ⅛"
2. Stella Walsh, Polish Falcons
3. Janet Dicks, Harrisburg, Pa.

Javelin throw
1. Frances Licata, N.Y. Police Athletic League   120' ½"
2. Amelia Bert, Little Rhody Club
3. Margaret Mates, Scanlon Playground, Chicago

Broad Jump
1. Stella Walsh, Polish Falcons   17' 3"
2. Nancy Phillips, German-American A.C.
3. Evelyn Lawler, Tuskegee Institute

Individual scores:
Nancy Phillips 24; Mary McNabb 20; Amelia Bert 19; Stella Walsh 18; Jean Patton 16; Catherine Hardy 16.

Team scores:
Tuskegee Institute 95; N.Y. Police Athletic League 66; German-American A.C. 40; Little Rhody, Providence, Rhode Island 34; Polish Falcons, Cleveland 18; Equitable Life Assurance Society, N.Y. 17; Tennessee State University 16; Fort Valley State Teachers College 16; Harrisburg A.A. 15.

The junior meet was held in conjunction with the senior championships. The outstanding star of this meet was also Mary McNabb. She bettered one American record and tied another in the 50 meters. Her third victory was in the 100 meters. The *New York Times* reported:

> The sturdy sprinter, who runs with driving arm action, won the 200 meters in 24.3, one-tenth of a second under the American citizens mark set by Miss Helen

Stephens in 1935. She took the 50 meter dash in 6.4 tying the American mark of Miss Alice Coachman, made in 1944. ... Dan Ferris, secretary-treasurer of the AAU termed the surprising Alabama Negro as "definitely Olympic material."

In all, the new sprinting flash ran eight races — two preliminaries and a final in the 50, the same in the 100, and a preliminary and final round in the 200. She won the 50 and 200 meters in the space of 15 minutes, and wasn't pressed at any time....

Miss McNabb is a clumsy starter but picks up ground in a hurry. She began her surprising afternoon by winning a 200 meter heat in what was announced as 23.7, only one-tenth of a second slower than the world record. It developed that this race was five yards short, but the rest were regulation distance....

Miss McNabb, whose parents live in Atlanta, Georgia received the James M. Roche Trophy as the outstanding athlete of the afternoon.

The Indoor Nationals

The senior women's indoor championship meet was held in New York City at the 102d Engineers Armory on February 12. The men's junior meet was held in conjunction with the women's meet. The *New York Times* story on February 13 reported the highlights of the men's meet and had the following sentence at the end of the article: "The distaff contribution to the games also was three meet records, with two others matched."

In a heat of the 100, Jean Patton set a meet record of 11.1, and Janet Moreau's standing broad jump record tied Helen Stephens' meet record from 1935.

50-yard dash
1. Catherine Hardy, Ft. Valley   6.3 MR
2. Dolores Dwyer, German-American A.C.
3. Janet Moreau, Little Rhody A.C.

100-yard dash
1. Jean Patton, Tennessee State   11.2
2. Dolores Dwyer, German-American A.C.
3. Janet Moreau, Little Rhody A.C.

220-yard dash
1. Mae Faggs, N.Y. Police Athletic League   26.9
2. Barbara Queary, N.Y. Police Athletic League
3. Harriet Norris, N.Y. Police Athletic League

50-yard hurdles
1. Nancy Phillips, German-American A.C.   7.2 ties MR
2. Constance Darnowski, German-American A.C.
3. Marilyn Vowles, Little Rhody A.C.

440-yard relay
1. N.Y. Police Athletic League, "A" team   52.7
   (Barfield, Norris, Taylor, Faggs)
2. German-American A.C.
3. N.Y. Police Athletic League, "B" team

280-yard shuttle hurdle relay
1. German-American A.C.   41.8
      (Darnowski, Blaul, Carmen, Phillips)
2. Little Rhody A.C.
3. German-American A.C., "B" team

440-medley relay (50-60-110-220)
1. N.Y. Police Athletic League   52.5 MR
      (Faggs, Barfield, Fleming, Spencer)
2. German-American A.C.
3. N.Y. Police Athletic League, "B" team

Basketball throw
1. Marian Twining Barone, Philadelphia Turners   93'
2. Ramona Massey, N.Y. Police Athletic League   88' 3"
3. Frances Kaszubski, Sandy's Club, Ohio   87' 9"

High jump
1. Nancy Phillips, German-American A.C.,   4' 10½"
      and Marion Boos, N.Y. Police Athletic League
3. Marilyn Vowles, Little Rhody A.C.,   4' 7½"
      Loretta Blaul, German-American A.C.,
      and Frances Kaszubski, Sandy's Club

Standing broad jump
1. Janet Moreau, Little Rhody A.C.   8' 8¼" ties MR
2. Nancy Phillips, German-American A.C.   8' 6⅞"
3. Ann Carmen, German-American A.C.   8' ¼"

8-lb. shot put
1. Frances Kaszubski, Sandy's Club   39' 1⅝"
2. Ramona Massey, N.Y. Police Athletic League   38' 9⅛"
3. Amelia Bert, Little Rhody A.C.   38'

Team scores:

N.Y. Police Athletic League 38⅓; German-American A.C. 35⅓; Sandy's Club 8⅓; Philadelphia Turners 6; Tennessee State College 6; Fort Valley State College 6; Chicago Catholic Youth Organization 3.

The Pan American Games

The first Pan American Games were held in Buenos Aires, Argentina, from February 25 to March 8. Eight women were members of the United States team.

	Event	Place	Performance
Bert, Amelia	Shot put	5	35' 6⅜"
	Javelin	2	124' 11¼"
Dwyer, Dolores	100m	DNQ	12.9
	200m	6	27.7
	400mr	1	48.7

Jackson, Nell	200m	2	25.7
	400mr	1	48.7
Kaszubski, Frances	SP	4	37' 2⅜"
	Discus	3	117' 7¼"
Lawler, Evelyn	80mh	6	12.6
	BJ	8	16' 2⅛"
Moreau, Janet	100m	4	12.7
	80mh	DNQ	12.7
	400mr	1	48.7
Patton, Jean	100m	2	12.3
	200m	1	25.3
	400mr	1	48.7
Phillips, Nancy	80mh	3	12.1
	BJ	5	16' 8"
Hall, Mrs. Evelyne	Coach and manager		

In the minutes of the 63d AAU Convention, Mrs. Hall stated: "The girls did their share in upholding the American supremacy in track and field. Each member of the team of eight girls gave her best performance or bettered it and the results were gratifying. Not only did the girls perform well in competition but they conducted themselves in a sportsmanlike manner and were so gracious and friendly they won the admiration of all." She also thanked the coaches of the girls on the team for putting forth a tremendous effort "in raising the necessary funds for the trip."

The *New York Times* on March 6 said:

> The second United States track championship of the day went to Miss Jean Patton, rangy Nashville (Tenn.) girl, who shaded a teammate, Miss Nell Jackson of Alabama's Tuskegee Institute, in the 200 meter run. It was the first track victory for the United States women.
>
> Miss Patton clipped a tenth of a second off the South American record when she breezed home in 25.3 seconds. Miss Jackson was just two strides back.

The 1951 All-America Women's Track and Field Team

50-meter dash	Mary McNabb
100-meter dash	Mary McNabb
200-meter dash	Jean Patton
50-yard hurdles	Nancy Phillips
80-meter hurdles	Nancy Phillips
High jump	Marion Boos
Running broad jump	Stella Walsh
Standing broad jump	Janet Moreau
Shot put	Amelia Bert
Discus	Frances Kaszubski
Javelin throw	Frances Licata
Baseball throw	Amelia Wershoven
Basketball throw	Marian Twining Barone

280-yard shuttle hurdle relay	Nancy Phillips, Evelyn Lawler, Constance Darnowski, Loita Mae Mauer
400-meter relay	Mary McNabb, Catherine Hardy, Janet Moreau, Jean Patton
440-yard medley relay	Mary McNabb, Catherine Hardy, Jean Patton, Mae Faggs

Mrs. Roxanne Atkins Andersen was the meet director of the national women's pentathlon championships at Berkeley, California, on July 14. Stella Walsh, in winning the title, placed first in the following four of five events: the running broad jump with a leap of 16' 3¾", the 60-meter dash in 8.2, the discus throw with a toss of 112' 2", and the 200-meter dash in 26.9. She placed second in the javelin throw, the fifth event. Her point total surpassed her 1950 total by three points.

1.	Stella Walsh, Polish Falcons	1932
2.	Doris Sutter, Glendale Lions	1394
3.	Norrine Westby, Dryer A.C.	1204½
4.	Mary Samuel, Dryer A.C.	776½
5.	Roberta Parks, Dryer A.C.	707
6.	Eleanor Repinski, Polish Falcons	653½
7.	Lois Dye, Dryer A.C.	648

Mrs. Evelyne Hall, chairman	Mrs. Catherine Donovan Meyer
Miss Florence Anderson	Mrs. Irvin Van Blarcon
Mrs. Kathryn Cradick	Miss Lucile Wilson
Mrs. Alice Arden Hodge	

The 1951 *A.A.U. Handbook* listed the members of the 1952 Olympic Women's Track and Field Committee.

Evelyne Hall, in her report at the annual AAU convention, suggested that the committee cooperate with the editor of the *Track and Field Guide* published by the National Section on Women's Athletics. She believed that this would increase interest in women's track. She also announced that an "Olympic collection" would be taken at the indoor nationals which would go towards funding the 1952 women's team.

Chapter 35

1952: The Helsinki Olympic Year

The 1952 Olympic Games were held in Helsinki, Finland, from July 19 through August 3. Our United States Olympic women's track and field team was composed of the following ten young women:

	Olympic Event	Olympic Place	Olympic Performance
Darnowski, Constance	80mh	DNQ	12.1
Dicks, Janet	SP	18	37' 6½"
Dwyer, Dolores	200m	DNQ	
Faggs, Mae	100m	6	12.1
	200m	DNQ	24.5
	400mr	1	45.9
Hardy, Catherine	100m	DNQ	12.1
	200m	DNQ	24.7
	400mr	1	45.9
Jones, Barbara	400mr	1	45.9
Landry, Mabel	BJ	7	18' 10½"
Larney, Marjorie	Javelin	13	133' 1¾"
McNabb, Mary	400mr	reserve	
Moreau, Janet	100m	DNQ	12.5
	400mr	1st	45.9
Lucile Wilson	Manager-Coach		

Finland's capital city of 400,000 hosted the record entry of 5,870 athletes in the Olympic Games, with the Soviet Union participating for the first time. The *New York Times* reported that "One American came through two rounds of the women's 100 meter dash heats, Mae Faggs of Bayside." Mae placed sixth in the final. On July 28, the *New York Times* said:

> Our women's 4 x 100 relay team scored an amazing victory in the world record time of 45.9 seconds. The triumph was all the more sensational because our women athletes during the entire games had tallied only one point, finishing sixth in the 100 meter dash.

1952 U.S. Olympic Champions, 400-meter relay, celebrating on the field after their world record victory in Helsinki, Finland. Mae Faggs, Barbara Jones, Janet Moreau and Catherine Hardy. (Author's photo.)

The winning team was composed of Mae Faggs of Bayside, Queens; Barbara Jones, 15 year old Chicago girl; Janet Moreau of Pawtucket, R.I., and Catherine Hardy of Georgia. They danced with glee with arms thrown around one another to the vast amusement of the crowd.

The Olympic Results

100 meters. In the 100 meters, Mae Faggs won heat two in the first round in 12.1. Janet Moreau was second in heat six in 12.5, and Catherine Hardy won heat seven in 11.9. There were twelve first-round heats. In the second round, Mae Faggs was third in 12.0 in the second heat, Moreau placed fifth in heat three in 12.5, and Hardy was fourth in 12.1 in heat four. In the semifinal round, on a water-soaked track, Mae was third in 12.1 in the first semifinal and sixth in the final in 12.1.

200 meters. In the 200 meters, Catherine Hardy ran 24.8 and finished second in heat three, Dolores Dwyer was in heat five and did not finish, and Mae Faggs ran 24.5 and placed third in heat six. In the semifinal round, Hardy was eliminated from the final round by placing fourth in 24.7 in heat two.

80-meter hurdles. Connie Darnowski, our only entry in the 80-meter hurdles, was eliminated in round one in heat five. She placed fifth in 12.1.

Discus and high jump. We had no entry in the high jump or discus throw.

Broad jump. Mabel Landry, our only entry in the broad jump, placed seventh with a jump of 18' 10½".

Shot put. Janet Dicks did not qualify for the finals in the shot put.

Javelin throw. Fifteen-year-old Marjorie Larney, our lone entry in the javelin throw, placed 13th.

Lucile Wilson, the team manager-coach, reported after the Games:

> Four days after the selection, the team flew to Helsinki. After eighteen hours of flight, they arrived at their destination, thus allowing a week for orientation and acclimation before competition commenced. The living quarters were very nice and the food was plentiful and well-prepared. A well-balanced diet for our athletes was not a problem....
>
> The ten-girl team worked and trained zealously even though women's track and field in the United States has been sadly neglected or ignored by the educational institutions throughout the country. If it had not been for the few women's athletic clubs, playground departments, and track coaches, the women would not have been represented in the Olympic Games of 1952....
>
> Our post–Olympic meets were in London, where the girls participated in both the British Games and the International Games, in Cologne, Dortmund, and Solingen, Germany and in Amsterdam, Holland.

Wilson's recommendations were:

1. A woman should be selected to serve as manager-chaperone and a second as coach.

2. The Olympic trials should be held at least one week prior to debarkation date.

3. Women competitors in this country should be provided with more national and international competition.

The Olympic Trials

The Olympic trials were held in Harrisburg, Pennsylvania, on July 4. Twelve hundred spectators sitting under a broiling sun watched as eight Olympic events were contested. The *New York Times* reported:

> Youth dominated a nine-woman track and field team chosen tonight to represent the United States at the Olympic Games in Helsinki later this month.
>
> The nine, approved by the Olympic Committee, including Mabel Landry of Chicago and Catherine Hardy of Fort Valley State College, Ga., who set new records for American citizens in the broad jump and the 200 meter dash, respectively, during the day's trials.
>
> Four other girls were recommended to make the trip. They were Janet Dicks, Harrisburg, who won the discus and shot put; Ora Lee Allen, Chicago, high jump winner; Theresa Manuel, Tuskegee, who took second in the hurdles, and Caroline McDermott, Norman, Oklahoma, third in the hurdles.
>
> The Olympic Committee will decide tomorrow in New York whether they will be added to the team....

Autographed cover of 1952 Olympic trial program. Autographs of Nell Jackson, Mae Faggs, Stella Walsh, Ernestine Hardy, Cynthia Robinson, Frances Newbern, Betty Coll, Connie Darnowski, Conrad Ford, Delores Queary, Charlie Setzer, Bobbie Hendrix, Dolores Dwyer, Mary McNabb, Barbara Husband and Marion Boos. (Author's collection.)

Miss Hardy, a triple winner in last weekend's National A.A.U. championships at Waterbury, Connecticut, broke the old record of 24.4 set in 1935 by Helen Stephens of Fulton, Missouri. Miss Landry's mark eclipsed Lula Mae Hyme's 1939 standard of 18 feet 1 1/2 inches.

However both records are below the best ever exhibited in America by the Polish-born Stella Walsh. Stella, who was barred from the tryouts because she twice competed for Poland, holds the world record of 23.6 and the American mark of 24.1 in the 200. She holds the American record of 19 feet 4⅛ inches in the broad jump....

Miss Faggs, who at 16 was the youngest member of the 1948 American team, won the 100 in the fast time of 12.1. She had turned in 11.9 — three tenths of a second off Miss Stephens' American record — in the semi-finals.

Twenty-year-old Mae broke from the blocks first and led all the way to the tape.

The *Patriot*, the Harrisburg newspaper, featured the local girl, Janet Dicks. Headlines read, "Janet Dicks Takes Two Events in Olympic Trials," and the story continued: "Janet Dicks, 19 year old Highland Park weight star, was the brightest light at the 1952 women's Olympic trials yesterday as the husky athlete was the lone double winner in the competition. ... The shy girl, a sophomore at East Stroudsburg State Teachers, topped her excellent showing by taking a third in the javelin, the best all-around effort of the day for any competitor."

100-meter dash
1. Mae Faggs, N.Y. Police Athletic League   12.1
2. Janet Moreau, Red Diamond A.C., Boston
3. Catherine Hardy, Fort Valley State College
4. Barbara Jones, Chicago Catholic Youth Organization
5. Mary McNabb, Tuskegee Institute

200-meter dash
1. Catherine Hardy, Fort Valley   24.3
2. Mae Faggs, N.Y. Police Athletic League
3. Dolores Dwyer, German-American A.C.

80-meter hurdles
1. Constance Darnowski, German-American A.C.   11.8
2. Theresa Manuel, Tuskegee Institute
3. Caroline McDermott, Norman, Oklahoma

Shot put
1. Janet Dicks, Harrisburg A.A.   39' 8¼"
2. Amelia Bert, Providence, R.I.   39' 5½"
3. Doris Sutter, Los Angeles   37' 2½"

High jump
1. Ora Lee Allen, Chicago Catholic Youth Organization   4' 11¾"
2. Loita Mauer, Pasadena, Calif.,   4' 10"
    and Marion Boos, N.Y. Police Athletic League

Discus throw
1. Janet Dicks, Harrisburg A.A.   108' 3½"

2. Marjorie Larney, Equitable Life   107' ¾"
3. Amelia Bert, Little Rhody A.A.   106' 7⅞"

Broad jump
1. Mabel Landry, Chicago Catholic Youth Organization   18' 3"
2. Joan Wolski, Equitable Life   16' 4¾"
3. Nancy Phillips, German-American A.C.   16' ½"

Javelin throw
1. Marjorie Larney, Equitable Life   133' 7½"
2. Amelia Wershoven, Ridgefield Park, N.J.   124'
3. Janet Dicks, Harrisburg A.A.   117' 1¼"

The Outdoor Nationals

The national AAU championship meet was held again in Waterbury, Connecticut, on June 29 at Municipal Stadium under adverse weather conditions. The star of the meet was one-hundred-pound Catherine Hardy. While winning the individual title in the meet, she tied the American 50-meter mark of 6.4 and won the 100 and 200 meter sprints.

50-meter dash
1. Catherine Hardy, Ft. Valley   6.4 ties AR
2. Barbara Jones, Chicago Catholic Youth Organization
3. Delores Queary, N.Y. Police Athletic League

100-meter dash
1. Catherine Hardy, Ft. Valley   12.3
2. Mae Faggs, N.Y. Police Athletic League
3. Cynthia Robinson, N.Y. Police Athletic League

200-meters
1. Catherine Hardy, Ft. Valley   25.5
2. Mae Faggs, N.Y. Police Athletic League
3. Janet Moreau, Red Diamond A.C., Boston

80-meter hurdles
1. Constance Darnowski, German-American A.C.   12.1
2. Nancy Phillips, German-American A.C.
3. Theresa Manuel, Tuskegee Institute

280-meter shuttle hurdle relay
1. Tuskegee Institute, "A" team   41.6
    (Bell, Hendrix, Lawler, Manuel)
2. German-American A.C.
3. N.Y. Police Athletic League

400-meter relay
1. N.Y. Police Athletic League "A" team   52.5
    (Husband, Queary, Robinson, Faggs)
2. Tuskegee Institute
3. Chicago Catholic Youth Organization

Broad jump
1. Mabel Landry, Chicago Catholic Youth Organization   18' 1½"
2. Nancy Phillips, German-American A.C.   17' 2¾"
3. Barbara Jones, Chicago Catholic Youth Organization   16' 5½"
   and Jean Simmons, unattached, Chicago

Baseball throw
1. Marion Brown, unattached, Texas   245' 11"
2. Amelia Wershoven, Equitable Life A.S.   237' 4¾"
3. Yvonne Macon, N.Y. Police Athletic League   227' 3½"

Discus throw
1. Janet Dicks, Harrisburg A.A.   114' 7½"
2. Stella Walsh, Dreyer A.C., Berkeley, Calif.   109' 3½"
3. Doris Sutter, unattached, Los Angeles   109' 2"

Javelin throw
1. Marjorie Larney, Equitable Life A.S.   126' 8⅞"
2. Amelia Wershoven, Equitable Life A.S.   125' 10⅛"
3. Janet Dicks, Harrisburg A.A.   110' 3½"
   and Theresa Manuel, Tuskegee Institute

8-lb. shot put
1. Amelia Bert, Little Rhody A.C.,   37' 9"
   and Janet Dicks, Harrisburg A.A.
3. Carolyn Nave, Little Rhody A.C.

High jump
1. Marion Boos, N.Y. Police Athletic League   4' 11⅝"
2. Lula Bell, Tuskegee Institute,   4' 10⅝"
   and Loita Mauer, unattached, Altadena, Calif.

Individual scores:
Catherine Hardy 30; Janet Dicks 24; Nancy Phillips 18; Mae Faggs 16.

Team scores:
N.Y. Police Athletic League 72; Tuskegee Institute 44; German-American A.C. 40;
Equitable Life Assurance Society 35.

The junior women's championship meet was held on June 28 in conjunction with the senior championships at Waterbury.

50-meter dash
1. Barbara Jones, Chicago Catholic Youth Organization   6.7
2. Janet Moreau, Red Diamond A.C.
3. Barbara Husband, N.Y. Police Athletic League

100-meter dash
1. Janet Moreau, Red Diamond A.C.   12.1 MR
2. Barbara Jones, Chicago Catholic Youth Organization
3. Edith Moten, Tuskegee Institute

200-meter dash
1. Betty Lawrence, Los Angeles   26.1

2. Josephine Gilmore, Tuskegee Institute
3. Rebecca Ayars, Chicago Catholic Youth Organization

80-meter hurdles
1. Caroline McDermott, Norman, Oklahoma   12.7
2. Lula Bell, Tuskegee Institute
3. Caroline Squires, Tustin, Calif.

400-meter relay
1. Red Diamond A.C.   50.4
   (Moreau, Anderson, Conners, MacDonnell)
2. N.Y. Police Athletic League, "A" team
   (Conners, McDaniel, Dunn, Mead)
3. Tuskegee Institute (Hendrix, Bell, Matthews, Moten)

280-meter shuttle hurdle relay
1. Equitable Life A.S.   43.0
   (Wolski, Painter, Leiser, Wershoven)
2. Tuskegee Institute
3. Little Rhody A.C.

Baseball throw
1. Marion Brown, Deer Park, Texas   255' 9" MR
2. Joan Stouffer, Harrisburg A.A.   239' 7"
3. Barbara Queary, N.Y. Police Athletic League   224' 5"

High jump
1. Carol Dunn, N.Y. Police Athletic League,   4' 7"
   and Ora Lee Allen, Chicago Catholic Youth Organization
3. Ella Spears, Tuskegee Institute   4' 5"
   and Elaine Strube, Chicago Catholic Youth Organization

8-lb. shot put
1. Nancy Reid, Little Rhody A.C.   36' ⅜"
2. Donnis Thompson, Chicago Catholic Youth Organization 35' 6½"
3. Joan Stouffer, Harrisburg A.A.   35' 1"

Discus throw
1. Pauline Ruppelt, Philadelphia Turners   105' 10½"
2. Marjorie Larney, Equitable Life A.S.   100' 3⅝"
3. Paula Deubel, Little Rhody A.C.   98' 1"

Broad jump
1. Barbara Jones, Chicago Catholic Youth Organization   18' 1⅞" MR
2. Joan Wolski, Equitable Life A.S.   16' 5½"
3. Frances Newbern, Tennessee A&I   16' 5½"

Javelin throw
1. Marjorie Larney, Equitable Life A.S.   127' 7½" MR
2. Rose Bory, Equitable Life A.S.   111' 2"
3. Marion Brown, Deer Park, Texas   107' 6½"

Individual scores:
Barbara Jones 28; Marjorie Larney 19; Janet Moreau 18; Marion Brown 6; Joan Stouffer 14.

Team scores:
Chicago Catholic Youth Organization 62; Equitable Life Assurance Society 60¼; Tuskegee Institute 57; N.Y. Police Athletic League 37.

The Indoor Nationals

The senior indoor championship meet was held on March 15 in Buffalo, New York, in the 174th Armory. The top performance "was turned in by Miss Dolores Dwyer of Brooklyn's German-American A.C. She bettered the AAU 50 yard indoor record three times, winning in 6.2, a tenth of a second under the recognized mark," reported the *New York Times* on March 16.

Mae Faggs defended her 220-yard dash title and won the 100 in 11.1, which equaled the meet record.

50-yard dash
1. Dolores Dwyer, German-American A.C.   6.2 MR
2. Janet Moreau, Red Diamond A.C.
3. Tiny Halloran, East York Track Club, Toronto

100-yard dash
1. Mae Faggs, N.Y. Police Athletic League   11.1 ties MR
2. Dolores Dwyer, German-American A.C.
3. Cynthia Robinson, N.Y. Police Athletic League

220-yard dash
1. Mae Faggs, N.Y. Police Athletic League   26.2
2. Constance Darnowski, German-American A.C.
3. Rebecca Ayars, Chicago Catholic Youth Organization

50-yard hurdles
1. Nancy Phillips, German-American A.C.   7.5
2. Caroline McDermott, unattached, Oklahoma
3. Joan Davis, Queen City Spikes, Toronto

280-yard shuttle hurdle relay
1. German-American A.C.   41.5 MR
   (Dwyer, Darnowski, Blaul, Phillips)
2. Queen City Spikes
3. N.Y. Police Athletic League

440-yard medley relay
1. N.Y. Police Athletic League, "A" team   52.1 MR
   (Husband, Robinson, Queary, Faggs)
2. German-American A.C.
3. N.Y. Police Athletic League, "B" team

440-yard relay
1. N.Y. Police Athletic League, "A" team   51.1
   (Husband, Robinson, Queary, Faggs)

2. East York T.C., Toronto
3. Chicago Catholic Youth Organization

High jump
1. Marion Boos, N.Y. Police Athletic League	5' ¾"
2. Ora Lee Allen, Chicago Catholic Youth Organization	4' 10"
3. Nancy Phillips, German-American A.C.	4' 9"

Standing broad jump
1. Janet Moreau, Red Diamond A.C.	8' 10"
2. Nancy Phillips, German-American A.C.	8' 4½"
3. Cynthia Robinson, N.Y. Police Athletic League	8' 1¼"

Basketball throw
1. Elizabeth Cipolt, Chicago Catholic Youth Organization	90' 6"
2. Ramona Massey, N.Y. Police Athletic League	88' 7⅝"
3. Amelia Bert, Little Rhody A.C.	88' 4⅞"

8-lb. shot put
1. Amelia Bert, Little Rhody A.C.	40' 11⅝"
2. Ramona Massey, N.Y. Police Athletic League	37' 3"
3. Carolyn Nave, Little Rhody A.C.	34' 8"

Individual scores:
Mae Faggs 10; Nancy Phillips 10; Janet Moreau 9; Dolores Dwyer 8; Amelia Bert 7; Ramona Massey 6.

Team scores:
N.Y. Police Athletic League 41; German-American A.C. 29; Chicago Catholic Youth Organization 14; Little Rhody A.C. 12; Red Diamond A.C. 9.

1952 All-America Women's Track and Field Team

50-yard dash	Dolores Dwyer
50-meter dash	Barbara Jones
100-yard dash	Mae Faggs
100-meter dash	Catherine Hardy
200-meter dash	Catherine Hardy
220-yard dash	Mae Faggs
50-yard hurdles	Nancy Phillips
80-meter hurdles	Constance Darnowski
High jump	Marion Boos
Broad jump	Mabel Landry
Standing broad jump	Janet Moreau
Shot put	Amelia Bert
Discus	Janet Dicks
Javelin	Marjorie Larney
Baseball throw	Marion Brown
Basketball throw	Betty Cipolt
280-yard shuttle hurdle relay	Constance Darnowski, Nancy Phillips, Caroline McDermott, Theresa Manuel

400-meter relay	Catherine Hardy, Mae Faggs,
	Janet Moreau, Barbara Jones
440-yard medley relay	Barbara Jones, Catherine Hardy,
	Janet Moreau, Mae Faggs

A senior national pentathlon championship meet was held on October 5 in Houston, Texas. Stella Walsh captured the crown again with 2,183 points. She won four of the five events, the long jump in 17' 6½", 60-meter dash in 7.8, discus with a toss of 100' 11¾", and the 200 meters in 24.9. She threw 95' 3" in the javelin, which placed her third. Jo Culver of Tomball, Texas, was second with 1,588 points, and Helen Hale of Houston was third with 1,585 points. All ten of the other competitors were from Texas. Walsh was the only out-of-state athlete.

Lucile Wilson was chairman of the track and field committee.

The metropolitan association conducted its first pentathlon championships.

Chapter 36

1953

The senior national outdoor championship meet was held on July 24 and 25 in San Antonio, Texas. The *New York Times* headlines read, "Miss Dwyer Takes A.A.U. Sprint Title." The article continued:

> Dolores Ann Dwyer, the 1952 United States Olympic star competing unattached, became the first champion crowned in the National Amateur Athletic Union Senior Track and Field Meet tonight when she captured the 200 meter dash.
>
> Miss Dwyer defeated another Olympic runner, Barbara Jones of the Chicago C.Y.O. The winner was timed in 24.4 seconds, just two-tenths of a second over the National A.A.U. record.
>
> Stella Walsh, who set the world record for the 200 meters eighteen years ago with a time of 23.6, finished a poor fourth.

Olympian Mabel Landry led the Chicago Catholic Youth Organization to the team title over Tuskegee Institute, winner of the championship crown for fourteen years out of the last sixteen championship meets. Landry in winning the 50-meter dash and the broad jump was the only double champion of the meet. She also placed third in the 100 meters and anchored her Chicago Catholic Youth Organization 400-meter relay team to victory in 49.7.

50-meter dash
1. Mabel Landry, Chicago Catholic Youth Organization   6.6
2. Annie McDonald, Gulf Coast A.C.
3. Esther Villalon, Mexico

100-meter dash
1. Barbara Jones, Chicago Catholic Youth Organization   11.9
2. Dolores Dwyer, unattached, NY
3. Mabel Landry, Chicago Catholic Youth Organization

200-meter dash
1. Dolores Dwyer, unattached, NY   24.4
2. Barbara Jones, Chicago Catholic Youth Organization
3. Calpurnia Jackson, Tuskegee Institute
4. Stella Walsh, Dreyer A.C.

80-meter hurdles
1. Nancy Phillips, German-American A.C.   12.2

2. Constance Darnowski, German-American A.C.
3. Barbara Mueller, Chicago Catholic Youth Organization

400-meter relay
1. Chicago Catholic Youth Organization, "A" team   49.7
   (Watkins, Lyman, Jones, Landry)
2. Tuskegee Institute, "A" team
3. Chicago Catholic Youth Organization, "B" team

800-meter relay
1. Tuskegee Institute, "A" team   1:46.4
   (McDaniel, Cantrell, Brown, Hendrix)
2. Chicago Catholic Youth Organization, "A" team
3. Gulf Coast A.C.

280-meter shuttle hurdle relay
1. Tuskegee Institute   41.9
   (McDaniel, Brown, Hendrix, Bell)
2. Chicago Catholic Youth Organization
3. Gulf Coast A.C.

High jump
1. Mildred McDaniel, Tuskegee Institute   5' 1½"
2. Lula Bell, Tuskegee Institute,   4' 10"
   and Jeanette Cantrell, Tuskegee Institute

8-lb. shot put
1. Amelia Bert, Little Rhody A.C.   40' 2½"
2. Paula Deubel, Little Rhody A.C.   39' 9¼"
3. Donnis Thompson, Chicago Catholic Youth Organization   39' 2"

Baseball throw
1. Marion Brown, Gulf Coast   268' 9"
2. Amelia Wershoven, Equitable Life A.S.   268'
3. Joan Wolski, Equitable Life A.S.   237' 8"

Discus throw
1. Janet Dicks, Harrisburg A.A.   123' 2"
2. Marjorie Larney, Equitable Life A.S.   118' 2"
3. Concepcion Villaneuva, Mexico   108' 6"

Broad jump
1. Mabel Landry, Chicago Catholic Youth Organization   18' 7½"
2. Nancy Phillips, German-American A.C.   17' 5"
3. Arlene Pugh, Tuskegee Institute   17' 1"
4. Stella Walsh, Dreyer A.C.   16' 5"

Javelin throw
1. Amelia Wershoven, Equitable Life A.S.   124' 7"
2. Marjorie Larney, Equitable Life A.S.   121' 11"
3. Janet Dicks, Harrisburg A.A.   118' ½"

Individual scores:
Mabel Landry 26; Barbara Jones 20; Janet Dicks 20; Nancy Phillips 19⅖.

Team scores:
Chicago Catholic Youth Organization 102⅖; Tuskegee Institute 86; Equitable Life
A.S. 4 ⅖; Gulf Coast A.C. 40⅖; German-American A.C. 27⅖.

The junior championship meet was held in conjunction with the senior meet.
The *New York Times* had a small article with headlines that read, "Tuskegee
Track Leader." The story highlighted two events, the 200 meters and 50 meters.
As a result of Edith Moten and Arlene Pugh finishing 1-2 in the 200-meter dash,
Tuskegee held a point lead at the end of the first two running events.

50-meter dash
1. Hazel Watkins, Chicago Catholic Youth Organization   6.7
2. Annie McDonald, Gulf Coast A.C.
3. Josephine Gilmore, Tuskegee Institute

100-meter dash
1. Josephine Gilmore, Tuskegee Institute   12.3
2. Arlene Pugh, Tuskegee Institute
3. Edith Moten, Tuskegee Institute

200-meter dash
1. Edith Moten, Tuskegee Institute   25.0
2. Arlene Pugh, Tuskegee Institute
3. Rebecca Ayars, Chicago Catholic Youth Organization

80-meter hurdles
1. Barbara Mueller, Chicago Catholic Youth Organization   12.0
2. Lula Bell, Tuskegee Institute
3. Nancy Reid, Little Rhody A.C.

280-meter shuttle hurdle relay
1. Chicago Catholic Youth Organization   43.0
      (Newbern, Robinson, Jordan, Mueller)
2. Tuskegee Institute
3. Little Rhody A.C.

400-meter relay
1. Chicago Catholic Youth Organization   50.7
      (Watkins, Martin, Ayars, Lyman)
2. Tuskegee Institute, "A" team
3. Gulf Coast "A" team

800-meter relay
1. Tuskegee Institute, "A" team   1:48.4
2. Chicago Catholic Youth Organization
3. Gulf Coast, "B" team

Baseball throw
1. Dueda McQueen, San Angelo   225' 7"
2. Barbara Jacket, Gulf Coast A.C.
3. Bertha Chiu, Mexico

High jump
1. Jeanette Cantrell, Tuskegee Institute   5' 1½"
    and Mildred McDaniel, Tuskegee Institute
3. Barbara Mueller, Chicago Catholic Youth Organization,
    and Joan Wolski, Equitable Life A.S.

8-lb. shot put
1. Paula Deubel, Little Rhody   38' 10½"
2. Donnis Thompson, Chicago Catholic Youth Organization
3. Lula Bell, Tuskegee Institute

Discus throw
1. Anne Gordon, Tuskegee Institute   108' 4"
2. Concepcion Villanueva, Mexico
3. Bertha Chiu, Mexico

Broad jump
1. Arlene Pugh, Tuskegee Institute   17' ¾"
2. Joan Wolski, Equitable Life A.S.
3. Anna Jordan, Chicago Catholic Youth Organization

Javelin throw
1. Bertha Chiu, Mexico   119'
2. Lula Bell, Tuskegee Institute
3. Mamalia Yubi, Mexico

Individual scores:
Arlene Pugh 26; Bertha Chiu 22; Lula Bell 20; Josephine Gilmore 17.

Team scores:
Tuskegee Institute 50; Chicago Catholic Youth Organization 89; Gulf Coast 56; Mexico 40; Little Rhody A.C. 28; Equitable Life Assurance Society 14.

The Indoor Nationals

The senior indoor championship meet was held in Buffalo, New York, on March 21. Six invitational men's events were contested. The *New York Times* headlines reported, "Grand Street Boys Set Relay Record." Towards the end of the article, the meet record that Nancy Phillips set in the hurdles was mentioned, along with an American record-equaling performance of 6.0 in a heat of the 50-yard dash by DePaul University junior Mabel Landry, the meet record set by the Police Athletic League in the 280-yard shuttle hurdle relay, and Janet Moreau's victory in the 220-yard dash.

50-yard dash
1. Mabel Landry, Chicago Catholic Youth Organization   6.3
2. Janet Moreau, Red Diamond A.C.
3. Delores Queary, N.Y. Police Athletic League

100-yard dash
1. Cynthia Robinson, N.Y. Police Athletic League   11.4

2. Barbara Jones, Chicago Catholic Youth Organization
3. Mildred Grosse, Toronto Silver Heels T.C.

220-yard dash
1. Janet Moreau, Red Diamond A.C.   26.5
2. Marilyn Connors, Red Diamond A.C.
3. Carol Dunn, N.Y. Police Athletic League

50-yard hurdles
1. Nancy Phillips, German-American A.C.   7.1 MR
2. Constance Darnowski, German-American A.C.
3. Carol Smith, Toronto Silver Heels T.C.

280-yard shuttle hurdle relay
1. N.Y. Police Athletic League   41.4 MR
   (McDaniel, Mead, Dunn, Connors)
2. Toronto Silver Heels T.C.
3. German-American A.C.

440-yard relay
1. N.Y. Police Athletic League   53.7
   (Connor, Robinson, Queary, Husband)
2. Chicago Catholic Youth Organization
3. Red Diamond A.C.

440-yard medley relay
1. N.Y. Police Athletic League, "A" team   53.0
   (Dunn, Robinson, Queary, Husband)
2. N.Y. Police Athletic League, "B" team
3. Chicago Catholic Youth Organization

High jump
1. Marion Boos, N.Y. Police Athletic League   5' 1¼"
2. Nancy Phillips, German-American A.C.   5' ¼"
3. Veronica Lewis, Red Diamond A.C.,   4' 8¼"
   Ora Lee Allen, Chicago Catholic Youth Organization,
   and Nancy Reid, Little Rhody A.C.

Standing broad jump
1. Janet Moreau, Red Diamond A.C.   8' 6¾"
2. Nancy Phillips, German-American A.C.   8' 6"
3. Cynthia Robinson, N.Y. Police Athletic League   8' 3¼"

Basketball throw
1. Ramona Massey, N.Y. Police Athletic League   95' 8"
2. Joan Dash, N.Y. Police Athletic League   95' 5"
3. Joan Stouffer, Harrisburg A.A.   90' 11¾"

8-lb. shot put
1. Amelia Bert, Little Rhody A.C.   40' 10½"
2. Janet Dicks, Harrisburg A.A.   37' 11½"
3. Paula Deubel, Little Rhody A.C.   37' 11¼"

Individual scores:
Janet Moreau 13; Nancy Phillips 11; Cynthia Robinson 7; Ramona Massey, Amelia Bert, Mabel Landry, Marion Boos 5.

1953 national indoor champions and American record holders in the shuttle hurdle relay from the New York Police Athletic League. *From left:* Marcella Conners, Carol Dunn, Louise Mead and Jesse McDaniel. (Author's photo.)

Team scores:
N.Y. Police Athletic League 42½; Red Diamond 20; Chicago CYO 17½; German-American A.C. 16; Little Rhody A.C. 11.

The 1953 All-America Women's Track and Field Team

50-yard dash	Mabel Landry
50-meter dash	Mabel Landry
100-yard dash	Cynthia Robinson
100-meter dash	Barbara Jones
200-meter dash	Dolores Dwyer
50-yard hurdles	Nancy Phillips
80-meter hurdles	Nancy Phillips
High jump	Mildred McDaniel
Broad jump	Mabel Landry
Standing broad jump	Janet Moreau
Shot put	Amelia Bert
Discus throw	Janet Dicks
Javelin throw	Amelia Wershoven
Basketball throw	Ramona Massey
Baseball throw	Marion Brown
280-yard shuttle hurdle relay	Nancy Phillips, Constance Darnowski, Barbara Mueller, Caroline McDermott
400-meter relay	Barbara Jones, Dolores Dwyer, Mabel Landry, Arlene Pugh
440-yard medley relay	Janet Moreau, Cynthia Robinson, Barbara Jones, Mabel Landry
800-meter relay	Dolores Dwyer, Barbara Jones, Calpurnia Jackson, Stella Walsh

Two regional pentathlon championships were held on the same day, October 18. Region 9 was held at Berkeley, California, and the Region 2 pentathlon was held at Victory Field, Queens, New York.

Stella Walsh captured the Region 9 pentathlon, winning all five of the events — broad jump, javelin, 60 meter, 200 meter, and discus. Dolores Dwyer, representing the Manhattan Catholic Youth Organization, won the Region 2 pentathlon. She led in three of the events. Stella's total score was 1944, and Dolores scored 1540 points.

Track and Field News featured a "Women's Best" list. Three American women were on the world list, which was at least ten deep for every event. Janet Moreau's 11.7 ranked her third, along with Shirley Strickland of Australia, in the 100 meters. Catherine Hardy's time of 11.8 was ranked with six other athletes for places five through eleven on the list. In the 200 meters, Hardy and Faggs ranked seven and eight with a time of 24.3.

The only other ranking from the United States was the time of 45.9 that the USA team ran in the 1952 Olympic Games 400-meter relay, which placed them number one in the world with Germany.

Chapter 37

1954

The national outdoor championship meet was staged at Fager Field, Harrisburg, Pennsylvania, on July 30–31. The headlines in the *New York Times* reported, "Tennessee State Sets Relay Mark in Women's A.A.U. Track Meet," and the article continued:

> Tennessee State University today set an American 800 meter relay record of 1:45.2 on the homestretch sprint of Mae Faggs....
>
> Lucinda Williams took the first 200 meter leg on the concrete-hard track by a small margin which was held by team-mate Isabelle Daniels.
>
> After maintaining a margin on the third leg, Cynthia Thompson gave the baton to the 22-year-old New York athlete. Miss Faggs put on a strong sprint to put Tennessee ahead of Tuskegee Institute at the finish by nearly 5 yards.
>
> Miss Faggs was the only American woman to score in the individual events in the 1952 Olympic Games at Helsinki, Finland. She also ran the anchor leg for the 1949 New York Police Athletic League squad that set the former 800 meter American record of 1:45.7....
>
> The dry track coupled with 93 degree heat, set performances on a sub-par basis, although another A.A.U. record was set in the 280 meter shuttle hurdles relay.
>
> The Equitable Life Assurance Society of New York was the other record breaker on the team performance of Lenore Leiser, Connie Painter, Joan Wolski and Lauretta Foley in 41.2....
>
> A crowd of fewer than 500 braved the heat to watch the events.

50-meter dash
1. Mabel Landry, Chicago Catholic Youth Organization   6.5
2. Barbara Lee, N.Y. Police Athletic League
3. Dolores Dwyer, N.Y. Catholic Youth Organization

100-meter dash
1. Barbara Jones, Chicago Catholic Youth Organization   12.0
2. Mabel Landry, Chicago Catholic Youth Organization
3. Delores Queary, N.Y. Police Athletic League

200-meter dash
1. Mae Faggs, Tennessee State   24.5
2. Betty MacDonnell, Liberty A.C.
3. Alfrances Lyman, Chicago Catholic Youth Organization

80-meter hurdles
1. Constance Darnowski, German-American A.C.   12.2

2. Lula Bell, Tuskegee Institute
3. Barbara Mueller, Chicago Catholic Youth Organization

280-meter shuttle hurdle relay
1. Equitable Life A.S. (Wolski, Painter, Foley, Leiser)   41.2
2. Tuskegee Institute
3. Chicago Catholic Youth Organization

400-meter relay
1. Chicago Catholic Youth Organization   49.0
   (Watkins, Lyman, Landry, Jones)
2. Tennessee State, "A" team
3. Tuskegee Institute, "A" team

800-meter relay
1. Tennessee State   1:45.2
   (Williams, Daniels, Thompson, Faggs)
2. Tuskegee Institute
3. Chicago Catholic Youth Organization

Baseball throw
1. Marion Brown, Gulf Coast   245' ½"
2. Amelia Wershoven, Equitable Life A.S.   244' 4½"
3. Joan Wolski, Equitable Life A. S.   232' 6"

Discus throw
1. Marjorie Larney, Equitable Life A.S.   120' 11½"
2. Janet Dicks, Harrisburg A.A.   107' 6"
3. Lois Testa, Red Diamond A.C.   101' 3½"

Shot put
1. Lois Testa, Red Diamond A.C.   41' 11¾"
2. Paula Duebel, Little Rhody A.C.   41' 8¾"
3. Joan Stouffer, Harrisburg A.A.   no mark

High jump
1. Jeanette Cantrell, Tuskegee Institute,   5' ¼"
   and Verneda Thomas, Chicago Catholic Youth Organization
3. Mildred McDaniel, Tuskegee Institute,   4' 10¼"
   Lula Bell, Tuskegee Institute,
   Veronica Lewis, Red Diamond A.C.,
   and Billie Jo Jackson, Gulf Coast

Broad jump
1. Mabel Landry, Chicago Catholic Youth Organization   17' 11"
2. Barbara Jones, Chicago Catholic Youth Organization   17' 9½"
3. Elvyra Siksnius, Lithuanian A.C.   16' 8"

Javelin throw
1. Karen Anderson, Mercury A.C.   127' 1"
2. Amelia Wershoven, Equitable Life A.S.   123' 4"
3. Lula Bell, Tuskegee Institute   121' 5½"

Team scores:
Chicago Catholic Youth Organization 110; Tuskegee Institute 59½; Equitable Life
Assurance Society 59; N.Y. Police Athletic League and Tennessee State University 31;
Red Diamond 21¼.

The Indoor Nationals

The senior national indoor championship meet was held on March 27 in New
York City at the 168th St. Armory. The *New York Times* on March 28 exclaimed,
"Chicago C.Y.O. Team Wins National A.A.U. Women's Track Crown." The com-
mentary continued: "Six first places in the eleven event show went to the Chicago
girls. ... The Chicago team's Barbara Mueller was the only double victor. She
took the 50 yard hurdles and the running high jump. Mabel Landry of Chicago
won the 50 yard dash, repeating her triumph of 1953."

50-yard dash
1. Mabel Landry, Chicago Catholic Youth Organization   6.1
2. Margaret Davis, Tennessee State
3. Barbara Lee, N.Y. Police Athletic League
4. Delores Queary, N.Y. Police Athletic League

100-yard dash
1. Barbara Jones, Chicago Catholic Youth Organization   11.5
   and Mae Faggs, Tennessee State
3. Dolores Dwyer, N.Y. Catholic Youth Organization
4. Rebecca Ayars, Chicago Catholic Youth Organization

220-yard dash
1. Mae Faggs, Tennessee State   26.5
2. Alfrances Lyman, Chicago Catholic Youth Organization
3. Betty MacDonnell, Liberty A.C.
4. Louise Mead, N.Y. Police Athletic League

50-yard hurdles
1. Barbara Mueller, Chicago Catholic Youth Organization   7.4
2. Lenore Leiser, Equitable Life A.S.
3. Joan Wolski, Equitable Life A.S.
4. Anna Jordan, Chicago Catholic Youth Organization

280-shuttle hurdle relay
1. Equitable Life A.S.   41.7
   (Wolski, Painter, Wershoven, Leiser)
2. Chicago Catholic Youth Organization
3. N.Y. Police Athletic League
4. Equitable Life A.S., "B" team

440-yard relay
1. Chicago Catholic Youth Organization   52.0
   (Landry, Jones, Ayars, Lyman)

2. Tennessee State
3. Equitable Life
4. N.Y. Police Athletic League

440-yard medley relay
1. Chicago Catholic Youth Organization   53.0
   (Ayars, Lyman, Jones, Landry)
2. N.Y. Catholic Youth Organization
3. N.Y. Police Athletic League, "B" team
4. N.Y. Police Athletic League, "A" team

8-lb. shot put
1. Paula Deubel, Little Rhody A.C.   39' 11¾"
2. Ramona Massey, N.Y. Police Athletic League   38' 8"
3. Amelia Bert, Little Rhody A.C.   38' 5½"
4. Lois Testa, Red Diamond A.C.   37' 7¼"

Standing broad jump
1. Cynthia Layne, N.Y. Police Athletic League   7' 10½"
2. Virginia Nagle, Equitable Life A.S.   7' 9⅛"
3. Mary Burns, Red Diamond A.C.   7' 8"
4. Amelia Wershoven, Equitable Life A.S.   7' 6"

High jump
1. Barbara Mueller, Chicago Catholic Youth Organization 4' 10¾"
2. Veronica Lewis, Red Diamond A.C.,   4' 9¾"
   and Marion Boos, N.Y. Police Athletic League
4. Elaine Strube, Chicago Catholic Youth Organization   4' 8¾"

Basketball throw
1. Catherine Walsh, Equitable Life A. S.   104' 3½"
2. Ann Flynn, N.Y. Catholic Youth Organization   103' 2½"
3. Joan Stouffer, Harrisburg A.A.   98' 9"
4. Joan Dash, N.Y. Police Athletic League   95' 3½"

Team scores:
Chicago Catholic Youth Organization 39; Equitable Life A.S. 22; N.Y. Police Athletic League 21½; Tennessee State University 14.

The senior national pentathlon championship was held on October 9 in Cleveland, Ohio.

Stella Walsh, forty-three, defended her fifth title against a field of thirty-eight women, but she won only one of the events, the discus throw. Her final score was 1,738 points. Betty MacDonnell of the Liberty A.C. placed second with 1,546 points, and Dolores Dwyer of the New York Catholic Youth Organization finished third with 1,516 points.

1954 All-America Women's Track and Field Team

50-yard dash	Mabel Landry
50-meter dash	Mabel Landry
60-meter dash	Dolores Dwyer

75-yard dash	Alfrances Lyman
100-yard dash	Barbara Jones
220-yard run	Betty MacDonnell
100-meter run	Barbara Jones
200-meter run	Mae Faggs
50-yard hurdles	Barbara Mueller
80-meter hurdles	Constance Darnowski
Broad jump	Mabel Landry
Standing broad jump	Cynthia Layne
High jump	Billie Jo Jackson
8-lb. shot put	Lois Testa
Discus throw	Marjorie Larney
Javelin throw	Karen Anderson
Baseball throw	Marion Brown
Basketball throw	Catherine Walsh

The track and field chairman was Frances Kaszubski of Cleveland, Ohio. The 1956 Olympic Committee chair was Roxy Andersen, and the members of her committee were Lucile Wilson, Dr. Cleve Abbott, Earl Flickinger, Alice Arden Hodge, Frances Kaszubski, and Catherine Donovan Meyer. All but Abbott, Flickinger, and Wilson were former national-level athletes.

Chairman Kaszubski's report at the 67th Annual AAU Convention in November in Miami Beach indicated that an effort was being made to stimulate interest in track and field by forming a positive relationship with the Division of Girls and Women's Sports.

The Knights of Columbus meet at the Boston Garden on January 16 included a 50-yard dash for women, which was listed as the women's indoor New England championship.

Chapter 38

1955

The national women's and girl's outdoor championship meet was held on June 17-18 in Ponca City, Oklahoma. *Track and Field News* had a small article announcing the breaking of three records and the equaling of the fourth in the meet: "Records were broken by Olympian Mae Faggs of Tennessee State University with a 10.7 for the 100 yards, Bertha Diaz of Cuba with 11.5 for 80 meter low hurdles, and Mildred McDaniel of Tuskegee Institute who high jumped 5' 6½", narrowly missing a world mark of 5' 8⅝". Isabelle Daniels of Tennessee State ran 5.8 for the 50 to equal the American record." Mae ran the 10.7 in a heat of the 100.

50-yard dash
1. Isabelle Daniels, Tennessee State   6.0 MR
2. Rebecca Ayars, Chicago Comets
3. Lucinda Williams, Tennessee State
4. Ella Turner, Tennessee State

80-meter hurdles
1. Bertha Diaz, Cuba   11.5 MR
2. Barbara Mueller, Chicago Comets
3. Nancy Phillips, German-American A.C.
4. Jeanette Cantrell, Tuskegee Institute

100-yard dash
1. Mae Faggs, Tennessee State   10.8
2. Martha Hudson, Tennessee State
3. Alfrances Lyman, Chicago Comets
4. Bertha Diaz, Cuba

Baseball throw
1. Amelia Wershoven, Equitable Life A.S.   249' 1¼"
2. Marion Brown, Wayland College   241' 8¾"
3. Pamela Kurrell, Laurel Track Club   238' 1¼"
4. Patricia Monsanto, Tennessee State   235' 7½"

Shot put
1. Wanda Wejzgrowicz, Polish Falcons   37' 4⅝"
2. Lois Testa, Red Diamond A.C.   36' 8"
3. Marjorie Larney, Equitable Life A.S.   35' 7¼"
4. Willie Ann Battie, Tuskegee Institute   33' 7"

440-yard relay
1. Tennessee State, "A" team   49.1 MR
   (Hudson, Williams, Daniels, Faggs)
2. Chicago Comets
3. Tennessee State, "B" team
4. Cuba

220-yard dash
1. Mae Faggs, Tennessee State   25.1 MR
2. Alfrances Lyman, Chicago Comets
3. Gayle Dierks, Englewood, Colorado
4. Charlsetta Reddick, Tennessee State

Discus
1. Alejandra Ilarra, Cuba   117' 8"
2. Marjorie Larney, Equitable Life A.S.   115' 1"
3. Patricia Monsanto, Tennessee State A.S.   113' 1"
4. Wanda Wejzgrowicz, Polish Falcons   107' 1¼"

Javelin
1. Karen Anderson, Mercury A.C.   150' 1¼" MR
2. Amelia Wershoven, Equitable Life A.S.   135' 4"
3. Marjorie Larney, Equitable Life A.S.   127' 5"
4. Nelsy Acosta, Chicago Comets   112' 4"

Broad jump
1. Nancy Phillips, German-American A.C.   17' 5¾"
2. Shirley Hereford, Holland A.C.   16' 6½"
3. Annie Smith, Tennessee State   16' 4⅞"
4. Margaret Matthews, Chicago Comets   15' 8⅛"

High jump
1. Mildred McDaniel, Tuskegee Institute   5' 6½" AR
2. Jo Jackson, Houston A.C.   5' ¾"
3. Verneda Thomas, Chicago Comets   4' 10¾"
4. Jeanette Cantrell, Tuskegee Institute,   4' 8¾"
   Kaye Bunting, Chicago Comets,
   and Freddie Dannhouse, Houston A.C.

Team scores:
Tennessee State University 87½; Chicago Comets 59⅓; Equitable Life A.S. 38; Cuba 33; Tuskegee Institute 27⅓; German-American A.C. 17.

Girls' Division

The *New York Times* reported that Tennessee State won the girls' championship by winning six of the eleven events. This meet was fifteen-year-old Wilma Rudolph's first national competition.

50-yard dash
1. Isabelle Daniels, Tennessee State   5.8 ties AR

2. Martha Hudson, Tennessee State
3. Lucinda Williams, Tennessee State
4. Jo Ann Baker, Woodward, unattached

50-yard hurdles
1. Jeanette Cantrell, Tuskegee Institute   7.4
2. Erol Linday Faucett, unattached, Oklahoma
3. Kaye Bunting, Chicago Comets
4. Shirley Crowder, Tuskegee Institute

Shot put
1. Willie Ann Battie, Tuskegee Institute   37' 2½"
2. Pamela Kurrell, Laurel T.C.   33' 1¼"
3. Melinda Roper, Chicago Comets   30' 8"
4. Ester Spickerman, Burnet, Texas   30' 6¾"

High jump
1. Jeanette Cantrell, Tuskegee Institute   4' 11⅝"
2. Kaye Bunting, Chicago Comets   4' 10⅝"
3. Freddie Dannhaus, Houston A.C.   4' 9⅝"
4. Nancy Barham, Kiwanis Club of Alva,   4' 7⅝"
     and Shirley Hereford, Holland Athletic Club

Discus
1. Gloria Myers, Tennessee State   108' 3"
2. Lorene Holmes, Tennessee State   103' 4½"
3. Pamela Kurrell, Laurel Track Club   100' 6½"
4. Doris Powell, Tennessee State   97' 7¾"

Javelin
1. Karen Anderson, Mercury A.C.   149' 4¾"
2. Melinda Roper, Chicago Comets   98' 5¾"
3. Ester Spickerman, Burnet, Texas   86' 4½"
4. Doris Powell, Tennessee State   78' 9½"

75-yard dash
1. Martha Hudson, Tennessee State   8.8
2. Lucinda Williams, Tennessee State
3. Jo Ann Baker, Woodward, unattached
4. Wilma Rudolph, Tennessee State

100-yard dash
1. Isabelle Daniels, Tennessee State   11.3
2. Wilma Rudolph, Tennessee State
3. Gayle Dierks, Englewood, Colo.
4. Anna Mae Sullifant, Michigan Girls Track Club

Baseball throw
1. Pamela Kurrell, Laurel Track Club   254' ⅜"
2. Melinda Roper, Chicago Comets   225' 10"
3. Charity Alker, Greenwich, Conn.   223' 9⅜"
4. Melba Robinson, Chicago Comets   220' 10"

300-yard relay
1. Tennessee State   34.7
    (Hudson, Rudolph, Williams, Daniels)
2. Tuskegee Institute
3. Chicago Comets
4. Burnet, Texas, H.S.

Broad jump
1. Annie Smith, Tennessee State   16' 10½"
2. Kaye Bunting, Chicago Comets   15' 10¾"
3. Gayle Dierks, Englewood, Colo.   15' 5"
4. Shirley Hereford, Holland A.C.   15' 3¾"

Team scores:
Tennessee State University 114; Chicago Comets 56½; Tuskegee Institute 47; Laurel Track Club 24; Burnet, Texas, High School 15; Englewood, Colo. 14; Mercury A.C. 10.

The Indoor Nationals

The senior national indoor meet was on February 5 in Chicago, Illinois, at the University of Chicago Field House. Two outdoor events added to the indoor program served as tryouts for the Pan American Games.

The *New York Times* featured an extensive story on the meet, its headlines proclaiming the victories of Marjorie Larney, eighteen, and Amelia Wershoven, twenty-three, in the two added events, the javelin and discus throw. The headlines read, "Misses Larney and Wershoven Win National A.A.U. Track Titles at Chicago." The article continued:

> A pair of New York girls established discus and javelin throw indoor records tonight — because there were no previous championship marks. ... Since this was the first time the javelin and discus were included in a championship indoor meet, each distance became a record.
>
> The national javelin throw record is 139 feet 3 inches set by Babe Didrikson Zaharias in 1932. The same year Ruth Osborn established the discus mark of 133' ¾" that still stands. Both, of course, were set outdoors....
>
> The six events determined the team that will fly the United States colors in the Pan-American games at Mexico City March 12-26.

60-meter dash
1. Isabelle Daniels, Tennessee State   7.9
2. Mae Faggs, Tennessee State
3. Margaret Davis, Tennessee State

100-meter dash
1. Barbara Jones, Chicago Comets   12.3
2. Mae Faggs, Tennessee State
3. Alfrances Lyman, Chicago Comets

80-meter hurdles
1. Nancy Phillips, German-American A.C.   12.0
2. Barbara Mueller, Chicago Comets
3. Constance Darnowski, German-American A.C.

220-yard dash
1. Alfrances Lyman, Chicago Comets   26.2
2. Stella Walsh, Montrose, California
3. Rebecca Ayars, Chicago Comets

440-yard relay
1. Chicago Comets   50.5 MR
   (Watkins, Lyman, Landry, Jones)
2. Tennessee A. & I.
3. East York Track Club, Canada

440-yard medley relay
1. Chicago Comets   52.8
   (Matthews, Landry, Ayars, Jones)
2. Tennessee A.& I.
3. East York Track Club, Canada

Basketball throw
1. Amelia Wershoven, Equitable Life A.S.   98' 2"
2. Pamela Kurrell, Laurel Track Club   96' 8¼"
3. Melba Robinson, Chicago Comets   93' ½"

4-kilo shot put
1. Lois Testa, Red Diamond A.C.   37' 6¾"
2. Marjorie Larney, Equitable Life A.S.   35' 11¼"
3. Wanda Wejzgrowicz, Polish Falcons   34' 6"

Standing broad jump
1. Shirley Hereford, Holland A.C.   8' 11¼" MR
2. Nancy Phillips, German-American A.C.   8' 7¼"
3. Barbara Mueller, Chicago Comets   8' 7¼"

High jump
1. Mildred McDaniel, Tuskegee Institute   5' 2"
2. Verneda Thomas, Chicago Comets   5' 1"
3. Jeanette Cantrell, Tuskegee Institute   4' 11¼"

Additional Pan-American tryout events

Discus throw
1. Marjorie Larney, Equitable Life A.S.   122' 2"
2. Pamela Kurrell, Laurel Track Club   117' 11"
3. Pat Monsanto, Tennessee State   114' 2"
4. Stella Walsh, Montrose, California   107' 11½"

Javelin throw
1. Amelia Wershoven, Equitable Life A.S.   138' 10"
2. Karen Anderson, Mercury A.C.   136' 4"
3. Marjorie Larney, Equitable Life A.S.   121' 6"
4. Lula Bell, Tuskegee Institute   no mark

The 1955 Pan-American team personnel, events, place, and performance follow. Mexico City hosted the Games from March 12 to March 26.

The 200 meters, shot put, and broad jump were not held.

	Event	Place	Performance
Anderson, Karen	Javelin	1	161' 3" (Pan American record)
Cantrell, Jeanette	HJ	4	5' 1⅜"
Daniels, Isabelle	60m	2	7.6
	400mr	1	47.0 (Pan American record)
Darnowski, Constance	80mh	6	no time given
Faggs, Mae	60m	5	7.7
	100m	2	11.8
	400mr	1	47.0 (Pan American record)
Jones, Barbara	100m	1	11.5 (Pan American record)
	400mr	1	47.0 (Pan American record)
Kurrell, Pamela	Discus	8	110' 2⅞"
Landry, Mabel	60m	3	7.6
	400mr	1	47.0 (Pan American record)
Larney, Marjorie	Javelin	4	132' 11¼"
	Discus	6	114' 8¾"
Lyman, Alfrances	100m	4	12.1
McDaniel, Mildred	HJ	1	5' 6¼" (Pan American record)
Monsanto, Patricia	Discus	11	104' 2¾"
Mueller, Barbara	80mh	5	11.9
Phillips, Nancy	80mh	DNQ	12.0
Thomas, Verneda	HJ	3	5' 2⅝"
Wershoven, Amelia	Javelin	3	141' 3¼"
Kaszubski, Frances	Manager		
Flickinger, Earl	Coach		

The *New York Times* headlined Mildred McDaniel's victory and record in the high jump in the Pan American Games. She smashed the record by nearly nine inches and just missed the world record.

Barbara Jones set a Pan American record in the 100 meters.

1955 All-America Women's Track and Field Team

50-yard dash	Isabelle Daniels
60-meter dash	Isabelle Daniels
100-yard dash	Mae Faggs
100-meter dash	Barbara Jones
220-yard dash	Mae Faggs
80-meter hurdles	Barbara Mueller
Standing broad jump	Shirley Hereford
Broad jump	Nancy Phillips
High jump	Mildred McDaniel
4-kilo shot put	Wanda Wejzgrowicz

Discus throw	Marjorie Larney
Javelin throw	Karen Anderson
Baseball throw	Pamela Kurrell
Basketball throw	Amelia Wershoven

A USA women's pentathlon championship was held on October 15 at Morristown, New Jersey. Barbara Mueller, competing in pouring rain all day, placed first with 3539 points, followed by Stella Walsh with 3,431 points.

Frances Kaszubski, in her report at the 68th Annual AAU Convention in December in Louisville, touched on the highlights of the year:

> The national championships indicate remarkable progress not only in this committee's first year of cooperation with the NSGWS, of AAHPER, but, also in the trend of public opinion which reflects the changing attitudes from anti track and field for girls to the new concept of the sport's techniques for necessary and fundamental skills....
>
> Beginning with the Pan American Games, in March, at University City, in Mexico, the U.S. women's track and field team, comprised of sixteen girls, won four out of seven gold medals for Pan American Championships. And, in addition to winning the lion's share of silver and bronze medals, the performances of two of our Pan American champions have been recognized as the best in the world for 1955. They are:
>
> | 100 meters | 11.5 | Barbara Jones |
> |---|---|---|
> | High jump | 5' 6¼" | Mildred McDaniel |
>
> Additionally, inter-collegiate competitions in the Southeastern Association, sponsored by Tennessee A. & I. University produced a new world record application for the 200 meter run by Mae Faggs, a senior at the University.
>
> Another highlight in the tremendous record of accomplishment in the sport of women's track and field became apparent when the Second Army conducted track and field competitions for the Women's Army Corps and, thanks to the cooperation of Col. D. F. Hull, fielded a team for the first time in the history of our sport at the national championships in Ponca City, Oklahoma.

Prior to this meet, Major Ingle, of Washington, D.C., stated that the entire Women's Army Corps would include a program of track and field for women in 1956.

During the national conference of leaders in July, the NSGWS discussed the benefits and reasons for including track and field skills in physical programs for girls in the United States.

A final first, reported Chairman Kaszubski, was the inclusion of the sport of track and field in the Helms Hall of Fame. Tennis, golf, swimming, and diving were the four sports previously recognized by the Hall.

The women's committee rejected a recommendation to include walking in the women's track and field program. It was suggested that amendments to the rules be submitted to read as follows, "Neither National or association competition may be held for women in cross country running nor walking."

The committee passed a resolution providing for greater cooperation with NSGWS. Approval was given to a motion that NSGWS be extended an invitation to affiliate with the AAU. The committee recommended that in any future research involving women's track and field, members of NSGWS be invited to serve as consultants.

Physical Education for High School Students was published this year; and included a chapter on track and field.

Chapter 39

1956: The Melbourne Olympic Year

The Olympic trials were held at American University in Washington, D.C., on August 25. At the conclusion, the following nineteen women were members of the 1956 Olympic track and field team that competed in the Olympic Games in Melbourne, Australia, from November 22 to December 8.

	Olympic Event	Olympic Place	Olympic Performance
Anderson, Karen	Javelin	8	157' 5½"
Ayars, Rebecca	400mr	reserve	
Brown, Mrs. Earlene	SP	6	49' 7¼"
	Discus	4	168' 5½"
Daniels, Isabelle	100m	4	11.8
	400mr	3	44.9
Darnowski, Constance	80mh	DNQ	11.9
Deubel, Paula	SP	16	40' 7½"
Ellis, Meredith	200m	DNQ	26.3
Faggs, Mae	100m	DNQ	12.2
	200m	DNQ	24.8
	400mr	3	44.9
Flynn, Ann Marie	HJ	19	5' 2½"
Kurrell, Pamela	Discus	18	132' 9⅝"
Larney, Marjorie	Javelin	11	148' 6"
	Discus	20	130' 11¼"
Matthews, Margaret	BJ	18	18' 8¼"
McDaniel, Mildred	HJ	1	5' 9¼" WR
Mueller, Barbara	80mh	DNQ	11.6
Robertson, Irene	80mh	DNQ	11.9
Rudolph, Wilma	200m	DNQ	24.6
	400mr	3	44.9
Testa, Lois	SP	14	42' 10"
Wershoven, Amelia	Javelin	15	145' 3½"
White, Willye	BJ	2	19' 11¾"

1956 United States Women's Olympic Track and Field Team. *Front row from left:* Pam Kurrell, Willye White, Amelia Wershoven, Mae Faggs, Karen Anderson, Connie Darnowski, Roxanne Andersen, manager-chaperone. *Second row from left:* Irene Robertson, Barbara Mueller, Isabelle Daniels, Rebecca Ayars, Lucinda Williams, Lois Testa, Margaret Matthews, Dr. Nell Jackson, coach. *Back row from left:* Wilma "Skeeter" Rudolph, Ann Flynn, Earlene Brown, Paula Deubel, Meredith Ellis, Marjorie Larney, Mildred McDaniel, Richmond "Boo" Morcom, field coach. (Courtesy of the U.S.O.C. Photo Library.)

Williams, Lucinda	100m	DNQ	12.0
	400mr	3	44.9
Andersen, Mrs. Roxanne	Manager-Chaperone		
Jackson, Nell	Coach		
Morcom, Richmond	Field coach		

The track and field chairman, Roxanne Andersen, reported in the *United States 1956 Olympic Book* that the committee which selected the "largest and best-performing" Olympic team was formed in 1953. Six meetings were subsequently held, and twenty-one bulletins were issued by the chairman at frequent intervals.

Andersen wrote, "For the first time in its history, the Olympic Women's Track and Field team was assembled for a pre–Olympic training period prior to departure for the Games. Athletes, coaches and manager checked into the Alexandria Hotel in Los Angeles by October 15."

Prior to departure for Australia, the team was divided into two groups, the field event group, which left on November 6 on Pan American Airways, and the track group, which left on November 11. The team made stopovers in Hawaii, Canton Island, and Fiji.

Our girls reached the finals in six events, in contrast to 1952, when we made only two finals.

Andersen noted that Australia and Russia, the leading countries, shared a similar attitude on the part of their educators towards women's competitive sport:

> Both countries go all out in discovering, encouraging and developing female athletic talent in schools, factories and clubs. In sharp contrast, the USA has only a handful of clubs and two women's colleges throughout a widely-scattered but very small proportion of the country.
>
> The American girl is still fighting the battle of mid–Victorian prejudice against participation by women in competitive sport. Many potential Olympic champions remain undiscovered because of our present system — or lack of it.

The Olympic Results

100 meters. In the 100-meter dash, Mae Faggs was third in the first heat in 12.2. Lucinda Williams was third in the second heat in 12.0. Neither qualified for the next round. Isabelle Daniels was second in the third heat in 11.6, third in the second semifinal in 11.7, and fourth in the final in 11.8. The placing between third and fourth was so close that originally the five foot, six inch Daniels had been brought to the victory stand for third. After the photo finish was studied, however, she was awarded fourth.

200 meters. In the 200 meters, Mae Faggs, the first American woman to make three Olympic teams, reached the semifinal round. Mae was second in the first heat in 24.9 and fifth in the second semifinal in 24.8. Wilma Rudolph, in her first Olympic appearance, finished third in the second heat in 24.6, and Meredith Ellis was fourth in the third heat in 26.3. Neither qualified for the next round.

400-meter relay. In the 400-meter relay, the United States team, all athletes from Tennessee State University, qualified for the final in 45.4 by placing second in the second heat. Wilma Rudolph said in her book, *Wilma,* "On the day of the relay, Mae Faggs was at her best. She was the motivator for us. ... She went around telling us, 'Let's go get 'em.' Mae Faggs started it off for us and got a good start. She came around about even in front and handed it off to Margaret Matthews. Margaret ran a decent leg, then passed it to me. It was a clean pass, and I got off well. I think I passed two people on my leg, then handed it to Isabelle Daniels, who ran anchor. She ran a fine leg and just missed getting us into second place." The team captured the bronze medal for third place.

Broad jump. In the broad jump, sixteen-year-old high school student Willye White qualified for the final round with a leap of 19' 8½" and set an American record with her silver medal, second-place jump of 19' 11¾". Margaret Matthews did not make the qualifying distance of 18' 8¼". Kieran and Daley stated in *The Story of the Olympic Games,* "Much more of a surprise was the achievement of Willye White of Tennessee State, ... who shattered the American record by doing 19 feet 11¾ inches for second place."

One report commented that Willye was nervous and read her Bible to relax

Mildred McDaniel, 1956 Olympic Champion and world record holder in the high jump (right) with Olympic coach, Nell Jackson (left) on their return to the United States from Melbourne. (Courtesy of the National Track & Field Hall of Fame Historical Research Library at Butler University.)

before the best jump of her life. She knew that there were only three steps on the victory stand, and she wanted to be on one of them. Elated about her final jump, she said that her grandfather would be so proud when he read about her in the paper.

High jump. Mildred McDaniel outclassed all of the competition in the high jump. Her winning height of 5' 9¼" was almost 4" higher than the next best jumps. Five girls jumped 5' 5¾", including the former world record holder of Romania, who finished fourth.

Mildred's win perpetuated the tradition of at least one gold medal victory from an American girl in each of the Games. "Mildred McDaniel was the outstanding star of the American team," Roxy Andersen said in her report. "She jumped to a new world record. Millie's competition fell by the wayside, thus putting her alone in the spotlight with some 110,000 people to groan when she knocked the bar down and then stand up and cheer as she went over the top to become the greatest woman high jumper in the world!"

80-meter hurdles. In the 80-meter hurdles, Connie Darnowski was fourth in the second heat in 11.9, Barbara Mueller was fourth in the first heat in 11.6, and Irene Robertson was sixth in the third heat in 11.9. None of the hurdlers qualified for the semifinals.

Javelin. Karen Anderson placed eighth in the javelin throw with a toss of 157' 5½". Marjorie Larney was eleventh, throwing 148' 6", and Amelia Wershoven was fifteenth with 145' 3½". In the qualifying round, Anderson threw 162' 10" and Larney 150' 3". The rules disallowed throws from the qualifying round to be carried over to the final round, however.

Discus throw. In the discus, Pam Kurrell threw 132' 9⅝", and Marjorie Larney's best was 130' 11¼". Neither qualified for the final round. Earlene Brown, on her second throw in the final round, tossed the platter 168' 5½". That distance, three inches short of the Olympic record, gave her a temporary first-place standing. Subsequently, she finished fourth, less than two feet from the bronze medal, an excellent achievement.

Shot put. In the shot put, Lois Testa qualified for the final with a toss of 44' 3¾" but finished fourteenth with a toss of 42' 10". Paula Deubel did not qualify for the final with her best put of 40' 7½". Earlene Brown finished sixth with a heave of 49' 7¼", within four inches of the old Olympic record, a second noteworthy accomplishment.

Two post-Olympic meets were held in Sydney, Australia, on December 2 and December 5. Isabelle Daniels sprinted the hundred yards in 10.5 in the first meet, the fastest time ever recorded for an American woman.

The Olympic Trials

"Mrs. Brown Betters Two Track Records" was the headline on the front page of the *New York Times* on August 26. Twenty-one-year-old Earlene set records in the shot and discus in winning both of the events in the tryouts for the Olympic team at American University in Washington, D.C., on August 25. Other records were set by Margaret Matthews in the broad jump and by Mae Faggs in the 200 meters as 6,000 spectators watched the history-making meet.

100-meter dash	
1. Isabelle Daniels, Tennessee State	12.0
2. Mae Faggs, Tennessee State	12.2
3. Lucinda Williams, Tennessee State	12.3
4. Rose Caccamise, Batavia, NY	12.5
200-meter dash	
1. Mae Faggs, Tennessee State	24.2
2. Wilma Rudolph, Tennessee State	24.2
3. Meredith Ellis, N.Y. Police Athletic League	25.2
4. Marcia Cosgrove, Renton, Washington	25.3
80-meter hurdles	
1. Barbara Mueller, Chicago Comets	11.9
2. Connie Darnowski, German-American A.C.	12.0
3. Irene Robertson, Los Angeles	12.1
4. Lenore Leiser, Equitable Life A.S.	12.3
Shot put	
1. Mrs. Earlene Brown, Los Angeles	46' 9½" AR

200-METER DASH

Time to equal or better to qualify for Olympic Team—25.3 seconds

World and Olympic Record: Marjorie Jackson (Australia)—23.4 seconds

**American Record: Nell Jackson (Tuskegee Institute) and
Mae Faggs (Tennessee State A&I) 24.2 seconds**

1—Barbara Kirkindall, Unattached, St. Louis, Mo.
7—Lucinda Williams, Tennessee State University Club
8—Isabelle F. Daniels, Tennessee State University Club
9—Mae Faggs, Tennessee State University Club
11—Martha B. Hudson, Tennessee State University Club
14—Charlesetta D. Reddick, Tennessee State University Club
15—Wilma G. Rudolph, Tennessee State University Club
18—Dolores A. Dwyer, Queens Mercurettes, New York City
23—Lenore Leiser, Queens Mercurettes, New York City
24—Mary McGovern, Queens Mercurettes, New York City
27—Sandra Lindquist, Holland A.C., Cleveland, Ohio
31—Pfc. Gloria A. Griffin, U. S. Marine Corps, San Francisco, Calif.
33—Vernell Golden, Tuskegee Institute A.C.
36—Shirley Crowder, Tuskegee Institute A.C.
38—Freddie Daniel, Tuskegee Institute A.C.
40—Mary Harris, Tuskegee Institute A.C.
47—Elizabeth McDonnell, Liberty A.C., Boston, Mass.

49—Hazel Watkins, Chicago Comets, Chicago, Ill.
51—Elmira Ulmer, Chicago Comets, Chicago, Ill.
55—Alfrances Lyman, Chicago Comets, Chicago, Ill.
56—Barbara Jones, Chicago Comets, Chicago, Ill.
58—Rebecca Jean Ayars, Chicago Comets, Chicago, Ill.
59—Marcia Cosgrove, Unattached, Renton, Wash.
76—Elaine Ellis, Police Athletic League, New York City
77—Lillian Greene, Police Athletic League, New York City
78—Louise Mead, Police Athletic League, New York City
79—Meredith Ellis, Police Athletic League, New York City
81—Cynthia Robinson, Police Athletic League, New York City
84—Gayle M. Dierks, Unattached, Englewood, Colo.
86—Audrey Patterson, Unattached, New Orleans, La.
88—Susan Deckman, Unattached, Yonkers, N. Y.
90—May Tait, So. Pacific Assn., Los Angeles, Calif.
91—Jane Ward, So. Pacific Assn., Los Angeles, Calif.
92—Stella Walsh, So. Pacific Assn., Los Angeles, Calif.

1st.............. 2nd.............. 3rd.............. 4th.............. Time..............
1st.............. 2nd.............. 3rd.............. 4th.............. Time..............
1st.............. 2nd.............. 3rd.............. 4th.............. Time..............
1st.............. 2nd.............. 3rd.............. 4th.............. Time..............
1st.............. 2nd.............. 3rd.............. 4th.............. Time..............

80-METER HURDLES

Time to equal or better to qualify for Olympic Team—12 seconds

World and Olympic Record: S. Strickland de la Huntey (Australia) 10.9 seconds

American Record: Bertha Diaz (Cuba) 11.1 seconds

17—Joan Wolski, Queens Mercurettes, New York City
19—Lauretta Foley, Queens Mercurettes, New York City
23—Lenore Leiser, Queens Mercurettes, New York City
30—Sylvia Zopf, Unattached, St. Louis, Mo.
34—Lulu Bell Smith, Tuskegee Institute Athletic Club
36—Shirley Crowder, Tuskegee Institute Athletic Club
41—Shirley Hereford, Holland A.C., Cleveland, Ohio

42—Caroline McDermott, Unattached, Norman, Okla.
52—Barbara Mueller, Chicago Comets, Chicago, Ill.
61—Nancy Phillips, German-American A.C., Brooklyn
62—Constance Darnowski, German-American A.C., Brooklyn
65—Alma Baskerville, Laurel T.C., Oakland, Calif.
93—Irene R. Robertson, So. Pacific Assn., Los Angeles, Calif.
94—Joan Gaertner, So. Pacific Assn., Los Angeles, Calif.
103—Doris McCaffrey, Red Diamond A.C., Providence, R. I.

1st.............. 2nd.............. 3rd.............. 4th.............. Time..............
1st.............. 2nd.............. 3rd.............. 4th.............. Time..............
1st.............. 2nd.............. 3rd.............. 4th.............. Time..............
1st.............. 2nd.............. 3rd.............. 4th.............. Time..............
1st.............. 2nd.............. 3rd.............. 4th.............. Time..............

Page from the program showing the entries in the 200-meter dash and 80-meter hurdles in the 1956 Olympic trials at American University, Washington, D.C., on August 25, with autographs from Mae Faggs, Isabelle Daniels and Barbara Mueller. (Author's collection.)

2. Lois Testa, Red Diamond A.C.   45' 6¾"
3. Paula Deubel, Little Rhody A.C.   41' 10"
4. Sharon Shepherd, Portland, Oregon   41' 4"

Discus throw
1. Mrs. Earlene Brown, Los Angeles   145' 4½" AR
2. Pamela Kurrell, San Francisco   141' 7½"
3. Marjorie Larney, Queens Mercurettes   130' 3½"
4. Lois Testa, Red Diamond A.C.   129' 3"

High jump
1. Mildred McDaniel, Tuskegee Institute   5' 4"
2. Ann Flynn, Mercurettes   5' 1"
3. Verneda Thomas, Chicago Comets   5' 0"
4. Kaye Bunting, Chicago Comets,   4' 11"
      and Billie Jo Jackson, unattached

Broad jump
1. Margaret Matthews, Tennessee State   19' 9¼" AR
2. Willye White, Tennessee State   19' 3¾"
3. Joan Wolski, Queens Mercurettes   18' ¼"
4. Kaye Bunting, Chicago   17' 2½"

Javelin throw
1. Karen Anderson, Lansdowne, Pa.   153' 5"
2. Marjorie Larney, Queens Mercurettes   143' 7½"
3. Amelia Wershoven, Queens Mercurettes   142' 4½"
4. Catherine Walsh, Queens Mercurettes   122' 10"

The Outdoor Nationals

The outdoor national championships was held at Franklin Field in Philadelphia on August 18. "Four Records Set in U.S. Women's Track," read the headlines in the *Philadelphia Inquirer* on August 19. The article continued: "First lady among the 139 Amazons making their last competitive stop before the Olympic trials next Saturday at Washington, D.C. was 24 year old Mae Faggs, a veteran of two Olympics, who is running for the last season. She plans to retire after visiting Melbourne."

Mae Faggs was featured in a photo on the front page of the *New York Times* on August 19, along with Pam Kurrell throwing the discus. The story stated: "Mae Faggs, tiny 24 year old sprint ace of the Tennessee University Club, won two events. ... She won the 100 meter dash in 11.7 and took the 200 meter dash in 24.6. In the 200 meter trial, which she won, she was clocked in 24.2, tying the meet record set by Nell Jackson of Tuskegee (Ala.) Institute in 1949."

Mae's third gold medal came from the first-place victory of Tennessee's relay team in the 400-meter relay. Mae's team was clocked in 47.1 seconds as she crossed the finish line running the anchor leg. The time clipped eight-tenths of a second off a twenty-three-year-old record set by the Illinois Women's Athletic Club.

50-meter dash
1. Isabelle Daniels, Tennessee State   6.4
2. Barbara Jones, Chicago Comets
3. Lucinda Williams, Tennessee State
4. Charlotte Gooden, Tuskegee Institute

100-meter dash
1. Mae Faggs, Tennessee State   11.7
2. Isabelle Daniels, Tennessee Stare
3. Charlotte Gooden, Tuskegee Institute
4. Rebecca Ayars, Chicago Comets

200-meters
1. Mae Faggs, Tennessee State   24.6
2. Wilma Rudolph, Tennessee State
3. Elaine Ellis, N.Y. Police Athletic League
4. Marcia Cosgrove, Renton, Washington

80-meter hurdles
1. Bertha Diaz, Cuba   11.2
2. Shirley Eckel, Toronto
3. Connie Darnowski, German-American A.C.
4. Irene Robertson, Los Angeles

400-meter relay
1. Tennessee State, "A" team   47.1 MR
    (Hudson, Rudolph, Daniels, Faggs)
2. Tennessee State, "B" team
3. N.Y. Police Athletic League, "A" team
4. Cuba

Broad jump
1. Margaret Matthews, Tennessee State   19' 4" AR
2. Willye White, Tennessee State
3. Phyllis Logan, Chicago Comets
4. Joan Wolski, Queens Mercurettes

Four-kilo Shot put
1. Earlene Brown, Compton, Calif.   45' AR
2. Jackie MacDonald, Toronto
3. Lois Testa, Little Rhody A.C.
4. Paula Deubel, Red Diamond A.C.

Discus
1. Pamela Kurrell, San Francisco   140' 11" AR
2. Jackie MacDonald, Toronto
3. Earlene Brown, Compton, Calif.
4. Marjorie Larney, Queens Mercurettes

High jump
1. Mildred McDaniel, Tuskegee Institute   5' 4"
2. Ann Flynn, Queens Mercurettes,
    and Verneda Thomas, Chicago Comets

4. Sondra Myers, Far Hills, N.J.,
   Billie Jo Jackson, Texas,
   and Hazel Ulmer, Chicago Comets

Baseball throw
1. Pamela Kurrell, San Francisco   269' 5½"
2. Jean Gaertner, Los Angeles
3. Amelia Wershoven, Queens Mercurettes
4. Catherine Walsh, Queens Mercurettes,
   and Yvonne Macon, Tennessee State

Javelin throw
1. Karen Anderson, Lansdowne, Pa.   159' 1" MR
2. Amelia Wershoven, Queens Mercurettes
3. Marjorie Larney, Queens Mercurettes
4. Melinda Roper, Chicago Comets

Team scores:
Tennessee State 95; Mercurettes 36; Chicago Comets 33⅓; Southern Pacific Amateur
Athletic Union 28; Tuskegee Institute 23; Laurel Track Club (San Francisco) 22.

Girls' Division

The meet was held on August 17 in conjunction with the senior national
championships.

50-meter dash
1. Martha Hudson, Tennessee State   6.4
2. Willye White, Tennessee State
3. Marcia Cosgrove, Renton, Wash.

75-yard dash
1. Martha Hudson, Tennessee State   8.5
2. Wilma Rudolph, Tennessee State
3. Rose Caccamise, Batavia, NY

50-meter hurdles
1. Shirley Crowder, Tennessee State   7.8
2. Doris McCaffrey, Little Rhody A.C.
3. Alma Baskerville, Laurel T.C.

300-yard relay
1. Tennessee State   32.4 MR
   (White, Scott, Hudson, Rudolph)
2. Tuskegee Institute
3. Texas Belles

Discus
1. Pamela Kurrell, Laurel T.C.   139' 1" MR
2. Helen Stratton, Philadelphia   114' 2"
3. Sally Pollock, Tuskegee Institute   106' 7"

Broad jump
1. Willye White, Tennessee State   18' 6"
2. Joann Mayweather, Pasadena, Calif.   16' 8½"
3. Kaye Bunting, Chicago Comets   6' 8"

High jump
1. Ann Flynn, Mercurettes   5' 2" MR
2. Kaye Bunting, Chicago Comets,   5'
   Jaqueline Oxley, Mass.,
   and Hazel Ulmer, Chicago Comets

Javelin
1. Pamela Kurrell, Laurel T.C.   118' 6½"
2. Charity Alker, Greenwich, Conn.   114' 8½"
3. Dixie Griffin, Calif.   110' 8½"

8-lb. shot put
1. Dixie Griffin, Calif.   37' 10½" AJR
2. Charity Alker, Greenwich, Conn.   36' 8½"
3. Sally Pollock, Tuskegee Institute   35' 3¼"

Baseball throw
1. Pamela Kurrell, Laurel T.C.   252' 8"
2. Jean Gaertner, Spartan A.C.   235' 7"
3. Elethea Hitchens, Philadelphia   223' 2"

Team scores:
Tennessee State University 86; Southern Pacific Amateur Athletic Union 52; Tuskegee Institute and Laurel Track Club 36; Chicago Comets 23.

The Indoor Nationals

The national indoor championship meet was held in Washington, D.C., on January 21, in conjunction with the ninth annual *Evening Star* Games. Isabelle Daniels was the star of the meet. The *New York Times* reported:

> Isabelle Daniels, this nation's leading hope for the women's Olympic sprint events, scored a double triumph tonight in the women's National A.A.U indoor track and field championships. She broke one record and equaled another.
> Miss Daniels, a tall, smooth-striding runner from Tennessee State A and I, bettered the women's world indoor mark for the 50 yard dash and tied the record for the 100....
> The 11.1 which Miss Daniels ran in the 100 tonight equaled the record shared by Jean Patton and Mae Faggs. Miss Faggs was a distant second tonight, a half stride ahead of 15 year old Marcia Cosgrove of Seattle.

50-yard dash
1. Isabelle Daniels, Tennessee State   6.2
2. Lucinda Williams, Tennessee State
3. Margaret Matthews, Tennessee State
4. Flora Lewis, N.Y. Police Athletic League

100-yard dash
1. Isabelle Daniels, Tennessee State   11.1 ties AR
2. Mae Faggs, Tennessee State
3. Marcia Cosgrove, unattached, Seattle
4. Cynthia Robinson, N.Y. Police Athletic League

220-yard dash
1. Mae Faggs, Tennessee State   26.6
2. Louise Mead, N.Y. Police Athletic League
3. Marcia Cosgrove, unattached, Seattle
4. Elaine Ellis, N.Y. Police Athletic League

70-yard hurdles
1. Constance Darnowski, German-American A.C.   9.7
2. Joan Wolski, Mercurettes
3. Lenore Leiser, Mercurettes
4. Barbara Mueller, Chicago Comets

440-yard relay
1. Tennessee State   52.2
   (Turner, Williams, Daniels, Faggs)
2. N.Y. Police Athletic League, "A" team
   (Lewis, Greene, Mead, Ellis)
3. Chicago Comets "A"
4. N.Y. Police Athletic League, "B" team

440-yard medley relay
1. Tennessee State   53.0
   (Turner, Matthews, Williams, Reddick)
2. N.Y. Police Athletic League, "A" team
3. Mercurettes
4. N.Y. Police Athletic League, "B" team

High jump
1. Mildred McDaniel, Tuskegee Institute   5' 4" MR
2. Ann Flynn, N.Y. Catholic Youth Organization   5' 1"
3. Jeanette Cantrell, Tuskegee Institute   4' 10¼"
   and Verneda Thomas, Chicago Comets

4-kilo shot put
1. Adele Tischler, Czechoslovakia   44' 4¼" MR
2. Jackie MacDonald, East York Track Club, Toronto   43' 9½"
3. Lois Testa, Red Diamond A.C.   40' 2"
4. Paula Deubel, Little Rhody A.C.   37' 9¾"

Basketball throw
1. Catherine Walsh, Mercurettes   101' 6"
2. Joan Dash, N.Y. Police Athletic League   99' 1"
3. Amelia Wershoven, Mercurettes   94' 7"
4. Wanda Weizgrowicz, Polish Falcons   93' 4"

Standing broad jump
1. Nancy Phillips, German-American A.C.   8' 2¼"

2. Barbara Mueller, Chicago Comets   7' 9½"
3. Shirley Hereford, Holland A.C., Cleveland   7' 9"
4. Margaret Matthews, Tennessee State   7' 8½"

Team scores:
Tennessee State 34; Mercurettes 15; N.Y. Police Athletic League 13; German-American A.C. 10; Chicago Comets 7½; Tuskegee Institute 6½.

For the first time in the history of girls track, two girls were selected to represent the United States on a team composed of men and women track athletes. Mae Faggs and Karen Anderson represented the United States on a trip to Nigeria and the Gold Coast in West Africa.

1956 All America Women's Track and Field Team

50-yard dash	Isabelle Daniels
50-meter dash	Barbara Jones
75-yard dash	Wilma Rudolph
100-yard dash	Isabelle Daniels
100-meter dash	Isabelle Daniels
220-yard dash	Mae Faggs
200-meter dash	Mae Faggs
50-meter hurdles	Shirley Crowder
70-yard hurdles	Barbara Mueller
80-meter hurdles	Barbara Mueller
Broad jump	Willye White
Standing broad jump	Nancy Phillips
High jump	Mildred McDaniel
8-lb. shot put	Dixie Griffin
4-kilo shot out	Earlene Brown
Discus throw	Earlene Brown
Javelin throw	Karen Anderson
Basketball throw	Catherine Walsh
Baseball throw	Earlene Brown
Pentathlon	Barbara Mueller

National Chairman Kaszubski reported that there was great progress in women's track and field this year because of an increase in participation, improvement in performances, and an awakening of public interest in competitive track and field for girls. A total of 195 girls competed in the outdoor championships, and 105 participated in the Olympic trials the following week.

Indoor competition produced four American records and six national championship records.

The girls' (junior) division produced nine championship records and five American records.

Five new American records fell at the senior nationals, and two American records were tied. Seven new championship records were established.

The chairman cited the six pages of *Sports Illustrated* publicity and attributed this to better public relations and cooperation between her organization and the National Section on Girls and Women's Sports for the past two years.

The program from January's Metropolitan Association AAU Senior Track and Field Championships included two women's events, the 100-yard dash and the 440-yard relay.

Dr. Rachel Bryant commented for the NSGWS saying interest in track and field in schools could be measured by the fact that in eight months (January through August), 12,000 NSGWS *Track and Field Guide's* for teachers had been sold and a chapter on track and field had been included in the high school text-book published by AAHPER.

Cooperation between the AAU and NSGWS was just beginning.

Track and Field Technique for Girls, the first book of its kind, written by Don Canham and Donnis Thompson, was published in 1956. The first films on the techniques of track and field for girls were produced with women instructors through a cooperative venture with NSGWS.

Willye B. White: Five-time Olympian

In an interview on August 31, 1995, Willye explained why she competed in athletics:

> I started in athletics because athletics was my flight to freedom. Freedom from the delta cotton fields, bias, and prejudice of the South. I had no other choice.
>
> At age ten, I was running varsity track. At age twelve, I was running varsity track and playing varsity basketball, and at thirteen, I won the high school state championship from then until I graduated. I ran, hurdled, high jumped, and long jumped. You know, in high school, they put you in everything, you ran anything you wanted too. I had the desire, and I wanted to win.
>
> When I was sixteen years old, the coach at Mississippi Valley College at that time was a fraternity brother of Ed Temple. He told Ed about the little girl in Mississippi who was so fast.
>
> The two schools that had "the pick of the litter" as far as athletes were concerned were Tennessee State and Tuskegee. The South was loaded with athletes because there was always a program for girls. There were basketball scholarships but no track scholarships.
>
> Temple invited me to Tennessee during the summer of 1956, when I was a freshman in high school. I was excited because that meant that I didn't have to go to the cotton fields and I'd be gone all summer. Our school let out May twenty-eighth. I was on the bus that day to Nashville, Tennessee. When I got to Tennessee State, I found out about the Olympic team. I knew I didn't want to go home, so I just decided to make that Olympic team. Temple said, "But the boat is going to sail without you." And I just decided, but shoot, I'm not going to let that boat sail without me. He told me that if I couldn't jump six-teen or seventeen feet with my flats on, that I was going home. I wasn't going home. So I jumped over nineteen feet and made the Olympic team.
>
> I worked hard that summer. I had never trained three times a day. We ran hills and mountains, and all that stuff. The first day at practice, we had run

this hill. I said, I don't believe this. There was nothing there but squirrels and raccoons. It was a farm, because Tennessee State was an agricultural school. So you run up one side of the hill where you hit the cows and you ran down the other side where there were chickens and pigs. It was unchartered territory. That was a shock.

Temple had six athletes on the Olympic team in nineteen fifty-six. I came home in September and left again in October because we had to go to the training camp.

In the summer of nineteen fifty-seven I came back to Tennessee, and in nineteen fifty-eight we went to Russia. That year I was hurt, I had twisted an ankle but they took me anyway. That was the first trip to Russia. I was very blessed on that one.

In nineteen fifty-nine, I made the Pan American team.

I like to think about all of the friends and people that I met throughout the years. We all had a common bond. We were doing what we wanted to do. We were not jealous of each other. We weren't envious of each other, and the friendships are lasting friendships. The world was a better place to live in. It was like an uncharted world, and I was very blessed to be a pioneer in so many different ways. I had the opportunity to travel to some beautiful places in the world without fear. It was very educational.

The nineteen seventy-two Games stand out in my mind more than any other Olympics. It was hard for me because when I went to the Olympics in nineteen fifty-six for the first time, I came out of a totally segregated area where that fourteen-year-old child had just been lynched in my hometown. Blacks and whites didn't associate. If they did meet, it was always in a confrontational manner, and the blacks would always lose. To get to the Olympic Games and go to the village and find blacks and whites living together, sleeping together, and being friends, it was just mind-boggling. I found out there were two worlds. Prior to that, I thought the whole world was like Mississippi, segregated and ugly. Had I not gone to the Olympic Games, I would have disliked all whites because I would have thought that they were all like the way they were in Mississippi. By traveling you find that there are only a few, and then you learn to judge people individually vs. a race of people or a group of people. That's why I spend so much of my time trying to give the children that I touch an opportunity to see what the world really looks like. There's a different world outside of your community.

In athletics there are no colors. And that's the thing that blew my mind in the seventy-two Olympic Games, to see the Olympic flag flying at half mast because someone had snuck into my house in the middle of the night and killed members of my family [the terrorist attack on Israeli athletes.] It was the only place in the world where there was total peace. And then a thief came in, in the middle of the night, and disrupted the world. It was a bomb that was heard around the world. I feel that I was invaded. Something that was very private and very special was taken away from me. The Olympic Games are not the same anymore.

My best long jump was in Hanford, California. That was really exciting. But I had worked real hard that year. When I jumped 21 feet it was so easy. That's the year, nineteen sixty-four, I jumped against the Russians and I really broke the world record. I jumped twenty-one feet, seven and three-quarters inches, wind aided. Then the Russian came back and jumped twenty-one feet, ten or eleven. I never had a chance to train like that again because they tore the track up, and they tore the stadium down. I did a lot of experimental training that year. That's how I did the twenty-one feet, seven and three-quarters inches.

Willye White long jumping. (Courtesy of Willye B. White.)

In Tokyo, I did so poorly because I never trained and ran in the rain before. I said, whoever wins this is going to be from a country where it rains all the time. When I got ready to jump, all I could see was the man who was an orange dot by the board. Water was up to your ankles. When you ran down the runway, you could hear the water going splat, splat, splat. It really takes your mind off it. The wind was blowing, and you couldn't see. And you say, what in the world is this? I never trained to be wet. I always trained to be dry. I said, if I get out of here, I'll never be caught like this anymore. That's the year when England, Poland, and Germany all placed in the long jump. They competed in the rain all the time. I talked to Ralph [Boston], and he said, when it rains on one, it rains on all. But, I said, it rains on some more than others. From that time on, every time it rained, I put my track gear on and I went to track practice.

Willye has a record of national and international competition that in the history of American women's track and field is unparalleled. She is the only American woman to compete in five Olympic Games. She was a finalist in all of them. She has two Olympic silver medals — a second place in the 1956 long jump and a second place from the 400-meter relay in 1964. In 1958, Willye made the first USA–USSR dual meet, and she made every one of them for ten years thereafter. She was on the 1959, 1963, 1967, and 1971 Pan American teams. In 1970, she was named "Athlete of the Year" and was presented with the Norm Saettel Award. Willye won thirteen national indoor and outdoor titles. Willye was a member of thirty-four international teams. In 1975, she was inducted into the Black Sports Hall of Fame. In 1981, she was inducted into the National Track and Field Hall of Fame.

Chapter 40

1957

The national championship meet was held August 9-10 at Shaker Heights, Ohio. Marjorie Larney's world-record-breaking performance in the javelin throw captured headlines on the front page of the *New York Times*. Twenty-year-old Marjorie threw the javelin 187' 8" using the Basque technique. This technique involved spinning with the javelin prior to its release. Controlling the javelin was a problem; it sometimes landed in the stands. The record was not submitted because the Basque style was never approved.

Barbara Jones was the only double winner in the championship in which four national meet records were broken.

50-yard dash
1. Barbara Jones, Tennessee State   6.2
2. Martha Hudson, Tennessee State
3. Annetta Anderson, Tennessee State
4. Shirley Crowder, Tennessee State

100-yard dash
1. Barbara Jones, Tennessee State   10.9
2. Isabelle Daniels, Tennessee State
3. Alfrances Lyman, Tennessee State
4. Rose Caccamise, unattached, Batavia, NY

220-yard dash
1. Isabelle Daniels, Tennessee State   24.7 MR
2. Margaret Matthews, Tennessee State
3. Alfrances Lyman, Tennessee State
4. Charlotte Gooden, Tuskegee Institute

80-meter hurdles
1. Shirley Crowder, Tennessee State   12.4
2. Doris McCaffrey, unattached, Pawtucket, R.I.
3. Lauretta Foley, Queens Mercurettes
4. Nancy Phillips, German-American A.C.

440-yard relay
1. Tennessee State, "A" team   47.0 MR
2. Tennessee State, "B" team
3. Tuskegee Institute
4. Cuba

Shot put
1. Earlene Brown, Southern Pacific AAU   43' ¼"
2. Lois Testa, Red Diamond A.C.   41' 1½"
3. Marjorie Larney, Queens Mercurettes   38' 10¼"
4. Georgia Benford, Sugarland, Tex.   34' 9½"

Broad jump
1. Margaret Matthews, Tennessee State   19' 5½" MR
2. Anna Lois Smith, Tennessee State   19' 3¼"
3. Willye White, Tennessee State
4. Rose Lovelace, Cleveland Recreation   18' 6¾"

Discus throw
1. Olga Fikotova Connolly, unattached, Boston   147' 8" MR
2. Earlene Brown, Southern Pacific AAU   141' 6½"
3. Marjorie Larney, Queens Mercurettes   136' 5"
4. Alejandriana Herrera, Cuba   129' 8¾"

High jump
1. Verneda Thomas, Chicago Comets,   4' 10"
   Hazel Ulmer, Chicago Comets,
   and Neomia Rogers, Tuskegee Institute
4. Lauretta Foley, Queens Mercurettes,
   Rose Robinson, Cleveland Recreation,
   and Ann Flynn, German-American A.C.

Javelin throw
1. Marjorie Larney, Queens Mercurettes   187' 8" WR
2. Amelia Wershoven, Queens Mercurettes   131' 9"
3. Annette Jenkins, Tuskegee Institute   116' 7"
4. Janet Dicks, Harrisburg A.A.   115' 11"

Baseball throw
1. Earlene Brown, Southern Pacific AAU   271' 10"
2. Amelia Wershoven, Queens Mercurettes   253' 5"
3. Yvonne Macon, Tennessee State   238' 10"
4. Barbara Jacket, Tuskegee Institute   233' 11"

Team scores:
Tennessee State University 143; Queens Mercurettes 48⅓; Tuskegee Institute 31; South Pacific Amateur Athletic Union 28; Chicago Comets 18.

Girls' Division

50-yard dash
1. Willye White, Tennessee State   6.1
2. Fronnie Tucker, Tennessee State
3. Amelia Puig, Cuba

75-yard dash
1. Wilma Rudolph, Tennessee State   8.6 AJR
2. Isobel Mitchell, Toronto Olympics
3. Fronnie Tucker, Tennessee State

100-yard dash
1. Wilma Rudolph, Tennessee State   11.2 AJR
2. Annetta Anderson, Tennessee State
3. Isobel Mitchell, Toronto Olympics

300-yard relay
1. Tennessee State   33.4
      (Hudson, Smith, White, Rudolph)
2. Chicago Comets, "A" team
3. Cleveland Recreation

50-yard hurdles
1. Isobel Mitchell, Toronto Olympics   7.2 AJR
2. Marcia Cosgrove, unattached, Renton, Wash.
3. Betty Scott, Tonkawa, Oklahoma

Discus throw
1. Mary Scott, Tonkawa, Oklahoma   106' 6"
2. Rita Jungmann, Cosmo Club, Topeka   79' 10"
3. Joanne Witmyer, Harrisburg A.A.

Broad jump
1. Willye White, Tennessee State   19' 3¼" MR
2. Mary Williams, Chicago Comets   17' 4"
3. Ann Roniger, Cosmo Club, Topeka   17' 2¾"

High jump
1. Ann Roniger, Cosmo Club   4' 8"
2. Mary Scott, Tonkawa, Oklahoma,
      and Wilma Turner, Columbus Recreation

Baseball throw
1. Wilma Turner, Columbus Recreation   252' 1½"
2. Alyce Smith, Cosmo Club   239' 8½"
3. Judy Girton, Gage Youth   234' 6"

Shot put
1. Joyce Binford, Sugarland, Tex.   34' 7½"
2. Betty Scott, Tonkawa, Oklahoma   34' 6"
3. Rita Jungmann, Cosmo Club,   33' 4"
      and Peggy Scholler, Queens Mercurettes

Javelin throw
1. Annette Jenkins, Tuskegee Institute   117' 1"
2. Peggy Scholler, Queens Mercurettes   110' 4"
3. Alyce Smith, Cosmo Club   106' 11"

Team scores:
Tennessee State University 78; Cosmo Club 44; Tonkawa, Okla. 30; Toronto Olympics 24; Cuba 21; Chicago Comets 21.

A total of twenty-one club affiliations were represented.

The Indoor Nationals

The senior indoor championship meet was held in the Cleveland Arena in Cleveland, Ohio, on April 6. Headlines read, "Tennessee State Takes 4th Straight Women's AAU Track Title" across the top of the page in the *New York Times* on April 7. Nineteen-year-old Isabelle Daniels set an American indoor record in the 50-yard dash in leading her Tennessee State team to the championship title. Two other records were set in the meet, one by the Tennessee State 440-yard relay team and another by twenty-five-year-old Amelia Wershoven in the basketball throw.

50-yard dash
1. Isabelle Daniels, Tennessee State   5.7 AR
2. Margaret Matthews, Tennessee State
3. Rose Caccamise, Buffalo
4. Charlotte Gooden, Tuskegee Institute

100-yard dash
1. Barbara Jones, Tennessee State   11.3
2. Margaret Matthews, Tennessee State
3. Alfrances Lyman, Tennessee State
4. Charlotte Gooden, Tuskegee Institute

220-yard dash
1. Lucinda Williams, Tennessee State   26.8
2. Alfrances Lyman, Tennessee State
3. Sandy Lindquist, Olympic Health Club
4. Ann Roniger, Topeka, Kansas

50-yard hurdles
1. Lauretta Foley, Queens Mercurettes   7.1 ties MR
2. Connie Darnowski, German-American A.C.
3. Nancy Phillips, German-American A.C.
4. Shirley Hereford, Cleveland Recreation

440-yard relay
1. Tennessee State   50.0 AR
   (Williams, Jones, Matthews, Daniels)
2. Hamilton Olympic Club
3. Cleveland Recreation, "A" team
4. Cleveland Recreation, "B" team

440-yard medley relay
1. Tennessee State   52.6
   (Daniels, Jones, Lyman, Williams)
2. Hamilton Olympic Club
3. Queens Mercurettes
4. Cleveland Recreation

High jump
1. Ann Flynn, German-American A.C.   5' 2"

2. Shirley Hereford, Cleveland Recreation
3. Nancy Phillips, German-American A.C.
4. Lauretta Foley, Queens Mercurettes

Shot put
1. Marjorie Larney, Queens Mercurettes   39' ½"
2. Yvonne Macon, Tennessee State
3. Bernice Holland, Cleveland Recreation
4. Dolores Melton, Cleveland Recreation

Standing broad jump
1. Shirley Hereford, Cleveland Recreation   8' 8¼"
2. Nancy Phillips, German-American A.C.
3. Ann Roniger, Topeka
4. Darlene Scott, Tennessee State

Basketball throw
1. Amelia Wershoven, Queens Mercurettes   105' 9½" AR
2. Catherine Walsh, Queens Mercurettes
3. Marjorie Larney, Queens Mercurettes
4. Bernice Holland, Cleveland Recreation

Team scores:
Tennessee State 40; Queens Mercurettes 23; Cleveland Recreation 17; German-American A.C. 15; Hamilton Olympic Club 6; Topeka Cosmo Club 3.

In February, *Track and Field News* carried a women's world list. Six American marks appeared:

Event	Athlete	Performance	World rank
100 yards	Isabelle Daniels	10.5	7
High jump	Mildred McDaniel	5' 9½"	1
Broad jump	Willye White	19' 11¾"	11
Shot put	Earlene Brown	49' 7¼"	8
Discus	Earlene Brown	168' 5"	6
400mr	USA	44.9	4

In November, *Track and Field News* reported the results of the pentathlon: "North Hollywood, Calif. October 20— Stella Walsh, 1932 Olympian, today bettered all American marks for the women's pentathlon, scoring 3809 to better Ann Roniger's 3803 made at Emporia, Kansas October 5th. Mrs. Walsh-Olson put the shot 32' 8¾", high jumped 4' 2¼", ran the 200 in 25.3, hurdled in 13.2, and broad jumped 18' 5½".

1957 All-America Women's Track and Field Team

50-yard dash	Willye White
75-yard dash	Wilma Rudolph
100-yard dash	Barbara Jones
220-yard dash	Isabelle Daniels

50-yard hurdles	Lauretta Foley
80-meter hurdles	Shirley Crowder
Standing broad jump	Shirley Hereford
Broad jump	Margaret Matthews
High jump	Ann Flynn
8-lb. shot put	Joyce Binford
4-kilo shot	Earlene Brown
Discus throw	Olga Connolly
Javelin throw	Amelia Wershoven
Baseball throw	Earlene Brown
Basketball throw	Amelia Wershoven
Pentathlon	Ann Roniger

An article in the *Amateur Athlete* in February 1958 stated: "During the 70th annual national convention of the A.A.U., two running events were added to the Women's Outdoor Track and Field Championships. These are the 440 and 880 yard runs. ... These events will be included for women only and will not be included in the girls' (14 to 17 years) championship program. ... The baseball throw has been eliminated from the women's outdoor program."

The *New York Times* reported that Montclair State Teacher's College was the winner of the metropolitan women's college track and field championships held on May 11 at Macombs Dam Park in the Bronx. Five colleges took part: Montclair, Hunter, Queens, St. Joseph's, and NYU. This first annual championship meet may have been the first intercollegiate track and field competition on the East Coast.

An article appeared in the April *Journal of Health-Physical Education-Recreation* entitled "On Your Mark, Get Set, Go!" It stated that anyone teaching a sound and wholesome program of physical education would be teaching track and field activities. A questionnaire was sent to fifty-one women teachers asking if they taught track and field. Thirty-two responded no. It was pointed out in the article that track and field is basic to all activity and suggested that teachers use the *Guide* to find reference material on the subject.

The booklet, *Amateur Athletic Union Study of Effect of Athletic Competition on Girls and Women*, written by Roxanne Andersen, was published this year. The fifty-two-page booklet provided answers to controversial questions about women's health and sport by nationally recognized physicians with years of experience in women's athletics. The issues of masculinity, child bearing, and menstruation were some of the topics covered because they were most frequently used in arguments about why women should not compete in vigorous competitive sport.

American Track Records

50y	5⅓*	Rosa Grosse	March 26, 1927
		Stella Walsh	March 12, 1930
			April 19, 1930
			February 12, 1931

		Mary Carew	April 19, 1930
			March 14, 1931
50y	5⅘	Elizabeth Robinson	July 27, 1929
50y	5.8	Isabelle Daniels	June 17, 1955
50y	5.7*	Isabelle Daniels	April 6, 1957
50y (dirt)	6.*	Elizabeth Robinson	March 19, 1931
50m	6.4	Claire Isicson	August 7, 1938
		Alice Coachman	July 8, 1944
		Mary McNabb	August 11, 1951
50m	6.4*	Helen Stephens	March 25, 1936
50m (dirt)	6.5*	Juanita Watson	April 24, 1948
60m	7.5	Mae Faggs	March 13, 1955
		Isabelle Daniels	March 13, 1955
75y	8.4	Martha Hudson	June 18, 1955
100y	10.7	Mae Faggs	June 18, 1955
100y	11.1*	Jean Patton	February 12, 1951
		Mae Faggs	March 15, 1952
		Isabelle Daniels	January 21, 1956
100m	11.5	Barbara Jones	March 16, 1955
200m	24.1	Stella Walsh (Poland)	August 18, 1932
200m	24.3c	Catherine Hardy	July 4, 1952
200m	25.8*	Stella Walsh	March 16, 1941
200m	25.9c*	Mae Faggs	March 26, 1949
200m (dirt)	26.4*	Audrey Patterson	April 24, 1948
220y	24.3	Stella Walsh	June 9, 1935
220y	24.6c	Betty MacDonnell	June 19, 1954
220y	25.8*	Stella Walsh	March 16, 1941
220y	25.9c*	Mae Faggs	March 26, 1949
50yh	7.0	Jeanette Cantrell	June 18, 1955
50yh	6.9*	Nancy Cowperthwaite	February 23, 1948
50mh	7.6*	Evelyne Hall	February 25, 1933
50mh (dirt)	7.4*	Theresa Manuel	April 24, 1948
60y	8.0	Josephine Schessler	1923
60yh	8.0	Helen Filkey	June 2, 1928
60yh	8⅖*	Hazel Kirk	February 13, 1926
80mh	11.1	Bertha Diaz (Cuba)	August 16, 1956
80mh	11.5c	Irene Robertson	August 31, 1957

* — indoor record
c — citizen's record

Chapter 41

1958

The outdoor track and field championship meet was held July 4-5 in Morristown, New Jersey. One American record was broken, one tied, and five meet marks were erased as the women qualified for the twenty-berth team that would compete in the first USSR-USA dual meet in Moscow. The *Newark Sunday News* on July 6 said the meet was

> one of the most confused championships ever held. The prize rhubarb was over disqualification of Lillian Greene of the New York PAL after winning the 880 yard run in 2:26.4, an American record.
>
> The foul, called by meet referee Frances Kaszubski of Cleveland, was for being paced over the last 220-yards by a teammate running in the crowded infield which had no policing or marshalling all through the competition....
>
> Why Mrs. Kaszubski chose to call the foul was a mystery. All was confusion, and even such leading officials as Dan Ferris and Jim Simms agreed that Miss Greene should not be penalized for the action of an excited teammate on an already crowded infield.

The women's track and field committee made the decision that Lillian Greene, a seventeen-year-old Hunter College sophomore, would go to Russia, but the committee was not allowed to overrule the foul. This was the first time that the 880-yard run had been included in a national championships in thirty years.

The first 440-yard run was won by Chris Slemon McKenzie, of the New York Police Athletic League.

The individual stars of the meet were Margaret Matthews and Earlene Brown. Both women won two events, and Margaret became the first American woman to jump over 20 feet in the broad jump in national competition, breaking Willye White's mark set in the 1956 Olympics.

Montclair State College served as the training camp location for the athletes for two weeks prior to their departure to Russia.

50-yard dash
1. Barbara Jones, Tennessee State   6.0
2. Martha Hudson, Tennessee State
3. Fronnie Tucker, Tennessee State
4. Amelia Puig, Cuba

100-yard dash
1. Margaret Matthews, Tennessee State   11.1

First national championship 880-yard run since 1928. Lillian Greene, second from left was the eventual winner. Flo McArdle, who finished second is on the far left. Stella Walsh, who placed fifth is on the right. The two Tennessee State runners are Anne Smith, second from right, and Alfrances Lyman, third from right. (Courtesy of Dr. Lillian Greene Chamberlain.)

2. Barbara Jones, Tennessee State
3. Martha Hudson, Tennessee State
4. Louise Mead, N.Y. Police Athletic League

220-yard dash
1. Lucinda Williams, Tennessee State   24.3
2. Isabelle Daniels, Tennessee State
3. Bertha Diaz, Cuba
4. Louise Mead, N.Y. Police Athletic League

440-yard run
1. Christine McKenzie, N.Y. Police Athletic League   61.6
2. Lydia Hernandez, Cuba
3. Amy Brown, Liberty A.C.
4. Harriet Douthitt, Cleveland Recreation

880-yard run
1. Flo McArdle, Queens Mercurettes   2:26.7
2. Grace Butcher, Cleveland Magyar A.C.
3. Christine McKenzie, N.Y. Police Athletic League
4. Josephine Abbott, Toronto Olympic Club

5. Mrs. Stella Walsh Olson, Southern Pacific Women's A.C.
6. Gloria Grifin, US Marines
   (Lillian Greene, N.Y. Police Athletic League finished first
   in 2:26.4 but was disqualified)

440-yard relay
1. Tennessee State   46.9 MR
   (Daniels, Williams, Jones, Matthews)
2. Tennessee State, "B" team
3. N.Y. Police Athletic Leagues, "B" team
4. Tuskegee Institute

Broad jump
1. Margaret Matthews, Tennessee State   20' 1" AR
2. Annie Smith, Tennessee State   19' 2¼"
3. Willye White, Tennessee State   18' 11"
4. Ann Roniger, Cosmopolitan Club, Topeka   17' 7¾"

Shot put
1. Earlene Brown, Southern Pacific Association   47' 5½" MR
2. Sharon Shepherd, Mapleton, Oregon   42' 3"
3. Wanda Wejzgrowicz, Polish Falcons   39' 5½"
4. Cynthia Wyatt, Williamsville, N.Y.   37' 2¾"

High jump
1. Barbara Browne, N.Y. Police Athletic League,   5' 2½"
   and Rose Robinson, Chicago
3. Verneda Thomas, Chicago Comets,   4' 11"
   Marva Mangrum, Chicago Comets,
   Ann Flynn, German-American A.C.,
   Neomia Rogers, Tuskegee Institute,
   Ann Roniger, Cosmopolitan Club, Topeka,
   and Darlene Everhart, Cosmopolitan Club, Topeka

Discus throw
1. Earlene Brown, Southern Pacific Assn.   152' 5½" MR
2. Marjorie Larney, Queens Mercurettes   137' 8½"
3. Alejandriana Herrera, Cuba   132' 5"
4. Pamela Kurrell, Laurel Track Club   130' 3"

Javelin throw
1. Marjorie Larney, Queens Mercurettes   153' 7½"
2. Amelia Wershoven, Queens Mercurettes   149' 1½"
3. Mary Jane Snyder, Harrisburg A.A.   128' 3½"
4. Annette Jenkins, Tuskegee Institute   123' 8"

80-meter hurdles
1. Bertha Diaz, Cuba   11.4
2. Lauretta Foley, Queens Mercurettes
3. Doris McCaffrey, Alumni A.C., Providence
4. Barbara Mueller, Chicago Comets

Team scores:
Tennessee State 110; Queens Mercurettes 46; N.Y. Police Athletic League 42; Cuba 37; Southern Pacific Association 26.

Girls' Division

50-yard dash
1. Fronnie Tucker, Tennessee State   6.2
2. Mary Williams, Chicago Comets
3. Gillian Bastian, Mount Royal A.C.

50-yard hurdles
1. Julie Padron, Cuban A.C.   7.2
2. Angela Wisdom, Seward Park
3. Marva Mangrum, Chicago Comets

75-yard dash
1. Annetta Anderson, Tennessee State   8.9
2. Fronnie Tucker, Tennessee State
3. Gillian Bastian, Mount Royal A.C.

100-yard dash
1. Annetta Anderson, Tennessee State   11.4
2. Mary Williams, Chicago Comets
3. Mamie Rallins, Chicago Comets

300-yard relay
1. Tennessee State   34.8
   (Tucker, Gaines, Alsup, Anderson)
2. Cleveland Recreation
3. Chicago Comets

8-lb. shot put
1. Cynthia Wyatt, unattached   39' 3½"
2. Betty Scott, unattached   38'
3. Peggy Scholler, Queens Mercurettes   35' 6"

Discus throw
1. Cynthia Wyatt, unattached   111' 3"
2. Amelia Puig, Cuban A.C.   99' 1"
3. Delores Melton, Cleveland Recreation   96' 10½"

Broad jump
1. Mary Williams, Chicago Comets   17' 4¾"
2. Marlene Pope, Cleveland Recreation   17' 1½"
3. Hazel Ulmer, Chicago Comets   16' 11½"

Javelin throw
1. Peggy Scholler, Queens Mercurettes   116' 5"
2. Jean Hofbauer, O'Hallaren Playground   109' 11"
3. Carol Kaufman, Queens Mercurettes   104' 5"

High jump
1. Marva Mangrum, Chicago Comets   5'
2. Marlene Pope, Cleveland Recreation   4' 11"
3. Josephine Spencer, unattached   4' 9"

Baseball throw
1. Nancy Svoboda, O'Hallaren Playground

Team scores:
Chicago Comets 70; Tennessee State 51; Cleveland Recreation 35; Cuban Athletic Club 31; Queens Mercurettes 30; O'Hallaren Playground 28.

The Indoor Nationals

The indoor national meet was held in Akron, Ohio, on March 22. The *New York Times* reported that Tennessee State won six of the twelve events in the Goodyear Gymnasium. Earlene Brown set American records in the shot put and basketball throw. The 440- and 880-yard runs were conducted as exhibition races. This was the first time that the 880 had been held on a national level since the Olympic trials in 1928.

50-yard dash
1. Isabelle Daniels, Tennessee State   5.8
2. Martha Hudson, Tennessee State
3. Margaret Matthews, Tennessee State
4. Shirley Crowder, Tennessee State

100-yard dash
1. Barbara Jones, Tennessee State   11.9
2. Martha Hudson, Tennessee State
3. Lucinda Williams, Tennessee State
4. Alfrances Lyman, Tennessee State

220-yard dash
1. Isabelle Daniels, Tennessee State   26.2
2. Lucinda Williams, Tennessee State
3. Alfrances Lyman, Tennessee State
4. Maureen Rever, McGill University

50-yard hurdles
1. Shirley Crowder, Tennessee State   7.0 MR
2. Irene Robertson, Southern Pacific Assn.
3. Doris McCaffrey, Springfield, Mass.
4. Lauretta Foley, Queens Mercurettes

440-yard relay
1. Tennessee State   51.3
   (Matthews, Smith, Hudson, Jones)
2. N.Y. Police Athletic League
3. Cosmopolitan Club, "A" team
4. Cosmopolitan Club, "B" team

440-yard medley relay
1. Tennessee State   52.5
   (Jones, Matthews, Williams, Daniels)
2. N.Y. Police Athletic League
3. Cosmopolitan Club, "B" team
4. Cosmopolitan Club, "A" team

4-kilo shot put
1. Earlene Brown, Southern Pacific Assn.   49' 6" AR
2. Marjorie Larney, Queens Mercurettes
3. Wanda Wejzgrowicz, Polish Falcons, St. Louis
4. Mary Magda, Cleveland Magyar A.C.

High jump
1. Barbara Browne, N.Y. Police Athletic League,   5' 2½"
   and Ann Flynn, German-American A.C.
3. Ann Roniger, Cosmopolitan Club
4. Marlene Pope, Cleveland Recreation,
   and Lauretta Foley, Queens Mercurettes

Standing broad jump
1. Shirley Hereford, Cleveland   9' ½" AR
2. Sandra Lindquist, Olympic Health Club
3. Ann Roniger, Cosmopolitan Club
4. Nancy Phillips, German-American A.C.

Basketball throw
1. Earlene Brown, Southern Pacific Assn.   135' 2" AR
2. Amelia Wershoven, Queens Mercurettes
3. Delia Burchfield, Cosmopolitan Club
4. Marjorie Larney, Queens Mercurettes

440-yard run (exhibition)
1. Annie Smith, Tennessee State   67.0
2. Jo Ann Abbott, Toronto Olympic Club
3. Stella Walsh Olson, Southern Pacific Assn.
4. Harriet Douthitt, Cleveland Recreation

880-yard run (exhibition)
1. Grace Butcher, Cleveland Magyar A.C.   2:48.6
2. Jo Ann Abbott, Toronto Olympic Club
3. Stella Walsh Olson, Southern Pacific Assn.
4. Lauretta Foley, Queens Mercurettes

Team scores:
Tennessee State 47; Southern Pacific Association 13; N.Y. Police Athletic League 10;
Cosmopolitan Club 9; Queens Mercurettes 8½; German-American A.C. 5.

The national pentathlon championship meet was held September 1, at Empo-ria, Kansas. Ann Roniger won the ten-woman event. She captured two of the five events — the broad jump in 16' 5¾" and the high jump with a leap of 4' 10" — and she finished with a point total of 3,762. Barbara Mueller was second with 3,729, and Betty Scott placed third with 3,398.

1958 All-American Women's Track and Field Teams

Indoor

50-yard dash	Isabelle Daniels
50-yard hurdles	Shirley Crowder
100-yard dash	Barbara Jones
220-yard dash	Isabelle Daniels
440-yard dash	Annie Lois Smith
880-yard run	Grace Butcher
4-kilo shot	Earlene Brown
Basketball throw	Earlene Brown
Standing broad jump	Shirley Hereford
High jump	Barbara Browne

Outdoor

50-yard dash	Barbara Jones
80-meter hurdles	Lauretta Foley
100-yard dash	Margaret Matthews
100-meter dash	Barbara Jones
220-yard dash	Lucinda Williams
200-meter dash	Isabelle Daniels
440-yard run	Chris McKenzie
400-meter run	Lillian Greene
880-yard run	Flo McArdle
800-meter run	Lillian Greene
High jump	Barbara Browne
Broad jump	Margaret Matthews
4-kilo shot put	Earlene Brown
Javelin throw	Marjorie Larney
Discus throw	Earlene Brown
Pentathlon	Ann Roniger

Girls' Division

75-yard dash	Annetta Anderson
Baseball throw	Nancy Svoboda
8-lb. shot put	Cynthia Wyatt

USA vs. USSR: Moscow, July 27-28

In the first USA-USSR dual track meet, our women set an American record in the 400-meter relay, and Lillian Greene eclipsed the 800 meter record. To the Russians' surprise, Earlene Brown won the shot put in an American record toss, and Lucinda Williams beat the Russian favorite in the 200 meters.

A postcard from our two javelin throwers said: "The Russians had us going but wait 'til next year. It was an extremely interesting experience but give us New York any day."

Certificate of Selection

1958 ALL AMERICA WOMEN'S TRACK AND FIELD TEAM
Selected by MRS. FRANCES KASZUBSKI, Chairman, Nat. A.A.U. Track and Field Committee

INDOOR

Event	Athlete	Team
50 Yard Dash	ISABEL DANIELS	Tenn. State
50 Yard Hurdles	SHIRLEY CROWDER	Tenn. State
100 Yard Dash	BARBARA JONES	Tenn. State
220 Yard Dash	ISABEL DANIELS	Tenn. State
440 Yard Dash	ANNIE LOIS SMITH	Tenn. State
880 Yard Run	GRACE BUTCHER	Cleveland Magyar
4 Kilo Shot Put	EARLENE BROWN	Southern Pacific WAC
Basketball Throw	EARLENE BROWN	Southern Pacific WAC
Standing Broad Jump	SHIRLEY HEREFORD	Unattached, Cleveland
Running High Jump	BARBARA BROWN	New York PAL

OUTDOOR

Event	Athlete	Team
50 Yard Dash	BARBARA JONES	Tenn. State
80 Meter Hurdles	LAURETTA FOLEY	Queens Mercurettes
100 Yard Dash	MARGARET MATTHEWS	Tenn. State
100 Meter Dash	BARBARA JONES	Tenn. State
220 Yard Dash	LUCINDA WILLIAMS	Tenn. State
200 Meter Dash	ISABEL DANIELS	Tenn. State
440 Yard Run	CHRIS McKENZIE	New York PAL
400 Meters	LILLIAN GREEN	New York PAL
880 Yard Run	FLORENCE McARDLE	Queens Mercurettes
800 Meters	LILLIAN GREEN	New York PAL
High Jump	BARBARA BROWN	New York PAL
Broad Jump	MARGARET MATTHEWS	Tenn. State
4 Kilo Shot Put	EARLENE BROWN	Southern Pacific WAC
Javelin Throw	MARJORIE LARNEY	Queens Mercurettes
Discus Throw	EARLENE BROWN	Southern Pacific WAC
Pentathlon	ANN RONIGER	Cosmo Club, Topeka

GIRLS

Event	Athlete	Team
5 Yard Dash	A. ANDERSON	Tenn. State
...all Throw	N. SVOBODA	O'Halloran Playground
...hot Put	CYNTHIA WYATT	Unattached, Wellsville, N. Y.

New York, January 1, 1959

PRESIDENT   SECRETARY-TREASURER   CHAIRMAN, WOMEN'S TRACK AND FIELD COMMITTEE

AAU certificate awarded to 1958 All-America Women's Track and Field Team athletes. (Courtesy of Dr. Lillian Greene Chamberlain.)

100-meter dash
1. Barbara Jones   11.6
3. Isabelle Daniels   11.6

200 meters
1. Lucinda Williams   24.4
3. Isabelle Daniels   24.5

800 meters
3. Lillian Greene   2:19.4 AR
4. Florence McArdle   2:24.9

80-meter hurdles
3. Lauretta Foley   11.9
4. Doris McCaffrey   12.0

400-meter relay
1. USA   44.8 AR
    (Daniels, Williams, Matthews, Jones)

High jump
3. Barbara Browne   5' 1"
4. Verneda Thomas   5' 1"

Discus
2. Earlene Brown   162' 1"
4. Pamela Kurrell   138' 5¼"

Shot put
1. Earlene Brown   54' 3"
4. Sharon Shepherd   44' 7¾"

Broad jump
3. Annie Smith   19' 1½"
4. Margaret Matthews   18' 8½"

Javelin
3. Marjorie Larney   159' 2½"
4. Amelia Wershoven   154' 11¼"

USSR 63 — USA 44

USA vs. Poland: Warsaw, August 1-2

100-meter dash
1. Barbara Jones   11.6
2. Margaret Matthews   11.8

200-meter dash
1. Isabelle Daniels   23.9
3. Lucinda Williams   24.0

800-meter run
3. Lillian Greene   2:18.8 AR
4. Florence McArdle   2:21.4

80-meter hurdles
2. Lauretta Foley   12.0
4. Doris McCaffrey   12.1

400-meter relay
1. USA   46.4
    (Daniels, Williams, Matthews, Jones)

Shot put
1. Earlene Brown   53' 4"
4. Sharon Shepherd   42' 9¼"

High jump
3. Verneda Thomas   4' 11"
4. Barbara Browne   4' 11"

Broad jump
1. Willye White   20' 2½" AR
4. Annie Smith   18' 2"

Discus throw
1. Earlene Brown   159' ½"
4. Pamela Kurrell   135' 9½"

Javelin
2. Marjorie Larney   156' 10½"
4. Amelia Wershoven   148' 7½"

Poland 54-USA 52

USA vs. Hungary: Budapest, August 5-6

100-meter dash
1. Isabelle Daniels   11.7
2. Martha Hudson   12.0
    (race held in two sections—final placing decided on time)

200-meter dash
1. Lucinda Williams   24.1
2. Isabelle Daniels   24.2

400-meter run
1. Lillian Greene   58.4 AR
6. Florence McArdle   62.2

800-meter run
3. Lillian Greene   2:18.6 AR
5. Florence McArdle   2:22.4

80-meter hurdles
5. Doris McCaffrey   11.9
6. Lauretta Foley   12.0

400-meter relay
1. USA   46.5
    (Daniels, Williams, Matthews, Hudson)

Discus throw
1. Earlene Brown   156' 7¾"
6. Pamela Kurrell   139' 1"

High jump
1. Barbara Browne   5' 2¾"
2. Verneda Thomas   5' ½"

Shot put
1. Earlene Brown   52' 11¼"
2. Sharon Shepherd   45' 2"

Broad jump
1. Margaret Matthews   20' 3½" AR
2. Willye White   19' 11¼"

Javelin throw
2. Marjorie Larney   150' 7½"
3. Amelia Wershoven   148' ¾"

USA vs. Greece: Athens, August 9-10

100-meter dash
1. Isabelle Daniels   11.9
2. Margaret Matthews   12.1

200-meter dash
1. Lucinda Williams   24.0
2. Isabelle Daniels   24.3

800-meter run
1. Lillian Greene   2:25.7
2. Florence McArdle   2:30.1

80-meter hurdles
1. Lauretta Foley   12.0
2. Doris McCaffrey   12.1

400-meter relay
1. USA   47.5
    (Daniels, Williams, Matthews, Hudson)

Broad jump
1. Willye White   19' 5"
2. Margaret Matthews   18' 8¼"

Discus throw
1. Earlene Brown   155' 8¾"
2. Pamela Kurrell   140' 2"

Shot put	
1. Earlene Brown	53' 3¼"
2. Sharon Shepherd	44' 2½"

High jump	
1. Barbara Browne	5' 1"
2. Verneda Thomas	5' 1"

Javelin throw	
1. Marjorie Larney	145' 1"
2. Amelia Wershoven	138' 9½"

The first world university games were held in Paris.

On the professional agenda, in the physical education circles, an article appeared in the March *Journal of Health, Physical Education and Recreation* entitled "On Intercollegiate Competition for Women." The author, Betty Hartman from Ohio State University, pondered the question of justifying intercollegiate competition, which she said had been a problem for many years. In the article, Hartman asked: "What does the average American man expect of women?" She continued:

> He expects the woman to be a "lady." Being ladylike does not, by any stretch of the imagination, mean a muscled Amazon who can literally hold her own with men. It means a woman who is well-groomed, a good mother, a competent homemaker; a woman who takes an interest in her husband's affairs; a woman who can play golf or tennis, fish, hunt or enjoy the out-of-doors with her family; a woman who, above all, displays more feminine than masculine qualities. Nowhere in analyses of the American woman is there a desire to have a woman be an Olympic champion, a professional golfer, or a great and outstanding athlete. ... Even though women have been given the right to vote, enter professions, and hold responsible business positions, women's successes remain in the shadow of a man's world....
>
> Men admire the good swimmer, golfer, and tennis player at the same time that they may sneer at the successful woman track star....
>
> With this in mind, the physical educator must realize that intercollegiate competition for the majority is limited to the socially accepted activities. Sports spectacles with women as participants will not be needed. ... Competition of an intercollegiate nature will appeal to the majority of women if the activities offered are those that women can feel comfortable in, from the standpoint of male recognition.

Lillian Greene

When Lil was eight, she won a field day race at P.S. 68 in Harlem in New York City and was "discovered" by Patrolman William Kelly. He introduced her to the 28th Precinct's Police Athletic League track program, and by the age of twelve she was the 28th Precinct's Track and Field Athlete of the Year.

Prior to her fourteenth birthday, Lil was training with the N.Y. Police Athletic League senior track team that competed on the national level.

In 1958, Lil became at seventeen the first American since 1928 to win an outdoor national championship in the newly added event, the 880-yard run. As a result, she was selected to represent the United States in the first USA-USSR dual meet in Moscow. During the years 1958 through 1961, Lil set American records in both the 400 and 800 meters and was named to the United States All-America Track and Field Team for three years.

In a conversation on August 17, 1995, Lil recalled her track history:

> Running the half mile was a fluke because I was a sprinter. In those days the two-twenty yards was the longest distance that we were allowed to run. We had a meet at Montclair State in New Jersey. It was an indoor meet, and I had a sore hamstring muscle at the time. I saw girls running a race and everybody appeared to be jogging; it seemed so slow. I asked my coach, Connie Ford, if I could run that race and he said no. He then went out to his car to get something for my teammate Barbara Browne, who was competing in the high jump. While he was gone, I entered myself in the next heat. That's how it happened. When the gun went off, I just thought, wow, they're really running slow. And all of a sudden I heard Connie shouting at me, "Get out of that race, get out of that race." I was having the time of my life. Not only was I leading, but I felt great. When I finished the race, they said that I had almost broken the record. I was shocked. Connie was not happy with me, but he was surprised. It was then that I knew that the eight hundred meters or the shorter four hundred meters were the races I wanted to run. Trials in the longer distances were being conducted at that time. I guess the AAU wanted to see whether we would faint or fall out while running those distances.
>
> By the time the outdoor season began, every time I ran, I broke the American record. I later learned that there was going to be an eight hundred meters in the outdoor national championships that year and that the AAU would be selecting a team to compete in Russia, Poland, Hungary, and Greece. This would be the first time that a United States track and field team would be competing behind the Iron Curtain, so I learned Russian phonetically.
>
> We got to the nationals, and when the race started I was leading, I was winning. Everyone was in the infield yelling and screaming. Many of the screaming athletes competed for Chicago's Mayor Daley Youth Foundation, as well as for my team, the New York PAL. Both teams wore bright green sweats. I won the race in two minutes, twenty-six point four seconds, an American record, Flo McArdle [Queens Mercurettes] was second, and Grace Butcher [Cleveland Magyars] was third. Only the first two places qualified for the team. Then all of a sudden the officials said I was disqualified because I had been paced by the athletes in the infield who were screaming and yelling. I never heard anybody. How can you pace somebody by screaming and yelling? Nobody was running along side me. I started crying and crying. I called my mother in New York, and she called our attorney. He called the *New York Times*. People started calling back, and I don't know what happened but they later told me that I was reinstated. The officials did not want to give me the record or the gold medal. Flo McArdle's father, however, was very fair. He asked Flo to give me the first place medal that was awarded to her. He said that I deserved it because I was not paced, I had done nothing wrong, and he was pleased that Flo made the team.
>
> That trip to the Soviet Union really opened my whole world. Because I was able to speak a little Russian, I saw things in Moscow that my other team members didn't see. I was taken to visit homes, and I saw how the Russian people lived. The Russians were surprised to see me because the only people with dark

skins that they saw were African students, and there were very few of them. They knew very little about how Americans lived. All they received was the propaganda of the late nineteen-fifties about us through their media, and they were shocked to see Americans, black and white, running and playing together and laughing and hugging each other.

Because my event was so new, no one really knew how to train a woman for that distance, so I trained with the white fellows from Oregon. We'd run through the park, and people would stare at us and their mouths would drop open. My ability to communicate with the people made all the difference. To be able to speak a few Russian words and phrases broke the ice, and people gave me gifts like bread, scarves, a violin, and Russian hats, which I still have. They touched my hair, they wanted to touch my face and asked lots of questions. They followed us all around.

But, I didn't know how to run the eight hundred meters. I didn't know that the two Russian women would run side by side. After the gun sounded, I ran up and jumped in front of them, and the crowd at Lenin Stadium was yelling and waving white handkerchiefs. That just made me crazy. I knew I was on my way. Then the two Russians ran right by me, so I quickly ran in front of them again. This comedy occurred several times, and by the time we reached the six hundred mark, I was tired. It was like a cat and mouse, and the spectators must have known that the Americans didn't really know how to tactically run the eight hundred meters. The people were chanting and going wild. All of my U.S. team mates were screaming at me and that just got me more excited because I was determined to win. That was my first international competition in the eight hundred meters. I placed third in the race behind the two Russians, and I broke my American record again.

I learned a lot from my race in Moscow. By the time I competed in the eight hundred meters in Warsaw, Poland, I ran a more tactical race and again broke my American record.

When we competed in Budapest, Hungary, I won the four hundred meters in an open All-Comers meet and set another American record of fifty-eight point four. I thought I had died and gone to heaven.

By the time we competed in Athens, Greece, the final country on our tour, running a "sane" race in the eight hundred meters produced a stadium and American record. For the first time, I enjoyed running the eight hundred meters.

Years later, while working for the United Nations in Paris, I traveled throughout the world and met people who I had been able to keep in touch with. One was a Russian woman, now a director of sports in Moscow, who reminded me that I had given her a tube of lipstick when we competed for our respective countries in nineteen hundred fifty-eight. This was more than twenty years later. She told me that the lipstick lasted for almost five years.

After the nineteen hundred fifty-eight European tour, I competed in the nineteen hundred fifty-nine Pan American games in an invitation four hundred meters as an exhibition event. After winning the race, I was asked to come out to Colorado State University to assist in promoting women's middle-distance running in the Midwest. At that time, I was a student at Hunter College in New York.

Although an injury kept me from performing well at the nineteen hundred sixty Olympic trials, I continued to compete during my days in Colorado, setting school and state records. After breaking the American record in winning the four hundred meters in the national indoor championships in nineteen hundred sixty-one, I decided to explore other frontiers and to focus on academic and career pursuits.

Nell Jackson (right, inscribed, "Love, Skeeter" by Wilma Rudolph) with Wilma Rudolph (left, inscribed, "Fondly, Nell" by Nell Jackson) and Lillian Greene at the 1987 Pan American Games in Indianapolis, Indiana. (Author's photo.)

Lil graduated from Colorado in 1963 and earned both her masters degree in 1974 and her Ph.D. in 1976 from Fordham University.

After working for more than a decade as a teacher and administrator in the New York City schools, Dr. Lillian Greene-Chamberlain in 1978 became the first woman and American to be appointed director of the 161-nation UNESCO Physical Education and Sport Program, headquartered in Paris, a position she held until 1988. In this capacity she used her expertise and pioneering spirit to enable other women to become pioneers in sport in many countries throughout the world.

Chapter 42

1959

The national championship meet was held in Cleveland, Ohio, at John Adams High School Field on June 28. The meet served as trials for the Pan American Games for the 202 athletes who were entered in the competition. The *New York Herald Tribune* on June 29 said, "Mrs. Earlene Brown, a 215 pound Los Angeles mother and Isabelle Daniels, one of Tennessee State's sprint sensations, were double winners today." The *New York Times* read, "Mrs. Brown, Miss Daniels Pace AAU Track."

This was the first outdoor national championships in which the 800 and 400 meter events were contested; consequently, the winners of both events established meet records. The 1958 national meet events were the 880 and 440 yard runs.

60-meter dash
1. Isabelle Daniels, Tennessee State   7.6
2. Barbara Jones, Tennessee State   7.6
3. Martha Hudson, Tennessee State   7.6
4. Lacey O'Neal, Mayor Daley Youth Foundation   7.8
5. Willye White, Tennessee State   7.9

100-meter dash
1. Wilma Rudolph, Tennessee State   12.1
2. Lucinda Williams, Tennessee State   12.1
3. Barbara Jones, Tennessee State   12.3
4. Martha Hudson, Tennessee State   12.4
5. Lacey O'Neal, Mayor Daley Youth Foundation   12.5

200-meter dash
1. Isabelle Daniels, Tennessee State   24.1 MR
2. Lucinda Williams, Tennessee State   24.4
3. Wilma Rudolph, Tennessee State   24.4
4. Charlotte Gooden, Tuskegee Institute   25.2
5. Louise Mead, N.Y. Police Athletic League   25.3

400-meter run
1. Kim Polson, Spartan A.C.   59.0 MR
2. Rose Lovelace, Cleveland Recreation   59.3
3. Isabelle Gonzalez, Hawaii X.D.R.   59.7
4. Elaine Ellis, N.Y. Police Athletic League   61.2
5. Patricia Baker, Takoma, Wa.   61.8

800-meter run
1. Grace Butcher, Cleveland Magyar A.C.   2:21.2 MR
2. Lillian Greene, N.Y. Police Athletic League   2:23.0
3. Florence McArdle, Queens Mercurettes   2:24.3
4. Diana Dade, Mayor Daley Youth Foundation   2:26.7
5. Anna Reid, Mayor Daley Youth Foundation   2:29.0

80-meter hurdles
1. Shirley Crowder, Tennessee State   11.7
2. Barbara Mueller, Mayor Daley Youth Foundation 11.7
3. JoAnn Terry, Tennessee State   11.8
4. Doris McCaffrey, Alumni A.C.   12.1
5. Cherrie Parrish, Laurel Track Club   12.3

400-meter relay
1. Tennessee State, "A" team   47.5
   (Hudson, Daniels, Rudolph, Williams)
2. N.Y. Police Athletic League   49.4
3. Mayor Daley Youth Foundation   49.4
4. Tuskegee Institute   49.5
5. Laurel Track Club   50.7

4-kilo shot
1. Earlene Brown, Spartan A.C.   46' 4¾"
2. Sharon Shepherd, Mapleton, Oregon   42' 3½"
3. Wanda Wejzgrowicz, St. Louis   40'
4. Betty Scott, Tonkawa, Okla.   39' 4¾"
5. Joan Whitehead, Montclair   38' 4¾"

Discus throw
1. Earlene Brown, Spartan A. C.   153' 8" MR
2. Pamela Kurrell, Laurel Track Club   136' 1½"
3. Marie Depree, Canada   134' 7"
4. Marjorie Larney, Queens Mercurettes   134' ½"
5. Mary Scott, Tonkawa, Okla.   125' 5½"

Javelin throw
1. Marjorie Larney, Queens Mercurettes   152' 9½"
2. Amelia Wershoven Wood, Mercurettes   151' 8"
3. Elsa Backus, Marshfield, Mass.   137' 2"
4. Peggy Scholler, Queens Mercurettes   134' 4½"
5. Mary Snyder, Harrisburg A.A.   127' 2½"

Broad jump
1. Margaret Matthews, Tennessee State   19' 4½"
2. Annie Smith, Tennessee State   19' 1½"
3. Willye White, Tennessee State   18' 9¾"
4. Ann Roniger, Cosmopolitan Club   17' 10¾"
5. Zlata Rozkosna, Mayor Daley Youth Foundation 17' 7"

High jump
1. Liz Josefsen, Spartan A.C.   5' 4"
2. Ann Roniger, Cosmopolitan Club   5' 3"

3. Rose Robinson, unattached, Chicago   5' 2"
4. Ann Flynn, German-American A.C.   5' 2"
5. Neomia Rogers, Tuskegee Institute   5'

Team scores:

Tennessee State 132; Spartan Women's A.C. 40; Queens Mercurettes 32; Mayor Daley Youth Foundation 30; N.Y. Police Athletic League 22; Cosmopolitan Club and Laurel Track Club 13.

Lil Greene and the author qualified for the first ten-day Olympic development track and field clinic in Cleveland. The first four Americans finalists qualified. After the clinic, the majority of the athletes traveled to Philadelphia to compete in the second USA-USSR dual meet on June 18–19.

Girls' Division

Fifteen-year-old Lacey O'Neal, who switched from swimming to track in 1958, was the individual star in the junior championships on June 27 in Cleveland. She set a meet record of 10.9 in the 100-yard semifinals and won the 100 and 75 yard finals with only a fifteen-minute rest in between.

50-yard dash
1. Rosie Bonds, Spartan A.C.   6.1
2. Kathy Krajewski, unattached, Buffalo   6.3
3. Theresa Weinkowitz, St. Anthony Catholic Youth Organization   6.3

75-yard dash
1. Lacey O'Neal, Mayor Daley Youth Foundation   8.4 ties MR
2. Sandra Smith, Mayor Daley Youth Foundation   8.7
3. Ernestine Pollards, Mayor Daley Youth Foundation   8.7

100-yard dash
1. Lacey O'Neal, Mayor Daley Youth Foundation   11.3 ties MR
2. Sandra Smith, Mayor Daley Youth Foundation   11.4
3. Kathy Krajewski, unattached, Buffalo   11.5

50-yard hurdles
1. Mary Kay Miller, De Kalb Young People's Club   7.3
2. Angela Wisdom, Mayor Daley Youth Foundation   7.4
3. Kaye Kittleson, DeKalb Young People's Club   7.5

300-yard relay
1. Mayor Daley Youth Foundation   34.0
   (O'Neal, Pollards, Rallins, Smith)
2. Cleveland Recreation, "B" team   36.1
3. De Kalb Young People's Club   36.3

Baseball throw
1. Jean Hofbauer, O'Hallaren Park, Chicago   271' 5" MR

2. Gladys Pate, Central Jersey Track Club   250' 6½"
3. Nancy Svoboda, O'Hallaren Park   246' 6"

8-lb. shot
1. Cynthia Wyatt, unattached   41' 2¾" MR
2. Annette Bayne, Hawaii X. D. R.   35' 5"
3. Neomia Rogers, Tuskegee Institute   35' 1"

Discus throw
1. Connie Smith, unattached   108' 7½"
2. Susan Schibanoff, Central Jersey Track Club   108' 5½"
3. Cynthia Wyatt, unattached   105' 1½"

Javelin throw
1. Carol Kaufman, Queens Mercurettes   121'
2. Nancy Frear, Montrose H.S.   118' 6"
3. Jean Hofbauer, O'Hallaren Park   103' 6"

Broad jump
1. Doris May, Mayor Daley Youth Foundation   16' 6¾"
2. Marlene Pope, Cleveland Recreation   16' 4¼"
3. Mamie Rallins, Mayor Daley Youth Foundation   16' 1½"

High jump
1. Neomia Rogers, Tuskegee Institute   5' 1"
2. Marlene Pope, Cleveland Recreation   5'
3. Susan Mehigan, unattached   4' 8"

Team scores:
Mayor Daley Youth Foundation 95; Cleveland Division of Recreation 35; De Kalb
Young People's Club 26; O'Hallaren Park, Chicago 22; Central Jersey Track Club
and Tuskegee Institute 20.

The Indoor Nationals

The indoor championship meet was held in Washington, D.C., on January
24. In the write-up the following day, the *Sunday Star* reported the exciting finishes
of the 880 and 440 yard runs. Harriet Douthitt, an eighteen-year-old high school
girl, won the 880 "by an eyelash" over Mrs. Grace Butcher, and Lil Greene, a
seventeen-year-old Hunter College sophomore, beat Alfrances Lyman by a half
step in the 440. This was the first official indoor 880 and 440. In 1958 these races
were exhibition runs.

50-yard dash
1. Wilma Rudolph, Tennessee State   6.2
2. Martha Hudson, Tennessee State
3. Margaret Matthews, Tennessee State

100-yard dash
1. Martha Hudson, Tennessee State   11.4

2. Isabelle Daniels, Tennessee State
3. Margaret Matthews, Tennessee State

220-yard dash
1. Lucinda Williams, Tennessee State   26.6
2. Isabelle Daniels, Tennessee State
3. Alfrances Lyman, Tennessee State

440-yard run
1. Lillian Greene, N.Y. Police Athletic League   63.4
2. Alfrances Lyman, Tennessee State
3. Louise Mead, N.Y. Police Athletic League

880-yard run
1. Harriet Douthitt, Cleveland Recreation   2:36.3
2. Grace Butcher, Cleveland Magyar A.C.
3. Elaine Ellis, N.Y. Police Athletic League

70-yard hurdles
1. JoAnn Terry, Tennessee State   9.7
2. Shirley Crowder, Tennessee State
3. Ann Flynn, German-American A.C.

440-yard relay
1. N.Y. Police Athletic League   52.4
      (Browne, Wood, Greene, Mead)
2. Tennessee State (Daniels, Williams, Matthews, Rudolph)
3. Queens Mercurettes

440-yard medley relay
1. Tennessee State   52.3
      (Rudolph, Crowder, Hudson, Williams)
2. N.Y. Police Athletic League (Mead, Greene, Ellis, Browne)
3. Cleveland Recreation

High jump
1. Ann Flynn, German-American A.C.   5' ½"
2. Marlene Pope, Cleveland Recreation,   5' ½"
      and JoAnn Terry, Tennessee State

Standing broad jump
1. JoAnn Terry, Tennessee State   8' 11"
2. Nancy Phillips, German-American A.C.   8' 8¾"
3. Annie Smith, Tennessee State   8' 7¼"

Basketball throw
1. Amelia Wood, Queens Mercurettes   101' 8½"
2. Marjorie Larney, Queens Mercurettes   100' 9½"
3. Nancy Freer, unattached   98' 8"

4-kilo shot put
1. Marjorie Larney, Queens Mercurettes   39' 7¼"
2. Joan Whitehead, Montclair Tr. College   37' 8½"
3. Carol Kaufman, Queens Mercurettes   33'

Team scores:
Tennessee State 61½; N.Y. Police Athletic League 18; Queens Mercurettes 18; Cleveland Recreation 13½; German-American A.C. 10.

The athletes who were on the 1959 Pan American team were selected from the outdoor nationals. The Pan American Games were held in the United States for the first time in Chicago at Soldier Field from August 27 to September 7.

	Event	Place	Performance
Brown, Earlene	Discus	1	161' 9½"*
	SP	1	48' 2"*
Crowder, Shirley	80mh	6	11.8
Daniels, Isabelle	60m	1	7.4*
	200m	2	24.8
	400mr	1	46.4*
Flynn, Ann	HJ	1	5' 3¼"
Hudson, Martha	60m	4	7.4
	100m	-	alternate
Jones, Barbara	60m	2	7.4
	100m	DNC	11.9#
Kurrell, Pamela	Discus	2	138' 5"
Larney, Marjorie	Discus	3	138' 4½"
	Javelin	2	143' 2½"
Matthews, Margaret	BJ	2	18' 9½"
Mead, Louise	200m	5	26.2
Mueller, Barbara	80mh	4	11.5
Rogers, Neomia	HJ	7	4' 9"
Roniger, Ann	HJ	4	4' 11"
Rudolph, Wilma	100m	2	12.3
	400mr	1	46.4
Scholler, Peggy	Javelin	4	130' 11"
Shepherd, Sharon	SP	2	44' 2¾"
Smith, Annie	BJ	1	18' 9¾"*
Terry, JoAnn	80mh	DNC	
Wejzgrowicz, Wanda	SP	3	43'
White, Willye	BJ	3	18' 8½"
Williams, Lucinda	100m	1	12.1
	200m	1	24.2*
Wood, Amelia	Javelin	3	140' 11½"
Temple, Edward	Coach		
Welch, Francis	Field coach		
West, Marilyn	Manager		

* Pan American record
# injured — did not complete event

1959 All-America Women's Track and Field Teams

Indoor

50-yard dash	Wilma Rudolph
70-yard hurdles	JoAnn Terry
100-yard dash	Martha Hudson
220-yard dash	Lucinda Williams
440-yard run	Lillian Greene
880-yard run	Harriet Douthitt
High jump	Ann Flynn
Standing broad jump	JoAnn Terry
Basketball throw	Amelia Wood
4-kilo shot put	Marjorie Larney

Outdoors

50-yard dash	Rosie Bonds
60-meter dash	Isabelle Daniels
75-yard dash	Lacey O'Neal
100-yard dash	Lacey O'Neal
100-meter dash	Barbara Jones
200-meter dash	Lucinda Williams
400-meter run	Kimberly Polson
800-meter run	Grace Butcher
50-yard hurdles	Mary Kay Miller
80-meter hurdles	Barbara Mueller
8-lb. shot put	Cynthia Wyatt
4-kilo shot put	Earlene Brown
Discus throw	Earlene Brown
Javelin throw	Marjorie Larney
High jump	Ann Flynn
Broad jump	Margaret Matthews
Penthathlon	Ann Roniger

The second USA-USSR meet and the first one on American soil was held at Franklin Field, Philadelphia, on July 18-19.

100-meter dash		
1. Barbara Jones	11.7	
4. Wilma Rudolph	12.3	
200-meter dash		
1. Lucinda Williams	23.4	
2. Isabelle Daniels	23.6	
800-meter run		
3. Grace Butcher	2:23.9	
4. Lillian Greene	2:24.9	
80-meter hurdles		
3. Barbara Mueller	11.5	
4. Shirley Crowder	11.7	

USA-USSR Dual Meet, July 18–19, 1959, Philadelphia. 800-meter run, American athletes Lillian Greene (second from left) and Grace Butcher (far left). (Courtesy of Dr. Lillian Greene Chamberlain.)

400-meter relay
2. USA   45.0
    (Daniels, Matthews, Jones, Williams)

High jump
3. Ann Flynn   5' 5"
4. Ann Roniger   5' 1"

Javelin
3. Marjorie Larney   150' 6"
4. Amelia Wood   148' 8½"

Discus
3. Earlene Brown   161' 6½"
4. Pamela Kurrell   143' 8½"

Shot put
2. Earlene Brown   51' 6½"
4. Sharon Shepherd   41' 4"

Broad jump
2. Margaret Matthews   20' 2"
4. Willye White   19' 7 1/2"

USSR 67 — USA 40

While women's track and field was growing in the country, support for the sport was still not there. The author wrote letters to meet directors of two large indoor meets in New York, the Millrose Games and the NYAC meet, requesting that a women's event be added to the program. Thomas Quinn, the meet director of the NYAC meet, replied on January 22, 1959: "It is absolutely impossible to do anything about having a girls event on the program of our indoor meet to be held on Saturday, February 14. There has never been a girls event at the New York A.C. Games in the past and we do not wish to deviate from our regular program at this late date."

In its "Of People and Things" column, *Track and Field News* published part of a letter from Grace Butcher, the United States women's champion in the 800 meters. It said, "Where are your women's results of the Russian meet? Oh honestly, I could just sit down and cry. There are a few of us girls in this country who are trying to do the impossible job of putting the U.S. on the map in women's athletics, and when the biggest meet of the year comes along you don't even indicate we were there."

Bert Nelson gave the following reply:

> So now what do we do? Since the question of coverage of women's track comes up every so often perhaps the best thing is to explain our policy.
>
> Every magazine has a space problem and *T&F N* is no exception. There is a great deal of news and features we would like to print. But there is just no room. So we must select the contents with the idea of trying to do the best possible job of coverage while keeping the most possible readers happy.
>
> If we add women's coverage, what do we leave out? Cut down on the high school section and we get complaints from those who point out that high school track takes in more than 10 times the number of athletes, coaches and fans as does the better publicized college track. Eliminate some of the world news — which already is undercovered — and we begin to lose some of the international flavor which makes track the great universal sport it is. Do away with some statistics and the fans and athletes cry out that they don't know what is going on. Eliminate some of the columns and features and we are panned for having only news and statistics. Cut out what little advertising we have and we remove a source of information for our subscribers while reducing important revenue that is needed to continually improve *T&F N*. And so it goes.
>
> The answer then, is this: We do our best to cover men's track and field in the U.S. and throughout the world. Road running, while a fine sport, is not strictly track and field. Neither is walking. And women's track definitely is not men's track. Since we do not now have the space to cover men's track as well as we would like we cannot sacrifice space on the "fringe" activities....
>
> But we continue to receive plenty of criticism on what little space we have devoted to the gals in *Track & Field News* and the "Track Nuts Newsletter."
>
> Personally, I can't get very excited about girlish athletics. Maybe it's the old fashioned streak in me. Or maybe it's that I'm so wrapped up in what the better known, more talented men are doing that there just isn't emotional room for the ladies. Whatever the reasons, I seem to feel about the same as 99% of the track fans I know.

The April edition of *Track and Field News* contained an advertisement for the *All-Time Woman's List*. The sixteen-page booklet selling for one dollar contained the best fifty marks of all time for all of the women's events. It was advertised as the "most completely detailed women's list yet available."

The *New York Times* on December 27, reporting the results of the Metropolitan Championships the night before, said, "In a special 880 race for women, Louise Mead of the Police Athletic League ran what was believed to be a record by an American woman indoors. She was clocked in 2:28.5 in the seldom run event."

Grace Butcher

In an interview on October 1, 1995, Grace told me how she became involved in track:

> I always loved running as a child and I always knew I could run fast. When I moved to Chardon, Ohio in nineteen forty-eight as a high school sophomore, I started haunting the coaches to start girls' track. They said, "Who would do it?" I said that I would get the girls, and I signed up all sorts of girls who wanted to throw and run and jump. Finally, the coaches said, "Well, to have girls' track in Chardon, you have to have girls' track somewhere else — and there isn't any — so there can't be any." I was really down about that.
>
> My mother had heard of Stella Walsh, the famous Olympic champion, and knew that she lived in Cleveland. Finally, one day she said, "I'll call Stella Walsh and see if she knows anything about a girls' track club." Come to find out, Stella had a team. She coached a little team for the Polish Falcons and invited me to come and run with them.
>
> The first day I went to the high school track, which was about forty miles from my home, Stella said, "What event would you like to do?" I said the mile, and she said, "Girls don't do that but you have nice long legs and you could be a hurdler." So I hurdled but never had the speed for it even though I won some medals.
>
> Stella moved away. I started college, then got married at the very young age of seventeen, and four years went by. I had my two sons, ran for fitness, and played basketball. One day in nineteen fifty-six I happened to turn on the television and a sports panel show was on with Harrison Dillard and Bernice Holland. Bernice was talking about coaching women's track. So I called her and went into Cleveland to run with her team, the Holland Athletic Club. There was still nothing longer than a two-twenty, so I sprinted, ran hurdles, and high jumped.
>
> The Cleveland Recreation Track Club hired Alex Ferenczy as a coach, to try to bring all of the little clubs together for national competitions. Alex, having just fled Hungary with his family, was surprised to learn that American girls did not run any longer than two hundred meters because in Europe they ran everything. Alex coached me, but his friend Julius Penzes, later my coach, ran with me. Then in nineteen fifty-seven, I ran the first exhibition eight-eighty in modern times at the Lake Erie District AAU meet — I think I ran a 2:57 and that was to prove women could run a half mile.
>
> Alex and I campaigned by writing letters, making phone calls, and arguing with officials to have the quarter and half mile events added to the national championship program.
>
> In the indoor national championships in nineteen fifty-eight in Akron, the

eight-eighty was held for the first time as an exhibition race. I won the race and Stella Walsh was third. That was the beginning.

The highlight of my track career was winning the eight hundred in nineteen fifty-nine in the outdoor nationals. That qualified me for the Russian dual meet in Philadelphia.

The biggest disappointment was not making the nineteen sixty Olympic team, but I had a foot injury which I later learned was a stress fracture.

I've never stopped running. I ran the early road races and then from nineteen seventy-seven on, the masters competitions, winning the silver medal in the fifty-five to fifty-nine age group at the Master's World Games in 1989.

It's been a great joy.

Grace taught English at Kent State University, Geauga Campus, for twenty-five years and retired in 1993. She has had five books of poetry published, the most recent, *Child, House, World*, which won her the Ohio Poet of the Year award in 1992. Grace has had articles in *Sports Illustrated* and *Runner's World*.

Chapter 43

1960:
The Rome Olympic Year

The Olympic trials were held in Abilene, Texas, at the Abilene Christian College stadium on July 15–16. The following became members of the 1960 Olympic team:

	Olympic Event	Olympic Place	Olympic Performance
Browne, Barbara	HJ	19	4' 11"
Brown, Earlene	SP	3	53' 10⅜"
	Discus	6	168' 3¼"
Connolly, Olga F.	Discus	7	167' 1⅞"
Crowder, Shirley	80mh	DNQ	12.3
Daniels, Billie Pat	800m		Disqualified
Gaertner, Jean	HJ	21	4' 11"
Hudson, Martha	100m	DNQ	12.2
	400mr	1	44.5
Jones, Barbara	100m	DNQ	11.7
	400mr	1	44.5
Kurrell, Pamela	Discus	19	138' 6"
Oldham, Karen Anderson	Javelin	13	152' 7½"
Pollards, Ernestine	200m	DNQ	24.5
Robertson, Irene	80mh	DNQ	11.6
Rogers, Neomia	HJ	14	5' 5"
Rudolph, Wilma G.	100m	1	11.0
	200m	1	24.0
	400mr	1	44.5
Smith, Anne L.	BJ	DNQ	
Terry, JoAnn	80mh	DNQ	11.4
White, Willye B.	BJ	16	18' 11¼"
Williams, Lucinda	200m	DNQ	25.0
	400mr	1	44.5
Kaszubski, Frances	Manager		
Temple, Edward S.	Coach of track		
Welch, Francis G.	Coach of field		

Photo of United States women's Olympic Track and Field team taken in Kansas during the training camp. *Front row from left*: Martha Hudson, Barbara Browne, Karen Anderson, Ernestine Pollards, Willye White, Pam Kurrell and Lucinda Williams. *Back row from left*: Ed Temple (coach), JoAnn Terry, Barbara Jones, Earlene Brown, Pat Daniels, Marie Wagner (chaperone), Jean Gaertner, Wilma Rudolph, Shirley Crowder, Anne Smith, Neomia Rogers, Irene Robertson and Fran Welch (field coach). (Author's photo.)

The heroine of the 1960 Rome Olympics, August 25–September 11, was Wilma Rudolph. The United States Olympic report stated:

> In a series of spectacular performances, Wilma Rudolph, a tall, Tennessee State University co-ed, established herself as the fastest woman ever by winning three gold medals in record fashion.
>
> The 20 year old flash from Clarksville, Tennessee, dominated the women's track and field program and shared the record-breaking honors with the Russian squad as every Olympic mark was wiped out.
>
> The 5' 11", 135 pound Wilma gained supremacy in the 100, 200 and 400 meter relay. She tied the world record of 11.3 seconds in the 100 semi-finals, and then jetted the final in 11.0 flat, although helped by a 2.75 meter per second wind which barred a world record.
>
> In the 200, she shattered the Olympic standard with 23.2 in the heat and romped to victory against the wind in the final in 24.0. And in the relay, she brilliantly anchored her Tennessee State team to a 44.4 world record in the heat and a 44.5 triumph in the final.

In *The Story of the Olympic Games*, Kieran and Daley wrote:

> The Americans even were to supply a dazzler in the distaff section. The dazzler was Wilma Rudolph, tall and willowy (5 foot 11, and 130 pounds) undergraduate at Tennessee State, the Negro University that was to supply half of the talent to the women's team.

Wilma Rudolph winning a round of the 100 meters in Rome, 1960. (Courtesy of the National Track & Field Hall of Fame Historical Research Library at Butler University.)

> Miss Rudolph, a female Jesse Owens, streaked 100 meters in her semifinal heat without even pressing the accelerator to the floor. She won, eased up, in 11.3 seconds to equal the women's world record. Then in the final she flew and ran away from the field. Her time of 11 seconds flat was first announced as a world record but then it was disallowed because the wind gauge showed a wisp of breeze that barely was above the limit.

Track and Field News printed a photo of Wilma crossing the finish line with headlines "Rudolph Wins Three Golds." Two brief paragraphs were devoted to her spectacular accomplishments. The bulk of the article carried all of the women's results.

The Olympic Results

100 meters. Wilma Rudolph topped the field of thirty-one women in every race. She won her first and second heats in 11.5 and then equaled the world and Olympic record with an 11.3 in the semifinals. In the six-girl final, after passing Russia's Maria Itkina at twenty-five meters, Wilma led the whole way. She won by three yards over Britain's Dorothy Hyman in 11 seconds flat. Because of a following wind of 2.75 meters, .75 over the allowable limit, her time was not allowed as a world record, but it was recognized as an Olympic record.

Wilma Rudolph winning the 100 meter final in Rome, 1960. (Courtesy of the National Track & Field Hall of Fame Historical Research Library at Butler University.)

In her book, *Wilma*, she said: "My start was relatively good. I came out second or third in the field, and my speed started increasing the farther I went. When I reached fifty meters, I saw that I had them all, and I was just beginning to turn it on. By seventy meters, I knew the race was mine, nobody was going to catch me."

Barbara Jones was second in her first two races in 11.7 and 11.9 but was eliminated in the semifinal, finishing a very close fourth in 11.7, the same time as the second and third place sprinters.

Martha Hudson, the third American also from Tennessee State University, was eliminated in the second round of heats, finishing fourth in 12.2.

200 meters. This was another victory for Wilma Rudolph, who won her heat in 23.2, bettering the Olympic record by two-tenths of a second, won her semifinal in 23.7, and won the final against a strong wind in 24.0. The track was slow from the first rain in Rome since April. She was in the lead all the way and won by four yards over Germany's Jutta Heine. With this triumph, Wilma became the first American woman to win the 200 meters.

She said in her book *Wilma* that before the final: "It was miserable out there, but I felt good, no real pressure. The 200 was mine, I loved it more than anything else. A little rain meant nothing to me. In fact, before the start of the race, I was saying to myself, as a way of psyching up, 'There's nobody alive who can beat you in the 200. Go get it' ... I really won that race a lot easier than I thought I would."

Lucinda Williams of Tennessee State was eliminated in the semifinals running 25.0, and Ernestine Pollards of Chicago was eliminated in the qualifying trials despite her time of 24.5.

400-meter relay. With Wilma Rudolph running sensational anchor legs, the USA team, all athletes from Tennessee State University, broke the world record of 44.5 by one-tenth of a second in the heats in running 44.4. In the final, after a quick team prayer, Wilma hit the tape three yards ahead of the German runner in 44.5.

The running order was Martha Hudson, Barbara Jones, Lucinda Williams, and Wilma Rudolph. The first three gained a two-yard lead, but the lead was lost as a result of a poor baton pass between Lucinda and Wilma. Lucinda said in *The Leaf-Chronicle* on November 18, 1994, "As I approached Wilma, I knew she wasn't taking off, so I yelled at her to go … and finally she took off, and it was like all the whirlwind had broke loose." It only took fifteen yards for Wilma to fly by Jutta Heine, Germany's anchor leg, and a runner from Australia and hit the finish line three yards ahead. That was Wilma's third gold medal, making her the first American woman to win three Olympic golds. Ed Temple said in his book, *Only the Pure in Heart Survive*:

> The stadium crowd bordered on hysterics. Over 100 photographers chased after Rudolph to get her picture. … Rudolph became such a celebrity that she couldn't leave the compound without creating a mob scene. Even tables were overturned in the dining hall by people trying to get to her. She was in all of the newspaper headlines — the Russians, who aren't usually very emotional, declared her the "Queen of the Olympics." The Africans called her the "Black Pearl," and the French referred to her as the "Black Gazelle."

With these four relay gold medals added to Wilma's previous two, Tennessee State University athletes returned home to Nashville with six gold medals.

800 meters. The only American entry, Billie Pat Daniels, seventeen, of California, was disqualified.

80-meter hurdles. The three American entries were eliminated in the qualifying heats. Irene Robertson placed fifth in the first heat in 11.6, JoAnn Terry placed fourth in heat three in 11.4, and Shirley Crowder placed fourth in heat six in 12.3.

Broad jump. Willye B. White, who placed second in the 1956 Olympic Games, cleared 20' 4¼" in the trials but jumped 18' 11¼" in the final round for sixteenth place in Rome. Annie Smith, another Tennessee State athlete, fouled out in the qualifying round.

Javelin throw. Karen Anderson Oldham, throwing with a sore elbow, finished eighth in 1956 but could only get a thirteenth place with her throw of 152' 7½", even though her throw in the qualifying round was 166' 1". Throws in that round did not carry over to the finals.

Shot put. Earlene led the field during the morning preliminary competition with a put of 52' 11¾". Her final put of 53' 10⅜" moved her into the bronze medal spot, a significant achievement for an American woman in a throwing event.

High jump. Neomia Rogers placed fourteenth with a jump of 5' 5". Our other entries, Barbara Browne and Jean Gaertner, failed to qualify.

Discus throw. The former Olympic champion, Olga Fikotova, now married to Harold Connolly and competing for the United States, threw 167' 1⅞" for seventh place. Pam Kurrell failed to qualify with a best throw of 141' 9⅞".

Earlene Brown finished sixth, throwing 168' 3¼".

Post-Olympic meets were held. The U.S.–British Empire and Commonwealth meet was held in London on September 14. The United States 400-meter relay team of Rudolph, Hudson, Jones, and Williams won in 46.1. Wilma Rudolph captured the 100-yard dash in a new record time of 10.6. Lucinda Williams was third in the 220-yard dash in 24.5, Billie Pat Daniels placed third in the 440-yard run in 58.0, and Earlene Brown won the shot put with a toss of 53'.

Athens hosted the USA–Greek meet on September 10-11. Wilma won the 100-meter dash in 11.8, and Barbara Jones was second in 12.1. Williams, and Hudson finished one-two in the 200 meters in 24.6 and 25.5 respectively. Billie Pat Daniels won the 800-meter run in 2:26.7. In the 80-meter hurdles, Irene Robertson was first in 11.4, and JoAnn Terry placed second in the same time. JoAnn also won the high jump with a leap of 5' 1" and the broad jump with a jump of 17' 2½". Earlene Brown won the shot with a toss of 52' 3½", the discus with a throw of 171' 3½", and the javelin with a throw of 118' 2½".

The Olympic Trials

The Olympic trials were held at Abilene Christian College in Texas on July 15-16, with a record entry of 136 women. *Track and Field News* featured an article in the August issue with the headline "White Jumps 20' 4½". The story read, "One American record was set, another tied ... as the United States' top track women battled for places on the Olympic Team."

The *New York Times* headlined Earlene Brown's discus throw of 176' 10½", which bettered the Olympic record.

100 meters	
1. Wilma Rudolph, Tennessee State	11.5 ties AR
2. Barbara Jones, Tennessee State	11.6
3. Martha Hudson, Tennessee State	11.7
4. Lucinda Williams, Tennessee State	11.8

200 meters	
1. Wilma Rudolph, Tennessee State	23.9
2. Lucinda Williams, Tennessee State	24.3
3. Ernestine Pollards, Mayor Daley Youth Foundation	24.5
4. Lacey O'Neal, Mayor Daley Youth Foundation	24.9

800 meters	
1. Billie Pat Daniels, San Mateo Girls' A.A.	2:15.6 AR
2. Rose Lovelace, Cleveland Recreation	2:15.7
3. Doris Severtsen, Northwest Mic-Mac Club	2:17.6
4. Louise Mead, N.Y. Police Athletic League	2:19.1

80-meter hurdles	
1. Shirley Crowder, Tennessee State	11.4w
2. JoAnn Terry, Tennessee State	11.4

3. Irene Robertson, Spartan Women's A.C.   11.4
4. Barbara Mueller, Mayor Daley Youth Foundation   11.5

Broad jump
1. Willye B. White, Mayor Daley Youth Foundation   20' 4½" AR
2. Sandra Smith, Mayor Daley Youth Foundation   18' 8"
3. Annie Smith, Tennessee State   18' 6"
4. Ann Roniger, Burdick, Kansas   18' 3¼"

High jump
1. Neomia Rogers, Tuskegee Institute   5' 4"
2. Barbara Browne, N.Y. Police Athletic League   5' 2¾"
3. Jean Gaertner, Spartan Women's A.C.   5' 2¾"
4. Darlene Everhart, Cosmopolitan Club   5' ¼"

Shot put
1. Mrs. Earlene Brown, Spartan Women's A.C.   50' 10¼"
2. Sharon Shepherd, Mapleton, Oregon   45' 10"
3. Cecilia Rutledge, Texas A.C.   43' 5"
4. Cindy Wyatt, Williamsville, N.Y.   42' 4"

Discus throw
1. Mrs. Earlene Brown, Spartan Women's A.C.   176' 10" AR
2. Olga F. Connolly, Spartan Women's A.C.   172' 4½"
3. Pamela Kurrell, Laurel Track Club   158' 8"
4. Sharon Shepherd, Mapleton, Oregon   140' 10"

Javelin throw
1. Karen A. Oldham, San Diego T&F Association   163' 5½" AR
2. Peggy Scholler, Queens Mercurettes   154' 6¼"
3. Karen Mendyka, San Fernando Women's A.C.   143' 8"
4. Marjorie Larney, Queens Mercurettes   139' 3"

A pre–Olympic training camp began on July 18 at Kansas State Teachers College in Emporia, Kansas. Meets were held to enable athletes to achieve the qualifying Olympic standards during the twenty-eight days that they were there.

The Outdoor Nationals

The national championship meet was held on July 9 in Corpus Christi, Texas. *Track and Field News* had a small article entitled "Rudolph Sets World Mark." The *New York Times* report featured Olga Connolly's win in the discus and her complaints about the discus throwing area. The last paragraph of the story was about the world record of 22.9 that Wilma Rudolph ran in the 200-meter final — a glimpse of things to come.

100-meter dash
1. Wilma Rudolph, Tennessee State   11.5
2. Barbara Jones, Tennessee State   11.7
3. Martha Hudson, Tennessee State   11.7

200-meter dash
1. Wilma Rudolph, Tennessee State — 22.9 WR
2. Lacey O'Neal, Mayor Daley Youth Foundation — 23.4
3. Lucinda Williams, Tennessee State — 23.4

80-meter hurdles
1. JoAnn Terry, Tennessee State — 11.4
2. Irene Robertson, Spartan Women's A.C. — 11.5
3. Shirley Crowder, Tennessee State — 11.6

400-meter run
1. Irene Robertson, Spartan Women's A.C. — 57.1
2. Rose Lovelace, Cleveland Recreation — 57.6
3. Ruth Ann Brand, Prescott, Arizona — 59.0

800-meter run
1. Billie Pat Daniels, San Mateo — 2:17.5
2. Rose Lovelace, Cleveland Recreation — 2:18.2
3. Ruth Brand, Prescott, Arizona — 2:20.2

400-meter relay
1. Tennessee State, "A" team — 46.1
   (Hudson, Williams, Jones, Rudolph)
2. Mayor Daley Youth Foundation — 47.5
3. Tennessee State, "B" team — 48.4

800-meter medley relay
1. Tennessee State — 1:47.3
2. Cleveland Recreation — 1:50.2
3. N.Y. Police Athletic League — 1:50.4

Discus throw
1. Olga F. Connolly, Spartan Women's A.C. — 159' 6½"
2. Earlene Brown, Spartan Women's A.C. — 152' 3½"
3. Pam Kurrell, Laurel Track Club — 146' 4"

4-kilo shot put
1. Earlene Brown, Spartan Women's A.C. — 49' 8½"
2. Sharon Shepherd, unattached, Oregon — 46' 6¾"
3. Cindy Wyatt, Williamsville, N.Y. — 40' 7½"

Broad jump
1. Willye White, Mayor Daley Youth Foundation — 19' 1½"
2. Sandra Smith, Mayor Daley Youth Foundation — 19' 1"
3. JoAnn Terry, Tennessee State — 18' 9"

Javelin throw
1. Marjorie Larney, Queens Mercurettes — 151' 10½"
2. Karen Mendyka, San Fernando Women's A.C. — 150' 5½"
3. Peggy Scholler, Queens Mercurettes — 147' 10½"

High jump
1. Liz Josefsen, Spartan Women's A.C. — 5' 5¼"
2. Neomia Rogers, Tuskegee Institute — 5' 4"
3. Jean Gaertner, Spartan Women's A.C. — 5' 2¼"

Team scores:
Tennessee State University 93; Spartan Women's A.C. 63; Mayor Daley Youth Foundation 46; Cleveland Division of Recreation 31; Queens Mercurettes 20; N.Y. Police Athletic League 14; San Mateo Girls' Track Club 14.

The Indoor Nationals

The indoor championship meet was held in Chicago on April 16.

50-yard dash
1. Wilma Rudolph, Tennessee State   5.9
2. Martha Hudson, Tennessee State   6.0
3. Lacey O'Neal, Mayor Daley Youth Foundation   6.2

100-yard dash
1. Wilma Rudolph, Tennessee State   10.7 MR
2. Barbara Jones, Tennessee State   11.2
3. Martha Hudson, Tennessee State   11.2

70-yard hurdles
1. JoAnn Terry, Tennessee State   9.5
2. Shirley Crowder, Tennessee State   9.6
3. Barbara Mueller, Mayor Daley Youth Foundation   9.6

220-yard dash
1. Wilma Rudolph, Tennessee State   25.7
2. Lucinda Williams, Tennessee State   26.0
3. Ernestine Pollards, Mayor Daley Youth Foundation   26.5

440-yard run
1. Rose Lovelace, Cleveland Recreation   62.1
2. Kathleen Krajewski, unattached   63.2
3. Kennie Hart, Tantivy A.C.   63.9

880-yard run
1. Grace Butcher, Magyar A.C.   2:26.8
2. Patricia Douthitt, Cleveland Recreation   2:28.6
3. Johnnie Ward, Tantivy A.C.   2:31.1

4-kilo shot put
1. Sharon Shepherd, unattached   45' 3¾"
2. Cel Rutledge, Texas A.C.   40' 11"
3. Wanda Wejzgrowicz, Polish Falcons   40' 4"

Standing broad jump
1. Sandra Smith, Mayor Daley Youth Foundation   9' 3¾"
2. Ann Roniger, Center H.S., Kansas   8' 10¼"
3. JoAnn Terry, Tennessee State   8' 9"

Basketball throw
1. Cel Rutledge, Texas A.C.   120' 10½"

2. Delia Burchfield, Cosomopolitan Club   110' 8"
3. Jean Hofbauer, O'Hallaren Playground   102' 2"

High jump
1. Darlene Everhart, Cosmopolitan Club   5' 3½"
2. Ann Flynn, Colorado State University   5' 3"
3. Ann Roniger, Center H.S., Kansas   4' 11"

440-yard relay
1. Tennessee State   49.6
   (Hudson, Crowder, Williams, Jones)
2. Mayor Daley Youth Foundation, "A" team   49.8
3. Mayor Daley Youth Foundation, "B" team   52.0

440-yard medley relay
1. Tennessee State   51.8 MR
   (Jones, Smith, Williams, Terry)
2. Mayor Daley Youth Foundation   54.1
3. Cleveland Recreation   54.3

Team scores:
Tennessee State University 49; Mayor Daley Youth Foundation 22; Cleveland Division of Recreation 10; Cosmopolitan Club 9.

1960 All-America Women's Track and Field Team

Indoor

50-yard dash	Wilma Rudolph
100-yard dash	Wilma Rudolph
220-yard dash	Wilma Rudolph
440-yard run	Rose Lovelace
880-yard run	Grace Butcher
50-yard hurdles	Mary Kay Miller
70-yard hurdles	JoAnn Terry
Shot put	Sharon Shepherd
High jump	Darlene Everhart
Standing broad jump	Sandra Smith
Basketball throw	Cel Rutledge

Outdoor

50-yard dash	Rosie Bonds
75-yard dash	Lacey O'Neal
100-yard dash	Wilma Rudolph
100-meter dash	Wilma Rudolph
200-meter dash	Wilma Rudolph
400-meter run	Irene Robertson
440-yard run	Irene Robertson
800-meter run	Pat Daniels
50-yard hurdles	Mary Kay Miller
80-meter hurdles	JoAnn Terry

Shot put (4 kilo)	Earlene Brown
Discus throw	Earlene Brown
Javelin throw	Karen Oldham
Broad jump	Willye White
High jump	Neomia Rogers
8-lb. shot put	Cel Rutledge
Pentathlon	JoAnn Terry
400-meter relay	Tennessee State

It was announced in a small article in *Track and Field News* that Frances Kaszubski would begin publishing *Track Talk*, a free monthly newsletter. In December, there was brief mention that Ed Temple might be named coach of the year. Wilma Rudolph, the article said, was an easy pick for best female athlete.

The pentathlon championship was held on August 5-6 in Emporia, Kansas. JoAnn Terry placed first with 4,249 points, Pat Daniels was second, and Shirley Crowder third.

The Helms World Trophy winners were announced. Wilma Rudolph won for North America.

The *New York Times* Sunday magazine section featured an article entitled "Venus Wasn't a Shot-Putter." Throughout the article the author expressed strong opinions about women in track:

> Now we find that their enthusiasm runs to presenting America's claims as having the best-muscled girls in the world. Next thing you know, we'll be bragging about having the best looking automobile wrecks in the world.
>
> Today, when we think of women athletes — if we think of them at all — we instinctively call to mind ... two cute young blonde swimmers. ... We do not instinctively think of shot putters and hurdlers, sprinters and discus throwers. Somehow they do not possess The Image....
>
> If the world is going to be divided according to muscle — and that is the point of the Olympics — then let the women engage in the muscle stretching sports and leave the muscle bunching sports to the men.

Wilma Glodean Rudolph

This was going to be a treasured interview, reminiscing about the days before and after her three gold medals, but it never will happen. Skeeter died on November 12, 1994, and flags flew at half-staff in Clarksville to honor her memory. Perhaps the comment made by her old teammate Mae Faggs Starr best expresses how I felt about her death, "It just blew my mind."

Ed Temple first noticed Wilma when he was refereeing basketball. She was tall and thin, and "she looked like she might have some potential in track," said Ed in his book, *Only the Pure in Heart Survive*. He made arrangements with her coach and parents to work with her in his summer training program in 1955. By the summer of 1956, she was on her first Olympic team, as Ed recounted in his book:

Wilma Rudolph on victory stand after the 100 meter final, being awarded the first of three Olympic gold medals in Rome, 1960. (Courtesy of the National Track & Field Hall of Fame Historical Research Library at Butler University.)

"But 1960 in Rome was her time and her year. She blossomed and surpassed all of her previous track accomplishments by winning an unprecedented three gold medals in the Olympics. ...The rest is history. She had the ability, the naive charm, and the charisma that endeared people to her. She, I suppose more than any other runner, opened up the modern door of track for women."

Wilma had to wear a brace on her right leg continuously between the ages of five and nine. In her book *Wilma*, she wrote: "When I first took off the brace and went out in public without it, I'll never forget it. I went to church, and I walked in without the brace, and I knew right off that people were looking at me, saying to themselves, 'Hey, there's Wilma, and she doesn't have the brace on her leg anymore'."The hospital treatments stopped when she was ten, but she wore the brace on and off until she was twelve when her leg bothered her.

Basketball was Wilma's first sport. Her older sister was already on the school team when she decided she wanted to join too. She sat on the bench for the seventh and eighth grades. When the basketball season was over that year, the coach started a track team and she joined that too.

Ninth grade was a repeat of the first two as far as basketball was concerned, but track was a different story. Although the school competition was informal and infrequent, she won all of the races that she entered.

In tenth grade, 5' 11" Wilma finally got to play in a basketball game. She recalled: "What I remember also about this season was this one referee. He worked a lot of our games, and people said he was the track coach at Tennessee State College. ... I liked him as a referee because he was always fair; I remember he always called me 'Rudolph,' never 'Number Such and Such' but always by my last name."

It was this summer in 1955 that Ed Temple came from Nashville to Clarksville and drove Wilma back to Tennessee State University for his summer program.

Wilma was now on her way to making history in Ed's successful program. She was up at 6 daily for a long morning run and back out twice again the same day for long runs during the two-week, cross-country part of his program. Then came the track work and a million points she learned and perfected and we all witnessed in Rome — the start, the baton pass, the body lean at the tape.

Wilma's first national championships were in 1955 in Ponca City, Oklahoma. She was fourth in the 75-yard dash and second to Isabelle Daniels in the 100-yard dash in the girls' division. She ran the second leg on the winning 300-yard relay.

In 1956, the national championships were held in Philadelphia. Wilma was second to Martha Hudson in the 75-yard dash in the girls' division and ran the anchor leg on the winning 300-yard relay team. In the senior division on August 18, she finished second to Mae Faggs in the 200 meters and ran second on the winning relay team.

One week later at the Olympic tryouts in Washington, D. C., Wilma placed a close second to Mae Faggs in the 200 meters again and qualified for the 1956 Olympic team. She ran a 24.6 seconds in Melbourne in the 200-meter trials and was eliminated but brought home a bronze medal after running the third leg on the all–Tennessee State University USA relay team.

In 1957, Wilma won the 75 and 100 yard dashes in the girls' division of the national championships and was named to the All-America Women's Track and Field Team for the 75-yard dash.

Wilma had her first daughter in 1958 and missed the first USA–USSR meet in Moscow.

In 1959, Wilma became national outdoor champion in the 100 meters and finished third in the 200 meters. Indoors she won the 50 meters. Ed was bringing her back slowly and pulled her out of the 200 meters in the Pan American Games in Chicago, but Wilma finished second in the 100 meters and in the USA–USSR meet that summer she placed fourth in the 100 meters.

The nationals were a week before the Olympic tryouts in Texas in 1960. In the nationals, Wilma ran a blistering 22.9 world-record-breaking clocking in the 200 meters and won the 100 in 11.5. Then in the tryouts, she repeated the wins in 23.9 and 11.5.

The rest is history. We were all so proud of her triumphs. Those of us that heard the news at home cried, and those who were teammates in Rome cried too.

My strong and lasting memories of Skeeter come from the time we spent in Texas in 1960 and the following three-week training camp in Kansas. Among other fond memories, I remember her reading her Bible one evening as she sat in bed. Every time I hear the following, I think of her reading it aloud:

> To every thing there is a season,
> and a time to every purpose
> under the heaven:
> A time to be born, and a time to
> die; a time to plant, and a time
> to pluck up that which is planted;
> A time to kill, and a time to heal;

> A time to break down, and a time
> to build up;
> A time to weep, and a time to laugh;
> A time to mourn, and a time to
> dance;
> A time to cast away stones, and
> a time to gather stones together; a
> time to embrace, and a time to
> refrain from embracing;
> A time to get, and a time to lose;
> A time to keep, and a time to cast
> away;
> A time to rend, and a time to sew; a
> time to keep silence, and a time to speak;
> A time to love, and a time to hate;
> A time of war, and a time of peace
>   [Ecclesiastes 2,3]

One of her high school classmates, Warren Keesee, said, "She was the best thing to ever happen to Clarksville." Wilma put the city of Clarksville on the map. The article from the front page of the November 18, 1994, *Leaf-Chronicle* recalled her role in the community:

> On one occasion after winning three medals, she poked fun at Muhammad Ali, who won only one.
> "She told him if he ever lost his one, she would give him one of her three," said Ed Crook, a 1960 Olympic gold medal winner in boxing.
> Officials describe her as one of the key threads that helped bring the city together during a time when racism and prejudice were prevalent throughout the South.

When Wilma returned home from Rome, Clarksville held a parade and an integrated banquet, one of the first of its kind in the history of the city. But only in May of 1992 did the city council vote to name a portion of U.S. 79 North after her. The ceremony unveiling the sign took place in January of 1994. Wilma said, "I've seen my name in a lot of different places, but it doesn't have the same meaning as this."

Skeeter, I stopped at the red brick church in Clarksville last December, and I heard you say, "Don't cry, Lou."

Edward Stanley Temple

Ed began his career as the greatest women's coach in the United States in 1950. In an interview on December 4, 1992, Ed said that he graduated from college in 1950, and he told me how he then began coaching:

> There was a small track team at Tennessee of four girls who were on work-aid. Tom Harris was the women's track coach at the time, but he was leaving to go to Virginia Union as athletic director. The president asked him who he would recommend to work with the women, so he recommended me. He thought that I could do a pretty good job. Now, I never worked with women. I was there on

a work-aid scholarship myself. I really had my mind set on working with football or basketball. I graduated in May, and I was staying there waiting for some kind of a job to come through. I wanted football or basketball. The placement bureau said hang around for a few weeks because jobs really come through. When the president called me over, he said, "Ed, Coach Tom Harris is leaving and he recommended you to take over the women's track team." I said, well, I was waiting for a football or basketball offer but so far I haven't had any. He said, "Well, I'll tell you what I'll do. I'll let you go to graduate school, give you one hundred and fifty dollars a month and let you run the post office." This is where the post office came in. So I said okay. At that time I didn't have anything. So that's how I got started. For one hundred and fifty dollars a month, I ran the post office and coached the women's track team. I got my master's in nineteen fifty-two and was then promoted to head the women's track team.

We didn't get an athletic scholarship until nineteen sixty-seven. That was the year that we got what is now called an athletic scholarship. All along with the Wilmas and the Tyuses we never had an athletic scholarship. They had work-aid. They had to work two hours a day in some office or something and do some type of work of that nature. We didn't get an athletic scholarship until nineteen sixty-seven, and I was about to leave then. A newspaper man, Fred Russell said, "I'm going to get an appointment for you with the governor." At that time the governor was Beaufort Ellerton, governor of the State of Tennessee. He said, "I want you to just go and talk with him." He got the appointment, and I went to see the governor. I told the governor, I said, "Governor Ellerton, I've been here seventeen years. We won gold medals, we set world records. We've done everything possible, and we don't have scholarships for women's track and field." He said, "Ed, I don't believe this." I said, "Football's got them, basketball's got them, but women's track doesn't have them. I've been to the president, I've been to the athletic director. I've been to everybody, and they tell me that they have no scholarships for women." He picked up the phone and by the time I got back out to the campus, because the capital is in Nashville, everything was jumping. I had scholarships, I had a new resurfaced track around my old cinder track. That's when things started to move. Everybody was mad at me. The president was mad because I went over his head, the athletic director was humming, but that's how I got started. I had to go to the governor, and the governor picked up that phone and he let them know. He said, "Ed Temple is not going anywhere. And you will have scholarships and you will do this and you will do that." He told them — because I was sitting right there. That's how I got them moving. All those years we never had an athletic scholarship. Wilma Rudolph never had an athletic scholarship. Wyomia Tyus never had an athletic scholarship. Edith McGuire never had an athletic scholarship. Manning had it, I think, in her last year. She was there when all this happened.

Most of the athletes that came to Tennessee came from state meets in Georgia. But you've got to realize this, that this was during the time of segregation. Some schools did give athletic scholarships like Alabama State, Tuskegee, and Philander Smith and various ones. In nineteen fifty-three, I would go to the Tuskegee Relays. I would go to Fort Valley, Georgia, to the state high school track meets. This was almost a national meet. All the state champions from Georgia, Alabama, and Tennessee would come to Tuskegee. It was the big thing. The colleges would run there also. It was almost like a black Penn Relays. Nell Jackson and Barbara Jacket came out of that program. I remember when Barbara was throwing the shot and javelin at Tuskegee. The program started with Cleve Abbott. He started it in the forties. This is how he made up the nineteen forty-eight Olympic team. Tuskegee was the mother of this type of program.

Cleve started women's track at Tuskegee. He put a lot of athletes on the nine-teen forty-eight Olympic team. That's where I got Lucinda Williams. That's where I got Isabelle Daniels. That's where I got Wyomia Tyus. I watched them, and then we had what we called a summer program. The summer program orig-inated at Tuskegee. The high school athletes pay their own way, we took care of the room and board. That's where I got my junior division. In other words, in the summer, we'd have a junior AAU division and a senior AAU division. Well, Mae Faggs and the older girls were the senior AAU division because they were in college. As the high school girls came in, they were the junior division, sixteen and under. In the summer we would take about ten high school girls, and we already had about eight or ten college girls there. We'd train together for one month three times a day. We practiced at five in the morning, ten-thirty in the morning and again at one-thirty. We'd work on basic fundamentals — arm movement, leg movement, how to get in the blocks, how to pass the baton, how to do all of these various things. But what helped me since I was the only coach was that the old girls showed the young girls. This is where Rudolph came in. Rudolph came into that program. All those girls from Wilma to Tyus started in the tenth grade. They came to Tennessee State in the summer, and then they'd go back home and run in their high school program. They would come back in the eleventh grade and then go back to their high school. They came back in the twelfth grade until they graduated. When they graduated and came to Ten-nessee, they had three years of good experience of being in the junior division and working with the senior girls — going to the national junior meets, because we had the junior and senior meets together at that time, and that's how they came along. They came along like a step ladder. As one would move out, the others would be coming along and move right on in. Out of the ten in a sum-mer, we didn't get all champions. About half of them turned out to be great, and the other half turned out to be good. Now they didn't make the Olympic team, but they were good. They were good. The summer program was like the training program in Colorado Springs. But mine was at the school, and I could keep control over them. I had the older ones like Faggs to help the others, to talk to them and say "no, we don't do it that way, we do it this way." As they came along, they learned the system. They passed it on. And it's a three-year program. You could see them each year. Now, they would play basketball in their high schools and they would run track, but you could see the times coming down, the distance going up. Everything was moving along.

The "mother" of the team at Tennessee was Mae Faggs. Mae came from Bay-side, New York. Mae came down to all of us country people. We didn't know anything. Faggs had run indoor track at Madison Square Garden. Faggs had made the nineteen forty-eight Olympic team. Faggs had made the nineteen fifty-two Olympics. Faggs came here, and we didn't even have a track. We had three-quarters of a track. Now, Mae came down to Tennessee, and in her first year she was so discouraged. Mae was indoor champion, and she couldn't even go up and defend her championship because the athletic director told her we didn't have any money to send anyone up to New York to run. So, her first two years were frustrating. She couldn't do anything because track was way down to minus zero here. They weren't going to give track anything. The athletic direc-tor wasn't paying any attention to track. We had a president named Dr. W. S. Davis. He reached out and gave women's track and field a hand. He wanted to give them a chance. Mae Faggs opened up the door for us. She said, "give me a chance and I'll help to bring this team along." So he gave her a chance, and the first time she got to compete was in her sophomore year. This is how she got to go. She wanted to run the two hundred, so our athletic director called Cleve

Abbott. He asked if Cleve was going to Madison Square Garden. Cleve said, "yes and we're going by train." So the athletic director said, when the train comes through Nashville, we're going to put Mae Faggs on the train and will you take care of her? That's how they were thinking. They thought that was the greatest thing in the world, put Mae Faggs on the train with Tuskegee.

After the nineteen fifty-two Olympics, Mae wanted to go to a school in New York, but none of the schools had women's track and field. She heard from Tuskegee and from Fort Valley. A fellow who was our business manager heard that she wanted to go to school. He wrote to her and told her about Tennessee. A fellow who worked for a Chicago newspaper knew Mae from the nineteen forty-eight and nineteen fifty-two Olympics. He called our president and told him this is a great track person. Now, I didn't know anything about it yet. When I found out, Mae was coming in. I didn't know anything about Mae Faggs. Mae Faggs helped me because, shoot, at that time, I didn't know anything about women's track. So, really, Mae Faggs taught me because she was already in the nineteen forty-eight and nineteen fifty-two Olympics. She knew way more than me. I hadn't been out of Tennessee. That's why we all call her the "mother" of the team, because she's the one that got us started.

From nineteen fifty to nineteen fifty-three, we went to one meet a year, the Tuskegee Relays. Then we went to two meets: the Alabama State Relays and the Tuskegee Relays until nineteen fifty-four.

In nineteen fifty-six, we put six on the nineteen fifty-six Olympic team: Wilma Rudolph, Margaret Matthews, Lucinda Williams, Isabelle Daniels, Mae Faggs, and Willye White. They won a bronze medal in Australia, and all four were on the relay team. [Willye won a silver in the broad jump.]

The first time that I was a national team coach was in nineteen fifty-eight. And I'll tell you how that came about. That was one of the weirdest things too. I guess out of all of the teams I had as far as depth, nineteen fifty-eight was the greatest team. I had Willye B. White on there and Margaret Matthews and Anne Lois Smith in the long jump. I had in the one hundred, Barbara Jones, Isabelle Daniels, and Lucinda Williams and also in the two hundred. I had Shirley Crowder in the hurdles. I put eight people on that team. We had the tryouts in Morristown, New Jersey. Frances Kaszubski was the national chairwoman. We won the junior division and we won the senior division and that was the second time we had a bus. In 1955, they chartered a bus for us to go to Ponca City, Oklahoma, because that was our first time running in a national track meet. All right, now this is nineteen fifty-eight, and we had a chartered bus to Morristown, New Jersey. We took one, two, and three in the one hundred. First and second in the two hundred, we had one and two in the long jump, and we won the hurdles. We had eight girls on the U.S. team. I asked Frances who was going to be the coach. Let's back track a little bit. I told my wife when we were leaving to pack my bags because the team is going to be picked to go to Moscow. We went to Poland, Hungary, and Greece. That was the first Russian trip. So I told my wife, pack my bags because I'm going to Russia. She said, "Have they written you?" I said no, they haven't, but pack my bags, I'm not coming back. She thought I was crazy everyone thought I was crazy. I even thought I was crazy at that time. But anyway, I said, Frances, let me tell you. She said "we're going in this tent and we're going to have a meeting and then I'll let you know." There was another coach of the PAL before Connie Ford, Bob Mangum, and he was the one that she was talking about that they were thinking about to have as coach. But I told her this. These are exactly the words I told her. I said, "Frances, I've got eight people that made this United States team. I have a chartered bus out there that's going to leave at seven o'clock in the morning. Now when you go in that room, I want you to say one thing. If I'm not on this team as coach, all eight will be on that bus going back to Nashville, Tennessee. Now you go in there and tell them that." I had all the sprinters, I had all the long jumpers, I had the team. She looked at me like I was crazy. You know, Frances was real tall, about six foot four, lookin' down at me. She looked at me and she went in there and she wasn't in there five minutes and she came out and she said, "Ed, you're the coach." I said thank you. That's how Ed Temple got started.

On that trip, Frances went also. She was the manager. We went over there, but they didn't even know we were there. All they were talking about was Rafer Johnson and Parry O'Brien. All of them were big superstars. The women were nothing. Russia had the Press sisters. The Press

Ed Temple, coach of 1960 Olympic team and Tennessee State University. (Author's photo.)

sisters had more whiskers than I had. We went over there and took the one hundred, we took the two hundred, we took the four by one hundred relay and even took the shot put. We even got Earlene Brown in shape. We practiced two weeks at Morristown. Then we went overseas. Then the next year, the Russians came over here to Philadelphia. I was the coach then. I didn't have any trouble then. I didn't have any trouble from that time on. I guess they said, he's crazy. Everything moved along pretty good.

A coach was able to do more coaching in those days on the teams. There were no agents. There were no personal coaches. I was the personal coach. What I told my eight, they passed on to the rest of them. That's what we did. We didn't have that pomp and circumstance. I didn't run into that until way down the line. I ran into some things about personal coaches, but that didn't phase me too much. In Mexico, especially, or some place that was close, if anybody wanted their personal coach, I told them to come. That was no problem.

I had two great Olympic wins, and I can't separate them because they each have great meaning to me. Number one was Rudolph's three gold medals in Rome. I had no idea this would happen. If you look back in the history, in the nineteen fifty-nine Pan American Games, Rudolph got third in the one hundred, and ran on the relay team. But Lucinda Williams won the three gold medals. She won the one hundred, two hundred, and ran the anchor leg on the four by one hundred. Then in nineteen sixty, Wilma just blossomed. If you look at the records, in nineteen fifty-nine in the USA versus Russia, Wilma took fourth place in the one hundred. There were four running. She took fourth place in the one hundred. In other words, she was coming along. But you have to realize too, that in nineteen fifty-eight she had a child. She had her first child. But people didn't know it. Nobody asked why Wilma was not on the nineteen fifty-eight team that went to Moscow. Well Wilma was having this child. That's why she wasn't on the fifty-eight team. She was having her first child. She didn't get back into running again until nineteen fifty-nine. Then she was beginning to come back. In sixty she gained her strength, and she was well on the move.

My second one was right up there with it. I'd have to say the nineteen sixty-four Olympics. And I'll tell you why I say that. Wyomia Tyus (who came up through the summer program like Edith McGuire) in the Olympic trials got third in the one hundred. Now, she was just coming into Tennessee State as a freshman. She had run in the juniors in the tenth, eleventh grade, right on up. McGuire was a sophomore going into her junior year that next year. But people were all talking about McGuire taking Wilma's place. She was our next one coming up in line. McGuire took the one hundred in Randall's Island, at the Olympic trials. She took the two hundred. Tyus got third. Well, I'm happy. I'm so happy with this that I don't know what to do because I'm saying that Tyus is just coming in and Tyus will get some exposure and everything and this will be good. So, when we got to Tokyo, after all my big problems with the starting blocks which you know about, they sent fifteen starting blocks and the men took all fifteen of them. We didn't have any blocks. We had to use the Japanese starting blocks which nobody knew how to put together. We didn't see an American starting block until we were in the Olympics. At that time they had about six different starting blocks at the start and the man said, "Pick the one you want." That's the first time we saw an American starting block. I went to Dan Ferris. I went to everybody I could go to and everybody tells me, well that's Giegengack, he's the coach. I said, "Now are we a part of the United States team. Hell, they sent fifteen blocks, only thing we want is three." We want three for the girls. Hell, we have U.S.A. on too. They looked at me like I was crazy.

To make a long story short, the other thing was when Tyus won the one hundred and McGuire took second. Now, when I talk to people and maybe you can do some research, have you ever heard of any school that took first and second in the Olympics, the first two coming from the same school? I don't know. Tyus got first in the one hundred, and McGuire took second. Now that was great. I was really happy about that. But then the thing that made me really happy was that McGuire came up to me and said, "Coach, I'm gonna win that 200." Now, I heard her and didn't hear her because I was so happy we got first and second, I was ready to pack up and go home then. I said, shoot, I'm not worried about the two hundred. Here we got first and second in the one hundred. But anyway, she came back and won that two hundred. Then they teamed up with Marilyn White and Willye B. White, and we got a second in the four by one hundred relay. Those two instances I'd have to put up there right together. And next close to it would be Manning winning the half mile in the sixty-eight Olympics and Tyus coming back and being the first person period, man or woman, to repeat in the sprints. She was the first person ever to do that. So those were, I'd say, really the highlights.

In 1960, I thought that the track was short and the watches were wrong in Corpus Christi, Texas, when Wilma won the two hundred. That's what I really thought. I said, there's no way this child could run twenty-two point nine. Nobody else had run twenty-three and hardly twenty-four. The twenty-four was the best they could run, and here she ran twenty-two point nine in Corpus Christi. When they announced the time, I told her, the track's just short, that's all. The track had to be two hundred ten yards, ten yards short. But then when she went to Abilene, she ran the same time. Well, then I said the watches were wrong. When we got to Rome, and they were seeding, when it came to twenty-two point nine for Wilma Rudolph, they said a girl never ran twenty-three. They just "tabled" it. That's a nice way of saying no. But, when she got to hummin on that track, they brought it "off the table." They brought it "off the table." When people ask me, I had no idea that this child was going to win three gold medals. I knew she was moving along. But, in the first place, I had never been to an Olympics. This was my first Olympics. So I didn't know what they did. It was Greek to me. She had more experience than me because she had gone to the fifty-six Olympics. Barbara Jones was at the fifty-two Olympics. Some of the others on the team had been to an Olympics, but this was my first Olympics.

In the one hundred, I was really nervous. But you see, I was in the warm-up area. I couldn't actually see Wilma run. I didn't see her run until the Olympics were over and I looked at it on film. I could see her start and the first fifteen yards. I was way over in some field some place, in the warm-up area. But she looked so good stretched out and everything. Before the final, she fell asleep. She fell asleep. She warmed-up and everything, and she was on the rub-down table. Then they said, "First call for the 100 finals" and here she's laying there sleeping. I'm about to have cardiac arrest. I'm pacing up and down. Well, she got off the table, and she was yawning and stretching. I told her to get out there and run like you did in the first and second round. I said, if you run like that, you're in good shape. I said, get out of your blocks. She got out of the blocks and swoosh. That was it. She won the one hundred, and we were all happy. I knew that the two hundred would be better than the one hundred because she can get rolling. I was pulling out my cigar now, ready to puff my cigar. Frances Kaszubski was walking like somebody about eight feet tall, talking about "her babies." She was talking about "her babies." Well, when she won the two hundred, she then wanted the relay. She wanted to win for her teammates. She wanted that relay. We knew all the rest of them had to get up and move to win the relay. She was determined. I'll tell you something, I wish they would have timed her split, in that four by one hundred after she got the stick, because we were really in third place. We were in a tight third place because Lucinda passed off to her and they kind of bubbled the pass. She didn't get in the first time, and she had to go back and hit it again. By that time, Australia and Germany were moving. That child the first seventy-five yards, it was just awesome, she chewed them up. She chewed them up like they were standing still. They looked like they were in slow motion, she jumped on them so fast. She jumped on them so fast and then from the seventy-five on, it was just a matter of her cruising.

The other stick passes were good. We were moving. She took off a little fast on Lucinda. Lucinda put it in there, but it didn't get in there good. Lucinda tried it again, and by that time we were moving through that zone pretty good. But when she got that stick it was awesome. It was almost like seeing Carl Lewis get it now. Zoom, gone. I knew this was going to be a race. But the way she jumped on them so quick, I couldn't believe it myself and I was looking at it. She caught them in seventy-five yards. She ran that like she was running a fifty-yard dash. There was no doubt about it. I wanted to time the splits.

I was bad on the splits, I'll never forget this. We were at the Tuskegee Relays, and we were running the four by one hundred. I caught myself on the back stretch because I was going to time the splits. So, we were running against Tuskegee, Alabama State, Mayor Daley, and Fort Valley. But I got to jumping up and down and hollering, and I was on a bench. I slipped and fell, and all I could see were legs flying. I fell on the ground and when I looked up, legs were flying. I said, I would never get this excited anymore.

We didn't use weights at that time. We ran a lot of hills. Lot of hills. Our school during that time had a great football team and a great basketball team. The girls had nothing. I would always stress to them that if the football team could win, you could win. I said, you're opening up the doors. I said, yes, we have no scholarships, yes, we're on work-aid, but if you make good, one of these days it's going to help people coming behind you. And I always stressed that to them. As I said before, Mae Faggs was a tremendous driving force. She told them that you could do it. She gave them that desire, that motivation. Once we started winning with Mae Faggs, we won our first national championship in nineteen fifty-five in Ponca City, Oklahoma. We won the junior division and the senior division. And, from that time on we won about twelve straight, right on through until about nineteen sixty-seven, indoor and outdoor. We were in indoor meets where the longest race was two hundred. And then we had to run around about six curves to get to the two hundred. That was when Earlene Brown threw the basketball. It was in a gym and she threw it up in the balcony and they didn't know where the basketball went. Those were the rough times. We went to the Coliseum one year, and we had more athletes than spectators. We ran some indoor meets where there were hardly any spectators. One of the things that opened up the doors for us was Wilma winning in nineteen sixty so we could have the men and women together. Now, the women are as much a headliner as the men. But it just goes to show you what they can do when given the opportunity. A door was opened, and they produced. I think that's the bottom line.

After Wilma won her three gold medals, she was on the cover of the Millrose Games program. That was the first time they ever put a woman on the cover. We went out to the *Los Angeles Times* meet, and she was featured. She got to go to a whole lot of things. All the indoor meets wanted her. All of them.

During the school year, we worked out one time a day. Only in the summer did we workout three times a day. Well, in the morning we would all come out and work on distance. At that time, we were running about two miles. You've got to realize that in the fifties they weren't thinking about long distance running. At the next session, we'd work on nothing but form. Arm action, leg action, getting into the blocks. We would come across the football field. We used the stripes to walk on to get the knees up, to get on the ball of the feet. We would go on back to work on the arms, so that they were moving their arms right, so that they were not coming across the body. We would work on basic fundamentals. We would assign a new girl to an old girl. That's the way we would operate. The old girl would work with the new girl. I knew if I got on somebody, they'd get nervous and wouldn't do anything but if you're there with an old girl you wouldn't get nervous and all tight.

At two o'clock, we would work on speed or baton passing or some other thing. We would do something different every day. We spent about eighty percent of the time on basic fundamentals and in the meantime, getting in good condition. My thought of getting hurt, if you're in good condition, is slimmer and slimmer, less and less. So we worked on conditioning a whole lot, getting those legs strong. But in the meantime, working on technology. We would do that, and the next year when they came in, boom, we start right back at that zero point again, like they never did it. But you could see that they were getting sharper and sharper. And the next year when they came back, boom, we'd start zero again. But they would have learned those two years. Now they're getting sharper and smoother all the time.

Track was still zero in high school. In Tennessee track was still separate. A few black schools would have only one or two track meets a year. They could care less. Most of my track people played basketball. Rudolph played basketball, Tyus played basketball, McGuire played basketball. Manning was about the first girl I had that actually didn't play basketball in high school. She came from Cleveland. They had the Cleveland Recreation, which was really good. Alex

Ferenczy trained her real good. She was my first girl that came to me that really knew what it was about when she came in. She had a good background, and it paid off.

I stopped with high school kids about twelve years ago, when we got in with the NCAA. The NCAA didn't open its doors until nineteen eighty. Now you had the AIAW, and all that stuff. When that began, we said, forget it. It messed up a good thing. It wouldn't work today. I was telling a reporter who asked, "Do you think you could coach the group today or do you think the coaches today could coach your group?" I said, I don't think either way would work. In the first place I could not coach up here today because there's too many agents, too many managers, too many mommas, too many girlfriends, too many husbands, too many wives, too many everything. I said, now, I don't have that kind of patience to deal with all that. The person who deals with all that ought to get a gold medal himself. But you take them down here to deal with me when I was coaching with one coach and a manager, hell, I had to do everything. We didn't have any training camp but about two weeks, we didn't have any premeets before the Olympics. Hell, we left the United States and went to the Olympics. There was not stopping over here and training three weeks, and had to do this, and the sun had to be right, and the right eating. Hell, we didn't know anything about this. We just went over and got the medal and came on home. Nike sent us two pair of shoes, and we thought that was the greatest thing in the world. Hell, we have two pairs of shoes. Nike sent me twelve pairs of shoes after Wilma Rudolph won the thing and man, I was struttin' around, I thought I hit a gold mine. They hadn't sent me a shoe string up to that time. I said, man, look at this, twelve pairs of shoes.

In nineteen sixty-seven, the first scholarship person might have been Cheeseborough. I had her three years in the summer. She was my last great person that I had three years in high school. She was the last one to come up "through the ranks." I got McMillan out of high school. Morehead was on scholarship.

In nineteen seventy-six the money started flowing. If you win, you get so much. The shoe companies started coming in. I could see there was going to be trouble because money does things to people, I don't care what you say. The money didn't go directly to the athletes. It went to the parents. There were some big bucks then. They didn't want momma and daddy to get it. Mom and daddy were sending them fifteen or twenty a month. That money belongs to me, it doesn't belong to them, I worked for it. Look, these are your parents, they're going to funnel it down to you. I want it. Well if you didn't have it, you didn't want it. But now that you have it, you want to act like a fool. The only person who didn't act a fool was Cheese. Cheese said, my momma needs it. She needs to get her furnace repaired, she needs a roof. After she finishes with all that when she sends me something, o.k. But, the others, I want my money now. I want my money. I shook my head and said oh, oh. I know it's trouble. I had no trouble at all with Rudolph and Tyus. There was nothing offered. I'll never forget, when Rudolph came home, somebody wanted to give her a black and white television. At that time they didn't have color. The president said, "That's against amateur rules, you can't do it. We don't want to give it to her, give it to her parents." No. You have to watch. I said to myself, my goodness, it was just a little television. They didn't have a television, they hardly had a radio with twenty-two kids. Hell, you didn't have a radio. I just shook my head. With the money that's coming along now, those girls would have been awesome. They'd have been awesome. If you look at the times they ran on a cinder track, eleven flat one hundred meters in nineteen sixty. With all the nice surfaces now and the shoes and everything else.

After my first trip in nineteen fifty-eight to Russia, the next one was the nine-teen sixty Olympics then the Tokyo Olympics. The next one was a European tour in nineteen seventy-one, to Russia and Romania. I picked up Mamie Rallins on the trip to Romania. She was older then. She was thirty. One morning we were eating and she came down and said, "One thing I regret is that I didn't get to go to college." I said, "Look, it's not too late. Did you graduate from high school?" She said yes. I said, "It's not too late." She went home and called Ralph Boston, who was her friend. She asked Ralph if I was serious or if I was kid-ding. She sent her transcript down. She came in as a thirty-one-year-old fresh-man and graduated with a degree in business. She got a job at Ohio State the next year. That's the only job she ever had. She jumped from boom to Ohio State. You can't ask for better than that. It's like going from zero to one hun-dred in one push. She had never coached in high school. The break was there. She had the experience and the education and the door opened. Of course, Mar-ilyn West helped her get the job.

Some of the other trips were small ones, the Pan American Games in Mexico and the first USA versus China trip in nineteen seventy-five. I had a weird expe-rience then. That was the only trip that I made that I didn't have any of my girls on the team. It was during school time. We stopped in Hong Kong. We prac-ticed there. We were in Hong Kong two days. I had eight sprinters. I'll never forget this experience. I had all the sprinters together. I said, "We're going to work on the four by one hundred. How many have ever run first leg?" and they all stood there and looked at each other. "How many have run second leg?" and they all stood there and looked at each other. I said, "How many have ever run third leg?" and they all stood there and looked at each other. "How many have run anchor?" and all eight raised their hand. I said, "I'll be damned, eight anchor legs." I had eight anchor legs. Nobody ever passed the baton. They said we just receive the baton. Nobody wanted to run first leg, and nobody wanted to run third leg. I had to go around for two days just begging people, please try this for us. We bumbled and stumbled, but we won over there. But it was not pretty at all, I tell you. China was just getting started. If it was anyone else, they would have killed us. We were running all over the top of each other. We just had the speed. That's all we had. All of them were anchor legs. It was the weirdest expe-rience I ever had.

This is it. You lead and you follow and then you get out of the way. It's time for me to get out of the way. I led for about thirty-five years, I followed for about five or six years, and now it's time to get on out of the way. I feel I've done everything I could possibly do in track. I have nothing to regret in track and field. Nothing at all. We started with zero and worked all the way up. The thing that I'm most proud of is that we put forty girls on the Olympic team. Thirty-five were on the United States Olympic teams, the other five were on teams from Panama, Jamaica, Bermuda, Bahamas, and Trinidad. Out of forty, thirty-nine graduated with their degrees and out of the thirty-nine we had twenty-five with masters and three with their Ph.D and one M.D. I'm happy with that. All of them are successful and working. No one's in jail, no one's on welfare. I see them quite a bit.

The NCAA has a silver anniversary award. That means that you have to be out twenty-five years, been great in your sport and made a contribution to your community and to society in the twenty-five years. Wilma was the first woman honored. McGuire got it two years ago. Tyus gets it this year. That makes me feel good. They've all done a good job. I have no regrets. I see them from time to time. Usually when they want something. Coach, will you send me my tran-script. But when I was sick this summer, they all called. Wilma was right there when I went into the hospital. I went into the hospital at six o'clock in the morning and when I went to my room to get prepared, Wilma was sitting there with my wife. Wilma was sitting there at six o'clock in the morning. And when I went in for surgery, she was sitting there when I came back out. Tyus called every day. McGuire called every day.

When I finish at Tennessee, I'll be out to pasture. What I'm going to be doing out in the pasture, I don't know. I be gnawing on some grass or something. I'll be coming to these conventions, sitting around and listening and giving my little two-cent word when I figure it's necessary, when I see them getting out of line. I'm gonna do that. This has been my life. This has been my life for forty-three years as of nineteen ninety-three. I started in nineteen fifty. A trillion changes have taken place.

I'm giving all my things to the library at Tennessee State. They are going to set up a room for me. Scrapbooks from nineteen fifty and all the various things we have won down through the years will be in this room. The history will be right there.

Wilma Rudolph wrote in the foreword to Ed's book, *Only the Pure in Heart Survive*, "His records speak for themselves."

Head coach, U.S. women's Olympic track and field team for two consecutive Olympiads, 1960 and 1964.

First coach ever to coach three U.S. Olympic teams, 1960, 1964, and 1980.

U. S. Pan American coach, 1959, 1975.

European tour coach, 1958 (first USA–USSR meet), 1960, and 1970.

Coach, first trip to China, 1975.

Member of U.S. Olympic Committee 1960, 1964, 1968, 1976, 1980.

Individual world records were held by six of his women athletes.

Olympic records were held by four of his women athletes, and the four athletes on the 1960 United States relay team were his women athletes from Tennessee State.

His Olympic medal winners won: 11 gold medals
                                         5 silver medals
                                         4 bronze medals.

His athletes have held twenty-seven indoor world records and sixteen outdoor records.

His athletes set thirty-six indoor and twenty-two outdoor American records.

Chapter 44

1961

The city of Gary, Indiana, hosted the women's national championships on July 1-2. Sixteen thousand spectators were attracted to the meet. Fifty-one clubs took part, breaking the previous record from 1960, when twenty-two teams competed. Unattached athletes also represented seven cities. The record number of participants skyrocketed from 206 to 264.

"Wilma Rudolph Takes AAU 100" read the headlines in the *New York Times* on July 3. The story continued:

> Wilma Rudolph, the Olympic champion, won the 100 yard dash in the National AAU women's track and field championships tonight.
> A winner of three Olympic gold medals in Rome last summer, Miss Rudolph was timed in 10.8 seconds. She had tied the AAU record of 10.7 in the semifinals earlier in the day. In the final, she ran against a wind of seven miles an hour.
> Lacey O'Neal of Chicago finished three yards behind Miss Rudolph.

100-yard dash
1. Wilma Rudolph, Tennessee State   10.8 ties MR
2. Lacey O'Neal, Mayor Daley Youth Foundation
3. Willye White, Mayor Daley Youth Foundation
4. Ernestine Pollards, Mayor Daley Youth Foundation

220-yard dash
1. Lacey O'Neal, Mayor Daley Youth Foundation   25.0
2. Ernestine Pollards, Mayor Daley Youth Foundation
3. Vivian Brown, Tennessee State
4. Janell Smith, Fredonia, Kansas

440-yard run
1. Jackie Peterson, N.Y. Police Athletic League   59.5 MR
2. Mary Rose, Abilene, Texas
3. Pat Douthitt, Cleveland Recreation
4. Ruth Ann Brand, Prescott, Ariz.

880-yard run
1. Billie Pat Daniels, San Mateo A.A.   2:19.2 MR
2. Leah Bennett, Oriole Track Club, Md.
3. Grace Butcher, Magyar A.C.
4. Judy Shapiro, Tujunga, Calif.

440-yard relay
1. Mayor Daley Youth Foundation, "A" team   47.0
      (White, O'Neal, May, Pollards)
2. Mayor Daley Youth Foundation, "B" team
3. Ohio Track Club
4. Texas Track Club

880-yard relay
1. San Mateo A.A.   1:49.0
      (Daniels, Mack, Duensing, Johnson)
2. Cleveland Recreation
3. Liberty Athletic Club, Boston
4. Ohio Track Club

Broad jump
1. Willye White, Mayor Daley Youth Foundation   19' 11½ "
2. Edith McGuire, Tennessee State
3. Flossie Wilcher, Tennessee State
4. JoAnn Terry, Tennessee State

4-kilo shot put
1. Earlene Brown, Spartan A.C.   47' 8½"
2. Cynthia Wyatt, Williamsville, N.Y.
3. Sharon Shepherd, Cleveland Recreation
4. Joan Whitehead, Montclair State College

Discus throw
1. Earlene Brown, Spartan A.C.   149' 4½"
2. Sharon Shepherd, Cleveland Recreation
3. Melody McCarthy, Los Angeles
4. Cynthia Wyatt, Williamsville, N.Y.

Javelin throw
1. Fran Davenport, Vista Chamber of Commerce   137' 8"
2. Karen Mendyka, unattached
3. Marjorie Larney, Queens Mercurettes
4. Cel Rutledge, Texas Track Club

High jump
1. Liz Josefson, Spartan A.C.   5' 1"
2. Rose Robinson, unattached
3. Barbara Browne, N.Y. Police Athletic League
4. Denise Parker, San Diego Track Club

80-meter hurdles
1. Cherrie Parrish, Laurel Track Club   11.5
2. JoAnn Terry, Tennessee State
3. Leontyne Reif, Mayor Daley Youth Foundation
4. Kay Miller, Mayor Daley Youth Foundation

Team scores:
Mayor Daley Youth Foundation 88; Tennessee State 44; Cleveland Recreation 30;
Spartan Women's A.C. 30; San Mateo Girls' A.A. 21; Texas Track Club 19; N.Y. Police
Athletic League 18.

Girls' Track and Field Championships

50-yard dash
1. Edith McGuire, Tennessee State   6.0
2. Janell Smith, Fredonia, Kans.   6.1
3. Flossie Wilcher, Tennessee State   6.1

75-yard dash
1. A. Miller, Tennessee State   8.4
2. Wyomia Tyus, Tennessee State   8.5
3. Carol Smith, unattached   8.6

100-yard dash
1. Edith McGuire, Tennessee State   11.0
2. Lacey O'Neal, Mayor Daley Youth Foundation   11.1
3. Wyomia Tyus, Tennessee State   11.1

50-yard hurdles
1. Tammy Davis, Frederick Track Club   7.3
2. Mary Rose, Texas Track Club   7.3
3. P. Watkins, Ohio Track Club

330-yard relay
1. Mayor Daley Youth Foundation   33.7
2. Cleveland Recreation   33.8
3. Ohio Track Club   no time

Baseball throw
1. L. Puckett, unattached   270' 6"
2. T. Bloodsaw, Cleveland Recreation   256' 1"
3. M. Hodge, Mayor Daley Youth Foundation   230' 2"

Broad jump
1. Flossie Wilcher, Tennessee State   19' 8½"
2. Edith McGuire, Tennessee State   19' 4¾"
3. Pat Daniels, San Mateo   19' 3¼"

High jump
1. Pat Daniels, San Mateo A.A.   5'
2. Estelle Baskerville, Ohio Track Club   4' 11"
3. Denise Parker, San Diego Track Club   4' 10"

8-lb. shot put
1. Cindy Wyatt, unattached   47' 9"
2. M. Clinchard, unattached   42' 7¾"
3. Gloria Kemp, Cosmopolitan Club   42' 7¼"

Discus
1. Cindy Wyatt, unattached   138' 2"
2. Melody McCarthy, San Fernando Valley Women's A.C.   131' 8"
3. Susan Schibanoff, Central Jersey Track Club   123' 7½"

Javelin
1. Fran Davenport, Vista Chamber of Commerce   130' 8"
2. C. Pulaski, Central Jersey Track Club   111' 5"
3. M. Clinchard, unattached   108' 6"

Team scores:
Tennessee State University 76; Mayor Daley Youth Foundation 34; Ohio Track Club 24; San Mateo Girls' A.A. 22; Cleveland Recreation Department 16; Central Jersey Track Club 15; Vista, California, Chamber of Commerce 12; Frederick Track Club, Md. 11; Texas Track Club 9.

The Indoor Nationals

The indoor nationals were held at Columbus, Ohio, on March 10. *Track and Field News* reported that Tennessee State, after a seven-year reign as indoor champion, was defeated by the Mayor Daley Youth Foundation. Six records were shattered. The article continued: "In an afternoon of surprises, Olympic sprinter Wilma Rudolph went home with only the 100 yard dash title. [Her winning time was 10.8.] She collapsed and needed medical attention for abdominal muscle spasms after running three events in succession." She lost her 220-yard dash crown to Tennessee State freshman Vivian Brown. Brown ran a 25.2 in the final but Wilma set an indoor record of 25.0 in a heat.

Track and Field News added: "It was in attempting to make up a six yard deficit on her anchor leg in the relay that Wilma strained herself. She got 4½ yards of it back as the Tigerbelles clocked 49.0 but the Chicago team posted a 48.8 for an American indoor mark."

Helen Shipley, a high school student from Wellesley, Massachusetts, won the 880-yard run. Running the first race of her career, she beat seasoned athletes who had each held the American record, at one time or another, for the event. In winning the 880, she set a new American record of 2:21.6. The best previous time was 2:24.8 by Rose Lovelace at the Mason-Dixon Games two weeks ago. Helen ran a practice half and had no kick. She felt that this would be the case today. So her plan was to go out fast and just keep going as long as she could.

The *New York Times* on March 11 added: "Lillian Greene, New Yorker representing Colorado State, cracked the old records as she led the quarter-mile qualifiers in 61.1. That was better than the American indoor record of 61.3 set by Louise Mead in 1960, and her own AAU mark of 63.4 set in 1959."

Standing broad jump
1. Sandra Smith, Mayor Daley Youth Foundation   8' 11"
2. Ann Roniger, Colorado State   8' 6¾"
3. Leontyne Reif, Mayor Daley Youth Foundation   8' 3"

Shot put
1. Cindy Wyatt, Williamsville, N.Y.   39' 11"
2. Gloria Kemp, Cosmopolitan Club   36' 7"
3. Joan Whitehead, Montclair State College

50-yard dash
1. Willye White, Mayor Daley Youth Foundation   6.0
2. Lorene Holmes, Tennessee State   6.1
3. Lacey O'Neal, Mayor Daley Youth Foundation   6.1

100-yard dash
1. Wilma Rudolph, Tennessee State   10.8
2. Willye White, Mayor Daley Youth Foundation   11.1
3. Vivian Brown, Tennessee State   11.4

220-yard dash
1. Vivian Brown, Tennessee State   25.2
2. Wilma Rudolph, Tennessee State   25.3
3. Ernestine Pollards, Mayor Daley Youth Foundation   25.4

440-yard dash
1. Lillian Greene, Colorado State   60.4 AR
2. Rose Robinson, Mayor Daley Youth Foundation   61.1
3. Anna Reid, Mayor Daley Youth Foundation   61.2

880-yard run
1. Helen Shipley, Liberty A.C.   2:21.6 AR
2. Sandra Pashkin, unattached   2:23.6
3. Grace Butcher, Magyar A.C.   2:23.8

70-yard hurdles
1. JoAnn Terry, Tennessee State   9.5
2. Kay Miller, DeKalb, Ill.   9.9
3. Rose Malenchuk, Colorado State   9.9

High jump
1. Rose Robinson, unattached   5' 4"
2. JoAnn Terry, Tennessee State   5' 3"
3. Estelle Baskerville, Ohio Track Club   5'

Basketball throw
1. Jean Hofbauer, O'Hallaren Playground   102' 5½"
2. Gloria Kemp, Cosmopolitan Club   97' 7½"

440-yard relay
1. Mayor Daley Youth Foundation, "A" team   48.8 AR
   (White, May, Pollards, O'Neal)
2. Tennessee State   49.0
3. Ohio Track Club   51.4

880-medley relay
1. Ohio Track Club   1:53.1
   (Long, Knott, Watkins, Fuller)
2. Mayor Daley Youth Foundation, "A" team   1:57.8
3. Liberty A.C.   1:58.8

Seventeen girls were selected from the outdoor championships to make up the United States team which competed in Russia, Germany, England, and Poland. Only five of the seventeen were veterans of the 1960 Olympic Games. Wilma Rudolph set a new world record in Germany of 11.2 for the 100 meters. Another world record was set in Russia by the 400-meter relay team. Willye White's consistent broad jumps of over 21 feet were a highlight of the team's performances.

USA vs. USSR: Moscow, July 15-16

The *New York Times* on July 16, reported:

> [Wilma was] clearly in command of the women's 100 meters after the first thirty meters. She sped home a comfortable winner. After the first race, she said: "I was very surprised to equal the record because I haven't been running that hard and haven't been too well — but I'm very pleased."

In the 400-meter relay Wilma was two yards behind at the baton pass. She caught the Soviet runner at 80 meters in a new world record time. "I guess the last leg was as fast as I ever ran," Miss Rudolph said.

100-meter dash
1. Wilma Rudolph   11.3 ties WR
4. Lacey O'Neal   12.0

200-meter dash
2. Ernestine Pollards   23.7
3. Vivian Brown   24.1

800-meter run
3. Billie Pat Daniels   2:16.2
4. Leah Bennett   2:21.0

80-meter hurdles
3. Cherrie Parrish   11.1
4. JoAnn Terry   11.1

400-meter relay
1. USA   44.3 WR
   (White, Pollards, Brown, Rudolph)

Shot put
3. Sharon Shepherd   44' 5¾"
4. Cindy Wyatt   44' 4¼"

Broad jump
2. Willye White   20' 11¾" AR
4. Edith McGuire   18' 5¼"

Javelin
3. Karen Mendyka   143' ¼"
4. Fran Davenport   133' ¾"

Discus
3. Sharon Shepherd   148' 1"
4. Melody McCarthy   129' 1½"

High jump
2. Barbara Browne   5' 4¾"
4. JoAnn Terry   4' 11"

USSR 68 — USA 36

USA vs. West Germany: Stuttgart, July 18-19

100-meter dash	
1. Wilma Rudolph	11.5
2. Willye White	11.7
200-meter dash	
2. Ernestine Pollards	24.3
3. Vivian Brown	24.5
800-meter run	
3. Billie Pat Daniels	2:13.1
400-meter relay	
USA disqualified for passing baton outside of zone	
80-meter hurdles	
3. Cherrie Parrish	11.4
High jump	
3. JoAnn Terry	5' 1¼"
Broad jump	
1. Willye White	21' ¼" AR
Shot put	
3. Sharon Shepherd	44' 11¼"
Discus	
2. Sharon Shepherd	149' 8¾"
Javelin	
3. Fran Davenport	151' 1"
West Germany 66 — USA 38	

USA vs. Great Britain: London, July 21-22

100-yard dash	
1. Willye White	10.9
2. Ernestine Pollards	11.0
220-yard dash	
1. Ernestine Pollards	24.2
2. Vivian Brown	24.6
80-meter hurdles	
3. Cherrie Parrish	11.3
4. JoAnn Terry	11.4
880-yard run	
3. Billie Pat Daniels	2:22.6
4. Sharon Shepherd	3:06
440-yard relay	
1. USA	45.5
(White, Pollards, Brown, Rudolph)	

High jump
3. Barbara Browne   5' 3"
4. Denise Parker   4' 9"

Shot put
2. Sharon Shepherd   45' 2¼"
3. Cindy Wyatt   44' 3½"

Javelin
3. Fran Davenport   144' 3½"
4. Karen Mendyka   134' ½"

Broad jump
1. Willye White   21' 1¾" AR
4. Edith McGuire   17' 5½"

Discus
1. Sharon Shepherd   154' 5"
4. Melody McCarthy   118' 7½"

USA 50— Great Britain 56

Colorado State University hosted the national pentathlon championships on September 30. The pentathlon was officially added to the Olympic program for 1964.

1961 All-America Women's Track and Field Teams

Outdoor

50-yard dash	Edith McGuire
50-yard hurdles	Tammy Davis
75-yard dash	A. Miller
80-meter hurdles	Cherrie Parrish
100-yard dash	Wilma Rudolph
100-meter dash	Wilma Rudolph
200-meter dash	Ernestine Pollards
220-yard dash	Lacey O'Neal
440-yard run	Jackie Peterson
800-meter run	Billie Pat Daniels
880-yard run	Billie Pat Daniels
400-meter relay	Willye White, Ernestine Pollards, Vivian Brown, Wilma Rudolph
Broad jump	Willye White
High jump	Barbara Browne
8-lb. shot put	Cynthia Wyatt
4-kilo shot put	Earlene Brown
Discus throw	Sharon Shepherd
Javelin throw	Fran Davenport
Baseball throw	L. Puckett
Pentathlon	Billie Pat Daniels

Indoor

50-yard dash	Willye White
70-yard hurdles	JoAnn Terry
100-yard dash	Wilma Rudolph
220-yard dash	Vivian Brown
440-yard run	Lillian Greene
880-yard run	Helen Shipley
Shot put	Cynthia Wyatt
High jump	Rose Robinson
Standing broad jump	Sandra Smith
Basketball throw	Jean Hofbauer

As a result of Wilma Rudolph winning three gold medals in the 1960 Olympic Games, meet directors added women's events to their programs. An illustration of this can be found in the Second Annual Los Angeles Invitational Indoor Track and Field Meet on January 21. Ed Temple was designated as the honorary meet referee, but even though two pages of the program were devoted to stories on Ed and Wilma, there was only one women's event: the 60-yard dash, featuring Wilma.

The first Annual Mason-Dixon Games in Louisville, Kentucky, featured Wilma Rudolph in a 70-yard dash. She set an indoor world record that evening with a time of 7.8. Rose Lovelace was the victor in 2:24.8 in the other women's event, the 880-yard run.

The Millrose Games, after thirty years of an all-male program, featured Wilma in a 60-yard dash which she won in 6.9, tying her two-week-old American and world record twice — once in the semifinal and again in the final. Vivian Brown was second, Barbara Browne third, and Louise Mead fourth.

The major outdoor meets showed the same pattern. During the First Annual Mt. San Antonio Relays on April 24-25, 1959, fifty-six events were contested on the two days; none were women's events. During the third Annual Mt. San Antonio relays, on April 28-29, 1961, however, 113 events were scheduled and one was a women's event, the 440-yard dash. Six women were entered: Ruth Ann Brand, Irene Robertson, Judy Shapiro, Doris Severtsen, Pat Daniels, and Gertie Derrington.

The history-making news of the year was the awarding of the Sullivan Trophy to Wilma Rudolph. Wilma was the first track and field woman to receive the prestigious award.

The *Amateur Athletic Union Handbook* reported on the award:

> Wilma Rudolph Ward, 100 meter world record holder and the outstanding woman track athlete in the United States, was voted the 1961 James E. Sullivan Award.
>
> A senior at Tennessee State, Wilma is a native of Clarksville, Tennessee.
>
> The Sullivan Award is presented annually by the Amateur Athletic Union of the United States to "the amateur athlete who, by performance, example, and good influence did the most to advance the cause of good sportsmanship during the year." It is in memory of James E. Sullivan, a founder of the AAU and a leader in its activities for over a quarter of a century.

The former Wilma Rudolph who recently announced her marriage, was named first on 205 of 676 ballots, second on 161 and received 119 votes for third for a total of 1627 points, based on a 5-3-1 scoring. Her total was the fourth highest number of points accumulated in the 32 years of balloting among former Sullivan Award winners, amateur sportsmen, sportswriters and sportscasters.

A year ago Wilma was runner-up to Rafer Johnson, 1960 Olympic decathlon champion. She is only the third woman to earn the nation's most coveted award for amateur athletes. Ann Curtis, a swimmer, was named in 1944, while Mrs. Patricia Keller McCormick earned the award five years ago....

Miss Rudolph equaled the world record for 100 meters in winning her specialty against the USSR at Moscow July 15, and then four days later in Stuttgart, Germany, was clocked in 11.2 seconds for a new record. She also anchored the United States women's 400 meter relay team to a world record of 44.3 seconds in defeating the USSR at Moscow.

Earlier this year Miss Rudolph was awarded the 1961 Columbus Award of the City of Genoa, Italy, for her outstanding contribution to athletics. The only other individual athlete to have been selected for this trophy was the Russian distance runner, Vladimir Kuts in 1958.

In an Associated Press poll this year, Wilma Rudolph was named Woman Athlete for 1961.

Frances Kaszubski's report at the 74th Annual AAU Convention in Washington, D.C., reaffirmed the cooperation between the AAU and the AAHPER's Division of Girls and Women's Sports. Both she and Wilma Rudolph were invited to demonstrate and teach track and field at the national convention in Atlantic City in March. Kaszubski said, "It is understood that this Section meeting was rated 'best' of the entire AAHPER convention."

Chairman Kaszubski said, "A majority of this committee's members are still trying to recover from the startling effects of Wilma Rudolph's triple gold medal victories in the Rome Olympics. As active members, they have been carried into still more activity within their districts. Several others, heretofore inactive, have been aroused by the din and clamor of girls asking for competition and teachers seeking not only competition for their outstanding students but requesting information and clinics."

Track Mirror, a four-page newsletter, was inaugurated in September 1961. Patricia Jones (Rico) was the editor, and Leo F. Larney was the manager.

Dr. Richard You, chairman of the track and field committee in Hawaii, was instrumental in having Cel Rutledge, Ernestine Pollards, Ann Roniger, Cindy Wyatt, and Anna Reid matriculate in 1961 at the University of Hawaii. All were freshman except Ann Roniger, who transferred from Colorado State University as a sophomore. Donnis Thompson joined the staff of the department of physical education at the school.

American Records

50y	5.7*	Isabelle Daniels	April 6, 1957
100y	10.5	Ernestine Pollards	June 11, 1960
100y	11.1*	Jean Patton	Feb. 12, 1951

		Mae Faggs	March 15, 1952
		Isabelle Daniels	January 21, 1956
100m	11.3	Wilma Rudolph	Sept. 2, 1960
200m	22.9	Wilma Rudolph	July 9, 1960
220y	24.3	Stella Walsh	June 9, 1935
220y	24.3	Lucinda Williams	July 5, 1958
220y	25.8*	Stella Walsh	March 16, 1941
220y	25.9	Mae Faggs	March 26, 1949
400m	56.7	Pat Daniels	August 12, 1960
440y	61.3*	Louise Mead	January 2, 1960
800m	2:14.4	Pat Daniels	August 5, 1960
880y	2:19.5	Doris Severtsen	June 11, 1960
880y	2:25.4*	Grace Butcher	February 13, 1960
50yh	6.9*	Nancy Cowperthwaite	February 23, 1948
70yh	9 3/5*	Helen Filkey	April 23, 1926
	9. 6*	Barbara Mueller	January 21, 1956
		Nancy Phillips	January 21, 1956
80mh	11.4	Barbara Mueller	August 31, 1959
		Shirley Crowder	July 16, 1960
		JoAnn Terry	July 9, 1960
		Irene Robertson	July 16, 1960
		JoAnn Terry	August 31, 1960
		JoAnn Terry	September 11, 1960
		Irene Robertson	September 11, 1960
HJ	5' 9¼"	Mildred McDaniel	December 1, 1956
	5' 4¾*	Rose Robinson	April 4, 1959
BJ	20' 4½"	Willye White	July 15, 1960
SBJ	9' ¼"*	Dorothy Lyford	January 25, 1933
SBJ	9' ½"*	Shirley Hereford	March 22, 1958
4K SP	54' 9"	Earlene Brown	September 22, 1960
	49' 6"*	Earlene Brown	March 22, 1958
Discus	176' 10"	Earlene Brown	July 16, 1960
Javelin	166' 1"	Karen Oldham	September 1, 1960
BB throw	135'2"*	Earlene Brown	March 22, 1958

Relays

400m	44.4	USA (TSU)	September 7, 1960
		(Hudson, Williams, Jones, Rudolph)	
440y	45.7	USA (TSU)	August 6, 1960
		(Hudson, Williams, Rudolph, Jones)	
440y	50.0*	Tennessee State University	April 6, 1957
		(Williams, Jones, Matthews, Daniels)	
800m med.	1:47.3	Tennessee State University	July 9, 1960
		(Crowder, Hudson, Jones, Hart)	

*Indoor record

Chapter 45

1962

The national senior and girls outdoor championship meet was held on July 7-8 at Los Angeles. Headlines in the *New York Times* featured Vivian Brown's new record of 24.1 in the 220-yard dash, Leah Bennett's record of 2:12.3 in the 880, and Wilma Rudolph's 100-yard dash victory.

Vivian Brown's time broke the record of 24.3 set by Stella Walsh in 1935 and equaled by Lucinda Williams in 1958.

Wilma Rudolph equaled her record of 10.7 in a heat of the 100.

100-yard dash
1. Wilma Rudolph, Tennessee State   10.8
2. Edith McGuire, Tennessee State   10.9
3. Vivian Brown, Tennessee State   11.1
4. Willye White, Mayor Daley Youth Foundation   11.1

880-yard run
1. Leah Bennett, University of Hawaii   2:12.3 AR
2. Sandra Knott, Cleveland Recreation   2:14.5
3. Suzanne Pfleiger, San Mateo A.A.   2:16.6
4. Doris Severtsen, Falcon Track Club   2:17.7

80-meter hurdles
1. Cherrie Parrish, Laurel Track Club   11.3
2. Ikuko Yoda, Japan   11.3
3. JoAnn Terry, Tennessee State   11.6
4. Karen Frisch, Falcon Track Club   11.7

220-yard dash
1. Vivian Brown, Tennessee State   24.1 AR
2. Carol Smith, California Spikers   24.8
3. Janell Smith, unattached, Kansas   25.0
4. Norma Harris, Mayor Daley Youth Foundation   25.2

440-yard dash
1. Suzanne Knott, Ohio Track Club   58.1
2. Carol Bush, Mayor Daley Youth Foundation   58.3
3. Ann Tegelius, Montclair College   58.7
4. Kathleen Krajewski, unattached, Buffalo   59.0

440-yard relay
1. Tennessee State   46.0 MR
   (Tyus, Rudolph, McGuire, Brown)
2. Mayor Daley Youth Foundation, "B" team   50.0
3. San Mateo Girls' A.A.   51.0
4. Texas Track Club   51.2

880-yard medley relay
1. Mayor Daley Youth Foundation, "A" team   1:47.1 AR
2. Mayor Daley Youth Foundation, "B" team   1:51.2
3. Laurel Track Club   1:52.1
4. Ohio Track Club   1:53.2

Shot put
1. Earlene Brown, California Spikers   48' 10¾"
2. Cynthia Wyatt, Univ. of Hawaii   48' 6"
3. Sharon Shepherd, Cleveland Recreation   48' 2½"
4. Cel Rutledge, Univ. of Hawaii   47' 10"

Broad jump
1. Willye White, Mayor Daley Youth Foundation   20' 3" MR
2. Fumiko Ito, Japan   19' 6½"
3. Sachiko Kishimoto, Japan   19' 6"
4. Edith McGuire, Tennessee State   18' 11½"

Discus
1. Olga Connolly, Pasadena Track Club   172' 2" MR
2. Earlene Brown, California Spikers   154' 5"
3. Seiko Obonai, Tokyo   150' 3"
4. Sharon Shepherd, Cleveland Recreation   147' 9½"

Javelin
1. Karen Mendyka, Univ. of Hawaii   158' 5"
2. RaNae Bair, San Diego Track and Field   152' 7"
3. Fran Davenport, Vista Chamber of Commerce   145' 8"
4. Cel Rutledge, Univ. of Hawaii   136' 9½"

High jump
1. Kinuko Tsutsumi, Japan   5' 3"
2. Barbara Browne, N.Y. Police Athletic League   5' 2"
3. Rose Robinson, unattached, Philadelphia   5' 2"
4. Billie Pat Daniels, San Mateo A.A.   5' 2"

Team scores:
Tennessee State University 64; Mayor Daley Youth Foundation 58; University of
Hawaii 42; Cleveland Recreation 28; California Spikers 27; San Mateo A.A., Ohio
Track Club, and Laurel Track Club 19.

Girls' Division

50-yard dash
1. Wyomia Tyus, Tennessee State   5.8 AJR

2. Debbie Thompson, Frederick Track Club   6.0
3. Flossie Wilcher, Tennessee State   6.2

75-yard dash
1. Wyomia Tyus, Tennessee State   8.3 AJR
2. Debbie Thompson, Frederick Track Club   8.5
3. Janell Smith, unattached, Kansas   8.5

100-yard dash
1. Wyomia Tyus, Tennessee State   11.0
2. Norma Harris, Mayor Daley Youth Foundation   11.4
3. Carol Bradshaw, Oakland Oakettes   11.5

220-yard dash (new event)
1. Norma Harris, Mayor Daley Youth Foundation   25.0 AJR
2. Janice Harris, Mayor Charcharis Youth Foundation 25.1
3. Wanda Fuller, Ohio Track Club   26.0

50-yard hurdles
1. Tamara Davis, Frederick Track Club   6.9 AJR
2. Susan Mack, San Mateo A.A.   7.2
3. Mary Rose, Texas Track Club   7.3

440-yard relay
1. Ohio Track Club, "A" team   49.0 AJR
   (Long, Williams, Fuller, Fears)
2. Oakland Oakettes   50.0
3. Mayor Charcharis Youth Foundation   50.2

Shot put
1. Glenda Etheridge, San Diego Track & Field   39' 1½"
2. Carol Moseke, Cedar Rapids   38' 11½"
3. Sally Sutton, Los Pocos Diablos   36' 8"

Discus
1. Melody McCarthy, San Fernando Women's A.C.   129' 6½"
2. Nancy Norberg, unattached, Palo Alto   119' 8"
3. Daryl Pennington, Los Pocos Diablos   113' 9½"

Baseball throw
1. Daryl Pennington, Los Pocos Diablos   253' 2½"
2. Kathleen Mirko, Los Pocos Diablos   233' 8"
3. Sally Sutton, Los Pocos Diablos   232' 6½"

Javelin
1. Kathleen Stevens, California Spikers   131' 2½"
2. Jan Kendrick, California Spikers   130' ½"
3. Judy Twenty, Frederick Track Club   120' 1"

Broad jump
1. Eleanor Montgomery, Cleveland Recreation   18' 1½"
2. Martha Watson, Long Beach Comets   18' 1"
3. Flossie Wilcher, Tennessee State   17' 10"

High jump
1. Lynette Jerry, Metairie, La.   5'
2. Estelle Baskerville, Ohio Track Club   5'
3. Denise Parker, unattached, San Diego   5'

Team scores:
Los Pocos Diablos 45; Tennessee State University 44; Frederick Track Club 40; Ohio Track Club 39; Oakland Oakettes 24; California Spikers 20.

The Indoor Nationals

The national indoor championship meet was held in Louisville, Kentucky, on February 17, 1962. "Four Records Set in Women's Track" proclaimed the *New York Times* on February 18: "Four world records fell today and tonight. ... Leah Bennett of the University of Hawaii ran the half mile in 2:17.5 to shatter the old mark of 2:21.1 by Grace Butcher of Cleveland in 1961."

Suzanne Knott, a Columbus, Ohio, high school senior set a record in the 440; JoAnn Terry broke a record in the hurdles, and Tennessee State established a new record in the 440-yard relay.

50-yard dash
1. Willye White, Mayor Daley Youth Foundation   5.9
2. Debbie Thompson, Frederick Track Club   6.0
3. Lorene Holmes, Tennessee State   6.0

100-yard dash
1. Willye White, Mayor Daley Youth Foundation   11.2
2. Lacey O'Neal, Univ. of Hawaii   11.3
3. Lorene Holmes, Tennessee State   11.6

220-yard dash
1. Vivian Brown, Tennessee State   25.5
2. Lacey O'Neal, Univ. of Hawaii   25.9
3. Lorraine Dunn, Tennessee State   26.6

440-yard run
1. Sue Knott, Ohio Track Club   58.2 AR
2. Carol Bush, Mayor Daley Youth Foundation   59.7
3. Pat Douthitt, Univ. of Hawaii   61.0

880-yard run
1. Leah Bennett, Univ. of Hawaii   2:17.5 AR
2. Sandra Knott, Cleveland Recreation   2:18.0
3. Sue May, Liberty A.C.   2:18.4

70-yard hurdles
1. JoAnn Terry, Tennessee State   9.2 AR
2. Cherrie Parrish, Chico State   9.4
3. Leontyne Reif, Mayor Daley Youth Foundation   9.4

440-yard relay
1. Tennessee State   46.0 AR
  (Holmes, Dunn, McGuire, Brown)
2. Ohio Track Club, "A" team   50.7
3. Mayor Daley Youth Foundation   51.0

880-yard medley relay
1. Ohio Track Club, "A" team   1:53.8
  (Davis, Long, Watkins, Fuller)
2. Ohio Track Club, "B" team   1:57.4
3. Mayor Chacharis Youth Foundation   1:58.4

4-kilo shot put
1. Sharon Shepherd, Cleveland Recreation   43' 9"
2. Cindy Wyatt, Univ. of Hawaii   43' 5"
3. Joan Whitehead, Montclair College   41' 8¾"

High jump
1. Estelle Baskerville, Ohio Track Club   5' 2"
2. JoAnne Terry, Tennessee State   5'
3. Eleanor Montgomery, Cleveland Recreation,   4' 10"
  L. Lewis, unattached, Miami,
  and H. Walker, Central Jersey

Basketball throw
1. Cindy Wyatt, Univ. of Hawaii   105' 7½"
2. Delia Burchfield, Cosmopolitan Club   100' 11"
3. Linda DeLong, Ohio Track Club   98' 4"

Broad jump
1. Willye White, Mayor Daley Youth Foundation   19' 6½"
2. JoAnn Terry, Tennessee State   18' 5¾"
3. Edith McGuire, Tennessee State   18' 5½"

Team scores:
Tennessee State University 30; Mayor Daley Youth Foundation 26; Ohio Track Club 24; University of Hawaii 21; Cleveland Division of Recreation 10; Topeka Cosmopolitan Club 4.

USA vs. USSR: Palo Alto, California, July 21-22

The meet was held in the Stanford University stadium before enthusiastic crowds of over 70,000 for both days.

In the 100 meters, Wilma Rudolph came from behind, and in the last twenty meters she passed the Russian athlete and won by eight feet.

100-meter dash
1. Wilma Rudolph   11.5
3. Edith McGuire   11.8

200-meter dash
1. Vivian Brown   23.7
4. Carol Smith   24.5

800-meter run
3. Leah Bennett   2:10.4 AR
4. Sandra Knott   2:11.6

400-meter relay
1. USA   44.6
    (White, McGuire, Brown, Rudolph-Ward)

80-meter hurdles
3. Cherrie Parrish   11.2
4. JoAnn Terry   11.3

Javelin throw
3. RaNae Bair   147' 1"
4. Karen Mendyka   142' 7½"

High jump
3. Barbara Browne   5' 3"
4. Estelle Baskerville   5' 1"

Discus
2. Olga Connolly   167' 1½"
4. Sharon Shepherd   151' 3"

Shot put
3. Earlene Brown   48' 11"
4. Cynthia Wyatt   46' 10¼"

Broad jump
2. Willye White   20' 3½"
4. Edith McGuire   18' 9½"

USSR 66 — USA 41

USA vs. Poland: Chicago, June 30–July 1

100-meter dash
2. Edith McGuire   11.8
4. Janell Smith   12.2

200-meter dash
1. Vivian Brown   23.9
3. Janell Smith   24.5

800-meter run
3. Leah Bennett   2:12.7
4. Sandra Knott   2:14.1

80-meter hurdles
2. Cherrie Parrish   11.2
4. JoAnn Terry   11.4

Broad jump
1. Willye White   19' 10½"
4. Edith McGuire   18' 3½"

High jump
2. Barbara Browne   5' 3¼"
4. Estelle Baskerville   5' 1"

Discus
3. Sharon Shepherd   145' 8½"
4. Melody McCarthy   141' 3"

Javelin
1. Fran Davenport   149' 9"
4. Karen Mendyka

Poland 61— USA 45

1962 All-America Women's Track and Field Teams

100-yard dash	Wilma Rudolph
100-meter dash	Wilma Rudolph
220-yard dash	Vivian Brown
200-meter dash	Vivian Brown
440-yard run	Suzanne Knott
400-meter run	Lacey O'Neal
880-yard run	Leah Bennett
800-meter run	Leah Bennett
80-meter hurdles	Cherrie Parrish
Javelin throw	Frances Davenport
Discus throw	Olga Connolly
Shot put	Cynthia Wyatt
Broad jump	Willye White
High jump	Barbara Browne
Pentathlon	Kathy Facciolli

Girls' Division

50-yard dash	Wyomia Tyus
75-yard dash	Wyomia Tyus
100-yard dash	Wyomia Tyus
220-yard dash	Norma Harris
50-yard hurdles	Tammy Davis
Javelin throw	Kathleen Stevens
Discus throw	Melody McCarthy
8-lb. shot put	Glenda Ethridge
Broad jump	Eleanor Montgomery
High jump	Lynette Jerry
Baseball throw	Daryl Pennington

A women's track and field top performance list, compiled by Lt. Col. Alvin Lloyd, appeared for the first time in the *Amateur Athletic Union Handbook*:

Willye White winning the 100-yard dash in the 1962 Penn Relays. This was the first women's event held. *From right:* Willye White (1), Barbara Browne (3), Darlene Tucker (4), Debbie Thompson (2), Claudette Littlejohn, Jackie Peterson, and Louise Mead (5). (Courtesy of Dave Johnson.)

100-yard dash	
10.7	Wilma Rudolph
10.8	Willye White
10.9	Janell Smith
10.9	Edith McGuire
10.9	Irene Obera

100-meters	
11.4	Wilma Rudolph
11.8	Edith McGuire
11.9	Irene Obera
12.1	Janice Rinehart
12.2	Carol Smith

220-yard dash	
24.1	Vivian Brown
24.3	Janell Smith
24.8	Carol Smith
25.2	Norma Harris
25.3	Janice Rinehart

200-meter dash	
23.7	Vivian Brown
24.5	Janell Smith
24.5	Carol Smith
25.2	Irene Obera
25.2	Jenny Lowe

440-yard run	
58.1	Sue Knott
58.3	Carol Bush
58.7	Ann Tegelius
59.0	Kathy Krajewski
59.6	Ruth Brand

400-meter run	
58.5	Lacey O'Neal
58.5	Leah Bennett
58.6	Sue Knott
60.0	Ruth Brand
61.2	Suzanne Pfleiger

880-yard run	
2:12.3	Leah Bennett
2:14.5	Sandra Knott
2:16.6	Suzanne Pfleiger
2:17.7	Doris Severtsen
2:18.4	Susan May

800-meter run
2:10.4   Leah Bennett
2:11.6   Sandra Knott
2:19.6   Suzanne Pfleiger
2:27.9   Judy Shapiro
2:29.0   A. Balasque

80-meter hurdles
11.2   Cherrie Parrish
11.3   JoAnn Terry
11.3w   Tammy Davis
11.7   Karen Frisch
11.7   Leontyne Reif

440-yard relay
46.0   Tennessee State
49.4   Mayor Daley Youth Foundation, "A" team
49.8   Ohio Track Club
50.0   Mayor Daley Youth Foundation, "B" team
50.2   Laurel Track Club

400-meter relay
44.6   USA (White, Rudolph, McGuire, Brown)
49.3   Laurel Track Club
49.4   Oakland Oakettes
50.3   Compton Track & Field Club
51.5   Texas Track Club

880-yard medley relay
1:47.1   Mayor Daley Youth Foundation, "A" team
1:52.2   Mayor Daley Youth Foundation, "B" team
1:52.1   Laurel Track Club
1:53.2   Ohio Track Club
1:53.4   Texas Track Club

Javelin		48' 6"	Cindy Wyatt
160' 4½"	Fran Davenport	48' 3¼"	Sharon Shepherd
158' 5"	Karen Mendyka	45' ¼"	Joan Whitehead
152' 7"	RaNae Bair	**Broad jump**	
140' 6"	Cel Rutledge	20' 5¾"	Edith McGuire
135' 9"	Daryl Pennington	20' 3½"	Willye White
Discus		18' 5¾"	JoAnn Terry
172' 2"	Olga Connolly	18' 5½"	Martha Watson
158' ½"	Sharon Shepherd	18'	Norma Harris
154' 5"	Earlene Brown	**High jump**	
147' 4½"	Helen Thayer	5' 3¼"	Barbara Browne
142' 10¼"	Cindy Wyatt	5' 2½"	Linda DeLong
4-kilo shot		5' 2"	Estelle Baskerville
49' 5¾"	Cel Rutledge	5' 2"	Rose Robinson
48' 11"	Earlene Brown	5' 2"	C. Ley

A listing was also compiled for the girls' division.

The 4th Annual Mt. San Antonio Relays were held on April 27-28 with 130 events listed for the two-day event. Two women's events, the discus throw and the 220-yard dash, were contested. This is one more women's event than the previous year.

The Mason-Dixon Games held in Louisville, Kentucky, on February 17 produced four women's indoor world records. Suzanne Knott won the 440-yard run in the record time of 58.2, JoAnn Terry captured the 70-yard hurdles in 9.2, Tennessee State blazed to victory in the 440-yard relay in 48.6, and Leah Bennett won the 880-yard run in 2:17.5.

Willye White tied Wilma Rudolph's world record in the 60-yard dash on February 24, before the largest crowd in the history of the men's nationals. The other women's event on the program was a 440-yard run won by Sue Knott.

For the first time, women's events were held in the *Los Angeles Times* Indoor Meet on February 10. The Southern California Spikers won the 640-yard relay. A girls' 320-yard relay was the second event.

Two events were held in the Cleveland Knights of Columbus Meet on March 16. Sandra Knott set a new 880-world record of 2:17.4 (bettering Bennett's mark set on February 17), and the Mayor Daley Youth Foundation set a new record in the four-lap relay.

The 68th Annual Penn Relays were held on April 27-28. For the first time since 1895, an invitational women's event was on the program. The 100-yard dash had nine "invited" competitors. Willye White won the event in 10.9. The author placed fifth.

At the bottom of a lengthy column, the March 1962 issue of *Track and Field News* reported, "Wilma Rudolph Ward has been named winner of the James E. Sullivan Award for 1961, which goes to the outstanding amateur of the year."

Another issue reported that "Grace Butcher recently clocked 5:04.0 for the mile in a workout. It is believed to be the first mile time ever posted by an American woman."

Chapter 46

1963

Welcome Stadium in Dayton, Ohio, was the site of the outdoor championships on July 6. The *Amateur Athletic Union Handbook* said that Welcome Stadium "proved just that" for Edith McGuire and Sharon Shepherd, who were double winners with outstanding performances. Two former champions, Vivian Brown and Suzanne Knott, retained their titles, while Sharon Shepherd, a five-year veteran of international teams, won her first two national crowns in the shot and discus. Sharon had been in the second-place spot for her past competitive years.

Three national marks were set. Suzanne Knott ran the 440 in 57 flat, sixteen-year-old Eleanor Montgomery, the Pan American champion, jumped 5' 8" to win the high jump, and Fran Davenport threw the javelin 166' 2½".

This was the largest entry ever in the women's and girls' championships.

100-yard dash
1. Edith McGuire, Tennessee State | 11.0
2. Wyomia Tyus, Tennessee State | 11.0
3. Marilyn White, L.A. Mercurettes | 11.0
4. Willye White, Mayor Daley Youth Foundation | 11.1

220-yard dash
1. Vivian Brown, Tennessee State | 24.4
2. Marilyn White, L.A. Mercurettes | 24.6
3. Diana Wilson, L.A. Mercurettes | 24.6
4. Norma Harris, Mayor Daley Youth Foundation | 24.8

440-yard run
1. Suzanne Knott, Ohio Track Club | 57.0 ties MR & AR
2. Myrtle Lowe, Oakland Oakettes | 57.2
3. Carol Bush, Mayor Daley Youth Foundation | 57.6
4. Jackie Peterson, N.Y. Police Athletic League | 58.0

880-yard run
1. Sandra Knott, Ohio Track Club | 2:12.5
2. Carol Mastronarde, L.A. Mercurettes | 2:12.9
3. Leah Bennett Ferris, Univ. of Hawaii | 2:16.1
4. Cynthia Hegarty, Univ. of Hawaii | 2:18.3

80-meter hurdles
1. Rosie Bonds, Laura Scudders   11.3
2. JoAnn Terry, Tennessee State   11.5
3. Chi Cheng, L.A. Mercurettes   11.8

220-yard low hurdles (did not count in team scoring)
1. Sally Griffith, Santa Clara Valley Track Club   29.5
2. Laura Voss, Ohio Track Club   30.3
3. Mary Rose, Texas Track Club   30.7
4. Cheryl Hoy, Frederick Track Club   31.5

440-yard relay
1. Tennessee State, "A" team   46.7
    (Wilcher, Tyus, Brown, McGuire)
2. Tennessee State, "B" team   47.7
3. Texas Track Club   48.8
4. Santa Ynez H.S.   48.9

880-yard medley relay
1. Mayor Daley Youth Foundation   1:46.9 AR
    (Robinson, May, Childred, Bush)
2. Compton Track Club   1:47.1
3. Oakland Oakettes   1:48.1
4. L.A. Mercurettes   1:49.9

Shot put
1. Sharon Shepherd, Cleveland Recreation   48' 3½"
2. Cynthia Wyatt, Univ. of Hawaii   46' 5½"
3. Earlene Brown, Laura Scudders   45' 5"
4. Joan Whitehead, Montclair Track Club   40' 5¾"

Discus throw
1. Sharon Shepherd, Cleveland Recreation   150' 6"
2. Cynthia Wyatt, Univ. of Hawaii   146' 9"
3. Melody McCarthy, San Fernando Valley W.A.C. 145' 9"
4. Earlene Brown, Laura Scudders   143' 10"

Javelin throw
1. Fran Davenport, U.S. Army   166' 2½" MR
2. RaNae Bair, San Diego Track & Field   153' 10½"
3. Gloria Wilcox, So. Pacific AAU   151' 11"
4. Elsa Backus, New England AAU   137' 10½"

High jump
1. Eleanor Montgomery, Cleveland Recreation 5' 8" MR
2. Pat Daniels, San Mateo Girls' A.A.   5' 6"
3. Estelle Baskerville, Ohio Track Club   5' 5"
4. Terrezene Brown, L.A. Mercurettes   5' 4"

Broad jump
1. Edith McGuire, Tennessee State   19' 4¾"
2. Willye White, Mayor Daley Youth Foundation 19' ¼"
3. Chi Cheng, L.A. Mercurettes   18' 8¾"
4. Pat Wilson, San Mateo Girls' A.A.   18' 7¼"

Team scores:
Tennessee State University 68; Los Angeles Mercurettes 48; Cleveland Recreation 40; Mayor Daley Youth Foundation 36; University of Hawaii 26; Laura Scudders 20; Ohio Track Club 18; San Mateo Girls' A.A. 16; Oakland Oakettes 14.

The national girls' championships were held at the same site on July 4-5. The 440-yard dash was held for the first time.

50-yard dash
1. Linda Bradshaw, Oakland Oakettes   5.9
2. Flossie Wilcher, Tennessee State   5.9
3. Diana Wilson, L.A. Mercurettes   5.9

75-yard dash
1. Wyomia Tyus, Tennessee State   8.3w
2. Dee Barnett, Santa Ynez H.S.   8.4
3. Debbie Thompson, Frederick Track Club   8.5

100-yard dash
1. Wyomia Tyus, Tennessee State   10.9 ties AJR
2. Nina Austin, Cleveland Recreation   11.2
3. Shirley Wilson, Compton Track Club   11.3

220-yard dash
1. Shirley Wilson, Compton Track Club   24.3 AJR
2. Norma Harris, Mayor Daley Youth Foundation 24.4
3. Diana Wilson, L.A. Mercurettes   24.7

440-yard dash
1. Sally Griffith, Santa Clara Valley   58.7 AJR
2. Carolyn Fumbanks, Mayor Daley Youth Foundation 59.0
3. Pat Elmore, Will's Spikettes   59.1

440-yard relay
1. Tennessee State   47.3 AJR
   (Wilcher, Render, Crews, Tyus)
2. Compton Track Club   48.3
3. Mayor Daley Youth Foundation   48.4

Baseball throw
1. Kathleen Mirko, Los Pocos Diablos   242' 5"
2. Daryl Pennington, Los Pocos Diablos   239' 8½"
3. Loretta Atkins, Denver Striders   238' 8½"

Javelin throw
1. Lurline Hamilton, Louisiana Track Club   139' 4½"
2. Daryl Pennington, Los Pocos Diablos   139' 0"
3. Sally Sutton, Los Pocos Diablos   131' 7"

8-lb. shot put
1. Sally Sutton, Los Pocos Diablos   40' ½"
2. Marilyn Cross, Rocky Mountain AAU   38' 4½"
3. Janis Filler, San Mateo Girls' A.A.   36' 3½"

Discus throw
1. Nancy Norberg, Pacific AAU   139'
2. Diane Congdon, Laurel Track Club   122' 7½"
3. Elinor Slack, San Mateo Girls' A.A.   120' 3½"

Broad jump
1. Martha Watson, Long Beach Comets   19' ¼"
2. Pat Wilson, San Mateo Girls' A.A.   18' 7¼"
3. Sonia Guss, Long Beach Comets   18' 4¼"

High jump
1. Eleanor Montgomery, Cleveland Recreation   5' 7" AJR
2. Terrezene Brown, L.A. Mercurettes   5' 6"
3. Sarah Cantrell, Tennessee State   5' 3"

Team scores:
Tennessee State University 54; Los Pocos Diablos 48; Compton Track Club 30; San Mateo Girls' A.A. 27; Cleveland Recreation 22; Los Angeles Mercurettes and Long Beach Comets 20; Oakland Oakettes 18; Frederick Track Club 17.

The Indoor Nationals

The indoor national meet was at French Field House, Columbus, Ohio, on March 22–23. The meet served as the trials for the Pan American Games.

50-yards
1. Willye White, Mayor Daley Youth Foundation   5.9
2. Debra Thompson, Frederick Track Club   6.0
3. Flossie Wilcher, Tennessee State   6.1

100-yard dash
1. Edith McGuire, Tennessee State   11.1
2. Willye White, Mayor Daley Youth Foundation   11.1
3. Marilyn White, L.A. Mercurettes   11.1

220-yard dash
1. Marilyn White, L.A. Mercurettes   24.8 AR
2. Norma Harris, Mayor Daley Youth Foundation   24.9
3. Vivian Brown, Tennessee State   25.5

440-yard dash
1. Suzanne Knott, Ohio Track Club   57.0 AR
2. Karen Davis, Ohio Track Club   58.2
3. Carol Bush, Mayor Daley Youth Foundation   58.2

880-yard run
1. Leah Bennett Ferris, Univ. of Hawaii   2:13.6 AR
2. Cynthia Hegarty, Univ. of Hawaii   2:14.4
3. Sandra Knott, Ohio Track Club   2:14.7

70-yard hurdles
1. Janell Smith, Mo. Valley AAU, Kansas   9.2 ties AR & MR

2. JoAnn Terry, Tennessee State   9.2
3. Tammy Davis, Frederick Track Club   9.3

440-yard relay
1. L.A. Mercurettes   48.3 AR
   (Wilson, Billingsley, Lawson, M. White)
2. Tennessee State   49.0
3. Ohio Track Club, "A" team   49.7

880-yard medley relay
1. Ohio Track Club, "B" team   1:50.6 AR
   (Knott, Thompson, Voss, Davis)
2. Mayor Daley Youth Foundation   1:51.1
3. Ohio Track Club   1:52.6

Shot put
1. Cynthia Wyatt, Univ. of Hawaii   47' 1¼"
2. Sharon Shepherd, Cleveland Recreation   46' 4¼"
3. Joan Whitehead, Montclair College   42' 8¾"

High jump
1. Eleanor Montgomery, Cleveland Recreation   5' 5½"
2. Estelle Baskerville, Ohio Track Club   5' 4½"
3. Billie Pat Daniels, San Mateo Girls' A.A.   5' 3½"

Broad jump
1. Edith McGuire, Tennessee State   19' 4"
2. Willye White, Mayor Daley Youth Foundation   19' 2"
3. Martha Watson, Long Beach Comets   18' 9"

Basketball throw
1. Linda DeLong, Ohio Track Club   103' 2"
2. Delia Burchfield, Cosmopolitan Club   102' 9"
3. Cynthia Wyatt, Univ. of Hawaii   101' 3"

Additional events for Pan American games:

Javelin throw
1. Frances Davenport, U.S. Army   147' 10½"
2. RaNae Bair, San Diego Track Club   145' 11"
3. Colette Freitas, Santa Clara Valley Track Club 127' 9"

Discus
1. Cynthia Wyatt, Univ. of Hawaii   149' ½"
2. Sharon Shepherd, Cleveland Recreation   144' 7½"
3. Melody McCarthy, San Fernando Valley A.C.   139' 9"

Team scores:
Ohio Track Club 26; Tennessee State University 23; Mayor Daley Youth Foundation 21; University of Hawaii 15; Los Angeles Mercurettes 14; Cleveland Recreation 10; Frederick Track Club 5.

The national pentathlon championship meet was held in Cleveland, Ohio, on July 10-11. Pat Daniels set a new American record with a total of 4,261 points.

Pat ran 12.7 for the 80-meter hurdles, 25.6 for the 200 meters, put the shot 38' ½", high jumped 5' 2", and broad jumped 17' 8¾". Barbara Browne of the New York Police Athletic League finished second with 4,192 points. Joyce Lawson of the Los Angeles Mercurettes was third with 3,901 points.

USA vs. USSR: Moscow, July 20-21

100 meters	
2. Edith McGuire	11.8
4. Wyomia Tyus	12.0
200 meters	
3. Vivian Brown	24.5
4. Diana Wilson	25.2
800 meters	
3. Cynthia Hegarty	2:18.0
Sandra Knott disqualified for two false starts	
80-meter hurdles	
JoAnn Terry did not finish	
Rosie Bonds disqualified for two false starts	
400-meter relay	
2. USA	45.2
(White, Tyus, V. Brown, McGuire)	
Javelin throw	
3. RaNae Bair	160' 5"
4. Fran Davenport	160' 2"
Discus throw	
3. Sharon Shepherd	147' 8½"
4. Cynthia Wyatt	138' 7"
Shot put	
3. Sharon Shepherd	46' 7¾"
4. Cynthia Wyatt	45' 10¾"
Broad jump	
3. Willye White	20'
4. Edith McGuire	18' 8"
High jump	
2. Eleanor Montgomery	5' 6¾"
4. Pat Daniels	5' 4¾"

USSR 75 — USA 28

USA vs. Poland: Warsaw, July 26-27

100 meters	
1. Edith McGuire	11.5
3. Wyomia Tyus	11.7
200 meters	
2. Vivian Brown	24.3
4. Diana Wilson	24.4
800 meters	
2. Sandra Knott	2:11.3
4. Cynthia Hegarty	2:16.8
80-meter hurdles	
3. JoAnn Terry	11.6
4. Rosie Bonds (disqualified)	
400-meter relay	
2. USA	46.2
(White, Tyus, McGuire, V. Brown)	
High jump	
1. Eleanor Montgomery	5' 8"
3. Pat Daniels	5' 4"
Broad jump	
1. Willye White	21' ¾"
4. Pat Daniels	18' 6¾"
Javelin throw	
1. Fran Davenport	166' 10¾" AR
3. RaNae Bair	156' 11"
Shot put	
2. Sharon Shepherd	46' 8¾"
3. Cynthia Wyatt	45' 6¼"
Discus throw	
3. Sharon Shepherd	148' 11¾"
4. Cynthia Wyatt	143' 6"

USA vs. West Germany: Braunschweig, July 30

100 meters	
1. Edith McGuire	11.6
3. Wyomia Tyus	11.8
200 meters	
2. Vivian Brown	24.6
4. Diane Wilson	25.1

400 meters
2. Suzanne Knott   56.3
3. Myrtle Lowe   56.4

800 meters
2. Sandra Knott   2:09.7
4. Cynthia Hegarty   2:13.7

80-meter hurdles
3. Tammy Davis   11.0 AR
4. Rosie Bonds   11.4

400-meter relay
2. USA   45.9
   (White, McGuire, Wilson, V. Brown)

Broad jump
1. Willye White   20' 9⅝"
4. Pat Daniels   17' 1"

High jump
1. Eleanor Montgomery   5' 7⅜"

Shot put
3. Sharon Shepherd   45' 9¼"
4. Cynthia Wyatt   44' 11"

Discus throw
3. Sharon Shepherd   147' 7¾"
4. Cynthia Wyatt   145' 7¼"

Javelin
3. Fran Davenport   165' ¼"
4. RaNae Bair   159' 10¼"

USA vs. Great Britain: London, August 3-5

100-yard dash
2. Edith McGuire   10.8
3. Wyomia Tyus   10.9

220-yard dash
3. Vivian Brown   24.3
4. Diana Wilson   24.6

440-yard dash
3. Myrtle Lowe   56.7
4. Suzanne Knott   56.8

880-yard run
1. Sandra Knott   2:10.7
4. Cynthia Hegarty   2:17.5

80-meter hurdles
1. Rosie Bonds   11.1
4. JoAnn Terry   11.3

440-yard relay
2. USA   45.7
  (White, Tyus, Wilson, McGuire)

Broad jump
2. Willye White   20' 9½"
4. JoAnn Terry   18' 4¼"

High jump
2. Eleanor Montgomery   5' 4"
  (tied for second place)
4. Pat Daniels   5' 4"

Discus throw
1. Sharon Shepherd   154' 6"
3. Cynthia Wyatt   145' 2½"

Shot put
1. Cynthia Wyatt   48' 4¼"
3. Sharon Shepherd   46' 8¼"

Javelin
2. Frances Davenport   161' ½"
3. RaNae Bair   160' 4"

Great Britain 65½— USA 51½

1963 All-America Women's Track and Field Teams

100 yards	Edith McGuire
220 yards	Diana Wilson
440 yards	Suzanne Knott
880 yards	Sandra Knott
800 meters	Leah Bennett Ferris
80-meter hurdles	JoAnn Terry
Javelin throw	Frances Davenport
Discus throw	Sharon Shepherd
Shot put	Cynthia Wyatt
High jump	Eleanor Montgomery
Pentathlon	Barbara Browne
Broad jump	Edith McGuire

Girls' Division

50 yards	Linda Bradshaw
75 yards	Dee Barnett
100 yards	Wyomia Tyus
220 yards	Shirley Wilson
440 yards	Sally Griffith
Javelin throw	Lurline Hamilton

50-yard hurdles	Tamara Davis
Discus throw	Nancy Norberg
Shot put	Sally Sutton
Broad jump	Martha Watson
High jump	Eleanor Montgomery
Baseball throw	Kathleen Mirko

The 1963 Pan American team that competed in São Paulo, Brazil, April 20– May 5 follows:

	Event	*Place*	*Performance*
Bair, RaNae	Javelin	no measurable throws	
Baskerville, Estelle	HJ	6	5' ¼"
Brown, Vivian	200m	1	23.9
	400mr	1	45.6
Davenport, Fran	Javelin	2	154' 11"
Ferris, Leah Bennett	800m	2	2:13.6
Grissom, JoAnn Terry	80mh	1	11.3
Harris, Norma	200m	4	25.3
	400mr	1	45.6
Hegarty, Cynthia	800m	4	2:17.4
McGuire, Edith	100m	1	11.5
	BJ	3	18' 8"
Montgomery, Eleanor	HJ	1	5' 6¼"
Shepherd, Sharon	SP	3	46' 3¼"
	Discus	3	155' 1⅛"
Smith, Janell	80mh	scratch	
White, Marilyn	100m	3	11.7
	400mr	1	45.6
White, Willye	BJ	1	20' 2¼"
	400mr	1	45.6
Wilson, Diana	SP	2	46' 9¾"
Wyatt, Cynthia	Discus	6	138' 10"

The 400-meter relay team composed of Willye White, Marilyn White, Norma Harris, and Vivian Brown finished first in 45.6.

Track and Field News in May reported that "the dolls dominated even more than the guys at Sao Paulo as the U.S. female brigade won six of ten events, finished second in three more, and won a bronze medal in the 10th affair. Only in the hurdles and javelin did both entries fail to make the first six."

A "ten deep" United States "top performance" list appeared in the *Amateur Athletic Union Handbook*. The top performer in each event appears in the following list:

100 yards	10.7	Edith McGuire
100 meters	11.5	Edith McGuire
220 yards	24.2	Diana Wilson

200 meters	23.8	Vivian Brown
440 yards	56.7	Myrtle Lowe
400 meters	56.3	Suzanne Knott
880 yards	2:10.7	Sandra Knott
800 meters	2:09.7	Sandra Knott
80-meter hurdles	11.0	Tammy Davis
440-yard relay	45.7	USA team
400-meter relay	45.2	USA team
880-yard medley relay	1:46.9	Mayor Daley "A" team
800-meter medley relay	1:47.7	Oakland Oakettes
4-kilo shot put	48' 4½"	Cynthia Wyatt
High jump	5' 8"	Eleanor Montgomery
Broad jump	21' ¾"	Willye White
Discus throw	155' 1¾"	Sharon Shepherd
Javelin throw	166' 10¾"	Frances Davenport
Pentathlon	4261	Pat Daniels

A girls' division list also appeared.

Track and Field News contained a few articles relating to women. One story reported a 2:52.8 half mile run by a tenacious nine year old. The writer, Bert Nelson, said, "I never expected to get a major kick from a 2:52.8 half-mile, as I did recently at one of our all-comers meets. It was during a girl's race, of all things, and ordinarily I would have been watching without seeing as I took the opportunity of a break in the program to talk."

The comments below were an answer to a letter written to *Track and Field News*. "Actually there is a lack of interest in women's track. We only have a pitiful handful of girls interested. True, more would be interested if there were a better organized program. Equally true, there would be a better program if more girls showed a demand for it."

Track and Field News reported the results of the Los Angeles Invitational. There were two women's events. Marilyn White won the 60 in 6.9, and Wilma Rudolph was third. Judy Shapiro won the 600 in 1:29.5. *Track Mirror* described Marilyn White as an eighteen-year-old freshman at UCLA, unknown before she beat the two fastest women in the world.

A women's 880 was run in the Massachusetts Knights of Columbus Meet. Cynthia Hegarty placed second in 2:20.9, and Louise Black of the N.Y. Police Athletic League was third in 2:36.8.

On February 2, the 19th Annual Philadelphia Games were held in Convention Hall. The two women's events contested were the 50-yard dash and the invitational 440-yard dash.

The 75th AAU Track and Field championships, which were held in St. Louis, Missouri, had two women's sprints as an "added feature."

The meet program included a photo of West German sprinter Jutta Heine, the featured sprinter in both the 100 and 220. She was also to lend her charm as "Queen of the Meet."

The write-up in the program next to Jutta's photo stated:

Women's track and field events are relatively undeveloped. ... Public interest and financial support of women's events were almost completely lacking until the joint holding of men's and women's events.

The exciting performances of such popular competitors as Jutta Heine of West Germany and Wilma Rudolph Ward of the U.S.A. has become a great attraction and for this reason, this event is being included in the St. Louis meet.

The Mason-Dixon Games produced a new world record for Tennessee State in the 440-yard relay of 48.3, bettering their time of the previous year.

The metropolitan AAU began conducting cross-country races for women at Van Cortlandt Park in the Bronx. The distance was 1¼ miles. The *New York Journal American* on October 29 reported, "Louise Mead of the Bronx, a 5 foot 7 inch blonde, 27 year old physical education teacher, won the one mile and a quarter cross country race for women in Van Cortlandt Park Sunday, by 60 yards." This was the first race of four to be run. The winning time was 7:51.5.

Merry Lepper ran the Western Hemisphere Marathon in Culver City, California, on December 16 in 3:37.07.

Jimmy Carnes started a Junior Champ track program during the summer of 1963 in Greenville, South Carolina, while he was coaching at Furman University. He designed it after a program run by the Jaycees throughout the nation. Both girls and boys had a daily training program which culminated in a competition every Friday. The Jaycees assisted in financing the program, which ran for eight to ten weeks.

Frances Kaszubski, the women's track and field chairman, wrote in her report presented at the 76th Annual AAU Convention in San Diego:

> The most significant development in this sport during 1963 occurred not in the ranks of the AAU but in another organization, DGWS. The Division of Girls and Women's Sports, a section of the American Association of Health, Physical Education and Recreation, outlawed the 40-years-old philosophy of anti-competitive sports for girls. This occurred in May during the AAHPER'S national convention. The new philosophy in physical education for girls in our educational institutions as of that date is "pro competitive." This action is the culmination of ten years of efforts on the part of AAU and DGWS Women's Track and Field Committees.
>
> To implement the "pro competitive" philosophy, the AAHPER and the USOC Olympic Development Committee (through its Women's Board) have conducted the first National Institute on Girls' Sports at the University of Oklahoma from November 4th through 9th. Over two hundred women educators attended from 50 states. The participants of the Institute learned not only how to teach track and field ... but, also, how to conduct clinics, workshops and state-wide institutes within their own states. It must be admitted even by the most conservative-minded opponent of competition for girls — that this new philosophy and the National Institute, in particular, is a giant step forward in the development of amateur athletics for girls and women in the United States.

In an article entitled, "The National Institute on Girls' Sports," Sara Staff Jernigan said: "One of the most exciting historical developments for the furtherance of girls and women's sports in the nation is the sports institute for girls planned for November 4-9. It is the first concrete effort of any sports organization in the history of the United States to meet the need to emphasize improvement of sports skills of all girls." Five needs were stated. One need was to improve the competence of physical educators in teaching and coaching track and field.

Sara Staff Jernigan, director of women's physical education at Stetson University, Deland, Florida, was named head of the nation's first National Institute on Girls' Sports. Mrs. Jernigan was chair of the Women's Board of the U.S. Development Committee. She was appointed one of four women on the newly formed women's advisory board to the United States Olympic Development Committee. It was the first time that women had functioned on this committee, the purpose of which was to develop potential Olympic competitors for the Tokyo Games in 1964. Mrs. Jernigan was appointed by Tom Hamilton of California, chairman of the United States Olympic Development Committee, and Kenneth Wilson. She assisted in selecting the other three members of the board: Mrs. Janet Bachna, Canton, Ohio, coach of the 1959 Pan American and 1960 Olympic women's gymnastic teams; Dr. Thelma Bishop, chairman, women's professional curriculum, Department of Health, Physical Education, and Recreation at Michigan State University, East Lansing; and Dr. Ann Paterson, chairman, women's physical education, San Francisco State College, California. Mrs. Jernigan was past vice president of the American Association for Health, Physical Education, and Recreation, a co-sponsor of the Institute. In December 1962, the plan for the Institute, devised by the Women's Board, was approved unanimously by the U.S. Olympic Board of Directors. The Women's Board then invited the DGWS to co-sponsor the Institute.

The Institute was an idea conceived by the Women's Board and became a reality through the joint efforts of the Women's Board and the DGWS.

Each state, as well as Hawaii, Alaska, and the Commonwealth of Puerto Rico, was invited to send three people to the Institute — a generalist in physical education, a teacher with an interest in track and field, and one interested in gymnastics, the other sport supported by the Institute. Each team signed a pledge to organize and conduct in its state a similar institute for teachers on all levels within seven months after the National Institute. Two hundred and fifty people were in attendance.

Dr. Nell Jackson, assistant professor of physical education at Illinois State Normal University, was chairman of track and field for the Institute.

The following track and field presentations were offered:

Contributions of Track and Field to the Development of Girls and Women	Nell C. Jackson
Principles of Training for Track and Field	Ken Doherty
Track and Field for Girls	Virginia Frank
Sprints and Middle Distance	John M. Cooper
Elementary Fundamentals in Sprint Relay Racing	Leroy T. Walker
Hurdle Progression	Barbara Mueller
Body Mechanics for the Javelin	Virginia Frank and Fran Davenport

Chapter 47

1964
The Tokyo Olympic Year

The Olympic trials were held in New York at Randall's Island in Downing Stadium on August 6–8. The largest women's team to that date, listed below, competed in the Tokyo Olympic Games from October 10 to October 24.

Name	Olympic Event	Olympic Place	Olympic Performance
Bair, RaNae	Javelin	13	153' 10"
Baskerville, Estelle	HJ	19	5' 5"
Bonds, Rosie	80mh	8	10.8
Brown, Earlene	SP	12	48' 6¾"
Brown, Terrezene	HJ	DNQ	
Brown, Vivian	200m	DNQ	24.3
Connolly, Olga	Discus	12	169' 2½"
Grissom, JoAnn Terry	LJ	19	19' 4¾"
Knott, Sandra	800m	DNQ	2:12.2
McGuire, Edith	100m	2	11.6
	200m	1	23.0
	400mr	2	43.9
Montgomery, Eleanor	HJ	8	5' 7¼"
O'Neal, Lacey	80mh	DNQ	10.9
Sherrard, Cherrie	80mh	DNQ	11.0
Smith, Janell	400m	DNQ	54.5
Thompson, Debbie	200m	DNQ	24.6
Tyus, Wyomia	100m	1	11.4
	400mr	2	43.9
Watson, Martha	LJ	18	19' 5¾"
White, Marilyn	100m	4	11.6
	400mr	2	43.9
White, Willye	LJ	12	19' 11"
	400mr	2	43.9
Winslow, Pat Daniels	Pentathlon	7	4724
Temple, Edward	Coach		

Wyomia Tyus, winning her first 100 meter Olympic title in 1964 in Tokyo. She became the first athlete, male or female to win the sprint in two successive Olympic Games when she successfully defended the 100 meter title again in 1968 in Mexico City. Edith McGuire was second, and Marilyn White, fourth. (Courtesy of the National Track & Field Hall of Fame Historical Research Library at Butler University.)

Griffin, Jack	Coach
Wilson, Lucile	Manager

The Olympic Results

100 meters. According to the report in *Olympic Games 1964*: "Temple has a girl who, in the preliminaries, breaks Wilma Rudolph's world record for the 100 meters, which the latter set at Stuttgart in 1961. ... She became Temple's 'girl for Tokyo.' Wyomia not only runs the distance in the preliminaries in 11.2 seconds, she also wins the finals one day later with 11.4 seconds."

Track and Field News said, "Wyomia Tyus tied the 100 record of 11.2 in a semi-final, then won the final in 11.4. Edith McGuire, a teammate at Tennessee State, was second to Tyus." Wyomia had a two-yard lead at the tape.

Wyomia said in *Tales of Gold* that she barely qualified for the team, but after Coach Temple told her that she might get a medal after winning her trial heats, she said to herself: "I have a good chance at the gold. ... I got off to a good start and was leading, but I kept thinking to myself, Where's Edith? At 80 or 90 yards she would always pull up and pass me by. But there was no Edith. I remember that Coach Temple always told me never to look around, so I just kept looking straight ahead."

Edith finished second in 11.6, and Marilyn White placed fourth in 11.6. With Tennesse State runners placing 1-2 and Marilyn White finishing fourth, this was the closest that the women of the United States came to a 1-2-3 sweep in an Olympic Games. It may be the only time in the history of the Games that two athletes from the same school finished 1-2 in an event said Ed Temple, who was very proud of this historical and almost impossible accomplishment.

Prior to the Games, *Track and Field News* predicted that twenty-year-old McGuire would win the 100 and 200. She was the only American selected as a 1-6 finalist in either sprint. Tyus, nineteen, was not on the list.

Lacey O'Neal, 1964 Olympian, 80-meter hurdles. (Courtesy of Lacey O'Neal.)

200 meters. The semifinals and finals were held on different days in 1964. "The favorite from Tennessee, Edith McGuire, performs a beautiful series of runs. In the first round she finishes after 23.4 seconds, in the semi-finals she takes 23.3 seconds to complete the 200 meters, and in the finals she ends in 23 seconds flat. She does not run as elegantly as Wilma Rudolph, but she is by no means slower than her predecessor. Edith set a new Olympic record with her last performance of 23.0 seconds," stated *Olympic Games 1964.*

Debbie Thompson and Vivian Brown did not qualify for the finals.

80-meter hurdles. *Track and Field News* reported that "Rosie Bonds of the US threatened an upset in the hurdles when she ran her heat in 10.6, but she pulled a muscle and finished last in the final." Rosie was the only American athlete to make the finals. Lacey O'Neal and Cherrie Sherrard ran 10.9 and 11.0 respectively in the earlier rounds.

400 meters. The 400-meter event was held for the first time in these Olympic Games. The only U.S. entry, Janell Smith, placed sixth in a semifinal round with a time of 54.5. She did not make the final.

800 meters. As in 1960, the United States had one athlete in the 800-meter run. Sandra Knott was sixth in heat two in round one in 2:12.2 and was eliminated.

400-meter relay. The U.S. team of Willye White, Wyomia Tyus, Marilyn White, and Edith McGuire finished a strong second for the silver medals in 43.9.

Edith McGuire, 1964 Olympic Champion, 200 meters. (Courtesy of U.S.O.C. Photo Library.)

High jump. Eleanor Montgomery finished eighth with a leap of 5' 7¼". Four women jumped this same height. Estelle Baskerville and Terrezene Brown did not qualify for the final round.

Long jump. Willye White jumped 19' 11" for twelfth place. Martha Watson and JoAnn Terry Grissom did not qualify for the final round.

Shot put. Earlene Brown, the only U.S. entrant in this event, placed twelfth with a put of 48' 6¾".

Discus throw. Olga Fikotova Connolly, the only U.S. entry in the discus throw, placed twelfth with a toss of 169' 2½".

Javelin throw. RaNae Bair, the only U.S. entry in the javelin, did not qualify for the final round.

Pentathlon. Pat Winslow, the only U.S. entry, finished seventh. Her score of 4,724 was just 73 points short of the fourth-place athlete.

The Olympic Trials

The Olympic trials were held on August 6–8 in Downing Stadium, Randalls Island, New York City.

100 meters
1. Edith McGuire, Tennessee State   11.3w
2. Marilyn White, L.A. Mercurettes   11.4
3. Wyomia Tyus, Tennessee State   11.5
4. Rosie Bonds, Pasadena A.A.   11.5
5. Debbie Thompson, Frederick Track Club   11.8

200 meters
1. Edith McGuire, Tennessee State   23.4
2. Debbie Thompson, Frederick Track Club   23.6
3. Vivian Brown, Tennessee State   23.7

400 meters
1. Janell Smith, Fredonia Track Club   55.6
2. Patricia Clark, N.Y. Police Athletic League   56.2
3. Valerie Carter, N.Y. Police Athletic League   57.1

800 meters
1. Sandra Knott, Cleveland Recreation   2:13.1
2. Leah Ferris, Univ. of Hawaii   2:14.8
3. Carol Mastronarde, L.A. Mercurettes   2:15.0

80-meter hurdles
1. Rosie Bonds, Pasadena A.A.   10.8w
2. Cherrie Sherrard, Laurel Track Club   10.9
3. Lacey O'Neal, Univ. of Hawaii   10.9

High jump
1. Eleanor Montgomery, Cleveland Recreation   5' 8"
2. Terrezene Brown, L.A. Mercurettes   5' 6"
3. Estelle Baskerville, Ohio Track Club   5' 6"

Long jump
1. Willye White, Mayor Daley Youth Foundation   21' 4"
2. Martha Watson, Long Beach Comets   21' 3"
3. JoAnn Grissom, Tennessee State   19' 11¼"

Shot put
1. Earlene Brown, Compton Track Club   49' 1¾"
2. Lynn Graham, So. Pacific AAU   44' 10½"
3. Cynthia Wyatt, Univ. of Hawaii   42' 7½"

Discus
1. Olga Connolly, L.A. Mercurettes   162' 9"
2. Earlene Brown, Compton Track Club   149' 4"
3. Sharon Shepherd, Ohio AAU   147' 1"

Javelin
1. RaNae Bair, San Diego Track & Field   176'
2. Virginia Husted, Falcon Track Club   148' 10½"
3. Lurline Hamilton, Louisiana Track Club   140' 7¼"

Pentathlon
1. Pat Winslow, San Mateo A.A.   4544

| 2. Sally Griffith, Santa Clara Track Club | 4225 |
| 3. Denise Paschal, Laurel Track Club | 4120 |

The Outdoor Nationals

The national outdoor championship meet was held on July 10–11 at Hanford, California.

100 meters
1. Wyomia Tyus, Tennessee State	11.5
2. Edith McGuire, Tennessee State	11.5
3. Rosie Bonds, Pasadena A.A.	11.5
4. Willye White, Mayor Daley Youth Foundation	11.5

200 meters
1. Edith McGuire, Tennessee State	23.6
2. Vivian Brown, Tennessee State	24.0
3. Shirley Wilson, Compton Track Club	24.0
4. Irene Piotrowski, Vancouver, B.C.	24.3

400 meters
1. Janell Smith, Fredonia Track Club	54.7
2. Una Morris, Jamaica	54.7
3. Patricia Clark, N.Y. Police Athletic League	56.5
4. Jenny Lowe, Oakettes	56.9

800 meters
1. Sandra Knott, Cleveland Recreation	2:10.4
2. Leah Bennett Ferris, Univ. of Hawaii	2:12.7
3. Carol Mastronarde, L.A. Mercurettes	2:12.9
4. Doris Severtsen Brown, Falcon Track Club	2:15.1

80-meter hurdles
1. Rosie Bonds, Pasadena A.A.	10.8
2. Cherrie Sherrard, Laurel Track Club	10.8
3. Tammy Davis, Frederick Track Club	11.1
4. Carmen Smith, Jamaica	11.6

200-meter hurdles (not an official event)
1. Sally Griffith, Santa Clara Track Club	28.2
2. Denise Paschal, Laurel Track Club	29.6
3. Laura Voss, Ohio Track Club	30.0
4. Janet Penn, Santa Ynez H.S.	30.4

400-meter relay
1. Compton Track Club, "A" team	47.2
2. Laurel Track Club	47.6
3. Mayor Daley Youth Foundation	47.7
4. Oakettes, "A" team	48.9

800-meter medley relay
| 1. Oakettes, "A" team | 1:45.5 |

2. Mayor Daley Youth Foundation   1:46.3
3. Compton Track Club, "B" team   1:47.1
4. San Mateo Girls' A.A.   1:48.7

High jump
1. Eleanor Montgomery, Cleveland Recreation   5' 8"
2. Terrezene Brown, L.A. Mercurettes   5' 6"
3. Pat Daniels Winslow, San Mateo Girls' A.A.   5' 6"
4. Marilyn Saling, Falcon Track Club,   5' 4"
    and Estelle Baskerville, Ohio Track Club

Long jump
1. Willie White, Mayor Daley Youth Foundation   21' 7"
2. Martha Watson, Long Beach Comets   19' 7"
3. Pat Daniels Winslow, San Mateo Girls' A.A.   19' 5¼"
4. Sonia Guss, Long Beach Comets   19' 1"

4-kilo shot put
1. Earlene Brown, Compton Track Club   46' 11"
2. Cynthia Wyatt, Univ. of Hawaii   44' 7½"
3. Lynn Graham, So. Pacific AAU, Pasadena   43' 4½"
4. Mary Peppler, L.A. Mercurettes   41' 7¾"

Discus throw
1. Olga Connolly, L.A. Mercurettes   158' 4"
2. Earlene Brown, Compton Track Club   156' 8"
3. Sharon Shepherd, Ohio AAU   143' 3"
4. Nancy Norberg, Pacific AAU, Palo Alto   141' 8"

Javelin throw
1. RaNae Bair, San Diego Track & Field   173' 4½"
2. Frances Davenport, U.S. Army and San Mateo   156' 4"
3. Lurline Hamilton, Louisiana Track Club   154' 10½"
4. Virginia Husted, Falcon Track Club   154' 4"

Team scores:
Compton Track Club 40; Tennessee State University 39; Los Angeles Mercurettes and Mayor Daley Youth Foundation 31; San Mateo Girls' A.A. 26; Cleveland Recreation 20; University of Hawaii, Laurel Track Club, and Oakettes 18.

The girls' championships were held on July 9-10 at the same site as the seniors.

50 yards
1. Linda Bradshaw, Oakettes A.C.   6.0
2. Debbie Thompson, Frederick Track Club   6.0
3. Matteline Render, Tennessee State   6.0

75 yards
1. Linda Bradshaw, Oakettes A.C.   8.4
2. Debbie Thompson, Frederick Track Club   8.4
3. Beverly Meadows, Compton Track Club   8.4

100 yards
1. Charlotte Cooke, Compton Track Club   11.0
2. Matteline Render, Tennessee State   11.0
3. Jenda Jones, Arizona O.C.   11.1

220 yards
1. Shirley Wilson, Compton Track Club   24.5
2. Charlotte Cooke, Compton Track Club   25.0
3. Karen Dennis, Detroit Track Club   25.3

440 yards
1. Shirley Wilson, Compton Track Club   58.5
2. Patricia Elmore, Will's Spikettes   59.0
3. Gloria Harper, Compton Track Club   59.2

880 yards
1. Francie Kraker, Ann Arbor Anns   2:17.4
2. Gloria Harper, Compton Track Club   2:17.9
3. Mary Anderson, San Mateo Girls' A.A.   2:18.0

50-yard hurdles
1. Tammy Davis, Frederick Track Club   6.6
2. LaVera Jordan, Cosmos Club   6.8
3. Denise Paschal, Laurel Track Club   7.1

440-yard relay
1. Compton Track Club, "A" team   47.7
2. Oakettes A.C., "A" team   48.5
3. Mayor Daley Youth Foundation   49.5

High jump
1. Terrezene Brown, L.A. Mercurettes   5' 7"
2. Eleanor Montgomery, Cleveland Recreation   5' 7"
3. Estelle Baskerville, Ohio Track Club   5' 6"

Long jump
1. Beatrice Blair, L.A. Mercurettes   18' 6¼"
2. Franzetta Parham, Isleton A.A.   17' 10¾"
3. Gloria Agee, Compton Track Club   17' 9½"

8-lb. shot put
1. Lynn Graham, So. Pacific AAU, Pasadena   45' 6¾"
2. Gretchen Walin, So. Pacific AAU, Pasadena   42' 4¾"
3. Joan Heater, Oregon AAU, Corvalis   41' 7"

Discus throw
1. Nancy Norberg, Pacific AAU, Palo Alto   142' 3½"
2. Lynn Graham, So. Pacific AAU, Pasadena   128' 1½"
3. Elinor Slack, San Mateo Girls' A.A.   112' 5"

Javelin throw
1. Lurline Hamilton, Louisiana Track Club   151' 7½"
2. Linda Haverlation, So. Pacific AAU   146' 9¼"
3. Louise Gerrish, Ann Arbor Anns   144' 8½"

Team scores:
Compton Track Club 75; Frederick Track Club 30; Oakettes A.C. 29; Los Angeles Mercurettes 20; San Mateo Girls' A.A. 19; Tennessee State University 18; Ann Arbor Anns 16; Will's Spikettes 15.

1964 All-America Women's Track and Field Teams

100 meters	Wyomia Tyus
200 meters	Edith McGuire
400 meters	Janell Smith
800 meters	Sandra Knott
80-meter hurdles	Rosie Bonds
Long jump	Willye B. White
High jump	Eleanor Montgomery
Shot put	Earlene Brown
Discus throw	Olga Connolly
Javelin	RaNae Bair
Pentathlon	Pat Daniels Winslow

Girls' Division

50 yards	Linda Bradshaw
75 yards	Debbie Thompson
100 yards	Charlotte Cooke
220 yards	Shirley Wilson
440 yards	Shirley Wilson
880 yards	Francie Kraker
50-yard hurdles	Tammy Davis
Long jump	Beatrice Blair
High jump	Terrezene Brown
Shot put	Lynn Graham
Discus throw	Nancy Norberg
Javelin throw	Lurline Hamilton

The first two finishers in the nationals were named to the USA team which competed against the Russians at the end of July. The team remained in Hanford, California, for a ten-day training period.

Track and Field News reported the results of the USSR–USA Meet held on July 25-26 at the Los Angeles Coliseum in Los Angeles.

Edith McGuire, a junior from Tennessee State University, was one of the standout performers in the sixth international dual meet. McGuire won both sprints and was the anchor leg on the victorious USA relay team.

The long jump proved to be an exciting event as Willye White took the lead on her fifth jump with a leap of 21' 6". Her final jump, which was wind-aided, was 21' 7¾", her all-time best. These two spectacular efforts were only good enough for second place, however.

For the first time in the history of the dual meets, our women finished 1-2 in the high jump. Eleanor Montgomery won with a leap of 5' 7¼", and Terrezene Brown finished second with a leap of 5' 5¼".

100 meters	
1. Edith McGuire	11.5
2. Wyomia Tyus	11.6
200 meters	
1. Edith McGuire	23.3
2. Vivian Brown	24.0
800 meters	
3. Leah Bennett Ferris	2:08.8
4. Sandra Knott	2:10.1
400-meter relay	
1. USA	44.4
(White, Bonds, Tyus, McGuire)	
Long jump	
2. Willye White	21' 7¾"
4. Martha Watson	19' 7¾"
High jump	
1. Eleanor Montgomery	5' 7¼"
2. Terrezene Brown	5' 5¼"
Shot put	
3. Earlene Brown	47' 6¾"
4. Lynn Graham	45' 7¼"
Discus throw	
3. Olga Connolly	169' 11½"
4. Earlene Brown	150' 2½"
Javelin throw	
3. RaNae Bair	171' 8"
4. Lurline Hamilton	155' 1"

USSR 58 — USA 48

A women's records committee was established for the first time on January 1, with Lt. Col. Alvin Lloyd as the chairman. All associations were asked to appoint records chairmen on a temporary basis until January 1, when they became members of the regular records committee. A position of statistician was created with the records committee.

Juner Bellew, the national women's track and field chairman, reported that the first national cross-country championships were held in Seattle at the end of November.

Herb Stockman was chair of the age-group committee, which had forty-one members. Ten–eleven and twelve–thirteen were the age groups in the program.

A top performance list was compiled by William Peck, statistician. Below are the best American performances in 1964:

100 yards	10.5	Edith McGuire
100 meters	11.2	Wyomia Tyus

220 yards	23.4	Edith McGuire
200 meters	23.0	Edith McGuire
440 yards	54.8	Janell Smith
400 meters	54.5	Janell Smith
880 yards	2:12.8	Carol Mastronarde
800 meters	2:08.8	Leah Bennett Ferris
80-meter hurdles	10.8	Rosie Bonds
220-yard hurdles	29.2	Sally Griffith
200-meter hurdles	28.2	Sally Griffith
High jump	5' 8"	Eleanor Montgomery
Long jump	21' 6"	Willye White
4-kilo shot	50' 7½"	Earlene Brown
Discus throw	184' 6½"	Olga Connolly
Pentathlon	4724	Pat Daniels Winslow

A girls' top performance list also appeared.

The Mason-Dixon Games produced three indoor world records. Tennessee State again bettered its 440-yard relay record by running 47.5, Wyomia Tyus won the 70-yard dash in the record time of 7.5, and Tammy Davis won the 70-yard hurdles in the record time of 9.1.

The 38th Annual Knights of Columbus meet held at the Boston Garden on January 11 featured one women's event, the "special invitation girls' 880-yard run." Ten years ago, this same meet had one event, the 50 yard dash. At that time eighteen girls were entered. This year, five girls were "invited" to run the 880.

Leo Larney, in his magazine *Cinderbelle,* said that this was the year for record breaking. Twenty-two new records were set, seventeen outdoors and five indoors. *Cinderbelle* was the first magazine in the United States devoted to women's track and field. Leo Larney was javelin-thrower Marjorie Larney's dad.

In the schools, the 1964-66 *Track and Field Guide,* edited by Eileen Goodnight, was published. It contained articles by outstanding women track and field athletes, notes on officiating, and latest official rules.

Track and Field for Girls and Women, written by Phebe M. Scott and Virginia R. Crafts, was published in 1964. In the history section of the book, the authors state: "Women in this country did not become leaders in the development of international competition for girls. On the contrary, professional women physical educators were largely responsible for discouraging this type of competition."

Kenneth D. Miller's *Track and Field for Girls* was published this year.

The April *Journal of Health, Physical Education and Recreation* featured an article on the first National Institute on Girls' Sports that stated: "It was unique in the true sense of the word in many ways." It was the first pilot project of the Women's Board of the United States Olympic Development Committee, and it was the first national track and field institute. Three leaders from each of fifty states assembled with the purpose of taking back to their states what they learned at the institute. It was the first project of this type to be funded by the United

States Olympic Development Committee, and it was a first also because it included male consultants, observers, and teachers of track and field.

The May *Journal* reported that Furman University was the site for the first National Institute on Girls' Sports ever held in South Carolina. Fifty delegates from all over the state convened on March 20 and 21. John Powell, an outstanding British track coach, and Jimmy Carnes, then a coach at Furman, headed the instructional staff.

Chapter 48

1965

The national championship meet was held in Columbus, Ohio, on July 2-3.

Wyomia Tyus, the 1964 Olympic champion in the 100 meters, led the final field in the 100-yard dash to the tape by two yards and tied, for the second time during the meet, her American record of 10.5.

The 200-meter Olympic champion, Edith Maguire, was well ahead at the finish of the 220-yard dash, and her time was a new meet record.

In the 440-yard relay, both McGuire and Tyus raced stride for stride as anchor legs on the Tennessee State "A" team and the Tennessee State "B" team. Both teams were given the same time, but the winning place was given to Tyus on the "B" team. The 1-2 finish in the relay also cinched the team title for Tennessee State.

This was the first time that the 1500-meter run was held in a national championship meet.

100-yard dash
1. Wyomia Tyus, Tennessee State   10.5
2. Diana Wilson, L.A. Mercurettes   10.8
3. Marilyn White, L.A. Mercurettes   11.0
4. Willye White, Mayor Daley Youth Foundation   11.1

220-yard dash
1. Edith McGuire, Tennessee State   23.6
2. Diana Wilson, L.A. Mercurettes   24.1
3. Barbara Ferrell, L.A. Mercurettes   24.5
4. Chris Iverson, Calif. Poly.   24.5

440-yard run
1. Janell Smith, Fredonia, Kans.   55.1
2. Norma Harris, Mayor Daley Youth Foundation   55.9
3. Jarvis Scott, L.A. Mercurettes   57.0
4. Pat Clark, N.Y. Police Athletic League   57.4

880-yard run
1. Marie Mulder, Will's Spikettes   2:11.1
2. Sandra Knott, Cleveland Recreation   2:12.1
3. Leah Ferris, Honolulu   2:14.0
4. Lori Schutt, Bloomington, Ill.   2:14.5

1500-meter run
1. Marie Mulder, Will's Spikettes — 4:36.5
2. Sandra Knott, Cleveland Recreation — 4:36.7
3. Susie Byersdorfer, Will's Spikettes — 4:41.0
4. Lori Schutt, Bloomington, Ill. — 4:41.2

100-meter hurdles
1. Cherrie Sherrard, Laurel Track Club — 13.7
2. Rosie Bonds, Riverside, Calif. — 13.9
3. Tammy Davis, Frederick Track Club — 14.0
4. Jennifer Wingerson, Toronto — 14.1

200-meter hurdles
1. Jennifer Wingerson, Toronto — 27.5
2. Mamie Rallins, Mayor Daley Youth Foundation — 27.7
3. Denise Paschal, Laurel Track Club — 28.5
4. Laura Voss, Columbus, Ohio — 28.6

440-yard relay
1. Tennessee State, "B" team — 46.5
   (Render, Rallings, Harvey, Tyus)
2. Tennesse State, "A" team — 46.5
3. L.A. Mercurettes — 46.6
4. Topeka, Kans., Cosmos — 48.8

880-yard relay
1. Cleveland Recreation — 1:43.9
   (Woods, McDonald, Allen, Manning)
2. Mayor Daley Youth Foundation — 1:44.2
3. L.A. Mercurettes — 1:44.5
4. Will's Spikettes — 1:47.2

High jump
1. Eleanor Montgomery, Cleveland Recreation — 5' 7"
2. Estelle Baskerville, Tennessee State — 5' 6"
3. Sarah Cantrell, Tennessee State — 5' 3"
4. Franzetta Parham, Isleton, Calif. — 5' 2"

Long jump
1. Willye White, Mayor Daley Youth Foundation — 20' 5½"
2. Sonia Guss, Tennessee State — 19' 3¾"
3. Bethe McBride, Liberty A.C., Mass. — 19' 3½"
4. Calanthia Rallings, Tennessee State — 19' 1¾"

Discus throw
1. Lynn Graham, L.A. Mercurettes — 157' 9"
2. Cynthia Wyatt, Buffalo, N.Y. — 152' 3"
3. Carol Moseke, Lincoln, Neb., Roadrunners — 150' 2½"
4. Nancy Norberg, Palo Alto — 148' 7½"

4-kilo shot
1. Lynn Graham, L.A. Mercurettes — 47' 7"
2. Cynthia Wyatt, Buffalo — 43' 11"

3. Carol Moseke, Lincoln, Neb., Roadrunners   42' 11¼"
4. Joan Whitehead, Indian Track Club, N.J.   42' 1½"

Javelin throw
1. RaNae Bair, San Diego Track and Field   175' ½"
2. Lurline Hamilton, Louisiana State   160' 6"
3. Virginia Husted, Falcon Track Club   160' 0"
4. Babs Brandin, Crown City Track Club   145' 1"

Team scores:
Tennessee State 68; Los Angeles Mercurettes 66; Mayor Daley Youth Foundation 39; Cleveland Recreation Division 36; Will's Spikettes, Sacramento 34.

The girls' championship meet on July 1-2 was held at the same site.

50-yard dash
1. Debbie Thompson, Frederick Track Club   5.9
2. Dorothy Myles, Tennessee State   6.0
3. Barbara Ferrell, L.A. Mercurettes   6.1

100-yard dash
1. Debbie Thompson, Frederick Track Club   10.7
2. Jenda Jones, Phoenix, Ariz.   10.8
3. Dorothy Myles, Tennessee State   10.8

220-yard dash
1. Jenda Jones, Phoenix, Ariz.   24.5
2. Barbara Ferrell, L.A. Mercurettes
3. Dixie Haywood, Oakland Oakettes   25.5

440-yard run
1. Madeline Manning, Cleveland   55.1
2. Dino Lowery, Will's Spikettes   56.8
3. Donnis White, L.A. Mercurettes   57.4

880-yard run
1. Cathy Catlin, Will's Spikettes   2:14.6
2. Susie Byersdorfer, Will's Spikettes   2:16.3
3. Pat Cole, Crown City Track Club   2:19.4

50-yard hurdles
1. LaVera Jordan, Topeka, Kans.   6.8
2. Ginger Smith, Delaware   7.1
3. Denise Paschal, Laurel Track Club   7.1

440-yard relay
1. Detroit Track Club   49.5
   (Colemen, Babridge, Gaines, White)
2. Frederick Track Club   49.5
3. Philadelphia   50.3

880-yard relay
1. Atoms Track Club, New York   1:43.2
   (Rusty, Birchette, Douglas, Lee)

2. Cleveland Recreation   1:44.5
3. Detroit Track Club   1:44.7

Discus throw
1. Lynn Graham, L.A. Mercurettes   146' ½"
2. Virginia Dearins, Santa Ynez, Calif.   132' 2½"
3. Toni Riddle, San Diego   127' 0"

Long jump
1. Beth McBride, Liberty Track Club   18' 7½"
2. Denise Paschal, Laurel Track Club   18' 3¾"
3. Barbara Emerson, Crown City Track Club   18' 3½"

Shot put
1. Lynn Graham, L.A. Mercurettes   48' 11 "
2. Maren Seidler, Atlanta, Georgia   43' 5¾"
3. Ruth Sackett, unattached   42' ¾"

High jump
1. Denise Paschal, Laurel Track Club   5' 3"
2. Franzetta Parham, Isleton, Calif.   5' 3"
3. Connie Peterson, Kalispell, Mont.   5' 0"

Javelin throw
1. Louise Gerrish, Southeastern Michigammes   141' 10½"
2. Babs Brandin, Crown City Track Club   137' 1"
3. Jean Sweeney, Ohio Track Club   136' 4"

Team scores:
Los Angeles Mercurettes 40; Will's Spikettes 34; Frederick Track Club 29; Laurel A.C. 24; Crown City Track Club 24; Tennessee State University 18; Cleveland Recreation 18; Detroit Track Club 16.

The Indoor Nationals

The national indoor championship meet was held on February 19-20 in New York City at Madison Square Garden, in conjunction with the men's championships for the first time.

The 440-yard run produced a tie when both Janell Smith and Norma Harris won their final sections in the same time.

60-yard dash
1. Wyomia Tyus, Tennessee State   6.8
2. Debbie Thompson, Frederick Track Club
3. Edith McGuire, Tennessee State
4. Barbara Ferrell, L.A. Mercurettes

60-yard hurdles
1. Chi Cheng, L.A. Mercurettes   7.9
2. Jennifer Wingerson, Toronto Track Club

3. Tammy Davis, Frederick Track Club
4. Lois Johnson, N.Y. Police Athletic League

200-yard dash
1. Edith McGuire, Tennessee State   21.9
2. Debbie Thompson, Frederick Track Club
3. Barbara Ferrell, L.A. Mercurettes
4. Pat Kraft, Long Island Mercurettes

880-yard run
1. Abby Hoffman, Toronto Olympic Club   2:11.8 MR
2. Antje Gleichfeld, Germany
3. Mrs. Nagy Szabo, Hungary
4. Marie Mulder, Will's Spikettes

440-yard run
1. Janell Smith, Fredonia, Kans.   56.5 MR
   and Norma Harris, Mayor Daley Youth Foundation
3. Abby Hoffman, Toronto Olympic Club
4. Pat Winslow, San Mateo Girls' A.A.

640-yard relay
1. Tennessee State   1:11.7
   (Tyus, Crews, Dunn, McGuire)
2. L.A. Mercurettes
3. Detroit Track Club

1060-yard relay
1. Mayor Daley Youth Foundation   2:14.0
   (Fumbanks, White, Hodge, Harris)
2. N.Y. Police Athletic League
3. Detroit Track Club
4. Atoms Track Club

High jump
1. Iolanda Balas, Romania   5' 9" MR
2. Eleanor Montgomery, Cleveland Recreation   5' 8"
3. Frances Slaap, England   5' 7"
4. Jaroslawa Bieda, Poland   5' 3"

Long jump
1. Mary Rand, England   20' 4" MR
2. Chi Cheng, L.A. Mercurettes   20' 2¼"
3. Martha Watson, Tennessee State   19' 4½"
4. Ingrid Becker, Germany   19' 3"

Shot put
1. Tamara Press, Soviet Union   57' 2½" MR
2. Lynn Graham, L.A. Mercurettes   49' 5"
3. Sharon Shepherd, Mansfield, Ohio, YWCA   42' 8½"
4. Jennifer Wingerson, Toronto Olympic Club   41' 9"

Basketball throw
1. Barbara Friedrich, Spring Lake, N.J.   107' 11"

2. Jean Sweeney, Ohio Track Club   107' 1"
3. Louise Gerrish, Ann Arbor, Michigan   98' 6"
4. Kay Johnson, Frederick Track Club   96' 0"

Team scores:
Tennessee State University 20; L.A. Mercurettes 15; Mayor Daley Youth Foundation and Frederick Track Club 9; N.Y. Police Athletic League and Detroit Track Club 4.

The national pentathlon championship meet was held at Lafayette, California, on June 25.

1. Pat Winslow, San Mateo Girls' A.A.	4399
2. Denise Paschal, Laurel Track Club	4220
3. Cherrie Sherrard, Laurel Track Club	4147
4. Janet Svendsen, San Mateo Girls' A.A.	3465

Pat ran the 80-meter hurdles in 12.3, put the 4-kilo shot 42' ¼", high-jumped 5' 2¾", long-jumped 17' 5¾", and ran 25.1 for the 200-meter dash.

The junior national women's outdoor championships was held in Monmouth, Oregon, on August 28.

100-meter dash
1. Evelyn Hamilton, Oakettes   11.9
2. Regina Wade, Ft. Worth Track Club   12.0
3. Shirley Emery, Oakettes   12.1

200-meter dash
1. Linda Crowder, Oakettes   26.2
2. Jenny Lowe, Oakettes   26.3
3. Willie Punch, Ft. Worth Track Club   26.4

400-meter run
1. Delores Stoneback, Seattle Olympic Club   58.6
2. Sharon Withers, Ft. Worth Track Club   59.7
3. Pat Van Wolvelaere, Angels Track Club   60.0

800-meter run
1. Susie Byersdorfer, Will's Spikettes   2:18.1
2. Violet Tittler, Richmond Track Club   2:18.1
3. Cindy Burns, Seattle Olympic Club   2:21.6

100-meter hurdles
1. Violet Dunn, unattached   14.3
2. Linda Crowder, Oakettes   14.6
3. Patricia McBurney, Seattle Olympic Club   15.5

400-meter relay
1. Oakettes (Lowe, Hamilton, Lee, Emery)   50.4
2. Ft. Worth Track Club   51.2
3. Seattle Olympic Club   51.3

1500-meter run
1. Susie Byersdorfer, Will's Spikettes   5:07.8
2. Pat Mills, Richmond Track Club   5:08.0
3. Carol Hughes, Will's Spikettes   5:08.2

800-meter medley relay
1. Seattle Olympic Club   1:51.5
  (Burns, Cooper, Kane, Stoneback)
2. Oakettes   1:53.6
3. Ft. Worth Track Club   1:55.6

High jump
1. Delores Stoneback, Seattle Olympic Club   5' 2¼"
2. Cylia Rico, Laurel Track Club   4' 10"
3. Bonnie Brown, unattached, Grant Pass   4' 8"

Long jump
1. Cylia Rico, Laurel Track Club   16' 5½"
2. Marie Spowage, Richmond Track Club   16' 4½"
3. Patricia McBurney, Seattle Olympic Club   15' 1"

Javelin
1. Joyce Humbel, Tacoma Track Club   136' 4½"
2. Michele Nance, Will's Spikettes   nm
3. Elinor Slack, San Mateo Girls' A.A.   nm

4-kilo shot
1. Janis Nay, San Mateo Girls' A.A.   35' 11¾"
2. Pauline Conwell, Angels Track Club   35' 9¼"
3. Michele Nance, Will's Spikettes   35' 2"

Discus
1. Helen Thayer, unattached   140' 5"
2. Gayle Davis, Falcon Track Club   129' 9"
3. Janis Nay, San Mateo Girls' A.A.   114' 8"

Team scores:
Seattle Olympic Club 72; Oakettes 63; Will's Spikettes 55; Ft. Worth Track Club 36; Richmond Track Club 26; Falcon Track Club 24; San Mateo Girls' A.A. 22; Laurel Track Club 18.

1965 All-America Women's Track and Field Teams

100-meter hurdles	Cherrie Sherrard
200-meter hurdles	Mamie Rallins
100-yard dash	Wyomia Tyus
220-yard dash	Edith McGuire
440-yard run	Janell Smith
880-yard run	Marie Mulder
1500-meter run	Marie Mulder
Long jump	Willye White
High jump	Eleanor Montgomery

4-kilo shot	Lynn Graham
Discus	Lynn Graham
Javelin	RaNae Bair
Pentathlon	Pat Winslow

Girls' Division

50-yard hurdles	Tammy Davis
50-yard dash	Debbie Thompson
100-yard dash	Debbie Thompson
220-yard dash	Jenda Jones
440-yard run	Madeline Manning
880-yard run	Cathy Catlin
Long jump	Bethe McBride
High jump	Denise Paschal
8-lb. shot	Lynn Graham
Discus	Lynn Graham
Javelin	Louise Gerrish

An article in the *AAU Handbook* stated that the United States women began preparing for the 1968 Olympics by performing well at the indoor meets at Wembley Stadium and in Berlin following the indoor season and in subsequent meets against Poland and West Germany. Ollan Cassell, the writer, noted, however, that for the seventh consecutive year, our women had lost to the USSR women's team.

Ollan stated that our sprinters seemed to hold their own, but they were not unbeatable. We had to improve in the other events, he said, if we were to have a well balanced team.

The outstanding performers in national and international competition this year, according to Ollan, were Wyomia Tyus and two teenage, middle-distance runners, Janell Smith and fifteen-year-old Marie Mulder.

Ollan noted that in preparation for the next Olympics in Mexico City, four middle-distance runners — Madeline Manning, Dino Lowery, Cathy Catlin, and Marie Mulder — had been selected to compete in the "Little Olympics" in Mexico City during the second week in October. Madeline Manning won the 400-meter run in 56.0 seconds.

USA vs. USSR: Kiev, July 31–August 1

The *New York Times* said that both McGuire and Tyus were magnificent in the 100 meters. Tyus bettered the listed world record of 11.2 that she shared with Wilma Rudolph and tied the pending mark set two weeks earlier by two Polish runners.

Fifteen-year-old Marie Mulder thrilled the crowd of 45,000 by finishing a close second in the 800 meters in a new American record. Marie started her kick at the final 200-meter point. She passed one Soviet runner and then pressed the other one to the finish line.

The *New York Times* featured Marie Mulder in an article saying that the lovely, slim, fifteen-year-old girl wearing baggy warm-ups had been running down the streets of Kiev. This youngest girl on the United States team had started running only a year and a half earlier.

100-meter dash	
1. Wyomia Tyus	11.1 WR
2. Edith McGuire	11.4
200-meter dash	
1. Edith McGuire	23.1
2. Wyomia Tyus	23.3
800-meter run	
2. Marie Mulder	2:07.3 AR
4. Sandra Knott	2:11.4
80-meter hurdles	
3. Rosie Bonds	10.9
4. Cherrie Sherrard	10.9
400-meter relay	
1. USA	44.4
(White, McGuire, Wilson, Tyus)	
Long jump	
3. Willye White	20' 8"
4. Sonia Guss	18' 11½"
Discus	
3. Cynthia Wyatt	140' 5"
4. Lynn Graham	139' 9"
Shot put	
3. Lynn Graham	50' 1"
4. Cynthia Wyatt	45' 11"
Javelin	
3. RaNae Bair	171' 9"
4. Lurline Hamilton	147' 0"
High jump	
2. Eleanor Montgomery	5' 8"
(tied with USSR competitor)	
4. Estelle Baskerville	5' 5"
USSR 63½— USA 43½	

USA vs. Poland: Warsaw, August 7-8

Twenty-one-year-old RaNae Bair set an American record in the javelin throw, and Janell Smith won the 400 meters in American record time.

The crowd of 35,000 applauded as fifteen-year-old Marie Mulder won the 800-meter run in 2:10.2. Sandy Knott set the pace for most of the race, but in the last 50 yards, with the crowd screaming for her, Marie Mulder passed Sandy Knott and a Polish runner for the win.

100-meter dash	
2. Wyomia Tyus	11.5
4. Diana Wilson	11.7
200-meter dash	
3. Edith McGuire	23.7
4. Wyomia Tyus	23.8
400-meter dash	
1. Janell Smith	53.7 AR
2. Madeline Manning	54.5
800-meter run	
1. Marie Mulder	2:10.2
2. Sandra Knott	2:10.4
80-meter hurdles	
1. Cherrie Sherrard	10.8
2. Tammy Davis	10.9
400-meter relay	
2. USA	
(White, McGuire, Wilson, Tyus)	
High jump	
1. Eleanor Montgomery	5' 7"
4. Estelle Baskerville	no mark
Long jump	
2. Willye White	20' 5⅜"
4. Sonia Guss	18' 9½"
Shot put	
1. Lynn Graham	50' 3½"
2. Cynthia Wyatt	46' 7¾"
Discus	
3. Cynthia Wyatt	155' 3"
4. Carol Moseke	151' 10"
Javelin	
1. RaNae Bair	184' 11½" AR
4. Lurline Hamilton	151' 5½"
USA 59 — Poland 57	

USA vs. West Germany: Munich, August 13

The *New York Times* headlines read, "American Women Triumph in Track." Edith McGuire won the 200, ran the second leg on the winning 400-meter relay team, and finished second to Wyomia Tyus in the 100 meters. The United States women won seven of the eleven events.

100-meter dash	
1. Wyomia Tyus	11.4
2. Edith McGuire	11.5

200-meter dash	
1. Edith McGuire	23.1
2. Diana Wilson	24.0

400-meter dash	
1. Janell Smith	54.0
2. Madeline Manning	54.6

800-meter run	
2. Sandra Knott	2:10.2
4. Marie Mulder	2:15.2

400-meter relay	
1. USA	44.9
(White, McGuire, Wilson, Tyus)	

80-meter hurdles	
2. Cherrie Sherrard	10.8
3. Tammy Davis	11.0

Long jump	
1. Willye White	21' 1½"
4. Sonia Guss	18' 6¾"

High jump	
1. Eleanor Montgomery	5' 5¾"
4. Estelle Baskerville	5' 3"

Javelin	
1. RaNae Bair	178' 3"
4. Lurline Hamilton	149' 11"

Shot put	
3. Lynn Graham	48' 7½"
4. Cynthia Wyatt	45' 8"

Discus	
3. Cynthia Wyatt	150' 11½"
4. Lynn Graham	142' 9"

USA 62 — West Germany 55

USA vs. Great Britain — Indoors: London, April 3-4

60-yard dash	
1. Barbara Ferrell	7.0
4. Marilyn White	7.1

60-yard hurdles
1. Tammy Davis   8.0
3. Lois Johnson   8.3

600-yard run
1. Janell Smith   1:25.2
4. Norma Harris   1:28.0

High jump
1. Pat Winslow   5' 6"
4. Kay Johnson   5' 0"

Invitation 880-yard run
1. Marie Mulder   2:15.0 (British record)

Long jump
2. Willye White   19' 10½"
4. Betty Holmes   18' 2"

Shot put
1. Lynn Graham   49' 7"
3. Sharon Shepherd   44' 7"

4 × 1 lap relay
2. USA   66.9
    (Reynolds, Carter, Ferrell, M. White)

USA 38½ — Great Britain 33½

USA vs. West Germany: West Berlin, April 7-8

The *New York Times* headlines on April 8 said, "U.S. Runners Set 2 Indoor Records." In the women's competition, both Janell Smith, the winner, and Norma Harris, who finished second, broke the existing world 400-meter run mark. Janell lowered the mark by 1.6 seconds.

60-yard hurdles
2. Tammy Davis   7.5
4. Lois Johnson   8.1

60-yard dash
1. Barbara Ferrell   6.7
3. Gladys Reynolds   6.9

400-meter dash
1. Janell Smith   54.0
2. Norma Harris   55.1

High jump
1. Pat Winslow   5' 4⅝"
4. Kay Johnson   4' 11"

Shot put
2. Lynn Graham   49' 1½"
4. Sharon Shepherd   44' 9¾"

4 × 1 lap relay
2. USA   1:35.6
    (Ferrell, Smith, Harris, White)

60-yard hurdles
1. Tammy Davis   7.6
4. Lois Johnson   8.1

60-yard dash
1. Marilyn White   6.8
2. Barbara Ferrell   6.8

Long jump
1. Willye White   20' 6¾"
4. Betty Holmes   18' 3"

800-meter run
2. Marie Mulder   2:08.3
3. Sandra Knott   2:10.9

4 × 1 lap relay
1. USA   1:31.1
    (Smith, Harris, Davis, White)

USA 61— West Germany 52

The 60-yard dash, 60-yard hurdles, and 4 × 1 lap relay were held on both days.

The national records committee compiled a "top performance" list for the year which appears below.

100 yards	10.3	Wyomia Tyus
100 meters	11.1	Wyomia Tyus
220 yards	23.6	Edith McGuire
200 meters	23.1	Edith McGuire
440 yards	54.3	Janell Smith
400 meters	53.7	Janell Smith
880 yards	2:10.2	Marie Mulder
800 meters	2:07.3	Marie Mulder
80-meter hurdles	10.8	Chi Cheng, Cherrie Sherrard
200-meter hurdles	27.6	Mamie Rallins
High jump	5' 8"	Eleanor Montgomery
Long jump	21' 1½"	Willye White
4-kilo shot	51' 1"	Nancy McCredie
Discus throw	157' 9"	Lynn Graham
Pentathlon	4399	Pat Winslow

Juner Bellew, the national chairman, wrote in her annual report:

Never before have so many opportunities been available to the U.S. women in track and field. Following is a list of 1965 invitations.

1) On the basis of performance at the combined Men & Women's Indoor Championships, sixteen girls were selected to participate in Indoor meets both in England and Germany.

2) The Australian AAA invited two girls Debbie Thompson and Willye White to Perth, Australia for their National Championships in March, as a return for the two girls from Melbourne who toured the U.S. on the indoor circuit.

3) Mexico extended invitations to several clubs for a meet held below the border in early May.

4) Toronto International Track Meet in June attracted several participants as did their Indoor meet.

5) Jamaica again invited six girls to Kingston for competition in mid–July.

6) Our outdoor nationals held in Columbus, Ohio where many records were rewritten, was also used to select the twenty-one athletes to compete against Russia, Poland, and West Germany.

7) The State Department sent four girls to several countries in South America for clinics, lectures, demonstrations and competitions.

8) Four of our longer distance runners were on hand to take part in a "Pilot Program" in Mexico City in October.

Willye White was awarded the international "fair play" trophy as the most sporting sports star of 1965.

Track and Field Techniques for Girls and Women written by Dr. Ken Foreman and Virginia Husted was published this year.

The Eastern Women's Track League was organized by Jack Griffin and included coaches Brooks Johnson from Washington, D.C., Connie Ford and Fred Thompson from New York, and Tim Hickey from Philadelphia. The League offered the opportunity for girls from the East Coast, from Maryland to Connecticut, to participate in an annual, organized schedule of cross-country, indoor, and outdoor track. Bill Mongovan, founder of the Gateway Track Club, praised the league and credited it with bringing him into the mainstream of women's track and field.

The Second National Institute on Girls' Sports was held at Michigan State University, East Lansing, from September 26 to October 1. The Institute was made possible through a grant from the Doris Duke Foundation. The track and field program follows:

Building on Basics	Virginia Crafts
Conditioning and Training for Competition	Nell Jackson
Good Track and Field Meets	Dorothy Harkins
Comments on Field Events	Olga Connolly
Coaching Beginners in the Shot, Discus, and Javelin	Olga Connolly
Shot Put and Discus Throw	Frances Wakefield
Teaching the Shot Put and Discus to Intermediate Performers	Frances Wakefield
Javelin and Softball Throws	Virginia Frank
Basketball Throw	Linda DeLong

Tips for a Long Jump	Bob Epskamp
Guidelines for Analysis and Correction of Faults in Hurdling	Kenneth Simmons
Sprinting, Middle Distance Running, and Long Distance Running	John M. Cooper
Warm-ups for Sprints, 440 and 880 Runs, 1500m Runs and Longer Races	John M. Cooper
Fundamentals of Relay Racing	Kenneth Simmons
How to Teach the Beginning Hurdler	Kenneth Simmons

Since the first Institute, 234 state workshops or clinics have been held, educating about 25,350 teachers in track and field and gymnastics.

Comments were made from the start that the results of the institutes would have far-reaching positive results for many years in track and field, and this seems to have been true.

Will Stephens

Will Stephens graduated from Franklin High in Portland, Oregon, in 1938 and then entered the Marine Corps. He later attended Lewis and Clark College, where he was named the outstanding senior athlete. During high school, through college, and in the masters program, he participated in track and field.

In 1954, Will returned to Franklin High as varsity track coach for a year and then served as assistant track coach until 1959.

Will then moved to California to become head cross-country and track coach at Encina High in Sacramento, a position he held until 1977. During this time he founded his nationally known club, Will's Spikettes. His team won 18 different national team titles, which earned him the distinction of being one of the best track coaches in the country.

Among the outstanding athletes he coached were Olympians Kathy Hammond, Kathy Weston, and Evelyn Ashford. Eight of his athletes won national championships, and twelve were named to United States national teams.

Stephens was named head coach at Oregon State in 1977, a year after he was inducted into the Sacramento Golden West Track and Field Hall of Fame. While at Oregon State University, he coached Kathy Weston, Robin Blaine, Kris Trom, and Kathy Costello, all national-level runners.

Stephens was appointed coach of several United States teams. In 1966, he coached the United States team which competed against the British Commonwealth team. In 1969, he coached the All-Stars, the American team at the World Cross-Country championships in Scotland, and the United States team at the World Games for the Deaf in Yugoslavia.

Will was selected on two occasions to coach the U.S. team that competed against the USSR. He also served as coach of the West team in the first Olympic Sports Festival in Colorado Springs in 1978. In 1979, he was the U.S. coach for the World Cup 11 in Montreal. Later that year he coached the U.S. team at the Jacques-Coeur Relays in France.

Cathy Catlin Van Leuven, who was the 1965 national girls' champion in the 880 yards, and was one of Will's Spikettes, shared with me some of her memories of her coach:

> I remember Will being a very kind, honest, and loving coach and father. He was strict and made us work hard, but I don't ever remember anyone complaining.
>
> He was always there for us, no matter what. I had a lot of personal problems with my father. I could always talk to Mr. Stephens. He would listen and help me work through them and even come over to the house and talk to my father.
>
> Will was a dedicated coach. He expected his runners to be dedicated too. He was so much like a father, we never wanted to disappoint him.
>
> I remember that he brought his movie camera to all our meets. He'd be filming our race and get so excited that he would be filming the sky and the grass instead of us running. After a while, he had to give that job to one of the parents.
>
> Mr. Stephens always encouraged us. He never made extreme demands. He just wanted us to work hard and have fun.
>
> In nineteen eighty, I knew he had become ill with cancer. I was out of town for a month and when I returned home I called his wife to see how he was. She told me he had died a few days earlier. I was devastated. I felt like I had lost my own father. I don't think there's a day that goes by that I don't think about him and all the good times I had as a member of Will's Spikettes.

Chapter 49

1966

The city of Frederick, Maryland, was the site of the national championship meet from June 30 to July 2. More than 450 athletes were entered in the meet directed by Jack Griffin of the Frederick Track Club, the greatest number to date.

The *New York Times* reported, "2 U.S. Women Marks Set in A.A.U. Track." During the semifinals, Tennessee State's 440-yard relay team composed of Wyomia Tyus, Edith McGuire, Marcella Daniel, and Matteline Render established a new American record of 45.9 seconds. This bettered their own mark of 46 seconds set in 1962 and tied in 1963. This mark is just .7 seconds slower than the world record.

Pat Van Wolvelaere set a 200-meter hurdle record of 27.4, surpassing Mamie Rallins' record of 27.6.

Track and Field News had a small article entitled "Women's AAU: Seagren Equals Own Vault Mark." The story proclaimed that the big event of the women's AAU meet was Bob Seagren's pole vault. The article contained nothing about the women's meet.

100-yard dash		
1. Wyomia Tyus, Tennessee State		10.5
2. Edith McGuire, Tennessee State		10.8
3. Barbara Ferrell, L.A. Mercurettes		10.9
220-yard dash		
1. Wyomia Tyus, Tennessee State		23.8
2. Barbara Ferrell, L.A. Mercurettes		23.9
3. Edith McGuire, Tennessee State		24.0
80-meter hurdles		
1. Cherrie Sherrard, Laurel Track Club		10.7
2. Mamie Rallins, Mayor Daley Youth Foundation		11.0
3. Tammy Davis, Tennessee State		11.1
200-meter hurdles		
1. Patty Van Wolvelaere, Angels Track Club		27.6
2. Mamie Rallins, Mayor Daley Youth Foundation		28.1
3. Kathryn Carlson, Westport Recreation		28.7
440-yard dash		
1. Charlotte Cooke, L.A. Mercurettes		53.4

2. Delores Stoneback, Seattle Olympic Club — 55.7
3. Chris Iverson, SFVR — 55.7

880-yard run
1. Charlotte Cooke, L.A. Mercurettes — 2:05.0
2. Madeline Manning, Cleveland Recreation — 2:06.2
3. Frances Kraker, Southeastern Michigammes — 2:10.9

1500-meters
1. Doris Brown Heritage, Falcon Track Club — 4:20.2
2. Marie Mulder, Will's Spikettes — 4:36.6
3. Frances Kraker, Southeastern Michigammes — 4:37.3

440-yard relay
1. Tennessee State, "A" team — 45.7
   (McGuire, Daniel, Render, Tyus)
2. Tennessee State, "B" team — 47.5
3. Detroit Track Club — 47.5

880-yard medley relay
1. Cleveland Recreation — 1:44.3
   (Woods, McDonald, Allen, Manning)
2. Westport Recreation — 1:46.9
3. Angels Track Club — 1:47.0

High jump
1. Eleanor Montgomery, Tennessee State — 5' 7"
2. Estelle Baskerville, Tennessee State — 5' 5"
3. Patricia Clark, N.Y. Police Athletic League — 5' 4"

Long jump
1. Willye White, Mayor Daley Youth Foundation — 20' 7½"
2. Martha Watson, Tennessee State — 19' 9¼"
3. Bethe McBride, Liberty A.C. — 19' 1½"

Shot put
1. Lynn Graham, L.A. Mercurettes — 47' 11¾"
2. Carol Moseke, Nebraska Track Club — 44' 5"
3. Maren Seidler, Greater Atlantic Track and Field — 43' 6"

Discus throw
1. Carol Moseke, Nebraska Track Club — 159' 8"
2. Cynthia Wyatt, unattached — 145' 6"
3. Nancy Norberg, unattached — 143' 9"

Javelin throw
1. RaNae Bair, San Diego M.B. — 174' 10"
2. Barbara Friedrich, Shore A.C. — 174' 3"
3. Louise Gerrish, Southeastern Michigammes — 159' 5"

Pentathlon
1. Pat Daniels, San Mateo Girls' A.A. — 4496 points

Team scores:
Tennessee State Univ. 86; Los Angeles Mercurettes 42; Mayor Daley Youth Foundation 26.

The Indoor Nationals

The *New York Times* headlined the setting of four world records in the indoor nationals. "Miss Tyus Snaps 60-Yard Record" and "Miss McGuire Sets Mark in 220, Mrs. Nagy-Szabo in 880, Miss Cooke in 440." The indoor national meet was held in Albuquerque, New Mexico, on March 4-5. Tyus and McGuire, the two Tennessee State Olympians, led the field on the record assault. Wyomia won the 60 in 6.5, which lowered the mark held by her and two others by one tenth of a second. The week before, in the *Telegram–Maple Leaf* Games in Toronto, she set a world record in the 50 with a time of 5.8.

Edith McGuire was presented with the Dieges Award.

60-yard dash
1. Wyomia Tyus, Tennessee State — 6.5 WR
2. Edith McGuire, Tennessee State — 6.7
3. Barbara Ferrell, L.A. Mercurettes — 6.8
4. Regina Wade, Ft. Worth, Texas — 6.9

220-yard dash
1. Edith McGuire, Tennessee State — 24.1 WR
2. Norma Harris, Mayor Daley Youth Foundation — 24.4
3. Wyomia Tyus, Tennessee State — 24.4
4. Karen Dennis, Detroit Track Club — 25.1

880-yard run
1. Mrs. Nagy-Szabo, Hungary — 2:08.6 WR
2. Marie Mulder, Camp Springs, Md. — 2:11.8
3. Sandra Knott, Cleveland Recreation — 2:12.3
4. Francie Kraker, Michigammes — 2:15.0

440-yard dash
1. Charlotte Cooke, L.A. Mercurettes — 54.2 WR
2. Una Morris, Jamaica — 55.6
3. Kathy Hammond, Will's Spikettes — 56.2
4. Diane Knight, Cullen Junior High — 58.6

60-yard hurdles
1. Chi Cheng, L. A. Mercurettes — 7.6
2. Cherrie Sherrard, Laurel Track Club — 7.6
3. Tammy Davis, Tennessee State — 7.8
4. Mamie Rallins, Mayor Daley Youth Foundation — 7.9

Sprint relay (704 yards — 4 lap)
1. Tennessee State — 1:18.5
   (McGuire, Render, Harvey, Tyus)
2. Lubbock Track Club — 1:22.0
3. Laurel Track Club — 1:22.0

1,060-yard medley relay
1. Mayor Daley Youth Foundation — 2:08.5
   (Loney, White, Rallins, Harris)

2. Detroit Track Club   2:09.9
3. Ohio Track Club   2:12.6

High jump
1. Eleanor Montgomery, Tennessee State   5' 8"
2. Estelle Baskerville, Tennessee State   5' 7"
3. Denise Paschal, Laurel Track Club   5' 2"
4. Connie Peterson, Kalispell Timberettes   5' 0"

Long jump
1. Chi Cheng, L.A. Mercurettes   19' 9½"
2. Willye White, Mayor Daley Youth Foundation   19' 6¼"
3. Martha Watson, Tennessee State   18' 8½"
4. Calanthia Rallings, Tennessee State   18' 6¼"

Basketball throw
1. Barbara Friedrich, Shore A.C.   134' 10"
2. Nancy Putman, Kalispell Timberettes   107' 11"
3. Louise Gerrish, Ann Arbor, Michigan   102' 8"
4. Shirley McCondichie, Chicago   100' 1"

Shot put
1. Joan Whitehead, Indian Track Club   40' 11¾"
2. Ann Kaufman, Topeka   40' 5½"
3. Janis Nay, Millbrae Lions   40' 5¼"
4. Sherry Calvert, S.C. Missiles   38' 1"

Team scores:
Tennessee State Univ. 33; Mayor Daley Youth Foundation 13; Laurel Track Club 7.

Women's events were held in Louisville, Kentucky, at the Mason-Dixon Games and in the Seventh Annual *Los Angeles Times* Meet in February. The Los Angeles meet reported a 60-yard dash, an 880-yard run, and a high jump. Wyomia Tyus won the 60 in 6.7, Marie Mulder was second in the 880 in 2:15.4 to an athlete from the USSR, and Eleanor Montgomery set an American record of 5' 8¾" in the high jump.

In Louisville, the women's events held were the 70-yard hurdles and 70-yard dash. A world record was set in the hurdles. Mamie Rallins was second in 9.0. Edith McGuire won the 70-yard dash in 7.9. A quote from the *New York Times* about the hurdle race said: "The students and fanciers of women's track were treated to a world record, too. It was authored by Inge Schell, a 26-year-old West German blonde of bathing-beauty proportions."

Juner Bellew's annual report stated that Willye White and Marie Mulder were invited to Israel to participate in the HAPOEL Games and a meet in Haifa.

Bellew also noted: "Five days before the Polish meet word came that both international matches were cancelled. Needless to say the athletes, both men and women, were most disappointed! ... These athletes participated in a quickly formed All-American meet in Berkeley which produced excellent performances. The Los Angeles meet was turned into a Commonwealth vs. USA spectacle, and it really was a fantastic competition for our girls."

The 10th Annual Marine Corps School Relays was held on May 6 and 7. Fourteen women's teams took part in two women's events. One event was an 880-yard run, which was listed as a new event. The race had twenty-seven competitors. The 440-yard relay with twelve teams entered was also listed as a new event.

June 4 was the date of the 24th Annual Compton Invitational Track Meet, which took place at the Los Angeles Coliseum. Two women's events were on the program, the 100- and the 440-yard run.

The 25th Anniversary–California Relays and State Junior College Track Championships were held on May 28 at Modesto Junior College Stadium. Forty-one events were listed and none of them women's events.

Cinderbelle's "Top Ten" list included:

11.5	Wyomia Tyus	100 meters
11.5	Barbara Ferrell	100 meters
23.6	Edith McGuire	200 meters
53.0	Charlette Cooke	400 meters
2:03.8	Charlette Cooke	800 meters
10.7	Cherrie Sherrard	80-meter hurdles
44.8	USA	400-meter relay
188' 11"	RaNae Bair	Javelin
183' 5"	Barbara Friedrich	Javelin

Cinderbelle had an article on cross-country growth in the United States. New York City and Michigan had full meet schedules. Meets were run for the first time in Indiana, Florida, upper New York State, and Pennsylvania, while Missouri, Illinois, Ohio, and New Jersey ran more meets than in 1965. The author said, "Those seeking to discredit cross-country as harmful are on shrinking grounds."

The January 1966–January 1968 *Track and Field Guide* was published by the Division for Girls and Women's Sports. Linda DeLong was the editor. Donnis Thompson had two articles on teaching sprinting, relay racing, and hurdling. Karen Anderson Oldham described javelin-throwing technique. This booklet was the "Bible" for physical education teachers and coaches in our nation's schools.

Another interesting article, "Kentucky High School Girls State Track Meet," indicated the progress of girls' track in Kentucky. For several years they had had invitational meets, play days, and sports days. For two years, wide area track and field meets had been held at Campbellsville College. Three clinics were held in February in different areas of the state, and regional meets were held at ten different sites. More than thirty high schools participated.

A request was made to use the track facility at Fort Campbell, Kentucky, for the first state girls' track meet. After influential people wrote letters of persuasion, permission was given to hold the meet at that location. First and second finishers from the regional meets were invited to participate in the 50, 75, 100,

Jack Griffin, founder and coach of Frederick Track Club, Frederick, Maryland, and coach of 1964, 1976 and 1984 Olympic teams. (Courtesy of Jack Griffin.)

220, and 440 yard dashes, the 50-yard hurdles, 440-yard relay, shot put, softball throw, high jump, long jump, and standing long jump.

Fran Davenport, the 1961 javelin champion, led a parade of athletes in the impressive opening ceremony. The meet was a success, and plans were made for sixty high schools to work towards the next year's meet to be held at the University of Kentucky on May 20. New events were planned, including the discus throw, the 660-yard run, and the 880-yard medley relay.

Another article dealt with encouraging girls in the Chicago area to compete in track meets and discussed the First Chicago Suburban Area Track and Field Meet for Girls. Fifty physical education teachers served as officials. Five hundred ninety-eight girls entered the meet, but 415 actually participated in twenty-four events. There were 80 entries from the elementary division, 221 from junior high school, and 114 high school age entries. The author, Mary Barnett, stated that some of the outcomes of the meet were significant: "Many of these girls gained additional knowledge of and enthusiasm for track and field. At the same time, information concerning forthcoming AAU track and field meets was distributed to participants. And finally, many physical education teachers have additional knowledge in how to organize and conduct track and field meets."

Girls' and women's track and field records were listed in the *Guine* for elementary school girls, junior high school, senior high school, college, and open and world records. All of the elementary and junior high records were from 1960 or later, the same for high school and college divisions, except for one in each category, the 50-yard dash which was set in 1959, in the high school category, and the basketball throw, also set in 1959, in the college and open category.

A most significant event took place in women's running on April 18, 1966. Twenty-three-year-old Roberta Gibb became the first woman to unofficially run the Boston Marathon.

Jack Griffin

Jack founded the Frederick Track Club, Frederick, Maryland, in 1957 and coached the women athletes for twenty-eight years. His athletes, including

Olympian Debbie Thompson and world-record-holder Tammy Davis, competed in eighteen countries as members of nine national teams. They held five world records, four indoor and one outdoor.

During the time that he taught and coached in the Frederick schools for thirty years, he was appointed coach of United States international teams:

1965 — U.S. team competing in Russia, Germany, and Poland

1972 — World cross-country team

1975 — U.S. team competing in Russia, Czechoslovakia, Poland, Romania, Pan-African

1978 — U.S. team competing in Russia, England, Germany

Jack was the assistant coach for the 1964 Olympic team, assistant coach for the 1976 Olympic team, and assistant coach for the 1984 Olympic team, becoming the only person besides Ed Temple receiving three Olympic coaching positions.

Chapter 50

1967

Santa Barbara, California, hosted the national track and field championships on July 1-2.

The *New York Times* headlines read, "Track Mark Tied by Miss Ferrell." In winning the 100-meter dash, Barbara Ferrell equaled the world 100-meter mark of 11.1 seconds.

Women's Track and Field World said Ferrell was off fast, was slightly ahead midway, and held the lead to the tape. Diana Wilson was a close second, and Tyus was two feet back. Wyomia's loss to Ferrell in the heat marked the end of her undefeated season. When Ferrell eased up slightly in the 200 meters, Wilson hit the tape first and won her first national championship.

Women's Track and Field World praised the strong field in the 400 meters and said that this field was faster and had greater depth than could be seen in any other country in the event. In the final, Hammond went out slowly, while Cooke, Johnson, and Burnett went out fast. Cooke had a substantial lead but began to fade. Hammond was closing the gap, and less than a yard separated them at the tape. Both times were under the old record. Charlotte Cooke shattered her own American record 400-meter mark by .8 of a second with her winning time of 52.5.

In the final of the 800 meters, Doris Brown was out fast and Manning trailed. By the 600-meter mark, Manning began to move up. *Women's Track and Field World* said, "Brown actually led the race for 799⅔ meters." Manning won by inches.

Tennessee State ran well in the heats of the 400-meter relay, setting a new record of 45.1. In the final, Matteline Render dropped the baton and after picking it up, could not do any better than sixth place.

In the high jump, Eleanor Montgomery had no misses until 5' 9¼". She was the only competitor to clear 5' 6¼". The other places were awarded on fewer attempts.

Pat Winslow's upset winning long jump was her lifetime best, although wind-aided. Another of her jumps, which was not wind-aided, was 20' 6", which also would have captured first place.

Sixteen-year-old Maren Seidler's win in the shot put was a big upset over Lynn Graham. On her final throw, Maren put a lifetime best of 46' 10".

The javelin throw was the most exciting of the field events. Barbara Friedrich set a new championship record in the trials with a throw of 183' 8". During the final throws, placing switched with almost every throw. RaNae Bair, in her second attempt in the finals, flung the spear 196' 3". Friedrich improved her mark to 191' 2" on her next throw, but neither athlete had good final attempts.

100-meter dash
1. Barbara Ferrell, L.A. Mercurettes   11.1 ties WR
2. Diana Wilson, Tennessee State   11.4
3. Wyomia Tyus, Tennessee State   11.6
4. Matteline Render, Tennessee State   11.6

200 meters
1. Diana Wilson, Tennessee State   23.6
2. Barbara Ferrell, L.A. Mercurettes   23.7
3. Wyomia Tyus, Tennessee State   24.0
4. Vilma Charlton, Pepperdine   24.1

400-meter dash
1. Charlotte Cooke, unattached   52.5 AR
2. Kathy Hammond, Will's Spikettes   52.6
3. Lois Drinkwater, Phoenix Valley   53.5
4. Janet Johnson, Falcon Track Club   53.6

200-meter hurdles
1. Pat Van Wolvelaere, Angels Track Club   27.8
2. Mamie Rallins, Mayor Daley Youth Foundation   28.0
3. Chris McFarland, Will's Spikettes   28.2
4. Kitty Carlson, Westport, Conn., Track Club   28.7

800-meter run
1. Madeline Manning, Tennessee State   2:03.6
2. Doris Brown, Falcon Track Club   2:03.6
3. Charlotte Cooke, unattached   2:08.3
4. Jarvis Scott, L.A. Mercurettes   2:10.3

1500-meter run
1. Natalie Rocha, Will's Spikettes   4:29.0
2. Vicki Foltz, unattached   4:29.5
3. Lori Schutt, Mayor Daley Youth Foundation   4:33.7
4. Kathy DeStout, San Diego Mission Belles   4:37.8

80-meter hurdles
1. Mamie Rallins, Mayor Daley Youth Foundation   10.9
2. Cherrie Sherrard, Laurel Track Club   11.0
3. Chi Cheng, unattached   11.0
4. Pat Van Wolvelaere, Angels Track Club   11.2

400-meter relay
1. Texas Southern   46.3
2. Mayor Daley Youth Foundation   47.3
3. Laurel Track Club   47.6
4. L.A. Mercurettes   48.3

800-meter medley relay
1. Tennessee State   1:41.7 AR
   (Morris, Daniel, Render, Manning)
2. Atoms Track Club, "A" team   1:44.6
3. San Diego Mission Belles   1:45.0
4. Orinda Track Club   1:45.2

High jump
1. Eleanor Montgomery, Tennessee State   5' 6¼"
2. Franzetta Parham, unattached   5' 5¼"
3. Estelle Baskerville, Tennessee State   5' 5¼"
4. Pat Winslow, Millbrae Lions   5' 5¼"

Long jump
1. Pat Winslow, Millbrae Lions   20' 8¼"w
2. Willye White, Mayor Daley Youth Foundation   20' 1"w
3. Martha Watson, Tennessee State   19' 7¼"w
4. RaNae Bair, San Diego Mission Belles   18' 11"w

Shot put
1. Maren Seidler, Shore A.C.   46' 10"
2. Lynn Graham, L.A. Mercurettes   46' 5"
3. Carol Moseke, Nebraska Track Club   43' 10"
4. Pat Winslow, Millbrae Lions   43' 8"

Discus throw
1. Carol Moseke, Nebraska Track Club   152' 5"
2. Ranee Kletchka, Nebraska Track Club   151' 7"
3. Helen Thayer, Falcon Track Club   144' 4"
4. Nancy Norberg, unattached   141' 9"

Javelin throw
1. RaNae Bair, San Diego Mission Belles   196' 3"
2. Barbara Friedrich, Shore A.C.   191' 2"
3. Jean Sweeney, Ohio Track Club   167' 1"
4. Roberta Brown, San Diego Mission Belles   163' 10"

Team scores:
Tennessee State U. 77; Mayor Daley Y.F. 40; Los Angeles Mercurettes 38; San Diego Mission Belles 29; Nebraska Track Club 24; Will's Spikettes 24; Millbrae Lions 19.

The Indoor Nationals

The New York Times carried an article on the indoor meet held in Oakland, California, on March 3-4. Two small paragraphs were devoted to the women's events. Pat Van Wolvelaere upset Cherrie Sherrard in the 60-yard hurdles, winning in 7.7, and Madeline Manning out-sprinted Doris Brown in the final 160 yards to win the women's 880 in 2:04.4, equaling the world indoor record.

Madeline was presented with the Dieges Award for her performance.

60-yard dash
1. Wyomia Tyus, Tennessee State   6.7
2. Barbara Ferrell, L.A. Mercurettes   6.7
3. Dee DeBusk, Santa Ynez Track Club   6.8

220-yard dash
1. Una Morris, Tennessee State   25.0
2. Karen Dennis, Detroit Track Club   25.3
3. Jane Burett, Valley of the Sun   25.7

440-yard dash
1. Kathy Hammond, Will's Spikettes   55.2
2. Jarvis Scott, L.A. Mercurettes   56.6
3. Jane Burnett, Sports International   57.5

880-yard run
1. Madeline Manning, Tennessee State   2:08.4 ties WR
2. Doris Brown, Falcon Track Club   2:09.2
3. Francie Kraker, Southeast Michigan   2:10.2

Mile run
1. Doris Brown, Falcon Track Club   4:43.3
2. Natalie Rocha, Will's Spikettes   5:01.5
3. Francie Kraker, Southeast Michigan   5:01.5

60-yard hurdles
1. Pat Van Wolvelaere, Angels Track Club   7.7
2. Cherrie Sherrard, Laurel Track Club   7.8
3. Denise Paschal, Laurel Track Club   7.9

Shot put
1. Lynn Graham, L.A. Mercurettes   46' 4¾"
2. Carol Moseke, Nebraska Track Club   43' 9"
3. Maren Seidler, Shore A.C.   43' 4¼"

High jump
1. Eleanor Montgomery, Tennessee State   5' 9"
2. Estelle Baskerville, Tennessee State   5' 7"
3. Fran Parham, Isleton A.C.   5' 6"

Long jump
1. Martha Watson, Tennessee State   20' 6½" MR
2. Pat Winslow, Millbrae Lions   20' 5¾"
3. Denise Paschal, Laurel Track Club   19' 10¼"

Basketball throw
1. Barbara Friedrich, Shore A.C.   131' 1½"
2. Carol Moseke, Nebraska Track Club   111' 10½"
3. Nancy Putman, Kalispell Track Club   111' 3"

Team scores:
Tennessee State University 33; Los Angeles Mercurettes 14; Will's Spikettes 11.

The Pan American Trials

The tryouts for the Pan American team were on July 15.

100 meters
1. Barbara Ferrell, L.A. Mercurettes   11.4
2. Janet MacFarlane, Santa Ynez Track Club   11.5
3. Dee DeBusk, Santa Ynez Track Club   11.6
4. Wyomia Tyus, Tennessee State   11.6
5. Matteline Render, Tennessee State   11.6

80 meter hurdles
1. Mamie Rallins, Mayor Daley Youth Foundation   10.8
2. Cherrie Sherrard, Laurel Track Club   10.9
3. Pat Van Wolvelaere, Angels Track Club   11.1

Discus throw
1. Carol Moseke, Nebraska Track Club   154' 6"
2. Ranee Kletchka, Nebraska Track Club   153' 3"
3. Nancy Norberg, unattached   150' 8"

Long jump
1. Martha Watson, Tennessee State   20' 10"
2. Willye White, Mayor Daley Youth Foundation   20' 1"
3. Janet MacFarlane, Santa Ynez Track Club   19' 4½"

High jump
1. Eleanor Montgomery, Tennessee State   5' 7"
2. Franzetta Parham, unattached   5' 6"
3. Estelle Baskerville, Tennessee State   5' 6"

800 meters
1. Madeline Manning, Tennessee State   2:06.2
2. Doris Brown, Falcon Track Club   2:06.5
3. Jarvis Scott, L.A. Mercurettes   2:06.5

Javelin throw
1. Barbara Friedrich, Shore A.C.   181' 11"
2. RaNae Bair, San Diego Mission Belles   179' 1"
3. Louise Gerrish, Michigammes   169' 5"

Shot put
1. Lynn Graham, L.A. Mercurettes   47' 9¾"
2. Maren Seidler, Mayor Daley Youth Foundation   47' 5¼"
3. Carol Moseke, Nebraska Track Club   45' 1¼"

200 meters
1. Barbara Ferrell, L.A. Mercurettes   24.0
2. Wyomia Tyus, Tennessee State   24.3
3. Jane Burnett, Sports International   24.3

The Pan American Games track competition began on July 29 in Winnipeg, Canada, at the University of Manitoba Stadium. The team, placing, and performance follow:

	Event	Place	Performance
Bair, RaNae	Javelin	2	169' 5"
Brown, Doris	800m	2	2:02.9
Burnett, Jane	400mr	DNQ	
DeBusk, Dee	400mr	DNQ	
Ferrell, Barbara	100	1	11.5
	200	2	23.8
	400mr	DNQ	
Friedrich, Barbara	Javelin	1	174' 9" (P.A. record)
Graham, Lynn	Shot	2	48' 9¾"
Johnson, Janet	Pentathlon	6	
Kletchka, Ranee	Discus	5	150' 2"
MacFarlane, Janet	100m	6	11.9
	400mr	DNQ	
Manning, Madeline	800m	1	2:02.3 (P.A. record)
Montgomery, Eleanor	HJ	1	5' 10" (P.A. record)
Moseke, Carol	Discus	1	161' 7"
Parham, Franzetta	HJ	3	5' 6½"
Rallins, Mamie	80mh	2	10.8
Seidler, Maren	SP	4	46' 3½"
Sherrard, Cherrie	80mh	1	10.8 (P.A. record)
Tyus, Wyomia	200m	1	23.7
Van Wolvelaere, Pat	80mh	DNQ	
Watson, Martha	LJ	4	20' 1½"
White, Willye	LJ	3	20' 3"
Winslow, Pat	Pentathlon	1	4860
Jim Bibbs	Coach, Track		
Dr. Harmon Brown	Coach, Field		
Dr. Maria Sexton	Manager-Chaperon		

USA vs. British Commonwealth: Los Angeles, July 8-9

In the 80-meter hurdles, Cherrie Sherrard and Mamie Rollins finished second and third, but they were closing fast on the winner. In the 400-meter dash, Charlotte Cook led at the halfway point, running the 200 meters in 25.5. With about five yards to go, Cook sustained an injury and dropped to fourth as she crossed the finish line.

In the long jump, Martha Watson had her lifetime best jump, and Willye White jumped her season best. Estelle Baskerville cleared 5' 8¼" on her last attempt in the high jump. Baskerville and the other remaining competitor had good efforts on two jumps at the next height of 5' 9½". This was one of the first times that Baskerville beat teammate Eleanor Montgomery.

In the javelin competition, RaNae Bair had one good throw to keep her winning streak intact. Barbara Friedrich, bothered by a knee injury, had a good throw on her second effort. Lynn Graham had her season best throw by nearly two feet, while sixteen-year-old Maren Seidler had two throws beyond her lifetime bests. Carol Moseke Frost also had three personal-best throws.

In the 100 meters, Barbara Ferrell, who set the world record of 11.1 a week earlier, led for the first 80 meters but finished in third, with Tyus a close fourth. Both ran the same time.

The 800 meter race was applauded as the most exciting event of the two-day competition. At the 200-meter mark, passed in 26 seconds, Jarvis Scott was leading, closely followed by Brown, Manning, and others. Brown took over at 400 meters, passing that point in 57.1. Manning was on her shoulder. "For the first time Manning was staying on the pace," said *Women's Track and Field World*. At the top of the final straightaway, Manning sprinted to a three-yard lead. She was challenged for the lead as the finish line loomed up but gave all her strength to hold the narrow lead for the victory in American record time. Doris Brown maintained third, and Jarvis Scott had her personal-best time for fourth place.

200-meter dash
4. Janet Johnson   23.8
5. Wyomia Tyus   24.0
6. Diana Wilson   24.4

80-meter hurdles
2. Cherrie Sherrard   10.8
3. Mamie Rallins   10.9
4. Pat Van Wolvelaere   11.2

400-meter dash
3. Kathy Hammond   53.9
4. Charlotte Cooke   54.1
5. Lois Drinkwater   55.1

Long jump
2. Martha Watson   20' 8½"
3. Willye White   20' 1"
6. Pat Winslow   18' 8½"

High jump
2. Estelle Baskerville   5' 8¼"
3. Eleanor Montgomery   5' 6¾"
6. Franzetta Parham   5' 4¾"

Javelin throw
1. RaNae Bair   187' 6"
2. Barbara Friedrich   182' 0"
5. Jean Sweeney   152' 7"

Discus throw
3. Carol Moseke   157' 10"
5. Helen Thayer   149' 6"
6. Ranee Kletchka   145' 7"

100 meters
3. Barbara Ferrell   11.7
4. Wyomia Tyus   11.7
5. Diana Wilson   11.9

800 meters
1. Madeline Manning   2:01.6 AR
3. Doris Brown   2:05.5
4. Jarvis Scott   2:06.7

400-meter relay
1. USA   44.6
    (Wilson, Render, DeBusk, Tyus)

Shot put
4. Lynn Graham   48' 3"
5. Maren Seidler   47' 4"
6. Carol Moseke   46' 5"

Commonwealth 125 — USA 102

The AAU held the first National Junior Olympic Swimming and Track and Field Meet this year. The track and field events were held at Calvin Coolidge High School in Washington, D.C.

The events for girls and women included the high jump, long jump, 50-yard low hurdles, for senior and intermediate girls; the 100-yard dash and 440-yard dash for senior girls; the 75 and 220 yard dashes for intermediate girls; and a 440-yard relay for both senior and intermediate girls.

A world list, compiled by *Women's Track and Field World* in the August issue, contained the following USA women (age, when available, is in parentheses):

100 meters
1. Barbara Ferrell (20)   11.1
7. Wyomia Tyus (22)   10.5y
   Diana Wilson (20)   11.4

200 meters
5. Barbara Ferrell   23.4
11. Diana Wilson   23.6

400 meters
1. Charlotte Cooke (19)   52.5
3. Kathy Hammond (16)   52.6
7. Lois Drinkwater (16)   53.8
12. Janet Johnson   54.5
15. Jane Burnett (15)   54.7

800 meters
2. Madeline Manning (19)   2:01.6
6. Doris Brown (25)   2:03.9
13. Charlotte Cooke   2:05.4

1500 meters/mile
6.	Natalie Rocha	4:29.0
8.	Vicki Foltz	4:29.5
12.	Lori Schutt	4:33.7

80-meter hurdles
11.	Cherrie Sherrard (29)	10.8

High jump
9.	Estelle Baskerville	5' 8"

Long jump
14.	Pat Winslow	20' 8½"

Javelin throw
1.	Barbara Friedrich (19)	198' 8"
2.	RaNae Bair (24)	196' 3"
11.	Louise Gerrish (19)	178' 10"

Pentathlon
1.	Pat Winslow	4832

400-meter relay
2.	USA	44.6
	(Wilson, Render, DeBusk, Tyus)	

Other interesting comments from *Women's Track and Field World* include a statement made by Dr. Maria Sexton to the effect that intercollegiate track competition for women was not far off. She noted that the matter was under consideration, and she projected that it would happen within five years.

Cinderbelle, published by Leo Larney, featured an article on Doris Brown's victory in the first Women's International Cross-Country Championship on March 18 at Barry, Wales. The 2½ mile race was run through fields and pastures on a cold, windy day. Two thousand spectators watched the race as the course wound around a "complex of 17 soccer fields and adjoining pastures" so that the entire race was visible to the spectators seated in the stadium. As she crossed the finish line in 14 minutes, 28 seconds, more than 100 yards ahead of the next runner, the spectators gave her a standing ovation."

Doris, a junior high school physical education teacher, and Dr. Ken Foreman, her coach, were impressed with the reception they received. The people were enthusiastic and knew more about her than she anticipated. She said that they were surprised that her training schedule sometimes included seventy-five miles a week. Twenty-four-year-old Doris was 5' 3" tall and weighed 105 pounds.

In Seattle, Doris was honored as the youngest woman ever named a "Woman of Achievement" by the Matrix Table of Seattle.

In 1967, K. Switzer, a twenty-year-old Syracuse University student, joined a carload full of Syracuse University cross-country runners and headed towards Boston in the snow. The Boston Marathon was on April 19. She got her number, dressed in heavy clothing, and started the race as the gun sounded. With number 261 pinned on her sweats, she ran with a boyfriend until Jock Semple, an official, jumped from the press bus and tried to tear the numbers off her. Because the cameras were operating nearby at the time, the incident became a worldwide news event.

Roberta Gibb was in the race for the second year. Her father dropped her off about 100 yards from the start, where she entered the race. Her unofficial time was 3:27:17.

After the race an official said, "I'm terribly disappointed that American girls force their way into something where they're neither eligible nor wanted."

Dr. Harmon Brown was appointed age-group chairman. At this time there were a handful of events for younger girls, none longer than 440 yards.

Madeline Manning (2:06.8) and Barbara Ferrell (11.6) captured first places in the World University Games.

Doris Severtsen Brown Heritage

In an interview on December 4, 1992, Doris told me about her track history:

> It must have been around nineteen fifty-seven when I got started in track. I was a junior playground leader, a volunteer, and the kids were going to a track meet. They had a fifty, a seventy-five and a long jump. I was young enough to compete so I entered. I was probably fifteen. I got second in the fifty — I was no sprinter — won the long jump and the seventy-five.
>
> I grew up out in the country with no athletic teams available for girls. There was a team in Tacoma where that meet was contested, and the coach asked me to be on his team. At that time my folks said no, they didn't want me getting involved in that kind of stuff — I was too much of a tomboy already. But about a year later they decided to let me do it. At that time I think the longest race in Olympic competition for women was two hundred meters, but I was somehow running the four hundred because it was run locally on occasion.
>
> My reason for starting track was that I wanted to be the first woman to climb Mt. Everest. I had that goal since the first grade. I was going to get in shape for this. The stadium that we worked out in had people training for mountain climbing. They were doing ropes and stuff off the edge. I was pretty excited about this stuff because they were among the world's best and had original ascents of Mt. Everest.
>
> In high school, I wasn't allowed on the track. There was a rule that girls were not allowed on the track. Our track was a square thing around the football field that had a ditch and cattails were growing out of it. The guys could train there but I couldn't. The coach would let me watch — sometimes he would let me run fifty-yard dashes with the guys, and he even let me go to one of the boy's track meets on the bus to watch because I was so interested.
>
> When the four hundred-meter girl on our team went to the nationals that year in Cleveland, Ohio, I ran the four hundred while she was away and set what would have been a national record. My time was fifty-nine point four.
>
> So then I ran the four hundred and did the long jump and ran some relays. That was what I did on this team with the coach. The team was called the Tacoma Mic Macs, and that name is after an Indian tribe in New York. The coach probably came from there. He was an old man, seventy-two years old,

and knew little about running. He had a neighbor girl who was very good, and he wanted her to have an opportunity. So he started doing this, and he did things like come out and help us dig a long jump pit in our garden. He worked through the Kiwanis Club and got us shoes and sweat suits, but he knew nothing about coaching. His idea of preparing us for a race was to rush out on the starting line and feed us a donut, a tablespoon of peanut butter, and send us off. That's really how we started, not warming up, nothing. But we thank him.

There were five girls on the team. One was a four hundred-meter runner, one was a javelin thrower, a fairly good javelin thrower, and the others must have been sprinters. We did things like starting out of the dirt holes (we didn't have starting blocks). I did that for a half hour with the sprinters. Then I long jumped for twenty minutes, and then I ran a quarter as hard as I could. So that was my work out once a week after church.

I just ran that one quarter. At home though I thought this was good stuff— I will train a little harder. So my dad measured off something near a quarter of a mile down the road. I'd get home from school, run down the road as hard as I could, be literally sick, turn around, run back again as hard as I could, and try things like standing upside down on the davenport to try to get rid of the stomach cramps, vowing I'd never run again. Then the next day I'd go through the same thing all over again, saying it wasn't that bad. Finally my mom took me to the doctor who said, "Well, are you warming up?" Warm-ups? What in the world is that? He said you have to go out and do whatever. I remember every day when I ran, I ran the same times I did in meets. It would vary between fifty-nine and sixty-one, and I couldn't understand why I didn't get better.

And somewhere along the line there was an eight hundred in our meets. Our meets at home had two divisions, junior and senior — so two of us would do every event in the junior and every event in the senior divisions.

My mother would bake us a can of cookies. She believed in healthy food, so she would put wheat germ in the oatmeal cookies. We would sit there and eat the whole can of cookies before the meet started.

I threw the javelin 30 feet — it was a men's javelin. It was hilarious. It was good training, but we didn't get better and I remember in the throwing events I was pathetic. I was good in the jumping events and running events — the longer the better. I lived on the beach, and I enjoyed taking ten-mile runs along the beach. There was a girl on our team who would win everything. When we finally had an eight hundred, I didn't want to beat her because she had been the star. Her family was the sports family of the state. I tried to tie her in that race, and I beat her. It was an awful feeling.

The first time that I ran the eight hundred my time was two-nineteen something. That was the national record. When Pat [Billie Pat Daniels, now Connelly] and I had the national record, it was around two-nineteen point two or something like that.

Our team took the train to the nationals and Olympic trials from Seattle to Texas. We stopped in Denver and ran a track meet there. I ran the four hundred. The first half was really easy, and then the last half was gross because of the altitude. But we had been on this train a long time, and we didn't even have beds or anything. We were sitting up the whole time, and it took us a week to get there. Can you believe such a thing?

I long jumped almost twenty feet, but I scratched. I was really excited about that. I did well in the eight hundred too. This is what I remember in the eight hundred in the nationals. Neither Pat nor I had ever run against anyone near us, and she had the inside lane. I ran outside her trying my best to pass her the whole

Doris Severtsen Brown Heritage (seated) in 1987 with the author at the Pan American Games in Indianapolis. (Author's photo.)

way. Going around behind the stand on the back stretch something happened to me and I passed out a few yards before the end of the race. A man later gave me a picture. He said she hit me in the stomach with her elbow and I passed out and fell on the track close to the finish line.

I don't remember the Olympic tryout eight hundred meters at all except I had to start in the ninth lane of an eight-lane track because I had not finished my race at the nationals. It was right next to the bleachers.

Remember the races we had in Kansas at the training camp? [The training camp was held for two purposes — one to train the Olympic team as a group and the second was to provide opportunity for second and third place finishers in the trials to qualify for the Olympic team by meeting the qualifying heights, times, or distances.] I left to go home by myself. I had never been on a plane and it was a prop then, there were no jets then. A man took me to the airport, and everyone else is going to Rome. He took me to the restaurant and gave me a big club sandwich. (I will never like them.) I tried to eat it, and I couldn't because I was so upset, so sad. He said, "You should have been on the trip to Rome. Others were taken care of that didn't meet the standard." (None of us made the 800 standard so only Pat went.)

On the plane I sat next to two Catholic nuns, and I'm not Catholic. They were sick and throwing up. It was a horrible plane ride — rough weather and no Olympics for me. Everyone was sick except me. I didn't get sick very easy. And that plane ride went on forever. The whole time I was thinking that I had just missed the Olympics and someone told me that I could have gone if. ... Later I realized I was lucky to go only when I had really earned it.

After the trials I went to college. My birthday is in September so I might have been sixteen. I went to Seattle Pacific, the Methodist school. Dr. Ken Foreman was there and I was a physical education major and it just happened that he was my adviser. I remember telling him I'm a runner, so I'm not going to be able to take swimming classes because swimming ruins runner's muscles. He didn't laugh at me or anything. I remember that. That's how my relationship with him started. He had just completed his doctorate at S.C. and someone else was coaching track that year.

I asked the other coach if I could run, and he said he wouldn't coach a woman but if the guys on the team didn't care, I could run with them. They said o.k. and I felt like I had to run with them and I ran way too hard. Every night my legs ached way too much to ever be able to sleep well. Finally, I developed serious shin splints and broke a bone in my foot. I couldn't walk back from the track. The workouts were absolutely awesome, but I couldn't race very well doing them, but I didn't have races anyway. I mean there weren't any more than maybe three a year for girls in our area.

I started running with coach Ken Foreman in nineteen sixty-two. Lots of things happened in those days that don't happen today. We really didn't have rights. An example of this was when I won the indoor national mile. The first indoor USA-USSR meet was held that year in Virginia, it was about nineteen seventy-one. I wanted to go to the cross-country meet because I had won it five times in a row and I really loved cross country and I won the trials by a lot. The team was staying in Seattle with us. That's where the trials were. I took them out and got them uniforms because we didn't have uniforms then, travel uniforms. The AAU people in track forced me to go to the USA-USSR meet instead of the cross-country world championship meet. I really felt a little bitter towards them. I ran my best time in the mile, but I took third. After an all-night flight, I had to run this race the day after I took my orals for my master's degree and it was poor timing.

I found out after a couple of years that I had been sent invitations to run in Europe. I hadn't been getting them because they went through our federation and the AAU people didn't pass them on. So when I was in Europe for the world cross-country championships, some people really berated me and told me what an awful person I was because I didn't even bother to answer their invitations. I didn't know that I was given them. When they found this out, they sent an invitation directly to me — it was to run in Kennedy Stadium in Ireland. After that I was invited to the Crystal Palace when it was quite new. This was early in the summer of nineteen sixty-eight. The Olympics would be that autumn, and I think that I had already qualified. I ran a two minutes and seven seconds at Compton Coliseum. The night before I was to leave, the AAU called me and said that I couldn't go unless I had a chaperone and that would require two weeks. If I went without a chaperone, I would not be able to compete anymore. They would take away my AAU card, and they would not issue me a travel permit if my way were paid. Because of this, I missed the first day of races. I had to borrow the money to go, and I was scared to death. In Ireland and England they offered me a lot of money, but I wouldn't take it. I never took a penny. In Ireland at Kennedy Stadium, I won my race by a lot. I also high jumped and won a set of Hungarian dishes. I ran a two minute, five second eight hundred meters on a cow pasture track. Then I went to the English championships at Crystal Palace and I was third but I ran my best time. I ran the last three hundred meters very hard, and that's the style I used thereafter, except when coaches of the U.S. team forced us to run using their style of running. I went home with all sorts of things. I had a blast. It was a peak experience. I met many great people and spent time with them. It took me years to pay back the money I borrowed for the trip.

In the Olympics in Mexico in nineteen sixty-eight, a girl from France grabbed my arm and kicked me and knocked me down. She took last so they didn't disqualify her. I spent four years replaying this every night. How could it happen? I had the best time in the world in that race, and I didn't even get a medal. My history in track must have been all downhill from there.

Four years later in nineteen seventy-two in Munich, the first Olympic fifteen hundred-meter run, we were on the warm-up track marching into the stadium. They had taken the curb out for the high jumpers, and a piece of it was hanging out in the lane. I was behind Francie Larrieu, and I didn't see it. I turned my foot over and broke five bones and tore a tendon in half. I was taken care of by some German doctors who just put me in a cast. The USA doctor was too busy. It wasn't until I got home that I had the operation to sew the tendon up. So, I've never had a successful Olympics. It's no wonder that I like cross-country the best.

After nineteen seventy-two my track years were pretty much over. I made some more cross-country teams, but I didn't ever win again. My last win was in nineteen seventy-one.

After that I started the Athletes' Advisory Committee and went to the nineteen seventy-six Olympics as the athlete's liaison. I was on the Olympic Committee, on the Executive Committee, and the House of Delegates.

But I sure met nice people and had great experiences. I can come away saying it was much better to have been there than not.

Chapter 51

1968: The Mexico City Olympic Year

The 1968 Olympic team that competed in Mexico City from October 12 to October 27, and the athlete's Olympic event, place, and performance follows:

	Olympic Event	Olympic Place	Olympic Performance
Bailes, Margaret	100m	5	11.31
	200m	7	23.18
	400mr	1	42.87 (WR)
Bair, RaNae	Javelin	11	174' 4"
Baskerville, Estelle	HJ	22	5' 3"
Brown-Heritage, Doris	800m	5	2:03.9
Callahan, Sharon	HJ	22	5' 3"
Connolly, Olga	Discus	6	173' 9"
Drinkwater, Lois	400m	DNQ	57.3
Dyer, Julia	80mh	DNQ	10.8
Ferrell, Barbara	100m	2	11.15
	200m	4	22.92
	400mr	1	42.87 (WR)
Friedrich, Barbara	Javelin	9	175' 4"
Hamblin, Cathy	Pentathlon	24	4330
Kraker, Francie	800m	DNQ	2:07.3
Manning, Madeline	800m	1	2:00.9 (WR)
Montgomery, Eleanor	HJ	16	5' 6"
Moseke, Carol	Discus	14	158' 5"
Netter, Mildrette	400mr	1	42.87 (WR)
Rallins, Mamie	80mh	DNQ	10.6
Scott, Jarvis	400m	6	52.7
Seidler, Maren	SP	11	48' 9"
Stroy, Esther	400m	DNQ	54.3
Tyus, Wyomia	100m	1	11.0
	200m	6	23.08
	400mr	1	42.87 (WR)
Van Wolvelaere, Pat	80mh	4	10.5

Watson, Martha	LJ	10	20' 4"
White, Willye	LJ	11	19' 11¼"
Winslow, Billie Pat	Pentathlon	6	4877
Ferenczy, Alex	Coach		
Ford, Conrad	Coach		

The Olympic Results

100 meters. Twenty-three-year-old Wyomia Tyus became the first person, man or woman, in Olympic Games history to defend successfully the 100-meter sprint title. Both times she set new Olympic and world records.

"For Miss Tyus, who comes from Tennessee, to have stayed at the top of the world and American sprinting for so long is a remarkable achievement since precociousness, in trans–Atlantic sprinting, is the order rather than an exception," said James Coote. "Despite this she has been consistently at the top. Her victory over her team mate Barbara Ferrell, her close rival throughout the last two years, was a fine feat, for Miss Tyus to a certain extent had been concentrating on 200 meters running."

Forty-one participants from twenty-one countries were entered. During the competition, the world record was broken twice and equaled five times.

Barbara Ferrell placed a close second in 11.1, with Margaret Bailes in fifth spot only .3 from the winner.

200 meters. This final was the seventh race for all of the USA sprinters within a five-day period. Wyomia took an early lead but faded in the home stretch and finished sixth in 23.0. Barbara Ferrell barely missed the bronze medal, placing fourth in 22.9. Margaret Bailes was seventh in 23.1.

400 meters. Jarvis Scott, recuperating from injuries, finished sixth in 52.7. Fourteen-year-old Esther Stroy, the youngest member of the team, was eliminated in the semifinal round.

800 meters. Madeline Manning ran down the final straightaway almost twenty yards ahead of the silver medalist. Her 2:00.9 was a new world record. Madeline became the first American winner of the 800 meters.

Madeline said in her book, *Running for Jesus*, that she was assigned to lane eight in the final. At the point where she cut in to the inside, she found herself way ahead. She slowed down a bit for about forty yards, then picked the pace back up. She said she felt very strong passing the 400-meter mark and forced herself to maintain her pace rather than run away from the field. She slowly began to pick up the pace down the backstretch, and at the final 200-meter mark, she began pulling away from everyone. She had a ten-meter lead with eighty meters to go and thought to herself, Madeline, you're all by yourself. During the last ten meters, she heard someone yell to her to break two minutes. That gave her the spark to push the last few meters. She just missed the two-minute mark by nine-tenths of a second, but the golden award was hers and history was made.

Madeline Manning, 1968 Olympic champion, 800 meters, on victory stand. (Courtesy of the National Track and Field Hall of Fame Historical Research Library at Butler University.)

Doris Brown-Heritage was fifth in 2:03.9.

80-meter hurdles. Pat Van Wolvelaere finished fourth in 10.5.

400-meter relay. The USA team won, as expected. Wyomia, the anchor leg, was five yards ahead of second place at the finish line. The team running the final was composed of Barbara Ferrell, Margaret Bailes, Mildrette Netter, and Wyomia Tyus. The final time of 42.87 was a new world record.

Long jump. Martha Watson placed tenth with a jump of 20' 4", and Willye White was eleventh in 19' 11½".

Discus throw. In a pouring rainstorm, in a slippery circle, Olga Connolly finished sixth with a toss of 173' 9". She was a mother of four, including twins, and this was the fourth Olympic Games for the gold medalist from 1956.

Javelin throw. Barbara Friedrich finished ninth and RaNae Bair eleventh.

Pentathlon. Pat Winslow placed sixth, scoring 4,877 points.

The Olympic Trials

Walnut, California, was the location of the Olympic trials on August 24-25.

100 meters	
1. Wyomia Tyus, Tennessee State	11.3
2. Margaret Bailes, Oregon Track Club	11.3
3. Barbara Ferrell, L.A. Mercurettes	11.4
4. Mildrette Netter, Alcorn A&M	11.6
5. Iris Davis, Tennessee State	11.6
200 meters	
1. Margaret Bailes, Oregon Track Club	23.5
2. Wyomia Tyus, Tennessee State	23.7
3. Barbara Ferrell, L.A. Mercurettes	23.7
400 meters	
1. Jarvis Scott, L.A. Mercurettes	53.5
2. Lois Drinkwater, Phoenix Track Club	54.0
3. Esther Stroy, Sports International	54.3

800 meters
1. Madeline Manning, Tennessee State   2:03.0
2. Doris Brown, Falcon Track Club   2:03.0
3. Jarvis Scott, L.A. Mercurettes   2:04.5

80-meter hurdles
1. Mamie Rallins, Mayor Daley Youth Foundation   11.0
2. Patty Van Wolvelaere, Angels Track Club   11.1
3. Janene Jaton, Angels Track Club   11.2

High jump
1. Sharon Callahan, Crown City Track Club   5' 7¼"
2. Eleanor Montgomery, Tennessee State   5' 7¼"
3. Estelle Baskerville, Tennessee State   5' 6"

Long jump
1. Martha Watson, Tennessee State   21' ¾"
2. Willye White, Mayor Daley Youth Foundation   21' 0"
3. Barbara Emerson, Crown City Track Club   19' 1½"

Shot put
1. Maren Seidler, Shore A.C.   50' 1¾"
2. Lynn Graham, L.A. Mercurettes   46' ½"
3. Sharon Shepherd, unattached   45' 7"

Discus
1. Olga Connolly, Culver City A.C.   175'
2. Carol Moseke, Nebraska Track Club   166' 5"
3. Nancy Norberg, unattached   152' 7"

Javelin
1. Barbara Friedrich, Shore A.C.   177' 5"
2. Sherry Calvert, Los Angeles   160' 7"
3. RaNae Bair, S.D. Lancers   158'

The pentathlon trial competition was held in Columbia, Missouri, on August 24-25. This was the only time that one Olympic trial event was held separate from the track and field tryouts.

1. Chi Cheng, Taiwan   4,823
2. Pat Winslow, Crown City Track Club   4,481
3. Barbara Emerson, Crown City Track Club   4,327

The Outdoor Nationals

The national championship meet was held in Aurora, Colorado, on August 17-18.

100 meters
1. Margaret Bailes, Oregon Track Club   11.1

2. Wyomia Tyus, Tennessee State   11.3
3. Chi Cheng, Crown City Track Club   11.3

200 meters
1. Wyomia Tyus, Tennessee State   23.5
2. Margaret Bailes, Oregon Track Club   23.7
3. Mildrette Netter, Alcorn A&M   24.1

400 meters
1. Jarvis Scott, L.A. Mercurettes   52.9
2. Lois Drinkwater, Phoenix Track Club   54.6
3. Gail Fitzgerald, Atoms Track Club   54.6

800 meters
1. Doris Brown, Falcon Track Club   2:05.1
2. Madeline Manning, Tennessee State   2:07.6
3. Francie Kraker, Michigammes   2:07.8

1500 meters
1. Jane Hill, Frederick Track Club   4:46.5
2. Maureen Dickson, Santa Monica A.A.   4:47.3
3. Judy Oliver, unattached   4:49.3

80-meter hurdles
1. Mamie Rallins, Mayor Daley Youth Foundation   10.6
2. Chi Cheng, Crown City Track Club   10.7
3. Pat Van Wolvelaere, Angels Track Club   11.0

200-meter hurdles
1. Pat Van Wolvelaere, Angels Track Club   27.3
2. Mamie Rallins, Mayor Daley Youth Foundation   27.5
3. Janene Jaton, Angels Track Club   27.6

High jump
1. Theresa Thresher, unattached   5' 6"
2. Eleanor Montgomery, Tennessee State   5' 6"
3. Sharon Callahan, Crown City Track Club   5' 6"

Long jump
1. Willye White, Mayor Daley Youth Foundation   20' 11¼"
2. Martha Watson, Tennessee State   20' 6"
3. Chi Cheng, Crown City Track Club   19' 11¼"

Shot put
1. Maren Seidler, Mayor Daley Youth Foundation   50' 3¾"
2. Lynn Graham, L. A. Mercurettes   47' 0"
3. Carmelita Capilla, Millbrae Lions   46' 1½"

Discus throw
1. Olga Connolly, Crown City Track Club   170' 10"
2. Carol Moseke, Nebraska Track Club   160' 10"
3. Nancy Norberg, unattached   158' 9"

Javelin throw
1. Barbara Friedrich, Shore A.C.   178' 10"

2. RaNae Bair, S.D. Lancers	166' 2"
3. Louise Gerrish, Michigammes	161' 8"

400-meter relay
1. Mayor Daley Youth Foundation	45.1
2. L.A. Mercurettes	45.6
3. Colorado Olympic Club	46.7

800-meter medley relay
1. L.A. Mercurettes	1:47.7
2. Motor City Track Club	1:44.1
3. Atoms Track Club	1:44.1

The Indoor Nationals

The indoor national championship meet on February 23-24 was held in Oakland, California. The *New York Times* on February 25 reported:

> World records were set or tied frequently in the woman's division. Pat Van Wolvelaere of the Los Angeles Track Club won the 60 yard low hurdles in 7.4 seconds, breaking the mark set in 1965 by Tammy Davis of the Frederick (Md.) Track Club by a tenth of a second.
>
> Three women's teams broke the world record in the 640 yard relay, with the Mayor Daley Youth Foundation team of Chicago timed in 1:11.9, half a second faster than the Detroit Track Club had set in the same arena last year.

Barbara Ferrell, Madeline Manning, and Eleanor Montgomery were the outstanding performers. The Dieges Award was presented to Eleanor Montgomery.

60-yard dash
1. Barbara Ferrell, L.A. Mercurettes	6.7
2. Vilma Charlton, Crown City Track Club	6.8
3. Willye White, Mayor Daley Youth Foundation	6.8

220-yard dash
1. Vilma Charlton, Crown City Track Club	25.1
2. Nancy Benson, Valley of the Sun Track Club	25.3
3. Jane Burnett, Sports International	25.4

One-mile run
1. Doris Brown, Falcon Track Club	4:50.1
2. Marie Mulder, Will's Spikettes	4:55.6
3. Vicki Foltz, Falcon Track Club	4:56.7

440-yard dash
1. Lois Drinkwater, Valley of the Sun Track Club	56.5
2. Jarvis Scott, L.A. Mercurettes	56.7
3. Jane Burnett, Sports International	56.8

880-yard run
1. Madeline Manning, Tennessee State	2:11.8
2. Francie Kraker, Southeast Michigan	2:13.0
3. Vicki Foltz, Falcon Track Club	2:13.0

60-yard hurdles
1. Pat Van Wolvelaere, Angels Track Club   7.4 WR
2. Cherrie Sherrard, Laurel Track Club   7.6
3. Mamie Rallins, Mayor Daley Youth Foundation   7.6

Basketball throw
1. Barbara Friedrich, Shore A.C.   135'
2. Simie Hollis, Crown City Track Club   110' 3"
3. Diane Franklin, Kalispell, Mont.   110'

Long jump
1. Tatiana Talisheva, USSR   20' 4½"
2. Martha Watson, Tennessee State   19' 10¼"
3. Willye White, Mayor Daley Youth Foundation   19' 9"

High jump
1. Eleanor Montgomery, Tennessee State   5' 10½"
2. T. Okorokova, USSR   5' 9"
3. Estelle Baskerville, Tennessee State   5' 8"

Sprint medley relay
1. L.A. Mercurettes   1:45.1 WR
   (Scott, Wilson, DeBusk, Ferrell)
2. Tennessee State   1:45.8
3. Laurel Track Club   1:49.9

Shot put
1. Maren Seidler, Shore A.C.   48' 9"
2. Lynn Graham, L.A. Mercurrettes   48' ¼"
3. Pat Winslow, Crown City Track Club   45' 9½"

4-lap relay (4 × 160 yards)
1. Tennessee State   1:10.8
   (Tyus, Daniel, Dennis, Render)

Team scores:
Tennessee State University 24; Los Angeles Mercurettes 19; Crown City Track Club 16; Valley of the Sun Track Club 10; Falcon Track Club 9.

The team competing at Kiel, West Germany, on March 20 (USA vs. W. Germany) was selected at the indoor nationals.

First places went to Mamie Rallins in the 50-meter hurdles, Jarvis Scott in the 400 meters, Cheryl Toussaint in the 800 meters, and Mildrette Netter in the 50 meters.

The Mason-Dixon Games produced a world record in the 70-yard hurdles; Mamie Rallins won the event in 8.7.

The 5th Annual Albuquerque Jaycee Invitational Meet, held on January 27 in Tingley Coliseum, featured a women's 200-meter dash, 60-yard low hurdles, 60-yard dash, 880-yard run, and a four-lap relay.

The San Diego Second Annual Indoor Games held at the San Diego International Sports Arena on February 3 listed two women's events in the twenty-one event program — the 60-yard dash and the 880-yard run.

Barbara Friedrich, 1968 Olympian, javelin.
(Courtesy of Barbara Friedrich.)

The Knights of Columbus Meet on January 13 had one women's event, the 440-yard dash.

The 9th Annual *L.A. Times* Indoor Games were held on February 10 at the Forum. The six women's events were the 60-yard dash won by Barbara Ferrell in 6.7, the 60-yard hurdles won by Cherrie Sherrard in 7.7, the long jump in which Martha Watson finished second, the 440 won by Kathy Hammond in 56.0, the 880 won by Madeline Manning in 2:10.9, and the high jump won by Eleanor Montgomery with a height of 5' 10".

The 5th Annual *Examiner* All-American Indoor Track and Field Meet was held at the Cow Palace on Friday, January 5. The women's events were the 60-yard hurdles, the 480-yard relay, and the sprint medley relay. There were twenty-two events on the program.

Nell Jackson, chairman of the women's track and field committee, reported on the foreign trips this year.

1. The international cross-country championships were in Blackburn, England, in March. Six girls, a coach, and manager represented the United States. Doris Brown was the individual winner, for the second year, and the United States won the team championship by one point.

2. The USSR indoor championships were held in February. Barbara Ferrell and Jane Burnett, along with Rosemary Reddich, as team manager, participated in the USSR indoor championships. Barbara Ferrell tied the world's indoor record in the 50-meter dash.

3. The Australian tour was held in March. Barbara Friedrich, Pat Van Wolvelaere, and Nancy Benson participated in several meets in Australia.

4. The Trinidad Invitational Meet was held in April. Wyomia Tyus and Pat Winslow were invited to participate in the international meet. Both of the girls won all of their events.

Nell reported that "the athletes held a meeting, for the first time, during the national outdoor championships."

The Division for Girls and Women's Sports published the 1968-70 *Track and Field Guide* and conducted the Fifth National Institute on Girls' Sports at the University of Illinois from January 21 to January 25.

Alex Ferenczy

In 1957, Alex became the coach for the Cleveland Division of Recreation Club one year after fleeing from his native Hungary in order to live in freedom.

The list of athletes he coached in the Cleveland area reads like a "who's who" in track and field. Perhaps his best-known athlete was Madeline Manning, 1968 gold medalist in the 800 meters. His other Olympians include Vivian Brown, Sandra Knott, and Eleanor Montgomery. Five of his athletes were Pan American champions, and fifteen women were national AAU champions. His athletes held seven world records and represented the United States forty-two times in international competition.

Alex was appointed the coach of the 1968 and 1976 women's Olympic teams, and in 1972 he was elected a member of the United States Olympic Committee.

Conrad A. Ford

Connie was born in Brooklyn, N.Y. His parents were from Barbados. His father was a great influence on his life because he taught him to set goals for himself.

While at Boys' High School, Connie ran the middle-distance events. He received his first degree from Brooklyn College, and his Master of Science in Social Work was earned at Columbia University. His running career continued through college and then with the famed New York Pioneer Club.

Connie started his career as a math teacher but switched professions and became a parole officer. During this time, in 1947, he began coaching girls' track for the Police Athletic League. His P.A.L. teams won eight indoor and outdoor championships, including five straight indoor titles.

In 1973, Connie was appointed executive director of the Police Athletic League, one of the largest youth service organizations in the United States. During his twelve years as executive director, he expanded Police Athletic League programs to include 60,000 New York City youngsters. During his thirty-five years as Police Athletic League coach, Connie made a deep and indelible impression on his athletes, his kids.

"He was like a second father to me," said 1980 Olympian Kim Thomas, twenty-five, a St. Albans neighbor who ran for him for thirteen years. "I really loved him so much. ... He kept me going. He was my inspiration. He gave me a lot of strength and courage. ... If it wasn't for him, I wouldn't have achieved the things I did in track — and in life."

There are a few times in life when you cross paths with someone and that crossing leads you towards another yet unventured pathway. I was a little kid of eleven in 1948 when I started running in the citywide Police Athletic League track and field program. We had Bronx borough indoor track meets in the Kingsbridge Armory and outdoor meets at Macombs Park, which is right across the street from Yankee Stadium. The meets culminated in the Bronx Championships and then the City Championships. It was during one of those meets at the Kingsbridge Armory, when I represented the 52nd Precinct in the Bronx, that Connie, who started all of the races, asked me to come to practice in Brooklyn and become a member of the "senior" Police Athletic League team. I was thirteen years old, but it seems like yesterday. It was September, and shortly I would be 14 and eligible to compete with the senior team in the AAU meets. That was the "crossing" and the start of my formal track

Connie Ford, coach of the 1968 Olympic team and New York City Police Athletic League. (Author's photo.)

life with the Police Athletic League and a lifelong pathway in track and field.

Connie was named coach of the 1968 Olympic team, 1963 Pan American coach, 1983 Pan American coach, and 1971 USA–Pan African Games coach. During ten summers he served as coach at the Empire Track and Field Camp for Girls.

On April 13, Connie was presented with the 1984 President's Award by the Metropolitan Athletics Congress at the 8th Annual Women's Olympic Development Track and Field Meet held at Tennessee State University, a meet which was dedicated to him.

Connie died on May 13, 1985, at the age of fifty-nine after returning home from yet another spring track meet.

Madeline Manning

Madeline began running in John Hay High School in Cleveland, Ohio, in the 10th grade at the age of 16. She won her first national title in the 440-yard dash in the girls' AAU championships in 1965. She also ran the 440-anchor leg on the women's 880-medley relay, running 52.5, which placed her on the national team representing the United States against Russia, Poland, and West Germany.

Highlights of her outstanding career include being the indoor and outdoor national 800-meter (880-yard) champion in 1967, 1968, 1969, and 1972 and the outdoor champion in 1975 and 1976. Her records include the following:

World Records

| 1966 | 880-yard indoor | 2:08.4 |
| 1968 | 800m | 2:00.9 |

Madeline Manning 1968 Olympic champion, 800 meters. (Author's photo.)

1969	800m	2:02.0

American Records

1967	800m	2:02.3
1975	800m	2:00.5
1976	800m	1:59.8
1976	800m	1:57.9

Madeline was a member of three United States Olympic teams and was the 1968 Olympic gold medalist in the 800 meters. She was the first American woman to break two minutes in that event.

The aspect of Madeline that goes far beyond her magnificent running talent documented above is perhaps summed up in what she wrote to me on a page in her book, *Running for Jesus*: "Thank you for the opportunity to share my love in Christ through coaching, singing, dancing, acting and being part of a great service to upcoming women athletes. Love, Madeline."

Chapter 52

1969

The outdoor national championship meet was held in Dayton, Ohio, on July 5-6.

The *New York Times* on July 7 featured Barbara Ferrell's double sprint wins in the 100 yards in 10.7 and the 220 in 23.8, making her the only double champion. In a meet delayed by rain, an American record was set by Eleanor Montgomery in the high jump of 5' 11".

Tennessee State won the team title.

100-yard dash
1. Barbara Ferrell, L.A. Mercurettes   10.7
2. Iris Davis, Tennessee State
3. Mildrette Netter, Alcorn A & M

220-yard dash
1. Barbara Ferrell, L.A. Mercurettes   23.8
2. Pam Greene, Denver All-Stars
3. Molly Hence, Alcorn A & M

440 yards
1. Kathy Hammond, unattached   54.4
2. Jarvis Scott, L.A. Mercurettes
3. Esther Stroy, Sports International Track Club

880 yards
1. Madeline Manning, Tennessee State   2:11.1
2. Nancy Shafer, Canton Track Club
3. Cheryl Toussaint, Atoms Track Club

1500 meters
1. Doris Heritage, Falcon Track Club   4:27.3
2. Francie Larrieu, San Jose Cindergals
3. Vicki Foltz, Falcon Track Club

100-meter hurdles
1. Chi Cheng, Taiwan   13.7
2. Mamie Rallins, Mayor Daley Youth Foundation
3. Jan Glotzer, Phoenix Track Club

200-meter hurdles
1. Pat Hawkins, Atoms Track Club   27.4

2. Janene Jaton, Seattle Angels
3. Cathy Hunter, Canada

440-yard relay
1. Mayor Daley Youth Foundation   46.4
2. Tennessee State
3. Atoms Track Club

One-mile relay
1. Seattle Angels   3:47.8
2. Atoms Track Club
3. Toledo Road Runners

880-yard medley relay
1. Tennessee State   1:42.4 AR
2. L.A. Mercurettes
3. Alcorn A & M

High jump
1. Eleanor Montgomery, Tennessee State   5' 11" AR
2. Debbie Brill, Canada
3. Audrey Reid, Jamaica

Long jump
1. Willye White, Mayor Daley Youth Foundation   19' 8¾"
2. Martha Watson, Tennessee State
3. Brenda Eisler, Canada

Shot put
1. Lynn Graham, Millbrae Lions Track Club   48' 11¾"
2. Maren Seidler, Mayor Daley Youth Foundation
3. Beth Smith, Oregon Track Club

Discus throw
1. Carol Moseke Frost, Nebraska Track Club   167' 3"
2. Ranee Kletchka, Nebraska Track Club
3. Nancy Norberg, unattached

Javelin throw
1. Kathy Schmidt, Long Beach Comets   177' 4"
2. Barbara Friedrich, Shore A.C.
3. Sherry Calvert, unattached

Pentathlon
1. Jan Glotzer, Phoenix Track Club   4,544 points

Tennessee State won the team title with 55 points.

The Indoor Nationals

The indoor national championships were held on March 1.

880-yard run
1. Madeline Manning, Tennessee State   2:07.9 AR

2. Abby Hoffman, Toronto Olympic Club — 2:09.0
3. Cheryl Toussaint, Atoms Track Club — 2:13.0

60-yard hurdles
1. Mamie Rallins, Mayor Daley Youth Foundation — 7.7 MR
2. Jan Glotzer, Phoenix Track Club — 7.8
3. Cheryl Rogers, Mayor Daley Youth Foundation — 7.8

60-yard dash
1. Barbara Ferrell, L.A. Mercurettes — 6.7
2. Matteline Render, Tennessee State — 6.8
3. Mildrette Netter, Alcorn A&M — 6.8

440-yard run
1. Jarvis Scott, L.A. Mercurettes — 56.4
2. Lois Drinkwater, Phoenix Track Club — 56.8
3. Esther Stroy, Sports International Track Club — 57.1

220-yard dash
1. Barbara Ferrell, L.A. Mercurettes — 27.5
2. Darlene Green, Phoenix Track Club — 27.6
3. Mildrette Netter, Alcorn A&M — 27.4
   (actual distance run was 240 yards)

One-mile run
1. Abby Hoffman, Toronto Olympic Club — 4:59.3
2. Cheryl Bridges, Indiana Univ. (Pa.) — 5:07.0
3. Jane Hill, Frederick Track Club — 5:14.7

640-yard relay
1. Tennessee State — 1:12.4
   (Render, Davis, Watson, Morris)
2. Atoms Track Club — 1:12.8
3. Phoenix Track Club — 1:13.3

Sprint medley relay
1. Tennessee State — 1:46.6
   (Manning, Render, Davis, Morris)
2. L.A. Mercurettes — 1:49.8
3. Ohio Track Club — 1:50.7

Shot put
1. Maren Seidler, Mayor Daley Youth Foundation — 48'
2. Pauline Thomas, Angels Track Club — 44' 4½"
3. Lee Ann Woitkowski, Florida State University — 41' 10½"

Basketball throw
1. Mary Boron, Canton Track Club — 108' 7"
2. Barbara Friedrich, Shore A.C. — 104' 9"
3. Simie Hollis, Crown City Track Club — 103' 6"

Long jump
1. Irena Kirszenstein Szewinska, Poland — 20' 3½"
2. Joan Hendry, Canada — 18' 9"
3. Brenda Eisler, Canada — 18' 7"

High jump
1.	Eleanor Montgomery, Tennessee State	5' 10"
2.	Estelle Baskerville, Tennessee State	5' 8"
3.	Debbie Brill, Canada	5' 6"

Nell Jackson reported: "Track and field had its most productive year in modern times. The increased participation on all levels — age-group, high school, colleges, and clubs, had a marked influence on the composition of team member and quality of performance throughout the year."

International competition

1. Doris Brown led the U.S. team, for the third year, to another championship at the International Cross Country Championships held in Scotland in March.

2. A full team was sent to the Soviet Union and West Germany for several indoor meets in March.

3. The summer triangular meet, USA–British Commonwealth–USSR, was held in Los Angeles. For the first time we were victorious over both countries.

4. A full team went to Europe and competed in Stuttgart, Germany; Augsburg, Germany; and London.

5. Ten girls participated in the Pacific Conference Games in Tokyo in late September.

The Second National Invitational Indoor Track Meet was held on January 10 at the Washington, D.C., Armory. The women's events were the invitational 60-yard dash, Catholic Youth Organization 4-lap relay, invitational 60-yard hurdles, invitational 440-yard run, invitational 880-yard run, and invitational 8-lap relay.

The Knights of Columbus meet on January 11 had the 440-yard dash, the same event as the previous year.

The 29th Knights of Columbus Annual Track Meet was held on February 22 in the Cleveland Arena. The women's events were the 880-yard relay, 50-yard dash, 880-yard run, high jump, and 440-yard dash.

A world indoor record was set in the Mason-Dixon Games in Louisville, Kentucky, by Tennessee State University in the 880-yard relay. They ran 1:40.2.

The first Olympic invitational meet was held on February 21 in Madison Square Garden. Barbara Ferrell, Los Angeles Mercurettes, won the 50-yard dash in 6.2, Jarvis Scott, Los Angeles Mercurettes, captured the 400 meters in 57.6, and Madeline Manning, representing Tennessee State University, ran a 2:09.1 in the 800 meters.

Track and Field for Girls and Women was published this year. A section on "Uniform and Grooming" offered advice:

> Probably no single factor has slowed the progress of women's track and field as much as the stereotyped image of the female track athlete. Right or wrong, many people still envision her as a muscular, masculine type with frowzy hair, no makeup and a baggy warm-up suit over an unattractive uniform. As a begin-

ning athlete, it is wise to give some consideration to your appearance on the track should you decide to compete.

Several uniform companies are now making very attractive racing uniforms of double knit nylon as well as slim, feminine warm-up suits. With proper care, these will serve you well and help you to feel like a girl as well as an athlete.

Careful grooming not only enhances your appearance but should match the activity in which you are engaged. For obvious reasons, nails should be kept short. Extreme hair styles will collapse with the first exertion so hair styling should be simple and neat rather than bouffant or flowing. A touch of makeup will suffice. A healthy skin will perspire under conditions of heat and exertion, so excessive amounts of makeup will not only give the face a streaky appearance but may lead to complexion problems as well.

Mamie Rallins

Mamie discussed her track history with me in an interview on December 3, 1992:

> I was born in Chicago on July 8, 1941. I started in track, just to stay off the streets. I ran with a club because the gym teacher that I had in school was with the club before and she asked her gym class if they wanted to go out for track. She had Barbara Jones and Alfrances Lyman in her class before me.
>
> The club was the Chicago Comets at the time and then the Mayor Daley Youth Foundation took over. Joe Robichaux and Donnis Thompson were coaching then. I was with the club for fifteen years.
>
> I was a sprinter and long jumper because I was so short. My mother died when I was thirteen and I did not eat properly after that and I stopped growing. I always wanted to hurdle, but the coach would say that I was too short. I got a little taller in my late teens after eating one meal a day at the coach's house. He finally said that I could try the hurdles. So I really started hurdling at age twenty-one.
>
> I went to Tennessee State University at age thirty when Coach Temple offered me a scholarship while I was with a USA team in Romania. I decided to take him up on the offer. After I graduated, I got the coaching position at Ohio State and have been here sixteen years now.
>
> My first international trip was in nineteen sixty-five and that began a ten-year span of international competition to nineteen seventy-five. I was second in the Pan American Games in nineteen sixty-seven, and in nineteen sixty-eight I made the Olympic team. In nineteen seventy-one our coach, Mr. Robichaux, died, and that's when I went to college. I made the nineteen seventy-two Olympic team. I competed until I was thirty-five.
>
> The highlights of my track career were making my first Olympic team at age twenty-seven and being number one or two in the country for about fifteen years. That was "old" back in those days, but now athletes are able to compete longer with the help of sponsors.
>
> At Ohio State, I coached Stephanie Hightower among many others, but she's the athlete that everyone would know about. She came in as a freshman the same year that I started. I coached her for thirteen years.

Chapter 53

1970

The outdoor national championship meet was held in Los Angeles on July 4. The Mayor Daley Youth Foundation won the team title.

100 yards
1. Chi Cheng, L.A. Track Club — 10.2
2. Iris Davis, Tennessee State — 10.4
3. Barbara Ferrell, L.A. Mercurettes — 10.4

220 yards
1. Chi Cheng, L.A. Track Club — 22.4w
2. Willie Mae Fergerson, West Coast Jets — 23.6
3. Pam Greene, Denver All-Stars — 23.7

440 yards
1. Mavis Laing, Phoenix Track Club — 52.9
2. Jarvis Scott, L.A. Mercurettes — 53.4
3. Gwen Norman, Sports International Track Club — 53.5

880 yards
1. Cheryl Toussaint, Atoms Track Club — 2:05.1
2. Francie Kraker Johnson, Michigammes — 2:05.3
3. Terry Hull, Knoxville Track Club — 2:05.5

100-meter hurdles
1. Mamie Rallins, Mayor Daley Youth Foundation — 13.4
2. Pat Johnson, Angels Track Club — 13.5
3. Jan Glotzer, Phoenix Track Club — 13.6

1500-meters
1. Francie Larrieu, San Jose Cindergals — 4:20.8
2. Doris Brown, Falcon Track Club — 4:24.3
3. Trina Hosmer, Falcon Track Club — 4:29.2

3,000-meter run
1. Beth Bonner, unattached — 9:48.1

200-meter hurdles
1. Pat Hawkins, Atoms Track Club — 26.1
2. Pat Johnson, Angels Track Club — 26.7
3. Pat Donnelly, L.A. Track Club — 27.3

High jump
1. Sally Plihal, Tyndall A.C.   5' 8"
2. Brenda Simpson, unattached   5' 8"
3. Toni Churchill, Nebraska Track Club   5' 6"

Long jump
1. Willye White, Mayor Daley Youth Foundation   21' 1"
2. Martha Watson, Tennessee State   20' ¾"
3. Vickie Betts, L.A. Track Club   19' 9½"

Shot put
1. Lynn Graham, Millbrae Lions   49' 10"
2. Maren Seidler, Mayor Daley Youth Foundation   49' 2¾"
3. Lynette Matthews, Falcon Track Club   48' 10½"

Discus throw
1. Carol M. Frost, Nebraska Track Club   172' 3"
2. Josephine Dela Vina, Mayor Daley Youth Foundation   159' 4"
3. Linda Langford, Millbrae Lions   158' 6"

Javelin throw
1. Sherry Calvert, unattached   184' 9"
2. Barbara Friedrich, N.J. Striders   174' 1"
3. Mary Boron, Oregon Track Club   157' 9"

440 relay
1. Tennessee State   45.2
2. Atoms Track Club   45.9
3. Mayor Daley Youth Foundation   46.0

Pentathlon
1. Pat Daniels, Los Angeles Track Club   4,735 points

The Indoor Nationals

The indoor national championship meet was held on February 27. Twenty-five-year-old Chi Cheng, a three-time Olympian and women's track and field athlete of the year, won the long jump and six races during the afternoon and evening competition.

880-yard run
1. Francie Kraker Johnson, Michigammes   2:10.5
2. Cheryl Toussaint, Atoms Track Club,   2:11.6
    and Nancy Shafer, College of Wooster   2:11.6

60-yard hurdles
1. Chi Cheng, Los Angeles Track Club   7.6
2. Pat Johnson, Angels Track Club
3. Mamie Rallins, Mayor Daley Youth Foundation

60-yard dash
1. Chi Cheng, Los Angeles Track Club   6.7

2. Iris Davis, Tennessee State
3. Barbara Ferrell, L.A. Mercurettes

440-yard run
1. Kathy Hammond, unattached	55.2
2. Gail Fitzgerald, Atoms Track Club	56.0
3. Jarvis Scott, L.A. Mercurettes	56.2

One-mile run
1. Kathy Gibbons, unattached	4:58.5
2. Maria Stearns, Santa Monica A.A.	5:03.0
3. Pam Bagian, Wolverine Parkettes	5:04.8

220-yard dash
1. Diane Kummer, Mayor Daley Youth Foundation	24.9
2. Laurie Barr, Ohio Track Club	25.0
3. Linda Reynolds, Atoms Track Club	25.0

Sprint medley relay
1. Atoms Track Club	1:46.3
(Fitzgerald, Reynolds, Cordy, Hawkins)	
2. Sports International	1:46.5
3. Ohio Track Club	1:49.7

640-yard relay
1. Mayor Daley Youth Foundation	1:12.3
(Jones, White, Kummer, Rallins)	
2. Atoms Track Club	1:12.6
3. Tennessee State	1:12.8

Shot put
1. Mary Jacobson, Oregon Track Club	46' 9"
2. Maren Seidler, Mayor Daley Youth Foundation	45' 5"
3. Denise Wood, New Jersey Striders	44' 9"

Long jump
1. Chi Cheng, Los Angeles Track Club	21' ¾" MR
2. Willye White, Mayor Daley Youth Foundation	20' 3¾"
3. Hiroko Yamashita, Japan	20' 3"

High jump
1. Debbie Brill, Canada	5' 11" MR
2. Debbie Van Kiekebelt, Scarborough Track Club	5' 7"
3. Vann Abram, Motor City Track Club	5' 6"

Team scores:
Mayor Daley Youth Foundation 20; Atoms Track Club 16; Los Angeles Track Club 15; Ohio Track Club 6; Oregon Track Club 5; Tennessee State U. 5.

In her report, Nell Jackson said that 1970 was another year of growth for women's track and field as shown by the increased number of girls competing and the records being set.

The city of Frederick, Maryland, hosted the Women's International Cross-

Country Championships. Doris Brown won the meet for the fourth consecutive year. The United States team placed second.

Two girls, Barbara Ferrell and Vann Abram, were invited to participate in a meet in Martinique in the spring.

Three dual meets were held during the summer with the USSR, West Germany, and Romania. After the meets, five girls continued on an extended tour of Sweden, West Germany, and Poland. Four girls were invited to participate in an invitational meet in Paris just before the West German dual meet. In September, two girls participated in a meet in Spain.

Eleanor Montgomery was the recipient of the 1969 Saettel Award, which is given to the young woman exhibiting the most outstanding performances throughout the year.

A world record was set in the Mason-Dixon Games in Louisville, Kentucky. The Atoms Track Club of New York broke Tennessee State's record in the 440-yard relay by one tenth of a second with a time of 47.4. Mamie Rallins, in winning the 70-yard hurdles, tied her previous record of 8.7.

The Sacramento Invitational Track and Field Championships were held at Hughes Stadium. The women's program was fairly extensive. It included the javelin, 440-yard club relay, discus, 200-meter hurdles, 880-yard run, 100-yard dash, long jump, 100-meter hurdles, mile run, high jump, 440-yard dash, 220-yard dash, shot put, and 880-yard medley relay.

The junior college track and field program in Southern California was addressed by Linda Garrison. She stated that the junior colleges had been involved in an intercollegiate program for the past seven years. The program began in May of 1963 with the first Southern California Junior College Invitational Women's Track and Field Meet. In the spring of 1965, a few junior colleges had dual and triangular meets. Garrison noted that by 1970 there was regularly scheduled competition from March until the final championships.

The Division for Girls and Women's Sports published the 1970-72 *Track and Field Guide*. Dr. Harmon Brown wrote "Long Distance Running for Young Girls," which appeared in the *Guide*. An asterisk appeared at the end of the title. The editor's note said: "We are cognizant of the fact that the distances Dr. Brown mentions in this article are not in keeping with the current DGWS rules. The DGWS Research Committee is currently conducting longitudinal studies to determine the effect of long distance running on young girls and women. Dr. Brown's article is included here to keep our readers informed of current medical opinion."

Dr. Brown referenced the well-known Swedish physiologist Astrand: "If they prepare their competition season carefully ... there are probably no physiological reasons why they should not compete in endurance events. ... From a physiological point of view females can participate in the same sports as males."

Dr. Brown stated that for the past five years, the AAU had conducted cross-country races of ¾ of a mile for 6-11 year olds, up to a mile for 12-13 year olds, and up to two miles for women 14 and over.

Gail Fitzgerald was presented the Vitalis Award for her outstanding performance in the U.S. Invitational. Sixteen-year-old Caroline Walker ran 3:02:53.0 on February 28 for a marathon world record in Seaside, Oregon, in the Trail's End Marathon.

In October the Road Runners Club of America (RRCA) sponsored a national women's marathon championship. Sara Mae Berman won the race.

Chapter 54

1971

The senior national AAU championship meet was held in Bakersfield, California, on July 9-10. The *New York Times* reported that the Atoms Track Club of Brooklyn set a world record in the mile relay. Anchored by Cheryl Toussaint, the Atoms team edged Sports International at the tape. Both teams were given the same time. The team of Denise Hooten, Linda Reynolds, Gail Fitzgerald, and Cheryl Toussaint broke its own record set the previous year.

Nineteen-year-old Pat Hawkins, also of the Atoms Track Club, set an American record in the 200-meter hurdles, and Lynn Olson of the Wolverine Parkettes of Michigan set an American record in the mile walk of 7:53.8, which bettered the old mark of 7:54.0.

100-meter dash
1. Iris Davis, Tennessee State   11.2
2. Raylene Boyle, Australia   11.3
3. Pat Hawkins, Atoms Track Club   11.5
4. Mavis Laing, Phoenix Track Club   11.5

200-meter dash
1. Raylene Boyle, Australia   23.1
2. Kathie Lawson, Liberty Athletic Club   23.3
3. Mable Fergerson, West Coast Jets   23.8
4. Rhonda McManus, Tennessee State   23.9

400-meter dash
1. Mable Fergerson, West Coast Jets   53.3
2. Gwen Norman, Sports International   53.8
3. Jane Burnett, Sports International   54.0
4. Nancy Benson, San Diego Metros   54.7

800-meter run
1. Cheryl Toussaint, Atoms Track Club   2:04.3
2. Terry Hull Crawford, Knoxville Track Club   2:05.3
3. Carol Hudson, Albuquerque Track Club   2:06.9
4. Cis Schafer, Millbrae Lions Track Club   2:07.5

1500-meter run
1. Kathy Gibbons, Glendale Track Club   4:19.2
2. Francie Johnson, Liberty A.C.   4:23.0

3. Barbara Lawson, Colorado Gold   4:23.8
4. Jennifer Orr, Australia   4:24.3

Two-mile run
1. Doris Brown, Falcon Track Club   10:07.0
2. Vickie Foltz, Falcon Track Club   10:34.1
3. Beth Bonner, South Jersey Chargers   10:34.4
4. Pam Bagian, Wolverine Track Club   10:48.1

100-meter hurdles
1. Pat Van Wolvelaere Johnson, Angels Track Club   13.5
2. Mamie Rallins, Mayor Daley Youth Foundation   13.6
3. Lacey O'Neal, Sports International   13.6
4. Pat Donnelly, San Diego Metros   13.8

200-meter hurdles
1. Pat Hawkins, Atoms Track Club   26.1 AR
2. Gayle Dell, Australia   27.1
3. Mamie Rallins, Mayor Daley Youth Foundation   27.6
4. Bobbette Krug, San Diego Metros   27.8

One-mile walk
1. Lynn Olson, Wolverine Parkettes   7:53.8 AR
2. Esther Marquez, Rialto Road Runners   8:22.2
3. Laurie Tucholski, Rialto Road Runners   8:22.3
4. Susan Brodock, Sports United   8:25.3

400-meter relay
1. Tennessee State University   44.8
2. Atoms Track Club   45.6
3. Phoenix Track Club   46.3
4. Prairie View A&M   47.1

One-mile relay
1. Atoms Track Club   3:38.8 WR
2. Sports International   3:38.8
3. Angels Track Club   3:53.1
4. Prairie View A&M   3:56.1

880-yard medley relay
1. Angels Track Club   1:43.5
2. Mickey's Missiles   1:44.7
3. Mayor Daley Youth Foundation   1:44.8
4. Atoms Track Club   1:45.7

High jump
1. Linda Iddings, Angels Track Club   5' 8"
2. Audrey Reid, Jamaica   5' 6"
3. Brenda Simpson, unattached,   5' 6"
      and Sandi Goldsberry, Lakewood Spartans

Long jump
1. Kim Attlesey, Lakewood Spartans   20' 8¾"
2. Willye White, Mayor Daley Youth Foundation   20' 8¼"

3. Martha Watson, Long Beach Comets   20' 1¼"
4. Diane Kummer, Mayor Daley Youth Foundation   18' 9¾"

Javelin
1. Sherry Calvert, unattached   179' 7"
2. Jean Sweeney, unattached   165' 6"
3. Barbara Friedrich, Shore Athletic Club   164' 6"
4. Diane Franklin, Kalispell Track Club   157' 4"

Discus
1. Josephine Dela Vina, Mayor Daley Youth Foundation   179' 6"
2. Carol Frost, Nebraska Track Club   164' 11"
3. Ranee Kletchka, Nebraska Track Club   159' 6"
4. Iva Wright, Fresno Elans   151' 11"

Shot put
1. Lynn Graham, Fresno Elans   52' 0"
2. Lynette Matthews, Falcon Track Club   50' 0"
3. Barbara Poulsen, New Zealand   49' 8½"
4. Maren Seidler, Mayor Daley Youth Foundation   49' 7"

Two-mile relay
1. San Jose Cindergals, "A" team   8:53.6
2. Wolverine Track Club   9:01.7
3. Falcon Track Club   9:05.8
4. Will's Spikettes, "A" team   9:08.2

The Indoor Nationals

The women's indoor championship meet was held at Madison Square Garden on February 26. The Atoms Track Club won the team title.

60-yard dash
1. Pat Hawkins, Atoms Track Club   6.9
2. Mavis Laing, Phoenix Track Club   6.9
3. Barbara Ferrell, L.A. Mercurettes

60-yard hurdles
1. Patty Johnson, Angels Track Club   7.8
2. Mamie Rallins, Mayor Daley Youth Foundation
3. Carol Thomson, Delaware Track Club

220-yard dash
1. Esther Stroy, Sports International   24.2
2. Jill Thomas, Kirkwood Track Club   24.8
3. Michele McMillan, Atoms Track Club   24.9

440-yard run
1. Jarvis Scott, L.A. Mercurettes   55.3
2. Kathy Hammond, Sacramento Road Runners   55.8
3. Gwen Norman, Sports International   56.7

880-yard run
1. Abby Hoffman, Canada   2:08.7
2. Cheryl Toussaint, Atoms Track Club   2:09.5
3. Terry Hull Crawford, Knoxville Track Club   2:10.3

One-mile run
1. Doris Brown, Falcon Track Club   4:47.9
2. Kathy Gibbons, unattached   4:55.6
3. Beth Bonner, Delaware Track Club   5:03.2

640-yard relay
1. Atoms Track Club   1:14.2
    (DeSandies, McMillan, Hooten, Merritt)
    (Three teams fell — only the Atoms finished)

880-sprint medley relay
1. Atoms Track Club   1:46.8
    (Fitzgerald, Smith-Brown, Hooten, Hawkins)
2. Mayor Daley Youth Foundation   1:50.9
3. Pioneer Athletic Club, Washington, D.C.   1:51.2

One-mile relay
1. Atoms Track Club   3:54.5
    (McMillan, Marshall, Fitzgerald, Toussaint)
2. Wolverine Parkettes   4:02.7
3. Mayor Daley Youth Foundation   4:03.2

Long jump
1. Marilyn King, Millbrae Lions Track Club   19' 10¾"
2. Willye White, Mayor Daley Youth Foundation   19' 10"
3. Vicki Betts, Lakewood Spartans   18' 6½"

High jump
1. Sezana Hrepevnik, Yugoslavia   6' ½"
2. Debbie Van Kiekebelt, Canada   5' 9"
3. Sally Plihal, Tyndall A.C.   5' 7"

Shot put
1. Lynette Matthews, Falcon Track Club   49' 7¾"
2. Maren Seidler, Mayor Daley Youth Foundation   48' 1½"
3. Denise Wood, New Jersey Striders   46' 1½"

Team scores:
Atoms Track Club 30; Mayor Daley Youth Foundation 12; Falcon Track Club 10; Los Angeles Mercurettes 7; Sports International 7.

The Junior National Championship meet was held in conjunction with the senior meet in Bakersfield, California, on July 6-7.

100-yard dash
1. Kathie Lawson, Liberty A.C.   10.5
2. Mavis Laing, Phoenix Track Club   10.6
3. Pam Greene, Denver All-Stars   10.7

220-yard dash
1. Rhonda McManus, Tennessee State   23.8
2. Mable Fergerson, West Coast Jets   24.0
3. Mavis Laing, Phoenix Track Club   24.0

440-yard dash
1. Mable Fergerson, West Coast Jets   54.2
2. Esther Stroy, Sports International   55.2
3. Sheila Ingram, LaMott Track Club   56.5

880-yard run
1. Carol Hudson, Albuquerque Olympic Club   2:08.4
2. Ann Gallagher, Phoenix Track Club   2:09.5
3. Sue Parks, Wolverine Track Club   2:11.7

Mile run
1. Eileen Claugus, Will's Spikettes   4:44.5
2. Debra Johnson, Rialto Road Runners   4:53.3
3. Brenda Webb, Kettering Striders   4:56.0

80-yard hurdles
1. Bobbette Krug, San Diego Metros   10.1
2. Lavonne Neal, Philadelphia Hawks   10.4
3. Janet Benford, Laurel Track Club   10.5

440-yard relay
1. Atoms Track Club   46.6
      (DeSandies, McMillan, Cordy, Johnson)
2. Denver All-Stars   47.2
3. La Jolla Track Club   47.4

880-yard medley relay
1. Atoms Track Club   1:39.0
2. Denver All-Stars   1:39.7
3. Pioneer Athletic Club   1:40.2

Mile relay
1. San Jose Cindergals   3:56.0
2. La Mirada Meteors   3:57.20
3. Denver Flyers   3:58.9

Long jump
1. Myra Albrecht, Del Norte Track Club   19' 5½"
2. Nora Johnson, La Jolla Track Club   19' 4½"
3. Diane Kummer, Mayor Daley Youth Foundation   19' 3¾"

High jump
1. Deanne Wilson, La Mirada Meteors   5' 4"
2. Connie Dorsey, Terre Haute,   5' 4"
       and Cindy Gilbert, La Jolla Track Club

Discus
1. Iva Wright, Fresno Elans   145' 6¾"

2. Kathy Schmidt, Long Beach Track Club   135' 7¼"
3. Dotty Barnes, Portland Track Club   134' 3¾"

Javelin
1. Karin Smith, La Jolla Track Club   154' 10"
2. Denise Sherrill, Lakewood Spartans   146' 0"
3. Debra Langevain, Lakewood Spartans   134' 9"

Shot put
1. Dotty Barnes, Portland Track Club   47' 4½"
2. Iva Wright, Fresno Elans   44' 8¾"
3. Suzanne Snider, unattached   44' 3½"

The Pan American Games

The 1971 Pan American Team that competed in Cali, Colombia, from July 30 to August 13 follows:

	Event	*Place*	*Performance*
Barr, Laurie	200m	DNQ	
Brown, Doris	800m	2	2:05.9
Brown, Orien	100m	4	11.4
	400mr	1	44.5
Brown, Roberta	Javelin	3	167' 1"
Calvert, Sherry	Javelin	2	169' 0"
Crawford, Terry	800m	4	2:09.0
Davis, Iris	100m	1	11.2 W
	400mr	1	44.5
Donnelly, Pat	100mh	DNQ	
Driscoll, Monette	Discus	DNQ	
Durham, Judy	Pentathlon	DNC injured	
Graham, Lynn	Shot put	1	51' 8"
Hawkins, Pat	400mr	1	44.5
King, Marilyn	Pentathlon	4	
Kletchka, Ranee	Discus	5	158' 6"
Lacy, Jean	LJ	6	19' 6¼"
Laing, Mavis	1600mr	1	3:32.4
Matthews, Lynette	Shot put	4	46' 5½"
Norman–Harris, Gwen	400m	7	55.4
Parks, Sue	HJ	7	5' 3"
Render, Matteline	400mr	1	44.5
Scott, Jarvis	400m	8	56.5
Simpson, Brenda	High jump	4	5' 5"
Stroy, Esther	200m	3	23.8
Toussaint, Cheryl	1600mr	1	3:32.4
Van Wolvelaere, Pat	100mh	1	13.4
White, Willye	Long jump	DNC injured	

The third United States Olympic Invitational Track and Field meet was held in Madison Square Garden on February 19. Three women's events were held: the Wilma Rudolph 50-meter dash, the Betty Robinson 400-meter run, and the Madeline Manning 800-meter run. Eighteen-year-old Cheryl Toussaint provided an exciting finish for the cheering crowd in the 800 meters. She won the race by out leaning a Soviet runner who had led for most of the race. She was voted the outstanding woman athlete of the meet.

Wilma Rudolph 50-meter dash
1. Iris Davis, Tennessee State — 6.2 ties MR
2. Pat Hawkins, Atoms Track Club
3. Barbara Ferrell, L.A. Mercurettes

Betty Robinson 400-meter run
1. Gail Fitzgerald, Atoms Track Club — 56.5
2. Jarvis Scott, L.A. Mercurettes — 56.9
3. Jane Burnett, Sports International — 58.1

Madeline Manning 800-meter run
1. Cheryl Toussaint, Atoms Track Club — 2:09.2
2. Nadezhka Kolesnikova, Soviet Union — 2:09.2
3. Ludmila Bragina, Soviet Union — 2:11.6

The senior national AAU women's cross-country championship meet was held at Cleveland, Ohio, on November 27.

1. Doris Brown, Falcon Track Club — 14:29.4
2. Beth Bonner, South Jersey Chargers — 14:44
3. Cheryl Bridges, L.A. Track Club — 14:49
4. Francie Larrieu, San Jose Cindergals — 14:53
5. Judy Graham, L.A. Track Club — 14:56

Team scores:
Oregon Track Club 78; Falcon Track Club 102; San Jose Cindergals 114.

The junior national AAU cross-country championship was held in Portland, Oregon, on November 13.

1. Caroline Walker, Oregon Track Club — 15:58
2. Debbie Roth, Oregon Track Club — 16:02
3. Holly Grayson, unattached — 16:33

The senior AAU pentathlon championship meet was held on June 12 in Los Alamos, New Mexico.

1. Marilyn King, Millbrae Lions — 4731
2. Judy Durham, Angels Track Club — 4525
3. Linda Iddings, Angels Track Club — 4392

Notes from Dr. Nell Jackson, chairman of the Women's Track and Field Committee, revealed that the committee named Doris Brown as a nominee for the Sullivan Award. The Saettel Award nominees were Iris Davis, Kathy Gibbons, Patty Johnson, Gwen Norman, Mamie Rallins, and Cheryl Toussaint.

In 1971, the New York City marathon had its first woman finisher. Beth Bonner completed the course in 2:55:22. A total of 246 runners entered the race, and 168 finished.

Patricia Rico was elected to serve as chairman of the Women's Track and Field Committee for 1972. Dr. Jackson retired from this position after serving four years. Dr. Jackson was nominated as representative to the women's commission of the IAAF.

Doris Brown won the world cross country title for the fifth consecutive year.

Patricia Jones Rico

For over thirty years, the women's track and field community has been fortunate to have Pat Rico as a consistent contributor and leader. As Brooks Johnson noted: "The role that Pat Rico has played in women's track and field has been pivotal. ... The growth and development of the sport was due to Pat and others as they led the sport from one generation to another."

Pat was an athlete in the 1950s. Her family was supportive, even though it was not common to have women throw the javelin at that time. Pat was always an individual and did what she thought she needed to do, not asking for the approval of those around her. In 1960, she participated in the Olympic trials, an athlete's dream for many.

In 1961, Pat was appointed by George T. Eastman, then president of the Metropolitan AAU and coach at Manhattan College, to the position of chairman of the Metropolitan Association women's track and field committee. In this position, she conducted more than twenty-five track meets a year with a full age-group program and a full program of open events. Thus began a long and illustrious career as an administrator in the women's track and field program in the United States.

In that same year, 1961, Pat was the cofounder and editor of *Track Mirror*, a publication devoted to women's track and field. She remained as a contributing editor to *Cinderbelle*, the magazine that followed *Track Mirror*.

During the sixties, Pat served as a member of the national women's track and field committee, and from 1967 to 1968 she was the chairman of the rules subcommittee. Pat directed or lectured at an average of three track and field clinics a year, promoting women's track and field to young people and their coaches. In 1969, she conducted what may have been the first women's track and field camp — Blue Mountain Sport Camp — with the staff of Lehigh University.

In 1971, Pat was elected chairman of the National AAU Women's Track and Field Committee, and she remained in that position until 1975. During this time

Patricia Jones Rico
(Courtesy of Patricia Jones Rico.)

she also became the chairman of the Women's Track and Field Committee of the United States Olympic Committee. From 1974 to 1978 she was an athletic adviser to the President's Commission on Amateur Sports, which culminated in the Amateur Sports Act of 1978.

Pat has served on the staff of many United States teams in the capacity of manager. She managed the European tour in 1970, the World Cup in 1977, the World University Games in 1983, and the 1984 Olympic Games. She served as deputy chief of mission of the first tour of China in 1975 and served as chief of mission for a 1973 trip to Europe and Africa, a 1975 trip to Europe and Africa, and the 1986 Goodwill Games. She was the first woman in track and field and perhaps in any sport to be the chief spokesperson for an official United States team abroad.

In 1976, there was a great need for strong leadership on the international scene. Pat responded to that call and became a member of the IAAF Women's Committee and is still serving in that capacity today. Europeans did not understand the United States and questioned its motives. A trust had to be built before progress could be made, and Pat took the time to build that trust. It has paid off for the sport because cooperation and trust have helped win acceptance for the women's marathon, the 10K, and the 10K race walk.

The development of athletes and concern for them are paramount when Pat looks at new programs, new legislation, and new opportunities. Secondarily, her focus is on unification — bringing together all aspects of the sport to help, encourage, and develop athletes. She is very sensitive to the vulnerability of athletes and concerned about the difficult decisions they face with respect to financial security, family ties, and coaching (college and club). She strives to create an atmosphere where athletes cannot just survive but thrive, and she encourages as a duty the concept to "put back into the sport." Pat believes that once you have been a receiver of the benefits, there comes a time to help others make the sport better. She has always encouraged athletes and new people in the sport — anyone who wants to take the time to be a part of women's track and field. She reminds us of where we have been and build how we can on it for the future. Wherever the future leads track and field, Pat Rico will be there.

Fred Thompson

Fred Thompson was honored in 1995 by the many young women whose lives he touched for his dedication to women's track and field for the past thirty-three years. Dr. Lillian Greene Chamberlain, master of ceremonies, elaborated on his many accomplishments:

> An attorney by profession, he is the founder and coach of the Atoms Track Club of Brooklyn, New York, one of the longest established, internationally respected groups in women's sports, for over thirty-three years. He is also currently the founder and meet director of the Colgate Women's Games....
>
> In 1963, Fred Thompson established the all-female Atoms Track Club and financed it with his personal resources. It wasn't long before he was able to bring the team to national prominence with core athletes like Linda Reynolds, Shelly Marshall, Pat Hawkins. Linda Cordy and Michele McMillan. ... Fred has guided several generations of runners to national championship victories, world records and international competitions. ... He has also coached a number of athletes who have gone on to Olympic fame, including Cheryl Toussaint, Gail Fitzgerald, Lorna Forde, Carmen Brown, Grace Jackson, Diane Dixon, Michelle Finn, Candy Young, Joetta Clark and Meredith Rainey.
>
> One of his greatest achievements ... is that he has inspired hundreds of young women to pursue higher education ... and an impressive number have gone on to establish successful careers as administrators, doctors, attorneys, entrepreneurs, teachers, coaches, therapists ... and an administrative law judge.

Fred's many USA-team coaching assignments included being an assistant coach of the United States women's track and field team at the 1988 Olympics in Seoul, Korea.

Chapter 55

1972: The Munich Olympic Year

The United States Olympic team that competed with athletes from 122 nations in Munich, Germany, from August 26 to September 10 follows:

	Olympic Event	Olympic Place	Olympic Performance
Attlesey, Kim	LJ	29	19' ¼"
Brown-Heritage, Doris	1500m	DNC (injured)	
Brown, Roberta	Javelin	19	157' 1"
Calvert, Sherry	Javelin	13	168' 7"
Connolly, Olga	Discus	16	169' 2"
Davis, Iris	100m	4	11.32
	400mr	4	43.39
Edwards-Armstrong, Debra	400m	DNQ	54.43
Fergerson, Mable	400m	5	51.96
	1600mr	2	3:25.15
Fergerson, Willa Mae	1600mr		alternate
Ferrell, Barbara	100m	7	11.45
	200m	DNQ	23.39
	400mr	4	43.39
Fitzgerald, Gail	Pentathlon	19	4206
Frederick, Jane	Pentathlon	21	4167
Gilbert, Cindy	HJ	32	5' 7"
Goldsberry, Sandi	HJ	38	5' 3"
Greene, Pam	200m	DNQ	23.85
Hammond, Kathy	400m	3	51.64 AR
	1600mr	2	3:25.15
King, Marilyn	Pentathlon	DNQ	
Koenig, Wendy	800m	DNQ	2:08.7
Kraker, Francie	1500m	DNQ	4:12.8
Larrieu, Francie	1500m	DNQ	4:15.3
Manning, Madeline	800m	DNQ	2:02.39
	1600mr	2	3:25.15
Netter, Mildrette	400mr	4	43.39

O'Neal, Lacey	100mh	DNQ	13.89
Rallins, Mamie	100mh	DNQ	13.75
Render, Matteline	100m	DNQ	11.67
	400mr	4	43.39
Schmidt, Kate	Javelin	3	196' 8"
Seidler, Maren	SP	14	53' 1"
Svendsen, Jan	SP	16	49' 1"
Thompson, Jackie	200m	DNQ	23.18
Toussaint, Cheryl	800m	DNQ	2:08.9
	1600mr	2	3:25.15
Van Wolvelaere, Pat	100mh	DNQ	13.26
Watson, Martha	LJ	23	19' 11¾"
	400mr	4	43.39
White, Willye	LJ	11	20' 7"
Wilson, Deanne	HJ	30	5' 7"

On September 6, 1992, the twentieth anniversary of the September 5 tragedy in which terrorists attacked and killed Israeli athletes in Munich, the *New York Times* reported the comments of Willye White offered years after this event that occurred during her fifth Olympic Games: "It is difficult for me to explain what it feels like to witness and be a part of a memorial service held in the Olympic Stadium watching the Olympic flag of peace flying at half mast."

The Olympic Results

100 meters. All three athletes, Matteline Render, Iris Davis, and Barbara Ferrell, made it to the quarter-final round, with Davis posting the best time in the heats of 11.34. Render was eliminated in the quarter-finals, placing sixth in the third race. Both Davis and Ferrell moved into the finals, with Iris Davis finishing fourth and Barbara Ferrell seventh.

200 meters. Two athletes, Barbara Ferrell and Jackie Thompson, made it to the semifinal round. Pam Greene was eliminated in the quarter-finals. Jackie Thompson had the best time of the trio of 23.18, placing sixth in the first semifinal.

400 meters. Kathy Hammond and Mable Fergerson ran three 400-meter races prior to placing third and fifth respectively in the final, breaking the American record three times. Debra Edwards did not qualify for the quarter-final round.

800 meters. Madeline Manning was the only athlete to qualify for the semifinal round. Both Wendy Koenig and Cheryl Toussaint placed sixth in their respective first round heats. Madeline barely missed the final. Both the fourth-place qualifier and Madeline, who was fifth, had the same time of 2:02.4. Her semifinal was won by the eventual 800-meter champion in 2:01.4.

1500 meters. Francie Kraker and Francie Larrieu got as far as the semifinal round. Larrieu ran her best time of 4:11.2 in the first round, and in the semi, Kraker ran her lifetime best of 4:12.8.

100-meter hurdles. All three hurdlers, Lacey O'Neal, Mamie Rallins, and

Patty Johnson, were eliminated in the semifinal round. Patty Johnson ran the fastest time of the U.S. hurdlers of 13.26 in the semifinals.

400-meter relay. The USA team of Martha Watson, Matteline Render, Mildrette Netter, and Iris Davis placed third in its heat with a time of 43.07 and was fourth in the finals in 43.39.

1600-meter relay. The USA team of Mable Fergerson, Madeline Manning, Cheryl Toussaint, and Kathy Hammond blazed to a silver-medal finish in 3:25.2.

High jump. Cindy Gilbert, Sandi Goldsberry, and Deanne Wilson did not qualify for the final.

Long jump. Willye White qualified for the final round with the fifth best jump in the trials of 20' 11½". Her longest jump in the final round was 20' 7", placing her eleventh. Neither Martha Watson nor Kim Attlesey qualified for the final.

Javelin. Kate Schmidt was third in the standing in the qualifying round with a best toss of 193'. She improved her distance to 196' 8" and retained the third position for the bronze medal.

American athletes entered in the shot put, discus throw, and pentathlon did not make the final round.

The Olympic Trials

The Olympic trials held in Frederick, Maryland, at the Governor Thomas Johnson High School field on July 7-8 attracted a crowd of 6,128. Three American records were broken. The record breakers were Patty Van Wolvelaere Johnson in the 100-meter hurdles, Kathy Hammond in the 400 meters, and Francie Larrieu in the 1500-meter run.

Patty Johnson made history as the twenty-two-year-old hurdler ran the 100-meter hurdles in 13 seconds flat. In the early rounds of competition, twenty-five-year-old Lacey O'Neal tied Mamie Rallins' old record of 13.1. In the final Lacey and Mamie finished two and three respectively.

Barbara Ferrell captured headlines in the *New York Times.* The twenty-four-year-old Los Angeles kindergarten teacher qualified for the 100 and 200 meter dashes with the fastest heat time in the hundred and finished fourth in the long jump.

Kate Schmidt threw the javelin 197' 9", just short of Barbara Friedrich's record of 198' 8" from 1969.

In the shot put, Maren Seidler came close to Earlene Brown's record of 54' 9" set in 1960. She was the only athlete to go over the qualifying mark with her toss of 53' 5".

Olga Connolly won the discus, making her fifth Olympic team (fourth U.S. team), but the 1956 Olympic gold medalist's throw of 170' 4" was under the qualifying standard of 180' 6".

The first three finalists in each event were invited to a training camp beginning August 3 at the University of Illinois. Those that finished in the top three and had not met the Olympic qualifying standards were given a chance to do so during the camp.

---

200 meters
1. Jackie Thompson, Mickey's Missiles   23.4
2. Barbara Ferrell, L.A. Mercurettes   23.4
3. Pam Greene, Denver All-Stars   23.7
4. Maureen Abare, Mickey's Missiles   23.9

800-meter run
1. Madeline Manning Jackson, Columbus   2:05.2
     Community Track Club
2. Cheryl Toussaint, Atoms Track Club   2:05.7
3. Carol Hudson, Albuquerque Olympettes   2:06.0
4. Nancy Shafer, Canton Track Club   2:06.7

100-meter hurdles
1. Patty Johnson, Angels Track Club   13.0 AR
2. Lacey O'Neal, Sports International   13.3
3. Mamie Rallins, Tennessee State   13.4
4. Pat Donnelly, L. A. Track Club   13.5

400-meter dash
1. Kathy Hammond, Sacramento Road Runners   51.8 AR
2. Debra Edwards, Houston Spikettes   53.3
3. Mable Fergerson, West Coast Jets   53.3
4. Madeline Manning Jackson, Columbus C. Track Club 53.3

100-meter dash
1. Barbara Ferrell, L.A. Mercurettes   11.3
2. Iris Davis, Tennessee State, Police Athletic League   11.3
     and Matteline Render, N.Y.   11.3
4. Mildrette Netter, Alcorn A&M   nt
5. Martha Watson, L.A. Track Club   nt

1500-meter run
1. Francie Larrieu, San Jose Cindergals   4:10.4 AR
2. Francie Johnson, Liberty A.C.   4:15.2
3. Doris Brown, Falcon Track Club   4:18.5
4. Eileen Claugus, Will's Spikettes   4:22.1

Shot put
1. Maren Seidler, Mayor Daley Youth Foundation   53' 5"
2. Lynn Graham, Fresno Elans Track Club   50' 2½"
3. Mary Jacobson, Oregon Track Club   48' 9½"
4. Jan Svendsen, Los Angeles Track Club   48' 8¾"

Javelin throw
1. Kathy Schmidt, Long Beach Track Club   197' 9"
2. Sherry Calvert, L.A. Track Club   178' 6"
3. Roberta Brown, San Diego Lancerettes   170' 7"
4. Barbara Friedrich, Shore A.C.   170' 7"

Discus throw
1. Olga Connolly, L.A. Track Club   170' 4"
2. Vivian Turner, L.A. Track Club   160' 1"
3. Denise Wood, New Jersey Striders   149' 0"
4. Monette Driscoll, L.A. Track Club   147' 8"

Long jump
1. Martha Watson, L.A. Track Club   20' 1½"
2. Willye White, Mayor Daley Youth Foundation   20' 1¼"
3. Kim Attlesey, L.A. Track Club   19' 3¾"
4. Barbara Ferrell, L.A. Mercurettes   18' 11¾"

High jump
1. Deanne Wilson, unattached   5' 9¼"
2. Sandi Goldsberry, L.A. Track Club   5' 9¼"
3. Cindy Gilbert, La Jolla Track Club   5' 7½"
4. Karen Moller, Delaware Sports Club   5' 6½"

The pentathlon trials were in Los Alamos, New Mexico, on June 23-24.

1. Jennifer Meldrum, Canada   4251
2. Penny May, Canada   4202
3. Jane Frederick, unattached   4189
4. Marilyn King, Milbrae Lions   4064
5. Gail Fitzgerald, Atoms Track Club   4034

The Outdoor Nationals

Kent State University in Canton, Ohio, hosted the championships on July 1-2. The *New York Times* had small articles for each of the two days of the meet. The first story announced that Wilma Rudolph's twelve-year-old, 200-meter meet record was broken by Alice Annum, a twenty-one-year-old freshman from Ghana attending the University of Tennessee. The 100-meter record was tied by Alice Annum and Iris Davis. Patty Johnson, twenty-two, broke the meet mark in a 100-meter hurdle semifinal by winning in 13.2.

The next day the newspaper proclaimed, "Miss White Jumps to 13th Track Title." Thirty-two-year-old Willye White won another championship title with a leap of 20' 6¼". Former Olympic medalist and four-time Olympian Olga Connolly finished second in the discus and tearfully spoke of retirement.

Three American records were set in the meet, and six meet marks were erased in preparation for the Olympic trials the following weekend in Frederick, Maryland.

100-meter dash
1. Alice Annum, Sports International   11.5 ties MR
2. Rose Allwood, Sports International   11.5 ties MR

3. Iris Davis, Tennessee State   11.5
4. Mildrette Netter, Alcorn A&M   11.5

200-meter dash
1. Alice Annum, Sports International   23.4 MR
2. Rose Allwood, Sports International   23.7
3. Pam Greene, Denver All-Stars   23.8
4. Jacqueline Thompson, Mickey's Missiles   24.0

400-meter dash
1. Kathy Hammond, Sacramento Road Runners   52.3
2. Mable Fergerson, West Coast Jets   54.2
3. Beth Warner, Ohio Track Club   54.6
4. Patricia Helms, Clippers   54.6

800-meter run
1. Carol Hudson, Albuquerque Olympettes   2:06.7
2. Cheryl Toussaint, Atoms Track Club   2:06.7
3. Cis Schafer, Millbrae Lions   2:07.5
4. Nancy Mullen, Sacramento Road Runners   2:09.0

1500-meter run
1. Francie Larrieu, San Jose Cindergals   4:18.4
2. Eileen Claugus, Will's Spikettes   4:24.0
3. Kathy Gibbons, Glendale Gauchos   4:28.2
4. Barbara Lawson, Colorado Gold   4:34.6

3000-meter run
1. Tena Anex, Will's Spikettes   9:42.6 AR
2. Brenda Webb, Kettering Striders   9:50.3
3. Ellyn Cornish, Frederick Track Club   9:59.3
4. Lynn Lovat, Wolverine Track Club   10:02.0

100-meter hurdles
1. Mamie Rallins, Tennessee State   13.5
2. Patty Van Wolvelaere Johnson, Angels Track Club   13.6
3. Lorna Tinney, La Jolla Track Club   13.6
4. Pat Donnelly, Los Angeles Track Club   13.7

200-meter hurdles
1. Pat Hawkins, Atoms Track Club   26.3
2. Patty Johnson, Angels Track Club   27.3
3. Nancy Kaiser, Texas Track Club,   28.0
   and Janet Reusser, Topeka Cosmos   28.0

1500-meter walk
1. Jeannie Bocci, Wolverine Track Club   6:59.1
2. Lynn Olson, Wolverine Track Club   7:06.0
3. Susan Brodock, Rialto Road Runners   7:14.1
4. Laura Tucholski, Toledo Road Runners   7:14.5

High jump
1. Audrey Reid, Texas Woman's University   6' ½" MR
2. Deanne Wilson, unattached   5' 8"

3. Sandi Goldsberry, Los Angeles Track Club   5' 8"
4. Karen Moller, Delaware Sports Club   5' 7"

Long jump
1. Willye White, Mayor Daley Youth Foundation   20' 6¼"
2. Martha Watson, Los Angeles Track Club   20' 4¼"
3. Brenda Bryan, Texas Track Club   19' 11¾"
4. Kim Attlesey, Los Angeles Track Club   19' 1½"

Shot put
1. Maren Seidler, Mayor Daley Youth Foundation   52' 9"
2. Lynn Graham, Fresno Elans   50' 7¼"
3. Lynette Matthews, Falcon Track Club   49' 6½"
4. Denise Wood, New Jersey Striders   49' 1¾"

Discus
1. Josephine Dela Vina, Mayor Daley Youth Foundation   172' 0"
2. Olga Connolly, Los Angeles Track Club   170' 8"
3. Monette Driscoll, Los Angeles Track Club   152' 10"
4. Vivian Turner, Los Angeles Track Club   150' 10"

Javelin
1. Sherry Calvert, Los Angeles Track Club   184' 0"
2. Roberta Brown, San Diego Lancerettes   181' 6"
3. Kate Schmidt, Long Beach Track Club   180' 0"
4. Barbara Friedrich, Shore A.C.   166' 1"

440-yard relay
1. Sports International   45.4
   (Annum, Allwood, Norman, O'Neal)
2. Tennessee State University   45.5
3. Atoms Track Club   45.8
4. Alcorn A&M   45.9

880-yard medley relay
1. Sports International   1:40.6 AR
   (Annum, O'Neal, Randolph, Allwood)
2. West Coast Jets   1:41.5
3. Mickey's Missiles   1:42.3
4. Pioneer A.C.   1:44.1

One-mile relay
1. Canton Track Club   3:45.3
   (Anderson, Boring, Stewart, Shafer)
2. Atoms Track Club   3:46.4
3. Columbus Community Track Club   3:49.7
4. Duke City Dashers   3:50.0

Two-mile relay
1. San Jose Cindergals   9:07.3
   (Poor, Cooper, Eberly, Larrieu)
2. Los Angeles Track Club   9:13.3
3. Kettering Striders   9:15.5
4. Suffolk A.C.   9:30.5

Team scores:
L.A. Track Club 64; Sports International Track Club 56; Atoms Track Club 34; Mayor Daley Youth Foundation 30; Tennessee State University 27.

International meets scheduled for this summer were a dual meet with Romania in early June and a USSR–West Germany and Canada-Cuba-Jamaica meet after the Olympic trials.

The Indoor Nationals

The indoor national championship meet was held in New York City at Madison Square Garden on February 25. Neil Amdur's lengthy write-up in the *New York Times* devoted one small paragraph to the women's events: "Confusion also necessitated a restart of the women's mile, won by Doris Brown. And the crowd of 14,341 never did learn who won the women's 220 (Esther Stroy) because the girls were not introduced."

60-yard dash
1. Iris Davis, Tennessee State   6.9
2. Martha Watson, Los Angeles Track Club
3. Alfreda Daniels, Motor City Police Athletic League

60-yard hurdles
1. Patty Johnson, Angels Track Club   7.5 AR
2. Lacey O'Neal, Sports International
3. Mamie Rallins, Tennessee State

220-yard dash
1. Esther Stroy, Sports International   24.6
2. Willie Mae Fergerson, West Coast Jets   24.7
3. Darlene Green, Phoenix Track Club   25.2

440-yard dash
1. Kathy Hammond, Sacramento Road Runners   54.9
2. Karen Lundgren, La Jolla Track Club   54.9
3. Jarvis Scott, L.A. Mercurettes   55.0

880-yard run
1. Cheryl Toussaint, Atoms Track Club   2:08.2
2. Carol Hudson, Albuquerque O.C.   2:09.5
3. Wendy Koenig, Colorado Gold   2:10.5

One-mile run
1. Doris Brown, Falcon Track Club   4:44.0
2. Debbie Heald, La Mirada Meteors   4:47.0
3. Glenda Reiser, Canada   4:48.8

Unseeded one-mile run
1. Ellyn Cornish, Frederick Track Club   5:05.0

| 2. Brenda Webb, Kettering Striders | 5:08.7 |
| 3. Roberta Austin, Alfred Atalantans | 5:06.9 |

640-yard relay
1. Atoms Track Club, "A" team	1:10.4 AR
(Reynolds, Cordy, Hawkins, Smith-Brown)	
2. N.Y. Police Athletic League	1:12.0
3. Phoenix Track Club	1:13.5

Sprint medley relay
1. L.A. Mercurettes	1:46.2
(Walker, Ferrell, Scott, Smallwood)	
2. Atoms Track Club	1:46.6
3. West Coast Jets	1:48.0

One-mile relay
1. N.Y. Police Athletic League	3:51.6 AR
(Simuel, Johnson, Carter, Bastian)	
2. Atoms Track Club	3:55.4
3. Canton Track Club	3:57.5

4-kilo shot put
1. Maren Seidler, Mayor Daley Youth Foundation	50' 11½" AR
2. Denise Wood, New Jersey Striders	47' 9½"
3. Mary Jacobson, Oregon Track Club	46' 7¾"

Long jump
1. Martha Watson, Los Angeles Track Club	20' 11¾" AR
2. Willye White, Mayor Daley Youth Foundation	20' 7½"
3. Gaylene Barber, Mayor Daley Youth Foundation	19' 5¾"

High jump
1. Debbie Van Kiekebelt, Canada	5' 8"
2. Alice Pfaff, Colorado Gold	5' 8"
3. Jane Frederick, Colorado Gold	5' 8"

Team scores:
Atoms Track Club 16; Mayor Daley Youth Foundation and Colorado Gold 10; Sports International 9; Los Angeles Track Club 8.

The senior national cross-country championships were held on November 25 in Long Beach, California. A record total of 830 girls finished the races in the five age divisions.

1. Francie Larrieu, San Jose Cindergals	13:27
2. Doris Brown, Falcon Track Club	13:34
3. Kathy McIntyre, Falcon Track Club	13:53
4. Valerie Eberly, San Jose Cindergals	13:56

The results of the senior national 5-kilometer race walk:

| 1. Stella Palamarchuk, Ambler Olympic Club, Philadelphia | 29:04 |

2. Beryl Robinson, Stockton, Calif.	29:21
3. Gail Bristow, Boulder, Colo.	31:58
4. Pamela Weigle, Boulder, Colo.	32:15.8
5. Ellen Minkow, Long Island, N.Y.	32:24.8

Other junior meets in 1972 included the pentathlon championships on June 24 in Poplar Bluff, Missouri. The winner was Janet Reusser, Topeka Cosmos, 3,546. The junior cross-country championships were held in Dayton, Ohio, on November 11. Winners in the different age groups were the following:

Women's open division	
Brenda Webb, Kettering Striders	15:25
14–17 age division	
Debbie Vetter, Blue Ribbon Track Club	12:06.6
12–13 age division	
Robin Campbell, Sports International	8:34.1
10–11 age division	
Donna Campbell, Sports International	7:31
9 and under	
Anne Berry, Fleet Feet Track Club	6:14.8

The first junior national championships meet was held in Poplar Bluff, Missouri, on June 23-24. The national girls' championship meet was held at Kent State University in Canton, Ohio, on June 28-29.

A postal meet was held in the age-group mile on June 3. Age group winners included:

9 and under	
Amy Russillo, Licthicum, Md.	5:52.3
10–11	
Donna Campbell, Sports International	5:30.6
12–13	
Mary Decker, California	5:04.1
14–15	
Doreen Ennis, Nutley Track Club	5:13.4

National chairwoman Patricia Rico's report included a summary of progress in race walking by Bruce MacDonald, chairman of the race walking committee. He stated that postal competitions at 1 mile, 3K, 2 mile, 5K, 5 miles, and 10K would be organized. Twenty-three athletes had competed in the 5K international postal competition. Sue Brodock was our best walker, with a time of 27:55.6. National competition was proposed at 1 mile, 2 miles, 5K, and 10K distances. It was proposed that the national outdoor competition distance should be changed to 2 miles and a 1-mile walk should be included in the indoor championships. Boulder, Colorado, was going to bid for the first national 5K walk.

After noting that Don Denoon had been the first national walk chairman, serving until he retired in 1972, Bruce McDonald stated:

> I took over. Our first international competition was postal. Competition was held around the country and the top five times at 5000 meters were sent to Denmark. This was a quick and inexpensive way to get the girls around the country thinking about international competition in walking. Through the postal meet I started making arrangements for the United States women to enter what was then the fore-runner to international competition. The first international competition was a dual meet with Canada in 1973.

Dr. Harmon Brown was chairman of the age-group committee and development subcommittee. He reported on a clinic attended by twenty-eight coaches and thirty-five athletes held at California State, Hayward.

Dr. Ken Foreman was chairman of the long distance running committee.

Lyle Knudsen reported a large increase in membership of the coaches' association. He distributed a newsletter in order to determine issues that were of concern to coaches and athletes.

Martha Watson, representative of the athletes, believed that athletes should be made aware of the top facilities in the country for training and that a listing of clinics should be made available.

Willye White said that we did poorly in the Olympics because of the poor conditions: lack of meets, lack of qualified coaches, and lack of fairness. For example, the nationals and Olympic trials were conducted on tracks that were not superior, and the team was not in Munich early enough to adjust to the climate and time changes.

Edward Temple was announced as the first winner of the Joseph Robichaux Memorial Award, and the following athletes were nominated for the Saettel Award: Kathy Hammond, Kathy Schmidt, Mable Fergerson, and Francie Larrieu. The national committee voted to name Willye White a nominee for the Sullivan Award.

Bob Seaman was appointed as the new standards chairman, and it was decided by vote to have qualifying standards in the indoor nationals.

Patricia Rico was elected national women's chairman for a two-year period.

Women's Track and Field World listed the following women from the United States in the world ranking:

100m	5	Iris Davis
	11	Barbara Ferrell
200m	11	Jackie Thompson
400m	3	Kathy Hammond
	5	Mable Fergerson
1500m	11	Francie Larrieu
100mh	11	Patty Johnson
	17	Lacey O'Neal
Long jump	14	Martha Watson and Willye White

1972 All-America Women's Track and Field Teams

100-yard dash	Iris Davis
220-yard dash	Pam Greene
440-yard dash	Kathy Hammond
880-yard run	Madeline Manning Jackson
1500-meter run	Francie Larrieu
100-meter hurdles	Patty Johnson
200-meter hurdles	Pat Hawkins
Two-mile run	Tena Anex
High jump	Deanne Wilson
Long jump	Willye White
Shot put	Maren Seidler
Discus	Olga Connolly
Javelin	Kathy Schmidt
440-yard relay	Tennessee State
880-medley relay	West Coast Jets
Mile relay	Canton Track Club
Two-mile relay	San Jose Cindergals
One-mile walk	Jeanne Bocci
Pentathlon	Jane Frederick

Girls' Division

100-yard dash	Jackie Thompson
220-yard dash	Jackie Thompson
440-yard dash	Debra Edwards
880-yard run	Ann Gallagher
1-mile run	Tena Anex
80-yard hurdles	Lavonne Neal
High jump	Sandi Goldsberry
Long jump	Gaylene Barber
Shot put	Iva Wright
Discus	Iva Wright
Javelin	Karin Smith
440-yard relay	Mickey's Missiles
880-yard relay	Mickey's Missiles
Mile relay	Duke City Dashers

Cross-Country

Eileen Claugus
Doris Brown
Beth Bonner
Caroline Walker
Tena Anex
Debbie Roth
Jane Hill

The 1972-74 *Track and Field Guide* published by the Division on Girls' and Women's Sports (DGWS) included cross-country.

The program of the 29th Annual *Times*/GTE Indoor Games for February 19 held at the Forum in Inglewood, California, listed the "Athletes of the Meet." The year 1972 marked the first time when both a man and a woman were given this recognition. Kathy Gibbons from Glendale, Arizona, was given this first honor. She won the 1000-yard run in 2:32.2.

February 18 was the date of the 4th United States Olympic Invitation Meet in New York. Three individual women's events were contested. The event and the first-place finishers were:

Wilma Rudolph 50-meter dash	Iris Davis
Betty Robinson 400-meter run	Esther Stroy
Madeline Manning 800-meter run	Cheryl Toussaint

The Dr. Martin Luther King, Jr., International Freedom Games in Philadelphia on May 14 had seven women's events:

100-yard dash	Rose Allwood, Sports International	10.6
100-meter hurdles	Mamie Rallins, Tennessee State	13.7
220 yards	Willie Mae Fergerson, West Coast Jets	23.5
440 yards	Jarvis Scott, L.A. Mercurettes	55.0
880 yards	Madeline Manning, Columbus, Ohio	2:02.0
440-yard relay	Tennessee State University	45.8
Long jump	Willye White, Mayor Daley Youth Foundation	20' ¾"

Nina Kuscsik was the first official women's winner of the Boston Marathon.

The all-women's L'eggs Mini Marathon inaugural race with seventy-eight entries was held in Central Park, New York. Jacqueline Dixon won the 6-mile event in 37:01.7.

Fifty-eight colleges indicating that they had track and field for women were sent questionnaires asking about their program. Only two of the colleges had track and field for women prior to 1960—Linfield College in Oregon and North West Nazarene in Idaho. Most of the colleges began programs in the late 1960s. Twenty-two colleges had an intercollegiate program with ten to twenty girls on a team.

Eileen Clauqus finished second in the world cross country championships.

Bob Seaman

I ran my last race at the July nineteen sixty-four AAU nationals, and I was just working out on a track in December when a Hungarian man asked me if I would help with the girls' track club over in Pasadena. I wasn't really that enthused, but I went over and you know how one thing leads to another and you start really getting involved. He subsequently left the club, and I became the head coach in about nineteen sixty-seven. The club was the Crown City Track Club.

We won the junior nationals and then in nineteen sixty-eight in Aurora, Colorado, a week or so before the Olympic trials, we won the senior nationals, defeating Tennessee State and all the other heavyweights. I think we squeaked out with a one or two point victory, but I have to say that Ed Temple, bless his heart, was resting some of his top people like Madeline Manning. Then after the trials we had our first Olympian, Sharon Callahan, who was a high jumper. We were very pleased.

The club then became the Los Angeles Athletic Club in about nineteen seventy and then later the Naturite Track Club. It was a very, very powerful team winning a number of national championships. Some of the athletes in the club were Jane Frederick, Jodi Anderson, Julie Brown, and Pam Spencer.

In December nineteen seventy-two, I was appointed by Pat Rico to be the national standards chairman, a position I held for twenty years. I've also managed a number of teams. Pat Rico opened it up for men to be managers in nineteen seventy-four. I went to Moscow in an indoor meet in nineteen seventy-four; two years later I managed a junior team to Europe. In nineteen seventy-nine I was head manager of the world cup team in Montreal. I almost forgot the other one that we had to pay our own way to in nineteen sixty-eight. I was the women's cross-country chairman, and we sent our first-ever women's cross-country team to a competition that was sort of an international competition among the British Isles, Wales, Scotland, Ireland, Great Britain, and the United States. We won by one point.

I've enjoyed other assignments as assistant manager for the nineteen eighty-four Olympic team and head manager for the nineteen eighty-eight Olympic team.

Chapter 56

1973

The *New York Times* carried a story on the national championships held in Irvine, California, on June 22-23. The small headline read, "Mable Fergerson Wins A.A.U. 220 and 440 in Upsets." Mable, who had recently graduated from high school, ran the 220 in a wind-aided 23.4, upsetting the favorite, and won the 440 in 54.1. Fran Sichting became the 220-yard dash favorite after she broke the American record by running 23.2 in lane nine during the early rounds.

The meet record was broken in the 880, when Wendy Koenig pulled away from the field and won in 2:04.7 by more than five yards.

Records were established for the new events — the 400-meter hurdles, mile walk, and mile run.

The first two Americans in each event were selected to compete on the national team which toured Europe and competed against the USSR.

400-meter hurdles
1. Gail Fitzgerald, Atoms Track Club   61.1 MR
2. Clydine Crowder, La Mirada Meteors   61.9
3. Janet Reusser, Topeka Track Club   63.0

One-mile run
1. Francie Larrieu, San Jose Cindergals   4:40.4 MR
2. Kathy Gibbons, Glendale Gauchos   4:40.5
3. Eileen Claugus, Will's Spikettes   4:40.7

440-yard dash
1. Mable Fergerson, West Coast Jets   54.1
2. Marilyn Neufville, L.A. Track Club   54.5
3. Kathy Hammond, Sacramento Road Runners   54.9

Two-mile run
1. Eileen Claugus, Will's Spikettes   10:19.4
2. Kathy Gibbons, Glendale Gauchos   10:33.0
3. Tena Anex, Will's Spikettes   10:34.0

Two-mile relay
1. San Jose Cindergals   9:08.2
      (Haughey, Eberly, Poor, Larrieu)
2. Kettering Striders   9:08.4
3. Blue Ribbon Track Club, Ohio   9:09.8

440-yard relay
1. Tennessee State   45.5
     (Hughes, Montgomery, Rallins, Davis)
2. Atoms Track Club   45.8
3. Prairie View A&M   46.1

One-mile relay
1. Albuquerque Olympettes   3:47.0
     (Gibbs, Ashby, Chiavaria, Hudson)
2. Atoms Track Club, "B" team   3:49.6
3. Micky's Missiles   3:50.1

220-yard dash
1. Mable Fergerson, West Coast Jets   23.4
2. Fran Sichting, unattached, Oregon   23.5
3. Jackie Thompson, L.A. Track Club   23.6

One-mile walk
1. Esther Marquez, Sports United   7:54.6 MR
2. Sue Brodock, Sports United   7:59.0
3. Cheryl Dotseth, Mayor Daley Youth Foundation   8:06.2

100-yard dash
1. Iris Davis, Tennessee State   10.3
2. Martha Watson, L.A. Track Club   10.4
3. Fran Sichting, unattached, Oregon   10.4

880-yard run
1. Wendy Koenig, Colorado Gold   2:04.7 MR
2. Mary Decker, Blue Angels Track Club   2:05.6
3. Cheryl Toussaint, Atoms Track Club   2:06.7

100-meter hurdles
1. Patty Johnson, Club Northwest   12.9 w
2. Debbie Lansky, San Luis Obispo   13.5
3. Pat Donnelly, San Luis Obispo   13.8

High jump
1. Deanne Wilson, South Coast Track Club   5' 9"
2. Audrey Reid, Texas Woman's University   5' 8"
3. Karen Moller, Delaware Sports   5' 8"

Long jump
1. Martha Watson, L.A. Track Club   21' 4¾" w
2. Willye White, Mayor Daley Youth Foundation   20' 5¼" w
3. Jane Frederick, unattached   20' 1¼" w

Shot put
1. Maren Seidler, Mayor Daley Youth Foundation   51' 8¼"
2. Denise Wood, unattached, Haledon, N.J.   49' ¾"
3. Jean Roberts, Delaware Sports Club   48' 11¾"

Discus
1. Jean Roberts, Delaware Sports Club   173' 3"

2. Josephine Dela Vina, Mayor Daley Youth Foundation   169' 9"
3. Monette Driscoll, L.A. Track Club   158' 10"

Javelin
1. Kate Schmidt, Long Beach Track Club   194' 6"
2. Barbara Friedrich, Shore A.C.   186' 3"
3. Lynn Cannon, Redwood City Striders   170' 11"

880-yard medley relay
1. West Coast Jets   1:43.2
2. Prairie View Track Club   1:44.0
3. Atoms Track Club   1:44.4

Team scores:
Los Angeles Track Club 44; Atoms Track Club 38; Mayor Daley Youth Foundation 34.

The Indoor Nationals

The indoor national championship meet was held on February 23 in Madison Square Garden.

Long jump
1. Irena Szewinska, Poland   20' 6"
2. Martha Watson, L.A. Track Club   20' 4¼"
3. Debbie Van Kiekebelt, Canada   18' 8"

High jump
1. Alice Pfaff, Colorado Track Club   5' 8"
2. Deanne Wilson, South Coast Track Club   5' 8"
3. Joni Huntley, Portland Track Club   5' 7"

One-mile walk
1. Lynn Olson, Ferris State   7:37.0
2. Ellen Minkow, unattached   8:06.6
3. Carol Mohanco, Kettering Striders   8:08.5

60-yard dash
1. Iris Davis, Tennessee State   6.6
2. Kathie Lawson, Liberty A.C.   6.8
3. Martha Watson, L.A. Track Club   6.8

440-yard run
1. Brenda Walsh, Canada   55.5
2. Kathy Hammond, Sacramento Road Runners   55.7
3. Marilyn Neufville, L.A. Track Club   56.2

60-yard hurdles
1. Patty Johnson, Club Northwest   7.5 ties MR
2. Mamie Rallins, Tennessee State   7.7
3. Lacey O'Neal, Sports International   7.7

One-mile run
1. Ludmila Bragina, Soviet Union   4:40.0 MR
2. Glenda Reiser, Canada   4:45.1
3. Debbie Heald, La Mirada Meteors   4:46.7

640-yard relay
1. N.Y. Police Athletic League   1:11.2
    (Render, Osborn, Wilson, Johnson)
2. Motor City Police Athletic League   1:12.8
3. Padukies   1:16.1

Sprint medley relay
1. Sports International   1:47.9
    (Campbell, O'Neal, Randolph, Stroy)
2. Atoms Track Club   1:49.1
3. Ambler Olympic Club   1:51.1

One-mile relay
1. Atoms Track Club   3:50.5 AR
    (DeSandies, McMillan, Fitzgerald, Toussaint)
2. N.Y. Police Athletic League   3:53.1
3. Canton Track Club   4:02.7

220-yard dash
1. Rosalyn Bryant, Los Angeles Mercurettes   24.6
2. Irena Szewinska, Poland   25.0
3. Janet Brown, Colorado Track Club   25.3

880-yard run
1. Cheryl Toussaint, Atoms Track Club   2:08.8
2. Robin Campbell, Sports International   2:08.9
3. Gayle Olinek, Toronto Olympic Club   2:10.9

Shot put
1. Jan Svendsen, unattached   50' ¼"
2. Jean Roberts, Delaware S.C.   49' 8¾"
3. Denise Wood, unattached   49' 5¾"

Team scores:
Atoms Track Club 14; Sports International 10; N.Y. Police Athletic League 9.

According to Bob Seaman, the last girls' and women's age-group pentathlon and race walk championship "package" was held at the University of California, Irvine, California, on June 17-24. Jane Frederick won the national pentathlon championship on June 17-18 in Irvine, California, with a score of 4,281. Gail Fitzgerald was second with 4,273 and Mitzi McMillan third with 4,109 points.

The national 5000-meter walk championship was won by Susan Brodock in the American record time of 27:39.9. Ellen Minkow was second and Esther Marquez third.

The late C. C. Jackson was named the recipient of the Robichaux Award for his many years of service to women's track. Martha Watson was named as the women's track and field committee nominee for the Sullivan Award.

After serving for six years as age-group chairman, Dr. Harmon Brown delivered his final report, stating that there were now over eighty events in four age divisions, with a balanced program of track and field events and distance running.

Women's Track and Field World reported that an "injury riddled, out of condition USA cross country team managed to finish third in the first IAAF sponsored International Cross Country Championships." Doris Brown was 15th, Francie Larrieu 16th, Vicki Foltz 29th, and Caroline Walker 30th. Doris Brown, who had won the championship title five times, was injured to the point where she was unable to work out properly. The race was held in Waregem, Belgium, on March 17.

The second indoor USSR–USA dual meet was held in March in Richmond, Virginia. The American women defeated the Soviet women for the second year in a row by a narrow margin. The final event, a medley relay, decided the win.

Robin Campbell, in a surprise upset, won the 880. The *New York Times* headlines read, "Girl Runner, 14, Leads U.S. Women to Victory." The article by Neil Amdur continued:

> Robin Campbell wowed 'em tonight, and no international debutante could have enjoyed a more satisfying coming-out party.
>
> Less than two hours after she outran a pair of veterans of international track competition in the 880 yard run, the 14 year old Washington schoolgirl anchored a United States women's team to a 20-yard medley relay victory over the Soviet Union in the final event of the second Indoor meet between the two countries.
>
> The relay triumph broke a 60-60 tie and brought the young American women's team a second consecutive upset victory, 65-62.

Martha Watson improved on her own American record in the long jump, and Americans Alice Pfaff and Deanne Wilson finished 1-2 in the high jump.

60-yard dash	
1. Iris Davis	6.6
4. Kathie Lawson	6.7
Triathlon (sp/hj/60yh)	
3. Gail Fitzgerald	3,614
(Svendsen was injured and did not finish)	
Long jump	
1. Martha Watson	21' 4¾" AR
4. Susan McLalin	18' 9½"
440-yard dash	
1. Kathy Hammond	55.3
2. Chris A'Harrah	55.6
60-yard hurdles	
1. Patty Johnson	7.6
2. Mamie Rallins	7.7

Shot put
3. Maren Seidler   48' 4½"
4. Denise Wood   48'

Two-mile run
3. Debbie Heald   10:34.2
4. Debbie Roth   10:59.0

600-yard run
1. Cheryl Toussaint   1:20.7
3. Jarvis Scott   1:22.3

880-yard run
1. Robin Campbell   2:11.1
4. Carol Hudson   2:12.3

High jump
1. Alice Pfaff   5' 7¼"
2. Deanne Wilson   5' 7¼"

Mile run
3. Mary Decker   4:40.1
4. Kathy Gibbons   4:52.1

Medley relay
1. U.S.   3:26.5
   (Render, Hammond, Toussaint, Campbell)

USA 65 — USSR 62

Munich, Germany, was the site of a triangular meet between the United States, Germany, and Switzerland on July 11-12. First-place finishers for the United States were:

200 meters	Jackie Thompson	23.08
100-meter hurdles	Patty Johnson	13.32
3000 meters	Francie Larrieu	9:16.0
Long jump	Martha Watson	6.53
Shot put	Maren Seidler	15.52

USA — 85 West Germany

A meet against Italy was held in Torino on July 17-18. The first-place finishers were:

100 meters	Jackie Thompson	11.5
200 meters	Jackie Thompson	23.3
400 meters	Chris A'Harrah	53.9
800 meters	Mary Decker	2:03.9
100-meter hurdles	Patty Johnson	13.2
Long jump	Martha Watson	6.11
Shot put	Maren Seidler	15.56
Javelin	Martha Pickel	50.06

400-meter relay	USA	44.3
(Watson, Montgomery, Thompson, Lawson)		
1600-meter relay	USA	3:37.8
(A'Harrah, Shafer, Sapenter, Hammond)		
USA 84 — Italy 49		

The USA–USSR meet was held on July 23-24 in Minsk. The first-place finishers for the United States were:

800 meters	Mary Decker	2:02.9
3000 meters	Francie Larrieu	9:30.0
100-meter hurdles	Patty Johnson	13.5
Long jump	Martha Watson	21' 7¼" AR
USA 51— USSR 95		

The seventh World University Games were held from August 16 to August 20 in Moscow at Lenin Stadium. The USA scored only one point on the track with a sixth place in the 400-meter relay. Kathy Schmidt placed second in the javelin.

The second woman named "Athlete of the Meet" at the Annual *Times/*GTE Indoor Games was Wendy Koenig. The Colorado Gold athlete won the 500 in 1:05.5.

Women's Track and Field World in January reported that four women's events were scheduled in the Sunkist meet in Los Angeles on January 13. The order of three of the women's events was switched at the last minute by ABC-TV. The women were ordered off the track at the point when they were waiting for the starter's commands. Francie Larrieu was so angered that she threw her shoes at the TV cameras when the mile was moved.

Track and Field Fundamentals for Girls and Women was published this year.

Kathy Hammond was named the North American Athlete of the Year. Mable Fergerson was awarded the first *Redbook* trophy as the outstanding female athlete at both the USA indoor and outdoor championships.

Bruce MacDonald reported that the first international competition in walking, a dual meet with Canada, was held in Montreal. Each country entered its five best women. Ellen Minkow of Port Washington won the 5000-meter walk in 26:31.8, and the United States won the team title. The girls had to raise their own money in order to compete. The United States swept the first four places.

American Outdoor Records

100y	10.3	Wyomia Tyus	1966
	10.2	Iris Davis	June 20, 1971
100m	11.0	Wyomia Tyus	October 15, 1968
200m	22.8	Barbara Ferrell	October 18, 1968
220y	23.4	Edith McGuire	August 13, 1964
400m	51.6	Kathryn Hammond	September 7, 1972

440y	52.2	Kathryn Hammond	August 12, 1972
800m	2:00.9	Madeline Manning	October 20, 1968
880y	2:02.0	Madeline Manning	1972
1500m	4:10.4	Francie Larrieu	July 8, 1972
One mile	4:39.6	Doris Brown	June 12, 1971
3000m	9:44.6	Doris Brown	1970
Two mile	10:07.0	Doris Brown	July 10, 1971
80mh	10.5	Cherrie Sherrard	August 20, 1967
	10.5	Pat Van Wolvelaere	October 18, 1968
100mh	13.0	Patty Johnson	July 8, 1972
200mh	26.1	Pat Hawkins	July 10, 1971
400mh	59.1	Wendy Koenig	1973

Race Walking
1500m	6:50.4	Jeannie Bocci	July 8, 1972
One mile	7:53.3	Jeannie Bocci	June 18, 1972
1K	5:11.2	Stella Palamarchuk	October 23, 1971
Marathon	2:49.90	Cheryl Bridges	1971

Field Events
HJ	5' 11"	Eleanor Montgomery	July 6, 1969
LJ	21' 6"	Willye White	July 26, 1964
	21' 6"	Martha Watson	May 27, 1972
4K shot	54' 9"	Earlene Brown	September 21, 1960
Discus	189'	Olga Connolly	May 27, 1972
Javelin	205' 6"	Kathy Schmidt	July 28, 1972
Pentathlon	4,305	Gail Fitzgerald	August 12-13, 1972

Relays
400m	42.8	USA	October 20, 1968
		(Ferrell, Bailes, Netter, Tyus)	
440y	44.7	Tennessee State Univ.	July 9, 1971
		(Hughes, Wedgeworth, Render, Davis)	
1600m	3:25.2	USA	September 10, 1972
		(Fergerson, Manning, Toussaint, Hammond)	
One mile	3:33.9	USA	August 12, 1972
		(Edwards, Jackson, Fergerson, Hammond)	
One mile	3:38.3	Atoms Track Club	July 10, 1971
		(McMillan, Reynolds, Fitzgerald, Toussaint)	
Two miles	8:53.6	San Jose Cindergals	July 10, 1971
		(Wooten, Cooper, Miller, Larrieu)	
880y medley	1:40.6	Sports International	July 2, 1972
(220-110-110-440)		(Annum, O'Neal, Randolph, Allwood)	

Robin Campbell

In an interview on December 2, 1992, Robin Campbell told me:

> I had four older brothers and they would always pick on me, so I wanted to
> learn how to defend myself. The recreation center happened to have a boxing

program for girls. I thought that was the best way for me to defend myself. I was a practical young kid. Then I was always getting hit at boxing so I decided that boxing was not for me. The other sport that was popular was track and field. So that's how I began my career in track and field in nineteen sixty-nine in Washington, D.C. I was nine years old.

My coach at the time was a school track coach, Mr. Clark. I ran for him for one year. Under his guidance I competed against other elementary schools.

I was at the dedication of the RFK Stadium in nineteen sixty-nine. Martha Watson and Brooks Johnson were there. Martha happened to see me compete in the sprints and asked me if I were interested in running and I said yes. She introduced me to Brooks, who gave me his card, told me about his track team, and said that I should talk to my parents about joining his team. Everything started from this.

The first year with Brooks I won the cross-country nationals and had a lot of competition in track in which I was very successful.

My first USA team was in nineteen seventy-three against the Russians, which I'm most known for. Brooks was the head coach, and Martha Watson was on the team. Most people remember me from nineteen seventy-two and nineteen seventy-three, when I was competing against Mary Decker. We ran against each other from nineteen seventy three through nineteen seventy-nine. It seemed like forever.

A year that I remember especially was nineteen seventy-five because I ran so many events. It was in the nationals in White Plains, N.Y. It was the first time that I ran more events than I wanted too. I ran the four by one relay, I anchored the four by four, I anchored the four by eight, and I got to run the open quarter. I was able to run in both the senior and junior divisions. I always thought that I was a sprinter until I ran the anchor leg on the four by one relay team. I was running against Chandra Cheeseborough, and she passed me like I was standing still. I guess I realized then that I was not as fast as I thought I was.

My best time for the quarter was fifty-two flat and twenty-three point five for the two hundred meters. My best time in the half was one fifty nine. I didn't like running the fifteen hundred because it was too many laps around the track.

One of my best memories was the trip to China in nineteen seventy-five and also all of my friends that I made in track and field. I spent most of my life, from fourteen to close to thirty, traveling with my track friends, we were like family.

My first Olympic team was in nineteen eighty, the boycotted games. I was third in the trials.

Sometimes it's hard watching the Olympic Games. I miss the competition and friends, but I'm still involved in track as a member of the board of directors of the Athletes' Advisory Committee.

Chapter 57

1974

The outdoor national championship meet was held on June 28-29 at Bakersfield College, Bakersfield, California. Two small paragraphs about the meet appeared in the *New York Times* at the bottom of the write-up about the junior USA–USSR meet. The article announced the equaling of the world 440-yard record by Debra Sapenter.

100-yard dash
1. Renaye Bowen, Lakewood International   10.4
2. Alice Annum, Sports International   10.4
3. Matteline Render, N.Y. Police Athletic League   10.4
4. Janet Brown, Texas Woman's University   10.5

100-meter hurdles
1. Patty Johnson, La Jolla Track Club   13.2 MR
2. Mamie Rallins, Tennessee State   13.3
3. Modupe Oshikoya, unattached   13.5
4. Debbie Lansky, Golden Triangle Track Club   13.6

220-yard dash
1. Alice Annum, Sports International   23.1
2. Francine Sichting, South Coast Track Club   23.4
3. Rhonda McManus, Southern University   23.7
4. Rosalyn Bryant, Mayor Daley Youth Foundation   23.7

440-yard dash
1. Debra Sapenter, Prarie View   52.2 ties WR, AR
2. Sheila Choates, Tennessee State   53.6
3. Marilyn Neufville, L.A. Track Club   53.6
4. Gwen Norman, Sports International   53.9

400-meter hurdles
1. Andrea Bruce, Prairie View A&M   59.7 MR
2. Michele Hopper, Premier Track Club   59.8
3. Janice Lester, Long Beach Comets   60.0
4. Linda Wright, Glendale Gauchos   61.0

880-yard run
1. Mary Decker, unattached   2:05.2
2. Robin Campbell, Sports International   2:05.9

3. Liane Swegle, Seattle Dynamics   2:07.4
4. Tecla Chemabwai, Chicago State Univ.   2:08.5

Mile walk
1. Sue Brodock, Rialto Road Runners   7:29.7 AR
2. Ellen Minkow, Syracuse Chargers   7:43.1
3. Esther Marquez, Rialto Roadrunners   7:53.6
4. Chris Sakelarios, Redwood City Flyers   8:06.9

Mile run
1. Julie Brown, L.A. Track Club   4:45.1
2. Judy Graham, San Jose Cindergals   4:46.0
3. Karen McHarg, Kettering Striders   4:50.2
4. Vicki Foltz, Falcon Track Club   4:50.4

Two-mile run
1. Lynn Bjorklund, Duke City Dashers   10:11.1
2. Clare Choate, L.A. Track Club   10:21.1
3. Marlene Harewicz, Mt. Lebanon Track Club   10:31.0
4. Debbie Johnson, Rialto Road Runners   10:40.3

440-yard relay
1. Texas Woman's University   45.6
      (Brown, Vaamonde, Davis, Reid)
2. Prairie View A&M   45.6
3. Sports International   45.6
4. Mayor Daley Youth Foundation   46.4

One-mile relay
1. Sports International   3:39.6
      (James, Norman, Campbell, Pastel)
2. Tennessee State   3:40.6
3. Atoms Track Club, "A" team   3:46.4
4. Dryades St. Track Club   3:47.5

Two-mile relay
1. San Jose Cindergals, "A" team   8:49.1 AR
      (Haughey, Graham, Haberman, Poor)
2. Kettering Striders   8:57.5
3. Falcon Track Club   8:53.3
4. L.A. Track Club   9:01.7

880-yard medley relay
1. Sports International   1:38.5 MR
      (Annum, Allwood, Norman, Pastel)
2. Prairie View A&M   1:40.1
3. Tennessee State Track Club   1:42.3

Shot put
1. Maren Seidler, Mayor Daley Youth Foundation   54' 3" MR
2. Cindy Reinhoudt, unattached   48' 4"
3. Jan Svendsen, La Jolla Track Club   47' 7¾"
4. Denise Wood, unattached   47' 6"

Javelin
1. Kathy Schmidt, L.A. Track Club   203' 2" MR
2. Lynn Cannon, Redwood City Striders   192' 1"
3. Sherry Calvert, Lakewood International   187' 4"
4. Barbara Friedrich, Shore A.C.   181' 0"

High jump
1. Joni Huntley, Oregon Track Club   6' 0"
2. Pam Spencer, Great Falls, Montana   5' 8"
    and Cindy Gilbert, La Jolla Track Club
4. Karen Moller, Delaware Sports Club   5' 8"

Long jump
1. Martha Watson, Lakewood International   21' 3½" MR
2. Willye White, Mayor Daley Youth Foundation   20' 11½"
3. Sherron Walker, Everett Chargers   20' 7½"
4. Modupe Oshikoya, unattached   20' 6½"

Discus
1. Joan Pavelich, La Jolla Track Club   173' 11"
2. Linda Langford, Mayor Daley Youth Foundation   164' 1"
3. Monette Driscoll, L.A. Track Club   161' 9"
4. Jean Roberts, Delaware Sports Club

Team scores:
Sports International 56; Prairie View A&M 45; Los Angeles Track Club 45; Mayor Daley Youth Foundation 37; La Jolla Track Club 34.

The Indoor Nationals

Madison Square Garden was the site of the indoor championships on February 22. Fifteen-year-old Mary Decker's record-breaking performance in the half mile captured the headlines in the *New York Times*. She set a world record of 2:02.4 the previous week and on this night repeated her winning performance in holding off the more experienced Abby Hoffman of Canada.

A second article in the *New York Times* on February 23 featured Joni Huntley's 6' high jump. Seventeen-year-old Joni broke the 6' barrier three times during the week and became the first American woman to clear 6'. The first record-breaking jump was the previous Saturday when she cleared 6' ½" to better the American mark by 2 inches.

60-yard dash
1. Theresa Montgomery, Tennessee State   6.7
2. Martha Watson, Lakewood International   6.8
3. Renaye Bowen, West Coast Jets Track Club   6.9
4. Janet Brown, Texas Woman's University   6.9

220-yard dash
1. Theresa Montgomery, Tennessee State,   25.0
    and Linda Cordy, Atoms Track Club

3. Esther Stroy, Sports International   25.1
4. Kathy Lawson, La Jolla Track Club   25.3

440-yard run
1. Brenda Nichols, Atoms Track Club   56.1
2. Tecla Chemabwai, Chicago State University   56.3
3. Gwen Norman, Sports International   58.0
4. June Smith, Sports International   58.8

880-yard run
1. Mary Decker, Blue Angels   2:07.1 MR
2. Abby Hoffman, Toronto Olympic Club   2:07.3
3. Cheryl Toussaint, Atoms Track Club   2:07.7
4. Wendy Koenig Knudson, Colorado Gold   2:10.9

One-mile run
1. Robin Campbell, Sports International   4:50.7
2. Doreen Ennis, Nutley Track Club   4:51.6
3. Kathy Gibbons, Glendale Gauchos   4:52.0
4. Debbie Quatier, Falcon Track Club   4:54.3

60-yard hurdles
1. Patty Johnson, La Jolla Track Club   7.7
2. Mamie Rallins, Tennessee State   7.7
3. Elizabeth Damman, Toronto   7.7
4. Debbie Lansky, Golden Triangle Track Club   8.0

One-mile walk
1. Susan Brodock, Rialto Road Runners   7:28.6
2. Ellen Minkow, Syracuse University   7:37.0
3. Judith Salkoski, Gateway Track Club   8:08.9
4. Marybeth Hayford, Gateway Track Club   8:09.1

Shot put
1. Maren Seidler, Mayor Daley Youth Foundation   54' 4"
2. Jane Haist, Ontario   50' ¾"
3. Jean Roberts, Delaware Sports Club   49' 10¼"
4. Denise Wood, Montclair, N.J.   48' 6¾"

Long jump
1. Martha Watson, Lakewood International   20' 9½"
2. Vicki Betts, Lakewood International   19' 11¾"
3. Celeste Johnson, Mayor Daley Youth Foundation   19' 1"
4. Sue McLalin, Golden Triangle Track Club   19' ½"

High jump
1. Joni Huntley, Oregon Track Club   6'
2. Cindy Gilbert, La Jolla Track Club,   5' 7"
      and Jil Hilgramson, Mayor Daley Youth Foundation
4. Cheryl Friesen, Tabor College   5' 7"

(Cindy Gilbert won the jump-off with Jil Hilgramson for 2d place to compete in USSR meet on March 2)

640-yard relay
1. Mayor Daley Youth Foundation   1:12.4
   (Bryant, Milan, Johnson, Hopkins)
2. Sports International   1:13.0
3. Atoms Track Club, "A" team   1:14.5
4. Atoms Track Club, "B" team   1:15.1

One-mile relay
1. Atoms Track Club, "A" team   3:48.3
   (McMillan, DeSandies, Fitzgerald, Nichols)
2. Sports International, "A" team   3:50.6
3. Atoms Track Club, "B" team   4:00.5
4. Ambler Olympics   4:14.1

The national cross country championships were held in Bellbrook, Ohio, on November 30.

1. Lynn Bjorklund, Los Alamos, New Mexico	17:31.7
2. Julie Brown, UCLA	17:41
3. Francie Larrieu, Pacific Coast Club	18:03
4. Debbie Quatier, Falcon Track Club	18:12

The first national AAU women's marathon championship race was held in San Mateo, California, on February 10. Fifty-seven women started the run. Ruth Anderson won the master's division with a time of 3:20:59.

1. Judy Ikenberry, Rialto Road Runners	2:55.17
2. Marilyn Paul, unattached	2:58.44
3. Peggy Lyman, West Valley Track Club	2:58.55
4. Nina Kuscsik, Suffolk A. C.	3:04.11

The national 10,000-meter run championships were held in New York City on May 18.

1. Marlene Harewicz, Mt. Lebanon Track Club	35:21.2 MR
2. Jackie Hansen, Beverly Hills, Calif.	38:03
3. Cathy Greene, L.I. Golden Spikes	39:18
4. Nina Kuscsik, Suffolk A.C.	39:50

The second international women's 10,000 meter championship race was held in Guayanilla, Puerto Rico, on November 3. The top American finishers were:

5. Marlene Harewicz	38:12:03
8. Doreen Ennis	39:01:18
9. Anita Scandurra	39:02:03

The national pentathlon championship meet was held in Bakersfield, California, on June 23-24.

1. Mitzi McMillan, Seattle, Wash.	405
2. Marilyn King, Millbrae Lions	403
3. Lisa Chiavaria, Albuquerque, N.M.	374
4. Lisa Kinimaka, San Jose Cindergals	370

For the first time, on August 3-4, pentathletes from the United States competed internationally as a team. Jane Frederick, Marilyn King, and Mitzi McMillan finished third in the meet in Tallin, Soviet Union.

Other junior and age-group meets were the national AAU women's junior division meet at Bakersfield College on June 25-26; the national AAU junior track and field championships at the University of Florida in Gainesville on June 14-15; the junior national open division track and field championships in Phoenix, Arizona, in June; the national junior pentathlon championships at Phoenix College, Phoenix, Arizona, on June 19; the national age-group invitational pentathlon classic at Drake Stadium, UCLA, on June 23-24; the junior national 5000-meter race walk at Belleville, Illinois, on June 1; and the AAU 13 and under 3000-meter race walking classic.

Bruce MacDonald reported on the first international race walking competition. In elaborating on the first competition, Bruce later wrote:

> As a result of the postal competition in 1972 contacts were made in Europe and arrangements were made for the United States team to compete in Stockholm, Sweden. Once again, the team was chosen from the national championships and once again each of the members of the party raised their own money to go. To cut expenses a three week stay was the least expensive air fare. The team spent the first two weeks in Denmark with a week in Copenhagen where they had two competitions and then traveled by train to Sdr Omme, Denmark for another week of training and one competition. A good portion of the stay in Denmark was picked up by the Danish Federation.
>
> The trip from Denmark was by train and boat to Stockholm. The team was housed in an old beautiful mansion for the week before the competition. Seven countries (Great Britain, Denmark, Germany, Norway, Sweden, Switzerland and the U.S.A.) had entries in the 5000 meter race. The competition was won by Sue Brodock from the United States breaking the world record with her win. The United States finished second in their first multi-international team effort.
>
> In taking advantage of the international gathering, I took the opportunity to assemble the team leaders to discuss the future of race walking covering three main topics:
>
> 1) How can more countries be encouraged to participate?
>
> 2) Can this competition become a world championship?
>
> 3) What can be done to have women's race walking included as one of the track events in the Olympics? These meetings continued each summer with the goal of fostering the growth of women's race walking. The meet was eventually recognized as a world championship.

The committee recommended that the marathon for women should be encouraged. The first national marathon team of nine women paid their own expenses to West Germany. The First International Women's Marathon was held in Waldniel on September 22; approximately forty-five women competitors participated. The team was composed of Judy Ikenberry, Marilyn Paul, Peggy Lyman, Nina Kuscsik, and Lucy Bunz, who placed 1-5 in the national championships in February, and Joan Ullyot, Jackie Hansen, Ruth Anderson, and Catherine Smith. Jackie Hansen finished fifth in 2:56:25 and was the first American.

The USA–USSR indoor meet was held in Moscow on March 2. The *New York Times* reported that the American women won two of the four field events but had only three victories in the running events. The greater part of the story was devoted to fifteen-year-old Mary Decker's anchor leg on the medley relay:

> She was in the lead ... but then dropped behind. The Russian cut in front of her and elbows flew. Mary, apparently thinking she had been fouled, slackened and threw her baton at Miss Shtula.
>
> Then Mary retrieved her baton and jogged on to the finish, where she tried again. Again, she missed.
>
> In sobs at the finish line, the American youngster screeched, "she hit me with the baton in the stomach."
>
> The judges disqualified the Soviet relay team for Miss Shtula's interference and did the same to the Americans for "unsportsmanlike conduct."

60-meter dash		
1. Martha Watson	7.1	
4. Theresa Montgomery	7.1	
60-meter hurdles		
2. Patty Johnson	8.4	
4. Mamie Rallins	8.5	
400-meter dash		
3. Brenda Nichols	56.1	
4. Gwen Norman	56.8	
600-meter run		
1. Robin Campbell	1:30.1	
2. Wendy Koenig	1:30.6	
800-meter run		
1. Mary Decker	2:04.5	
3. Cheryl Toussaint	2:05.8	
1500-meter run		
3. Kathy Gibbons	4:25.6	
4. Doreen Ennis	4:28.3	
3000-meter run		
3. Debbie Quatier	9:29	
4. Brenda Webb	10:00	

2000-meter medley relay
Both teams disqualified, the USSR for bumping and the USA for unsportsmanlike conduct.

High jump		
1. Joni Huntley	5' 11¼"	
4. Cindy Gilbert	5' 7"	

Long jump
1. Martha Watson   20' 8"
4. Vicki Betts   19' ¾"

Shot put
3. Maren Seidler   53' 6¼"
4. Denise Wood   46' 4¼"

Triathlon
3. Mitzi McMillan   2417
4. Lorna Tinney   2016

The outdoor USA–USSR meet was held at Duke University in Durham, North Carolina, on July 5-6. Premeet articles in the *New York Times* featured stories on Mary Decker, remembering her tearful conclusion in the relay in the indoor meet. The Soviets confirmed the fact that the Soviet runner involved was not on the outdoor team. According to the *New York Times* article:

> Miss Decker, the 15 year old national half mile champion and American record holder, burst onto the international scene during this meet last summer when she upset Niele Sabaite, the Olympic silver medal winner, in the 800 meter run. Both are back for Saturday's race and will be joined by Robin Campbell, the talented Washington, D.C., teenager.
> "Mary's ready, and so is Robin," said Will Stephens, the coach of the American women's team, which has won only one of the 11 duals in the Soviet series. "It should be a great race."
> The women's 800 was the highlight for the American women. Mary took the lead on the final turn, lost it in the stretch to the charging Miss Sabaite and somehow regained it with a finishing kick that stunned the red-shirted Soviet athlete. Miss Decker's winning time was 2:02.3.
> At 5 feet 4 inches and 98 pounds, still wearing braces, Miss Decker hardly looks the part of a competitive tiger who eats spaghetti as a pre-race meal. But she is intensely competitive (I like to be first, I don't like to be second) and seems to fire up best under adversity.

100 meters		3000 meters	
1. Renaye Bowen	11.62	3. Clare Choate	9:39.67
4. Matteline Render	11.78	4. Marlene Harewicz	9:45.27
200 meters		100-meter hurdles	
1. Fran Sichting	23.17	2. Mamie Rallins	13.2
3. Rhonda McManus	24.00	3. Patty Johnson	13.4
400 meters		High jump	
1. Debra Sapenter	52.13	1. Joni Huntley	6'
4. Sheila Choates	54.3	4. Pam Spencer	5' 8"
800 meters		Long jump	
1. Mary Decker	2:02.29 MR	1. Martha Watson	21' 4"
4. Robin Campbell	2:04.40	2. Willye White	21' 2½"
1500 meters		Shot put	
3. Julie Brown	4:26.7	3. Maren Seidler	55' 9¾"
4. Judy Graham	4:30.1	4. Cindy Reinhoudt	47' 11¾"

Discus			Javelin		
3. Monette Driscoll	161' 1"		2. Kathy Schmidt	191' 2"	
4. Linda Langford	157' 9"		4. Lynn Cannon	172'	

The USA–USSR Junior Championships were held at the University of Texas, Austin, on June 28-29.

The *New York Times* reported that "little 16 year old Kathy Weston anchored the American women to a 10 yard mile-relay victory after she had broken the 800 meter meet mark."

The third winner of the women's "Athlete of the Meet" in the Annual *Times*/GTE Indoor Games in California was Mary Decker. The Blue Angels Track Club athlete won the 880 in 2:06.7.

The 11th Annual Albuquerque Jaycee Meet was held on February 2. Events for women were the 60-yard hurdles, 60-yard dash, mile relay, 300-yard dash, 440-yard dash, and 880-yard run. In a six-year period since 1968, one additional event for women had been added.

The 8th Annual San Diego Indoor Games on February 17 showed an increase in women's events from six years earlier (1968). Added to the 60-yard dash and the 880-yard run were the 640-yard relay, 60-yard high hurdles, two-mile run, which in 1974 was unique in indoor programs for women, sprint medley relay, and high jump.

The National Track and Field Hall of Fame was founded this year. Two women, Mildred "Babe" Didrikson and Wilma Rudolph, were the first women enshrined in the Hall of Fame.

Women's Track and Field World published an "athletes of the year" article; the only American in the group was Kathy Schmidt.

Juner Bellew won the Robichaux Award, and Martha Watson was the track and field committee's choice for the Sullivan Award nomination.

California's 56th state meet included girls' state competition in eleven events for the first time this year. In a survey sent to twelve state athletic associations, it was found that New Jersey, Texas, Michigan, Iowa, Indiana, Colorado, Alabama, and Connecticut already conducted state girls' championships. Ohio and New York planned their first state meet for girls in 1975.

Chapter 58

1975

The White Plains high school track, White Plains, New York, was the location of the national championships on June 27-28. In its "Steve Talk" column, *Women's Track and Field World* commented, "Never before had there been such a fine assemblage of female athletes collected for one competition in the United States. Meet and American records fell by the wayside as if women's track were in its infancy. In many ways that may not be far from the truth. It becomes very apparent that the women's track and field program is entering a phase of tremendous change." Six American records were either broken or tied.

100-meter dash
1. Rosalyn Bryant, Mayor Daley Youth Foundation   11.6
2. Martha Watson, Lakewood International   11.6
3. Renaye Bowen, Lakewood International,   11.6
    and Rochelle Davis, Texas Woman's Univ.

200-meter dash
1. Debra Armstrong, Sports International   23.0
2. Rosalyn Bryant, Mayor Daley Youth Foundation   23.2
3. Pamela Jiles, New Orleans Superdames   23.5
4. Lorna Forde, Atoms Track Club   23.8

400-meter run
1. Debra Sapenter, Prairie View A&M   51.6 ties AR
2. Lorna Forde, Atoms Track Club   52.6
3. Robin Campbell, Sports International   52.7
4. Pat Helms, Padukies   53.3

800-meter run
1. Madeline Manning Jackson, Cleveland Track Club   2:00.5 AR
2. Kathy Weston, Will's Spikettes   2:02.9
3. Cheryl Toussaint, Atoms Track Club   2:03.1
4. Kathie Hall, Oak Park, Ill.   2:04.4

1500-meter run
1. Julie Brown, L.A. Track Club   4:13.5 MR
2. Jan Merrill, Age Group A.A.   4:14.4
3. Cindy Bremser, Wisconsin Track Club   4:25.0
4. Cyndy Poor, San Jose Cindergals   4:17.2

3000-meter run
1. Lynn Bjorklund, Duke City Dashers   9:10.6 AR
2. Cindy Bremser, Wisconsin Track Club   9:13.4
3. Peg Neppel, Iowa State Track Club   9:17.4
4. Julie Brown, L.A. Track Club   9:19.4

100-meter hurdles
1. Jane Frederick, L.A. Track Club   13.8
2. Deby LaPlante, unattached   13.9
3. Pat Donnelly, Lakewood International   14.2
4. Carol Thomson, Delaware Sports Club   14.3

400-meter hurdles
1. Debbie Esser, Nebraska Track Club   57.3 AR
2. Pat Collins El, Atoms Track Club   57.4
3. Mary Ayers, Prairie View   59.3
4. June Smith, Sports International   59.4

400-meter relay
1. Tennessee State   45.8
2. Sports International   45.8
3. Lakewood International   46.0
4. New Orleans Superdames

880-yard sprint medley relay
1. Sports International   1:40.0
2. New Orleans Superdames
3. Wilt's Wonder Women   1:43.3
4. Tennessee State   1:44.3

Mile relay
1. Atoms Track Club   3:37.9 MR
   (Nichols, Blaine, Forde, Toussaint)
2. New Orleans Superdames   3:42.5
3. Atoms Track Club, "B" team   3:45.0
4. Premier Track Club   3:45.4

Two-mile relay
1. Blue Ribbon Track Club   8:46.4 AR
   (Dianne Vetter, Stibbe, J. Vetter, Debbie Vetter)
2. Sports International   8:49.8
3. San Jose Cindergals   8:50.6
4. L.A. Track Club   8:53.2

1500-meter walk
1. Lisa Metheny, Rialto Road Runners   6:46.6 AR
2. Susan Brodock, Rialto Road Runners   6:58.1
3. Linda Brodock, Rialto Road Runners   7:03.4
4. Christine Sakelarios, Redwood City Flyers   7:26.0

High jump
1. Joni Huntley, Oregon Track Club   6'
2. Susan Hackett, New Orleans Superdames   5' 10"

3. Pam Spencer, Great Falls, Mont.   5' 9"
4. Jane Frederick, Los Angeles Track Club   5' 9"

Long jump
1. Martha Watson, Lakewood International   21' 3"
2. Kathy McMillan, Tennessee State   20' 6½"
3. Sherron Walker, Falcon Track Club   20' 5½"
4. Jodi Anderson, Premier Track Club   19' 11¾"

Shot put
1. Maren Seidler, Mayor Daley Youth Foundation   53' 2½"
2. Denise Wood, Haledon, N.J.   49' 1½"
3. Mary Jacobson, unattached   49' 1"
4. Emily Dole, Lakewood International   48' 11¾"

Javelin
1. Kathy Schmidt, L.A. Track Club   209' 7" AR
2. Sherry Calvert, Lakewood International   178' 10"
3. Karin Smith, L.A. Track Club   178' 2"
4. Lynn Cannon, Millbrae Lions   176' 4"

Discus
1. Jean Roberts, Delaware Sports Club   159' 9"
2. Jan Svendsen, Wilt's Wonder Women   155' 9"
3. Joan Pavelich, Wilt's Wonder Women   154' 11"
4. Linda Langford, Mayor Daley Youth Foundation   151' 6"

Team scores:
Los Angeles Track Club 55; Sports International and Lakewood International 47; Atoms Track Club 46; Mayor Daley Youth Foundation 32; New Orleans Superdames 28; Rialto Road Runners 24.

The junior championship competition was held in White Plains, New York, in conjunction with the senior meet. The junior women's meet replaced the girls' competition. Tennessee State won the championship title with just four girls competing.

100-meter dash
1. Brenda Morehead, Tennessee State   11.4 ties AJR
2. Chandra Cheeseborough, Tennessee State   11.5
3. Sandra Howard, Long Beach Comets   11.5
4. Evelyn Ashford, Will's Spikettes   11.7

200-meter dash
1. Brenda Morehead, Tennessee State   23.3 MR
2. Chandra Cheeseborough, Tennessee State   23.4
3. Bernadine Given, New Orleans Superdames   24.0
4. Isabel Hartford, New Orleans Superdames   24.2

400-meter run
1. Robin Campbell, Sports International   53.4
2. Pat Helms, Klub Keystone   54.2

3. Sharon Dabney, Clippers   54.9
4. Debbi Pastel, Sports International   55.3

800-meter run
1. Jan Merrill, Age Group A.A.   2:06.1 MR
2. Debbie Vetter, Blue Ribbon Track Club   2:06.9
3. Johanna Forman, Falmouth Track Club   2:07.7
4. Susan Vigil, Duke City Dashers   2:08.3

1500-meters
1. Doreen Ennis, Nutley Track Club   4:23.1
2. Hilary Noden, Shore A. C.   4:23.4
3. Margaret Groos, Nashville Whippets   4:24.8
4. Eryn Forbes, Portland Track Club   4:25.8

3000-meter run
1. Lynn Bjorklund, Duke City Dashers   9:29.4
2. Kathy Mills, Syracuse Chargers   9:48.6
3. Suzanne Keith, Rialto Road Runners   9:49.0
4. Doreen Ennis, Nutley Track Club   9:50.2

100-meter hurdles
1. Rhonda Brady, Mayor Hatcher Youth Foundation   13.8 AJR
2. Sonya Hardy, Boulder Track Club   13.9
3. Jeanine Shepherd, Gazelle Track Club   13.9
4. Deborah Jacobsen, Crescent City Track Club   14.3

400-meter hurdles
1. Tonetta Rumph, Atoms Track Club   59.8 MR and ties AJR
2. Debbie Vetter, Blue Ribbon Track Club   60.9
3. Sue White, Sports International   61.7
4. Patty Cape, Long Beach Comets   62.6

440-yard relay
1. Tennessee State   45.8 MR
2. Millbrae Lions Track Club   46.4
3. Mayor Daley Youth Foundation   46.7
4. Long Beach Comets   47.3

880-yard medley relay
1. Tennessee State   1:42.2 AJR
2. Sports International   1:43.1
3. Peoria Pacettes   1:46.9
4. Atoms Track Club, "A" team   1:47.1

One-mile relay
1. New Orleans Superdames   3:43.7 AJR
2. Atoms Track Club, "A" team   3:44.3
3. Police Athletic League, "A" team   3:45.0
4. Nebraska Track Club   3:45.3

Two-mile relay
1. Blue Ribbon Track Club   8:50.8
2. Sports International   9:01.4

3. San Jose Cindergals   9:02.2
4. Madison Badger Jettes   9:02.2

1500-meter walk
1. Susan Brodock, Rialto Road Runners   6:50.4
2. Lisa Metheny, Rialto Road Runners   7:03.9
3. Linda Brodock, Rialto Road Runners   7:16.5
4. Cynthia Johnson, Blue Angels   7:24.2

Long jump
1. Lorraine Ray, Community Youth Club   20' 1½"
2. Karen Elmore, Millbrae Lions   19' 5½"
3. Jodi Anderson, Premier Track Club   19' 4"
4. Sandra Howard, Long Beach Comets   18' 8"

High jump
1. Joni Huntley, Oregon Track Club   6' 2"
2. Paula Girvin, Sports International   6' 1"
3. Pam Spencer, Great Falls, Mont.   5' 9"
4. Susan Hackett, River Ridge, La.   5' 8"

Shot put
1. Ann Turbyne, Gilly's Gym   48' 1"
2. Emily Dole, Lakewood International   47' 5¾"
3. Marcia Mecklenburg, Gazelle Track Club   46' 2¼"
4. Kathy Devine, San Diego Lancerettes   46' 1½"

Javelin
1. Cathy Sulinski, Millbrae Lions   177' 3" MR
2. Nadine Bowers, San Jose Cindergals   163' 3"
3. Kelly Fuiks, Cactus Wrens   145' 2"
4. Lisa Kirk, Central Point, Oregon   156' 3"

Discus
1. Lorna Griffin, Kalispell, Mont.   153' 9"
2. Terry Sabol, L.A. Track Club   146' 6"
3. Mary Stevenson, Malin, Oregon   138' 6"
4. Jackie Gordon, Sports International   138' 3"

Team scores:
Tennessee State University 56; Sports International 52; Rialto Road Runners 30; Blue Ribbon Track Club and Millbrae Lions 26.

The Indoor Nationals

The indoor championship meet was held in Madison Square Garden, New York, on February 28. The highlights in the women's events were Rosalyn Bryant's 23.6 world indoor record in the 220-yard dash, Sue Brodock's American record in the mile walk, and Martha Watson's meet record in the long jump.

60-yard dash
1. Alice Annum, Sports International | 6.6
2. Angel Doyle, Ambler Olympic Club | 6.7
3. Martha Watson, Lakewood International | 6.8

220-yard dash
1. Rosalyn Bryant, Mayor Daley Youth Foundation | 23.6 WR
2. Rose Allwood, Sports International | 24.3
3. Theresa Montgomery, Baton Rouge Track Club | 24.5

440-yard dash
1. Robin Campbell, Sports International | 55.1
2. Rosemarie Giampalmo, Staten Island Jets | 55.5
3. Debra Sapenter, Prairie View | 55.7

880-yard run
1. Kathy Weston, Will's Spikettes | 2:07.6
2. Cheryl Toussaint, Atoms Track Club | 2:07.9
3. Wendy Knudson, Colorado State | 2:08.2

One-mile run
1. Francie Larrieu, Pacific Coast Club | 4:42.8
2. Julie Brown, UCLA | 4:43.8
3. Jan Merrill, Age Group A.A., Conn. | 4:49.4

Two-mile run
1. Brenda Webb, Kettering Striders | 10:22.0
2. Kate Keyes, UCLA | 10:31.2
3. Debbie Heald, La Mirada Meteors | 10:44.4

Hurdles
1. Modupe Oshikoya, Sports International | 7.6
2. Deby LaPlante, Inkster, Mich. | 7.7
3. Patty Van Wolvelaere, Wilt's Wonder Women | 7.7

One-mile walk
1. Susan Brodock, Rialto Road Runners | 7:22.5 AR
2. Linda Brodock, Rialto Road Runners | 7:25.7
3. Esther Marquez, Rialto Road Runners | 7:25.7

High jump
1. Joni Huntley, Oregon Track Club | 6'
2. Andrea Bruce, Prairie View A&M | 5' 10"
3. Susan Hackett, New Orleans Superdames | 5' 8"

Long jump
1. Martha Watson, Lakewood International | 21' 2" MR
2. Willye White, Chicago State | 19' 11½"
3. Sherron Walker, Falcon Track Club | 19' 6"

4-kilo shot put
1. Faina Melnik, USSR | 55' 7"
2. Maren Seidler, Mayor Daley Youth Foundation | 51' 3"
3. Denise Wood, Haledon, N.J. | 49' 4"

640-yard relay
1. Sports International ..... 1:10.4 ties MR
   (Annum, Allwood, Norman, Armstrong)
2. Atoms Track Club, "B" team 1:10.8
3. Atoms Track Club, "A" team 1:13.7

880-yard medley relay
1. Atoms Track Club ..... 1:43.2 MR
   (Toussaint, Collins El, Cordy, Forde)
2. Sports International 1:45.0
3. New Orleans Superdames 1:48.9

One-mile relay
1. Atoms Track Club, "A" team 3:51.2
   (McMillan, DeSandies, Evans, Nichols)
2. Atoms Track Club, "B" team 3:52.4
3. Sports International 3:55.2

Team scores:
Sports International 29; Atoms Track Club 25; Mayor Daley Youth Foundation 11; Rialto Road Runners 10.

The national women's pentathlon championships were held in Los Alamos, New Mexico, on June 20-21.

1. Jane Frederick, Los Angeles ..... 4676 AR
2. Diana Jones, Saskatoon, Canada 4442
3. Gail Fitzgerald, Atoms Track Club 4334

Junior Women

1. Nancy Kindig, Nebraska Track Club 3854
2. Cindy Mitchell, Cactus Wrens 3727
3. Patsy Walker, Thurston Striders 3698

The Pan American Games were held in Mexico City from October 12 to October 26. The trials were held at UCLA on August 30-31. The team was composed of the following members:

	Event	Place	Performance
Bowen, Renaye	100m	5	11.50
Bremser, Cindy	1500m	4	4:31.73
Calvert, Sherry	Javelin	1	179' 5½"*
Cannon, Lynn	Javelin	3	159' 7"
Cheeseborough, Chandra	200m	1	22.77
	400mr	1	42.90*
Collins, Dana	Pentathlon	6	
Dabney, Sharon	400m	5	52.68
	400mr	2	3:30.64
Donnelly, Pat	100mh	4	13.90
Fitzgerald, Gail	Pentathlon	2	4486

Hall, Kathie	800m	3	2:07.56
Helms, Pat	1600mr	2	3:30.64
Huntley, Joni	HJ	1	6' 2½"*
Jacobson, Mary	SP	6	49' 1"
Jiles, Pam	200m	2	22.81
	400mr	1	42.90*
	100m	1	11.38
La Plante, Deby	100mh	2	13.68
McMillan, Kathy	LJ	3	21' 3½"
Merrill, Jan	1500m	1	4:18.32*
Morehead, Brenda	400mr	1	42.90*
Sabol, Terry	Discus	8	143' 10¾"
Sapenter, Debra	400m	2	52.22
	1600mr	2	3:30.64
Seidler, Maren	SP	5	53' 7¾"
Spencer, Pam	HJ	6	5' 9¾"
Svendsen, Jan	Discus	5	160' 6¾"
Watson, Martha	LJ	2	21' 6¾"
	400mr	1	42.90*
Weston, Kathy	800m	1	2:04.93
	1600mr	2	3:30.64

* Pan American Games record

The indoor USA–USSR track meet was held in Richmond Coliseum, Richmond, Virginia, on March 3.

60-yard dash
1. Angel Doyle   6.6 ties MR
2. Martha Watson   6.7

440-yard dash
1. Robin Campbell   55.1
2. Debra Sapenter   55.6

880-yard run
1. Cheryl Toussaint   2:08.6
2. Kathy Weston   2:08.7

One-mile run
1. Francie Larrieu   4:28.5 WR
2. Julie Brown   4:38.8

Two-mile run
2. Kate Keyes   10:16.8
4. Brenda Webb   10:48.8

60-yard hurdles
1. Pat Van Wolvelaere   7.5
2. Deby LaPlante   7.5

High jump
1. Joni Huntley   6' 2½" WR
4. Susan Hackett   5' 6"

Long jump
1. Martha Watson   21' ½"
2. Willye White   20' ¾"

Shot put
2. Maren Seidler   52' 5½"
4. Denise Wood   47' 3½"

Triathlon
1. Jane Frederick   2902 MR
4. Gail Fitzgerald   2628

Medley relay
1. USA   3:25.3
    (Doyle, Bryant, Campbell, Weston)

USA 73-USSR 44

On May 16 the United States team left San Francisco airport bound for Hong Kong. The final destination was Canton, China. The team visited three cities in China: Canton, Shanghai, and Peking. This was the first United States track team allowed to enter Red China. Ed Temple served as coach, and the team members were selected based on their indoor national performances.

It poured on the first day of competition in Canton. Ten thousand people filled the stadium to capacity on both days of competition. Many others peered into the stadium from rooftops and apartment house balconies. The United States won 14 of the 15 events.

From there, the team went to Shanghai. There were 30,000 spectators for the meet, and it rained both days. Again, aside from the javelin and discus throws, the United States won all of the events.

International friendship was the theme of all three of the competitions, and no score was kept. The tour was a success.

The USA–USSR outdoor meet was held in Kiev, Soviet Union, on July 4-5. A team from Bulgaria competed in the women's events.

100-meter dash
3. Rosalyn Bryant   11.7
6. Pat Collins El   12.0

200 meters
3. Rosalyn Bryant   23.8
6. Debra Armstrong   DNC

400 meters
3. Robin Campbell   52.3
4. Debra Sapenter   52.4

800-meter run
1. Madeline Manning Jackson   2:00.3 AR
4. Kathy Weston   2:03.4

1500-meter run
5. Julie Brown   4:19.8
6. Jan Merrill   4:23.6

3000-meter run
3. Lynn Bjorklund   9:08.6 AR
6. Cindy Bremser   9:30.0

100-meter hurdles
4. Deby LaPlante   13.7
5. Pat Donnelly   14.0

400-meter relay
2. USA   44.2
    (Armstrong, Collins El, Bryant, Jiles)

1600-meter relay
2. USA   3:30.7
    (Campbell, Toussaint, Manning-Jackson, Sapenter)

High jump
1. Joni Huntley   6' ½" MR
4. Susan Hackett   5' 9"

Long jump
2. Sherron Walker   21' 3"
6. Kathy McMillan   19' 7"

Shot put
5. Denise Wood   45' 5¾"
6. Emily Dole   44' 8½"

Discus throw
5. Monette Driscoll   153' 10"
6. Jan Svendsen   149' 8"

Javelin throw
2. Kathy Schmidt   197' 10"
6. Sherry Calvert   164' 1"

USSR 96 — USA 49

The USA–USSR junior track and field competition was held at the University of Nebraska, Lincoln, Nebraska, on July 4-5.

100-meter dash
1. Brenda Morehead   11.4 MR
2. Chandra Cheeseborough   11.4

200-meter dash
1. Brenda Morehead   23.2 MR
2. Chandra Cheeseborough   23.4

400-meter dash
1. Pat Helms   53.1
2. Sharon Dabney   54.3

Denise Wood, USA team to China, USA–USSR indoor and outdoor meet, USA-Poland-Czech, USA–Germany–Pan Africa, and 1975 All-American, shot put. (Author's photo.)

800 meters
1. Susan Vigil   2:07.5
2. Johanna Forman   2:08.0

1500 meters
1. Hillary Noden   4:26.6
4. Doreen Ennis   4:41.1

100-meter hurdles
1. Sonya Hardy   14.0
2. Rhonda Brady   14.2

High jump
1. Paula Girvin   6' ties MR
3. Pam Spencer   5' 9"

Long jump
1. Jodi Anderson   19' 10½"
3. Karen Elmore   19' ¾"

Shot put
3. Marcia Mecklenburg   47' 5"
4. Ann Turbyne   46' 4"

Discus
3. Terry Sabol   154' 6"
4. Mary Ann Stevenson   139' 9"

Javelin
1. Cathy Sulinski   177' 1"
4. Nadine Bowers   159' 2"

440-yard relay
1. USA   44.8 MR
   (Cheeseborough, Morehead, Given, Ashford)

One-mile relay
1. USA   3:37.9 MR
   (Given, Pastel, Esser, Helms)

Pentathlon
1. Nancy Kindig   3,918
4. Cindy Mitchell   3,576

USA 88 — USSR 58

A USA-Poland-Czech meet was held in Prague, Czechoslovakia, on July 7-8.

---

100 meters
2. Rosalyn Bryant   11.5
5. Pat Collins El   11.9

200 meters
1. Pam Jiles   23.2
2. Rosalyn Bryant   23.5

400 meters
1. Debra Sapenter   52.0
2. Robin Campbell   52.5

800 meters
1. Madeline Manning Jackson 2:01.9
4. Kathy Weston   2:04.1

1500-meter run
2. Julie Brown   4:14.8
3. Jan Merrill   4:16.3

3000-meter run
1. Cindy Bremser   9:21.8
3. Lynn Bjorklund   9:25.0

100-meter hurdles
3. Deby LaPlante   13.8
5. Pat Donnelly   14.0

400-meter relay
2. USA   44.2
   (Bryant, Collins El, Campbell, Jiles)

1600-meter relay
1. USA   3:31.0
   (Campbell, Toussaint, Manning Jackson, Sapenter)

High jump
2. Joni Huntley   5' 11¼"
3. Susan Hackett   5' 10"

Long jump
1. Kathy McMillan   21' 7"
5. Sherron Walker   20' 7¾"

Shot put
5. Denise Wood   46' 5½"
6. Emily Dole   44' 11"

Discus throw
5. Monette Driscoll   155' 10"
6. Jan Svendsen   150' 11"

Javelin throw
1. Kathy Schmidt   207'
6. Sherry Calvert   172' 7"

USA 86 — Czechoslovakia 148
USA 189 — Poland 70

The USA–Germany–Pan Africa track meet was held at Duke University, Durham, North Carolina, on July 18-19.

100-meter dash
4. Rosalyn Bryant   11.60
6. Pat Collins El   11.82

200-meter dash
2. Pam Jiles   23.12
5. Rosalyn Bryant   23.69

400-meter dash
1. Debra Sapenter   52.06
4. Robin Campbell   53.19

800-meter run
1. Madeline Manning Jackson   2:01.60
4. Kathy Weston   2:03.70

1500-meter run
3. Jan Merrill   4:24.88

3000-meter run
2. Lynn Bjorklund   9:12.50
4. Cindy Bremser   9:17.87

100-meter hurdles
4. Deby LaPlante   13.64
5. Pat Donnelly   13.8

440-yard relay
2. USA   44.20 AR
    (Watson, Collins El, Bryant, Jiles)

Mile relay
2. USA   3:30.86 AR
    (Campbell, Toussaint, Jackson, Sapenter)

High jump
3. Joni Huntley   5' 10¾"
4. Susan Hackett   5' 8¾"

Long jump
1. Kathy McMillan   21'

Shot put
2. Emily Dole   47' 5"
3. Denise Wood   47' 2¼"

Discus throw
2. Monette Driscoll   150' 10"
3. Jan Svendsen   148' 3"

Javelin throw
1. Kathy Schmidt   199' 10"
3. Sherry Calvert   176' 8"

USA 99 — West Germany 131— Pan Africa 40

1975 All-Americans

100-yard dash
  Rosalyn Bryant
  Martha Watson
  Renaye Bowen
220-yard dash
  Debra Armstrong
  Rosalyn Bryant
  Pam Jiles
440-yard dash
  Debra Sapenter
  Robin Campbell
  Sharon Dabney
880-yard run
  Madeline Manning Jackson
  Kathy Weston
  Cheryl Toussaint
One-mile run
  Julie Brown
  Janice Merrill
  Cindy Bremser
  Francie Larrieu
Two-mile run
  Lynn Bjorklund

  Cindy Bremser
  Peg Neppel
100-meter hurdles
  Deby LaPlante
  Jane Frederick
  Pat Donnelly
400-meter hurdles
  Debbie Esser
  Pat Collins El
  Mary Ayers
One-mile walk
  Lisa Metheny
  Susan Brodock
  Linda Brodock
10,000-meter run
  Carol Cook
  Julie Brown
  Peg Neppel
Long jump
  Martha Watson
  Kathy McMillan
  Sherron Walker

High jump
  Joni Huntley
  Susan Hackett
  Pam Spencer
Shot put
  Maren Seidler
  Denise Wood
  Mary Jacobson
Discus
  Jan Svendsen
  Monette Driscoll
  Linda Langford
Javelin
  Kathy Schmidt
  Sherry Calvert
  Karin Smith
Pentathlon
  Jane Frederick
  Gail Fitzgerald
  Dana Collins
Marathon
  Jackie Hansen
  Kim Merritt
  Miki Gorman
5-K race walk
  Sue Brodock
  Lisa Metheny
  Esther Marquez
10-K race walk
  Sue Brodock

  Chris Sakelarios
  Sandy Brisco
440-yard relay
  Tennessee State
  Lakewood International
  New Orleans Superdames
880-yard medley relay
  New Orleans Superdames
  Wilt's Wonder Women
  Tennessee State University
One-mile relay
  New Orleans Superdames
  Atoms Track Club
  Premier Track Club
  Falmouth Track Club
Two-mile relay
  Blue Ribbon Track Club
  Sports International
  San Jose Cindergals
Cross country
  Lynn Bjorklund
  Doris Brown
  Julie Brown
  Sue Kinsey
  Eryn Forbes
  Cindy Bremser
  Debbie Quatier
  Judy Graham
  Peg Neppel
  Cheryl Bridges

Three women were inducted into the National Track and Field Hall of Fame: Alice Coachman Davis, Helen Stephens, and Stella Walsh.

Joni Huntley, with a high jump of 6' 2½", won the fourth women's "Athlete of the Meet" award for the best performance in the *Times*/GTE Indoor Games in California.

The Colgate Women's Games were founded by Colgate-Palmolive Company this year. Five thousand young women from the New York metropolitan area participated. Fred Thompson, founder of the Atoms Track Club, was the meet director. Anyone over the age of six could compete. The preliminaries were held at the 168th Street Armory in Manhattan, and Madison Square Garden was the site of the finals. Colgate-Palmolive established an awards format of educational grants-in-aid to top finishers.

Conrad A. Ford, longtime coach of the New York Police Athletic League, was awarded the Joseph Robichaux Award. Madeline Manning Jackson was awarded the Mobil Cup, and Joni Huntley was named the North American Athlete of the Year.

New York State conducted the first New York State outdoor track and field championships for girls at West Point, New York.

Julie Brown won the world cross country championship in Rabat, Morocco.

Martha Watson

Martha was born on August 19, 1946, in Long Beach, California. Her distinguished career started while she was in school and led her to become a four-time Olympian—1964, 1968, 1972, and 1976. She was a member of the 1967 and 1975 Pan American teams, winning a silver medal in the long jump and a gold medal as a member of the 400-meter relay in 1975. Internationally, she competed on the United States team in the following competitions:

1964–1974	USA vs. USSR
1964–1970	USA vs. British Commonwealth
1970	USA vs. Romania
1969–1977	USA vs. West Germany
1970–1977	USA vs. Italy
1975	USA vs. Peoples Republic of China
1978	Sports Festival

Among Martha's many notable honors for her outstanding career in women's track and field were being enshrined in the National Track and Field Hall of Fame, being nominated for the Sullivan Award, and being named the *Los Angeles Times* Woman of the Year in 1975.

Since retiring from competition in 1980, Martha has managed six United States women's teams; her seventh assignment is to be the head manager for the 1996 Olympic team.

Dave Rodda

In a conversation in December 1992 Dave remarked:

> I started coaching women's track and field, ironically, in my profession. I'm currently the Director of Recreation and Community Services in the City of Lakeland a community of about seventy-five thousand residents in the Southeast corner of Los Angeles County. Back in nineteen sixty-three, I realized there was an inequity in recreational track and field for girls, both in the number of meets and events in which they could compete. In our area all that was available was a Jaycee meet and the only events for girls were the standing long jump and fifty-yard dash, while the guys had a full menu of events. The inequity was brought to the attention of my superiors and I proposed to put on a meet at a local park.

Understanding that most of the running events would be on a grass straight-away and the long jump would be in the play area and I would have to find pits for the high jump, I still felt the need was there. My proposal was not received enthusiastically, but they did allow me to proceed with the full knowledge I would fail. To make a long story short, three hundred girls showed up on a Saturday and from that time on the City of Lakewood was at the forefront of recreation track and field.

From this competition four young ladies in the ten-eleven years age group really stood out and their parents indicated interest in pursuing track and field further. This was the beginning of my coaching career. In nineteen sixty-three and sixty-four we organized the Lakewood Recreation Track Club. The official uniform was bare feet, white blouses with a large red "L" my wife cut out and cut off jeans. In my zeal to find competition someone told me about an organization called the AAU. I found out there was a meet at our local university and we went. I had no idea what AAU meant and upon arrival a very officious official greeted me with, "Do you have AAU cards" and asked, "How could I bring these cute little tow headed girls to compete against the teams the likes of the L.A. Mercurettes, Compton Track Club, Long Beach Comets and Pasadena Track Club?" As a caveat he stated this was a district meet, which in essence meant the local championships. I indicated to this very large person, that although bare footed these young ladies were pretty good. We proceeded to buy the AAU cards and entered the ten-eleven year old division. Well, we won the team title and all four girls set a number of district records. I was now hooked!

The following year I connected with the Long Beach Comets and Ron Allice. This lasted for a year then I organized the Lakewood Spartans and the club dominated age group track and field in the late sixties. As the seventies rolled around I began to get older athletes and the club started to compete in the national junior and senior championships. In nineteen seventy-two the club consolidated with L.A. Naturite for funding purposes, this lasted a year and in nineteen seventy-three I formed Club International and began working with Martha Watson, who became an athlete I coached, and also one of my best friends. Martha's competitive career began in Long Beach, then she went to Tennessee State and then came back to Long Beach in nineteen seventy-one. By the time she returned Martha was a two time Olympian. Since the long jump was my specialty the connection worked well and Martha's jumping and sprinting moved to a higher level and she dominated the jumps in the USA from nineteen seventy-three until nineteen seventy-six. At one time she held the world record for the sixty meter dash.

Nineteen seventy-two was my introduction to the international arena. Three of my athletes, Kim Attlesey and Sandi Goldsberry, along with Martha, made the Olympic team. In nineteen seventy-three I received my initial international assignment as an assistant coach with the first USA junior team to tour Europe. This team was made up of a number of young women, who went on to achieve great things on the national and international scene in track and field over the next ten years. Some of the athletes from this junior team moved to the Long Beach area and worked with me through nineteen eighty-four. A few come quickly to mind — Joni Huntley in the high jump, Karin Smith the four time Olympian in the javelin and Mitzi McMillan who won the national pentathlon title in nineteen seventy-four.

After the nineteen seventy-three assignment, I served on the staffs of the nineteen seventy-five Pan American Team and the nineteen seventy-seven World Cup Team. In the seventies, the nineteen seventy-six Olympic trials, in my opinion, was the most significant meet and competition for my athletes and women's track and field in general. This was the first combined men's and women's national level meet in Eugene, Oregon before sixteen thousand enthusiastic fans daily who appreciated the accomplishments of the women athletes as much as the men. Women's track and field had arrived in the United States. I took seven athletes to Eugene and five made the team. I also lost about ten pounds, lost hair and started turning grey in the process.

I was on the Olympic staff in nineteen eighty. My last assignments were the nineteen eighty-one Junior Pan American Team, the nineteen eighty-five USA vs West Germany Dual meet, the nineteen eighty-eight Olympics, the nineteen ninety-one world championships and the nineteen ninety-five Pan American team.

Chapter 59

1976: The Montreal Olympic Year

The following women athletes represented the United States in the 1976 Olympic Games in Montreal, Canada, from July 17 through August 1:

	Olympic Event	Olympic Place	Olympic Performance
Armstrong-Edwards, Debra	200m	DNQ	23.16
	400mr	7	43.35
Ashford, Evelyn	100m	5	11.24
	400mr	7	43.35
Brady, Rhonda	100mh	DNQ	13.84
Bryant, Rosalyn	400m	5	50.65
	1600mr	2	3:22.81
Calvert, Sherry	Javelin	15	168' 7"
Cheeseborough, Chandra	100m	6	11.31
	200m	DNQ	23.20
	400mr	7	43.35
Donnelly, Patrice	100mh	DNQ	13.71
Fitzgerald, Gail	Pentathlon	13	4263
Frederick, Jane	Pentathlon	7	4566
Gainer, Arthurene	Reserve		
Girven, Paula	HJ	18	6' ½"
Huntley, Joni	HJ	5	6' 2¼"
Ingram, Sheila	400m	6	50.90
	1600mr	2	3:22.81
Jackson, Madeline Manning	800m	DNQ	2:07.25
Jiles, Pamela	400mr	2	3:22.81
King, Marilyn	Pentathlon	17	4165
Knudson, Wendy Koenig	800m	DNQ	2:02.31
LaPlante, Debra	100mh	DNQ	13.36
Larrieu-Smith, Francie	1500m	DNQ	4:09.07
McMillan, Kathy	LJ	2	21' 10¼"
Merrill, Janice	1500m	8	4:08.54
Morehead, Brenda	100m	DNQ	11.38
	200m	Scratch	

Poor, Cyndy	1500m	DNQ	4:08.89
Sapenter, Debra	400m	8	51.66
	1600mr	2	3:22.81
Schmidt, Kathy	Javelin	3	209' 10"
Seidler, Maren	SP	12	51' 2¼"
Smith, Karin	Javelin	8	188' 8"
Spencer, Pamela	HJ	24	5' 7"
Walker, Sherron	LJ	14	20' 4½"
Watson, Martha	LJ	25	19' 5½"
	400mr	7	43.35
Weston, Kathy	800m	DNQ	2:03.31
Winbigler-Anderson, Lynne	Discus	14	158' 2"
Sandor "Alex" Ferenczy	Coach		
Dr. Harmon Brown	Assistant coach		
Jack Griffin	Assistant coach		
Brooks Johnson	Assistant coach		
Dr. Evie Dennis	Manager		

The United States women won three medals, which barely improved upon their performances in Munich, where the women's team won one silver and two bronze medals. In Montreal they won two silvers and one bronze. The 1600-meter relay team composed of Debra Sapenter, Sheila Ingram, Pam Jiles, and Rosalyn Bryant repeated the silver medal finish of Munich. Kathy McMillan jumped to a second place finish in the long jump, and Kathy Schmidt repeated her bronze medal throw of four years earlier in the javelin.

The Olympic Results

100 meters. Evelyn Ashford placed fifth in 11.31, and seventeen-year-old Chandra Cheeseborough was sixth in 11.24. Brenda Morehead suffered a muscle pull in the heats while running an 11.30. With a heavily taped thigh, she ran 11.38 in the semifinals but finished sixth.

200 meters. Debra Armstrong and Chandra Cheeseborough each finished sixth in their semifinal races. Debra ran a 23.16 and Chandra 23.20. Brenda scratched from the event.

400 meters. Rosalyn Bryant finished fifth in the final in 50.65. Sheila Ingram was sixth in 50.90, and Debra Sapenter placed eighth in 51.66.

800 meters. No American reached the final in this event. Wendy Koenig Knudson ran 1:59.91 in the first round. She then ran 2:02.31 in the semifinal round, but it was only good for seventh place. Three-time Olympian and 1968 gold medalist Madeline Manning Jackson ran 2:00.62 in the first round but in the semifinal round finished eighth in 2:07.25. Kathy Weston, just eighteen years old, was fifth in her heat in 2:03.31.

1500 meters. Jan Merrill was eighth in the finals. Her time was 4:08.54. In the semifinals she set an American record of 4:02.61. Both Francie Larrieu-Smith and Cyndy Poor were sixth in their heats. Francie ran 4:07.21 and Cyndy 4:08.89.

100-meter hurdles. None of the American women made the finals. Deby LaPlante ran 13.36, which placed her sixth in her semifinal. Pat Donnelly and Rhonda Brady were both sixth in their heats. Pat ran 13.71 and Rhonda 13.84.

400-meter relay. Martha Watson, Evelyn Ashford, Debra Armstrong, and Chandra Cheeseborough made up the relay team that finished seventh in 43.35.

1600-meter relay. Debra Sapenter, Sheila Ingram, Pam Jiles, and Rosalyn Bryant composed this relay team. Their time of 3:22.81 easily captured the silver medal.

High jump. Nineteen-year-old Joni Huntley cleared 6' 2¼" for fifth place. Paula Girvin, eighteen, cleared 6' ½" and finished 18th. Pam Spencer, also eighteen, did not qualify for the finals with her jump of 5' 7".

Long jump. Eighteen-year-old Kathy McMillan was the lone silver medal winner for the United States. Her leap of 21' 10¼" was 2" short of first place. Sherron Walker jumped 20' 4½" and Martha Watson 19' 5½". Both failed to qualify for the finals.

"Miss McMillan, who was jumping 17 feet in ninth grade, set an American record of 22' 3" last month," reported the *New York Times* on July 24. "She was almost not an Olympic finalist. She needed 20' 8" in the morning qualifying round and managed only 20' 6". But because just four jumpers met the qualifying standard, the next eight were added to get a 12 woman field. She was one of the eight."

Shot put. Maren Seidler was the only U.S. entrant in this event. She placed 12th with a toss of 51' 2¼".

Discus throw. Lynne Winbigler did not qualify for the finals. Her best throw was 158' 2½".

Javelin throw. With her last throw of the competition, Kathy Schmidt again captured the bronze medal. She hurled the javelin 209' 10". Karin Smith, with a throw of 188' 8", did not qualify for the final round.

Pentathlon. The same three athletes that were in Munich in 1972 were in Montreal. Jane Frederick placed seventh, with 4,566 points. Gail Fitzgerald was 13th with 4,263 points, and Marilyn King was 17th with 4,165 points.

The Olympic Trials

The combined Olympic trials, staged for the first time in conjunction with the men, were held in Eugene, Oregon, from June 19 to June 27.

Long jump	
1. Kathy McMillan, Tennessee State	22' 3" w
2. Sherron Walker, Falcon Track Club	21' 8¼" w
3. Martha Watson, Lakewood International	21' 6"

Kathy Weston, 1976 Olympian, 800 meters. (Author's photo.)

Javelin throw
1. Kate Schmidt, L.A. Track Club   213' 5"
2. Sherry Calvert, Lakewood International   191' 7"
3. Karin Smith, UCLA   187' 9"

100-meter dash
1. Brenda Morehead, Tennessee State   11.08
2. Chandra Cheeseborough, Tennessee State   11.13
3. Evelyn Ashford, U.C.L.A.   11.22
4. Pam Jiles, New Orleans Superdames   11.31
5. Rosalyn Bryant, L.A. Mercurettes   11.47

800-meter run
1. Madeline Manning Jackson, Cleveland Track Club   1:59.81 AR
2. Cyndy Poor, San Jose Cindergals   2:00.55
3. Kathy Weston, Will's Spikettes   2:00.73

Pentathlon
1. Jane Frederick, L.A. Track Club   4,622
2. Gail Fitzgerald, Atoms Track Club   4,417
3. Marilyn King, Millbrae Lions   4,374

High jump
1. Paula Girvin, unattached, Virginia   6' 1¾"
2. Joni Huntley, Oregon Track Club   6' ½"
3. Pam Spencer, Falcon Track Club   5' 11¼"

200-meter dash
1. Brenda Morehead, Tennessee State   22.49 w
2. Chandra Cheeseborough, Tennessee State   22.64
3. Debra Armstrong, Grambling   22.74

400-meter dash
1. Sheila Ingram, Pioneer A.C.   52.69
2. Debra Sapenter, Prairie View A&M   52.73
3. Rosalyn Bryant, L.A. Mercurettes   52.76

Discus throw
1. Lynne Winbigler, Oregon Track Club   166' 2"
2. Jan Svendsen, San Jose Stars   164' 11"
3. Monette Driscoll, L.A. Naturite Track Club   160' 6"

100-meter hurdles
1. Rhonda Brady, Mayor Hatcher Youth Foundation   13.25 w
2. Deby LaPlante, unattached, Michigan   13.27
3. Pat Donnelly, Lakewood International   13.36

Shot put
1. Maren Seidler, Mayor Daley Youth Foundation   53' 3¾"
2. Kathy Devine, Emporia State University   50' 11¾"
3. Mary Jacobson, unattached   48' 3¼"

1500-meter run
1. Cyndy Poor, San Jose Cindergals   4:07.32 AR
2. Jan Merrill, Age Group A.A.   4:07.35
3. Francie Larrieu, Pacific Coast Club   4:08.08

Thirty athletes assembled on July 6 to attend the Olympic training camp at Plattsburg, New York.

The National Championships

The national championships were held at UCLA's Drake Stadium in Westwood, California, on June 10-12. This was the first combined men's and women's national championship meet.

100-meter dash
1. Chandra Cheeseborough, Tennessee State   11.34
2. Rosalyn Bryant, L.A. Mercurettes   11.43
3. Renaye Bowen, Lakewood International   11.49

200-meter dash
1. Brenda Morehead, Tennessee State   22.94 ties MR
2. Debbie Armstrong, Florida Track Club   23.19
3. Rosalyn Bryant, L.A. Mercurettes   23.40

400-meter dash
1. Lorna Forde, Atoms Track Club   52.30

2. Sheila Ingram, Pioneer A.C.   52.52
3. Shirley Williams, Prairie View A&M   52.53

800-meter run
1. Madeline Manning Jackson, Cleveland Track Club   2:01.00
2. Kathy Weston, Will's Spikettes   2:03.52
3. Jan Merrill, Age Group A.A.   2:03.85

1500-meter run
1. Francie Larrieu, Pacific Coast Club   4:09.93 MR
2. Cindy Bremser, Wisconsin Track Club   4:10.8
3. Julie Brown, L.A. Track Club   4:14.14

3000-meter run
1. Jan Merrill, Age Group A.A.   8:57.17
2. Teri Anderson, Athletes in Action   9:19.55
3. Peg Neppel, Iowa State   9:22.65

100-meter hurdles
1. Jane Frederick, L.A. Track Club   13.29
2. Deby LaPlante, Inkster, Mich.   13.32
3. Sonya Hardy, Boulder Cinderbelles   13.50

400-meter hurdles
1. Arthurine Gainer, Prairie View A&M   57.24 AR
2. Debbie Esser, Iowa State   57.56
3. Mary Ayers, Prairie View A&M   58.53

5000-meter walk
1. Susan Brodock, Rialto Road Runners   25:28.68
2. Laura Tucholski, Ohio Track Club   25:55.4
3. Susan Liers, Island Track Club   26:29.8

High jump
1. Joni Huntley, Oregon Track Club   6' 2" MR
2. Pam Spencer, Falcon Track Club   6' ½"
3. Ann Gilliland, Albuquerque, N.M.   5' 9"

Long jump
1. Kathy McMillan, Raeford, N.C.   22' 3" AR
2. Sherron Walker, Falcon Track Club   21' 4¼"
3. Martha Watson, Lakewood International   20' 11¾"

Shot put
1. Maren Seidler, Mayor Daley Youth Foundation   54' 4" MR
2. Kathy Devine, Emporia State University   51' 4¾"
3. Marcia Mecklenburg, Falcon Track Club   50' 3"

Discus throw
1. Lynne Winbigler, Oregon Track Club   174' 1"
2. Jan Svendsen, San Jose Stars   169' 10"
3. Linda Langford, Millbrae Lions   166' 9"

Javelin throw
1. Kathy Schmidt, L.A. Track Club   218' 3" AR

2. Karin Smith, Lakewood International	203' 10"
3. Sherry Calvert, Lakewood International	190' 5"

440-yard relay
1. Tennessee State	44.97 MR
2. Prairie View A&M	45.34
3. Texas Southern University	45.54

880-yard medley relay
1. L.A. Mercurettes	1:38.69
2. Tennessee State	1:41.62
3. Klub Keystone	1:42.83

One-mile relay
1. Prairie View A&M	3:33.85 MR
2. Atoms Track Club	3:35.72
3. N.Y. Police Athletic League	3:44.96

Two-mile relay
1. L.A. Track Club, "A" team	8:34.44 AR
2. Falcon Track Club	8:36.83
3. Blue Ribbon Track Club	8:40.33

Team champion — Los Angeles Track Club
Redbook Award — Kathy Schmidt

The Indoor Nationals

The national indoor championship meet was held in Madison Square Garden, New York City, on February 27. Nineteen-year-old Jan Merrill set two meet records in the mile and two mile runs with only thirty minutes rest in between. Her two-mile time made history. It was the first time that an American woman had gone below ten minutes in that event.

60-yard dash
1. Lisa Hopkins, Chicago Mercurettes	6.7
2. Alice Annum, D.C. Striders	6.8
3. Veronica Harris, Chicago Zephyrs	6.8

60-yard hurdles
1. Deby LaPlante, Belleville, Mich.	7.7
2. Carol Thomson, Delaware State College	7.8
3. Rhonda Brady, Mayor Hatcher Youth Foundation	7.9

220-yard dash
1. Pamela Jiles, New Orleans Superdames	24.0
2. Rosalyn Bryant, L.A. Mercurettes	24.0
3. Linda Cordy, Atoms Track Club	24.2
(Bryant set an AR record of 23.5 in semi)	

440-yard run
1. Lorna Forde, Atoms Track Club	54.6

2. Sharon Dabney, Clippers Track Club   54.7
3. Yolanda Rich, L.A. Mercurettes   55.2

880-yard run
1. Johanna Forman, Falmouth Track Club   2:07.9
2. Kathy Weston, Will's Spikettes   2:08.7
3. Wendy Knudson, Colorado State Univ.   2:08.8

One-mile run
1. Janice Merrill, Age Group A.A.   4:38.5 MR
2. Julie Brown, L.A. Track Club   4:38.5
3. Abby Hoffman, Canada   4:43.7

Two-mile run
1. Janice Merrill, Age Group A.A.   9:59.6 MR
2. Katy Schilly, Syracuse Chargers   10:19.4
3. Doreen Ennis, Nutley Track Club   10:23.0

One-mile race walk
1. Susan Brodock, Rialto Road Runners   7:12.7 MR
2. Laura Tucholski, Ohio Track Club   7:39.6
3. Cindy Johnson, Blue Angels   7:46.1

High jump
1. Julie White, Canada   6' 1" MR
2. Pam Spencer, Seattle Pacific College   6'
3. Joni Huntley, Oregon Track Club   6'

Long jump
1. Martha Watson, Lakewood International   20' 9½"
2. Cathy Newman, Collins, La.   19' 2¼"
3. Lorraine Ray, Community Youth Club   19' 1"

4-kilo shot put
1. Ann Turbyne, Gilly's Gym   51' 5¼"
2. Kathy Devine, Emporia State University   49' 10¼"
3. Denise Wood, Haledon, N.J.   49' 4¼"

640-yard relay
1. Atoms Track Club, "A" team   1:09.7 AR
   (McMillan, Collins El, Cordy, Brown)
2. New Orleans Superdames   1:11.8
3. Cavalette Track Club   1:14.5

880-yard medley relay
1. Atoms Track Club, "A" team   1:46.2
   (Toussaint, Collins El, Cordy, Forde)
2. Jackson State   1:48.2
3. Klub Keystone   1:52.8

One-mile relay
1. Atoms Track Club, "A" team   3:50.6
   (Blaine, Toussaint, Jones, McMillan)
2. Klub Keystone   3:51.0
3. Falmouth Track Club   3:52.0

Team scores:
Atoms Track Club 23; Age Group A.A. 10; New Orleans Superdames 8; Falmouth Track Club 7.

Outstanding performer:
Redbook Trophy — Janice Merrill

The national indoor pentathlon championship meet was held in Pocatello, Idaho, on February 14. Jane Frederick won the competition with a score of 4,400, Marilyn King placed second with 4,296, and Dana Collins was third with 4,117.

The national senior and junior outdoor pentathlon championships were held at Santa Barbara, California, on May 28-29. Jane Frederick placed first with a score of 4,677, which was a new American record, Marilyn King was second with 4,233, and Gail Fitzgerald was third with 4,193.

Kerry Zwart of the Los Angeles Track Club won the junior title with a score of 3,871, Nancy Kindig of the Nebraska Track Club was second with 3,845, and Terry Seippel of the Kettering Striders was third with 3,838.

The USA-USSR indoor dual meet was held in Leningrad on March 6.

60-meter dash	
3. Veronica Harris	7.45
4. Lisa Hopkins	7.46
400-meter run	
1. Sharon Dabney	54.75
4. Yolanda Rich	55.72
600-meter run	
1. Wendy Knudson	1:29.50
4. Johanna Forman	1:37.23
800-meter run	
2. Kathy Weston	2:10.2
3. Johanna Forman	2:11.3
1500-meter run	
1. Jan Merrill	4:16.0
3. Kate Keyes	4:24.0
3000-meter run	
2. Jan Merrill	9:14.0
4. Katy Schilly	9:44.0
60-meter hurdles	
3. Carol Thomson	8.59
4. Rhonda Brady	8.61
2000-meter relay	
1. USA	
(Jiles, Armstrong, Knudson, Weston)	4:53.8
High jump	
2. Paula Girvin	5' 10¼"
3. Pamela Spencer	5' 10¼"

Long jump
3. Cathy Newman   19'
4. Lorraine Ray   18' 9½"

Shot put
3. Ann Turbyne   50' 4¾"
4. Denise Wood   47' 8"

Triathlon
3. Judy Fontaine   2,177
4. Lori West   2,119

The USA–USSR outdoor meet was held at College Park, Maryland, on August 6-7.

100 meters
3. Martha Watson   11.75
4. Linda Cordy   11.95

200 meters
3. Debra Sapenter   23.6
4. Linda Cordy   24.8

400 meters
3. Sheila Ingram   52.14
4. Sharon Dabney   52.88

800 meters
3. Madeline Jackson   1:57.9
4. Kathy Weston   2:04.3

1500 meters
3. Francie Larrieu Lutz   4:06.20
4. Cyndy Poor   4:06.83

3000 meters
3. Francie Larrieu Lutz   8:54.95
4. Teri Anderson   9:33.20

100-meter hurdles
3. Deby LaPlante   13.58
4. Carol Thomson   14.40

400-meter relay
2. USA   44.56
      (Watson, Sapenter, Cordy, Ingram)

High jump
3. Joni Huntley   6'
4. Paula Girvin   6'

Long jump
2. Kathy McMillan   21' ¾"
3. Sherron Walker   20' 1¼"

Shot put
3. Maren Seidler   51' 4¼"
4. Kathy Devine   48' ¾"

Discus throw
3. Jan Svendsen   159' 4"
4. Lynne Winbigler   151' 4"

Javelin throw
3. Sherry Calvert   190' 11"
4. Karin Smith   187' 4"

USA 42 — USSR 104

The national junior meet was held at Drake Stadium, UCLA, Westwood, California, on June 14-15.

100-meter dash
1. Kathy Crawford, Central Jersey Track Club   11.61
2. Evelyn Ashford, UCLA   11.67
3. Pam Waters, Premier Track Club   11.84

200-meter dash
1. Stephanie Brown, Metroplex Striders   24.13
2. Gwen Smith, Texas Southern University   24.35
3. Freida Cobbs, Berkeley East Bay Track Club   24.38

400-meter dash
1. Sharon Dabney, Clippers Track Club   53.04
   (new meet record by Dabney in heat — 53.01)
2. Robin Campbell, Florida Track Club   53.93
3. Chris Mullen, Falmouth Track Club   54.18

800-meter run
1. Lynn Hollins, unattached   2:07.1
2. Susan Vigil, New Mexico Int. Track Club   2:07.1
3. Karel Jones, Atoms Track Club   2:08.0

1500-meter run
1. Debbie Quatier, Falcon Track Club   4:22.5 MR
2. Joan Benoit, Liberty A.C.   4:26.3
3. Julie Shea, Junior Striders   4:26.5

3000-meter run
1. Aileen O'Connor, Washington, D.C.,
   Catholic Youth Organization   9:34.0
2. Karen Cramond, New Mexico Int. Track Club   9:39.8
3. Joan Benoit, Liberty A.C.   9:44.8

100-meter hurdles
1. Rhonda Brady, Mayor Hatcher Youth Foundation   13.53 MR
2. Sonya Hardy, Boulder Cinderbelles   13.54
3. Karen Wechsler, Indy Chevettes   13.76

400-meter hurdles
1. Debbie Esser, Iowa State — 58.34 MR
2. Teresa Wierson, Portland Track Club — 59.27
3. Stephanie Vega, Atoms Track Club — 60.63

3000-meter race walk
1. Lisa Metheny, Rialto Road Runners — 14:50.2 MR (new event)
2. Tracy Trisco, Blue Angels Track Club — 15:30.7
3. Becky Villavazo, Rialto Road Runners — 15:49.33

440-yard relay
1. Indy Chevettes — 46.74
2. Metroplex Striders — 46.77
3. Klub Keystone — 46.89

880-yard medley relay
1. Klub Keystone, "A" team — 1:43.46
2. Klub Keystone, "B" team — 1:43.91
3. Motor City Track Club — 1:44.45

One-mile relay
1. Atoms Track Club — 3:41.9 MR
2. Klub Keystone — 3:42.2
3. N.Y. Police Athletic League — 3:44.3

Two-mile relay
1. L.A. Track Club — 8:51.6
2. Berkeley Track Club — 8:59.8
3. Metroplex Striders — 9:00.0

High jump
1. Ann Gilliland, unattached, New Mexico — 5' 10"
2. Kari Grosswiller, Salem Track Club — 5' 10"
3. Denise Cornell, Salinas Valley Track Club — 5' 8½"

Long jump
1. Jodi Anderson, unattached, Los Angeles — 19' 9½"
2. Karen Elmore, Millbrae Lions Track Club — 19' 6¾"
3. Lisa Kinimaka, San Jose Cindergals — 19' 5¾"

Shot put
1. Kathy Devine, Emporia State University — 50' 7" MR
2. Marcia Mecklenburg, Falcon Track Club — 49' 2"
3. Emily Dole, Lakewood International — 47' 2½"

Discus throw
1. Debbie Stephens, Kettering Striders — 142' 11"
2. Mary Ann Stevenson, Oregon Track Club — 142' 10"
3. Gina Piatt, West Penn Track Club — 141' 4"

Javelin throw
1. Cathy Sulinski, Millbrae Lions — 163' 5"
2. Marilyn White, Valley of the Sun Track Club — 154' 2"
3. Keri Camarigg, Shore A.C. — 149' 4"

Team scores:
Klub Keystone 32; Metroplex Striders 28; Atoms Track Club 25; Millbrae Lions Track Club 22; Falcon Track Club 20; Los Angeles Track Club 20.

The USA–USSR junior team competition was held in Tallin, Estonia (USSR), on July 2-3.

100-meter dash
1. Kathy Crawford   11.5
4. Elaine Parker   11.8

200-meter dash
3. Freida Cobbs   23.9
4. Gwen Smith   24.1

400-meter dash
2. Kim Thomas   54.5
3. Chris Mullen   55.1

800-meter run
2. Lynn Hollins   2:08.5
3. Karel Jones   2:09.4

1500-meter run
3. Margaret Groos   4:25.2
4. Julie Shea   4:28.4

100-meter hurdles
3. Lori Dinello   13.9
4. Karen Wechsler   14.0

400-meter relay
1. USA   45.4
   (Crawford, Smith, Cobbs, Loud)

1600-meter relay
1. USA   3:39.4
   (Jones, Mullen, Golden, Thomas)

High jump
2. Ann Gilliland   5' 9"
4. Denise Cornell   5' 3"

Long jump
3. Karen Elmore   19' 5½"
4. Lisa Kinimaka   19' 1½"

Shot put
3. Deanna Patrick   41' 10¾"
4. Kerry Zwart   41' 2"

Discus
3. Mary Ann Stevenson   115' 5"
4. Gina Piatt   114' 9"

Javelin
3. Keri Camarigg	141' 3"
4. Jacque Nelson	136' 6½"

Pentathlon
3. Nancy Kindig	3,928
4. Kerry Zwart	3,791

USA 54 — USSR 90

The team then competed in Leudenscheid, West Germany, on July 7-8.

A national postal one-hour run was held through July 30. The winner was Mary Shea, Raleigh Junior Striders. She ran 10 miles, 121 yards within the hour.

A national 10-K championship was held in San Francisco on September 12. The winner was Cyndy Poor, San Jose Cindergals, with a time of 34:32.4. Second place was captured by Judy Graham, unattached, San Jose, California, with a time of 34:57.

The national marathon championship was held on October 16 in Crowley, Louisiana. Dorothy Doolittle of the Austin Runner's Club placed first in 2:55.38. Second and third places respectively were Sue Ellen Trapp of Ft. Myers YMCA in 3:10.32 and Peggy Kokevnot in 3:25.46.

The Mason-Dixon Games held in Louisville, Kentucky, produced an indoor world record in the women's pole vault. Susie Brutscher won the event with a vault of 7'.

The 8th annual U.S. Olympic Invitational meet was held on February 20. Matteline Render won the 50-yard dash in 6.3, Debra Armstrong was first in the 400 meters in 55.1, and Francie Larrieu ran the 1500 meter run in 4:20.1.

The March *womenSports* reported that a "three mile cross country race became the first athletic championship event for female students of the City University of New York (C.U.N.Y.)."

Dr. Donald P. Cohen, president of the Board of Governors of the National Track and Field Hall of Fame, initiated the National Track and Field Youth Program sponsored by the Hershey Foods Corporation. The West Virginia Recreation and Parks Association and the Hall of Fame conducted the program for 10,000 West Virginia youngsters.

Roxanne Andersen was awarded the fifth annual Joseph Robichaux Award, and the inductees into the National Track and Field Hall of Fame were Dee Boeckmann and Mae Faggs Starr.

Wendy Koenig Knudson

Wendy was born in Boulder, Colorado, on May 28, 1955. In an interview on December 4, 1991, Wendy related her track history:

> I started in track because a physical education teacher in junior high school, who knew I was good in sports, gave me information about a pentathlon competi-

First coaching staff in 1976 of the Empire Track and Field Camp for Girls, Westport, N.Y. *Front row, from left:* Kathy Weston, Madeline Manning, Denise Wood, Joni Huntley, Lacey O'Neal. *Back row, from left:* Norm Tate, Bruce MacDonald, Al Bonney, Connie Ford and Alex Ferenczy. (Author's photo.)

tion. My dad taught me how to throw the shot and hurdle a couple of days before I competed. I tried it, and to make a long story short, I qualified for the national standard by five points. That was in 1970. One month later I competed in the regional Junior Olympics in the high jump in Albuquerque, and about a month later I was on a plane to Knoxville, Tennessee, as a high jumper in the Junior Olympics. I was fortunate to have had success so quickly.

I was a pentathlete for about a year with the Colorado Gold, a team that Lyle Knudson was just starting. I began running the four hundred-meter hurdles when it was an experimental event for women. I was the first woman in the world to run the four hundred-meter hurdles under sixty seconds. I ran it in fifty-nine seconds, proving that women could run it under sixty seconds. We never could get the meet director to verify my time, so it has always been an unofficial world record of fifty-nine point ninety-one.

I saw an article in *Women's Track and Field World* about the first woman in Germany, Hildegard Falck, who ran under two minutes for the half mile. I said, hey, dad, that would be easy to do. I can run a quarter in fifty-four point seven you know, and I should be able to cruise to a two-minute eight hundred and eighty-yard run. He said, "I'll give you two hundred dollars if you can do it." When Lyle called to see what event I wanted to run in a meet, I said, the eight hundred and I'm going to run it in under two minutes. There was a pause on the phone, and then he said, "how are you going to do that?"

Well, I told Lyle I'd run it in two minutes or less by coming through the four hundred meters in fifty-eight seconds. That time would give me four seconds of rest, and I could still come back in sixty-two seconds. Yeah! So he said, "Okay,

I'll put you in the event." I said, all I want you to do is to stand on the corner and tell me if I'm on pace for fifty-eight seconds.

I came through the first lap in fifty-seven point five, and I was two hundred or three hundred yards ahead of the field. As I came around the five hundred curve, I suddenly began slowing way down and I ran the last lap in about seventy-two seconds. I ran a two-ten, and all of a sudden I was the fourth fastest eight hundred and eighty yard runner in the United States. I was surprised I hadn't run faster. And I had new respect for Hildegard Falck. I was fifteen at the time.

It took me six years of running the eight hundred meters to finally run under two minutes. Four years later in nineteen seventy-two, I ran two minutes, four point seven seconds and qualified for the Munich Olympics. I ran one minute fifty-nine point ninety-one in nineteen seventy-six, in Montreal, and my dad didn't come through with the two hundred dollars. He said it took me too long, and he'd spent more than two hundred dollars getting me to meets. I'm real proud of the accomplishment.

I semi-retired after Montreal, and two of my three children were born. Then I started training again for nineteen eighty-four, but I got injured.

After I stopped competing, I served as vice chairman of the Athletes' Advisory Committee, and some day I'd like to be women's chairman. That will happen after my kids get a little older.

Kate Schmidt

Kate was inducted into the National Track and Field Hall of Fame on December 3, 1994. In an early morning meeting with her on December 4, the two-time Olympic bronze medalist told me how she became interested in track and field:

I started when I was thirteen. Some of the stories were told last night. It's interesting, ask my mom. I had a vision when I was very young, I don't know if I actually saw this or it was in my imagination, of hundreds of spears vertically stuck in the ground at Long Beach State College right in front of the track. That's where all the guys used to throw. It was sort of a javelin throwing center back in the sixties. I lived right across the street. I had to do this. I saw these things that people were throwing. And I knew I was going to do that. I had too. And I did.

I played softball then. I had a coach that said don't throw the softball, you should throw things officially. Something that's a real throwing event. There were spears at the park, this is unheard of kind of stuff in California because it's just not really done very much at a Parks and Rec. To have javelins sort of sitting in someone's office is very unusual. So I was set up with one of the other players on the team who was a javelin thrower, Robbie Stewart, a left-hander, which explains a lot about my technique — I learned the first of what I learned from a left-hander. We went over to Ron Allice of the Long Beach Comets. They were working out at Wilson High School, and he said, "Sure, be on the team, go over there and throw, go over there and learn how to throw." So he sent us out in the field. We did that for a little while, and then Robbie would schlep me up to Pasadena and we worked out. Those are the very earliest memories I have. I was thirteen when I started with Robbie. So it was a year of a little bit of Pasadena, tennis shoes, grass, sticking the thing — I don't know how long it was before I took my arm back or before I ran on the runway — it was all, I think, in a matter of a year.

Then I won the girls' nationals when I was fourteen. When I was fifteen, in nineteen sixty-nine, I won the women's nationals. I don't believe I competed when I was thirteen, but I was introduced, we were introduced. I loved it immediately. It's just one of those things, the more I did, the more I had to do. I think it was a means to get out of my family, to have my own identity, to do my own thing.

One thing led to another. Dave Pearson and I sort of learned the event together. We did films and started weight training. When I was fourteen, I was in the Olympic trials. I came in fourth in the nineteen sixty-eight Olympic trials at Mt. Sac. So that would have been silly to go to an Olympics. I barely knew which end of the javelin went in the dirt. The first national team I made was when I was fifteen. We went to Germany and England for some dual meets.

It was all club stuff, no school stuff. I sort of did it at UCLA half heartedly, but at the time I

Two-time Olympic bronze medalist and world record holder in the javelin, Kate Schmidt. (Courtesy of Kate Schmidt.)

was there it was a political mess. I came up through the clubs — Comets, Naturite Track Club in Los Angeles, Pacific Coast Club. With Dave Pearson, it was the South Coast Track Club. In nineteen seventy-one, this was funny, in one of the nationals in Ohio, we made team T-shirts. This was before anyone really knew anything. It said on the front "Steroids," on the back "Breakfast of Champions." And we wore those to the meet. I have the shirt, but it's not so funny anymore. But then, we had heard of this thing people did, and it wasn't real to us.

So, eighteen years old, Munich; I'm pretty sure it was a surprise bronze medal. I was still pretty young for a medal in a field event. For me it was all about loving to throw and having fun. I could not have had more fun. I loved throwing, and I loved having fun with the parties after. We worked hard, and we partied hard. That's what I did for eighteen years.

All the lost years in between Olympics, I don't remember them very well; life was on a four-year calendar. By nineteen seventy-six, I was getting sort of official about it, you know, doctors and harder training, two a day. You can't work because you have to train so hard. You go to the doctors half the day, and you go to train the rest of the day. By Montreal I was co-favorite for the gold with Ruth Fuchs from East Germany. She, of course, won and I, of course, got the bronze — that was the story of our lives. I was disappointed, I was always disappointed. Even if I won, I was disappointed, I never threw far enough. It was never far enough. As enjoyable as it was, it was never far enough.

In nineteen seventy-seven, I broke Ruth's world record, which made me very happy. Unfortunately, not against her, and I don't think I ever beat her. The record lasted a season or so. Then everybody was taking stuff, and the record went crazy. I still sort of have a hunch, I don't say it very often — it sounds like sour grapes — but I think my throw was one of the longest ever nonsteroid throws. I personally and quietly feel very good about that. Then it all got out of control. By nineteen eighty I was hurt. In nineteen seventy-eight I first dislocated my shoulder, which led to the surgery, but not until nineteen eighty-five. I threw in a lot of pain for a few years. Through the nineteen eighty Olympics I was injured. I made that team, but I wasn't throwing very well.

I moved to Canada to train with Lionel Pugh and Debbie Brill. I finally decided to be coached. For my whole life, people had been saying, you throw so far, if only you had a coach. So I went up to work with him, and it didn't go very well only because I was injured. I came back and sort of thought about quitting, and then the 1984 trials came around and I had nothing better to do, which is the worst reason in the world to come out of retirement, even though I wasn't in retirement. And I said, well, one more, why not? So I trained again hurt and finished fourth in that trials. I think that was my last meet.

I'm real sketchy on stuff, on data. I remember all of the sensations. I remember the smell of the grass and the color of the sky and a good throw. I don't know how far I threw in places or how many times I broke the records. I read it, and it sort of sounds familiar. That's pretty much the highlights. It's been so long since I was in that mode of thinking. I used to always think about the times between big meets. And I'm out of that habit now. That was my life. What are you doing between the World Championships and the Olympics?

The dream throw within one of the six — every meet is like that — your whole life is like that. I did a bunch of different things in 1976 to try to get an edge. One of them was working with a hypno-therapist. I wanted to get some of those more distasteful aspects of training to have a more pleasant feel to them, and one of them was all of the running I had to do. We worked on key words — one of them had to be like a kinesthetic kind of a word — it was about visual imaging and sensations that you wanted to feel to make a perfect throwing situation. What would a perfect throwing day taste like, smell like, feel like, look like, and how would you feel on a perfect throwing morning? All of that. I would go through this process before long runs and stuff, and I think powerful and relaxed were some of my key words. A lot of it was about being able to duplicate all of those kinds of feelings of effortlessness in competition after having done all the work. The whole paradox of throwing is to pull off a completely relaxed physical effort for something that takes enormous strength and power. The king was Janis Lusis as far as I'm concerned. He was an amazing athlete. He could come down the runway in a position that everybody else would have to strain to get into, and his muscles would be so supple and so loose. Throwing was all about getting incredibly strong and then having a touch, and being delicate, and being relaxed, and so throwers to me are pretty amazing athletes. They used to have a standing long jump competition in the Stockholm meet, and Al Feuerbach won it every year against the long jumpers. Brian Oldfield used to win indoor sprints sometimes against the sprinters. So you work on this part of the throw and that part of the throw and break it down from September until February, March. It's parts of the throw, it's this part of the run and that part of the run, it's the left foot, it's the right foot, it's the hand and the ankle and the elbow and the shoulder and the head. It gets broken down into so many little pieces, and then you have to put it back together and hopefully end up with the right thing by the time you've got to go down the runway in the spring and let go.

Hopefully, you've done enough distance work and enough power work and enough speed work. That's what all the events are about, but then you just get six throws. You may have had a perfect throw that whole year in practice, maybe not. You may have ten important meets coming up. That's only sixty throws, and to get a perfect throw is very unlikely. It's always very unlikely, but it's always why you're there.

The world record day in nineteen seventy-seven, in Furth, Germany, was the end of the longest competitive summer I had had in Europe, I think twenty-seven meets, and I was sick of track. I was fifteen pounds underweight. I'd been sick. In April, I visited my parents. I was watching a football game with Maren Seidler. I ran outside and broke my wrist. I had to be casted for seven weeks in April, right when everything's supposed to be coming together. I thought, that's it — I had been training quite hard. I thought that was the end of that. But I went to Europe in June, and we were there until September. I'd had one suitcase, and I just wanted to go home. That week we'd been to three meets, three countries. We had just come from Belgium. Sabina Airlines lost my spears. I wound up with Kurt Benlein's javelin, he's a German decathalete, a very handsome boy. It was really a nice little meet. It was an adorable stadium. Everybody I knew was there. Eleven thousand people were there. But all of my friends were there. The whole Pacific Coast Club was there. Mac [Wilkins] and Al [Feuerbach] were there, Dwight [Stones] and all the girls. The women's javelin was right after the men's discus, and they hadn't put out any sector lines yet. My clothes were all dirty, and I had to wear a little red T-shirt. I remember how upset Tom [Jennings] was afterwards that I didn't have a Pacific Coast Club jersey on [laugh].

I always loved throwing men's spears because it always gave me really good kinesthetic tips. It forced me to keep my hand higher, forced me to pull back further because of the weight and the length. It made me more conscious of the right things to do. The women's javelin is too small and light. You can't feel it. So it was a good warm-up, and I had some good feelings. Because I was light weight and because I was sick of it, because I never wanted to see another track again, I was quite reckless. I was more reckless than usual. The last meet of the year, nothing to lose. I went a little faster on the runway, I was a little quicker because of the weight, with slightly more abandon than I would normally have. I don't even remember what throw it was, I think it was the third or fourth throw, and I don't know what the series was. There were only three or four women in the meet. I had to borrow a spear. I think it was a fifty-five-meter Held javelin. It was a perfect throw. I came down the runway with good acceleration, and when I let go of it I hadn't felt anything. I immediately knew that that's what a perfect throw meant. It was perfectly efficient. There was nothing in the wrong place. Because everything was in the right place, I didn't feel anything. I didn't feel the effort. I didn't feel any pain. It was all perfect. I could hardly see the javelin. Where's the spear? Because there was no vibration, all I could see was the little tiny bit of the back tip of the spear. There was no vibration. It was really — I was so impressed, right away looking at it. It felt good. And I heard the announcer say "neun und sechzig" — that's 69 meters something — and I knew the world record was sixty-nine point ten, but I wasn't sure of the centimeters that he said. Was the world record thirty-two or ten, what is the world record? And then he said "neu worldt record" or however they say it, and I screamed — I think I screamed like someone who lost emotional control. I screamed and everybody came down and I got lots of hugs. My heart was pounding, it was very exciting. The party afterwards is legendary now amongst a whole new generation of reporters. It started out in the swimming pool on the ninth floor of the hotel we were staying in. It just kept getting worse. We were up all night until seven thirty in the morning, when I left to get a flight to Boston. When I tried to find some clothes, remember my clothes were so dirty, I hand-washed some things to wear on the plane and they hadn't dried. So I put the top, it was a velour top, on the lamp to dry it, and it burned a hole through the front and a little hole through the back. I had this islandy batik skirt, burnt top, one Adidas sandal. I couldn't find the other one. I got on the bus like this and went to the Frankfurt airport to go home. I was in another world. I had this world record. I had this great party. I had to go home. There was so much going on in my head. All the papers in the airport had my picture all over them. I was always popular in Germany because of my name. I was mobbed in the airport. I wasn't very presentable [laughter]. It wasn't my best moment [more laughter].

It was a long flight home. But that was it. That was the world record. Two eighteen had been my best throw. I had thrown two hundred and twenty-eight in practice. That [227' 5"] was, I think, as good as I was capable of throwing. To do it in a meet, you're just lucky. It's just luck. I was capable of doing it. Lucky me. And I always say medals and records weren't the thing ever for me. But that's easy to say because I get to say that I have them both. It's easier to go through life being able to say Olympics and world record than not. But still, the pleasure was exactly the way I said it last night, a bucket of ice tea, a sunny afternoon at UCLA, and a bunch of spears.

Brooks Johnson

In an interview on December 3, 1992, Brooks told me about his track and field experiences:

I got started in women's track and field because of an experience I had in nineteen fifty-six when I was a law student at the University of Chicago. I went to the field house and was training with Ted Hayden and there was Joe Robichaux and the Mayor Daley's Youth Foundation. Because of the atmosphere there, the men and women basically trained together. It was as if there was no big deal, which was one of the few times where I saw that kind of gender integration. So that's basically where I got exposed, up close and personal, to women's track and field.

I went to work for the State Department, and by nineteen sixty-three I was stationed in Washington, D.C. I continued to run and made the Pan American team in nineteen sixty-three.

In nineteen sixty-five, I was coaching a bunch of kids at American University and this red-headed girl came over. She had been a gymnast and a diver and her father said, "My daughter Jane would like to run." This was the summer of nineteen sixty-five. So she came out and started training. She was the first female athlete I had ever coached.

By nineteen sixty-eight, Esther Stroy had made the Olympic team at fourteen, and Jane Burnett was an alternate on that team. She made the Pan American team in nineteen sixty-seven. That's basically what started it.

The program grew for both men and women. I've always coached people of both genders. It's just that you get stereotyped and you become identified as being a women's coach but I always coached both genders. The Stanford University program was a combined program.

I continued to coach in Washington, D.C. As a matter of fact, one of the people I coached on the other side of the gender thing was Al Gore. I was at St. Albans School, which is where he attended school. Evan Bayh, who is the governor of the state of Indiana, was there too with a lot of kids like that. It was a pretty interesting experience getting these kids from the wrong side of the tracks and integrating with these kids that came from very prominent political and economic families. We did that in Washington until nineteen seventy-five, when I went to the University of Florida. In nineteen seventy-nine, I left Florida and went to Stanford, and in nineteen ninety-two, I left Stanford, and went to Cal Poly, San Luis Obispo.

With the team in Washington, we would jump into vans, cars, and station wagons — I remember driving eighteen hours straight to go to the national cross-country championships in St. Louis once. The kids got out and they won and got back in the cars and we drove back through a snow storm on the Pennsylvania Turnpike. Half of the cars got marooned — that was typical of those days. The actual standard for track and field for women, particularly at the high school and sub–high school level was much greater than it is now. If you look at the high school times, on an average, in most events they are going backwards. The emphasis is not there. Then everybody was coaching kids for the national team, to make national teams, to be internationalists. Now they're coaching kids to win high school conference meets, high school regionals, and perhaps the state meet. The point is all of us would throw our kids from our teams into vans and set out for these big meets.

In nineteen seventy-two, I had twelve athletes in the Olympics, eight from Stanford in eighty-eight, seven from Stanford in ninety-two. I've had an Olympian on every Olympic team except for nineteen sixty-four, starting in nineteen sixty. The overwhelming majority, starting in nineteen sixty-eight, have been women.

All of the years have been very interesting for me. I'm a people-person, and you get a chance to see people at their very best and oftentimes at their very worst. It's been an on-going, hands-on education for me. It's hard for me to single out one interesting phenomenon because it's all interesting. I sit in the hall and watch these kids go by, and I've seen them evolve. There have been some highlights — Olympic champions, world records — but after a while it all sort of blends in.

What has women's track and field done for me and what have I tried to do by way of reciprocation? I was involved with the women's development at a time when it was pretty critical.

One of the other things I was very active in that I'm probably most proud of was to fight off efforts by certain men to become chairman of women's track and field. The other thing that I'm very proud of are the efforts that I and others put into making sure that the last two Olympic coaches were women and pretty much trying to assure that the next Olympic coach is going to be a woman.

Brooks was a coach of the 1976 Olympic team.

Chapter 60

1977

More than 10,000 fans witnessed the second combined men's and women's national championships at Drake Stadium on the campus of UCLA from June 9 to June 11. The meet served as the qualifying meet for the first World Cup championships in Dusseldorf, West Germany, from September 2 to September 4. Only the winner of each event made the World Cup team.

The only double winner of the meet was Evelyn Ashford. Mary Ayers set an American record in the 400-meter hurdles. Kate Schmidt won her fifth straight national championship in the javelin and Joni Huntley her fourth in the high jump. Evelyn Ashford was chosen as the outstanding performer. She was presented with the *Redbook* Award. The *womenSports* team trophy was awarded to the Los Angeles Mercurettes.

5000-meter walk
1. Sue Brodock, Rialto Road Runners   24:10.1 AR
2. Susan Liers, Island Track Club   25:30.9
3. Joyce Brodock, Rialto Road Runners   26:01.1

Two-mile relay
1. L.A. Naturite Track Club   8:41.5
    (Antoniewicz, Mullins, Warner, Brown)
2. Atoms Track Club   8:44.9
3. Falcon Track Club   8:46.4

10,000-meter run
1. Peg Neppel, Iowa State   33:15.1 WR
2. Karen Bridges, Texas Track Club   34:27.9
3. Lori Ann Thrupp, unattached   34:40.5

400-meter hurdles
1. Mary Ayers, Prairie View Track Club   56.61 AR
2. Debbie Esser, Iowa State   56.90
3. Sandra Levinski, Texas Woman's University   57.9

1500-meter run
1. Francie Larrieu Lutz, Pacific Coast Club   4:08.2 MR
2. Jan Merrill, Age Group A.A.   4:09.3
3. Cindy Bremser, Wisconsin Track Club   4:11.8

400-meter dash
1. Sharon Dabney, Clippers Track Club   51.55 MR
2. Lorna Forde, Atoms Track Club   52.0
3. Rosalyn Bryant, unattached   53.44

440-yard relay
1. Tennessee State   45.44
   (Morehead, McMillan, Fuller, Cheeseborough)
2. L.A. Mercurettes   45.85
3. Texas Southern   45.86

100-meter dash
1. Evelyn Ashford, Maccabi Track Club   11.14 w
2. Brenda Morehead, Tennessee State   11.19
3. Chandra Cheeseborough, Tennessee State   11.36

200-meter dash
1. Evelyn Ashford, Maccabi Track Club   22.62
2. Deborah Jones, Tennessee State   23.05
3. Chandra Cheeseborough, Tennessee State   23.20

800-meter run
1. Sue Latter, Michigan State University   2:03.8
2. Julie Brown, L.A. Naturite Track Club   2:04.0
3. Tecla Chemabwai, Maccabi Track Club   2:04.7

100-meter hurdles
1. Patty Van Wolvelaere, L.A. Naturite Track Club   13.15
2. Deby LaPlante, unattached, Michigan   13.21
3. Modupe Oshikoya, Maccabi Track Club   13.45

3000-meter run
1. Jan Merrill, Age Group A.A.   9:00.2
2. Cindy Bremser, Wisconsin Track Club   9:04.0
3. Francie Larrieu Lutz, Pacific Coast Club   9:16.7

High jump
1. Joni Huntley, Oregon Track Club   6' 1"
2. Louise Ritter, Texas Woman's University   5' 11"
3. Paula Girven, D.C. Striders   5' 11"

Javelin throw
1. Kate Schmidt, unattached   200' 7"
2. Sherry Calvert, Lakewood International   191' 2"
3. Lynn Cannon, Millbrae Lions   188' 5"

Long jump
1. Jodi Anderson, L.A. Naturite Track Club   21' 9¼"
2. Kathy McMillan, Tennessee State   21' 5⅛"
3. Lorraine Ray, Florida   21' 2½"

Shot put
1. Maren Seidler, Mayor Daley Youth Foundation   54' 1¼"
2. Jane Frederick, L.A. Naturite Track Club   51' ¼"
3. Kathy Devine, Emporia State University   49' 6¾"

Discus throw
1. Jane Haist, Canada   193' 6"
2. Lynne Winbigler, Oregon Track Club   187' 2" AR
3. Jan Svendsen, Quest Club   175' 10"

The Indoor Nationals

The indoor championship meet was held on February 25 in Madison Square Garden. Francie Larrieu Lutz was voted the outstanding athlete and won the *Redbook* Award. *WomenSports* magazine presented the team championship trophy to the Los Angeles Mercurettes.

The indoor national team that competed in the USA–USSR–Canadian meet was selected from this meet.

One-mile walk
1. Sue Brodock, Rialto Road Runners   7:05.9 AR
2. Susan Liers, Island Track Club   7:19.3
3. Tracy Trisco, Blue Angels   7:33.4

60-yard dash
1. Brenda Morehead, Tennessee State   6.6
2. Jeanette Bolden, L.A. Mercurettes   6.7
3. Rhonda Brady, Mayor Hatcher Youth Foundation   6.9

60-yard hurdles
1. Jane Frederick, Los Angeles Track Club   7.3 AR
2. Deby LaPlante, Great Lakes A.C.   7.4
3. Rhonda Brady, Mayor Hatcher Youth Foundation   7.7

Two-mile run
1. Francie Larrieu Lutz, Long Beach, Calif.   9:58.2 MR
2. Jan Merrill, Age Group A.A.   9:59.2
3. Carol Cook, Iowa State   10:02.2

440-yard run
1. Lorna Forde, Atoms Track Club   53.6 MR
2. Yolanda Rich, L.A. Mercurettes   54.8
3. Sharon Dabney, Clippers Track Club   55.2

One-mile run
1. Francie Larrieu Lutz, Long Beach, Calif.   4:43.1
2. Julie Brown, L.A. Track Club   4:45.4
3. Lynn Jennings, Liberty A.C.   4:50.6

220-yard dash
1. Rosalyn Bryant, L.A. Mercurettes   23.4 AR
2. Pam Jiles, New Orleans Superdames   24.7
3. Kim Robinson, L.A. Mercurettes   24.7

880-yard run
1. Cyndy Poor, Athletes in Action   2:06.7 MR

2. Robin Campbell, Florida Track Club   2:07.5
3. Wendy Knudson, Colorado State   2:09.5

640-yard relay
1. West Suburban Track Club   1:12.6
   (Gutowski, Dinello, Blanchard, Kulovitz)
2. Jackson State Flying Tigers   1:13.3
3. Cavalette Track Club   1:13.5

880-yard medley relay
1. L.A. Mercurettes   1:42.6 AR
   (Bryant, Rich, Robinson, Loud)
2. Atoms Track Club   1:44.3
3. Klub Keystone, "A" team   1:48.6

One-mile relay
1. D.C. Striders   3:45.8 AR
   (Davy, Smith, Norman, Bruce)
2. N.Y. Police Athletic League   3:49.7
3. Atoms Track Club   3:50.1

Long jump
1. Kathy McMillan, Tennessee State   21' 4¼" MR
2. Diane Kummer, Maccabi Union Track Club   20' 2½"
3. Jodi Anderson, L.A. Track Club   20' 1¾"

Shot put
1. Maren Seidler, Mayor Daley Youth Foundation   52' 3¾"
2. Jane Frederick, L.A. Track Club   49' 9½"
3. Jane Haist, Univ. of Tennessee   49' 1¾"

High jump
1. Joni Huntley, Long Beach, Calif.   6'
2. Pam Spencer, Seattle Pacific College   6'
3. Paula Girvin, Univ. of Maryland   5' 10"

Team scores:
Los Angeles Mercurettes 19; Los Angeles Track Club 14; Tennessee State University 10; Atoms Track Club 10; West Suburban Track Club 6; Athletes in Action 5.

The performances of the United States women in the first World Cup championships in West Germany from September 2-4 follow:

100 meters		Shot put	
5. Evelyn Ashford	11.48	4. Maren Seidler	50' 10¼"
200 meters		400-meter dash	
4. Evelyn Ashford	23.14	4. Sharon Dabney	51.96
800-meter run		3000-meter run	
5. Sue Latter	2:05.0	3. Jan Merrill	8:46.6
100-meter hurdles		400-meter relay	
5. Pat Van Wolvelaere	13.54	USA did not finish	

Long jump		Discus throw	
7. Jane Frederick	20' 1½"	5. Lynne Winbigler	174' 5"

The United States women finished sixth in the 1600-meter relay and fourth in the point standing.

Twenty-four women on the indoor national team competed in Maple Leaf Garden, Toronto, on March 3-4 in a tricountry track meet with the Soviet Union and Canada. The *New York Times* headlines announced, "Jane Frederick Wins Triathlon and Hurdles." Despite an injury incurred while high jumping, twenty-four-year-old Jane Frederick continued competing and won the triathlon and the 50-yard hurdles. She hit her foot on the metal high jump standard and sustained a deep gash which required eight stitches.

880-yard run
1. Wendy Koenig Knudson   2:06.3
2. Cyndy Poor   2:06.7

One-mile run
1. Francie Larrieu Lutz   4:36.0
2. Julie Brown   4:41.1

50-yard hurdles
1. Jane Frederick   6.3
2. Deby LaPlante   6.4

Triathlon
1. Jane Frederick   2887
   (SP 50' 11½", HJ 5' 9¼", 50H 6.3)
4. Dana Collins   2600

USA 36 — Soviet Union 19
USA 38 — Canada 17

The cross-country team competed in Germany. The USA team took second in the competition.

The 10,000-meter run was added to the senior championships.

The indoor pentathlon championship was held in Sterling, Illinois, and the outdoor pentathlon championship was held in Dayton, Ohio. On May 1, the 800-meter run replaced the 200 meters as the final event in the pentathlon.

The senior team competed in the Jacques Coeur Relays in France; Turin, Italy; Gelsenkirchen, West Germany; and Sochi, USSR.

The two American women on the world list were Kathy Hammond and Debra Sapenter for a 52.2 clocking in the 440-yard dash.

The girls' outdoor championships were held at UCLA on June 13-14. The junior team was selected from the meet to compete in Richmond, Virginia, against the USSR. They defeated the Russians for the second time in the history of the meet.

For the first time, the junior team competed against the Japanese junior team at UCLA on August 20.

Rosalyn Bryant won the 400 meter (52.10) in the World University Games.

Irene Spieker broke the world indoor record in the pole vault in the Mason-Dixon Games in Louisville, Kentucky, with a vault of 8' ¼".

The 1977 inductee into the National Track and Field Hall of Fame was Betty Robinson, the 100-meter Olympic gold medalist from 1928.

The second annual National Track and Field Youth Program, sponsored by Hershey's, was held on August 6. More than 250,000 boys and girls, ages ten to fifteen, participated in this program. Meets were held in ten southeastern states, and more than 500 winners competed in the finals at Marshall University in Huntington, West Virginia. Expanding the program to include all fifty states was considered.

Dr. Harmon C. Brown was awarded the sixth annual Joseph Robichaux Award. The Woman of the Year Award presented for outstanding contributions and service to long distance running was presented to Miki Gorman. This was the first time it was awarded. The first Otto Essig Award for meritorious service to masters' long distance running was presented to Ruth Anderson.

American Outdoor Records

60m	7.3	Barbara Ferrell	8/25/68
100y	10.2	Iris Davis	6/20/71
100m	11.0(ET)	Wyomia Tyus	10/15/68
200m	22.8	Barbara Ferrell	10/18/68
	22.8	Chandra Cheeseborough	10/16/75
	22.8	Pam Giles	10/16/75
220y	23.3	Mable Fergerson	6/22/73
400m	50.6(ET)	Rosalyn Bryant	7/28/76
440y	52.2	Kathy Hammond	8/12/72
	52.2	Debra Sapenter	6/29/74
800m	1:57.9	Madeline M. Jackson	7/7/76
880y	2:04.6	Charlotte Cooke	7/23/66
	2:04.6	Mary Decker	5/18/74
1500m	4:02.6(ET)	Janice Merrill	7/29/76
Mile	4:33.1	Francie Larrieu	6/8/74
3000m	8:54.9(ET)	Francie Larrieu Lutz	8/7/76
2 miles	10:02.8	Francie Larrieu	6/3/73
3 miles	16:32.8	Clare Choate	1/12/74
5000m	16:28.5	Peg Neppel	4/24/76
6 miles	33:52.8	Julie Brown	3/29/75
10,000m	34:18.9(ET)	Peg Neppel	5/22/76
100mh	13.0	Patty Johnson	7/8/72
400mh	57.3	Debbie Esser	6/28/75
HJ	6' 2¾"	Joni Huntley	1/26/75
LJ	22' 3"	Kathy McMillan	6/12/76
SP	56' 7"	Maren Seidler	6/1/74
DT	185' 3"	Olga Connolly	5/27/72
JT	218' 3"	Kate Schmidt	6/12/76

Pentathlon	4677	Jane Frederick	5/28-29/76
400mr	42.8	USA (Ferrell, Bailes, Netter, Tyus)	10/20/68
440yr	44.2	USA (Watson, Collins El, Bryant, Jiles)	7/18/75
800m	1:35.5	USA (Tyus, Brown, Thompson, McGuire)	10/25/64
1600mr	3:22.8(ET)	USA (Sapenter, Ingram, Jiles, Bryant)	7/31/76
Mile relay	3:30.9	USA (Campbell, Toussaint, M. Jackson, Sapenter)	7/19/75
1000m walk	5:11.2	Stella Palamarchuk	10/23/72
1500m walk	6:46.6	Lisa Metheny	6/28/75
Mile walk	7:20.1	Susan Brodock	2/2/74
5000m walk	25:28.8	Susan Brodock	6/11/76
10,000m walk	52:03.0	Susan Brodock	8/29/75

ET — electronically timed

Chapter 61

1978

The outdoor track and field championship meet was held on June 8-10 at UCLA. Jodi Anderson was selected as the outstanding performer and was presented with the *Redbook* Award. Tennessee State University won the *womenSports* trophy for the team championship.

A meet record was established in the 10,000-meter walk because this is the first time that the event was contested.

5000-meter walk
1. Sue Liers, Island Track Club   25:46.8
2. Sue Brodock, So. Calif. Road Runners   26:20.4
3. Chris Shea, N.Y. Police Athletic League   26.29.4

Two-mile relay
1. San Jose Cindergals   8:41.8
   (Regan, Figliomeni, Wetherspoon, Williams)
2. Liberty A.C.   8:42.2
3. L.A. Naturite Track Club   8:45.8

10,000-meter run
1. Ellison Goodall, Duke A.A.   33:40.2
2. Sue Kinsey, L.A. Naturite Track Club   33:42.7
3. Karen Bridges, Oklahoma State   34:17.3

1500-meter run
1. Jan Merrill, Age Group A.A.   4:09.4
2. Debbie Heald, San Fernando Valley Track Club   4:10.9
3. Cindy Bremser, Wisconsin Track Club   4:11.1

10,000-meter walk
1. Sue Brodock, So. Calif. Road Runners   52:18.2 MR
2. Paula Mori, California Walkers   53:00.9
3. Susan Liers, Island Track Club   53:29.0

Javelin throw
1. Sherry Calvert, Lakewood International   203' 7"
2. Kate Schmidt, Pacific Coast Club   198' 5"
3. Lynn Cannon, Millbrae Lions   181' 5"

Long jump
1. Jodi Anderson, L.A. Naturite Track Club   22' 7½" AR

2. Kathy McMillan, Tennessee State   22' ¾"
3. June Griffith, Adelphi University   20' 8¼"

200-meter dash
1. Evelyn Ashford, Maccabi Track Club   22.66
2. Brenda Morehead, Tennessee State   22.88
3. Chandra Cheeseborough, Tennessee State   23.55

100-meter dash
1. Leleith Hodges, Texas Woman's University   11.23
2. Brenda Morehead, Tennessee State   11.25
3. Evelyn Ashford, Maccabi Track Club   11.30

400-meter dash
1. Lorna Forde, Atoms Track Club   51.04 MR
2. Patricia Jackson, Prairie View A&M   51.11
3. Sharon Dabney, Clippers Track Club   51.31

800-meter run
1. Ruth Caldwell, Citrus College   2:02.0
2. Essie Kelley, Prairie View A&M   2:03.0
3. Mary Decker, University of Colorado   2:03.1

High jump
1. Louise Ritter, Texas Woman's University   6' 1¼"
2. Pam Spencer, Falcon Track Club   6' 1¼"
3. Debbie Brill, Pacific Coast Club   6'

3000-meter run
1. Jan Merrill, Age Group A.A.   8:56.4 MR
2. Kathy Mills, New Jersey A.A.   9:03.3
3. Cindy Bremser, Wisconsin Track Club   9:11.8

400-meter hurdles
1. Debbie Esser, Iowa State Track Club   57.85
2. Ellie Mahal, East York Track Club   58.60
3. June Smith, D.C. International   58.62

Shot put
1. Maren Seidler, San Jose Stars   59' 8" MR
2. Ann Turbyne, Gilly's Gym   52' 4½"
3. Kathy Devine, Emporia State University   50' 10"

100-meter hurdles
1. Deby LaPlante, unattached, N.J.   13.19 MR
2. Patty Van Wolvelaere, L.A. Naturite Track Club   13.22
3. Mary Smith, Texas Southern   13.50

440-yard relay
1. Texas Woman's University   44.61 MR
    (Hodges, Brown, Holmes, Simpson)
2. Tennessee State   45.04
3. L.A. Naturite Track Club   45.59

880-yard medley relay
1. Tennessee State   1:37.7 WR
   (Morehead, Davis, Cheeseborough, Jones)
2. Prairie View A&M   1:39.2
3. Texas Southern University   1:39.7

Discus throw
1. Lynne Winbigler, Oregon Track Club   178' 6"
2. Lorna Griffin, Falcon Track Club   176' 2"
3. Helene Connell, Atlantic Coast Track Club   171' 0"

One-mile relay
1. Prairie View A&M   3:34.9
   (Melrose, Kelley, Dudley, Jackson)
2. Atoms Track Club   3:35.4
3. Colorado Flyers   3:36.5

The Indoor Nationals

The indoor championship meet was again held in Madison Square Garden on February 24 before more than 13,000 fans.

Francie Larrieu set a meet record in the mile run. Larrieu and Jan Merrill had a ten-yard lead on the rest of the field with a lap and a half to go. Francie's strong finishing kick enabled her to win by five yards in 4:37.0.

A meet record was set by twenty-six-year-old Maren Seidler in the shot put. Her throw of 61' was almost 4' better than her previous best put.

Kim Thomas, eighteen, upset the favorites in the 440-yard dash.

Deby LaPlante was selected the outstanding athlete and received the *Redbook* Award. Tennessee State University won the team championship and the trophy presented by *womenSports*.

60-yard dash
1. Brenda Morehead, Tennessee State   6.73
2. Evelyn Ashford, Maccabi Track Club   6.80
3. Chandra Cheeseborough, Tennessee State   6.86

60-yard hurdles
1. Deby LaPlante, Englewood, N.J.   7.53 WR
2. Patty Van Wolvelaere, L.A. Naturite Track Club   7.54
3. Esther Rot, Maccabi Union Track Club   7.59

One-mile walk
1. Susan Brodock, Rialto Road Runners   7:01.7 AR
2. Susan Liers, Island Track Club   7:34.9
3. Tracy Trisco, L.A. Naturite Track Club   7:39.2

Two-mile run
1. Brenda Webb, Knoxville Track Club   9:55.8 MR

2. Kathy Mills, Penn State University   10:01.9
3. Sue Kinsey, L.A. Naturite Track Club   10.03.5

440-yard run
1. Kim Thomas, St. John's University   55.53 AR
2. Sharon Dabney, Clippers Track Club   55.81
3. Rosalyn Bryant, L.A. Mercurettes   56.19

220-yard dash
1. Freida Nichols, D.C. Striders   24.23
2. Theresa Montgomery, Memphis-Shelby Track Club   24.73
3. Valerie Brisco, L.A. Mercurettes   25.06

One-mile run
1. Francie Larrieu, Long Beach, Calif.   4:37.0 MR
2. Jan Merrill, Age Group A.A.   4:37.6
3. Lynn Jennings, Liberty A.C.   4:39.0

640-yard relay
1. Tennessee State   1:09.4 AR
   (Morehead, Davis, Cheeseborough, Jones)
2. L.A. Mercurettes   1:10.4
3. D.C. Striders   1:12.6

880-yard medley relay
1. Atoms Track Club   1:44.3
   (Forde, Brown, Cummings, James)
2. Klub Keystone   1:47.8
   (Tennessee State finished first but was disqualified)

One-mile relay
1. L.A. Mercurettes   3:51.7
   (Winlock, Wallin, Gardner, Roberson)
2. Atoms Track Club   3:54.1

880-yard run
1. Debbie Vetter, Iowa State   2:08.8
2. Kathy Weston, L.A. Naturite Track Club   2:09.8
3. Darlene Beckford, Liberty A.C.   2:10.5

High jump
1. Debbie Brill, Canada   6' 2" MR
2. Joni Huntley, Long Beach, Calif.   6' 1"
3. Paula Girvin, Univ. of Maryland   5' 10"

Long jump
1. Modupe Oshikoya, Maccabi Union Track Club   20' 6¼"
2. Kathy McMillan, Tennessee State   20' 3¾"
3. Jodi Anderson, L.A. Naturite Track Club   20' 3¼"

Shot put
1. Maren Seidler, San Jose Stars   61' 0" MR
2. Caryl Van Pelt, Univ. of Washington   49' 6¼"
3. Diane Patrick, Kentucky Blue Diamond   48' 8¼"

The women's national team was selected from the indoor meet. They competed in Milan, Italy, on March 14 against the European All-Stars. Brenda Morehead bettered the American record in the 60 meters in finishing third in 7.32. Sharon Dabney set an American record of 53.27 in the 400-meter run and placed second. Deby LaPlante bettered the American record in the 60-meter hurdles, clocking 8.25 to place third. The USA 1600-meter relay team consisting of Kim Thomas, Liz Hatz, Pam Jiles, and Sharon Dabney finished second but set an American record of 3:38.6 for the distance.

The IAAF world cross-country meet was held in Glasgow, Scotland, on March 25. Julie Shea was fourth in 17:12, and Jan Merrill ran 17:17 to place seventh. The United States finished second. The team was selected from the nationals. In that meet, Julie Brown was the winner in 16:32.6, followed by Jan Merrill in 16:35.1 and Julie Shea in 16:41.8.

The indoor pentathlon championship was held in Albuquerque, New Mexico, on February 2-3. Ann Gilliland won with 3,839 points, Karen Page of New Zealand was second, and Linda Cornelius was third.

The outdoor pentathlon championship was held at Tempe, Arizona, on June 4-5. Jodi Anderson was the first American and finished third with 4,197 points, Judy Fontaine was fourth, and Denise Cornell was fifth.

The first indoor dual pentathlon meet was held at the Air Force Academy between U.S. pentathletes and Canada's on March 11. Linda Cornelius finished in third place and was the top American. Five pentathletes went to Europe in June for competition in Russia, Poland, and France.

The USA–USSR dual meet was held at Berkeley on July 7-8. With gold medal performances in the 100 meters in 11.22 and in the 200 meters in 22.69, the outstanding performer at the meet was Evelyn Ashford. Other United States gold medal performers were Pat Jackson in the 400 meters in 51.2, Louise Ritter in the high jump with a leap of 6' 1¾", Jodi Anderson in the long jump in 21' 9½", Sherry Calvert in the javelin with a best toss of 207' 11", and the 1600-meter relay team composed of Sharon Dabney, Kim Thomas, Patricia Jackson, and Essie Kelley in 3:28.6.

For the first time, the women's junior meet was combined with the men's junior meet on June 24-25 at the University of Indiana, Bloomington. The junior tour consisted of competitions with West Germany, Great Britain, and the USSR.

The national race walking team competed in Fredrickstad, Norway, in August.

Dr. Evie Dennis was the national chairwoman.

The first United States Olympic Festival was held this year at the Air Force Academy at Colorado Springs. The winners were:

100 meters	11.45	Karen Hawkins
200 meters	23.35	Liz Young
400 meters	52.33	Essie Kelley
800 meters	2:05.42	Ruth Caldwell
1500 meters	4:24.26	Debbie Heald
100-meter hurdles	13.52	Mary Smith

400-meter relay	44.30	South team
1600-meter relay	3:34.28	South team
High jump	6' 0"	Paula Girvin
Long jump	20' 8½"	Sheila Pettit
Shot put	51' 4¼"	Ann Turbyne
Discus	167' 7"	Lorna Griffin
Javelin	188' 6"	Sherry Calvert
Pentathlon	3,895	Judy Pollion

The Eight Nations Track and Field Games was held in Tokyo on September 25. Maren Seidler was the only gold medal winner, with a toss of 58' 6" in the shot put. Sherry Calvert was third in the javelin with a throw of 188' 8", and Louise Ritter placed third in the high jump with a leap of 6' 2".

The September 1978-79 *NAGWS Track and Field Guide* was published this year. Dr. Bert Lyle and Dr. Nell Jackson were on the rules committee.

Women's Track World printed a report from Pat Rico, representative from the USA at the meeting of the IAAF Congress in Puerto Rico. Despite harassment from the IAAF president, Pat fought to have the 3000-meter event for women added to international competition. She requested approval for the marathon and 10,000 meters and asked that the 5000 replace the 3000 meters. These suggestions were not allowed to be brought up before the Congress, however.

The Mason-Dixon Games produced three world indoor records. Tennessee State's 880-yard relay team lowered its time to 1:38.5, Jackson State won the sprint medley relay in 4:11.5, and Irene Spieker raised her pole vault record to 8' 6¼".

Jan Merrill and Jodi Anderson were awarded the first C.C. Jackson Awards provided by Brooks Johnson and Jack Griffin as a tribute to the outstanding pioneer work done by Jackson in America for women's track and field. Jan was selected as the most outstanding woman runner, and Jodi as the most outstanding athlete in the field events this year. Dr. Ken Foreman was awarded the Joseph Robichaux Award, and Deby LaPlante and Jodi Anderson were awarded the Mobil Cup. Nina Kuscsik was presented with the second Woman of the Year Award, and Pat Bessell was awarded the second Otto Essig Award for service to masters' long distance running.

Bert Lyle

In an interview in December 1994, Dr. Bert Lyle told me how he became involved in coaching:

> During the Korean War I was in the Air Force and volunteered to do something in athletics while stateside to fill the time. They needed track coaches because they were getting ready for the Pan American Games. Some women athletes also came out and worked with the men, so I just took them under my wing. We went to the national championships held for both men and women. The women's AAU championships in Ponca City, Oklahoma, in nineteen fifty-five was my introduction to women's track and field.

After completing my doctorate at the University of Texas, I went to Texas Woman's University, mainly because a good friend of mine who had preceded me there told me, "You could come up here and you can do anything that you want [smile], as long as it's constructive." So I envisioned going up there to continue my research and teaching. Dr. John Guinn, president of TWU, summoned me one day and said: "We need an athletic program. I have here a letter from the coach of a girl who has jumped 5' 6" [which in those days was close to the national record] and she wants to come here." Without much choice in the matter I said, well, all right. We began informally at first in nineteen sixty-seven. Then we competed in the emerging DGWS meets and won first place in the first national track and field college championship for women in nineteen sixty-nine. We won two more national college championships as well as two seconds, two or three thirds, over the next few years. Our team had some truly fine sprinters and jumpers and fielded some excellent relays in improving on the collegiate records throughout the seventies.

As I was teaching a full load, guiding graduate studies, and serving on committees, I intended to get out of it. At one point, I resigned. But instead, Dr. Quinn put me in charge of the athletic department and provided a staff. That's another story, but that's how I got into collegiate women's track.

Dr. Lyle's best-known athlete was Louise Ritter, the 1988 Olympic high jump champion. He has been a coach on the staff of many USA teams; his last assignment was as assistant coach of the 1992 Olympic team.

Chapter 62

1979

The last national outdoor championship meet held under the auspices of the Amateur Athletic Union took place in Walnut, California, on June 15-17. The AAU had been the governing body for women since 1923.

The first day of competition saw an exciting finish of the 10,000-meter run. Eighteen-year-old Mary Shea nipped Joan Benoit at the finish for the win. Both were given the same time.

1. Mary Shea, Cardinal Gibbons H.S.	32:52.5
2. Joan Benoit, Liberty A.C.	32:52.5

In the 100 meters, twenty-two-year-old Evelyn Ashford won the sprint, and in the semifinal, she set an American record of 10:97, becoming the first American to break the 11-second barrier.

1. Evelyn Ashford, Maccabi Track Club	11:01
2. Brenda Morehead, Tennessee State	11.13
3. Chandra Cheeseborough, Tennessee State	11.33

Deby LaPlante won the 100-meter hurdles in American record time. It was also the first time that the thirteen-second barrier had been broken. Seventeen-year-old Candy Young was second in a world junior record.

1. Deby LaPlante, KCBQ Track Club	12.86 AR
2. Candy Young, unattached, Pennsylvania	12.95 WJR
3. Stephanie Hightower, Ohio State	13.09

Twenty-eight-year-old Maren Seidler won her tenth national outdoor shot put title with an American record toss.

1. Maren Seidler, San Jose Stars	62' 7¾" AR
2. Ann Turbyne, Gilly's Gym	55' 9¼"
3. Kathy Devine, Texas Track Club	52' 8¼"

Evelyn Ashford's wind-aided time in the 200 meters was the fastest ever run by an American.

1. Evelyn Ashford, Maccabi Track Club	22.07 w
2. Valerie Brisco, Naturite Track Club	22.53
3. Brenda Morehead, Tennessee State	22.75

Francie Larrieu's finishing kick propelled her past Mary Decker in the final straightaway for the win and a new meet record in the 1,500-meter run.

1. Francie Larrieu, Pacific Coast Club	4:04.6 MR
2. Mary Decker, unattached	4:06.8
3. Julie Brown, Naturite Track Club	4:09.4

Francie set her second meet record of the day by out-kicking Jan Merrill in the last 80 meters of the 3,000-meter run.

1. Francie Larrieu, Pacific Coast Club	8:53.8 MR
2. Jan Merrill, Age Group A.A.	8:54.0
3. Julie Brown, Naturite Track Club	8:58.3

400-meter hurdles
1. Edna Brown, Temple University	57.60
2. Debra Melrose, Prairie View A&M	58.33
3. Debbie Esser, Iowa State	58.68

800-meter run
1. Essie Kelley, Prairie View A&M	2:02.3
2. Julie Brown, Naturite Track Club	2:02.6
3. Madeline Manning, Oral Roberts Track Club	2:02.8

400-meter run
1. Patricia Jackson, Prairie View A&M	52.21
2. Sharon Dabney, Clippers Track Club	52.37
3. Sherri Howard, L.A. Mercurettes	52.54

400-meter relay
1. Tennessee State	43.68 MR
2. L.A. Mercurettes	44.76
3. Naturite Track Club	45.19

800-meter medley relay
1. Prairie View A&M	1:38.2
2. Naturite Track Club	1:38.8
3. Texas Southern	1:39.3

10,000-meter walk
1. Sue Brodock, So. Calif. Road Runners	50:32.8 AR
2. Sue Liers, Island Track Club	51:13.2
3. Chris Sakelarios, So. Calif. Road Runners	51:33.0

5000-meter walk
| 1. Sue Brodock, So. Calif. Road Runners | 24:07.6 |

1600-meter relay
1. Prairie View A & M   3:32.8 MR
2. Tennessee State   3:33.4
3. N.Y. Police Athletic League   3:38.7

Discus throw
1. Lynne Winbigler, Oregon Track Club   189' 5"
2. Lorna Griffin, Sportswest   185' 7"
3. Ria Stalman, Sportswest   181' 10"

Long jump
1. Kathy McMillan, Tennessee State   21' 3½"
2. Jane Frederick, Pacific Coast Club   21' 1½"
3. Pat Johnson, Wisconsin-United   20' 10"

Javelin throw
1. Kate Schmidt, Pacific Coast Club   206' 1"
2. Cathy Sulinski, Millbrae Lions   179' 3"
3. Lynn Cannon, Millbrae Lions   173' 4"

High jump
1. Debbie Brill, Pacific Coast Club   6' 4" MR
2. Louise Ritter, Texas Woman's University   6' 2½"
3. Pam Spencer, Naturite Track Club   6'

The Indoor Nationals

The indoor nationals were held on February 23 in Madison Square Garden. Neil Amdur's article in the *New York Times* on February 24 said:

> A star was born in Madison Square Garden last night. Her name is Canzetta Young, but Candy will do just fine; she is 16 years old and lives in Beaver Falls, Pa., and set a world indoor record in the women's 60 yard high hurdles.
> Gertie Young, mother of eight daughters and one son, was among the 13,087 spectators who watched daughter #4 run 7.50 seconds ... to outlean Mrs. Deby LaPlante, the defending champion.

For the first time, a mile was walked in under seven minutes. Chris Shea did it and set a new American record of 6:58.9.

Chandra Cheeseborough and Evelyn Ashford joined the record club. "Cheese" set a new world record for automatic timing in the 220-yard dash, and Evelyn ran 6.71 in the 60-yard dash to edge out Brenda Morehead for the win and the world record.

One-mile walk
1. Chris Shea, Georgetown University   6:58.9 AR
2. Susan Brodock, So. Calif. Road Runners   7:12.1
3. Christine Sakelarios, So. Calif. Road Runners   7:21.7

Long jump
1. Kathy McMillan, Tennessee State   21' 3"

2. Jodi Anderson, Naturite Track Club   21' 2¾"
3. Martha Watson, Club International   20' ¼"

Shot put
1. Trixi Philipp, West Germany   56' 11"
2. Maren Seidler, San Jose Stars   56' 9"
3. Marcia Mecklenburg, Sportswest   52' 1"

High jump
1. Louise Ritter, Texas Woman's University   6' 1"
2. Paula Girven, Univ. of Maryland   6'
3. Pam Spencer, Naturite Track Club   5' 11"

60-yard hurdles
1. Candy Young, Beaver Falls, Pa.   7.50 WR
2. Deby LaPlante, San Diego State   7.53
3. Rhonda Brady, Tennessee State   7.72

60-yard dash
1. Evelyn Ashford, Maccabi Union   6.71 WR
2. Brenda Morehead, Tennessee State   6.72
3. Leleith Hodges, Texas Woman's University   6.78

Two-mile run
1. Julie Brown, Naturite Track Club   9:46.1 MR
2. Jan Merrill, Age Group A.A.   9:46.1
3. Cindy Bremser, unattached, Wisconsin   9:49.0

440-yard run
1. June Griffith, Adelphi University   54.0
2. Yolanda Rich, So. Calif. Cheetahs   54.8
3. Sherri Howard, L.A. Mercurettes   55.0

One-mile run
1. Francie Larrieu, unattached, L. A.   4:39.2
2. Jan Merrill, Age Group A.A.   4:39.6
3. Debbie Heald, Golden Bear Track Club   4:41.2

220-yard dash
1. Chandra Cheeseborough, Tennessee State   23.93 AR
2. Gwen Gardner, L.A. Mercurettes   24.06
3. Rosalyn Bryant, Muhammad Ali Track Club   24.21

880-yard run
1. Wendy Knudson, Athletes International   2:07.3
2. Karel Jones, Atoms Track Club   2:08.6
3. Joetta Clark, unattached   2:08.7

640-yard relay
1. Tennessee State   1:10.6
    (Brady, McMillan, Jones, Cheeseborough)
2. L.A. Mercurettes   1:11.4
3. Naturite Track Club   1:12.7

880-yard medley relay
1. Tennessee State   1:44.5
    (Blake, Jones, McMillan, Morehead)
2. Flashette Track Club   1:45.8
3. Grambling State   1:47.4

One-mile relay
1. Prairie View A & M   3:43.0 WR
    (Melrose, Jackson, Dudley, Kelley)
2. Atoms Track Club   3:43.4
3. Tennessee State   3:44.0

Team scores:
Tennessee State 26; Naturite Track Club 13; Los Angeles Mercurettes 8; Texas Woman's University 8; Atoms Track Club 8.

The U.S. team competed against the Soviet team indoors in the seventh indoor dual meet on March 3 in Fort Worth, Texas. Chandra Cheeseborough finished second in the 60 yards, setting a new American record of 6.68.

The following Pan American team competed in San Juan, Puerto Rico, from July 1 to July 15:

	Event	*Place*	*Performance*
Anderson, Jodi	Pentathlon	2	4434
Winbigler-Anderson, Lynne	Discus	6	169' 6"
Ashford, Evelyn	100m	1	11.07
	200m	1	22.24
	400mr	1	43.30
Brisco, Valerie	200m	4	22.84
	400mr	1	43.30
Brown, Julie	800m	2	2:01.20
	1500m	2	4:06.40
	3000m	2	8:59.90
Bryant, Rosalyn	1600mr	1	3:29.40
Cannon, Lynn	Javelin	2	185' 3"
Cheeseborough, Chandra	400mr	1	43.30
Dabney, Sharon	400m	1	51.81
	1600mr	1	3:29.40
Decker, Mary	1500m	1	4:05.7
Frederick, Jane	Pentathlon	DNC	
	LJ	5	20' ¼"
Griffin, Lorna	Discus	4	177' 5"
Hawkins, Karen	400mr	1	43.30
Jackson, Pat	400m	3	52.32
Kelley, Essie	800m	1	2:00.35
	1600mr	1	3:29.40
LaPlante, Deby	100mh	2	13.68
McMillan, Kathy	LJ	1	21' 2¼"
Merrill, Jan	3000m	1	8:53.06

Morehead, Brenda	100m	2	11.11
	400mr	1	43.30
Ritter, Louise	HJ	1	6' 4"
Seidler, Maren	SP	2	60' 11¼"
Spencer, Pamela	HJ	2	6' 1¾"
Sulinski, Cathy	JT	3	185' 2"
Turbyne, Ann	SP	4	53' 11½"
Young, Candy	100mh	4	13.67

The results of the second Olympic Sports Festival held from July 27 to August 1 at Colorado Springs, Colorado, follow:

100m	Brenda Morehead, Toledo, Ohio	11.40
200m	Liz Young, Washington, D.C.	23.6
400m	Sherri Howard, Los Angeles, Calif.	51.09
800m	Joetta Clark, Maplewood, N.J.	2:05.43
1500m	Darlene Beckford, Massachusetts	4:27.34
3000m	Cindy Bremser, Madison, Wisconsin	9:41.3
100mh	Stephanie Hightower, Columbus, Ohio	13.43
High jump	Paula Girvin, Dale City, Virginia	6' 1"
Javelin	Lynn Cannon, Chico, California	182' 1"
Shot put	Jill Stenwall, Winside, Nebraska	51' 1½"
Discus	Julie Hansen, Seattle, Washington	158' 7"
Long jump	Jodi Anderson, Van Nuys, California	22' 7¼"
Pentathlon	Linda Waltman, College Station, Tex.	3865 pts.
400m relay	South team	43.80
1600m relay	West team	3:30.79
Team	West	

On August 25-26, the World Cup championships took place in Montreal, Canada. Evelyn Ashford won the 100 and 200 meter runs. Her time in the 100 meters was 11.06, and her time in the 200 was 21.83. The United States women were fourth in the point scoring.

The national junior men's and women's championships were held in Bloomington, Indiana, on June 22-24.

The junior and senior pentathlon championships were held at UCLA on June 10. The pentathlon became a one-day event.

The 1979 inductee into the National Track and Field Hall of Fame was Edith McGuire Duvall.

The 10th Annual Dartmouth Relays were held at Dartmouth College, Hanover, New Hampshire, on January 13-14. This was the first time that a woman shared the cover of the program. Jan Merrill was the woman.

Sports Illustrated published *Running for Women* this year. Information gleaned from the publication included a first of its kind training camp held at Squaw Valley for twenty-five of the top female distance runners in the country. The United States Olympic Committee organized and financed the camp in 1977.

Irene Spieker again broke her indoor world record in the pole vault with a jump of 10' ¼" in the Mason-Dixon Games.

The C.C. Jackson Awards were presented to Evelyn Ashford, track, and Maren Seidler, field. Eileen Goodnight was awarded the Joseph Robichaux Award, and the Mobil Cup was presented to Evelyn Ashford. Doris Brown Heritage won the third annual Woman of the Year Award.

Lyle Knudson

Lyle was the head women's coach of the Pan American team in 1979. In an interview in December 1991, he told me about his history as a coach:

> In nineteen sixty-eight, the Colorado Gold track club was formed. Jane Frederick, Wendy Koenig, and Alice Pfaff were our first international team members in nineteen seventy-two, and then Jane and Wendy made the Olympic team that summer. Things really happened very quickly as far as the success of the team was concerned.
>
> I'd never heard of Jane Frederick when she showed up at a track meet one day. She told some of the girls on the team that she was interested in participating on our team.
>
> In nineteen seventy-two we called the team the University of Colorado track club even though there was no formal "official" team at the school. I had to pay the entry fee into the AIAW championships. Our total budget was zero. When we went to the national meet in nineteen seventy-three, I paid all of the transportation, housing, bought uniforms, everything out of my own pocket.
>
> In nineteen seventy-five, I got paid seven hundred dollars for coaching, and our budget was three thousand dollars. We had a formal athletic program, but there were no scholarships.
>
> During the twenty-four years I've coached, I've had thirty-seven athletes make international teams and five Olympians. I have been a coach on ten U.S. teams.

Among many other contributions to the sport, Lyle chaired the United States Women's Track Coaches' Association from 1972 to 1980 and the Women's Multiple Event Committee from 1974 to 1980.

Chapter 63

1980: The Olympic Year That Wasn't

The 1980 Olympic team that suffered as a result of the boycott was selected at the Olympic trials at Eugene, Oregon, from June 21 to June 29.

	Olympic Event	*Olympic Place*	*Olympic Performance*
Anderson, Jodi	LJ		
	Pentathlon		
	400mr		
Anderson-Winbigler, Lynne	Discus		
Belle, Roberta	1600mr		
Bolden, Jeanette	400mr		
Brown, Alice	100m		
	400mr		
Brown, Julie	800m		
	1500m		
Campbell, Robin	800m		
Cheeseborough, Chandra	100m		
	200m		
	400mr		
Dabney, Sharon	1600mr		
Decker-Slaney, Mary	1500m		
Fitzgerald, Benita	100mh		
Gardner, Gwen	400m		
	1600mr		
Girvin-Pittman, Paula	HJ		
Greene, Pam	200m		
Griffin, Lorna	SP		
	Discus		
Harmon, Marlene	Pentathlon		
Hawkins, Karen	200m		
Hightower-Leftwich, Stephanie	100mh		
Howard, Denean	400m		
	1600mr		

Howard, Sherri	400m
	1600mr
King, Marilyn	Pentathlon
Larrieu, Francie	1500m
Lewis, Carol	LJ
Manning, Madeline	800m
McMillan, Kathy	LJ
Morehead, Brenda	100m
	400mr
Osborne, Mary	Javelin
Ritter, Louise	HJ
Schmidt, Kathy	Javelin
Seidler, Maren	SP
Smith, Karin	Javelin
Sokolitz, Karen	200m
Spencer, Pamela	HJ
Thomas, Kim	1600mr
Turbyne, Ann	SP
Waltman, Linda	Pentathlon
Williams, Diane	400mr
Young, Candy	100mh

The Olympic Trials

The United States Olympic trials were held from June 21 to June 29 at Haywood Field at the University of Oregon, Eugene, Oregon.

The *New York Times* reported on June 22: "The first three finishers in each event make the United States Olympic team. Even though the United States is boycotting the Moscow Olympics because of Soviet intervention in Afghanistan, Olympic teams are being selected in all Olympic sports. The track team will compete in at least six European meets in July and August."

More than 13,000 enthusiastic spectators daily watched the nine-day spectacle under fair skies in 70-degree temperatures.

Intense competition ensued in the pentathlon between Jane Frederick, twenty-eight, and Jodi Anderson, twenty-two. After three events, which Anderson had personal "bests" in, Jane Frederick was ahead 2,781 points to Anderson's 2,756. However, because of a strained left hamstring muscle, five-time national pentathlon champion Jane Frederick was forced to drop out of the competition prior to the long jump. With two events left, Anderson jumped 21' 8½" and ran the 800 meters in a 2:11.42 to win the event. Linda Waltman ran 2:09.30 in the 800 meters for a pentathlon 800-meter world record and made the team. Marilyn King placed second and became the first pentathlete to make three Olympic teams.

1. Jodi Anderson, Naturite Track Club	4,697
(13.5, 2:11.42, 5' 10½", 21' 8¼", 44')	
2. Marilyn King, Millbrae Lions	4,199
(14.2, 2:23.73, 5' 7", 19' 6¼", 42' 11¼")	
3. Linda Waltman, Texas Track Club	4,191
(14.5, 2:09.30, 5' 7", 18' 8¾", 36' 11¾")	
4. Marlene Harmon, Cal. H.S.	4,189
(14.0, 2:12.29, 5' 7", 20' 2¼", 31' 2¾")	

Shot put
1. Maren Seidler, San Jose Stars	58' 9½"
2. Ann Turbyne, Gilly's Gym	56' 8"
3. Lorna Griffin, ACA	52' 1½"
4. Sandy Burke, Northeastern University	51' 7"

100 meters
1. Alice Brown, Naturite Track Club	11.32
2. Brenda Morehead, Tennessee State	11.43
3. Chandra Cheeseborough, Tennessee State	11.45
4. Jodi Anderson, Naturite Track Club	11.52
5. Diane Williams, Michigan State	11.61
6. Jeanette Bolden, Naturite Track Club,	11.65
and Michele Glover, Willingboro Track Club	

On a cool and rainy day, thirty-two-year-old Madeline Manning won the 800-meter run in 1:58.30, the second fastest time by an American. The fastest time was her 1:57.90 in 1976. Madeline led the race from the start and hit the tape eighteen meters ahead of the second-place Julie Brown.

1. Madeline Manning, Oral Roberts Track Club	1:58.30 MR
2. Julie Brown, Naturite Track Club	2:00.96
3. Robin Campbell, Stanford Track Club	2:01.23
4. Delisa Walton, Knoxville Track Club	2:01.93

Javelin
1. Karin Smith, Am. Council on Athletics	208' 5"
2. Kate Schmidt, Pacific Coast Club	207' 4"
3. Mary Osborne, Stanford Track Club	181' 3"
4. Jeanne Eggart, Sportswest	169' 11"

100-meter hurdles
1. Stephanie Hightower, Ohio State	12.90
2. Benita Fitzgerald, Univ. of Tennessee	13.11
3. Candy Young, Ryan's Angels	13.30
4. Lori Dinello, Shore A.C.	13.52

400-meter dash
1. Sherri Howard, Ali Track Club	51.48
2. Gwen Gardner, L.A. Mercurettes	51.68
3. Denean Howard, Ali Track Club	51.70
4. Sharon Dabney, Clippers Track Club	52.00

200-meter dash
1. Chandra Cheeseborough, Tennessee State   22.70w
2. Karen Hawkins, Texas Southern   23.04
3. Pam Greene, Boulder, Colo.   23.21
4. Florence Griffith, Naturite Track Club   23.25

10,000-meter run (not an Olympic event)
1. Kristin Bankes, Reading Athletic Attic   33:45.6
2. Judi St. Hilaire, Liberty A.C.   33:45.7
3. Ellen Hart, Liberty A.C.   33:47.4
4. Anne Sullivan, Brown University   34:01.4

Long jump
1. Jodi Anderson, Naturite Track Club   22' 11¾" AR
2. Kathy McMillan, Tennessee State   22' 2¼"
3. Carol Lewis, Willingboro Track Club   21' 6¼" w
4. Lorraine Ray, unattached   20' 11½" w

Mary Decker finished first in the 1500 meters with a 15-meter lead over second-place Julie Brown.

1. Mary Decker, Athletics West   4:04.91
2. Julie Brown, Naturite Track Club   4:07.13
3. Leann Warren, Oregon   4:15.16
4. Francie Larrieu, Pacific Coast Club   4:15.32

3000-meter run (not an Olympic event)
1. Julie Shea, North Carolina State   15:44.12
2. Mary Shea, North Carolina State   16:07.50
3. Rocky Racette, Minnesota   16:12.28
4. Carol Urish, Houston A.C.   16:13.28

400-meter hurdles
1. Esther Mahr, KCBQ Track Club   56.56
2. Kim Whitehead, Iowa State   57.46
3. Debra Melrose, Prairie View   59.13
4. Tammy Etienne, Univ. of Texas   59.71

Discus throw
1. Lorna Griffin, Am. Council on Athletics   197' 6"
2. Lynne Anderson, Oregon Track Club   184' 11"
3. Lisa Vogelsang, Am. Council on Athletics   176' 0"
4. Denise Wood, unattached   175' 8"

High jump
1. Louise Ritter, Pacific Coast Club   6' 1¼"
2. Paula Girven, University of Maryland   6' 1¼"
3. Pam Spencer, Naturite Track Club   6'
4. Kari Gosswiller, CS North   6'

On June 30, the *New York Times* reported: "The team includes two sisters (18 year old Sherri and 15 year old Denean Howard), a sister and brother (19 year old Carl and 16 year old Carol Lewis) and a husband and wife (Colin and Lynne Winbigler Anderson). It has two four time Olympians (Madeline Manning and Maren Seidler) and five others who made their third Olympic team (Randy Williams, John Powell, Al Feuerbach, Kate Schmidt and Marilyn King)."

The Amateur Athletic Union was no longer the custodian of track and field in the United States. Our national championships were now called The Athletic Congress Senior Men's and Women's Track and Field Championships, and the first meet was held June 13-15 at Walnut, California, on the famous Mt. San Antonio College track.

The Outdoor Nationals

There were many surprises, and only three champions successfully defended their titles: Francie Larrieu in the 1500 meters, twenty-nine-year-old Maren Seidler in the shot, and Sue Brodock in the two walks. Brodock was the only double winner. This was Maren's ninth straight national shot put title and her eleventh in fourteen years.

Twenty-six-year-old Kate Schmidt was beaten by Karin Smith in the javelin throw. Kate had won the championship six times in the previous seven years and seven times in eleven years.

Thirty-two-year-old Madeline Manning, the 1968 Olympic 800-meter champion, provided an outstanding performance in her race before a crowd of 6500. She passed the halfway point in 57 seconds. She led the whole race and finished in 1:58.8, the second fastest time by an American, which was her fifth national outdoor title.

100 meters
1. Alice Brown, Naturite Track Club   11.21
2. Brenda Morehead, Tennessee State   11.30
3. Karen Hawkins, Texas Southern   11.40

200 meters
1. Karen Hawkins, Texas Southern   22.80w
2. Brenda Morehead, Tennessee State   22.80w
3. Chandra Cheeseborough, Tennessee State   23.04w

400 meters
1. Sherri Howard, Muhammad Ali Track Club   51.51
2. Sharon Dabney, Clippers Track Club   52.35
3. Gwen Gardner, L.A. Mercurettes   52.35

800-meter run
1. Madeline Manning, Oral Roberts Track Club   1:58.8
2. Robin Campbell, Stanford Track Club   2:01.6
3. Mary Decker, Athletics West   2:02.3

1500 meters
1. Francie Larrieu, Pacific Coast Club   4:12.8

2. Cindy Bremser, Wisconsin-United Track Club   4:13.7
3. Linda Goen, UCLA   4:14.2

3000 meters
1. Julie Brown, Naturite Track Club   9:07.9
2. Julie Shea, North Carolina State   9:11.4
3. Rose Thompson, Univ. of Wisconsin   9:26.1

10,000 meters
1. Judi St. Hilaire, Liberty A.C.   33:31.1
2. Carol Urish, Houston Harriers   33:33.1
3. Betty Springs, North Carolina State   33:34.9

100-meter hurdles
1. Stephanie Hightower, Ohio State   13.14
2. Benita Fitzgerald, Knoxville Track Club   13.23
3. Linda Weekly, Texas Southern   13.59

400-meter hurdles
1. Esther Mahr, KCQB Track Club   56.3
2. Kim Whitehead, Iowa State   57.2
3. Debra Melrose, Prairie View   58.2

400-meter relay
1. Naturite Track Club   43.81
   (Bolden, Anderson, Brown, Griffith)
2. Tennessee State   44.31
3. Berkeley East Bay Track Club   45.84

1600-meter relay
1. Muhammad Ali Track Club   3:34.2
   (Bryant, D. Howard, Rich, S. Howard)
2. D.C. International   3:37.6
3. MS A.C.   3:37.8

800-meter medley relay
1. Muhammad Ali Track Club   1:37.4
   (Lair, Bryant, Pusey, D. Howard)
2. Naturite Track Club   1:39.1
3. N.Y. Police Athletic League   1:40.5

3200-meter relay
1. Naturite Track Club   8:32.3
   (Jacobs, Antoniewicz, Mullins, Brown)
2. Sportswest   8:36.1
3. San Jose Cindergals   8:36.4

High jump
1. Colleen Reinstra, Sun Devil Sports   6' 4"
2. Pam Spencer, Naturite Track Club,   6' 2"
   and Louise Ritter, Texas Woman's University

Long jump
1. Jodi Anderson, Naturite Track Club   21' 9¾"

2. Kathy McMillan, Tennessee State   21' 9" w
3. Shonel Ferguson, D.C. International   21' 2¾"

Shot put
1. Maren Seidler, San Jose Stars   59' 1"
2. Lorna Griffin, American Council on Athletics   53' 10½"
3. Mary Jacobson, Oregon Track Club   50' 11½"

Discus
1. Lorna Griffin, ACA   191' 9"
2. Denise Wood, unattached   179' 11"
3. Lisa Vogelsang, ACA   173' 3"

Javelin
1. Karin Smith, ACA   199' 1"
2. Kate Schmidt, Pacific Coast Club   197' 6"
3. Donna Mayhew, Glendale College   166' 9"

5000-meter walk
1. Sue Brodock, So. Calif. Road Runners   23:19.1 AR
2. Susan Liers-Westerfield, Island Track Club   24:38.7
3. Bonnie Dillon, Cupertino Yearlings   24:40.3

10,000-meter walk
1. Sue Brodock, So. Calif. Road Runners   51:01.0
2. Susan Liers-Westerfield, Island Track Club   52:33.6
3. Esther Lopez, So. Calif. Road Runners   52:40.6

Team scores:
Naturite Track Club 77; Tennessee State 42; Muhammad Ali Track Club 37; ACA 35; Southern California Road Runners 30; Pacific Coast Club 29; Texas Southern 22; Wisconsin-United 20; North Carolina State 19.

More than 50 teams scored.

The Indoor Nationals

The indoor national championship meet was held on February 28 at Madison Square Garden. On March 1, the *New York Times* reported that Evelyn Ashford had capped an unbeaten season by coming from behind to beat Brenda Morehead in the 60-yard dash. Evelyn commented on the Olympic boycott, saying that it had caused her to lose her desire to run fast times.

Rosalyn Bryant's 440-yard win in 53.92 was a new record for automatic timing.

One-mile walk
1. Susan Brodock, So. Calif. Road Runners   7:06.9
2. Susan Liers, Island Track Club   7:11.3
3. Esther Lopez, So. Calif. Road Runners   7:21.8

60-yard hurdles
1. Stephanie Hightower, Ohio State   7.4
2. Candy Young, unattached, Pennsylvania   7.4
3. Sharon Collyer, Boston University   7.6

60-yard dash
1. Evelyn Ashford, American Council on Athletics   6.76
2. Brenda Morehead, Tennessee State   6.76
3. Chandra Cheeseborough, Tennessee State   6.93

Two-mile run
1. Cindy Bremser, Wisconsin-United Track Club   9:45.0 MR
2. Brenda Webb, Knoxville Track Club   9:52.2
3. Margaret Groos, Univ. of Virginia   9:52.3

440-yard run
1. Rosalyn Bryant, Mohammad Ali Track Club   53.92 MR
2. Gwen Gardner, L.A. Mercurettes   54.20
3. Yolanda Rich, Mohammad Ali Track Club   54.50

One-mile run
1. Maggie Keyes, Maccabi Union Track Club   4:39.3
2. Cindy Bremser, Wisconsin-United Track Club   4:42.3
3. Rose Thompson, Univ. of Wisconsin   4:42.6

220-yard dash
1. Wanda Hooker, Memphis State   24.0
2. Deborah Jones, Tennessee State   24.0
3. Merlene Ottey, Univ. of Nebraska   24.1

880-yard run
1. Madeline Manning, Oral Roberts Track Club   2:04.5 MR
2. Robin Campbell, Stanford Track Club   2:04.7
3. Joetta Clark, unattached, New Jersey   2:07.7

640-yard relay
1. D.C. International   1:09.5 AR
   (Jackson, Bernard, McRoy, Allwood)
2. University of Florida   1:10.9
3. Naturite Track Club   1:13.0

880-yard medley relay (440-110-110-220)
1. L.A. Mercurettes   1:45.0
   (Paige, Evans, Washington, Gardner)
2. D.C. International   1:46.1
3. Tennessee State   1:46.9

One-mile relay
1. Muhammad Ali Track Club   3:41.0 AR
   (Rich, D.Howard, S. Howard, Bryant)
2. D.C. International   3:44.3
3. L.A. Mercurettes   3:44.8

Long jump
1. Pat Johnson, Univ. of Wisconsin   20' 11½"

2. Carol Lewis, Willingboro Track Club   20' 10½"
3. Kathy McMillan, Tennessee State   20' 7"

Shot put
1. Maren Seidler, San Jose Stars   57' ¼"
2. Ann Turbyne, Gilly's Gym   53' 5¾"
3. Lorna Griffin, unattached, California   53' 2¼"

High jump
1. Louise Ritter, Texas Woman's University   6' 3"
2. Sharon Burrill, Univ. of Nebraska   6' 3"
3. Paula Girvin, Houston Track Club   6'

Team scores:
Tennessee State 13; Muhammad Ali Track Club 12; D.C. International 11; Los Angeles Mercurettes 11.

The junior men's and women's championships were held on June 16-17 at Knoxville, Tennessee.

The first Pan American junior meet was held in Sudbury, Ontario. Joetta Clark won the 800 meters in 2:05.65, and Jackie Joyner long jumped 20' 3½" to win that event.

The junior and senior pentathlon championships were held on June 8 at the University of California at Santa Barbara.

On February 23, Mary Decker set a world 880 record of 1:59.7 in the San Diego Invitational track meet. Twenty-one-year-old Mary led all the way to break her old mark by more than 2 seconds.

The age-group program became Youth Athletics with a separate sports committee.

On December 6, the *New York Times* obituary page announced: "While buying ribbons for a welcoming ceremony for the Polish Olympic women's basketball team, Stella (Walsh) was shot and killed. Sixty nine year old Stella was in a shopping center parking lot when she was shot in the abdomen at about 8:45 P.M. She died on December 4."

On December 10, the *New York Times* headlines read, "Slain Athlete's Sex Questioned." The article continued:

> In reports broadcast yesterday, two Cleveland television stations, WEWS and WKYC, said they had been informed that the Cuyahoga County coroner's office was trying to determine the sex of Miss Walsh....
>
> County Coroner Samuel R. Gerber would not discuss with The Associated Press the issue of whether Miss Walsh was genetically male or female....
>
> The coroner's office was bringing in other people to talk about gender determination.

The *Plain Dealer*, a Cleveland newspaper, on December 16 featured an article by W. C. Miller entitled "Angry Stella Walsh friends push suit to clear her." The article said, "WKYC's report, telecast the night before Walsh's funeral, said an autopsy would show that Walsh had male sex organs." The following night,

WKYC ran an interview with one of Walsh's friends, who said Walsh had both male and female organs. "A chromosome test was done with results not expected for several weeks." On January 22, 1981, the Cayahoga County coroner's office issued a statement that Walsh had male sex organs.

The 1980 inductee into the National Track and Field Hall of Fame was Wyomia Tyus.

A *NAGWS Guide in Track and Field* was published for 1980-81.

The Sudafed International Women's Sports Hall of Fame was founded this year. Mildred "Babe" Didrikson Zaharias was one of the first six inductees in the "Pioneer" category. Wilma Rudolph was one of three inductees in the "contemporary" category, and Dr. Nell Jackson was one of two in the "coach" category.

The third annual C. C. Jackson Awards were presented to Mary Decker, track, and Karin Smith, field. The ninth annual Joseph Robichaux Award was presented to Dr. Nell Jackson, and the 1980 Mobil Cup Awards went to Cindy Bremser and Madeline Manning Mims. Dr. Joan Ullyot won the Woman of the Year Award. Dr. Evie Dennis, Dr. Nell Jackson, Dr. Harmon Brown, Dr. Bert Lyle, and Heliodoro Rico were awarded President's Awards established for the first time this year to honor those individuals "whose dedication and support have been an inspiration to the members of this Congress, and whose leadership has played so vital a role in the fruition of our purposes and programs."

American Records

100	10.97	Evelyn Ashford	1979
200	21.83	Evelyn Ashford	1979
400	50.62	Rosalyn Bryant	1976
800	1:57.9	Madeline Manning	1976
1500	3:59.43	Mary Decker	1980
Mile	4:21.7	Mary Decker	1980
2 Mile	9:49.6	Jan Merrill	1978
3000	8:42.6	Jan Merrill	1978
5000	15:33.8	Jan Merrill	1979
10000	32:52.5	Mary Shea	1979
100mh	12.86	Deby LaPlante	1979
400mh	56.61	Mary Ayers	1977
HJ	6' 4¾"	Louise Ritter	1980
LJ	22' 11½"	Jodi Anderson	1980
SP	62' 7¾"	Maren Seidler	1979
DT	207' 5"	Lorna Griffin	1980
JT	227' 5"	Kate Schmidt	1977
Pent.	4708	Jane Frederick	1979
Marathon	2:35:15	Joan Benoit	1979
400mr	42.87	USA	1968
800mr	1:32.6	USA	1979
1600mr	3:22.8	USA	1976
3200mr	8:19.9	USA	1979

Louise Ritter

In an interview on October 2, 1995, Louise Ritter told me about her athletic history:

> I started track briefly when I was in the fourth grade and I entered a track and field play day. Then in nineteen seventy-two, right before my freshman year in high school, I started in a summer track program in Red Oaks, Texas. An ex-track star from the University of Texas started a little track program in our hometown. That's how it all began.
>
> I immediately became successful as a high jumper. In high school I won the state championships. I gravitated toward the field events, and I also won the state meet in the long jump and triple jump. I continued winning all of the high school meets and received a scholarship to Texas Woman's University.
>
> At TWU I began specializing in the high jump and looking towards a future of becoming an Olympic champion. I started dreaming about that when I was seventeen.
>
> The first Olympic team that I made was in nineteen eighty, the boycotted Games. The biggest thing that I learned at that point was that no matter how much you work and how much you think you're in an individual sport, and you do it for yourself, you find out that somebody always has control over what's happening to you. In that instance, I felt like I had put in the time and the work and had done everything I needed to do and was one of the favorites, and I had no control. I think that was the first time in my life I realized that it doesn't matter what you do, someone else always has more control over it than you do.
>
> I won the high jump in the Olympic trials, and I was in the top five in the world in nineteen eighty. In the Olympic Games, I would have been one of the top six, and I like to think that I would have been in the top three.
>
> Nothing replaced the Games that summer. We went to the White House, and that was supposed to be our consolation prize. We were the only ones sacrificed in the whole thing. We got the brunt of it all.
>
> Fortunately for me, I was a very young athlete at the time. I was twenty-one, but there were a lot of people that weren't as fortunate as I was. The nineteen eighty Games was their one-shot deal, and they never got a chance to do it again. It was such a big disappointment and a total letdown. The entire season was just a wash.
>
> Eight years later, I became the Olympic champion. But I still feel resentment from nineteen eighty because in nineteen eighty-four, I feel that I would have placed a lot higher if I had the experience of the nineteen eighty Games. Instead, I had to pay the price when I was older to get the Olympic experience. The ideal time for me to have jumped well was in nineteen eighty-four, but I walked in there very inexperienced. I hadn't had an Olympics under my belt. It's a very different feeling from an everyday meet. So I had to draw on the experience from nineteen eighty-four to help me win in nineteen eighty-eight.
>
> When you only have a four-year plan, and you're waiting for four years to do something and they pull the rug out from under you, it takes eight years to do something that you wanted to do in four. It kind of throws a monkey wrench into the rest of your career. I had to learn in nineteen eighty-four what I should have learned in nineteen eighty.
>
> In nineteen eighty-eight, the last twenty minutes of the competition was pretty interesting. I felt a complete sense of relief when I wasn't going to be eighth place. I had gotten eighth in nineteen eighty-four and eighth in the world championships. When I counted and found that there were only seven competitors

left, the curse was off. I felt like there was nothing to stop me now. I had some pretty bad luck in the last two big meets with eighth, so once I passed that I really relaxed a little and got into the competition. It was a moral victory. Then when I was in the top three and knew I was going to be a medalist, another sense of relief came through because any time you're in the top three you can look at yourself and say, O.K., I finally accomplished as an athlete and a person what I can do. So then I said, let's just win it all. It was almost like three competitions in one. It was that vivid in my mind, each time I hit a different barrier. I could feel the difference of a weight being lifted off my shoulder. So in reality, as the bar got higher and fewer people remained, it became easier for me to compete.

When it came down to the two of us, we both cleared six feet seven inches on our first attempts and then went to the next height at six feet eight inches and both missed all three times. We had the same exact jumps across the board, so we were tied. We jumped again at the last height and she missed and I cleared it on my fourth attempt.

We [Dr. Bert Lyle and I] both felt completely prepared for this competition and were as good as we could be. He and I had spent twelve years in a coach-athlete relationship. I can't say enough about how much he meant to my career and where I went. So to me it wasn't like I won. It was, we won.

Halls of Fame

Black Sports Hall of Fame Enshrinees

Cleveland Abbott	Wilma Rudolph
Alice Coachman	Willye White

Helm's Hall of Fame Enshrinees

1955	Mae Faggs	1960	Wilma Rudolph

National Track and Field Hall of Fame Enshrinees

1974-1980	
1974	Mildred Didrikson (Zaharias)
	Wilma Rudolph
1975	Alice Coachman (Davis)
	Helen Stephens
	Stella Walsh
1976	Mae Faggs (Starr)
	Dee Boeckmann
1977	Elizabeth Robinson (Schwartz)
1979	Edith McGuire (DuVall)
1980	Wyomia Tyus (Simberg)

The National Track and Field Hall of Fame Historical Research Library

The National Track and Field Hall of Fame was founded in 1974 in Charleston, West Virginia. It housed a small historical research library. When the Hall moved to Indianapolis in 1983, a new home was sought for the research collection. In May of 1986 an agreement was reached with the Irwin Library, But-

649

ler University, to house and maintain the track and field materials as a special collections within the Department of Rare Books and Special Collections.

Gisela Schlüter Terrell, Rare Books and Special Collections librarian, began the collection in 1986 with some 250 books and old meet programs donated by Dr. J. Kenneth Doherty. By 1991, the collection contained more than 25,000 books, periodicals, meet programs, photographs, research papers, films, archives, and other materials. It is the largest collection in the nation specializing in track and field information.

The annual Ken Doherty Fellowship was established by the library committee to encourage and promote the publishing of research in track and field. A special thank-you is extended to Gisela Schlüter Terrell and her committee for giving me, the second recipient of the fellowship, the opportunity to spend time in 1992 at Butler University collecting treasured historical data which was the basis for this book.

Sudafed International Women's Sports Hall of Fame Enshrinees

	Pioneer	*Contemporary*	*Coach*
1980	Mildred Didrikson	Wilma Rudolph	Dr. Nell Jackson
1981		Wyomia Tyus	

Awards

C. C. Jackson Awards

	Track	Field
1978	Jan Merrill	Jodi Anderson
1979	Evelyn Ashford	Maren Seidler
1980	Mary Decker	Karin Smith

The Dieges Awards

1966	Edith McGuire
1967	Madeline Manning
1968	Eleanor Montgomery

Gwilym Brown Awards

1978	Irene Obera
1979	JoAnn Terry Grissom
1980	Judy Fox

Mobil Cup Awards

1973	Mable Fergerson
1975	Madeline Manning Jackson
1976	Jan Merrill
1977	Francie Larrieu
	Evelyn Ashford
1978	Deby LaPlante
	Jodi Anderson
1979	Evelyn Ashford

1980	Cindy Bremser
	Madeline Manning Mims

North American Athletes of the Year

1967	Madeline Manning	1973	Kate Schmidt
1968	Wyomia Tyus	1975	Joni Huntley
1969	Madeline Manning	1976	Kathy McMillan
1970	Iris Davis	1977	Kate Schmidt
1972	Kathy Hammond	1979	Evelyn Ashford

Saettel Awards

1965	Wyomia Tyus	1971	Iris Davis
1968	Madeline Manning	1973	Martha Watson
1969	Eleanor Montgomery		

Joseph Robichaux Awards

1972	Edward Temple	1977	Dr. Harmon Brown
1973	C. C. Jackson	1978	Dr. Ken Foreman
1974	Juner Bellew	1979	Eileen Goodnight
1975	Conrad Ford	1980	Dr. Nell Jackson
1976	Roxanne Andersen		

Sullivan Awards

1960	Wilma Rudolph

President's Awards

1980	Dr. Evie Dennis
	Dr. Nell Jackson
	Dr. Bert Lyle
	Heliodoro Rico
	Dr. Harmon Brown

Team Championship Awards

1974	Atoms Track Club
1975	Sports International Track Club

1976	Atoms Track Club
1977	Los Angeles Mercurettes
1978	Tennessee State University
1979	Los Angeles Naturite Track Club
1980	Los Angeles Naturite Track Club

Vitalis Awards of Excellence

1970	Gail Fitzgerald	1976	Robin Campbell
1971	Cheryl Toussaint	1977	Jeanette Bolden
1972	Cheryl Toussaint	1978	Francie Larrieu
1973	Cheryl Toussaint	1979	Jan Merrill
1974	Francie Larrieu	1980	Evelyn Ashford
1975	Francie Larrieu		

Women's Long Distance Running Awards

1977	Miki Gorman	1979	Doris Brown Heritage
1978	Nina Kuscsik	1980	Dr. Joan Ullyot

Olympic Gold Medalists, 1928–1980

1928

Elizabeth Robinson	100 meters

1932

Mildred Didrikson	100-meter hurdles
	Javelin
Lillian Copeland	Discus throw
Jean Shiley	High jump
Mary Carew	400-meter relay
Evelyn Furtsch	400-meter relay
Annette Rogers	400-meter relay
Wilhelmina Von Bremen	400-meter relay

1936

Helen Stephens	100-meters
	400-meter relay
Elizabeth Robinson	400-meter relay
Harriet Bland	400-meter relay
Annette Rogers	400-meter relay

1948

Alice Coachman	High jump

1952

Mae Faggs	400-meter relay
Barbara Jones	400-meter relay
Janet Moreau	400-meter relay
Catherine Hardy	400-meter relay

1956

Mildred McDaniel	High jump

1960

Wilma Rudolph	100 meters
	200 meters
	400-meter relay
Martha Hudson	400-meter relay
Lucinda Williams	400-meter relay
Barbara Jones	400-meter relay

1964

| Wyomia Tyus | 100 meters |
| Edith McGuire | 200 meters |

1968

Wyomia Tyus	100 meters
	400-meter relay
Madeline Manning	800 meters
Barbara Ferrell	400-meter relay
Margaret Bailes	400-meter relay
Mildrette Netter	400-meter relay

1972

None

1976

None

1980

No participation

Two Olympic Gold Medals

Elizabeth Robinson
Mildred Didrikson
Helen Stephens
Annette Rogers
Barbara Jones

Three Olympic Gold Medals

Wilma Rudolph
Wyomia Tyus

Marathon Winners

Boston Marathon

1966	Roberta Gibb	(unofficial)	3:21:40
1967	Roberta Gibb	(unofficial)	3:27:17
1968	Roberta Gibb	(unofficial)	3:30:00
1969	Sara Mae Berman	(unofficial)	3:22:46
1970	Sara Mae Berman	(unofficial)	3:05:07
1971	Sara Mae Berman	(unofficial)	3:08:30
1972	Nina Kuscsik		3:10:26
1973	Jacqueline Hansen		3:50:59
1974	Miki Gorman		2:47:11
1975	Liane Winter (Germany)		2:42:24
1976	Kim Merritt		2:47:10
1977	Miki Gorman		2:48:33
1978	Gayle Barron		2:44:52
1979	Joan Benoit		2:35:15
1980	Jacqueline Gareau (Montreal)		2:34:28

L'eggs Mini Marathon

Year	*Entries*	*Time*	*Winner*
1972*	78	37:01.7	Jacqueline Dixon
1973*	103	36:48.7	Katherine Schrader
1974*	157	35:45.6	Doreen Ennis
1975	304	35:56.6	Charlotte Lettis
1976	492	35:04.8	Julie Shea
1977	2277	34:15.3	Peg Neppel
1978	4346	33:29.7	Martha White
1979	5807	31:15.4	Grete Waitz (Norway)
1980	5417	30:59.8**	Grete Waitz (Norway)

* race was six miles
** world road-racing record

New York Marathon

1970	No woman finisher	
1971	Beth Bonner	2:55:22
1972	Nina Kuscsik	3:08:42
1973	Nina Kuscsik	2:57:08
1974	Katherine Switzer	3:07:29
1975	Kim Merritt	2:46:15
1976	Miki Gorman	2:39:11
1977	Miki Gorman	2:43:10
1978	Grete Waitz (Norway)	2:32:30
1979	Grete Waitz (Norway)	2:27:33
1980	Grete Waitz (Norway)	2:25:41

Chronologies of Women's Events

Millrose Games

60-yard dash (50 yards before 1961; 60 yards 1961 on)

1923	Marion McCartie	6.7
1924	Rosa Grosse	6.6
1925	Frances Ruppert	6.6
1926	Rosa Grosse	6.2
1927	Rosa Grosse	6.4
1928	Myrtle Cook	6.4
1929	Myrtle Cook	6.4
1930	Stella Walsh	6.0 WR
1931	Stella Walsh	6.2
1932	Mary Carew	6.2
1961	Wilma Rudolph	6.9 WR
1963	Jutta Heine	6.9
1965	Wyomia Tyus	6.9
1969	Carmen Smith	7.1
1971	Iris Davis	6.8
1972	Matteline Render	7.0
1973	Matteline Render	6.9
1974	Matteline Render	7.0
1975	Alice Annum	6.7
1976	Alice Annum	6.7
1977	Freida Davy	6.7
1978	Andrea Lynch	6.8
1979	Brenda Morehead	6.78
1980	Brenda Morehead	6.87

High jump

1930	Jean Shiley	5' 2¾"
1976	Joni Huntley	6' 2¼"
1977	Paula Girvin	5' 10"
1978	Joni Huntley	6' 3"

| 1979 | Debbie Brill | 6' 1" |
| 1980 | Joni Huntley | 6' 4¾" AR |

Women's 440 (except where noted)

1963	Maria Jeilbmann	59.8
1965	Judith Amoore	55.6 WR
1972	Cheryl Toussaint	56.6
1973	Cherly Toussaint	1:21.1 (600 yards)
1974	Brenda Nichols	1:24.0 (600 yards)
1975	Robin Campbell	
	Pat Helms	1:27.7 (600 yards)
1976	Sharon Dabney	1:23.8 (600 yards)
1977	Rosalyn Bryant	53.5 WR
1978	Lorna Forde	54.7
1979	June Griffith	54.04 WR
1980	June Griffith	
	Gwen Gardner	53.31 (11-lap indoor record)

880-yard run (except where noted)

1966	Roberta Picco	2:13.0
1967	Francie Kraker	2:11.8
1968	Madeline Manning	2:13.8
1969	Madeline Manning	2:11.9
1970	Cheryl Toussaint	2:13.5
1971	Cheryl Toussaint	2:10.0
1974	Mary Decker	2:17.4 (1000 yards)
1975	Francie Larrieu	2:26.8 (1000 yards)
1976	Kathy Weston	2:10.1
1977	Lorna Forde	2:06.5
1978	Jan Merrill	2:10.1
1979	Jan Merrill	2:08.2
1980	Madeline Manning	2:05.6

60-yard hurdles

1978	Patty Van Wolvelaere	7.7
1979	Deby LaPlante	7.59
1980	Stephanie Hightower	7.47 WR

1500-meter run

1976	Jan Merrill	4:15.2
1977	Francie Larrieu	4:15.8
1978	Jan Merrill	4:19.7
1979	Francie Larrieu	4:15.0
1980	Mary Decker	4:00.8 WR

Mile relay

1975	Sports International	3:47.6
1976	Florida Track Club	3:48.0
1977	Atoms Track Club	3:47.5
1978	Atoms Track Club	3:49.2
1979	Atoms Track Club	3:45.0
1980	Tennessee State	3:41.5 WR

Penn Relays

1962	Women's invitational 100-yard dash
1963	Women's 440-yard relay
1964	Women's 440-yard relay
1965	High school girls' 440-yard relay
1966	High school girls' 440-yard relay Olympic development women's 440-yard relay
1967	High school girls' 440 yard relay Olympic development women's 440-yard relay Women's 100-yard dash Women's 440-yard dash
1968	High school girls' 440-yard relay Olympic development women's 440-yard relay championship Women's 440-yard relay Women's 440-yard dash Women's 100-yard dash
1969	High school girls' 440-yard relay Olympic development women's 440-yard relay championship Women's 440-yard relay Women's 440-yard dash
1970	High school girls' 440-yard relay Olympic development women's 440-yard relay Women's 440-yard relay Women's 440-yard dash
1971	High school girls' 440-yard relay Olympic development women's 440-yard relay Olympic development women's mile relay
1972	High school girls' 440-yard relay 100-yard dash Women's 440-yard relay championship Women's 440-yard relay Women's mile relay
1973	High school girls' 440-yard relay Women's 440-yard relay

Women's 440-yard relay championship
Women's mile relay
Women's 100-yard dash

1974   Philadelphia junior high school 440-yard relay
Women's 440-yard relay championship
Women's 440-yard relay
Women's mile relay
Women's 100-yard dash

1975   Philadelphia JHS 440-yard relay
Parochial schools 440-yard relay
Women's club–college 440-yard relay
Women's club–college mile relay
High school girls' 440-yard relay

1976   PIAA girls' 400-meter relay
Philadelphia JHS 400-meter relay
Parochial girls' 400-meter relay
Women's sprint-medley relay
Women's club–college 1600-meter relay
Women's 1500 meters
Women's 100 meters

1977   PIAA girls' 400-meter relay
Philadelphia JHS 400-meter relay
Philadelphia girls' 400-meter relay
Parochial schools 400-meter relay
Women's 1500-meter run
Women's 100 meters
Women's 400-meter hurdles
Women's high jump
Women's club 400-meter relay
Women's club–college 1600-meter relay
Women's sprint medley relay
H.S. 400-meter relay
Women's college 400-meter relay championship

1978   High school girls

One-mile run	400-meter relay
Two-mile run	1600-meter relay
High jump	3200-meter relay
Long jump	
Shot put	

Junior high school
     400-meter relay (four divisions)

Olympic development
     400-meter relay
     1600-meter relay
     Sprint-medley relay

100 meters
1500 meters
3000 meters
400-meter hurdles

College events
Javelin   400-meter relay
1500 meters   1600-meter relay
3000 meters   3200-meter relay
400-meter hurdles
High jump
Long jump
Shot put
Discus throw

1979   Girls' relays
400-meter relay   Philadelphia JHS
400-meter relay   Philadelphia Middle Schools
400-meter relay   PIAA JHS
400-meter relay   Parochial schools

High school events
400-meter relay
3200-meter relay
One-mile run
Two-mile run
1600-meter relay
Long jump
Shot put
High jump

Women's championships
400-meter relay
3200-meter relay
One-mile run
Two-mile run
High jump
Long jump
Shot put

College women's events
400-meter hurdles
400-meter relay
3200-meter relay
3000-meter run
1500-meter run
1600-meter relay
High jump
Javelin
Discus
Shot put
Long jump

Women's Olympic development events
    1500-meter run
    3000-meter run
    400-meter hurdles
    400-meter relay
    1600-meter relay
    Sprint medley relay
    100-meter hurdles
    100-meter dash
    Marathon

Bibliography

Chapter 1

Ballintine, Harriet Isabel. "Out-of-Door Sports for College Women." *American Physical Education Review*, March 1898: 38–43.
____. "The Value of Athletics to College Girls." *American Physical Education Review*, June 1901: 151–153.
"The Call's Dipsea Race for Girls Proves Athletic Classic." *The San Francisco Call and Post*, April 22, 1918: 14.
"Examinations Given January, 1913 to Play Leaders in Los Angeles, California." *American Physical Education Review*, October 1913: 493–494.
"Fine Athletic Sports." *The Montclair Times.* May 30, 1903.
"First Annual Field Day of the Cambridge Public Schools." *American Physical Education Review*, November 1912: 650–653.
"Games for Scotchmen." *New York Times*, July 6, 1886: 8.
"Girl Makes Pole Vault Record." *New York Times*, May 21, 1915: 10.
"Girls in Athletic Meet." *New York Times*, May 30, 1903: 4.
"Girls Learn How to Rest at Wisconsin." *American Physical Education Review*, October 1911: 477.
"Grand Rapids Annual Playground Festival." *American Physical Education Review*, November 1911: 540–542.
Hill, Lucille Eaton, ed. *Athletics and Out-Door Sports for Women.* New York: The MacMillan Company, 1903.
Kindervater, A.E. "Our First Public School Field Day." *American Physical Education Review*, October 1910: 538–547.
"New York Girl Athlete." *New York Times*, June 14, 1910: 15.
"Preble County, Ohio, Play Day Festival." *American Physical Education Review*, May 1915: 331–333.
"The Pretty Pedestrians." *The National Police Gazette*, April 12, 1879: 11.
Redmond, Gerald. *The Caledonian Games in Nineteenth-Century America.* Teaneck, N.J.: Fairleigh Dickinson University Press, 1971.
"Report of the Committee on Track Athletics." *American Physical Education Review*, February 1911: 120–122.
"Report of the Convention of the Public School Physical Training Society." *American Physical Education Review*, September 1906: 149–186.
Requa, August M. "The Object, Means, Difficulties and Successes in Introducing Physical Education into the Public Schools of the Boroughs of Manhattan and the Bronx, New York City." *American Physical Education Review*, September 1898: 208–211.
Spitz, Barry. *Dipsea: The Greatest Race.* San Anselmo, California: Potrero Meadow, 1993.
Stecher, William A. "Course of Study in Physical Training for Boys' and Girls' High

Schools, Philadelphia, Pennsylvania." *American Physical Education Review*, November 1913: 551–555.

____. "Third Field Day of the Public Schools of Philadelphia, Pennsylvania." *American Physical Education Review*, June 1910: 472–475.

"Strong Gotham Girls." *The National Police Gazette*, January 26, 1895: 7.

Sullivan, James E., ed. *Spalding's Official Athletic Almanac*. New York: American Sports, 1904, 1908, 1909, 1910, 1911, 1912.

"University of Wisconsin News Notes." *American Physical Education Review*, January 1915: 43.

"Vassar Record Beaten." *New York Times*, May 19, 1915: 10.

"Vassar Student's First Field Day." *Mind and Body*, November 1895: 180.

Walder, Barbara. "Walking Mania." *womenSports*, June 1976: 16–17.

"Wisconsin Physical Education Society." *American Physical Education Review*, March 1904: 57.

Chapter 2

"Athletic Girls of Vassar." *New York Tribune*, November 10, 1895: 3.

"Athletics at Vassar." *Poughkeepsie News Telegraph*, November 16, 1895: 7.

Ballintine, Harriet Isabel. "Annual Report of the Department of Physical Training." 1897: 4–8.

____. *The History of Physical Training at Vassar College 1865–1915*. Poughkeepsie, New York: Lansing and Broas, 1915.

____. "Out-of-Door Sports for College Women." *American Physical Education Review*, March 1898: 38–43.

Blossom, May. "Vassar Girls and Their Mettle." *Poughkeepsie News Telegraph*, May 22, 1897: 3.

Bridgman, Anna J. "Annual Report of the Department of Physical Training." 1890–91.

"Field Day at Vassar." *New York Times*, November 10, 1895.

"Field Day — Vassar College." *The Herald*, November 10, 1895.

"Field Sports at Vassar." *New York Tribune*, May 16, 1897: 8.

"First Woman's Field Day." *Poughkeepsie Daily Eagle*, November 11, 1895: 6.

"Ha! Rah! Rah! Vassar." *Poughkeepsie News Telegraph*, May 23, 1896: 6.

Harvard University. *The Harvard University Catalogue 1896–97*. Cambridge: Published by the University, 1896.

____. *Summer School Announcement of Courses of Instruction 1896*. Cambridge: Published by the University, 1896.

"Notes from Various Organizations." *The Vassar Miscellany*, May 1896: 388.

Raymond, C. "Vassar College History." 1896. Handwritten Observations from Special Collections of the Vassar College Libraries.

Tappan, Lillian. "Annual Report of the Department of Physical Training." 1876–77.

Thelberg, Dr. Elizabeth. "Annual Report to the President of Vassar College." 1888.

____. "Annual Report to the President of Vassar College." 1889.

Unidentified newspaper fragment from Special Collections of Vassar College Libraries, November 1895.

"Vassar Athletes in Competition." *The World*, May 1899.

Vassar College. *Letters from Old-Time Vassar*. Poughkeepsie, N.Y.: Vassar College, 1915.

"Vassar College Field Day." *New York Tribune*, May 16, 1899.

Vassar Student Scrapbooks. Laura Beach, Florence Bernd, Elizabeth Bishop, Mary Vida Clark, Ethel Hintov Elsworth, Lillian Bayless Green, Grace Hartley Howe, Alice M. Howland, Sara Elizabeth Hughes, Eleanor Belknap Humphrey, Jean Eleanor James, Bina Seymour (Special Collections of Vassar College Libraries).

"Vassar Students' First Field Day." *Mind and Body*, November 1895: 180.
Vassarion (The Vassar College Yearbook), 1899, 1900, 1901, 1908.

Chapter 3

Ainsworth, Dorothy S. *The History of Physical Education in Colleges for Women*. New York: A. S. Barnes, 1930.
McCabe, Lida Rose. *The American Girl at College*. New York: Dodd, Mead, 1893.
Morgan, Mary C., ed. "Girls and Athletics." *Spalding's Athletic Library*. New York: American Sports, 1917.

Elmira College

Brown, S.W., ed. *The Elmira Iris*, 1903.
Physical Education at Elmira College. Typed paper from Elmira College Library.
Rockwell, Rena, ed. *The Iris*, 1904.
Numerous other untitled typed papers courtesy of the Elmira College Library.

Mount Holyoke College

"Athletic Notes." *The Mount Holyoke*, June 1897: 29.
"Athletics." *Student's Handbook. Mount Holyoke College 1898–99*: 31.
"Department Notes." *The Mount Holyoke*, October 1903: 113.
Howard, Mildred S. *History of Physical Education at Mount Holyoke College 1837–1955*: 2–8.
_____. *Physical Education at Mount Holyoke College 1837–1974*: 5–9.
Llamarada, 1898: 124.
Llamarada, 1905: 130.
McCurdy, Persis Harlow. "The History of Physical Training at Mount Holyoke College." *American Physical Education Review*, March 1909: 138–150.
Mount Holyoke College Field Day Program, May 23, 1925.
Student's Handbook. Mount Holyoke College, 1904: 51–52.
Student's Handbook. Mount Holyoke College, 1906: 57.

Wellesley College

"Field Day." *Boston Evening Record*, May 16, 1899.
"Field Day." *College News*, November 12, 1902: 1.
Field Day Program, 1903.
Hill, Lucille Eaton. "The New Athletics." *College News*, October 29, 1902: 1.
Smith, M. C. "Athletics." *The Wellesley Magazine*, 1900: 144.

Randolph-Macon Woman's College

Cornelius, R. D. *History of Randolph-Macon Woman's College*, 1951.
"Field Day." *The Sun Dial*, May 7, 1920: 1.
"Field Day Program." *The Sun Dial*, April 29, 1915: 1–3.
Helianthus, 1899, 1903, 1912, 1914, 1918, 1925.
"Two Records Broken." *The Sun Dial*, May 7, 1926: 1.

Bryn Mawr College

Fortnightly Philistine, April 28, 1899.
Lantern, 1892, 1907, 1912, 1913, 1915, 1916.
Philadelphia Inquirer, September 22, 1972.
Tipyn-O-Bob. Typed fact sheet.

Barnard College

Barnardiana. Barnard College Alumnae Monthly, November 1935: 8.
Field Day. *Barnard Bulletin*, May 17, 1906: 1.
Field Day Celebration. *Barnard Bulletin*, April 25, 1904: 1.
Field Day Sports. *Barnard Bulletin*, May 8 1905: 1–3.

Northwestern University

"New Record Hung Up by Northwestern Girl." *Daily Northwestern*, March 31, 1915.
Paulison, Walter. "Women in Athletics." *The Tale of the Wildcats*. Evanston, Ill.: Northwestern University Alumni Association, 1951: 158–160.

Mills College

History of the Mills College Athletic Association, 1899–1927.
The Chimes, 1915, 1920, 1922, 1923, 1930.

University of Nebraska

Cornhusker, 1915, 1917.
Lee, Mabel. *75 Years of Professional Preparation in Physical Education for Women at the University of Nebraska, 1898–1973.*

Sweet Briar College

Stohlman, Martha Lou L. *The Story of Sweet Briar College*. Princeton, N.J.: Princeton University Press, 1956.

Skidmore College

"8th Spring Field Day." *Skidmore Athletic Association Program*, June 3, 1922.
"Fall Field Day." Typed fact sheet, November 4, 1922.
Herald, June 26, 1916.
Skidmore School of Arts, first field day program, June 21, 1915.
Unidentified newspaper articles, June 6, 1922; November 7, 1922.

Syracuse University

Onodagan, 1919, 1923, 1924, 1925, 1927, 1928.
Syracuse Daily Orange, May 11, 13, 16, 1914.
"Women's Day Revels Favored by Weather and Big Attendance." *Syracuse Daily Orange*, May 18, 1914: 1, 4.

Oregon State University

"Co-ed Track Stars Training for Meet." *Daily Barometer*, May 8, 1926: 5.
"Girls to Hold Athletic Meet." *O. A. C. Barometer*, December 11, 1917.
"Track." *Beaver*, 1927.
"Track, Archery, Tennis, and Fencing." *O. A. C. Alumnus*, March 1925: 150.

Florida State University

Flastacowo, Yearbook of the Junior and Senior Classes of the Florida State College for Women, 1922.
Florida Flambeau, April 19, 1919; March 6, 1920; March 20, 1920; March 5, 1921; April 2, 1921.

University of Illinois–Urbana

Catalogue, 1923–24.
Women's track and field meet program, May 15, 1923.

University of Chicago

Cap and Gown, University of Chicago Junior Class, 1919, 1920.

Rockford College

Cupola, 1919, 1920, 1927.
Rockford College Catalogue, 1918.

University of Wisconsin–Madison

Badger, 1923.

University of Arizona

Desert, 1923.

University of Kansas

Jayhawker, 1926.
"Telegraphic Meet Is First of Kind to Be Held Here." *University Daily Kansan*, May 20, 1926.

Stanford University

Cashel, Patricia. *History and Function of the Women's Athletic Association at Stanford University*, 1946.
Stanford Quad, 1926, 1928.
Stanford Register, 1893–94; 1915–16; 1916–17; 1918–19; 1920–21; 1921–22; 1922–23; 1926–27.
"Women's Track Meet Should Prove Big Sensation of Athletic World." *Daily Palo Alto*, April 20, 1923: 4.
Zimmerli, Elizabeth. *A History of Physical Education for Women at Stanford University and a Survey of the Department of Physical Education for Women in 1943–44.*

Smith College

"Intercollegiate Marks Broken at Smith Field Day." *Springfield Republican*, May 17, 1928.
Physical Education Bulletin, 1931–32.
Smith Alumnae Quarterly, November 1930.
Smith College News, May 26, 1929.
Smith College Weekly, spring 1917; June 3, 1926; May 1927.
Track meet result sheet, May 26, 1926; May 18, 1927.

Louisiana State University

Gumbo, 1925.

Louisiana Tech University

Lagniappe, 1925, 1927.

Winthrop University

"Cutting the Corners." *Johnsonian*, May 20, 1927: 3.
"Telegraphic Meet." *Charlotte Observer*, May 8, 1927.
Fleming, Rhonda. *History of the Department of Physical Education at Winthrop College 1886–1970*, 1973.
Johnsonian, April 18, 25, May 2, 1925; May 1, 1926.
"State Track Meet Will Be Held Here." *Johnsonian*, February 14, 1925: 1.

Ohio Wesleyan University

Transcript, May 12, 26, June 2, 9, 1926; May 20, 25, June 1, 1927; February 21, 28, April 24, May 29, 1928; May 7, 24, June 7, 18, 1929.
"Women's Track to Start Soon." *Transcript*, April 21, 1926: 5.

Humboldt State College

Forbes, Joseph M. *History of Athletics Humboldt State College 1914–1968*, 1968.

Mississippi State College for Women

American Physical Education Review, October 1929.

Earlham College

Sargasso, 1924, 1925.

Chapter 4

"Athletic Notes." *Mamaroneck Paragraph*, May 16, 1918: 4.
"Athletic Notes." *Mamaroneck Paragraph*, May 15, 1919: 1.
Burrell, Florence C. "Intercollegiate Athletics for Women in Coeducational Institutions." *American Physical Education Review*, January 1917: 17–19.
"Conference of Women's Athletic Association of the Middle West." *American Physical Education Review*, June 1917: 386–387.
"High School's May Festival." *Mamaroneck Paragraph*, June 3, 1920: 1.
"Inter-Year Track Meet." *Mamaroneck Paragraph*, May 20, 1921: 8.
"New Broad Jump Record." *American Physical Education Review*, October 1916: 432.
"Oaksmere Field Day." *Mamaroneck Paragraph*, May 19, 1921: 1.
Stewart, Harry E., M.D. "A Survey of Track Athletics for Women." *American Physical Education Review*, January 1916: 13–21.
_____. "A Survey of Track Athletics for Women." *American Physical Education Review*, February 1916: 98–108.
_____. "Track Athletics for Women." *American Physical Education Review*, May 1922: 207–211.
_____. "Track Athletics for Women." *American Physical Education Review*, June 1922: 280–288.
_____. "Women's Athletic Records." *Spalding's Official Athletic Almanac*, 1916: 176–179.
_____. "Women's Athletic Records." *Spalding's Official Athletic Almanac*, 1919: 155–160.
_____. "Women's Athletic Records." *Spalding's Official Athletic Almanac*, 1920: 160–165.

Chapter 5

"American Girls Are Second in Olympics." *New York Times*, August 21, 1922: 7.

"America's Girl Athletes Sail for Paris Olympics." *Newark Evening News*, August 1, 1922: 1.

"Athletic Girls Break Records." *Mamaroneck Paragraph*, May 18, 1922: 1.

Batson, Mead, Voorhees, Voorhees Award. Alumni Weekend, May 12, 1978. Typed paper courtesy of Choate Rosemary Hall Archives, The Andrew Mellon Library.

"Camelia Sabie Honored." *New York Times*, September 13, 1922: 17.

Chepesiuk, Ron. "Lucile Godbold, South Carolina's First Olympic Competitor." Reprint from *The Charlotte Observer*. Courtesy of the Winthrop University Archives and Special Collections.

"Committee Is Appointed." *New York Times*, July 17, 1922: 10.

Crampton, C. Ward. "Women's Athletic Committee Report." *American Physical Education Review*, February 1923: 68–69.

"Eleanor Smith, a Runner." *New York Times*, May 24, 1920: 19.

Ferris, Daniel J., ed. *The Athlete*, December 1921.

"Flora Batson Is Injured on Track." *New York Times*, August 10, 1922: 22.

"Girl Athletes Depart." *New York Times*, August 2, 1922: 14.

"Girl Athletes to Sail on *Aquitania*." *New York Times*, August 1, 1922: 16.

"Girls Set Relay Record." *New York Times*, September 11, 1922: 14.

"High School Girl Sets World Mark." *New York Times*, May 14, 1922: 28.

Johnson, Dr., President of Winthrop College. (Speeches.) Courtesy of Winthrop University Archives and Special Collections.

"Miss Sabie Breaks Two World's Marks." *New York Times*, September 24, 1922: 3.

"Our Ludy Comes Home." *The Winthrop College News*, October 20, 1922: 1, 3.

"Rye Girl Goes to Europe as Member of U.S. Track Team." *Port Chester Daily Item*, July 26, 1922.

"Set Two Records in Women's Games." *New York Times*, September 17, 1922: 2.

Stewart, Harry E., M.D. "Track Athletics for Women." *American Physical Education Review*, June 1922: 280–288.

"To Go After Record." *New York Times*, September 22, 1922: 12.

"U.S. Girl Athletes Get Big Welcome." *New York Times*, August 9, 1922: 23.

"Vassar Record Beaten." *New York Times*, May 19, 1915: 10.

"Will Hold Third Meet." *New York Times*, September 20, 1922: 17.

"Women Athletes Back from Paris." *New York Times*, September 3, 1922: 17.

"Women Athletes Hold Their First International Congress." *New York Times*, August 19, 1922: 8.

"Women Athletes in Paris." *New York Times*, August 21, 1922.

"Women Athletes Ready for Pistol." *New York Times*, August 20, 1922: 24.

"Women's Meet to Be Held by Amateur Athletic Union." *New York Times*, July 20, 1922: 12.

"Women's Olympic Games Tomorrow." *New York Times*, August 19, 1922: 8.

Chapter 6

"Amateur Athletic Union Firmly Entrenched." *Amateur Athletic Union of the United States — Bulletin No. 1*, November 24, 1923: 1.

Klein, Martin. "Report of the Women's Athletic Committee." *Minutes of the Metropolitan Association of the Amateur Athletic Union*, 1923–24: 14–15.

"An Oakesmere Girl Breaks Record." *Mamaroneck Paragraph*, May 24, 1923: 1.

Obertubbesing, Herman. "Women's Athletics." *Minutes of the Metropolitan Association of the Amateur Athletic Union*, 1923–24: 4.

Program of the Conference on Athletics and Physical Recreation, April 6–7, 1923, Washington, D.C.

"Roy Runs Fast Mile in Meet at Stadium." *New York Times*, September 9, 1923: 1.

Somers, Florence. "Subcommittee on Field and Track." *American Physical Education Review*, February 1923: 184.

Steers, Fred L. "Women's Athletics." *Amateur Athletic Union Bulletin*, December 3, 1923: 9–10.

Trilling, Blanche M. "Report of the Committee on Organization of the Conference of Athletics and Physical Education for Women and Girls, April 6 and 7, 1923 at Washington, D.C." *American Physical Education Review*, June 1923: 284–289.

Women Athletes Set New Records." *New York Times*, September 30, 1923: 5.

"Women Break Four Marks" (subtitle). *New York Times*, September 4, 1923: 20.

Chapter 7

"Athletic Carnival at Armory Tonight." *Paterson Morning Call*, April 4, 1924: 19.

Burdick, William. "All Girls Baltimore News Meet." *American Physical Education Review*, September 1924: 432.

Burstyn, Joan, ed. *Past and Promise: Lives of New Jersey Women*. Metuchen, N.J.: Scarecrow Press, 1990.

Ferris, Daniel J., ed. *Amateur Athletic Union Bulletin*, February 23, 1924; December 12, 1924.

"Invaders from Over The Board: American Girls." *New York Times*, September 21, 1924.

Jable, J. Thomas. "Eleanor Egg: Paterson's Track and Field Heroine." *New Jersey History*, fall-winter 1984: 69–84.

Lee, Mabel. "The Case for and Against Intercollegiate Athletics for Women and the Situation as It Stands Today." *American Physical Education Review*, January 1924: 13–17.

Schoedler, Lillian. National Amateur Athletic Federation of America — letter, May 21, 1924.

_____. "The Women's Division of the National Amateur Athletic Federation." Booklet, 1924: 2–5.

Sibley, Katharine. "First Report of the Subcommittee on Track and Field Athletics, April 15, 1924." *American Physical Education Review*, October 1924: 461–462.

"Standards for a Field Meet." Paper prepared by the Women's Division of the National Amateur Athletic Federation. *Newsletter*, February 19, 1924.

"Two Records Go in Meet at the Armory." *Paterson Morning Call*, April 5, 1924: 1.

"Women's National Champions." *Spalding's Official Athletic Almanac*, 1925.

Chapter 8

Emery, Lynne. "The Pasadena Athletic Club and Sport for Southern California Women in the 1920's." *Paper Presented to the Western Association of Women Historians Conference XVII*, May 11, 1986.

"Girl Athletes Set 3 World Marks." *New York Times*, July 19, 1925: 5.

"Girl Star Breaks World Hurdle Record." *Pasadena Evening Post*, July 11, 1925: 1.

"Greatest of Meets Will Be July 11." *Pasadena Evening Post*, July 6, 1925: 8.

Johnson, Bessie. "Sports Fail to Conquer Femininity." *Pasadena Evening Post*, July 9, 1925: 1, 12.

"Kansas City Public School Athletic Association Indoor Track Meet Records." *American Physical Education Review*, January 1925: 49.

"Large Crowd Is Expected for Meet." *Pasadena Star-News*, July 10, 1925: 15.

Lindsay, Dorothy. "Women in Sports." *Boston Herald*, December 1, 1925.

"Louisiana Sends Girl Athletes to Pasadena." *Pasadena Evening Post*, July 8, 1925: 1.

"Members and Endorsers." *Women's Division, National Amateur Athletic Federation*, 1925.

"Metropolitan Amateur Athletic Union Engages Coaches for Embryo Athletes." *Amateur Athletic Union Bulletin*, February 1925.

"Miss Filkey Sets 3 World Records." *New York Times*, July 12, 1925: 6.

"More Than Six Thousand to Cheer Girl Track Athletes at Paddock Field Saturday." *Pasadena Evening Post*, July 7, 1925: 1.

"Noted Men Will Judge Track Meet." *Pasadena Evening Post*, July 8, 1925: 8.

"Officials of Girls' Meet Selected." *Pasadena Star-News*, July 8, 1925: 15.

"Pasadena Is Winner of Big Meet." *Pasadena Star-News*, July 13, 1925: 13.

Sargent, L.W. "A Method of Instruction in Hurdling." *American Physical Education Review*, May 1925: 348–352.

Schoedler, Lillian. "Report of Second Annual Meeting." *Women's Division, National Amateur Athletic Federation of America*, 1925: 14.

"Southland Sunshine Turns Invalid Into Girl Track Champion." *Pasadena Evening Post*, July 13, 1925: 1.

Steers, Fred L. "Report on the Committee on Women's Athletics." *Minutes of the Annual Meeting Amateur Athletic Union*, November 1925: 100–112.

"Thirty-four Fair Athletes to Limber Up Tomorrow on Track in Tournament Park." *Pasadena Evening Post*, July 7, 1925: 1.

"Women Stars Start Last Training." *Pasadena Star-News*, July 8, 1925: 13.

"World Title Captured by Pasadena Girls in Meet, Records Tumble." *Pasadena Evening Post*, July 13, 1925: 8.

Chapter 9

Becht, June Wuest. "High Jump Still Interests 1928 Olympian." *St. Louis Post-Dispatch*, June 3, 1985: 8.

"California State Board of Education, Department of Physical Education." *American Physical Education Review*, February 1926: 680.

Cassidy, Rosalind. "A Successful College Play Day." *American Physical Education Review*, February 1926: 124–125.

"Catherine Maguire and Sisters Honored at Reception by Pacific Citizens," from Catherine Maguire's scrapbook courtesy of Dan Maguire and Sandra Maguire Weaver.

"Catherine Maguire Breaks World's Record," from Catherine Maguire's scrapbook courtesy of Dan Maguire and Sandra Maguire Weaver.

Coops, Helen L. "Sports for Women." Paper published by the *Women's Division, National Amateur Athletic Federation*, April 1926.

"Former Olympic Performer Serves as Parade Marshall Here." *The Meramec Valley Transcript*, October 13, 1982: 12.

Kelley, Robert F. "2 More Records Set in Women's Meet." *New York Times*, July 11, 1926: 1.

Lindsay, Dorothy. "Women in Sports." *Boston Herald*, April 10, 1926.

____. "Women in Sports." *Boston Herald*, November 9, 1926.

Maguire, Dan. "My Sister, Kay." Written and sent to the author by Dan Maguire, November 1993.

Mueller, Anita. "Miss Catherine Maguire…" *Globe-Democrat*, from Catherine Maguire's scrapbook. Courtesy of Dan Maguire and Sandra Maguire Weaver.

Schoedler, Lillian. "Report of the Third Annual Meeting." *Women's Division, National Amateur Athletic Federation*, May 1926.

Small, Clare H. "Leadership of State Universities in the Field of Athletics for Girls." Paper presented at the Third Annual Meeting of the *Women's Division, National Amateur Athletic Federation*, May 1926.

"Steers and Benedetto Visit Texas." *Amateur Athletic Union Bulletin*, June 1927: 2.

"3 U.S. Marks Fall in Women's Games." *New York Times*, July 11, 1926: 1.

"Women's Athletics." *Amateur Athletic Union Bulletin*, December 1926: 4.

"Women's Outdoor Track and Field." *Spalding's Athletic Library*. New York: American Sports, 1927.

Chapter 10

Aller, Aileen. "World's Champions." *Pasadena Sportland*, March 25, 1925: 10.

Amateur Athletic Union Bulletin, Report on Women's Track and Field Championships, June 1927.

"Girls National Track and Field Meet." *Minutes of the Annual Meeting of the Amateur Athletic Union*, November 21–23, 1927.

"Miss Filkey Clips World Record Time." *New York Times*, September 4, 1927: 2.

Steers, Fred L. "Women's Athletics Committee Report." *Minutes of the Annual Meeting of the Amateur Athletic Union*, November 21–23, 1927: 79–83.

"Women's Outdoor Track and Field." *Spalding's Official Athletic Almanac*. New York: American Sports, 1928.

"Women's Track Championships at Eureka." *Amateur Athletic Union Bulletin*, September 1927.

Chapter 11

"American Olympic Team and Cabin Passengers on the President Roosevelt." *United States Lines*, July 11, 1928.

Becht, June Wuest. " 'The Dutchess' Enters Sports Hall of Fame." *St. Louis Globe-Democrat*, May 21, 1978: 26–34.

Beckmann (Boeckmann), Dee. Fact sheet on accomplishments obtained at the U.S.A. Track and Field Hall of Fame Historical Reach Library, Butler University.

Castellano, Joe. "Dee Boeckmann Was a Pioneer in Women's World of Athletics." *St. Louis Globe-Democrat*, March 20–21, 1976: 4.

Field, Bryan. "U.S. Olympic Team Sails for Holland." *New York Times*, July 12, 1928: 18.

"Girls Athletics." *American Physical Education Review*, March 1928: 204.

Hodak, George A. "Anne Vrana O'Brien." *Amateur Athletic Foundation of Los Angeles*, printed taped interview, 1988.

Lerner, Marsha. "Mary Washburn Conklin." Correspondance: June 1993.

Lindsay, Dorothy. "Women in Sports." *Boston Herald*, December 29, 1928.

McGeehan, W.O. "Glorified Tomboys." *Ladies' Home Journal*, July 1928: 25, 72.

"Miss Cartwright Wins Three Titles." *New York Times*, July 5, 1928: 15.

"Miss Copeland Sets Mark in Shot Put." *New York Times*, August 13, 1928: 12.

"Olympic Ship Sails from Southampton; Athletes to Drill Aboard for Meets Here." *New York Times*, August 15, 1928: 15.

"Olympic Results." *New York Times*, August 2, 1928: 17.

"Olympic Results." *New York Times*, August 3, 1928: 11.

"Olympic Results." *New York Times*, August 5, 1928: 8.

"Olympic Results." *New York Times*, August 6, 1928: 22.

Perrin, Ethel. *Report to the Members of the Women's Division, National Amateur Athletic Federation*, November 22, 1928.

"Report of the Women's Division." *American Physical Education Review*, April 1928: 256–260.

Rice, Jack. "Meet Miss Marco Polo — Career Girl — Dee Boeckmann Now Home as Globe-Hurdler." *St. Louis Post-Dispatch*, November 7, 1957: 2.

Rogers, Frederick Rand. "Physical Education Programs for Girls." *American Physical Education Review*, May 1928: 112–114.

Schmidt, P.F. "Rochester, Minnesota Has Every Childs Track Meet." *American Physical Education Review*, February 1928: 112–114.

Schroeder, Louis C. "The Amsterdam Olympic Games." *American Physical Education Review*, November 1928: 608–611.

Sheppard, Melvin W. "Report of the American Olympic Committee." *American Olympic Committee*, 1928: 156–161.

"Three World Marks Set in Women's Meet." *New York Times*, March 11, 1928: 7.

"Track Meet Results." *Spalding's Official Athletic Almanac*. New York: American Sports, 1929.

"U.S. Record in 440 Yard Relay." *New York Times*, June 24, 1928: 3.

Williams, Wythe. "American's Capture 2 Olympic Events, Setting New Marks." *New York Times*, August 1, 1928: 1, 16.

"Women's Track Test for Olympic Today." *New York Times*, July 4, 1928: 11.

Chapter 12

Belding, Alice. "Track and Field Committee of Women's Athletic Committee." *American Physical Education Review*, June 1929: 364–366.

"Five World Marks Broken by Women." *New York Times*, July 28, 1928: 4.

Klein, Martin A. "Women's Athletic Committee Report." *Minutes of Meetings, Metropolitan Association of the Amateur Athletic Union*, September 12, 1929: 70–74.

MacFadden, Bernarr. "Athletics for Women Will Help Save the Nation." *Amateur Athletic Union Bulletin*, February–July 1919: 7–8.

"Miss Swetlik Takes Slovak Olympic Title." *Schenectady Gazette*. July 17, 1929: 19.

National Amateur Athletic Federation, Women's Division. *Newsletter*, February, March, November, December 1929.

"Records in Field and Track for Mississippi State College for Women." *American Physical Education Review*, October 1929: 473.

Sackett, Ada Taylor. "Women in Athletics." *Amateur Athletic Union Bulletin*, August 1929: 6.

"Southern Women's Championship a Big Success." *Amateur Athletic Union Bulletin*, February–July 1920: 8.

Steers, Fred L. "Five Records Fall in Women's Title Meet in Chicago." *Amateur Athletic Union Bulletin*, August 1929: 4.

"Third International Track Meet for Women in Prague Next Year." *Amateur Athletic Union Bulletin*, February–July 1929.

"Women's Indoor Track and Field." *Spalding's Official Athletic Almanac*. New York: American Sports, 1930: 109.

"Women's Outdoor Track and Field." *Spalding's Official Athletic Almanac*. New York: American Sports, 1930: 107, 215, 225, 231.

"Women's Track Championships at Chicago." *Amateur Athletic Union Bulletin*, February–July 1919: 8.

Chapter 13

"Around the Country with J.E. Rogers." *The Journal of Health and Physical Education*, June 1930: 30.

Athletic Activities for Women and Girls. Spalding's Athletic Library. New York: American Sports, 1930–31.

"Babe Didrikson, Local Girl, Named Member American Team for International Track Go." *Dallas Morning News*, July 20, 1930.

"Big Doings in the Allegheny Mountain Association." *The Amateur Athlete*, June 1930: 11.

"A Classified Listing of Our Latest Publications." *The Journal of Health and Physical Education*, September 1930: 31.

Coops, Helen L. "A Study of Intramural Point Systems on a State Basis for Girls' Athletics in the High Schools of Five States — Alabama, Illinois, Kansas, Nebraska and Oregon." Typed paper from *Women's Division, National Amateur Athletic Federation*, July 1930.

"Feminine Fleetness on Display in Pru Meet Tonight." *Newark Evening News*, February 19, 1930: 9.

"Fourth Annual Indoor Track Meet of Columbus Council, 126 Knights of Columbus." *Official Program*, January 4, 1930.

Menke, Frank G., ed. *All-Sports Record Book*. Brooklyn, N.Y.: Guide, 1931.

Moore, Walter. "Records Tumble as Chicago Team Retains Title." *The Dallas Morning News*, July 5, 1930: 14.

"National Amateur Athletic Federation, Women's Division." *Newsletter*, February 1930: 1–3.

"National Amateur Athletic Union Women's Track and Field Meet." *The Dallas Morning News*, July 4, 1930.

"A New Contribution to the Athletics for Women Series." *The Journal of Health and Physical Education*, June 1930.

"No Furs Here." *Daily News*, January 30, 1930.

Parker, Bill. "6 New Records Made in National Track Go." *The Times Herald*, July 5, 1930: 5.

_____. "Track Meet Starts at 3 o'Clock." *The Times Herald*, July 4, 1930.

"A Pioneer Among the Ladies." *The Amateur Athlete*, March 1930: 3.

"Prague Scene of 3rd World Ladies Games in September." *The Amateur Athlete*, July 1930: 2.

"Records Break in Women's Championships." *The Amateur Athlete*, May 1930.

Somers, Florence A. *Principles of Women's Athletics*. New York: A.S. Barnes, 1930.

"Stella Walsh." *The Amateur Athlete*, January 1931: 13.

"Stella Walsh Feted." *The Amateur Athlete*, November 1930: 7.

"Three World Marks Set by Miss Walsh." *New York Times*, July 5, 1930: 10.

"Two Important Books Which Will Be Ready This Summer." *The Journal of Health and Physical Education*, April 1930: 29.

Vreeland, George. "New Jersey Girls Real Record-Breakers." *The Amateur Athlete*, June 1930: 3.

"Where Are the Stars of Yesterday?" *The Amateur Athlete*, July 1930: 6.

"Women Track Athletes Increase." *The Amateur Athlete*, January 1931: 3.

"Women's Outdoor Track and Field." *Spalding's Official Athletic Almanac*. New York: American Sports, 1931: 55, 57, 83, 85, 101, 107, 110, 123, 131, 137, 150, 155, 159, 169, 179, 199, 201.

"Women's Track and Field Committee Report." *Minutes of the Annual Amateur Athletic Union Meeting*, November 16–18, 1930: 316.

Chapter 14

"Annual Report of the National Section on Women's Athletics." *The Journal of Health and Physical Education*, September 1931: 42.

"Babe Didrikson Excels in National Women's Meet." *The Amateur Athlete*, August 1931: 6.

"Central Association Marks Lowered in Women's Track and Field Meet." *The Amateur Athlete*, August 1931: 7.

Daley, Arthur. "World's Mark Set by Miss Didrikson." *New York Times*, July 26, 1931: 1, 10.
"Discus Hits Onlooker; Woman Athlete Held." *New York Times*, July 26, 1931: 25.
"Miss Mearls Breaks Record." *The Amateur Athlete*, May 1931: 6.
Smith, Helen N. "Evils of Sports for Women." *The Journal of Health and Physical Education*, January 1931: 8, 9, 50.
Steers, Fred L. "Women's Track and Field." *Minutes of the Annual Meeting of the Amateur Athletic Union*. November 15–17, 1931: 309.
"This Is Their Day." *The Amateur Athlete*, September 1931: 7.
"235 Compete Today in Women's Meet." *New York Times*, July 25, 1931: 10.
"Women's Division, National Amateur Athletic Federation." *Newsletter*, January 1, 1931; February 1, 1931.

Chapter 15

Adams, Evelyn Hall. Biographical material sent to the author by Evelyne Hall Adams: November 1991.
Anderson, Thomas J. "Girls and Modern Athletics." *The New York Amsterdam News*, July 6, 1932: 9.
"Babe Didrikson Zaharias." *New York Times*, September 28, 1956: 28.
"Betty Robinson Training Again for Anticipated Olympic Honors." *The Amateur Athlete*, April 1932: 5.
Carlson, Lewis H. and John J. Fogarty. *Tales of Gold*. Chicago; New York: Contemporary Books, 1987.
"Chicago Girl in Olympics." *The Chicago Defender*, July 23, 1932: 9.
"Chords... Evelyn Furtsch Ojeda." *Tustin Weekly*, November 22, 1991: A9.
"The Didrikson Case." *The Amateur Athlete*, January 1933: 8.
"Five First Places to Miss Didrikson." *New York Times*, July 17, 1932: 1.
Himmelberg, Michele. "A Dashing Grandmother: Ojeda Joins Hall of Fame Tonight." *The Register*, March 4, 1985.
Kieran, John and Arthur Daley. *The Story of the Olympic Games*. New York: F.A. Stokes, 1969.
Lockwood, Wayne. "Olympian's Memories, Not Medals, Are Golden." *The San Diego Union*, June 30, 1991: 1, 13.
"Meadowbrook Club Captures Women's National Indoor Track Championship." *New York Times*, March 13, 1932: 6.
"National Women's Indoor Title Captured by Meadowbrook Team." *The Amateur Athlete*, April 1932: 5.
Rice, Grantland. *The Tumult and the Shouting*. New York: A.S. Barnes, 1954.
"Salem Bests the Mercurys." *The New York Amsterdam News*, July 20, 1932: 9.
Scrapbook of Tenth Olympiad, from National Track and Field Hall of Fame Library, Butler University. Scrapbook revealed newspaper articles written during the Olympic Games about women athletes.
Steers, Fred L. "Report of the Manager of the American Women's Track and Field Team." *The American Olympic Committee Report*, 1932: 121–127.
_____. "Report of Track and Field Committee Women." *Minutes of the Annual Meeting of the Amateur Athletic Union*, November 1932: 100–102.
_____. "Spirit." *The Amateur Athlete*, October 1932: 7, 12.
"Stella Walsh States." *Silver Anniversary Games Program*, February 6, 1932: 51.
"Throng Attends Zaharias Rites." *New York Times*, September 29, 1956: 19.
Wayman, Agnes. "Women's Division of the National Amateur Athletic Federation." *The Journal of Health and Physical Education*, March 1932: 3–6.
"Women's Division, National Amateur Athletic Federation." *Newsletter*, June; July; 1932.

"Women's Division, National Amateur Athletic Federation." *Program Eighth Annual Meeting*, July 21–23, 1932.
"Women's Division Notes." *The Journal of Health and Physical Education*, June 1932: 46.
Zaharias, Babe Didrikson. *This Life I've Led*. New York: A.S. Barnes, 1955.
Zaharias, Babe Didrikson — A Record of Achievement. Flyer published by the Babe Didrikson Foundation, Inc., Beaumont, Texas.

Chapter 16

"Illinois Women's Athletic Club Captures National Title in Chicago Meet." *New York Times*, July 1, 1933.
"National Women's Sports Committee Report." *Minutes of the Annual Meeting of the Amateur Athletic Union*, November 20–22, 1933: 141–142.
Rogers, J.E. "Around The Country." *The Journal of Health and Physical Education*, November 1933: 14.
"Women's Athletic Section." *The Journal of Health and Physical Education*, December 1933: 40–41.
"Women's Division, National Amateur Athletic Federation." *Newsletter*, February, November, December 1933.
"Women's Track and Field Committee Report." *Minutes of the Annual Meeting of the Amateur Athletic Union*, November 20–22, 1933: 81–84.

Chapter 17

Abramson, J.P. "Women's Track Championships." *The Amateur Athlete*, May 1934: 9.
Becker, Olga. "Ex Champion Now Chairman." *The Amateur Athlete*, February 1934: 11.
Boeckmann, Dee. "Women's Sports Committee Report." *Minutes of the Annual Meeting of the Amateur Athletic Union*, December 1934: 154–157.
Do You Know That —. *The Amateur Athlete*, January 1934: 15.
Do You Know That —. *The Amateur Athlete*, March 1934: 15.
Do You Know That —. *The Amateur Athlete*, August 1934: 15.
Effrat, Louis. "Miss Walsh Clips World Dash Mark." *New York Times*, April 15, 1934: 1.
Hazelton, Helen W. "Seventeen Years of Progress." *The Journal of Health and Physical Education*, April 1934: 11–13.
Howland, Amy. "The New 1933–1934 Athletic Handbook of the Women's Athletic Section of the American Physical Education Association." *The Journal of Health and Physical Education*, March 1934: 55.
Steers, Fred L. "Women's Track and Field Committee Report." *Minutes of the Annual Meeting of the Amateur Athletic Union*, December 1934: 150–152.
Werden, Lincoln. "Women in Sports." *New York Times*, August 12, 1934: 3.

Chapter 18

Boeckmann, Dee. "Helen Stephens Again." *The Amateur Athlete*, October 1935: 12.
_____. "A Potential Olympic Champion." *The Amateur Athlete*, May 1934: 4, 9.
_____. "Women's Track and Field Committee Report." *Minutes of the Annual Meeting of the Amateur Athletic Union*, December 1935: 65–66.
"Ellerbe Stars in Tuskegee's Meet." *The Chicago Defender*, May 18, 1935: 16.

Gates, Edith M. "The Women's Division, National Amateur Athletic Federation, in 1935." *The Journal of Health and Physical Education*, April 1935: 27, 62.

"Helen Stephens." *The Amateur Athlete*, October 1935: Front Cover Photo.

"Miss Walsh Bows in 50-Meter Dash." *New York Times*, March 23, 1935.

"Miss Walsh Shatters 60-Yard Dash Record." *New York Times*, May 12, 1935.

"Publications of the Rules and Editorial Committee of the Women's Athletic Section." *The Journal of Health and Physical Education*, September 1935: 41.

Vinson, Maribel Y. "World Record Set by Miss Stephens." *New York Times*, September 15, 1935: 1.

"Women's Athletics." *Amateur Athletic Union Official Handbook*. New York: American Sports, 1935: 114.

Chapter 19

Birchall, Frederick T. "Gloom Descends on Joyous Crowd as Germans Drop Baton in Relay." *New York Times*, August 10, 1936: 12.

Boeckmann, Dee. "National Women's Track and Field Committee Report." *Minutes of the Annual Meeting of the Amateur Athletic Union*, December 1936: 36, 37.

____. "Women's Track and Field." *The Amateur Athlete*, January 1936: 6.

Burnes, Robert L. "The Forgotten Champion." *St. Louis Globe-Democrat*, February 28, 1978.

Daley, Arthur J. "Owens Captures Olympic Title, Equals World 100-Meter Record." *New York Times*, August 4, 1936: 1, 23.

Epstein, Charlotte. "Women's Sports." *The Amateur Athlete*, January 1936: 5.

Flachsbart, Harold. "Helen Stephens Breaks Two U.S. Track Records." *St. Louis Daily Globe-Democrat*, February 18, 1936: 4B.

____. "Six Champions to Defend Titles in National Women's Meet Tonight." *St. Louis Daily Globe-Democrat*, February 12, 1936: 7A.

"Die Frauenwettbewerbe." *XI Olympiade Berlin 1936–Amtlicher Bericht*: 609.

Hahn, Reno. "Helen Stephens Again Lowers Record for 100 Meters." *St. Louis Post-Dispatch*, June 15, 1936: 1.

Kerby, Damon. "Helen Stephens Breaks U.S. Record in 50-Meter Dash." *St. Louis Post-Dispatch*, February 13, 1936: 2B.

____. "Helen Stephens Hopes to Break Two Records Tonight." *St. Louis Post-Dispatch*, February 12, 1936: 2B.

"Male of Species Not Alone in Waiting for Glory as Member of U.S. Team." *The New York Amsterdam News*, July 3, 1936.

Noyes Elizabeth. "Recreational Activities for Women." *The Journal of Health and Physical Education*, February 1936: 106, 107, 127.

Nutter, Joe. "Helen Stephens Wins Top Honors at Brown Field." *The Providence Sunday Journal*, July 5, 1936: 1.

____. "Nation's Girl Track Stars to Compete at Brown Today." *Providence Journal*, July 4, 1936: 1.

____. "U.S. Entries Will Be Chosen in 6 Events at Brown Field." *Providence Journal*, July 4, 1936: 1.

Sackett, Ada Taylor. "Women's Sports Committee Report." *Minutes of the Annual Meeting of the Amateur Athletic Union*, December 1936: 80.

Steers, Fred L. "Track and Field Athletics — Women." *Report of the American Olympic Committee*, 1936: 151–160.

"They'll Represent Nation." *The New York Amsterdam News*, July 8, 1936: 14.

"Three Titles Won by Miss Stephens." *New York Times*, February 13, 1936: 28.

"Track and Field." *New York Times*, August 3, 1936: 19.
"Track and Field Committee — Women." *Amateur Athletic Association Handbook*. New York: American Sports, 1936.
"Women's Division, National Amateur Athletic Federation." *Newsletter*, June 1, 1936.
"World Record Set by Miss Stephens." *New York Times*, July 5, 1936: 1, 2.

Chapter 20

Allison, (Mrs.) E.J. "Women's Sports Committee Report." *Minutes of the Annual Meeting of the Amateur Athletic Union*, November 1937: 132.
Boeckmann, Dee. "Women's Sports Committee Report." *Minutes of the Annual Meeting of the Amateur Athletic Union*, January 1937: 6.
"Fleet Tuskegee Fems Capture Cinder Title." *The New York Amsterdam News*, May 15, 1937: 15.
Howland, Amy. "Women's Athletic Section News." *The Journal of Health and Physical Education*, March 1937: 182,
_____. "Women's Athletic Section News." *The Journal of Health and Physical Education*, June 1937: 385.
"National Women's Amateur Athletic Union Track and Field Titles at Stake Here Today." *Trenton Evening Times*, September 26, 1937: 13.
"National Women's Track Meet Here Yields All New Champs." *Trenton Times*, September 27, 1937.
"Over 100 Entries Listed for National Women's Meet Here Tomorrow." *Trenton Evening Times*, September 24, 1937: 29.
Sefton, Alice Allene. "Must Women in Sports Look Beautiful?" *The Journal of Health and Physical Education*, October 1937: 481, 510.
"Tuskegee Sends 9 to Women's Meet." *The New York Amsterdam News*, September 25, 1937: 17.
"Tuskegee Takes Women's Track Championship." *Trenton Sunday Times-Advertiser*, September 26, 1937: 1.
"U.S. Track Crown to Tuskegee Girls." *New York Times*, September 26, 1937: 10.
Vreeland, George. "National Women's Track and Field Championships." *The Amateur Athlete*, September 1937: 9.
_____. "National Women's Track and Field Committee Report." *Minutes of the Annual Meeting of the Amateur Athletic Union*, November 1937: 105–107.
_____. "Women's Track Championships." *The Amateur Athlete*, November 1937: 6.
"Women's Division, National Amateur Athletic Federation." *Executive Committee Annual Report*. 1936–1937.
"Women's Division, National Amateur Athletic Federation." *Newsletter*, February, November 1937.
"Women's Division, National Amateur Athletic Federation." *Program of the Fourteenth Annual Meeting*, April 21, 1937.

Chapter 21

Boeckmann, Dee. "Women's Track and Field Committee Report." *Minutes of the 50th Annual Meeting of the Amateur Athletic Union*, December 1938: 63–65.
"Femme Track Title." *The New York Amsterdam News*, August 6, 1938: 5.
Landon, Alice Lord. "Women's Sport Committee Report." *Minutes of the 50th Annual Meeting of the Amateur Athletic Union*, December 1938: 147–148.

"Mercury Athletic Club Track Meet Next Month at Macombs." *The New York Amsterdam News*, May 28, 1938: 19.

Mullaney, Ruth. "Play Streets." *The Journal of Health and Physical Education*, September 1938: 434–435, 456.

"Official Sports Library for Women." *The Journal of Health and Physical Education*, October 1938: 497.

Palmer, Gladys E. "Policies in Women's Athletics." *The Journal of Health and Physical Education*, November 1938: 565–567, 586–587.

"Track and Field Committee." *Amateur Athletic Union Handbook*. New York: American Sports, 1938: 170.

"Tuskegee Girls Smash Records." *The New York Amsterdam News*, May 21, 1938: 15.

"Tuskegee Women Keep Track Title." *New York Times*, August 8, 1938: 18.

"Women's Division, National Amateur Athletic Federation." *Newsletter*, April 1, 1938; October 1, 1938; February 1, 1938.

"Women's Division, National Amateur Athletic Federation." *Report of the Fifteenth Annual Meeting*, April 1938.

"Women's Records." *The Amateur Athlete*, June 1938: 13.

"Women's Track Title." *The Amateur Athlete*, September 1938: 6.

Chapter 22

Amateur Athletic Union Official Handbook. Athletic Rules, Amateur Athletic Union of United States, 1939.

Benton, Rachel Jane. "Women's Athletic Section News." *The Journal of Health and Physical Education*, February 1939: 133.

_____. "Women's Athletic Section News." *The Journal of Health and Physical Education*, October 1939: 482.

"Club Annexes Metropolitan Femme Titles." *The New York Amsterdam News*, July 8, 1939: 14.

Goldstein, Sol. "Women's Track Performances." *The Amateur Athlete*, September 1938: 12.

"Interscholastic Athletic Standards for Boys." *The Journal of Health and Physical Education*, September 1939: 374, 423.

"Miss Walsh Breaks Record in Broad Jump; Tuskegee Keeps Women's U.S. Track Title." *New York Times*, September 4, 1939: 26.

O'Donnell, William P. "Stella Walsh Tops Own Running Broad Jump Mark to Feature Amateur Athletic Union Meet." *Waterbury Republican*, September 4, 1939: 8.

Thompson, Nellie. "The Ohio State University Sports Clinic." *The Journal of Health and Physical Education*, October 1939: 477.

"Women's Track." *The Amateur Athlete*, September 1939: 4.

"Women's Track." *The Amateur Athlete*, October 1939: 13.

"Women's Track-Field Championships Today." *The Sunday Republican*, September 4, 1939: 8.

Chapter 23

Meyer, Catherine Donovan. "Women's Track and Field Committee Report." *Minutes of the 52nd Annual Meeting of the Amateur Athletic Union*, December 1940: 122, 123.

_____. "Women's Track Title." *The Amateur Athlete*, August 1940: 4.

"Miss Walsh Stars in National Meet." *New York Times*, July 7, 1940: 4.

Schrwer, Alice C. "Track and Field Survey." *The Journal of Health and Physical Education*, February 1940: 87, 120.

"Track and Field Committee — Women." *Amateur Athletic Union of the United States Official Track and Field Handbook*. New York: The Amateur Athletic Union, 1940.
"Track Coaches' Convention." *Proceedings*, December 1940.
"When Stella Walsh's Reign Was Ended." *The New York Amsterdam News*, July 20, 1940: 1.
"Women's National Track Meet at Ocean City Today." *Atlantic City Press*, July 6, 1940: 13.
"Women's Track." *The Amateur Athlete*, July 1940.

Chapter 24

"Jean Lane Cracks Women's 200-Meter Dash Record." *Atlantic City Press*, July 6, 1941: 7, 8.
"Jean Lane Cracks World Record." *Atlantic City Press*, April 13, 1941: 7.
Meyer, Catherine Donovan. "Women's Track and Field Committee Report." *Minutes of the Annual Meeting of the Amateur Athletic Union*, November 1941: 99–101.
____. "Women's Track Title." *The Amateur Athlete*, August 1941: 13.
"Miss Lane Breaks U.S. Sprint Record." *New York Times*, July 6, 1941: 1, 4.
"Miss Lane Breaks World 200-Meter Mark in Women's U.S. Track Championship." *New York Times*, April 13, 1941: 4.
"Women's American Records." *Amateur Athletic Union of the United States Official Track and Field Handbook*. New York: The Amateur Athletic Union, 1942.
"Women's Outdoor Track and Field Championships." *Amateur Athletic Union of the United States Official Track and Field Handbook*. New York: The Amateur Athletic Union, 1942.
"Women's Title Track." *The Amateur Athlete*, May 1941: 11.
"Women's U.S. Track Classic in Ocean City." *Atlantic City Press*, July 5, 1941: 11.

Chapter 25

Meyer, Catherine Donovan. "Women's Track and Field Committee Report." *Minutes of the Annual Meeting of the Amateur Athletic Union*, December 1942: 88.
Moulton, Gertrude E. "Track and Field in a Program of Physical Education for Girls." *The Journal of Health and Physical Education*, February 1942: 89, 108, 109.
Smith, Ann Avery. "For Fitness, Run." *The Journal of Health and Physical Education*, March 1942: 182.
Steers, Fred L. "The Hand That Rocks the Cradle." *The Amateur Athlete*, November 1942: 9.
"Stella Walsh Carries Off Three U.S. Track Titles." *Atlantic City Press*, July 5, 1942: 7, 8.
"Three Events Won by Stella Walsh." *New York Times*, July 6, 1942: 5.
"Women's American Records." *Amateur Athletic Union of the United States Official Track and Field Handbook*. New York: The Amateur Athletic Union, 1943.
"Women's National Amateur Athletic Union Track Meet at Ocean City." *Atlantic City Press*, July 4, 1942: 7.

Chapter 26

"All America Women's Track and Field Team." *Amateur Athletic Union of the United States Official Track and Field Handbook*. New York: The Amateur Athletic Union, 1943.
Meyer, Catherine Donovan. "Women's Track and Field Committee Report." *Minutes of the Annual Meeting of the Amateur Athletic Union*, December 1943: 105.

"Three Events Won by Stella Walsh." *New York Times*, August 16, 1943: 22.

"Women's Track and Field." *Amateur Athletic Union of the United States Official Track and Field Handbook*. New York: The Amateur Athletic Union, 1944.

"Women's Track Title." *The Amateur Athlete*, September 1943: 9.

Chapter 27

"All America Women's Track and Field Team." *Amateur Athletic Union of the United States Official Track and Field Handbook*. New York: The Amateur Athletic Union, 1945.

"Dee Ran G.I. Athletics in Iceland." *The Amateur Athlete*, November 1944: 6.

"Laurel Ladies Club Photo." *The Amateur Athlete*, August 1944: cover photo.

Meyer, Catherine Donovan. "Women's Track and Field Committee Report." *Minutes of the Annual Meeting of the Amateur Athletic Union*, December 1944: 86.

"National Senior Outdoor Track and Field Championships, Women." *The Amateur Athlete*, August 1944: 11.

"3 U.S. Track Titles Go to Miss Walsh." *New York Times*, July 9, 1944: 1, 2.

"Women's American Records." *Amateur Athletic Union of the United States Official Track and Field Handbook*. New York: The Amateur Athletic Union, 1945.

"Women's Athletic Section News." *The Journal of Health and Physical Education*, June 1944: 332.

"Women's Sport Committee." *Minutes of the Annual Meeting of the Amateur Athletic Union*, 1944: 86.

"Women's Track Title." *The Amateur Athlete*, August 1944: 2.

Yocom, Rachel B. "Track and Field for Girls in Secondary Schools." *The Journal of Health and Physical Education*, October 1944: 441, 442, 460.

Chapter 28

"Alabaman Sets Women's Track Pace." *The Amateur Athlete*, August 1945: 9.

Campbell, Rosy Atkins. "Fashions in Feminine Sport." *The Amateur Athlete*, March 1945: 7, 39.

"Do You Know That —." *The Amateur Athlete*, November 1945: 15.

"Do You Know That —." *The Amateur Athlete*, December 1945: 13.

Meyer, Catherine Donovan. "Women's Track and Field Committee Report." *Minutes of the Annual Meeting of the Amateur Athletic Union*, December 1945: 83, 84, 85.

"Miss Walsh Wins Easily." *New York Times*, July 1, 1945: 3.

"National Senior Indoor Track and Field Championships — Women." *Amateur Athletic Union of the United States Official Track and Field Handbook*. New York: The Amateur Athletic Union, 1945.

"Rafferty Is First in Mile at Buffalo." *New York Times*, April 1, 1945: 1, 2.

Chapter 29

Feeney, Bob. "'Don't Like to Run,' Say Women Stars of Title Track Meet." *Buffalo Evening News*, August 5, 1946: 23.

Lurie, Dora. "Women in Track and Field." *Souvenir Program* (of the Second Annual Philadelphia Inquirer Invitation Indoor Track Meet), January 25, 1946: 24, 25.

Meyer, Catherine Donovan. "Alice Coachman Again Dominates Women's Track." *The Amateur Athlete*, September 1946: 10, 16.

_____. "Tuskegee Girls Again Win Indoor Track." *The Amateur Athlete*, May 1946: 20.

_____. "Women's Track and Field Committee Report." *Minutes of the Annual Meeting of the Amateur Athletic Union*, December 1946: 86, 87.

"Miss Walsh to Compete in National Meet Today." *New York Times*, August 4, 1946: 2.

"National Amateur Athletic Union Women's All-America Track and Field Team." *The Amateur Athlete*, March 1947: 25.

"National Senior Indoor and Outdoor Track and Field Championships." *Amateur Athletic Union of the United States Official Track and Field Handbook*. New York: The Amateur Athletic Union, 1947.

"One Shoe Off, One Shoe On, Society Ace Clears Bar." *Buffalo Evening News*, August 5, 1946: 23.

Sauerbrei, Harold. "Tuskegee Girls Snare National Track Title." *Cleveland Plain Dealer*, April 1, 1946.

"Second Annual Philadelphia Inquirer Invitation Indoor Track Meet." *Souvenir Program*, January 25, 1946.

Sheehan, Joseph M. "U.S. Crushes Canada in Resumption of International Track Competition." *The Amateur Athlete*, September 1946: 8, 9.

Stedler, Bob. "Sport Comment." *Buffalo Evening News*, August 5, 1946: 23.

"Tuskegee Women Keep Track Title." *New York Times*, April 1, 1946: 21.

Chapter 30

"All-America Women's Track and Field Team." *Amateur Athletic Union of the United States Official Track and Field Handbook*. New York: The Amateur Athletic Union, 1948: 11.

Meyer, Catherine Donovan. "Women's Track and Field Committee Report." *Minutes of the Annual Meeting of the Amateur Athletic Union*, December 1947: 91–93.

"Miss Walsh Keeps 200-Meter Crown." *New York Times*, June 29, 1947: 6.

"National Junior Outdoor Track and Field Championship — Women." *Amateur Athletic Union of the United States Official Track and Field Handbook*. New York: The Amateur Athletic Union, 1947: 57.

Peebles, Dick. "5 New National Track Queens Crowned." *San Antonio Express*, June 29, 1947: 1C.

_____. "Tuskegee Girls Top National Amateur Athletic Union Juniors." *San Antonio Express*, June 28, 1947: 1.

"Senior Outdoor Track and Field Championships — Women." *Amateur Athletic Union of the United States Official Track and Field Handbook*. New York: The Amateur Athletic Union, 1948: 41, 56.

"Walsh, Coachman Again Dominate Women's Track." *The Amateur Athlete*, August 1947: 12, 13.

Chapter 31

"Admiral Brown to Administer Olympic Oath at Tryouts." *The Providence Journal*, July 6, 1948: 10.

"Alice Coachman Jump Winner." *The New York Amsterdam News*, July 17, 1948.

"All-American Women's Track and Field Team." *Amateur Athletic Union of the United States Official Track and Field Handbook*. New York: The Amateur Athletic Union, 1949: 10.

"American Indoor Track and Field Championships." *Official Program*, February 21, 1948: 22, 31.

"American Olympians Arrive Photo." *The New York Amsterdam News*, July 31, 1948: 15.

Bennett, Roscoe D. "National Women's Track Meet Under Way." *The Grand Rapids Press*, July 6, 1948: 20.

_____. "Record Crowd Sees Track Queens Crowned." *The Grand Rapids Press*, July 7, 1948: 26.

"Best Marks by Women." *Track and Field News*, February 1948: 8.

Carroll, Ted. "City PAL Centers Put Emphasis in Sportsmanship, Clean Living." *The New York Amsterdam News*, June 12, 1948: 28.

Clapp, Charles L. "Women's Amateur Athletic Union Track Meet Preps Olympic Hopefuls." *Grand Rapids Herald*, July 7, 1948: 8.

D'Aviso, Richmondo. "The Alice Coachman Olympic Story." Booklet on her accomplishments courtesy of Richmond Davis, her son.

"Girls' Track Team Photo." *The New York Amsterdam News*, July 31, 1948: 7.

Jackson, Nell C. "Biographical Abstract." Also other articles sent to the author courtesy of her brother, Dr. Burnett Jackson.

Kiernan, John and Arthur Daley. *The Story of the Olympic Games*. New York: F.A. Stokes, 1969.

McCarron, Rosemary. "The New Outlook." *Souvenir Program of the 4th Annual Philadelphia Inquirer Track Meet*, February 1948: 20, 21, 32.

Madden, Barney. "Georgia College Star Shatters American Amateur Athletic Union High Jump Marks." *The Providence Journal*, July 13, 1948: 1, 8.

_____. "74 Women Track Hopes Try for 24 U.S. Olympic Spots." *The Providence Journal*, July 12, 1948: 1, 8.

_____. "Top Women Athletes Here for Olympic Trials." *The Providence Journal*, July 11, 1948: 11.

Marmor, Milton. "341 U.S. Athletes Set Sail for Olympic Games Today." *The Providence Journal*, July 14, 1948: 8

Meyer, Catherine Donovan. "Women's Indoor Amateur Athletic Union Track Championship." *The Amateur Athlete*, June 1948: 14.

_____. "Women's Track and Field." *Report of the United States Olympic Committee*. New York: United States Olympic Association, 1948: 106–113.

_____. "Women's Track and Field Committee Report." *Minutes of the Annual Meeting of the Amateur Athletic Union*, December 1948: 44–45.

"Miss Alice Coachman Is Lone U.S. Woman Champ; Dixie City to Honor Her." *The New York Amsterdam News*, August 21, 1948: 15.

"Miss Walsh Gains 3 Amateur Athletic Union Crowns." *New York Times*, July 7, 1948: 28.

"Mrs. Kaszubski Annexes Shot Put, Discus Throw in Olympic Tests." *New York Times*, July 13, 1948: 24.

Musel, Robert. "American Athletes Fail in First Three Olympic Finals but Dominate in Preliminaries of Several Other Events." *The Providence Journal*, July 31, 1948: 4.

"National Championship — Special Events Results." *The Amateur Athlete*, April 1948: 11.

"National Senior Indoor and Outdoor Track and Field Championships." *Amateur Athletic Union of the United States Official Track and Field Handbook*. New York: The Amateur Athletic Union, 1949: 102.

"Olympic News." *The Amateur Athlete*, August 1948: 9.

Reemes, Jackie. "Brooklyn Sports Highlights." *The New York Amsterdam News*, May 22, 1948: 20.

"Results of Invitation Meet Held at Paris, August 15, 1948 — Women's Events." *The Amateur Athlete*, September 1948: 15.

Sheehan, Joseph M. "U.S. Sends Abroad 'Best Squad Ever.'" *New York Times*, July 15, 1948: 28.

"Stella Walsh Now American Citizen." *The Amateur Athlete*, February 1948: 9.

"Stetson Wins 2nd Place in Florida Olympic Meet Saturday." *Deland Sun News*, May 2, 1948: 16.

"Summaries of Paris Events." *New York Times*, August 16, 1948: 15.

"U.S. Olympic Officials Busy Processing Athletes for London Trip." *New York Times*, July 13, 1948: 24.

"U.S. Wins a Relay, Loses 400 in Foul." *New York Times*, August 8, 1948: 3.

"Women Erase 6 Marks in Meet." *The New York Amsterdam News*, May 8, 1948: 27.

Chapter 32

"All-America Women's Track and Field Team." *Amateur Athletic Union of the United States Official Track and Field Handbook*. New York: The Amateur Athletic Union, 1950: 10.

Meyer, Catherine Donovan. "16-Year Old Beats Famed Stella Walsh." *The Amateur Athlete*, May 1949: 12.

_____. "Women's Track and Field Committee Report." *Minutes of the Annual Meeting of the Amateur Athletic Union*, December 1949: 88–89.

"Miss Robinson Sets Track Mark." *The Amateur Athlete*, September 1949: 11.

"National Women's Amateur Athletic Union Track Meet Opens Tonight." *The Odessa American*, August 2, 1949: 7.

Schellberg, Ruth M. "National Section on Women's Athletics." *The Journal of Health and Physical Education*, February 1949: 111.

_____. "Women's Athletic News." *The Journal of Health and Physical Education*, October 1949: 526.

Snider, Dick. "Tuskegee Takes Amateur Athletic Union Crown." *The Odessa American*, August 14, 1949: 1.

"Stella Walsh Will Retire After Amateur Athletic Union Track Meet." *New York Times*, August 12, 1949: 24.

Summers, John. "New Entries Received for National Amateur Athletic Union Track Meet." *The Odessa American*, August 2, 1949: 7.

"Tuskegee Women Take Track Title." *New York Times*, August 14, 1949: 5.

Chapter 33

"American Indoor Track and Field Championships." *Official Program*, February 18, 1950.

Andersen, Roxy Atkins. "Girls Thrive on Sport." *The Amateur Athlete*, November 1950: 24, 28.

_____. "So You Want to Be a Coach." *The Amateur Athlete*, October 1950: 24.

_____. "What's New in the Amateur Athletic Union." *The Amateur Athlete*, December 1950: 28.

Cottrell, Elmer B. "Pennsylvania." *The Journal of Health and Physical Education*, April 1950: 250.

"Did You Know That —." *The Amateur Athlete*, December 1950: 18.

"Girl's Interscholastic Track Meet." *The Journal of Health and Physical Education*, September 1950: 56.

Hall, Evelyne. "Report of Women's Track and Field Committee." *Minutes of the Annual Meeting of the Amateur Athletic Union*, December 1950: 44.

_____. "Women's Track and Field Needs Promotion." *The Amateur Athlete*, September 1950: 22.

"Name 14 New National Amateur Athletic Union Chairmen for 1950." *The Amateur Athlete*, February 1950: 16.

"National Women's Junior Outdoor Track and Field Championships." *Amateur Athletic Union of the United States Official Track and Field Handbook*. New York: The Amateur Athletic Union, 1951: 78.

"National Women's Senior Outdoor Track and Field Championships." *Amateur Athletic*

Union of the United States Official Track and Field Handbook. New York: The Amateur Athletic Union, 1951: 77.

"1950 All-America Women's Track and Field Team." *Amateur Athletic Union of the United States Official Track and Field Handbook*. New York: The Amateur Athletic Union, 1950: 10.

"1952 Olympic Women's Track and Field Committee." *Amateur Athletic Union of the United States Official Track and Field Handbook*. New York: The Amateur Athletic Union, 1950: 15.

"Ninth National Crown for Nancy Phillips." *The Amateur Athlete*, April 1950: 8.

"Records Accepted and Rejected at National Amateur Athletic Union Convention." *The Amateur Athlete*, February 1950: 14, 15, 22.

Sheehan, Joseph M. "Manhattan Team Virtually Clinches Crown in National Amateur Athletic Union Junior Title." *New York Times*, February 14, 1950: 34.

"Stella Walsh Wins Amateur Athletic Union Pentathlon." *The Amateur Athlete*, November 1950: 9.

"Tuskegee Annexes Title." *New York Times*, August 27, 1950: 8.

"Tuskegee Women Keep Track Title." *New York Times*, August 28, 1950: 22.

"2,000 Athletes in New York Junior Olympics." *The Amateur Athlete*, October 1950: 17.

"Women's Senior Pentathlon Championship." *Amateur Athletic Union of the United States Official Track and Field Handbook*. New York: The Amateur Athletic Union, 1951: 79.

Chapter 34

"Cuban Beats Bragg in 100 Meter Race." *New York Times*, March 1, 1951: 35.

Hall, Evelyne. "Report of the Women's Track and Field Committee." *Minutes of the Annual Meeting of the Amateur Athletic Union*, November 1951: 53, 70, 71.

"Miss McNabb Gains Sweep in Sprints." *New York Times*, August 13, 1951: 24.

"Miss McNabb Sets U.S. Track Record." *New York Times*, August 12, 1951: 24.

"N.S.W.A. Guides." *The Journal of Health, Physical Education, and Recreation*, June 1951: 43.

"National Amateur Athletic Union U.S.A. Women's Indoor Track and Field Championships." *Official Program*, February 1951.

"The National Section on Women's Athletics." *The Journal of Health, Physical Education, and Recreation*, January 1951: 42.

Sheehan, Joseph M. "Manhattan Keeps Amateur Athletic Union Track Title." *New York Times*, February 13, 1951: 38.

"Southern District." *The Journal of Health, Physical Education, and Recreation*, May 1951: 57.

"Summaries of Games at Buenos Aires." *New York Times*, March 2, 1951: 29.

"Summaries of Games at Buenos Aires." *New York Times*, March 3, 1951: 9.

"Summaries of Games at Buenos Aires." *New York Times*, March 4, 1951: 2.

"Summaries of Games at Buenos Aires." *New York Times*, March 5, 1951: 27.

"Summaries of Games at Buenos Aires." *New York Times*, March 6, 1951: 33.

"Summaries of Games at Buenos Aires." *New York Times*, March 7, 1951: 44.

"U.S.A. Senior Women's Track and Field Championships." *Amateur Athletic Union of the United States Official Track and Field Handbook*. New York: The Amateur Athletic Union, 1951: 75, 76, 77.

"USA Women's Pentathlon Championship." *Amateur Athletic Union of the United States Official Track and Field Handbook*. New York: The Amateur Athletic Union, 1951: 79.

Chapter 35

"Amateur Athletic Union Indoor Track and Field Championships." *Official Program*, February 16, 1952.

Blackburn, Rachel. "Women in Athletics." *The Journal of Health, Physical Education, and Recreation*, October 1952: 50.

Bushnell, Asa S., ed. *United States 1952 Olympic Book*. New York: U.S. Olympic Association, 1953.

Delmonaco, Antonio, ed. *Women's Amateur Sport News*, Published @ P.O. Box 1918, Waterbury, Connecticut, 1952.

"Miss Hardy Ties 50-Meter Record." *New York Times*, June 30, 1952: 25.

"Nine Women Named to U.S. Squad After Harrisburg Track Tryouts." *New York Times*, July 5, 1952: 11.

"Senior National Women's Pentathlon Championships." *Amateur Athletic Union of the United States Official Track and Field Handbook*. New York: The Amateur Athletic Union, 1952–53: 107.

"Summaries of Olympic Games." *New York Times*, July 22, 1952: 29.

"Summaries of Olympic Games." *New York Times*, July 23, 1952: 27.

"Summaries of Olympic Games." *New York Times*, July 28, 1952: 19.

"Track and Field Tryouts for Women." *1952 U.S. Olympic Souvenir Book*, July 4, 1952.

"U.S.A. Senior and Junior Women's Track and Field Championships." *Amateur Athletic Union of the United States Official Track and Field Handbook*. New York: The Amateur Athletic Union, 1952–53: 103, 104, 105.

"University of Delaware News." *The Journal of Health, Physical Education, and Recreation*, May 1952: 57.

Wilson, Lucile. "Women's Track and Field Committee Report." *Minutes of the Annual Meeting of the Amateur Athletic Union*, December 1952: 63–64.

"Wilt Easily Takes Mile Race in 4:101." *New York Times*, March 16, 1952: 3.

"Women's Track and Field." *Amateur Athletic Union of the United States Official Track and Field Handbook*. New York: The Amateur Athletic Union, 1952: 234, 235, 236, 237.

Chapter 36

"C.Y.O. Women Win U.S. Track Title." *New York Times*, July 27, 1953: 22.

"Grand Street Boys Set Relay Record." *New York Times*, March 22, 1953: 1, 5.

"Miss Dwyer Takes Amateur Athletic Union Sprint Title." *New York Times*, July 26, 1953: 9.

"1953 All-America Women's Track and Field Team." *Amateur Athletic Union of the United States Official Track and Field Handbook*. New York: The Amateur Athletic Union, 1954: 10.

"Official Sports Library." *The Journal of Health, Physical Education, and Recreation*, April 1953: 33.

"Region 2 and 9 Women's Pentathlon Championship." *Amateur Athletic Union of the United States Official Track and Field Handbook*. New York: The Amateur Athletic Union, 1954: 63.

"Senior and Junior National Women's Track and Field Championships." *Amateur Athletic Union of the United States Official Track and Field Handbook*. New York: The Amateur Athletic Union, 1954: 59, 60, 62.

"Senior National Women's Indoor Track and Field Championships." *Amateur Athletic Union of the United States Official Track and Field Handbook*. New York: The Amateur Athletic Union, 1953: 100.

"Women's American Records." *Amateur Athletic Union of the United States Official Track and Field Handbook.* New York: The Amateur Athletic Union, 1954: 30, 31.

"Women's Best." *Track and Field News*, January 1953: 4.

Chapter 37

"All-America Women's Track and Field Team." *Amateur Athletic Union of the United States Official Track and Field Handbook.* New York: The Amateur Athletic Union, 1955: 10.

Blunk, Frank M. "Chicago C.Y.O. Team Wins National Amateur Athletic Union Women's Track Crown." *New York Times*, March 28, 1954: 8.

Kaszubski, Frances. "Report of the Women's Track and Field Committee." *Minutes of the Annual Meeting of the Amateur Athletic Union*, November 1954: 24.

"Massachusetts State Council Knights of Columbus 28th Annual Athletic Games." *Official Program*, January 16, 1954.

"1956 Olympic Women's Track and Field Committee." *Amateur Athletic Union of the United States Official Track and Field Handbook.* New York: The Amateur Athletic Union, 1954: 12.

"Senior National Amateur Athletic Union Women's Pentathlon Championship." *Amateur Athletic Union of the United States Official Track and Field Handbook.* New York: The Amateur Athletic Union, 1955: 73.

"Senior National Outdoor and Indoor Women's Track and Field Championships." *Amateur Athletic Union of the United States Official Track and Field Handbook.* New York: The Amateur Athletic Union, 1955: 56, 62, 63.

"Tennessee State Sets Relay Mark in Women's Amateur Athletic Union Track Meet." *New York Times*, August 1, 1954: 4.

Chapter 38

"All-America Women's Track and Field Team." *Amateur Athletic Union of the United States Official Track and Field Handbook.* New York: The Amateur Athletic Union, 1956: 11.

Kaszubski, Frances. "Women's Track and Field Committee Report." *Minutes of the Annual Meeting of the Amateur Athletic Union*, December 1955: 20, 78.

"Miss McDaniel High Jump Victor." *New York Times*, March 18, 1955: 37.

"Misses Larney and Wershoven Win National Amateur Athletic Union Track Titles at Chicago." *New York Times*, February 6, 1955: 7.

"Pan American Games Summaries." *New York Times*, March 17, 1955: 82.

"Physical Education for High School Students." *The Journal of Health, Physical Education, and Recreation*, March 1955: 47.

"Senior National Women's and Girls' Outdoor Track and Field Championships." *Amateur Athletic Union of the United States Official Track and Field Handbook.* New York: The Amateur Athletic Union, 1956: 59, 60.

"Summaries in Mexico City Games." *New York Times*, March 16, 1955: 44.

"Tennessee State Girls Win." *New York Times*, June 19, 1955: 4.

"Women Break Records." *Track and Field News*, July 1955: 5.

Chapter 39

"All-America Women's Track and Field Team." *Amateur Athletic Union of the United States Official Track and Field Handbook.* New York: The Amateur Athletic Union, 1957: 11.

Beglane, Bernie. "Dolores Dwyer's Olympic Fate May Hinge on Senior Meet." *Long Island Star Journal*, August 4, 1956.

Bushnell, Asa S., ed. *United States 1956 Olympic Book*. New York: United States Olympic Association, Inc.

Jokl, E., M. Karvonen, J. Kihlberg, A. Koskela and L. Noro. "Research on Olympic Athletes." *The Journal of Health, Physical Education, and Recreation*, September 1956: 61–62.

Kaszubski, Frances T. "Women's Track and Field Committee Report." *Minutes of the Annual Meeting of the Amateur Athletic Union*, October 1956: 71, 72.

Kiernan, John and Arthur Daley. *The Story of the Olympic Games*. New York: F.A. Stokes, 1969.

"Mae Faggs Excels in 3 Track Events." *New York Times*, August 18, 1956: 1, 10.

"Mrs. Brown Betters Two Track Records." *New York Times*, August 26, 1956: 1, 7.

"Senior and Girls' National Amateur Athletic Union Women's Outdoor Track and Field Championships." *Amateur Athletic Union of the United States Official Track and Field Handbook*. New York: The Amateur Athletic Union, 1957: 82, 84.

"Senior National Indoor Women's Track and Field Championships." *Amateur Athletic Union of the United States Official Track and Field Handbook*. New York: The Amateur Athletic Union, 1957: 86.

Chapter 40

Adams, Lucinda Williams. "My Olympic Experiences." *The Journal of Health, Physical Education, and Recreation*, March 1988: 35, 36.

"All-America Women's Track and Field Team." *Amateur Athletic Union of the United States Official Track and Field Handbook*. New York: The Amateur Athletic Union, 1958: 11.

Andersen, Roxanne. *AAU Study of Effect of Athletic Competition on Girls and Women*, Third Revision, Amateur Athletic Union of the United States: May 1960.

Briordy, William J. "Miss Larney Sets 3 AAU Records." *New York Times*, August 19, 1957.

Mayer, Eleanor and Martha Haverstick. "On Your Mark, Get Set, Go!" *The Journal of Health, Physical Education, and Recreation*, April 1957: 17, 69.

"Miss Larney Sets U.S. Javelin Mark." *New York Times*, August 11, 1957: 1, 3.

"Senior National Women's and Girls' Outdoor Track and Field Championships." *Amateur Athletic Union of the United States Official Track and Field Handbook*. New York: The Amateur Athletic Union, 1958: 48, 50.

"Senior Women's Indoor Track and Field Championships." *Amateur Athletic Union of the United States Official Track and Field Handbook*. New York: The Amateur Athletic Union, 1958: 57.

"Stella Walsh in Pentathlon." *Track and Field News*, November 1957.

"Tennessee State Takes 4th Straight Women's Amateur Athletic Union Track Title." *New York Times*, April 7, 1957: 4.

"Women's World List." *Track and Field News*, February 1957: 9.

Chapter 41

Abramson, Jesse. "Moscow-Bound Track Stars Set Unofficial Records Here." *New York Herald Tribune*, July 20, 1958: 4.

_____. "1 American, 5 AAU Marks Shattered in Women's Track." *New York Herald Tribune*, July 6, 1958.

"All-America Women's Track and Field Team." *Amateur Athletic Union of the United States Official Track and Field Handbook*. New York: The Amateur Athletic Union, 1959: 11.

"Editor's Mail." *The Journal of Health, Physical Education, and Recreation*, May-June 1958: 6.

Friel, Ed. "Girl Loses Race, Wins Team Berth." *Newark Sunday News*, July 6, 1958.

Hartman, Betty G. "On Intercollegiate Competition for Women." *The Journal of Health, Physical Education, and Recreation*, March 1958: 24.

McGowen, Deane. "U.S. Girls' Team Drills for Meet with Russia." *New York Times*, July 16, 1958.

Means, Clarence G. "Let the Girls Play, Too." *The Journal of Health, Physical Education, and Recreation*, May-June 1958: 22.

"Meet Summaries." *New York Times*, August 3, 1958: 5.

"Meet Summaries." *New York Times*, August 7, 1958: 32.

"Moscow Track Summaries." *New York Times*, July 29, 1958: 27.

"1958 National Amateur Athletic Union Women's Pentathlon Championships. *Amateur Athletic Union of the United States Official Track and Field Handbook*. New York: The Amateur Athletic Union, 1959: 40.

"The Prince Philip Lecture: The Changing World of Physical Education and Sport." *The Physical Education of Great Britain and Northern Ireland*, December 2, 1982.

"Summaries in Budapest Track." *New York Times*, July 28, 1958: 17.

"U.S.A. Women's Track and Field Championships." *Amateur Athletic Union of the United States Official Track and Field Handbook*. New York: The Amateur Athletic Union, 1959: 17, 19.

Chapter 42

"All-America Women's Track and Field Team." *Amateur Athletic Union of the United States Official Track and Field Handbook*. New York: The Amateur Athletic Union, 1960–61: 12.

"All-Time Woman's List." *Track and Field News*, April 1959.

Kaszubski, Frances. "Track Talk." July 1959.

Nelson, Bert. "Of People and Things." *Track and Field News*, September 1959: 7.

Quinn, Thomas. Meet Director of New York Athletic Club Games. Personal Correspondence: January 22, 1959.

Sheehan, Joseph M. "Norton Ties World Dash Record in Pan-American Track." *New York Times*, September 1, 1959: 26.

_____. "West Indies Sweeps 400-Meter Run at Chicago." *New York Times*, September 2, 1959: 26.

"USA Senior Women's Indoor Track and Field Championships." *Amateur Athletic Union of the United States Official Track and Field Handbook*. New York: The Amateur Athletic Union, 1960–61.

"USA Women's and Girls' Outdoor Track and Field Championships." *Amateur Athletic Union of the United States Official Track and Field Handbook*. New York: The Amateur Athletic Union, 1960–61: 14, 16.

"Women's Track and Field Committee." *Amateur Athletic Union of the United States Official Track and Field Handbook*. New York: The Amateur Athletic Union, 1959: 7.

Chapter 43

"All America Women's Track and Field Team." *Amateur Athletic Union of the United States Official Track and Field Handbook*. New York: The Amateur Athletic Union, 1961: 12.

Campbell, Darwin. "City Says Goodbye to One of the Greats." *The Leaf-Chronicle*, November 18, 1994: 1, 8.

"Greek-USA Meet." *Amateur Athletic Union of the United States Official Track and Field Handbook*. New York: The Amateur Athletic Union, 1961: 41.

Kaszubski, Frances. *Track Talk*, March 1960.

_____. *Track Talk*, June 1960.

Kiernan, John and Arthur Daley. *The Story of the Olympic Games*. New York: F.A. Stokes, 1969.

Lentz, Arthur, ed. *United States 1960 Olympic Book*. New York: United States Olympic Association, 1961.

"N.Y. Meet Summaries." *Track and Field News*, January 1960: 11.

"National Amateur Athletic Union Outdoor Women's and Girls' Track and Field Championships." *Amateur Athletic Union of the United States Official Track and Field Handbook*. New York: The Amateur Athletic Union, 1961: 49, 51.

Nelson, Bert. "Of People and Things." *Track and Field News*, June 1960: 7.

Nelson, Cordner. "Track Talk." *Track and Field News*, December 1960.

"Records Change Needed." *Track and Field News*, February 1960: 10.

Rudolph, Wilma. *Wilma*. New York: New American Library, 1977.

"Rudolph Sets World Mark." *Track and Field News*, August 1960.

"Rudolph Wins Three Golds." *Track and Field News*, September 1960.

Temple, Ed. *Only the Pure in Heart Survive*. Nashville, Tenn.: Broadman Press, 1980.

"U.S.–British Empire and Commonwealth Meet." *Amateur Athletic Union of the United States Official Track and Field Handbook*. New York: The Amateur Athletic Union, 1961: 39.

Walker, Teresa M. "Rudolph Teammate Has Fond Memories." *The Leaf-Chronicle*, November 18, 1994: 1, 4.

"White Jumps 20' 4-1/2." *Track and Field News*, August 1960.

"Wilma Rudolph Win for U.S. in Olympics." *New York Times*, September 3, 1960.

"Women's American Records." *Amateur Athletic Union of the United States Official Track and Field Handbook*. New York: The Amateur Athletic Union, 1961: 32.

Chapter 44

Abramson, Jesse. "Wadsworth, Surprise Star, Voted Top Millrose Athlete." *New York Herald Tribune*, February 5, 1961: 2.

"All America Women's Track and Field Team." *Amateur Athletic Union of the United States Official Track and Field Handbook*. New York: The Amateur Athletic Union, 1962: 14.

"Butcher, Grace." *Track and Field News*, September 1961: 18.

Jones, Patricia, ed. *Track Mirror*, December 1961.

Kaszubski, Frances. "Women's Track and Field Committee Report." *Minutes of the Annual American Athletic Union Meeting*, November 1961: 22, 23.

"Meet Summaries." *Track and Field News*, March 1961.

"National Amateur Athletic Union Senior Women's and Girls' Track and Field Championships." *Amateur Athletic Union of the United States Official Track and Field Handbook*. New York: The Amateur Athletic Union, 1962: 13, 15.

"Second Annual Los Angeles Invitational Track and Field Meet." *Official Program*. January 21, 1961.

"Senior National Amateur Athletic Union Women's Indoor Track and Field Championships." *Amateur Athletic Union of the United States Official Track and Field Handbook*. New York: The Amateur Athletic Union, 1962: 19, 21.

"Tennessee State Upset." *Track and Field News*, March 1961.

"Track Summaries at Moscow." *New York Times*, July 16, 1961: 3.

"Track Summaries at Moscow." *New York Times*, July 17, 1961.

"Wilma Rudolph Wins Sullivan Award." *Amateur Athletic Union of the United States Official Track and Field Handbook*. New York: The Amateur Athletic Union, 1962: 15.

"Women Track Stars Here to Attend University of Hawaii." *Honolulu Star Bulletin*, September 10, 1961: 13.

"Women's American Records." *Amateur Athletic Union of the United States Official Track and Field Handbook*. New York: The Amateur Athletic Union, 1962: 34.

Chapter 45

"All American." *Amateur Athletic Union of the United States Official Track and Field Handbook*. New York: The Amateur Athletic Union, 1963: 4.

Bateman, Hal. "On Your Marks." *Track and Field News*, March 1962: 17.

____. "On Your Marks." *Track and Field News*, September 1962: 17.

"The 4th Annual Mt. San Antonio Relays." *Official Program*, April 27–28, 1962.

Jones, Patricia, ed. *Track Mirror*, January 1962.

____. *Track Mirror*, March 1962.

Lloyd, Lt. Col, Alvin. "Women's Track and Field Top Performances." *Amateur Athletic Union of the United States Official Track and Field Handbook*. New York: The Amateur Athletic Union, 1963: 22, 23.

"Meet Summaries." *New York Times*, July 22, 1962: 3.

"National Amateur Athletic Union Senior and Girls' Outdoor Championships." *Amateur Athletic Union of the United States Official Track and Field Handbook*. New York: The Amateur Athletic Union, 1963: 13, 15.

"The 32nd Annual Mason Dixon Games." *Official Program*, February 1992.

"United States vs. Poland International Meet." *Amateur Athletic Union of the United States Official Track and Field Handbook*. New York: The Amateur Athletic Union, 1963: 12.

"United States vs. Soviet Union International Dual Meet." *Amateur Athletic Union of the United States Official Track and Field Handbook*. New York: The Amateur Athletic Union, 1963: 12.

"Vivian Brown's 0:24.1 in 220 Lowers U.S. Record on Coast." *New York Times*, July 9, 1962: 26.

Chapter 46

"Amateur Athletic Union All American Track and Field Teams." *Amateur Athletic Union of the United States Official Track and Field Handbook*. New York: The Amateur Athletic Union, 1964: 183.

"Edith McGuire and Sharon Shepherd Score Double Victories in Women's Championships." *Amateur Athletic Union of the United States Official Track and Field Handbook*. New York: The Amateur Athletic Union, 1964: 198.

"Great Britain vs. United States." *Amateur Athletic Union of the United States Official Track and Field Handbook*. New York: The Amateur Athletic Union, 1964: 211.

Jernigan, Sara Staff. "The National Institute on Girls' Sports." *The Journal of Health, Physical Education, and Recreation*, June 1963.

Kaszubski, Frances T. "Women's Track and Field Committee Report." *Minutes of the Annual Meeting of the Amateur Athletic Union*, December 1963: 40.

Lloyd, Lt. Col. Alvin. "Women's and Girls' Track and Field Top Performances in 1963." *Amateur Athletic Union of the United States Official Track and Field Handbook*. New York: The Amateur Athletic Union, 1964: 212–215.

"Los Angeles Invitational." *Track and Field News*, January 1963: 2.

"Massachusetts Knights of Columbus." *Track and Field News*, January 1963: 2.

National Amateur Athletic Union Women's and Girls' Track and Field Championships." *Amateur Athletic Union of the United States Official Track and Field Handbook.* New York: The Amateur Athletic Union, 1964: 199–201.

National Amateur Athletic Union Women's Indoor Track and Field Championships." *Amateur Athletic Union of the United States Official Track and Field Handbook.* New York: The Amateur Athletic Union, 1964: 202, 203.

Nelson, Bert. "Of People and Things." *Track and Field News,* March 1963: 24.

____. "Of People and Things." *Track and Field News,* December 1963: 24.

"Poland vs. United States." *Amateur Athletic Union of the United States Official Track and Field Handbook.* New York: The Amateur Athletic Union, 1964: 210.

"Proceedings — First National Institute on Girls' Sports." American Association for Health, Physical Education and Recreation. November 4–9, 1963.

"75th Amateur Athletic Union Track and Field Championships." *Official Program,* February 1963.

"U.S.S.R. vs. United States." *Amateur Athletic Union of the United States Official Track and Field Handbook.* New York: The Amateur Athletic Union, 1964: 209–210.

"West Germany vs. United States." *Amateur Athletic Union of the United States Official Track and Field Handbook.* New York: The Amateur Athletic Union, 1964: 210, 211.

"Women Win Six Events." *Track and Field News,* May 1963.

Chapter 47

"All America Track and Field Teams." *Amateur Athletic Union of the United States Official Track and Field Handbook.* New York: The Amateur Athletic Union, 1965: 183.

"Amateur Athletic Union Track Summaries." *New York Times,* February 23, 1964: 9.

Bellew, Juner. "Women's Track and Field Committee Report." *Minutes of the Annual Meeting of the Amateur Athletic Union,* December 1964: 29.

Carlson, Lewis H. and John J. Fogerty. *Tales of Gold.* Chicago and New York: Contemporary Books, 1987.

"Girls Sports Institute in South Carolina." *The Journal of Health, Physical Education, and Recreation,* May 1964: 93.

Lechenperg, Harald, ed. *Olympic Games 1964.* New York: A.S. Barnes, 1964.

Peck, William. "Women's and Girl's Track and Field Top Performances in 1964." *Amateur Athletic Union of the United States Official Track and Field Handbook.* New York: The Amateur Athletic Union, 1965: 215, 216.

"Presses Eye 4 Golds." *Track and Field News,* September 1964.

"Records Rewritten." *Track and Field News,* October/November 1964: 37.

Smith, Hope. "The First National Institute on Girls' Sports." *The Journal of Health, Physical Education, and Recreation,* April 1964: 31, 32, 58.

"Summaries of Women's and Girl's National Championships." *Amateur Athletic Union of the United States Official Track and Field Handbook.* New York: The Amateur Athletic Union, 1965: 201–204.

"Track and Field for Girls." *The Journal of Health, Physical Education, and Recreation,* May 1964: 93.

"Track and Field for Girls and Women." *The Journal of Health, Physical Education, and Recreation,* September 1964: 49.

Watman, Melvyn. "Tokyo Olympic Report." *Athletics Weekly.* November 7, 1964.

Chapter 48

"American Women Triumph in Track." *New York Times*, August 14, 1965: 17.

Bellew, Juner. "Women's Track and Field Committee Report." *Minutes of the Annual Meeting of the Amateur Athletic Union*, December 1965: 33.

Cassell, Olana. "United States Women Win Four International Dual Meets." *Amateur Athletic Union of the United States Official Track and Field Handbook*. New York: The Amateur Athletic Union, 1966: 53, 54.

Crawford, Elinor. "D.G.W.S. Cooperates with National Sports Organizations." *The Journal of Health, Physical Education, and Recreation*, January 1965: 25, 86.

Durdin, Tillman. "Hayes Runs 100-Yard Dash in 0:09.6 in His First Pro Start and Earns $500." *New York Times*, April 4, 1965: 7.

"880-Yard Crown to Marie Mulder." *New York Times*, July 4, 1965: 7.

Foreman, Ken and Virginia Husted. *Track and Field Techniques for Girls and Women*. Dubuque, Iowa: Wm. C. Brown, 1965.

Grose, Peter. "Girl Quarterback Now a Top Runner." *New York Times*, August 1, 1965: 4.

Larney, Leo, ed. *Cinderbelle*. February 1965, March 1965, May 1965.

"Larrabee Sets World Indoor 400-Meter Record." *New York Times*, April 9, 1965: 25.

"McGuire and T. Press Standouts in USA–USSR Meet." *Amateur Athletic Union of the United States Official Track and Field Handbook*. New York: The Amateur Athletic Union, 1965: 213.

"National Amateur Athletic Union Indoor Championships." *Amateur Athletic Union of the United States Official Track and Field Handbook*. New York: The Amateur Athletic Union, 1966: 57.

"National Amateur Athletic Union Women's and Girls' Outdoor Championships." *Amateur Athletic Union of the United States Official Track and Field Handbook*. New York: The Amateur Athletic Union, 1966: 60, 61.

"National Amateur Athletic Union Women's Pentathlon Championship." *Amateur Athletic Union of the United States Official Track and Field Handbook*. New York: The Amateur Athletic Union, 1966: 57.

"Soviet Men Lead U.S. by a Point in Track at Kiev." *New York Times*, August 1, 1965: 1, 4.

"U.S. Men Lead Poles in Track." *New York Times*, August 8, 1965: 1.

"U.S. Men's and Women's Track Teams Triumph Over Poles at Warsaw." *New York Times*, August 9, 1965: 30.

"U.S. Runners Set 2 Indoor Records." *New York Times*, April 8, 1965: 51.

"Will Stephens." *The Oregon State University Coaching Staff—1982 Press Guide*. Oregon State University Archives.

"Women's and Girls' Track and Field Top Performances in 1965." *Amateur Athletic Union of the United States Official Track and Field Handbook*. New York: The Amateur Athletic Union, 1966: 69.

Chapter 49

"Conference on Olympic Development." *The Journal of Health, Physical Education, and Recreation*, November-December 1966: 77.

DeLong, Linda B., ed. *Track and Field Guide*. Washington, D.C.: American Association for Health, Physical Education and Recreation, 1966.

"Miss McGuire to Retire After Soviet Track Meet." *New York Times*, July 4, 1966: 22.

"Pennel Betters Pole-Vault Mark." *New York Times*, February 13, 1966: 2, 3.

"Saturday Track Summaries." *New York Times*, February 14, 1966.

"10th Annual Marine Corps. Schools Relays." *Official Program*, May 6-7, 1966.

"24th Annual Compton Invitational Track Meet." *Official Program*, June 4, 1966.

"25th Anniversary — California Relays and State Junior College Track Championships."
    Official Program, May 28, 1966.
"2 U.S. Women Marks Set in Amateur Athletic Union Track." *New York Times*, July 3,
    1966: 12.
"Women's Amateur Athletic Union: Seagren Equals Own Vault Mark." *Track and Field
    News*, July 1966: 2.
"Women's World Indoor Marks Set in Four Track Events at Amateur Athletic Union
    Meet." *New York Times*, March 6, 1966: 8.

Chapter 50

"Finals of Women's Amateur Athletic Union Track." *New York Times*, July 4, 1967: 14.
Larney, Leo F., ed. *Cinderbelle*, February-May 1967.
"Pan-American Games Results." *New York Times*, July 30, 1967: 8.
"Pan-American Games Results." *New York Times*, July 31, 1967: 32.
"Pan-American Games Results." *New York Times*, August 2, 1967: 29.
"Pan-American Games Results." *New York Times*, August 3, 1967: 39.
"Pan-American Games Results." *New York Times*, August 5, 1967: 18.
"Pan-American Games Results." *New York Times*, August 6, 1967: 6.
Reel, Vince, ed. *Women's Track and Field World*. August 1967.
"Summaries of Coast Track Meet." *New York Times*, July 10, 1967: 37.
"Track Mark Tied by Miss Ferrell." *New York Times*, July 3, 1967: 23.
"Tracy Smith Breaks Indoor 3-Mile Mark." *New York Times*, March 5, 1967: 3.

Chapter 51

"Amateur Athletic Union Summaries." *New York Times*, February 25, 1968: 3.
Carlson, Lewis H. and John J. Fogarty. *Tales of Gold*. New York: Contemporary Books,
    1987.
Coote, James. *Olympic Report 1968*, London: Robert Hale, 1969.
"5th Annual Examiner All-American Games Indoor Track and Field Meet." *Official Pro-
    gram*, January 5, 1968.
Harkins, Dorothy, ed. *Track and Field Guide*. Washington, D.C.: American Association
    for Health, Physical Education and Recreation, 1968.
Jackson, Madeline Manning. *Running for Jesus*. Waco, Texas: Word Books, 1977.
Jackson, Nell C. "Women's Track and Field Committee Report." *Minutes of the Annual
    Meeting of the Amateur Athletic Union*, 1968: 43, 44.
1968 United States Olympic Book. New York: United States Olympic Committee, 1969.
"9th Annual Los Angeles Times Indoor Games." *Official Program*, February 10, 1968.
Reel, Vince, ed. *Women's Track and Field World*. October 1968.
"San Diego Second Annual Indoor Games." *Official Program*, February 10, 1968.
"Young Upsets Tracy at 3 Miles — Two Records Set." *New York Times*, February 25, 1968: 1.

Chapter 52

"Barbara Ferrell Takes 2 Sprints." *New York Times*, July 7, 1969: 39.
Jackson, Nell C. "Report of the Women's Track and Field Committee." *The Journal of Health,
    Physical Education, and Recreation*, December 1969: 56.
"Miss Cheng Sets U.S. Hurdle Mark." *New York Times*, July 6, 1969: 9.

Parker, Virginia and Robert Kennedy. *Track and Field for Girls and Women*. Philadelphia: W.B. Saunders, 1969.

"Summaries of Women's Track Events." *New York Times*, March 2, 1969: 6.

"29th Annual Knights of Columbus Annual Indoor Track Meet." *Official Program*, January 11, 1969.

Chapter 53

Jackson, Nell C. "Women's Track and Field—Annual Report." *Minutes of the Annual Meeting of the Amateur Athletic Union* , 1970: 60, 61.

"Summaries of the Indoor Championships." *New York Times*, February 28, 1970: 32.

Wienke, Phoebe. ed. *Track and Field Guide*, Washington, D.C.: American Association for Health, Physical Education and Recreation, 1970.

Chapter 54

"Amateur Athletic Union Track Summaries." *New York Times*, February 27, 1971: 16.

Chamberlain, Lillian Greene. "Fred Thompson." Biographical sketch, written for presentation at Thompson's award ceremony. 1995.

"Here's to You—General." *The Athletics Congress Newsletter*, November 1988: 1–2.

Jackson, Dr. Nell. "Women's Track and Field Committee." *Minutes of the Annual Meeting of the Amateur Athletic Union*, 1971: 38.

"Miss Falck Sets World Record in 800-Meter Run." *New York Times*, July 12, 1971: 37.

"Pat Hawkins Sets U.S. Hurdle Mark." *New York Times*, July 11, 1971: 4.

Reel, Vince, ed. *Women's Track and Field World*, September/October 1972.

Smelkinson, Marsha. *Amateur Athlete 1971: The Official Amateur Athletic Union Yearbook*. Indianapolis: Amateur Athletic Union, 1972.

"Summaries of Olympic Meet." *New York Times*, February 20, 1971: 18.

"United States Olympic Invitational Track and Field Meet." *Official Program*, February 1971.

Chapter 55

Amdur, Neil. "Meriwether Takes A.A.U. 60; Dyce and Evans Win Crowns." *New York Times,* February 26, 1972: 21, 22.

____. "Munich 1972: Tragic Blur on Olympic Family Memory." *New York Times* September 6 1992: 15.

"Athletes of the Meet." *29th Annual Times/GTE Indoor Games Program*. February 19, 1988.

"Ghana Sprinter Sets A.A.U. Mark." *New York Times* July 2, 1972: 7.

Harvin, Al. "Miss Ferrell Gains in 3 Events at U.S. Olympic Final Trials." *New York Times*, July 8, 1972: 22.

____. "3 U.S. Records Are Shattered in Windup of Women's Olympic Track Trials." *New York Times,* July 9, 1972: 5.

"Miss White Jumps to 13th Track Title." *New York Times,* July 3, 1972: 13.

"Olympic Games Summaries." *New York Times*, September 8, 1972: 22, 23.

"Olympic Games Summaries." *New York Times*, September 10, 1972: 2–3.

"Olympic Games Summaries." *New York Times*, September 1, 1972: 10.

"Olympic Games Summaries." *New York Times*, September 2, 1972: 10.

"Olympic Games Summaries." *New York Times*, September 3, 1972: 2.

"Olympic Games Summaries." *New York Times*, September 4, 1972: 10.

"Olympic Games Summaries." *New York Times*, September 5, 1972: 48–49.
"Olympic Games Summaries." *New York Times*, September 8, 1972: 22.
"Olympic Games Summaries." *New York Times*, September 9, 1972.
Rico, Pat. "Women's Track and Field Committee Report." *Minutes of the Annual Meeting of the Amateur Athletic Union*, November 29, 1972: 50–52.
Smelkinson, Marsha, ed. *Amateur Athlete 1972: The Official AAU Yearbook*. Indianapolis: Amateur Athletic Union of the United States, 1973.
Wakefield, Frances. *Track and Field Guide*. Washington, D.C.: American Association for Health, Physical Education, and Recreation, 1972.

Chapter 56

Amateur Athlete 1973: The Official AAU Yearbook. Indianapolis: Amateur Athletic Union of the United States, 1974.
Amdur, Neil. "Girl Runner, 14, Leads U.S. Women to Victory." *New York Times*, March 17, 1973: 23, 25.
"England Wins XC Title; USA Third." *Women's Track and Field World*, March/April 1973: 1–12.
"Mable Ferguson Wins A.A.U. 220 and 440 in Upsets." *New York Times*, June 24, 1973: 4.
Popper, Jan. "World University Games." *Women's Track and Field World*, September/October 1973: 1, 4.
"The Race of the Meet." *Women's Track and Field World*, June 1973: 9.
Rico, Pat. "Report of the Women's Track and Field Committee." *Minutes of the Annual Meeting of the Amateur Athletic Union*, November 1973: 52–55.
"Summaries of Meet." *New York Times*, February 24, 1973: 22.
"U.S. Downs Russians." *Women's Track and Field World*, March/April 173: 1.
Wakefield, Frances, Dorothy Harkins and John M. Cooper. *Track and Field Fundamentals for Girls and Women*. Saint Louis: C.V. Mosby, 1973.

Chapter 57

Amateur Athlete 1974: The Official Amateur Athletic Union Yearbook. Indianapolis: Amateur Athletic Union of the United States, 1975.
Amdur, Neil. "Miss Decker Is Ready to Test Soviet Runners." *New York Times*, July 5, 1974: 27, 29.
_____. "Soviet Men, Women Lead U.S. in Track." *New York Times*, July 6, 1974: 11, 13.
Bateman, Hal. "National Track and Field Hall of Fame." *Grand Opening and Dedication Reception Booklet*, January 12, 1986.
Eskenazi, Gerald. "Joni Huntley Clears 6 Feet in High Jump; Mile-Walk Record Set by Miss Brodock." *New York Times*, February 23, 1974: 21, 22.
_____. "Mary Decker Eclipses Amateur Athletic Union Record for Half-Mile; New Zealanders Excel." *New York Times*, February 23, 1974: 21.
Reel, Vince, ed. "Athletes of the Year." *Women's Track and Field World*. January/February 1974: 4–5.
_____. "Outdoor Records." *Women's Track and Field World*," April 1974: 12.
_____. "Soviets Pin Double Loss on Yanks." *Women's Track and Field World*, August 1974: 10, 12.
_____. "U.S. in First-Ever International Pentathlon." *Women's Track and Field World*, September 1974: 3.
Rico, Pat. "Report of the Women's Track and Field Committee." *Minutes of the Annual Meeting of the Amateur Athletic Union*, October 15, 1974: 28–29.

"Summaries of US–USSR Track Meet." *New York Times*, July 7, 1974: 4.

Thompson, Donnis H., ed. *Track and Field Guide*. Washington, D.C.: American Association for Health, Physical Education, and Recreation, 1974.

"U.S. Defeats Russians in Junior Track Meet." *New York Times*, June 30, 1974: 4.

"U.S.–Soviet Track Summaries." *New York Times*, March 3, 1974: 3.

Chapter 58

Amateur Athlete 1975: The Official Amateur Athletic Union Yearbook. Indianapolis: Amateur Athletic Union of the United States, 1976.

Amdur, Neil. "Williams, Miss Rudolph Shed Leg Braces in Sprint to Fame." *New York Times*, May 20, 1975: 30.

"American Girl, 16, First at 200 Meters." *New York Times*, October 17, 1975: 41, 43.

"Colgate Women's Games." *Fact Sheet*. New York: Forman, Cohen, Walsh.

"Colson, Joni Huntley Win." *New York Times*, October 18, 1975: 35, 37.

"Jan Merrill Triumphs in Pan-Am Test." *New York Times*, September 1, 1975: 10.

"Pan-Am Games Summaries." *New York Times*, October 18, 1975: 37.

"Pan American Games Summaries." *New York Times*, October 22, 1975: 33.

Reel, Vince, ed. *Women's Track and Field World*. January/February 1975.

____. *Women's Track and Field World*. March 1975.

____. *Women's Track and Field World*. July 1975.

____. *Women's Track and Field World*. August 1975.

____. *Women's Track and Field World*. September 1975.

____. *Women's Track and Field World*. October 1975.

____. *Women's Track and Field World*. November 1975.

____. *Women's Track and Field World*. December 1975.

"79th Annual Drake Relays. *Official Program*, April 1975.

"Shanghai Winners." *New York Times*, May 25, 1975: 44.

"Summaries of Pan-American Games." *New York Times*, October 15, 1975: 29.

"Summaries of Pan-American Games." *New York Times*, October 16, 1975: 52.

"Summaries of Pan-American Games." *New York Times*, October 17, 1975: 43.

"Summaries of Pan-American Games." *New York Times*, October 21, 1975: 32.

"Track and Field Summaries." *New York Times*, October 14, 1975: 50.

"Track and Field Summaries." *New York Times*, October 20, 1975: 49.

"U.S. Captures 4 of 5 Finals in Pan-Am Swimming Events." *New York Times*, October 20, 1975: 47, 49.

"U.S. Scores on China Track." *New York Times*, May 19, 1975: 36.

"U.S. Sweep Is Cheered by Chinese." *New York Times*, May 20, 1975: 30.

Watson, Martha. "Outstanding Accomplishments in Track and Field." Typed biographical material from Martha Watson, October 1, 1995.

White, Gordon S., Jr. "Chinese Women Victors of U.S. in Javelin." *New York Times*, May 23, 1975: 44.

Chapter 59

Amateur Athlete 1976: The Official Amateur Athletic Union Yearbook. Indianapolis: Amateur Athletic Union of the United States, 1977.

"Athletes' Feats." *womenSports*, March 1976: 64

"Athletes of the Year." *Women's Track and Field World*, January/February 1976.

Dennis, Dr. Evie G. "Women's Track and Field Committee Report." *Minutes of the Annual Meeting of the Amateur Athletic Union*, December 1976: 105, 106.
"Foster Wins Hurdles Trials." *New York Times*, June 25, 1976: 18.
Litsky, Frank. "East German Woman Triumphs in Long Jump, with U.S. Next." *New York Times*, July 24, 1976: 17.
1976 United States Olympic Book. United States Olympic Committee: 1976.
"1976 U.S. Olympic Track and Field Trials." *Official Souvenir Program*, June 1976.
"Olympic Track Team." *New York Times*, June 29, 1976: 38.
"Summaries of Olympic Track Trials." *New York Times*, June 27, 1976: 4.
"Summaries of Olympic Track Trials." *New York Times*, June 28, 1976: 37.
"Summaries of Olympic Trials." *New York Times*, June 20, 1976: 11.
"Summaries of Olympic Trials." *New York Times*, June 21, 1976.
"Summaries of Olympic Trials." *New York Times*, June 23, 1976: 30.
"Summaries of U.S. Track Trials." *New York Times*, June 22, 1976: 45.
"Summaries of U.S. Track Trials." *New York Times*, June 26, 1976: 13.
"United States Olympic Team." *Information for the Press-Television-Radio*, 1976.
Wennerstrom, Steve. "Out of the Past." *Women's Track and Field World*, March 1976: 16.
_____. "Out of the Past." *Women's Track and Field World*, April 1976: 12.

Chapter 60

"Amateur Athletic Union Track Summaries." *New York Times*, February 26, 1977: 16.
Amdur, Neil. "Jane Frederick Wins Triathlon and Hurdles." *New York Times*, March 4, 1977: A17, A23.
Dennis, Dr. Evie G. "Women's Track and Field Committee Report." *Minutes of the Annual Meeting of the Amateur Athletic Union*, December 1976: 105, 106.
"Fact Sheet." *National Track and Field Youth Program*. Pittsburgh, Penn.: Ketchum, MacLeod & Grove, 1977.
Koppett, Leonard. "Moses Sets World 400 Hurdles Mark." *New York Times*, June 12, 1977: 1, 7.
_____. "World Cup Qualifying Spices Competition in Amateur Athletic Union Track." *New York Times*, June 10, 1977: A22, A25.
"Track and Field." *New York Times*, June 10, 1977: 22.
"Track and Field." *New York Times*, June 11, 1977: 16.
"Track and Field." *New York Times*, June 12, 1977: 7.
"World Cup Track Summaries." *New York Times*, September 4, 1977: 4.
"World Cup Track Summaries." *New York Times*, September 5, 1977: 15.

Chapter 61

Dennis, Evie. "Women's Track and Field Committee Report." *Minutes of the Annual Meeting of the Amateur Athletic Union*, 1978: 75.
Ede, Rich. "High School Track." *Women's Track World*, spring 1978: 25–28.
Hansen, Jacqueline. "The World's Marathon Movement." *Women's Track World*, November 1978: 21–22
"Let's Hear It for Pat Rico." *Women's Track World*, December 1978: 23.
"McTear Runs 6.04 in Dash for World Indoor Mark." *New York Times*, February 25, 1978: 13.
Polvino, Geri, ed. *NAGWS Track and Field Guide*. Washington, D.C.: American Alliance for Health, Physical Education, and Recreation, 1978.

"Track and Field." *New York Times*, February 25, 1978: 14.
"Track and Field." *New York Times*, June 9, 1978: A20.
"Track and Field." *New York Times*, June 10, 1978: 12.
"Track and Field." *New York Times*, June 11, 1978: 8.
U.S. Olympic Festival—'89: Record Book. United States Olympic Committee, 1989.
Weiss, Martin E., ed. *Amateur Athlete 1978: The Official Amateur Athletic Union Yearbook*. Indianapolis: Amateur Athletic Union of the United States, 1975.

Chapter 62

"Amateur Athletic Union National Track and Field Champions." *New York Times*, June 17, 1979: 6.
Amdur, Neil. "Miss Ashford Breaks a Barrier." *New York Times*, June 17, 1979: 1, 6.
_____. "Miss Young, 16, Sets Indoor Hurdles Mark." *New York Times*, February 24, 1979: 11.
_____. "Swift Rise of Candy Young Defies U.S. Amateur Athlete Pattern." *New York Times*, February 25, 1979: 4S.
Heinonen, Janet. *Sports Illustrated Running for Women*. New York: J.B. Lippincott, 1979.
Perelman, Rich, ed. "Media Guide." *1979 Cross Country Handbook*.
Reel, Vince, ed. *Women's Track World*, October 1979.
_____. *Women's Track World*, December 1979.
"Track and Field." *New York Times*, February 24, 1979: 12.
"Track and Field." *New York Times*, June 18, 1979: 11.
"Track Team Announced." *New York Times*, February 25, 1979: 4.
"Vault Mark Set by Ripley." *New York Times*, March 4, 1979: 6.

Chapter 63

Amdur, Neil. "Coghlan Sets Record in 3 Mile at 13:02.8." *New York Times*, March 1, 1980: 15, 17.
"$5,000 Reward in Walsh Killing." *Cleveland Press*, December 10, 1980: 1.
Litsky, Frank. "Miss Anderson Is Triumphant in Pentathlon at Olympic Trials." *New York Times*, June 22, 1980: 6.
_____. "Nehemiah Takes Hurdle Title." *New York Times*, June 15, 1980: 3.
_____. "Scott 1,500 Winner as Paige Drops Out." *New York Times*, June 30, 1980: 7.
McLaughlin, Dick. "Stella Walsh Lives on in Hearts of Friends." *Cleveland Press*, December 6, 1980: A4.
Miller, W.C. "Angry Stella Walsh Friends Push Suit to Clear Her." *Plain Dealer*, December 16, 1980: 6A.
"Miss Decker's 1:59.7 Sets World 880 Mark." *New York Times*, February 23, 1980: 18.
Nano, Stephanie. "Olympic Star Is Shot to Death." *Cleveland Press*, December 5, 1980: 1.
Reel, Vince, ed. "TAC Championships." *Women's Track World*, July 1980: 21, 23–24.
_____. *Women's Track World*, January 1980.
_____. *Women's Track World*, March 1980.
_____. *Women's Track World*, September 1980.
_____. *Women's Track World*, December 1980.
"Secret Witness Sought in Stella Walsh Slaying." *Cleveland Press*, December 8, 1980: A1.
"Slain Athlete's Sex Questioned." *New York Times*, December 10, 1980: B12.
"Stella Walsh Slain: Olympic Track Star." *New York Times*, December 6, 1980.
"Tip on Walsh Murder Could Lead to Reward." *Cleveland Press*, December 13, 1980: A23.
"Track and Field." *New York Times*, June 14, 1980.
"Track and Field." *New York Times*, June 15, 1980: 8.

"Track and Field." *New York Times*, June 16, 1980: 12.
"Track and Field." *New York Times*, June 22, 1980: 10.
"Track and Field." *New York Times*, June 23, 1980: 11.
"Track and Field." *New York Times*, June 24, 1980: 12.
"Track and Field." *New York Times*, June 25, 1980: 6.
"Track and Field." *New York Times*, June 26, 1980: 18.
"Track and Field." *New York Times*, June 28, 1980: 14.
"Track and Field." *New York Times*, June 29, 1980: 10.
"Track and Field." *New York Times*, June 30, 1980: 11.
"Track and Field Summaries." *New York Times*, March 1, 1980: 16.

Index